Lecture Notes in Computer Science 2303

Edited by G. Goos, J. Hartmanis, and J. van Leeuwen

T0223730

Springer
Berlin
Heidelberg
New York
Barcelona
Hong Kong
London
Milan
Paris
Tokyo

Mogens Nielsen   Uffe Engberg (Eds.)

Foundations of Software Science and Computation Structures

5th International Conference, FOSSACS 2002
Held as Part of the Joint European Conferences
on Theory and Practice of Software, ETAPS 2002
Grenoble, France, April 8-12, 2002
Proceedings

 Springer

Series Editors

Gerhard Goos, Karlsruhe University, Germany
Juris Hartmanis, Cornell University, NY, USA
Jan van Leeuwen, Utrecht University, The Netherlands

Volume Editors

Mogens Nielsen
Uffe Engberg
University of Aarhus
BRICS, Department of Computer Science
Ny Munkegade Bldg. 540, 8000 Aarhus C, Denmark
E-mail: {mn/engberg}@brics.dk

Cataloging-in-Publication Data applied for

Die Deutsche Bibliothek - CIP-Einheitsaufnahme

Foundations of software science and computation structures : 5th
international conference ; proceedings / FOSSACS 2002, held as part of the
Joint European Conferences on Theory and Practice of Software, ETAPS 2002,
Grenoble, France, April 8 - 12, 2002. Mogens Nielsen ; Uffe Engberg (ed.). -
Berlin ; Heidelberg ; New York ; Barcelona ; Hong Kong ; London ; Milan ;
Paris ; Tokyo : Springer, 2002
      (Lecture notes in computer science ; Vol. 2303)
      ISBN 3-540-43366-X

CR Subject Classification (1998): F.3, F.4.2, F.1.1, D.3.3-4, D.2.1

ISSN 0302-9743
ISBN 3-540-43366-X Springer-Verlag Berlin Heidelberg New York

Springer-Verlag Berlin Heidelberg New York
a member of BertelsmannSpringer Science+Business Media GmbH

http://www.springer.de

© Springer-Verlag Berlin Heidelberg 2002
Printed in Germany

Typesetting: Camera-ready by author, data conversion by Steingräeber Satztechnik GmbH
Printed on acid-free paper   SPIN 10846490   06/3142   5 4 3 2 1 0

Foreword

ETAPS 2002 is the fifth instance of the European Joint Conferences on Theory and Practice of Software. ETAPS is an annual federated conference that was established in 1998 by combining a number of existing and new conferences. This year it comprises five conferences (FOSSACS, FASE, ESOP, CC, TACAS), thirteen satellite workshops (ACL2, AGT, CMCS, COCV, DCC, INT, LDTA, SC, SFEDL, SLAP, SPIN, TPTS and VISS), eight invited lectures (not including those that are specific to the satellite events), and several tutorials.

The events that comprise ETAPS address various aspects of the system development process, including specification, design, implementation, analysis and improvement. The languages, methodologies and tools which support these activities are all well within its scope. Different blends of theory and practice are represented, with an inclination towards theory with a practical motivation on one hand and soundly-based practice on the other. Many of the issues involved in software design apply to systems in general, including hardware systems, and the emphasis on software is not intended to be exclusive.

ETAPS is a loose confederation in which each event retains its own identity, with a separate programme committee and independent proceedings. Its format is open-ended, allowing it to grow and evolve as time goes by. Contributed talks and system demonstrations are in synchronized parallel sessions, with invited lectures in plenary sessions. Two of the invited lectures are reserved for "unifying" talks on topics of interest to the whole range of ETAPS attendees. The aim of cramming all this activity into a single one-week meeting is to create a strong magnet for academic and industrial researchers working on topics within its scope, giving them the opportunity to learn about research in related areas, and thereby to foster new and existing links between work in areas that were formerly addressed in separate meetings.

ETAPS 2002 is organized by Laboratoire Verimag in cooperation with

Centre National de la Recherche Scientifique (CNRS)
Institut de Mathématiques Appliquées de Grenoble (IMAG)
Institut National Polytechnique de Grenoble (INPG)
Université Joseph Fourier (UJF)
European Association for Theoretical Computer Science (EATCS)
European Association for Programming Languages and Systems (EAPLS)
European Association of Software Science and Technology (EASST)
ACM SIGACT, SIGSOFT and SIGPLAN

The organizing team comprises

Susanne Graf - General Chair
Saddek Bensalem - Tutorials
Rachid Echahed - Workshop Chair
Jean-Claude Fernandez - Organization

Alain Girault - Publicity
Yassine Lakhnech - Industrial Relations
Florence Maraninchi - Budget
Laurent Mounier - Organization

Overall planning for ETAPS conferences is the responsibility of its Steering Committee, whose current membership is:

Egidio Astesiano (Genova), Ed Brinksma (Twente), Pierpaolo Degano (Pisa), Hartmut Ehrig (Berlin), José Fiadeiro (Lisbon), Marie-Claude Gaudel (Paris), Andy Gordon (Microsoft Research, Cambridge), Roberto Gorrieri (Bologna), Susanne Graf (Grenoble), John Hatcliff (Kansas), Görel Hedin (Lund), Furio Honsell (Udine), Nigel Horspool (Victoria), Heinrich Hußmann (Dresden), Joost-Pieter Katoen (Twente), Paul Klint (Amsterdam), Daniel Le Métayer (Trusted Logic, Versailles), Ugo Montanari (Pisa), Mogens Nielsen (Aarhus), Hanne Riis Nielson (Copenhagen), Mauro Pezzè (Milano), Andreas Podelski (Saarbrücken), Don Sannella (Edinburgh), Andrzej Tarlecki (Warsaw), Herbert Weber (Berlin), Reinhard Wilhelm (Saarbrücken)

I would like to express my sincere gratitude to all of these people and organizations, the programme committee chairs and PC members of the ETAPS conferences, the organizers of the satellite events, the speakers themselves, and finally Springer-Verlag for agreeing to publish the ETAPS proceedings. As organiser of ETAPS'98, I know that there is one person that deserves a special applause: Susanne Graf. Her energy and organizational skills have more than compensated for my slow start in stepping into Don Sannella's enormous shoes as ETAPS Steering Committee chairman. Yes, it is now a year since I took over the role, and I would like my final words to transmit to Don all the gratitude and admiration that is felt by all of us who enjoy coming to ETAPS year after year knowing that we will meet old friends, make new ones, plan new projects and be challenged by a new culture! Thank you Don!

Lisbon, January 2002

José Luiz Fiadeiro
Steering Committee Chairman
ETAPS 2002

Preface

The present volume contains the proceedings of the international conference *Foundations of Software Science and Computation Structures (FOSSACS) 2002*, held in Grenoble, France, April 10–12, 2002. FOSSACS is an event of the *Joint European Conferences on Theory and Practice of Software (ETAPS)*. The previous four FOSSACS conferences took place in Lisbon (1998), Amsterdam (1999), Berlin (2000), and Genova (2001).

FOSSACS presents papers, which offer progress in foundational research with a clear significance to Software Sciences. Central objects of interest are the algebraic, categorical, logical, and geometric theories, models, and methods which support the specification, synthesis, verification, analysis, and transformation of sequential, concurrent, distributed, and mobile programs and software systems. This volume contains research contributions to a wide spectrum of topics within this scope, many of which are motivated by recent trends and problems in the practice of software and information technology.

These proceedings contain 29 papers. The first one accompanies the invited lecture *Semantical Evaluations as Monadic Second-Order Compatible Structure Transformations* delivered by Bruno Courcelle, University of Bordeaux. The other 28 are contributed papers, selected from a total of 67 submissions. I would like to sincerely thank all members of the FOSSACS 2002 Program Committee for the excellent job they did in the difficult selection process. Also I would like to thank all the sub-referees for their invaluable contributions to this process.

Thanks also to the co-editor of this volume, Uffe H. Engberg, for his assistance in handling and preparing the files for the publisher. And special thanks to Pawel Sobocinski for his excellent administrative handling of the conference web page, the electronic submissions, the reviewing, and the notification process. Thanks also to Rich Gerber for allowing us to use his conference management system START. And finally thanks to the ETAPS 2002 Organizing Committee chaired by Susanne Graf, and the Steering Committee of ETAPS for their efficient coordination of all the activities leading up to FOSSACS 2002.

Aarhus, January 2002

Mogens Nielsen
Program Chair
FOSSACS 2002

Program Commitee

David Basin (Freiburg, Germany)
Julian Bradfield (Edinburgh, UK)
Thomas Erhard (Marseille, France)
Marcelo Fiore (Cambridge, UK)
Carl Gunter (U. Pennsilvania, USA)
Furio Honsell (Udine, Italy)
Mogens Nielsen
         (Aarhus, Denmark, chair)

Fernando Orejas (Barcelona, Spain)
Antoine Petit (Cachan, France)
Frank Pfenning (CMU, USA)
Sanjiva Prasad (IIT Delhi, India)
Vladimiro Sassone (Sussex, UK)
Andrzej Tarlecki (Warsaw, Poland),
Frits Vaandrager
         (Nijmegen, The Netherlands)
Martin Wirsing (Munich, Germany)

Referees

Luca Aceto
Alessandro Aldini
Fabio Alessi
Albert Atserias
Paolo Baldan
Andrej Bauer
Hubert Baumeister
Joffroy Beauquier
Arnold Beckmann
Marek A. Bednarczyk
Nick Benton
Béatrice Bérard
Stefano Berardi
Martin Berger
Andrew Bernard
Karthikeyan Bhargavan
Michel Bidoit
Chiara Bodei
Andrzej M. Borzyszkowski
Tomasz Borzyszkowski
Ahmed Bouajjani
Ilaria Castellani
Didier Caucal
Maura Cerioli
Iliano Cervesato
Sagar Chaki
Piotr Chrząstowski
Nicoletta Cocco
Thomas Colcombet
Paolo Coppola
Roberto Di Cosmo

John N. Crossley
Olivier Danvy
Stéphane Demri
Josée Desharnais
Deepak D'Souza
E. Allen Emerson
Berndt Farwer
Hugues Fauconnier
Andrzej Filinski
Juliana Küster Filipe
Cedric Fournet
Thom Fruehwirth
David de Frutos Escrig
Carsten Führmann
Kim Gabarró
Pietro Di Gianantonio
Paola Giannini
Stephen Gilmore
Alwyn Goodloe
Andy Gordon
Serge Grigorieff
Martin Grohe
Stefano Guerrini
Robert Harper
Rolf Hennicker
Miki Hermann
Jane Hillston
Daniel Hirschkoff
Yoram Hirshfeld
Hans Hüttel
Subramanian Iyer

David Janin
Dirk Janssens
Henrik Ejersbo Jensen
Jens Bæk Jørgensen
Jan Johannsen
Felix Klaedtke
Josva Kleist
Bartek Klin
Alexander Knapp
Mikołaj Konarski
Piotr Kosiuczenko
Marcin Kubica
K. Narayan Kumar
Martin Lange
Sławomir Lasota
Marina Lenisa
Pierre Letouzey
Ugo de' Liguoro
Sylvain Lippi
Kamal Lodaya
Denis Lugiez
Monika Maidl
Jean-Yves Marion
Narciso Martí-Oliet
Michael McDougall
Massimo Merro
Stephan Merz
Marino Miculan
Giuseppe Milicia
Oliver Möller
Eugenio Moggi
Madhavan Mukund
Anca Muscholl
Nikos Mylonakis
Peter O'Hearn
Yolanda Ortega-Mallén
Vincent Padovani
Prakash Panangaden
Paritosh K. Pandya
Dirk Pattinson
Wiesław Pawłowski
Alberto Pettorossi
Ricardo Peña

Marco Pistore
Andrew Pitts
Jeff Polakow
John Power
Christophe Raffalli
Julian Rathke
Jakob Rehof
Bernhard Reus
Salvatore Riccobene
Simona Ronchi Della Rocca
Jan Rutten
Ivano Salvo
Davide Sangiorgi
Don Sannella
Claus Schröter
Dana Scott
Peter Selinger
Natarajan Shankar
Pawel Sobocinski
Stefan Sokołowski
Dieter Spreen
Christoph Sprenger
Jiří Srba
Ian Stark
Colin Stirling
Mathieu Turuani
Paweł Urzyczyn
Frank Valencia
Daniele Varacca
Björn Victor
Luca Vigano
Igor Walukiewicz
Markus Wenzel
Lucian Wischik
Burkhart Wolff
James Worrell
Zhe Yang
Julia Zappe
Guo-Qiang Zhang
Wieslaw Zielonka
Pascal Zimmer
Peter Csaba Ölveczky

Table of Contents

Invited Paper

Contributed Papers

Semantical Evaluations
as Monadic Second-Order Compatible
Structure Transformations

Bruno Courcelle

LaBRI (CNRS, UMR 5800), Université Bordeaux-I,
351 cours de la Libération, F-33405 Talence, France
courcell@labri.fr
http://dept-info.labri.fr/~courcell/ActSci.html

Abstract. A transformation of structures τ is *monadic second-order compatible* (*MS-compatible*) if every monadic second-order property P can be effectively rewritten into a monadic second-order property Q such that, for every structure S, if T is the transformed structure $\tau(S)$, then $P(T)$ holds iff $Q(S)$ holds.

We will review *Monadic Second-order definable transductions* (*MS-transductions*): they are MS-compatible transformations of a particular form, *i.e.*, defined by monadic second-order (MS) formulas.

The unfolding of a directed graph into a tree is an MS-compatible transformation that is not an MS-transduction.

The MS-compatibility of various transformations of semantical interest follows. We will present three main cases and discuss applications and open problems.

Overview of the Lecture

Our working logical language is *Monadic Second-Order Logic*, *i.e.*, the extension of First-Order Logic with variables denoting sets of elements of the considered structures. It enjoys a number of interesting properties regarding decidability and construction of polynomial algorithms [4].

We consider certain semantical evaluations that can be formalized as transformations of discrete structures like graphs or trees (and not as mappings from terms to values belonging to semantical domains as this is usual in denotational semantics).

Our main concern will be to identify transformations such that the verification of an MS property P, of a structure $T = \tau(S)$ reduces to the verification of an MS property Q of the input structure S, where Q depends only on τ and P and, of course, of the fixed relational signatures of S and T.

In such a case, if the MS theory of an infinite structure S is decidable (which means that there exists an algorithm that decides whether a monadic second-order formula is true or not in S), then so is that of $T = \tau(S)$. We say that τ is *Monadic Second-order compatible* (*MS-compatible*).

M. Nielsen and U. Engberg (Eds.): Fossacs 2002, LNCS 2303, pp. 1–4, 2002.

Monadic Second-order definable transductions (*MS-transductions* in short) have been surveyed in [2]. The idea is that $T = \tau(S)$ if T is defined by MS formulas inside the structure formed of k disjoint copies of S (where k and these MS formulas are fixed and constitute the logical specification of τ). That an MS-transduction is MS-compatible is pretty clear for those familiar with the notion of interpretation in model theory.

An obvious consequence of the definition is that the size of the domain of $T = \tau(S)$ is at most k times the size of that of S. In particular the *unfolding* operation which transforms a finite graph into an infinite tree is not an MS-transduction. However, the unfolding operation is MS-compatible [3,6].

Let us consider some examples and their semantical motivations.

Example 1. The structure S is a finite or infinite *transition system*, i.e., a directed labelled graph, given with a special vertex called the *initial state*. The *unfolding* of S from the initial state is a tree (usually infinite), the tree of finite paths starting from the initial state, that represents the behavior of the transition system.

Example 2. S is here a finite or infinite *directed acyclic graph* representing a finite or infinite term with *shared* subterms. Labels attached to vertices and edges make unambiguous the description of such a term by a graph. *Unsharing*, the operation that reconstructs the term, is a special case of unfolding.

As an example of such a graph, we can take $f \Rightarrow f \Rightarrow f \Rightarrow a$ with f a binary function symbol and a a constant.

It unshares into the term $f(f(f(a,a), f(a,a)), f(f(a,a), f(a,a)))$.

By looking at sizes, one can see that unsharing is not an MS-transduction.

Example 3. S is here a *recursive applicative program scheme*, as those considered in [1], and T is the infinite term called an *algebraic tree*. It is the infinite term resulting from a certain form of unfolding, involving term substitutions. Here is an example, consisting of a single equation:

$$\varphi(x) = f(x, \varphi(g(x))$$

This scheme unfolds into the algebraic tree:

$$f(x, f(g(x), f(g(g(x)), f(g(g(g(x))), ...)))).$$

The scheme is actually not given by a graph, but a graph representation fitting our formal framework is easy to build. The transformation from graphs representing schemes (consisting of several mutually recursive equations) with function symbols of bounded arity to algebraic trees is MS-compatible. It follows in particular that the MS theory of an algebraic tree is decidable [3,5].

Example 4. Hyperalgebraic trees are defined as algebraic trees except that the "unknown functions" in schemes may take parameters of function type. Such schemes have been first investigated by W. Damm [7] and more recently by Knapik et al. [8,9].

Example 5. We introduce new symbols to represent first-order substitutions. It is proved in [5] that the mapping from terms to terms that evaluates substitutions, *i.e.*, that eliminates substitution symbols is MS-compatible.

Here is an example. $Sub_{x,y}$ denotes the ternary function such that $Sub_{x,y}(t, t_1, t_2)$ evaluates into the term $t[t_1/x, t_2/y]$, *i.e.*, the result of the simultaneous substitution of t_1 for x and t_2 for y in t.

For instance, the term

$$Sub_{x,y}(Sub_{x,u}(f(x, x, x, u), a, y), b, c)$$

evaluates to $Sub_{x,y}(f(a, a, a, y), b, c)$ and then to $f(a, a, a, c)$. Note that b disappears because the variable x has no occurrence in the term $f(a, a, a, c)$.

A central result is the MS-compatibility of the unfolding mentioned in Examples 1 and 2. The case of Example 5 is proved in [5] and the results of Examples 3 and 4 follow.

Actually, the main result behind all this is the MS-compatibility of a transformation of structures defined by Muchnik (improving a definition by Shelah and Stupp), which builds a kind of tree $Tree(S)$ over any structure S. (If S is a set of two elements, then $Tree(S)$ is the infinite complete binary tree). This result is proved in [10]. It subsumes the case of unfolding and we think it may help to solve some open questions in [8,9].

We will discuss applications and open problems related to Example 5.

Full texts of submitted or unpublished papers and other references can be found from: `http://dept-info.labri.fr/~courcell/ActSci.html`.

References

1. B. Courcelle: Recursive Applicative Program Schemes, chapter 9 of *Handbook of Theoretical Computer Science, Volume B*, J. Van Leeuwen ed., Elsevier 1990, pp. 459–492.
2. B. Courcelle: Monadic second order graph transductions: A survey. *Theoretical Computer Science*, **126**, (1994) 53–75.
3. B. Courcelle: The Monadic Second-Order Logic of Graphs, IX: Machines and their behaviours, *Theoret. Comput. Sci.* **151**, (1995) 125–162.
4. B. Courcelle: The expression of graph properties and graph transformations in monadic second-order logic, Chapter 5 of the "Handbook of graph grammars and computing by graph transformations, Vol. 1: Foundations", G. Rozenberg ed., World Scientific (New-Jersey, London), 1997, pp. 313–400.
5. B. Courcelle, T. Knapik: The evaluation of first-order substitution is monadic second-order compatible, 2001, *Theoret. Comput. Sci.*, to appear.
6. B. Courcelle, I. Walukiewicz: Monadic second-order logic, graph coverings and unfoldings of transition systems, *Annals of Pure and Applied Logic*, **92** (1998) 35-6-2.
7. W. Damm: The IO- and OI hierarchies, *Theoret. Comput. Sci.* **20** (1982) 95–208.
8. T. Knapik, D. Niwinski, P. Urzyczyn: Deciding monadic theories of hyperalgebraic trees, in *Typed lambda-calculi and applications*, Lec. Notes Comp. Sci., **2044** (2001) 253–267.

9. T. Knapik, D. Niwinski, P. Urzyczyn: Higher-order pushdown trees are easy, FOS-SACS 2002, this volume.

10. I. Walukiewicz: Monadic second-order logic on tree-like structures. Proceedings STACS'96, Lec. Notes Comp. Sci. **1046** (1996) 401–414. (Full paper to appear).

Verification
for Java's Reentrant Multithreading Concept

Erika Ábrahám-Mumm[1], Frank S. de Boer[2],
Willem-Paul de Roever[1], and Martin Steffen[1]

[1] Christian-Albrechts-Universität zu Kiel, Germany
eab,wpr,ms@informatik.uni-kiel.de
[2] Utrecht University, The Netherlands
frankb@cs.uu.nl

Abstract. Besides the features of a class-based object-oriented language, *Java* integrates concurrency via its thread-classes, allowing for a *multithreaded* flow of control. The concurrency model offers *coordination* via lock-synchronization, and *communication* by synchronous message passing, including re-entrant method calls, and by instance variables shared among threads.

To reason about multithreaded programs, we introduce in this paper an *assertional proof method* for $Java_{MT}$ (*"Multi-Threaded Java"*), a small concurrent sublanguage of *Java*, covering the mentioned concurrency issues as well as the object-based core of *Java*, i.e., object creation, side effects, and aliasing, but leaving aside inheritance and subtyping.

1   Introduction

The semantical foundations of *Java* [15] have been thoroughly studied ever since the language gained widespread popularity (see e.g. [4,29,12]). The research concerning *Java*'s proof theory mainly concentrated on various aspects of *sequential* sublanguages (see e.g. [20,33,27]). This paper presents a proof system for *multithreaded Java* programs. Concentrating on the issues of concurrency, we introduce an abstract programming language $Java_{MT}$, a subset of *Java* featuring object creation, method invocation, object references with aliasing, and specifically concurrency. Threads are the units of concurrency and are created as instances of specific Thread-classes.

As a mechanism of concurrency control, methods can be declared as *synchronized*, where synchronized methods within a single object are executed by different threads mutually exclusive. A call chain corresponding to the execution of a single thread can contain several invocations of synchronized methods within the same object. This corresponds to the notion of re-entrant monitors and eliminates the possibility that a single thread deadlocks itself on an object's synchronization barrier.

The assertional proof system for verifying safety properties of $Java_{MT}$ is formulated in terms of *proof outlines* [24], i.e., of annotated programs where Hoare-

M. Nielsen and U. Engberg (Eds.): Fossacs 2002, LNCS 2303, pp. 5–20, 2002.
© Springer-Verlag Berlin Heidelberg 2002

style assertions [14,18] are associated with every control point. Soundness and completeness of the proof system is shown in [3].

Recall that the global behaviour of a *Java* program results from the concurrent execution of method bodies, that can interact by shared-variable concurrency, synchronous message passing for method calls, and object creation. In order to capture these features, the proof system is split into three parts.

The execution of a single method body in isolation is captured by *local correctness* conditions that show the inductiveness of the annotated method bodies.

Interaction via synchronous message passing and via object creation cannot be established locally but only relative to assumptions about the communicated values. These assumptions are verified in the *cooperation test*. The communication can take place within a single object or between different objects. As these two cases cannot be distinguished syntactically, our cooperation test combines elements from similar rules used in [8] and in [22] for CSP.

Finally, the effect of shared-variable concurrency is handled, as usual, by the *interference freedom test,* which is modeled after the corresponding tests in the proof systems for shared-variable concurrency in [24] and in [22]. In the case of *Java* it additionally has to accommodate for reentrant code and the specific synchronization mechanism. To simplify the proof system we reduce the potential of interference by disallowing public instance variables in $Java_{MT}$.

The assertion language consists of two different levels: The local assertion language specifies the behaviour on the level of method execution, and is used to annotate programs. The global behaviour, including the communication topology of the objects, is expressed in the global language used in the cooperation test. As in the Object Constraint Language (OCL) [34], global assertions describe properties of object-structures in terms of a navigation or dereferencing operator.

This paper is organized as follows: Section 2 defines the syntax of $Java_{MT}$ and sketches its semantics. After introducing the assertion language in Section 3, the main Section 4 presents the proof system. In Section 5, we discuss related and future work.

2   The Programming Language $Java_{MT}$

In this section we introduce the language $Java_{MT}$ (*"Multi-Threaded Java"*). We start with highlighting the features of $Java_{MT}$ and its relationship to full *Java*, before formally defining its abstract syntax and sketching its semantics.

$Java_{MT}$ is a multithreaded sublanguage of *Java*. Programs, as in *Java*, are given by a collection of classes containing instance variable and method declarations. *Instances* of the classes, i.e., *objects,* are dynamically created and communicate via *method invocation,* i.e., synchronous message passing. As we focus on a proof system for the concurrency aspects of *Java*, all classes in $Java_{MT}$ are thread classes in the sense of *Java*: Each class contains a start-method that can be invoked only once for each object, resulting in a new thread of execution. The new thread starts to execute the start-method of the given object while the initiating thread continues its own execution.

All programs are assumed to be well-typed, i.e, each method invoked on an object must be supported by the object, the types of the formal and actual parameters of the invocation must match, etc. As the static relationships between classes are orthogonal to multithreading aspects, we ignore in $Java_{MT}$ the issues of *inheritance*, and consequently subtyping, overriding, and late binding. For simplicity, we also do not allow method *overloading*, i.e., we require that each method name is assigned a unique list of formal parameter types and a return type. In short, being concerned with the verification of the run-time behavior, we assume a simple *monomorphic* type discipline for $Java_{MT}$.

2.1 Abstract Syntax

Similar to *Java*, the language $Java_{MT}$ is strongly typed. We use t as typical element of types. As built-in primitive types we restrict to integers and booleans. Besides the built-in types Int and Bool, the set of user-definable types is given by a set of class names C, with typical element c. Furthermore, the language allows pairs of type $t_1 \times t_2$ and sequences of type list t. Methods without a return value will get the type Void.

For each type, the corresponding value domain is equipped with a standard set F of operators with typical element f. Each operator f has a unique type $t_1 \times \cdots \times t_n \to t$ and a fixed interpretation f, where constants are operators of zero arity. Apart from the standard repertoire of arithmetical and boolean operations, F also contains operations on tuples and sequences like projection, concatenation, etc.

Since $Java_{MT}$ is strongly typed, all program constructs of the abstract syntax are silently assumed to be well-typed. In other words, we work with a type-annotated abstract syntax where we omit the explicit mentioning of types when no confusion can arise.

For variables, we notationally distinguish between *instance* and *local* variables, where instance variables are always private in $Java_{MT}$. They hold the state of an object and exist throughout the object's lifetime. Local variables play the role of formal parameters and variables of method definitions. They only exist during the execution of the method to which they belong and store the local state of a thread of execution.

The set of variables $Var = IVar \mathbin{\dot\cup} TVar$ with typical element y is given as the disjoint union of the instance and the local variables. Var^t denotes the set of all variables of type t, and correspondingly for $IVar^t$ and $TVar^t$. As we assume a monomorphic type discipline, $Var^t \cap Var^{t'} = \emptyset$ for distinct types t and t'. We use as typical elements $x, x', x_1, \ldots$ for $IVar$ and $u, u', u_1, \ldots$ for $TVar$.

Table 1 contains the abstract syntax of $Java_{MT}$. Since most of the syntax is standard, we mention only a few salient constructs and restrictions. We distinguish between side-effect-free expressions $e \in Exp_c^t$ and those with side effects $sexp \in SExp_c^t$, where c is the class in which the expression occurs and t is its type. We will use similar conventions concerning sub- and superscripts for other constructs. Methods can be declared as *non-synchronized* or *synchronized*. The body of a method m of class c we denote by $body_{m,c}$. As mentioned earlier, all classes in $Java_{MT}$ are thread classes; the corresponding start- and run-methods are denoted by $meth_{start}$ and $meth_{run}$. The main class $class_{main}$ contains as entry point of the program execution the specific method $meth_{main}$ with body $body_{main}$.

To simplify the proof system, we make the following additional restrictions: Method invocation and object creation statements may not refer to instance variables. We also disallow assignments to formal parameters. For methods, we assume that their bodies are terminated by a single return statement.

Table 1. $Java_{MT}$ abstract syntax

$exp ::= x \mid u \mid \textsf{this} \mid \textsf{nil} \mid f(exp,\ldots,exp)$	$e \in Exp$	expressions
$sexp ::= \textsf{new}^c \mid exp.m(exp,\ldots,exp)$	$sexp \in SExp$	side-effect exp
$stm ::= sexp \mid x := exp \mid u := exp \mid u := sexp$		
$\quad\mid \epsilon \mid stm; stm \mid \textsf{if } exp \textsf{ then } stm \textsf{ else } stm$		
$\quad\mid \textsf{while } exp \textsf{ do } stm\ldots$	$stm \in Stm$	statements
$modif ::= \textsf{nsync} \mid \textsf{sync}$		modifiers
$rexp ::= \textsf{return} \mid \textsf{return } exp$		
$meth ::= modif\ m(u,\ldots,u)\{\ stm; rexp\}$	$meth \in Meth$	methods
$meth_{run} ::= modif\ \textsf{run}()\{\ stm; \textsf{return }\}$	$meth_{run} \in Meth$	run-meth.
$meth_{start} ::= \textsf{nsync start}()\{\ \textsf{this.run}(); \textsf{return }\}$	$meth_{start} \in Meth$	start-meth.
$meth_{main} ::= \textsf{nsync main}()\{\ stm; \textsf{return }\}$	$meth_{main} \in Meth$	main-meth.
$class ::= c\{meth\ldots meth\ meth_{run}\ meth_{start}\}$	$class \in Class$	class defn's
$class_{main} ::= c\{meth\ldots meth\ meth_{run}\ meth_{start}\ meth_{main}\}$	$class_{main} \in Class$	main-class
$prog ::= \langle class\ldots class\ class_{main}\rangle$		programs

2.2   Semantics

States and configurations.   For each type t, Val^t denotes its value domain, where Val is given by $\bigcup_t Val^t$. Specifically, for class names $c \in \mathcal{C}$, the set Val^c with typical elements $\alpha, \beta, \ldots$ denotes an infinite set of *object identifiers*, where the domains for different class names are assumed to be disjoint. For each class name c, the constant $nil^c \notin Val^c$ defines the value of nil of type c. In general we will just write nil when c is clear from the context. We define Val^c_{nil} as $Val^c \cup \{nil^c\}$, and correspondingly for compound types; the set of all possible values Val_{nil} is given by $\bigcup_t Val^t_{nil}$.

A *local state* $\tau \in \Sigma_{\textsf{loc}}$ of type $TVar \cup \{\textsf{this}\} \rightharpoonup Val_{nil}$ holds the values of the local variables. Especially it contains a reference $\textsf{this} \in dom(\tau)$ to the object in which the corresponding thread is currently executing. A *local configuration* (τ, stm) specifies, in addition to a local state, the point of execution. A *thread configuration* ξ is a non-empty stack $(\tau_0, stm_0)(\tau_1, stm_1)\ldots(\tau_n, stm_n)$ of local configurations, representing the chain of method invocations of the given thread. An *instance state* $\sigma^c_{inst} \in \Sigma_{inst}$ of type $IVar \rightharpoonup Val_{nil}$ assigns values to the instance variables of class c. In the following we write σ_{inst} when the class c is clear from the context. A *global state* $\sigma \in \Sigma$ is a partial function of type $(\bigcup_{c \in \mathcal{C}} Val^c) \rightharpoonup \Sigma_{inst}$ and stores for each currently *existing* object $\alpha \in Val^c$ its object state σ_{inst}^c. The state of an existing object α in a global state σ is given by $\sigma(\alpha)$. The set of existing objects of type c in a state σ is given by $dom^c(\sigma)$. We define $dom^{\mathsf{Int}}(\sigma)=\mathsf{Int}$ and $dom^{\mathsf{Bool}}(\sigma)=\mathsf{Bool}$, and correspondingly for compound types, where $dom(\sigma) = \bigcup_t dom^t(\sigma)$. We write $dom_{nil}^c(\sigma) = dom^c(\sigma) \cup nil^c$. For compound types t the set dom_{nil}^t is defined analogously, and $dom_{nil}(\sigma)$ is given by $\bigcup_t dom_{nil}^t$. A *global configuration* $\langle T, \sigma \rangle$ consists of a set T of thread configurations describing the currently executing threads, and a global state σ describing the currently existing objects.

Operational semantics.   Computation steps of a program are represented by transitions between global configurations. In the informal description we concentrate on the object-oriented constructs and those dealing with concurrency. The formalization as structural operational semantics is given in [3]. Executing $u:=\mathsf{new}^c$ creates a new object of type c and initializes its instance variables, but does not yet start the thread of the new object. This is done by the first invocation of the **start**-method, thereby initializing the first activation record of the new stack. Further invocations of the **start**-method are without effect.

The invocation of a method extends the call chain by creating a new local configuration. After initializing the local state, the values of the actual parameters are assigned to the formal parameters, and the thread begins to execute the body of the corresponding method. Synchronized methods of an object can be invoked only if no other threads are currently executing any synchronized methods of the same object. This mutual exclusion requirement is expressed in terms of a predicate on a set of thread configurations. This way, the semantics abstracts from any particular implementation of the synchronization mechanism.

When returning from a method call, the callee evaluates its return expression and passes it to the caller which subsequently updates its local state. The execution of the method body then terminates and the caller can continue. Returning from a method without return value is analogous. Returning from the body of the **main**-method or of a **start**-method is treated differently in that there does not exist an explicit local configuration of the caller in the stack.

The initial configuration $\langle T_0, \sigma_0 \rangle$ of a program satisfies the following: $T_0 = \{(\tau_{nil}, body_{\mathsf{main}})\}$, where c is the type of the main class, $\alpha \in Val^c$, and τ_{nil} is the initial local state assigning α to **this**, and nil, 0, and *false* to class-typed, integer, and boolean variables, and correspondingly for composed types. Moreover, $dom(\sigma_0)=\{\alpha\}$ and $\sigma_0(\alpha)=\sigma_{inst}^{nil}$, where σ_{inst}^{nil} is the initial object state assigning initial values to variables as in τ_{nil}. We call a configuration $\langle T, \sigma \rangle$ *reachable* iff there exists a computation $\langle T_0, \sigma_0 \rangle \longrightarrow^* \langle T, \sigma \rangle$, where $\langle T_0, \sigma_0 \rangle$ is the initial configuration and $\longrightarrow^*$ is the reflexive transitive closure of $\longrightarrow$.

3   The Assertion Language

In this section we define two different assertion languages. The *local* assertion language is used to annotate methods directly in terms of their local variables and of the instance variables of the class to which they belong. The *global* assertion language describes a whole system of objects and their topology, and will be used in the cooperation test.

In the assertion language, we introduce as usual a countably infinite set $LVar$ of well-typed *logical variables* disjoint from the instance and the local variables occurring in programs. We use z as typical element of $LVar$, and write $LVar^t$ when specific about the type. Logical variables are used as bound variables in quantifications and, on the global level, to represent the values of local variables. To be able to argue about communication histories, we add the type Object as the supertype of all classes into the assertion language.

Table 2 defines the syntax of the assertion language. *Local expressions* $exp_l \in LExp_c^t$ of type t in class c are expressions of the programming language possibly containing logical variables. In abuse of notation, we use $e, e' \ldots$ not only for program expressions of Table 1, but also for typical elements of local expressions. *Local assertions* $ass_l \in LAss_c$ in class c, with typical elements p, q, and r, are standard logical formulas over local expressions, where unrestricted quantification $\exists z(p)$ is only allowed for integer and boolean domains, i.e., z is required to be of type Int or Bool. Besides that, $\exists z \in e(p)$, resp., $\exists z \sqsubseteq e(p)$ assert the existence of an element denoted by $z \in LVar^t$, resp., a subsequence $z \in LVar^{\text{list } t}$ of a given sequence $e \in LExp_c^{\text{list } t}$, for which a property p holds. Restricted quantification involving objects ensures that the evaluation of a local assertion indeed only depends on the values of the instance and local variables.

Global expressions $exp_g \in GExp^t$ of type t with typical element E are constructed from logical variables, nil, operator expressions, and qualified references $E.x$ to instance variables x of objects E. *Global assertions* $ass_g \in GAss$, with typical elements P, Q, and R, are logical formulas over global expressions. Different to the local assertion language, quantification on the global level is allowed for all types. Quantifications $\exists z(P)$ range over the set of *existing* values only, i.e., the set of objects $dom_{nil}(\sigma)$ in a global configuration $\langle T, \sigma \rangle$. The semantics of the assertion languages is standard and omitted (cf. [6]).

Table 2. Syntax of assertions

$exp_l ::= z \mid x \mid u \mid \text{this} \mid \text{nil} \mid f(exp_l, \ldots, exp_l)$	$e \in LExp$	local expressions
$ass_l ::= exp_l \mid \neg ass_l \mid ass_l \wedge ass_l$		local assertions
$\quad \mid \exists z(ass_l) \mid \exists z \in exp_l(ass_l) \mid \exists z \sqsubseteq exp_l(ass_l)$	$p \in LAss$	
$exp_g ::= z \mid \text{nil} \mid f(exp_g, \ldots, exp_g) \mid exp_g.x$	$E \in GExp$	global expressions
$ass_g ::= exp_g \mid \neg ass_g \mid ass_g \wedge ass_g \mid \exists z(ass_g)$	$P \in GAss$	global assertions

The verification conditions defined in the next section involve the following substitution operations: By $p[\vec{e}/\vec{y}]$ we denote the standard capture-avoiding substitution. The effect of assignments to instance variables is expressed on the *global* level by the substitution $P[\vec{E}/z.\vec{x}]$, which replaces in P the instance variables $\vec{x}$ of the object referred to by z by the global expressions $\vec{E}$. To accommodate properly for the effect of assignments, though, we must not only syntactically replace the occurrences $z.x_i$ of the instance variables, but also all their *aliases* $E'.x_i$, when z and the result of the substitution applied to E' refer to the same object. As the aliasing condition cannot be checked syntactically, we define the main case $(E'.x_i)[\vec{E}/z.\vec{x}]$ of the substitution by the conditional expression if $E'[\vec{E}/z.\vec{x}]=z$ then E_i else $(E'[\vec{E}/z.\vec{x}]).x_i$ fi [6]. We also use $P[\vec{E}/z.\vec{y}]$ for arbitrary variable sequences $\vec{y}$, where local variables are untouched. To express on the global level a property defined by a local assertion p, we define the substitution $p[z, \vec{E}/\text{this}, \vec{u}]$, where the logical variable z is assumed to occur neither in p nor in $\vec{E}$, by simultaneously replacing in p all occurrences of the self-reference this by z, transforming all occurrences of instance variables x into qualified references $z.x$, and substituting all local variables u_i by the given global expressions E_i. For unrestricted quantifications $(\exists z'(p))[z, \vec{E}/\text{this}, \vec{u}]$ the substitution applies to the assertion p. Local restricted quantifications are transformed into global unrestricted ones where the relations $\in$ and $\sqsubseteq$ are expressed at the global level as operators. For notational convenience, we sometimes view the local variables occurring in $p[z/\text{this}]$ as logical variables. Formally, these local variables should be replaced by fresh logical variables.

4   Proof System

This section presents the assertional proof system for reasoning about $Java_{MT}$ programs, formulated in terms of *proof outlines* [24,13], i.e., where Hoare-style pre- and postconditions [14,18] are associated with each control point. The proof system has to accommodate for shared-variable concurrency, aliasing, method invocation, synchronization, and dynamic object creation.

To reason about multithreading and communication, first we define a program transformation by introducing new communication statements that model explicitly the communication mechanism of method invocations, then augment the program by auxiliary variables, and, finally, introduce critical sections.

4.1   Program Transformation

To be able to reason about the communication mechanism of method invocations, we split each invocation $u:=e_0.m(\vec{e})$ of a method different from the start-method into the sequential composition of the *communication statements* $e_0.m(\vec{e})$ and receive u. Similarly for methods without a return value, $e_0.m(\vec{e})$ gets replaced by $e_0.m(\vec{e})$; receive.

Next, we augment the program by fresh *auxiliary* variables. Assignments can be extended to multiple assignments, and additional multiple assignments to auxiliary variables can be inserted at any point. We introduce the specific auxiliary variables callerobj, id, lock, critsec, and started to represent information about the global configuration at the proof-theoretical level. The local variables callerobj and id are used as additional formal parameters of types Object and Object × Int, resp. The parameter callerobj stores the identity of the caller object, where id stores the identity of the object in which the corresponding thread has begun its execution, together with the current depth of its stack. Each statement $e_0.m(\vec{e})$ gets extended to $e_0.m(\text{this}, callee(\text{id}), \vec{e})$, where $callee(\alpha, n) = (\alpha, n+1)$. If m is the start-method, the method call statement is extended to $e_0.m(\text{this}, (e_0, 0), \vec{e})$, instead. The formal parameter lists get extended correspondingly. The variables callerobj and id of the thread executing the main-method in the initial configuration are initialized to nil and $(\alpha, 0)$, resp., where α is the initial object. The auxiliary instance variable lock of the same type $\textsf{Object} \times \textsf{Int}$ is used to reason about thread synchronization: The value $(nil, 0)$ states that no threads are currently executing any synchronized methods of the given object; otherwise, the value (α, n) identifies the thread which acquired the lock, together with the stack depth n, at which it has gotten the lock. The auxiliary variable lock will be only used to indicate who owns the lock, i.e., it is *not* used to *implement* the synchronization mechanism (e.g. by means of semaphores and the like). The meaning of the boolean auxiliary instance variable critsec will be explained after the introduction of critical sections. The boolean instance variable started states whether the object's start-method has already been invoked.

Finally, we extend programs by *critical sections,* a conceptual notion, which is introduced for the purpose of proof and, therefore, does not influence the control flow. Semantically, a critical section $\langle stm \rangle$ expresses that the statements inside are executed without interleaving with other threads. To make object creation and communication observable, we attach auxiliary assignments to the corresponding statements; to do the observation immediately after these statements, we enclose the statement and the assignment in critical sections. The formal replacement of communication and object creation statements, and method bodies is defined in Table 3.

Table 3. Critical sections

Replace each statement of the form	by
$e_0.m(\vec{e})$	$\langle e_0.m(\vec{e}); \vec{y}_1 := \vec{e}_1 \rangle$
method body $stm; rexp$	$\langle \vec{y}_2 := \vec{e}_2 \rangle; stm; \langle rexp; \vec{y}_3 := \vec{e}_3 \rangle$
receive u	$\langle \text{receive } u; \vec{y}_4 := \vec{e}_4 \rangle$
receive	$\langle \text{receive}; \vec{y}_4 := \vec{e}_4 \rangle$
$u := \text{new}$	$\langle u := \text{new}; \vec{y} := \vec{e} \rangle$
new	$\langle \text{new}; \vec{y} := \vec{e} \rangle$

Critical sections of method call and return statements, representing the sending parts of communication, contain the assignments $\textsf{critsec} := (e_0 = \textsf{this})$ and $\textsf{critsec} := (\textsf{callerobj} = \textsf{this})$, resp. Correspondingly for the receiver part, the critical sections at the beginning of method bodies and that of receive statements include the assignment $\textsf{critsec} := \textsf{false}$. I.e., critsec states whether there is a thread currently communicating within the given object, i.e., executing some self-calls or returning from a method within the object, such that the observation of the sender part is already executed but not yet that of the receiver part. Critical sections at the beginning of start-methods contain additionally the assignment started:=true; in case of a synchronized method, $\vec{y}_2:=\vec{e}_2$ and $\vec{y}_3:=\vec{e}_3$ include the assignments lock:=getlock(lock, id) representing lock reservation and lock:=release(lock, id) representing lock release, where $getlock(lock, id)$ is given by $lock$ if $lock\neq(nil, 0)$ and id, otherwise; correspondingly, $release(lock, id)$ equals $lock$ if $lock\neq id$ and $(nil, 0)$, otherwise. The vectors $\vec{y}, \vec{y}_1, \ldots, \vec{y}_4$ from above are auxiliary variable sequences; the values of the auxiliary variables callerobj, id, lock, critsec, and started are changed only in the critical sections, as described.

As auxiliary variables do not change the control flow of the original program, we can schedule the execution order of the augmented program as follows: For method call statements, after communication of the parameters, first the auxiliary assignment of the caller and then that of the callee is executed. Conversely, for return, the communication of the return value is followed by the execution of the assignment of the callee and then that of the caller, in this order. Note that these three steps for method invocation and return may not be interleaved by other threads. Control points within a critical section and at the beginning of a method body, which we call *non-interleaving* points, do not change the program behaviour. All other control points we call *interleaving* points.

To specify invariant properties of the system, the transformed programs are *annotated* by attaching local assertions to all control points. Besides that, for each class c, the annotation defines a local assertion I_c called *class invariant*, which refers only to instance variables, and expresses invariant properties of the instances of the class. Finally, the *global invariant* $GI \in GAss$ specifies the communication structure of the program. We require that for all qualified references $E.x$ in GI with $E \in GExp^c$, all assignments to x in class c are enclosed in critical sections. An annotated transformation of $prog$, denoted by $prog'$, is called a *proof outline*. For annotated programs, we use the standard notation $\{p\}\, stm\, \{q\}$ to express that p and q are the assertions in front of and after the statement stm. We call $pre(stm)=p$ and $post(stm)=q$ the *pre-* and *postconditions* of stm.

4.2   Proof System

The proof system formalizes a number of *verification conditions* which ensure that in each reachable configuration all preconditions are satisfied, and that the class and global invariants hold. To cover concurrency and communication, the verification conditions are grouped into local correctness conditions, an interference freedom test, and a cooperation test.

Before specifying the verification conditions, we first fix some auxiliary functions and notations. Let $InitValue : Var \rightarrow Val$ be a function assigning an initial value to each variable, that is nil, $false$, and 0 for class, boolean, and integer types, respectively, and analogously for composed types, where sequences are initially empty. For each class c, let $IVar_c$ be the set of instance variables in class c, and let $Init(z)$ denote the global assertion $\bigwedge_{x \in IVar_c} z.x = InitValue(x)$, for all $z \in LVar^c$, expressing that the object denoted by z is in its initial object state. The predicate $samethread((\alpha_1, n_1), (\alpha_2, n_2))$, defined by $\alpha_1 = \alpha_2$, characterizes the relationship between threads. Similarly, the relation $<$ of the same type is given by $(\alpha_1, n_1) < (\alpha_2, n_2)$ iff $\alpha_1 = \alpha_2$ and $n_1 < n_2$.

Initial correctness. *Initial correctness* means that the precondition of the main statement is satisfied by the initial object and local states, where $\mathsf{id} = (\mathsf{this}, 0)$ and all other variables have their initial values. Furthermore, the global invariant is satisfied by the first reachable stable configuration, i.e., by the global state after the execution of the critical section at the beginning of the main-method.

Definition 1. *A proof outline prog$'$ is initially correct, if*

$$\models_{\mathcal{L}} pre(body_{\mathsf{main}})[(\mathsf{this}, 0)/\mathsf{id}][InitValue(\vec{y})/\vec{y}], \tag{1}$$

$$\models_{\mathcal{G}} \exists z \Big(z \neq \mathsf{nil} \wedge Init(z) \wedge \forall z'(z' = \mathsf{nil} \vee z = z') \Big) \rightarrow \exists z \left(GI[\vec{e}_2/z.\vec{y}_1] \right), \tag{2}$$

where $body_{\mathsf{main}} = \langle \vec{y}_1 := \vec{e}_1 \rangle$; stm is the body of the main-method, $\vec{y}$ are the variables occurring in $pre(body_{\mathsf{main}})$, z is of the type of the main class, and $z' \in LVar^{\mathsf{Object}}$.

Local correctness. A proof outline is *locally correct*, if the usual verification conditions [7] for standard sequential constructs hold: The precondition of a multiple assignment must imply its postcondition after the execution of the assignment. For assignments occurring outside of critical sections, $\neg\mathsf{critsec}$ expresses the enabledness of the assignment. Furthermore, all assertions of a class are required to imply the class invariant. Inductivity for statements involving object creation or communication are verified on the global level in the cooperation test.

Definition 2. *A proof outline is* locally correct, *if for each class c with class invariant I_c, all multiple assignments $\vec{y} := \vec{e}$ and $\vec{y}_{crit} := \vec{e}_{crit}$ occurring outside and inside of critical sections, resp., and all statements stm in class c,*

$$\models_{\mathcal{L}} pre(\vec{y} := \vec{e}) \wedge \neg\mathsf{critsec} \rightarrow post(\vec{y} := \vec{e})[\vec{e}/\vec{y}] \tag{3}$$

$$\models_{\mathcal{L}} pre(\vec{y}_{crit} := \vec{e}_{crit}) \rightarrow post(\vec{y}_{crit} := \vec{e}_{crit})[\vec{e}_{crit}/\vec{y}_{crit}] \tag{4}$$

$$\models_{\mathcal{L}} (pre(stm) \rightarrow I_c) \wedge (post(stm) \rightarrow I_c). \tag{5}$$

The interference freedom test. In this section we formalize conditions that ensure the invariance of local properties of a thread under the activities of other threads. Since we disallow public instance variables in *Java$_{MT}$*, we only have to deal with the invariance of properties under the execution of statements within the same object. Containing only local variables, communication and object creation statements do not change the state of the executing object. Thus we only have to take assignments $\vec{y} := \vec{e}$ into account.

Satisfaction of a local property of a thread at an *interleaving* point may clearly be affected by the execution of assignments by a *different* thread in the same object (Eq. (6)). If, otherwise, the property describes the *same* thread that executes the assignment, the only interleaving points endangered are those waiting for a return value earlier in the current execution stack, i.e., we have to show the invariance of preconditions of receive statements (Eq. (7)). Since an object can call a method of itself, the preconditions of method bodies and the postconditions of receive statements, representing *non-interleaving* points, must be proven interference free, as well: For method invocation, after communication, the caller executes the assignment of its critical section $\langle e_0.m(\vec{e}); \vec{y}_1 := \vec{e}_1 \rangle$, which may affect the precondition of the body of the called method (Eq. (8)). Likewise when returning from a method, after communicating the return value, first the callee executes the multiple assignment of its critical section $\langle rexp; \vec{y}_3 := \vec{e}_3 \rangle$, which can affect the postcondition of the receive statement of the caller (Eq. (9)).

Definition 3. *A proof outline is* interference free, *if for all classes c the following conditions hold, where we denote by p' the assertion p with each local variable u different from* this *replaced by a fresh one denoted by u':*

- *For all statements $\vec{y} := \vec{e}$ in a critical section and all assertions p representing an interleaving point in class c, if not both the statement and the assertion occur in a synchronized method, then*

$$\models_{\mathcal{L}} p' \wedge pre(\vec{y} := \vec{e}) \wedge \neg samethread(\mathsf{id}', \mathsf{id}) \rightarrow p'[\vec{e}/\vec{y}]. \tag{6}$$

For statements $\vec{y} := \vec{e}$ in critical sections we have the additional antecedent $\neg$critsec.

- *For all statements $\vec{y} := \vec{e}$ in a critical section and all assertions p in c, if p is the precondition of a receive statement, then*

$$\models_{\mathcal{L}} p' \wedge pre(\vec{y} := \vec{e}) \wedge \mathsf{id}' < \mathsf{id} \rightarrow p'[\vec{e}/\vec{y}]. \tag{7}$$

If $\vec{y} := \vec{e}$ occurs outside of critical sections, we have the additional antecedent $\neg$critsec.

- *For all statements $\langle e_0.m(\vec{u}); \vec{y} := \vec{e} \rangle$ in c with $e_0 \in Exp_c^c$, if p is the precondition of the body of $m \neq$start in c, then*

$$\models_{\mathcal{L}} p' \wedge pre(\vec{y} := \vec{e}) \wedge e_0 = \mathsf{this} \wedge \mathsf{id}' = callee(\mathsf{id}) \rightarrow p'[\vec{e}/\vec{y}]. \tag{8}$$

If $m =$start, then $\mathsf{id}' = (\mathsf{this}, 0)$ replaces $\mathsf{id}' = callee(\mathsf{id})$.

- *For all statements $\langle rexp; \vec{y} := \vec{e} \rangle$ in a method m of c, if p is the postcondition of a receive statement preceded by a critical section invoking method m of $e_0 \in Exp_c^c$, then*

$$\models_{\mathcal{L}} p' \wedge pre(\vec{y} := \vec{e}) \wedge e_0' = \mathsf{this} \wedge \mathsf{id} = callee(\mathsf{id}') \rightarrow p'[\vec{e}/\vec{y}]. \tag{9}$$

Note that we have to replace the local variables different from this occurring in p to avoid name clashes with those in $\vec{y} := \vec{e}$ and its associated precondition.

The cooperation test. Whereas the verification conditions associated with local correctness and interference freedom cover the effects of assigning side-effect-free expressions to variables, the *cooperation test* deals with method call and object creation. Since different objects may be involved, it is formulated in the global assertion language. We start with the cooperation test for method invocations.

In the following definition, the logical variable z denotes the object calling a method and z' refers to the callee. The cooperation test assures that the local assertions at both ends of the communication hold, immediately after the values have been communicated. When calling a method, the postcondition of the method invocation statement and the precondition of the invoked method's body must hold after passing the parameters (Eq. (10)). In the global state prior to the call, we can assume that the global invariant, the precondition of the method invocation at the caller side, and the class invariant of the callee hold. For synchronized methods, additionally the lock of the callee object is free, or the lock has been acquired in the call chain of the executing thread. This is expressed by the predicate $isfree(z'.\mathsf{lock}, \mathsf{id})$ defined as $z'.\mathsf{lock}{=}(\mathsf{nil}, 0) \lor z'.\mathsf{lock} \leq \mathsf{id}$, where id is the identity of the caller. Equation (11) works similarly, where the postconditions of the corresponding return- and receive-statements are required to hold after the communication when returning from a method. Note that we rename the local variables of the callee in order to avoid name clashes with that of the caller.

The global invariant GI, which describes invariant properties of a program, is not allowed to refer to instance variables whose values are changed outside of critical sections. Consequently, it will be automatically invariant over the execution of statements outside of critical sections. For the critical sections themselves, however, the invariance must be shown as part of the cooperation test. A difference between the treatment of the local assertions and the global invariant is, that the latter does not necessarily hold immediately after communication, but only after the accompanying assignments to the auxiliary variables of both the caller and callee have been completed. This is reflected in the two substitutions applied to the global invariant on the right-hand sides of the implications.

Invoking the start-method of an object whose thread is already started, or returning from a start-method or from the first execution of the main-method does not have communication effects; Equations (12) and (13) take care about the validity of the postconditions and the invariance of the global invariant.

Definition 4. *A proof outline satisfies the* cooperation test *for* communication, *if for all classes c and statements $\langle e_0.m(\vec{e}); \vec{y}_1{:=}\vec{e}_1 \rangle; \langle \mathsf{receive}\, v; \vec{y}_4{:=}\vec{e}_4 \rangle$ in c with $e_0 \in Exp_c^{c'}$, where method m of c' with formal parameter list $\vec{u}$ is synchronized with $body_{m,c'}{=}\langle \vec{y}_2{:=}\vec{e}_2 \rangle; stm; \langle \mathsf{return}\, e_{ret}; \vec{y}_3{:=}\vec{e}_3 \rangle$,*

$$\models_{\mathcal{G}} GI \land pre(e_0.m(\vec{e}))[z/\mathsf{this}] \land I_{c'}[z'/\mathsf{this}] \land e_0[z/\mathsf{this}]{=}z' \land isfree(z'.\mathsf{lock}, \mathsf{id})$$
$$\rightarrow post(e_0.m(\vec{e}))[z/\mathsf{this}] \land pre'(body_{m,c'})[z', \vec{E}/\mathsf{this}, \vec{u}] \land$$
$$GI[\vec{E}_2/z'.\vec{y}_2][\vec{E}_1/z.\vec{y}_1] \tag{10}$$

$$\models_{\mathcal{G}} GI \wedge pre'(\mathsf{return}\ e_{ret})[z', \vec{E}/\mathsf{this}, \vec{u}] \wedge pre(\mathsf{receive}\ v)[z/\mathsf{this}] \wedge\ e_0[z/\mathsf{this}]=z'$$
$$\to post'(\mathsf{return}\ e_{ret})[z', \vec{E}/\mathsf{this}, \vec{u}] \wedge post(\mathsf{receive}\ v)[z, E_{ret}/\mathsf{this}, v] \wedge$$
$$GI[\vec{E}_4/z.\vec{y}_4][\vec{E}_3/z'.\vec{y}_3], \tag{11}$$

where $z \in LVar^c$ and $z' \in LVar^{c'}$ are distinct fresh logical variables, and id is the auxiliary local variable of the caller viewed as logical variable on the global level. The assertion $pre'(body_{m,c'})$ is $pre(body_{m,c'})$ with every local variable except the formal parameters and this, of class, boolean, or integer type replaced by nil, false, or 0, respectively, and correspondingly for composed types; $pre'(\mathsf{return}\ e_{ret})$, $post'(\mathsf{return}\ e_{ret})$, and e'_{ret} denote the given assertions and expressions with every local variable except the formal parameters and this replaced by a fresh one. Furthermore, $\vec{E}_1=\vec{e}_1[z/\mathsf{this}]$, $\vec{E}_j=\vec{e}_j[z', \vec{E}/\mathsf{this}, \vec{u}]$ for $j=2,3$, $\vec{E}_4=\vec{e}_4[z, E_{ret}/\mathsf{this}, v]$, where $\vec{E}=\vec{e}[z/\mathsf{this}]$ and $E_{ret} = e'_{ret}[z', \vec{E}/\mathsf{this}, \vec{u}]$. For the invocation of non-synchronized methods, the antecedent $isfree(z'.\mathsf{lock}, \mathsf{id})$ is dropped. The verification conditions for methods without return value are analogous. For invocations of start-methods, only (10) applies with the additional antecedent $\neg z'.\mathsf{started}$. For the case that the thread is already started,

$$\models_{\mathcal{G}} GI \wedge pre(e_0.\mathsf{start}(\vec{e}))[z/\mathsf{this}] \wedge I_{c'}[z'/\mathsf{this}] \wedge e_0[z/\mathsf{this}]=z' \wedge z'.\mathsf{started}$$
$$\to post(e_0.\mathsf{start}(\vec{e}))[z/\mathsf{this}] \wedge GI[\vec{E}_1/z.\vec{y}_1] \tag{12}$$

have to be satisfied. Finally, for statements $\langle \mathsf{return}; \vec{y}_3:=\vec{e}_3 \rangle$ in the main-method or in a start-method,

$$\models_{\mathcal{G}} GI \wedge pre(\mathsf{return})[z'/\mathsf{this}] \wedge \mathsf{id}=(z', 0)$$
$$\to post(\mathsf{return})[z'/\mathsf{this}] \wedge GI[\vec{E}_3/z'.\vec{y}_3]. \tag{13}$$

The substitution of $\vec{u}$ by $\vec{E}$ in the condition $pre'(body)[z', \vec{E}/\mathsf{this}, \vec{u}]$ reflects the parameter-passing mechanism, where $\vec{E}$ are the actual parameters $\vec{e}$ represented at the global assertional level. This substitution also identifies the callee, as specified by its formal parameter id. Note that the actual parameters do not contain *instance* variables, i.e., their interpretation does not change during the execution of the method body. Therefore, $\vec{E}$ can be used not only to logically capture the conditions at the entry of the method body, but at the exit of the method body, as well, as shown in Equation (11).

Furthermore, the cooperation test needs to handle critical sections of object creation taking care of the preservation of the global invariant, the postcondition of the new-statement, and the new object's class invariant. The extension of the global state with a freshly created object is formulated in a strongest postcondition style, using existential quantification to refer to the old, changed value, i.e., z' of type $LVar^{\mathsf{list\ Object}}$ represents the existing objects prior to the extension. Moreover, that the created object's identity is fresh and that the new instance u is properly initialized is captured by the global assertion $Fresh(z', u)$ defined as $u \neq \mathsf{nil} \wedge u \notin z' \wedge Init(u) \wedge \forall v(v \in z' \vee v=u)$, where $z' \in LVar^{\mathsf{list\ Object}}$, and $Init(u)$ is as defined in Section 4.2. To have quantifications on the left-hand side of the implication to refer to the set of existing objects *before* the new-statement, we need to *restrict* any existential quantification to range over objects from z', only. For a global assertion P we define its restriction $P \downarrow z'$ by replacing all quantifications $\exists z(P')$ in P by $\exists z(z \in z' \wedge P')$, when z is of type c or Object, and by $\exists z(z \sqsubseteq z' \wedge P')$, when z is of type list c or list Object, and correspondingly for composed types.

Definition 5. *A proof outline satisfies the* cooperation test *for object creation, if for all classes c' and statements $\langle u{:=}\mathsf{new}^c; \vec{y}{:=}\vec{e}\rangle$ in c':*

$$\models_{\mathcal{G}} \exists z' \Big(Fresh(z', u) \wedge (GI \wedge \exists u(pre(u{:=}\mathsf{new}^c)[z/\mathsf{this}])) \downarrow z' \Big) \qquad (14)$$
$$\rightarrow post(u{:=}\mathsf{new}^c)[z/\mathsf{this}] \wedge I_c[u/\mathsf{this}] \wedge GI[\vec{E}/z.\vec{y}],$$

with fresh logical variables $z \in LVar^{c'}$ and $z' \in LVar^{\mathsf{list\ Object}}$, and $\vec{E}{=}\vec{e}[z/\mathsf{this}]$.

Theorem 1. *The proof method is sound and relative complete.*

The soundness of our method is shown by a standard albeit tedious induction on the length of the computation. Proving its completeness involves the introduction of appropriate assertions expressing reachability and auxiliary *history variables*. The details of the proofs can be found in [3].

5   Conclusion

In this paper we introduce an assertional proof method for a multithreaded sub-language of *Java*. In [2] the basic ideas have been introduced for proof outlines by means of a modular integration of the interference freedom and the cooperation test for a more restricted version of *Java*. The present paper offers such an integration for a more concrete version of *Java* by incorporating *Java*'s *reentrant* synchronization mechanism. This requires a non-trivial extension of the proof method by a more refined mechanism for the identification of threads. Its soundness and completeness is proved in [3]. As such, our paper presents a first assertional proof method for reasoning about threads in Java which is complete in the sense that it forms a basis for extending our proof method to more specific Java-synchronization methods, such as wait(), notify(), and notifyAll(), and the important feature of exception handling [20].

Most papers in the literature focus on *sequential* subsets of Java [28,10,26,27], [11,31,1,32,33]. Formal semantics of *Java*, including multithreaded execution, and its virtual machine in terms of abstract state machines is given in [29]. A structural operational semantics of multithreaded *Java* can be found in [12].

Currently we are developing in the context of the European Fifth Framework RTD project Omega and the bilateral NWO/DFG project MobiJ a front-end tool for the computer-aided specification and verification of *Java* programs based on our proof method. Such a front-end tool consists of an editor and a parser for annotating *Java* programs, and of a compiler which translates these annotated *Java* programs into corresponding verification conditions. A theorem prover (HOL or PVS) is used for verifying the validity of these verifications conditions. Of particular interest in this context is an integration of our method with related approaches like the LOOP project [17,23].

More in general, our future work focuses on including more features of multithreading, inheritance, and polymorphic extensions involving behavioral subtyping [5].

Acknowledgment

This work was partly supported by the bilateral NWO/DFG project MobiJ. We also thank the reviewers for their helpful comments.

References

1. M. Abadi and K. R. M. Leino. A logic of object-oriented programs. In Bidoit and Dauchet [9], pages 682–696.
2. E. Ábrahám-Mumm and F. de Boer. Proof-outlines for threads in Java. In Palamidessi [25].
3. E. Ábrahám-Mumm, F. de Boer, W.-P. de Roever, and M. Steffen. Verification for Java's reentrant multithreading concept: Soundness and completeness. Technical Report TR-ST-01-2, Lehrstuhl für Software-Technologie, Institut für Informatik und praktische Mathematik, Christian-Albrechts-Universität Kiel, 2001.
4. J. Alves-Foss, editor. *Formal Syntax and Semantics of Java*. LNCS State-of-the-Art-Survey. Springer, 1999.
5. P. America. A behavioural approach to subtyping in object-oriented programming languages. Technical report 443, Phillips Research Laboratories, 1989.
6. P. America and F. Boer. Reasoning about dynamically evolving process structures. *Formal Aspects of Computing*, 6(3):269–316, 1993.
7. K. R. Apt. Ten years of Hoare's logic: A survey – part I. *ACM Transact. on Progr. Lang. and Syst.*, 3(4):431–483, 1981.
8. K. R. Apt, N. Francez, and W.-P. de Roever. A proof system for communicating sequential processes. *ACM Transact. on Progr. Lang. and Syst.*, 2:359–385, 1980.
9. M. Bidoit and M. Dauchet, editors. *Theory and Practice of Software Development, Proc. of the 7th Int. Joint Conf. of CAAP/FASE, TAPSOFT'97*, volume 1214 of *LNCS*. Springer, 1997.
10. R. Breu. *Algebraic Specification Techniques in Object Oriented Programming Environments*. PhD thesis, Universität Passau, 1991. See also Springer LNCS 562.
11. P. A. Buhr, M. Fortier, and M. H. Coffin. Monitor classification. *ACM Computing Surveys*, 27(1):63–107, 1995.
12. P. Cenciarelli, A. Knapp, B. Reus, and M. Wirsing. An event-based structural operational semantics of multi-threaded Java. In Alves-Foss [4].
13. W.-P. de Roever, F. de Boer, U. Hannemann, J. Hooman, Y. Lakhnech, M. Poel, and J. Zwiers. *Concurrency Verification: Introduction to Compositional and Non-compositional Proof Methods*. Cambridge University Press, 2001.
14. R. W. Floyd. Assigning meanings to programs. In J. T. Schwartz, editor, *Proc. Symp. in Applied Mathematics*, volume 19, pages 19–32, 1967.

15. J. Gosling, B. Joy, and G. Steele. *The Java Language Specification*. Addison-Wesley, 1996.
16. C. Hankin, editor. *Programming Languages and Systems: Proc. of ESOP '98, Held as Part of ETAPS '98*, volume 1381 of *LNCS*. Springer, 1998.
17. J. Hensel, M. Huisman, B. Jacobs, and H. Tews. Reasoning about classes in object-oriented languages: Logical models and tools. In Hankin [16].
18. C. A. R. Hoare. An axiomatic basis for computer programming. *Communications of the ACM*, 12:576–580, 1969. Also in [19].
19. C. A. R. Hoare and C. B. Jones, editors. *Essays in Computing Science*. International Series in Computer Science. Prentice Hall, 1989.
20. M. Huisman. *Java Program Verification in Higher-Order Logic with PVS and Isabelle*. PhD thesis, University of Nijmegen, 2001.
21. H. Hussmann, editor. *Fundamental Approaches to Software Engineering*, volume 2029 of *LNCS*. Springer, 2001.
22. G. M. Levin and D. Gries. A proof technique for communicating sequential processes. *Acta Informatica*, 15(3):281–302, 1981.
23. The LOOP project: Formal methods for object-oriented systems. http://www.cs.kun.nl/~bart/LOOP/, 2001.
24. S. Owicki and D. Gries. An axiomatic proof technique for parallel programs. *Acta Informatica*, 6(4):319–340, 1976.
25. C. Palamidessi, editor. *CONCUR 2000*, volume 1877 of *LNCS*. Springer, 2000.
26. A. Poetzsch-Heffter. *Specification and Verification of Object-Oriented Programs*. Technische Universität München, 1997. Habilitationsschrift.
27. A. Poetzsch-Heffter and P. Müller. A programming logic for sequential Java. In Swierstra [30], pages 162–176.
28. B. Reus, R. Hennicker, and M. Wirsing. A Hoare calculus for verifying Java realizations of OCL-constrained design models. In Hussmann [21], pages 300–316.
29. R. Stärk, J. Schmid, and E. Börger. *Java and the Java Virtual Machine*. Springer, 2001.
30. S. Swierstra, editor. *Proc. of ESOP '99*, volume 1576 of *LNCS*. Springer, 1999.
31. D. von Oheimb. Axiomatic sematics for Java^{light} in Isabelle/HOL. In S. Drossopoulo, S. Eisenbach, B. Jacobs, G. Leavens, P. Müller, and A. Poetzsch-Heffter, editors, *Formal Techniques for Java Programs*, number 269, 5/2000 in Technical Report. Fernuniversität Hagen, 2000.
32. D. von Oheimb. Hoare logic for Java in Isabelle/HOL. *Concurrency – Practice and Experience*, 2001. To appear.
33. D. von Oheimb and T. Nipkow. Hoare logic for NanoJava: Auxiliary variables, side effects and virtual methods revisited. Submitted for publication, 2002.
34. J. B. Warmer and A. G. Kleppe. *The Object Constraint Language: Precise Modeling With Uml*. Object Technology Series. Addison-Wesley, 1999.

On the Integration
of Observability and Reachability Concepts [*]

Michel Bidoit[1] and Rolf Hennicker[2]

[1] Laboratoire Spécification et Vérification (LSV), CNRS & ENS de Cachan, France
[2] Institut für Informatik, Ludwig-Maximilians-Universität München, Germany

Abstract. This paper focuses on the integration of reachability and observability concepts within an algebraic, institution-based framework. We
develop the essential notions that are needed to construct an institution
which takes into account both the generation- and observation-oriented
aspects of software systems. Thereby the underlying paradigm is that the
semantics of a specification should be as loose as possible to capture all
its correct realizations. We also consider the so-called "idealized models"
of a specification which are useful to study the behavioral properties a
user can observe when he/she is experimenting with the system. Finally,
we present sound and complete proof systems that allow us to derive
behavioral properties from the axioms of a given specification.

1 Introduction

Reachability and observability concepts are both equally important in system
specifications. Reachability concepts focus on the specification of generation
principles usually presented by a set of constructors. Most algebraic specification languages incorporate features to express reachability like, for instance,
the CASL language [1]. Observability concepts are used to specify the desired observable properties of a program or software system (see, e.g., [17, 18, 15, 16, 8]).
Particular institutions which formalize the syntactic and semantic aspects of observability were introduced in [10] (hidden algebra) and in [11] (observational
logic). In [5] we have shown that by dualization of observational logic one obtains
a novel treatment of reachability, called the constructor-based logic institution.
Both frameworks capture, *either* from the observability *or* from the reachability
point of view, the idea that the model class of a specification SP should describe
all correct realizations of SP. In many examples, however, both aspects have to
be considered simultaneously. The aim of this paper is therefore to integrate our
novel treatment of reachability *and* observational logic in a common, powerful
institution, called the constructor-based observational logic institution.

Of course, we are aware that many approaches in the literature already cover
in some way reachability and/or observability. However, most of them either are
not based on a loose semantics (like [16]) or are too restrictive w.r.t. the interpretation of reachability in the sense that only reachable models are admitted.

---

[*] This work is partially supported by the German DFG-project InopSys and by the
German BMBF-project GLOWA-Danube.

M. Nielsen and U. Engberg (Eds.): Fossacs 2002, LNCS 2303, pp. 21–36, 2002.
© Springer-Verlag Berlin Heidelberg 2002

Thus standard implementations which simply contain junk (like the realization of the natural numbers by the integers) are ruled out from the models of a specification. The ultra-loose approach of [20], the notion of behavioral specification w.r.t. a partial observational equality in [6, 12] and the hidden algebra approach are closely related to our framework. The main difference to [20] is that no explicit notion of observer or constructor operation is used there while in our approach they are the basic ingredients of a signature which lead to a specification methodology and to an institution tailored to observability and reachability. The partial observational equality of [6] does not take into account a distinguished set of observer and constructor operations which in our case facilitates proofs and leads to a powerful notion of signature morphism. The main difference to the presentation of hidden algebra in [10] is that there the reachable values are given by a fixed data universe while in our approach constructors can be defined for arbitrary sorts and hence also for hidden state sorts which we believe is important to deal with reachable states.

We assume that the reader is familiar with the basic notions of algebraic specifications (see, e.g., [14, 2]), like the notions of (many-sorted) *signature* $\Sigma = (S, OP)$ (where S is a set of *sorts* and OP is a set of *operation symbols* $op : s_1, \ldots, s_n \to s$), *(total) Σ-algebra* $A = ((A_s)_{s \in S}, (op^A)_{op \in OP})$, class $\text{Alg}(\Sigma)$ of all Σ-algebras, *Σ-term algebra* $T_\Sigma(X)$ over a family of variables X and *interpretation* $I_\alpha : T_\Sigma(X) \to A$ w.r.t. a *valuation* $\alpha : X \to A$. We implicitly assume throughout this paper that the carrier sets of an algebra are not empty.

2   The Constructor-Based Observational Logic Institution

In this section we develop, step by step, the syntactic and semantic notions which lead to the constructor-based observational logic institution, called COL for short. We start by considering so-called COL-signatures which provide the syntactic basis to integrate reachability and observability concepts in algebraic system specifications. Technically, a COL-signature consists of a standard algebraic signature together with a distinguished set of constructor operations and a distinguished set of observer operations. Intuitively, the constructors determine those elements which are of interest from the user's point of view while the observers determine a set of observable experiments that a user can perform to examine hidden states. Thus we can abstract from junk elements and also from concrete state representations whereby two states are considered to be "observationally equal" if they cannot be distinguished by observable experiments.

Definition 1 (COL-signature). *A* constructor *is an operation symbol cons :* $s_1, \ldots, s_n \to s$ *with* $n \geq 0$. *The result sort s of cons is called a* constrained sort. *An* observer *is a pair* (obs, i) *where obs is an operation symbol obs :* $s_1, \ldots, s_n \to s$ *with* $n \geq 1$ *and* $1 \leq i \leq n$. *The distinguished argument sort* s_i *of obs is called a* state sort *(or* hidden sort*).*

A COL-signature $\Sigma_{\text{COL}} = (\Sigma, OP_{\text{Cons}}, OP_{\text{Obs}})$ *consists of a signature* $\Sigma = (S, OP)$, *a set* $OP_{\text{Cons}} \subseteq OP$ *of constructors and a set* OP_{Obs} *of observers* (obs, i) *with* $obs \in OP$.

The set $S_{\text{Cons}} \subseteq S$ of constrained sorts *(w.r.t. OP_{Cons}) consists of all sorts s such that there exists at least one constructor in OP_{Cons} with range s. The set $S_{\text{Loose}} \subseteq S$ of* loose sorts *consists of all sorts which are not constrained, i.e.* $S_{\text{Loose}} = S \setminus S_{\text{Cons}}$.

The set $S_{\text{State}} \subseteq S$ of state sorts *(or* hidden sorts, *w.r.t. OP_{Obs}) consists of all sorts s_i such that there exists at least one observer (obs, i) in OP_{Obs}, $obs : s_1, \ldots, s_i, \ldots, s_n \to s$. The set $S_{\text{Obs}} \subseteq S$ of* observable sorts *consists of all sorts which are not a state sort, i.e. $S_{\text{Obs}} = S \setminus S_{\text{State}}$.*

An observer $(obs, i) \in OP_{\text{Obs}}$ with profile $obs : s_1, \ldots, s_i, \ldots, s_n \to s$ is called a direct observer *of s_i if $s \in S_{\text{Obs}}$, otherwise it is an* indirect observer.

Note that in many examples state sorts are also constrained sorts which allows us to deal with reachable states. We implicitly assume in the following that whenever we consider a COL-signature Σ_{COL}, then $\Sigma_{\text{COL}} = (\Sigma, OP_{\text{Cons}}, OP_{\text{Obs}})$ with $\Sigma = (S, OP)$ and similarly for Σ'_{COL} etc.

Example 1. As a running example we consider the following COL-signature $\Sigma_{\text{COL}} = (\Sigma, OP_{\text{Cons}}, OP_{\text{Obs}})$ for containers of natural numbers where:
$\Sigma = (S, OP)$, $S = \{ bool, nat, container \}$
$OP = \{ true : \to bool, false : \to bool,$
$\qquad 0 : \to nat, succ : nat \to nat, add : nat \times nat \to nat,$
$\qquad empty : \to container, insert : container \times nat \to container,$
$\qquad remove : container \times nat \to container, isin : container \times nat \to bool \}$
$OP_{\text{Cons}} = \{ true, false, 0, succ, empty, insert \}$
$OP_{\text{Obs}} = \{ (isin, 1) \}$
Hence, in this example, all sorts are constrained, *container* is the only state sort and the observable sorts are *bool* and *nat*.   ◇

Any set OP_{Cons} of constructor symbols (and hence any COL-signature) determines a set of constructor terms.

Definition 2 (Constructor term). *Let Σ_{COL} be a COL-signature, and let $X = (X_s)_{s \in S}$ be a family of countably infinite sets X_s of variables of sort s. For all $s \in S_{\text{Cons}}$, the set $\mathcal{T}(\Sigma_{\text{COL}})_s$ of constructor terms with "constrained result sort" s is inductively defined as follows:*
1. *Each constant $cons : \to s \in OP_{\text{Cons}}$ belongs to $\mathcal{T}(\Sigma_{\text{COL}})_s$.*
2. *For each constructor $cons : s_1, \ldots, s_n \to s \in OP_{\text{Cons}}$ with $n \geq 1$ and terms $t_1, \ldots, t_n$ such that t_i is a variable $x_i : s_i$ if $s_i \in S_{\text{Loose}}$ and $t_i \in \mathcal{T}(\Sigma_{\text{COL}})_{s_i}$ if $s_i \in S_{\text{Cons}}$, $cons(t_1, \ldots, t_n) \in \mathcal{T}(\Sigma_{\text{COL}})_s$.*
The set of all constructor terms is denoted by $\mathcal{T}(\Sigma_{\text{COL}})$. We implicitly assume in the following that for any constrained sort $s \in S_{\text{Cons}}$, there exists a constructor term of sort s.

Note that only constructor symbols and variables of loose sorts are used to build constructor terms. In particular, if all sorts are constrained, i.e., $S_{\text{Cons}} = S$, the constructor terms are exactly the (S, OP_{Cons})-ground terms which are built by the constructor symbols. This is the case, for instance, in the above example.

The syntactic notion of a constructor term induces, for any Σ-algebra A, the definition of a family of subsets of the carrier sets of A, called reachable part, which consists of all elements which are reachable (from the loose sorts, if any) with respect to the given constructors. In the following considerations the reachable part plays a crucial role since it represents those elements which are of interest from the user's point of view.

Definition 3 (Reachable part). *Let Σ_{COL} be a COL-signature. For any Σ-algebra $A \in \text{Alg}(\Sigma)$, the* reachable part *(w.r.t. OP_{Cons}) $\mathcal{R}_{\Sigma_{\text{COL}}}(A) = (\mathcal{R}_{\Sigma_{\text{COL}}}(A)_s)_{s \in S}$ of A is defined by:*
1. $\mathcal{R}_{\Sigma_{\text{COL}}}(A)_s = A_s$, if $s \in S_{\text{Loose}}$.
2. $\mathcal{R}_{\Sigma_{\text{COL}}}(A)_s = \{a \in A_s \mid$ there exists a term $t \in \mathcal{T}(\Sigma_{\text{COL}})_s$ and a valuation $\alpha : X \to A$ such that $I_\alpha(t) = a\}$, if $s \in S_{\text{Cons}}$.

Definition 4 (Reachable algebra). *Let Σ_{COL} be a COL-signature. A Σ-algebra A is called* reachable *(w.r.t. OP_{Cons}) if it coincides with its reachable part.*

Example 2. Consider the signature Σ_{COL} of Example 1 and the following Σ-algebra A with carriers:
$A_{bool} = \{T, F\}$, $A_{nat} = \mathbb{Z}$ (set of the integers),
$A_{container} = \mathbb{Z}^* \times \mathbb{Z}^*$ (pairs of finite lists of integers)
and with operations:
$true^A = T$, $false^A = F$, $0^A = 0$, $succ^A(a) = a + 1$, $add^A(a, b) = a + b$,
$empty^A = (<>, <>)$,
$insert^A((< a_1, \ldots, a_n >, < b_1, \ldots, b_m >), a) =$
$\quad (< a, a_1, \ldots, a_n >, < b_1, \ldots, b_m >)$ if $a \neq a_i$ for $i = 1, \ldots, n$,
$insert^A((s, t), a) = (s, t)$ otherwise,
$remove^A((< a_1, \ldots, a_n >, < b_1, \ldots, b_m >), a) =$
$\quad (< a_1, \ldots, a_{i-1}, a_{i+1}, \ldots, a_n >, < a, b_1, \ldots, b_m >)$ if $a_i = a$ and $a_j \neq a$ for
$\quad j = 1, \ldots, i - 1$,
$remove^A((s, t), a) = (s, t)$ otherwise,
$isin^A((< a_1, \ldots, a_n >, t), a) = F$ if $a \neq a_i$ for $i = 1, \ldots, n$,
$isin^A((s, t), a) = T$ otherwise.
The above Σ-algebra A can be considered as an implementation of containers of natural numbers whereby the natural numbers are implemented by the integers and containers are implemented by two finite lists s and t such that s stores the elements which are actually in the container and t is a "trash" which stores those elements that have been removed from the container. The *remove* operation is defined in an efficient way: only one occurrence of a given element is deleted from the actual elements of a container. This is sufficient since the *insert* operation only stores an element if it does not already belong to the actual elements of a container. The reachable part $\mathcal{R}_{\Sigma_{\text{COL}}}(A)$ of A consists of the following sets:
$\mathcal{R}_{\Sigma_{\text{COL}}}(A)_{bool} = \{T, F\}$,
$\mathcal{R}_{\Sigma_{\text{COL}}}(A)_{nat} = \mathbb{N}$ (set of the natural numbers),
$\mathcal{R}_{\Sigma_{\text{COL}}}(A)_{container} = \{(s, <>) \mid s \in \mathbb{N}^*$ and each element of s occurs only once
$\qquad \qquad \qquad$ in $s\}$. $\diamond$

Let us now focus on the set OP_{Obs} of observers declared by a COL-signature Σ_{COL}. The observers determine a set of observable contexts which represent the observable experiments. In contrast to the inductive definition of constructor terms, observable contexts are defined in a coinductive style.

Definition 5 (Observable context). *Let Σ_{COL} be a COL-signature, let $X = (X_s)_{s\in S}$ be a family of countably infinite sets X_s of variables of sort s and let $Z = (\{z_s\})_{s\in S_{\text{State}}}$ be a disjoint family of singleton sets (one for each state sort). For all $s \in S_{\text{State}}$ and $s' \in S_{\text{Obs}}$ the set $\mathcal{C}(\Sigma_{\text{COL}})_{s\to s'}$ of observable Σ_{COL}-contexts with "application sort" s and "observable result sort" s' is inductively defined as follows:*

1. *For each direct observer (obs, i) with $obs : s_1,\ldots,s_i,\ldots,s_n \to s'$ and pairwise disjoint variables $x_1{:}s_1,\ldots,x_n{:}s_n$,*
   $obs(x_1,\ldots,x_{i-1},z_{s_i},x_{i+1},\ldots,x_n) \in \mathcal{C}(\Sigma_{\text{COL}})_{s_i\to s'}$.
2. *For each observable context $c \in \mathcal{C}(\Sigma_{\text{COL}})_{s\to s'}$, for each indirect observer (obs, i) with $obs : s_1,\ldots,s_i,\ldots,s_n \to s$, and pairwise disjoint variables $x_1{:}s_1,\ldots,x_n{:}s_n$ not occurring in c,*
   $c[obs(x_1,\ldots,x_{i-1},z_{s_i},x_{i+1},\ldots,x_n)/z_s] \in \mathcal{C}(\Sigma_{\text{COL}})_{s_i\to s'}$
   where $c[obs(x_1,\ldots,x_{i-1},z_{s_i},x_{i+1},\ldots,x_n)/z_s]$ denotes the term obtained from c by substituting the term $obs(x_1,\ldots,x_{i-1},z_{s_i},x_{i+1},\ldots,x_n)$ for z_s.

The set of all observable contexts is denoted by $\mathcal{C}(\Sigma_{\text{COL}})$. We implicitly assume in the following that for any state sort $s \in S_{\text{State}}$ there exists an observable context with application sort s.

Note that only the observer operations are used to build observable contexts For instance, the context $isin(z_{container}, x)$ is (up to renaming of the variable x) the only observable context in the container example.

The syntactic notion of an observable context will be used to define, for any Σ-algebra A, a semantic relation, called observational equality, which expresses indistinguishability of states. As already pointed out, the observable contexts represent observable experiments which can be applied to examine states. Then two states are observationally equal if they cannot be distinguished by these experiments.

If there is no constructor symbol, this intuitive idea can easily be formalized as done in the observational logic framework, see [11]. However, if we integrate observability and reachability concepts, we have to be careful with respect to the role of constructors in observable experiments. For instance, in the container example, the observable context $isin(z_{container}, x)$ represents a set of observable experiments on containers which depend on the actual values of the variable x of sort nat. Since nat is a constrained sort, from the user's point of view the only relevant values are representable by a constructor term (and hence belong to the reachable part). This leads to the following definition of the observational equality which depends, in contrast to the pure observational approach in [11], not only on the observers but also on the chosen constructors.

Definition 6 (Observational equality). *Let Σ_{COL} be a COL-signature. For any Σ-algebra $A \in \text{Alg}(\Sigma)$, the observational Σ_{COL}-equality on A is denoted* by $\approx_{\Sigma_{\mathrm{COL}},A}$ and defined as follows. For all $s \in S$, two elements $a, b \in A_s$ are observationally equal w.r.t. Σ_{COL}, i.e., $a \approx_{\Sigma_{\mathrm{COL}},A} b$, if and only if

1. $a = b$, if $s \in S_{\mathrm{Obs}}$,
2. for all observable sorts $s' \in S_{\mathrm{Obs}}$, for all observable contexts $c \in \mathcal{C}(\Sigma_{\mathrm{COL}})_{s \to s'}$, and for all valuations $\alpha, \beta : X \cup \{z_s\} \to A$ with $\alpha(x) = \beta(x) \in \mathcal{R}_{\Sigma_{\mathrm{COL}}}(A)$ if $x \in X$, $\alpha(z_s) = a$ and $\beta(z_s) = b$, we have $I_\alpha(c) = I_\beta(c)$, if $s \in S_{\mathrm{State}}$.

Definition 7 (Fully-abstract algebra). Let Σ_{COL} be a COL-signature. A Σ-algebra A is called fully abstract (w.r.t. Σ_{COL}) if the observational Σ_{COL}-equality $\approx_{\Sigma_{\mathrm{COL}},A}$ on A coincides with the set-theoretic equality.

Example 3. Consider the signature Σ_{COL} of Example 1 and the algebra of containers defined in Example 2 where a container is represented by a pair (s, t) of finite lists of integers. Two containers $(s1, t1)$ and $(s2, t2)$ are observationally equal, $(s1, t1) \approx_{\Sigma_{\mathrm{COL}},A} (s2, t2)$, if for all natural numbers n, $isin^A((s1, t1), n) = isin^A((s2, t2), n)$ holds. By definition of $isin^A$, this means that the same natural numbers occur in $s1$ and in $s2$. Thus the observational equality abstracts not only from the ordering and multiple occurrences of elements, but also from the occurrences of negative integers and from the content of each "trash" $t1$ and $t2$. This expresses exactly our intuition according to the given constructors and observers. For instance, the following container representations are observationally equal: $(< 1, 2 >, <>) \approx_{\Sigma_{\mathrm{COL}},A} (< 2, -7, 2, -3, 1 >, < 6, -4 >)$.   ◇

Up to now the syntactic notion of a COL-signature Σ_{COL} has lead to the semantic concepts of a reachable part (determined by the constructors) and of an observational equality (determined by the observers but with an impact of the constructors) which both have been defined for an arbitrary algebra over the underlying signature Σ. As we will see in the following discussion, the constructors and the observers induce also certain constraints on algebras which lead to the notion of a COL-algebra.

In traditional approaches to reachability, constructor symbols are used to restrict the admissible models of a specification to those algebras which are reachable with respect to the given constructors (i.e. to reachable algebras, see Definition 4). We do not adopt this interpretation since, as many examples show, it is too restrictive if the semantics of a specification is expected to capture all correct realizations. For instance, the container algebra of Example 2 is not reachable w.r.t. the given constructors but should be usable as a correct realization of containers. As a consequence, we are interested in a more flexible framework where the constructor symbols are still essential, but nevertheless non-reachable algebras can be accepted as models if they satisfy certain conditions. Since the reachable part represents the elements of interest, one could simply require that no further elements should be constructible by the non-constructor operations. Indeed, if we are working in a pure constructor-based framework, this condition fits perfectly to our intuition (see [5], Section 3). However, if we deal simultaneously with observability, this requirement is still too strong because from the user's point of view it doesn't matter if a non-constructor operation yields an element *outside* the reachable part as long as this element is observationally equal to some other element *inside* the reachable part. Formally, this condition is expressed by the following reachability constraint.

Definition 8 (Reachability constraint). *Let* Σ_{COL} *be a COL-signature. For any* Σ-*algebra* $A \in \mathrm{Alg}(\Sigma)$, $\langle \mathcal{R}_{\Sigma_{\mathrm{COL}}}(A) \rangle_\Sigma$ *denotes the smallest* Σ-*subalgebra of* A *which includes the reachable part* $\mathcal{R}_{\Sigma_{\mathrm{COL}}}(A)$. [1]

A Σ-*algebra* A *satisfies the reachability constraint induced by* Σ_{COL}, *if for any* $a \in \langle \mathcal{R}_{\Sigma_{\mathrm{COL}}}(A) \rangle_\Sigma$ *there exists* $b \in \mathcal{R}_{\Sigma_{\mathrm{COL}}}(A)$ *such that* $a \approx_{\Sigma_{\mathrm{COL}},A} b$.

Example 4. Let A be the container algebra of Example 2. It is obvious that the reachable part of A is not closed under the operation $remove^A$. For instance, $remove^A((< 1, 2 >, <>), 1) = (< 2 >, < 1 >) \notin \mathcal{R}_{\Sigma_{\mathrm{COL}}}(A)_{container}$. In fact, we have $\langle \mathcal{R}_{\Sigma_{\mathrm{COL}}}(A) \rangle_{\Sigma,container} = \{(s,t) \mid s, t \in \mathbb{N}^*$ and each element of s occurs only once in $s\}$. However, any element $(s, t) \in \langle \mathcal{R}_{\Sigma_{\mathrm{COL}}}(A) \rangle_{\Sigma,container}$ is observationally equal to $(s, <>)$ (see Example 3) which is an element of the reachable part. Considering the sort nat, the reachable elements (which are just the natural numbers) are preserved under add^A, i.e. $\langle \mathcal{R}_{\Sigma_{\mathrm{COL}}}(A) \rangle_{\Sigma,nat} = \mathcal{R}_{\Sigma_{\mathrm{COL}}}(A)_{nat} = \mathbb{N}$. Thus A satisfies the reachability constraint induced by Σ_{COL}.   ◇

Let us now discuss the constraints on a Σ-algebra A that are induced by the observers OP_{Obs} of a COL-signature Σ_{COL}. Since the declaration of observers determines a particular observational equality on any Σ-algebra A, the (interpretations of the) non-observer operations should respect this observational equality, i.e. a non-observer operation should not contribute to distinguish states. For this purpose one could simply require that the observational equality is a Σ-congruence on A. Indeed, if we are working in a pure observational framework, this condition fits perfectly to our intuition (see [11]). However, if we deal simultaneously with reachability, this requirement is too strong because computations performed by a user can only lead to elements in the Σ-subalgebra $\langle \mathcal{R}_{\Sigma_{\mathrm{COL}}}(A) \rangle_\Sigma$. As a consequence, it is sufficient to require the congruence property on this subalgebra which is expressed by the following observability constraint.

Definition 9 (Observability constraint). *Let* Σ_{COL} *be a COL-signature. A* Σ-*algebra* A *satisfies the observability constraint induced by* Σ_{COL}, *if* $\approx_{\Sigma_{\mathrm{COL}},A}$ *is a* Σ-*congruence on* $\langle \mathcal{R}_{\Sigma_{\mathrm{COL}}}(A) \rangle_\Sigma$.

Example 5. The container algebra A of Example 2 satisfies the observability constraint of the given COL-signature for containers. Note, however, that $\approx_{\Sigma_{\mathrm{COL}},A}$ is only a Σ-congruence on $\langle \mathcal{R}_{\Sigma_{\mathrm{COL}}}(A) \rangle_\Sigma$ but not on the whole algebra A since $remove^A$ does not respect the observational equality for *all* elements of A. Consider, for instance, the element $(< 1, 1 >, <>) \notin \langle \mathcal{R}_{\Sigma_{\mathrm{COL}}}(A) \rangle_{\Sigma,container}$. $(< 1, 1 >, <>) \approx_{\Sigma_{\mathrm{COL}},A} (< 1 >, <>)$ but since $remove^A((< 1, 1 >, <>), 1) = (< 1 >, < 1 >)$, it is *not* observationally equal to $remove^A((< 1 >, <>), 1) = (<>, < 1 >)$.   ◇

---

[1] Indeed $\langle \mathcal{R}_{\Sigma_{\mathrm{COL}}}(A) \rangle_\Sigma$ is the Σ-subalgebra of A generated by the operations OP over the carrier sets A_s with loose sort s.

Definition 10 (COL-algebra). *Let Σ_{COL} be a COL-signature. A Σ_{COL}-alge-bra (also called COL-algebra) is a Σ-algebra A which satisfies the reachabil-ity and the observability constraints induced by Σ_{COL}. The class of all Σ_{COL}-algebras is denoted by $\mathrm{Alg}_{\mathrm{COL}}(\Sigma_{\mathrm{COL}})$.*

Note that the satisfaction of the two constraints is essential for defining the black box semantics of COL-specifications considered in Section 3 and hence for guaranteeing the soundness of the proof systems in Section 4. In particular the instantiation rule and the congruence rule of the equational calculus would not be sound w.r.t. the COL-satisfaction relation defined below without assuming both the reachability and observability constraints. The following notion of COL-morphism is a generalization of standard Σ-homomorphisms.

Definition 11 (COL-morphism). *Let $A, B \in \mathrm{Alg}_{\mathrm{COL}}(\Sigma_{\mathrm{COL}})$ be two Σ_{COL}-algebras. A Σ_{COL}-morphism (also called COL-morphism) $h : A \to B$ is an S-sorted family $(h_s)_{s \in S}$ of relations $h_s \subseteq \langle \mathcal{R}_{\Sigma_{\mathrm{COL}}}(A) \rangle_{\Sigma,s} \times \langle \mathcal{R}_{\Sigma_{\mathrm{COL}}}(B) \rangle_{\Sigma,s}$ with the following properties, for all $s \in S$:*
1. *For all $a \in \langle \mathcal{R}_{\Sigma_{\mathrm{COL}}}(A) \rangle_{\Sigma,s}$, there exists $b \in \langle \mathcal{R}_{\Sigma_{\mathrm{COL}}}(B) \rangle_{\Sigma,s}$ such that $a\ h_s\ b$.*
2. *For all $a \in \langle \mathcal{R}_{\Sigma_{\mathrm{COL}}}(A) \rangle_{\Sigma,s}$, $b, b' \in \langle \mathcal{R}_{\Sigma_{\mathrm{COL}}}(B) \rangle_{\Sigma,s}$, if $a\ h_s\ b$, then $(a\ h_s\ b'$ if and only if $b \approx_{\Sigma_{\mathrm{COL}},B} b')$.*
3. *For all $a, a' \in \langle \mathcal{R}_{\Sigma_{\mathrm{COL}}}(A) \rangle_{\Sigma,s}$, $b \in \langle \mathcal{R}_{\Sigma_{\mathrm{COL}}}(B) \rangle_{\Sigma,s}$, if $a\ h_s\ b$ and $a \approx_{\Sigma_{\mathrm{COL}},A} a'$, then $a'\ h_s\ b$.*
4. *For all $op : s_1, \ldots, s_n \to s \in OP$, $a_i \in \langle \mathcal{R}_{\Sigma_{\mathrm{COL}}}(A) \rangle_{\Sigma,s_i}$, $b_i \in \langle \mathcal{R}_{\Sigma_{\mathrm{COL}}}(B) \rangle_{\Sigma,s_i}$, if $a_i\ h_{s_i}\ b_i$ for $i = 1, \ldots, n$, then $op^A(a_1, \ldots, a_n)\ h_s\ op^B(b_1, \ldots, b_n)$.*

For any COL-signature Σ_{COL}, the class $\mathrm{Alg}_{\mathrm{COL}}(\Sigma_{\mathrm{COL}})$ together with the Σ_{COL}-morphisms is a category which, by abuse of notation, will also be denoted by $\mathrm{Alg}_{\mathrm{COL}}(\Sigma_{\mathrm{COL}})$.

In the next step we generalize the standard satisfaction relation of first-order logic by abstracting with respect to reachability and observability. First, from the reachability point of view, the valuations of variables are restricted to the elements of the reachable part only.[2] From the observability point of view, the idea is to interpret the equality symbol = occurring in a first-order formula φ not by the set-theoretic equality but by the observational equality of elements.

Definition 12 (COL-satisfaction relation). *The COL-satisfaction relation between Σ-algebras and first-order Σ-formulas (with variables in X) is denoted by $\models_{\Sigma_{\mathrm{COL}}}$ and defined as follows. Let $A \in \mathrm{Alg}(\Sigma)$.*
1. *For any two terms $t, r \in T_\Sigma(X)_s$ of the same sort s and for any valuation $\alpha : X \to \mathcal{R}_{\Sigma_{\mathrm{COL}}}(A)$, $A, \alpha \models_{\Sigma_{\mathrm{COL}}} t = r$ holds if $I_\alpha(t) \approx_{\Sigma_{\mathrm{COL}},A} I_\alpha(r)$.*
2. *For any arbitrary Σ-formula φ and for any valuation $\alpha : X \to \mathcal{R}_{\Sigma_{\mathrm{COL}}}(A)$, $A, \alpha \models_{\Sigma_{\mathrm{COL}}} \varphi$ is defined by induction over the structure of the formula φ in the usual way. In particular, $A, \alpha \models_{\Sigma_{\mathrm{COL}}} \forall x{:}s.\, \varphi$ if for all valuations $\beta : X \to \mathcal{R}_{\Sigma_{\mathrm{COL}}}(A)$ with $\beta(y) = \alpha(y)$ for all $y \neq x$, $A, \beta \models_{\Sigma_{\mathrm{COL}}} \varphi$.*

---

[2] This idea is related to the ultra-loose approach of [20] where the same effect is achieved by using formulas with relativized quantification.

*3. For any arbitrary Σ-formula φ, $A \models_{\Sigma_{\mathrm{COL}}} \varphi$ holds if for all valuations $\alpha :$
$X \to \mathcal{R}_{\Sigma_{\mathrm{COL}}}(A)$, $A, \alpha \models_{\Sigma_{\mathrm{COL}}} \varphi$ holds.*

The notation $A \models_{\Sigma_{\mathrm{COL}}} \varphi$ is extended in the usual way to classes of algebras and sets of formulas. Note that the COL-satisfaction relation is defined for arbitrary Σ-algebras though it will only be used in this paper for COL-algebras. Note also that for COL-algebras, the COL-satisfaction relation would be the same if we would have used valuations "$\alpha : X \to \langle \mathcal{R}_{\Sigma_{\mathrm{COL}}}(A)\rangle_{\Sigma}$" instead of "$\alpha : X \to \mathcal{R}_{\Sigma_{\mathrm{COL}}}(A)$" in the above definition.

Definition 13 (Basic COL-specification). *A basic COL-specification $\mathrm{SP}_{\mathrm{COL}}$ $= \langle \Sigma_{\mathrm{COL}}, \mathrm{Ax} \rangle$ consists of a COL-signature $\Sigma_{\mathrm{COL}} = (\Sigma, OP_{\mathrm{Cons}}, OP_{\mathrm{Obs}})$ and a set Ax of Σ-sentences, called axioms. The semantics of $\mathrm{SP}_{\mathrm{COL}}$ is given by its signature $\mathrm{Sig}_{\mathrm{COL}}(\mathrm{SP}_{\mathrm{COL}})$ and by its class of models $\mathrm{Mod}_{\mathrm{COL}}(\mathrm{SP}_{\mathrm{COL}})$ which are defined by:*

$$\mathrm{Sig}_{\mathrm{COL}}(\mathrm{SP}_{\mathrm{COL}}) \overset{\mathrm{def}}{=} \Sigma_{\mathrm{COL}}$$
$$\mathrm{Mod}_{\mathrm{COL}}(\mathrm{SP}_{\mathrm{COL}}) \overset{\mathrm{def}}{=} \{A \in \mathrm{Alg}_{\mathrm{COL}}(\Sigma_{\mathrm{COL}}) \mid A \models_{\Sigma_{\mathrm{COL}}} \mathrm{Ax}\}$$

In the following, $\mathrm{SP}_{\mathrm{COL}} \models_{\Sigma_{\mathrm{COL}}} \varphi$ means $\mathrm{Mod}_{\mathrm{COL}}(\mathrm{SP}_{\mathrm{COL}}) \models_{\Sigma_{\mathrm{COL}}} \varphi$. According to the flexible satisfaction relation, the model class of a COL-specification $\mathrm{SP}_{\mathrm{COL}}$ describes all algebras which can be considered as correct realizations of $\mathrm{SP}_{\mathrm{COL}}$.

Example 6. The following specification extends the COL-signature of Example 1 by appropriate axioms for containers of natural numbers.[3]

spec CONTAINER =
    sorts *bool, nat, container*
    ops *true, false : bool;*
           0 : nat; succ : nat $\to$ nat; add : nat $\times$ nat $\to$ nat;
           empty : container; insert : container $\times$ nat $\to$ container;
           remove : container $\times$ nat $\to$ container;
           isin : container $\times$ nat $\to$ bool;
    constructors *true, false, 0, succ, empty, insert*
    observer *(isin, 1)*
    axioms
    $\forall x, y : nat;\ c : container$
    %% standard axioms for booleans and natural numbers, plus

- $isin(empty, x) = false$ (1)
- $isin(insert(c, x), x) = true$ (2)
- $x \neq y \Rightarrow isin(insert(c, y), x) = isin(c, x)$ (3)
- $remove(empty, x) = empty$ (4)
- $remove(insert(c, x), x) = remove(c, x)$ (5)
- $x \neq y \Rightarrow remove(insert(c, y), x) = insert(remove(c, x), y)$ (6)

end

---

[3] We use here a syntactic sugar similar to the one of CASL.

It is important to note that the declaration of constructors and observers leads to corresponding specification methods. As usual, non-constructor operations can be defined by a complete case distinction w.r.t. the given constructors. For instance, the axioms (1) - (3) define the non-constructor *isin* by a complete case analysis w.r.t. *empty* and *insert* and, similarly, *remove* is specified by a constructor complete definition according to the axioms (4) - (6).

On the other hand, also the observers give rise to a specification method whereby the observable effect of the non-observer operations can be defined by a complete case distinction w.r.t. the given observers. For instance, axiom (1) can be considered as an observer complete definition of *empty* and axioms (2) and (3) can be considered as an observer complete definition of *insert* (see [3] for a general schema of observer complete definitions). Thus the axioms (1) - (3) can be seen from both sides, from the observational or from the reachability point of view, the result is the same.

However, this is not the case for the axioms (4) - (6) that specify *remove* (which is neither a constructor nor an observer). In this case we have chosen a constructor style, but we can ask whether we couldn't use just as well an observer style with the same semantic result. Indeed it is simple to provide an observer complete definition of *remove* by the following two formulas:

- $isin(remove(c, x), x) = false$ (7)
- $x \neq y \Rightarrow isin(remove(c, x), y) = isin(c, y)$ (8)

Obviously, with a standard interpretation, the formulas (7) and (8) are quite different from the axioms (4) - (6). However, in the COL framework developed in this paper it turns out that indeed the axioms (4) - (6) could be replaced by the formulas (7) and (8) without changing the semantics of the container specification. A formal proof of this fact (using the proof systems developed in Section 4) is provided in [4].

Let us still point out that the container algebra A of Example 2 is a model of CONTAINER. Thereby it is essential that the COL-satisfaction relation interprets the equality symbol by the observational equality. Otherwise, axiom (5) would not be satisfied by A. For instance, if we interpret c by the empty container $(<>, <>)$ and x by 1, we have $remove^A((<>, <>), 1) = (<>, <>)$ and $remove^A(insert^A((<>, <>), 1), 1) = remove^A((< 1 >, <>), 1) = (<>, < 1 >)$ where the results $(<>, <>)$ and $(<>, < 1 >)$ are not the same but are observationally equal.

On the other hand, if we would use (7) and (8) for specifying *remove* then it is essential that the COL-satisfaction relation interprets variables by values in the reachable part. Otherwise, axiom (7) would not be satisfied by the container algebra A. For instance, if we would interpret c by the non reachable container $(< 1, 1 >, <>)$ and x by 1, we would obtain:
$isin^A(remove^A((< 1, 1 >, <>), 1), 1) = isin^A((< 1 >, < 1 >), 1) = true.$ $\diamond$

The definitions stated above provide the basic ingredients for defining the *constructor-based observational logic institution*. Thereby it is particularly important to use an appropriate morphism notion for COL-signatures which guarantees encapsulation of properties with respect to the COL-satisfaction relation (formally expressed by the satisfaction condition of institutions, see [9]). To ensure that the satisfaction condition holds, the crucial idea is to require that neither "new" constructors nor "new" observers are introduced for "old" sorts when composing systems via signature morphisms. This requirement is formally captured by the following definition.

Definition 14 (COL-signature morphism).
Let $\Sigma_{\text{COL}} = (\Sigma, OP_{\text{Cons}}, OP_{\text{Obs}})$ and $\Sigma'_{\text{COL}} = (\Sigma', OP'_{\text{Cons}}, OP'_{\text{Obs}})$ be two COL-signatures with $\Sigma = (S, OP)$ and $\Sigma' = (S', OP')$. A COL-signature morphism $\sigma_{\text{COL}} : \Sigma_{\text{COL}} \to \Sigma'_{\text{COL}}$ is a signature morphism $\sigma : \Sigma \to \Sigma'$ such that:
1. If $op \in OP_{\text{Cons}}$, then $\sigma(op) \in OP'_{\text{Cons}}$.
2. If $op' \in OP'_{\text{Cons}}$ with $op' : s'_1, \ldots, s'_n \to s'$ and $s' \in \sigma(S)$, then there exists $op \in OP_{\text{Cons}}$ such that $op' = \sigma(op)$.
3. If $(op, i) \in OP_{\text{Obs}}$, then $(\sigma(op), i) \in OP'_{\text{Obs}}$.
4. If $(op', i) \in OP'_{\text{Obs}}$ with $op' : s'_1, \ldots, s'_n \to s'$ and $s'_i \in \sigma(S)$, then there exists $op \in OP$ such that $(op, i) \in OP_{\text{Obs}}$ and $op' = \sigma(op)$.

As a consequence of the definition, for all $s \in S$, the following holds:
$s \in S_{\text{Cons}}$ if and only if $\sigma(s) \in S'_{\text{Cons}}$, $s \in S_{\text{Loose}}$ if and only if $\sigma(s) \in S'_{\text{Loose}}$, $s \in S_{\text{State}}$ if and only if $\sigma(s) \in S'_{\text{State}}$, $s \in S_{\text{Obs}}$ if and only if $\sigma(s) \in S'_{\text{Obs}}$.

COL-signatures together with COL-signature morphisms form a category which has pushouts. Moreover, to any COL-signature morphism $\sigma_{\text{COL}} : \Sigma_{\text{COL}} \to \Sigma'_{\text{COL}}$ is associated a reduct functor $\_\_|_{\sigma_{\text{COL}}} : \text{Alg}_{\text{COL}}(\Sigma'_{\text{COL}}) \to \text{Alg}_{\text{COL}}(\Sigma_{\text{COL}})$. One can also show that the satisfaction condition holds, i.e., for any Σ'_{COL}-algebra $A' \in \text{Alg}_{\text{COL}}(\Sigma'_{\text{COL}})$ and Σ-sentence φ: $A' \models_{\Sigma'_{\text{COL}}} \sigma(\varphi)$ if and only if $A'|_{\sigma_{\text{COL}}} \models_{\Sigma_{\text{COL}}} \varphi$.

Thus we obtain the *constructor-based observational logic institution* in a straightforward way. This institution provides also a suitable framework for instantiating the institution-independent specification-building operators introduced in [19] and hence for defining structured COL-specifications (which will not be detailed here).

3   Logical Consequences of Specifications: The Black Box View

So far we have emphasized the fact that the model class $\text{Mod}_{\text{COL}}(\text{SP}_{\text{COL}})$ of a COL-specification SP_{COL} reflects all its correct realizations. In the following we will refer to $\text{Mod}_{\text{COL}}(\text{SP}_{\text{COL}})$ as the *glass box semantics* of the specification SP_{COL}. Glass box semantics is appropriate from an implementor's point of view.

Of equal importance are the logical consequences of a given specification. In this section we focus on the properties φ that can be inferred from a given specification SP_{COL}. This means that we are interested in statements of the form $\text{SP}_{\text{COL}} \models_{\Sigma_{\text{COL}}} \varphi$.

For this purpose it is convenient to *abstract* the models of a specification into "idealized" models, such that the consequences of the actual models of a COL-specification are exactly the consequences of its idealized models, in *standard* first-order logic. Hence to any specification SP_{COL} we will associate the class of its "idealized" models (which lie in the standard algebraic institution), and this class will be called the *black box semantics* of the specification. Black box semantics is appropriate from a client's point of view.

Let Σ_{COL} be a COL-signature and A be a Σ_{COL}-algebra. As pointed out in the previous section, $\langle \mathcal{R}_{\Sigma_{COL}}(A) \rangle_\Sigma$ represents the only elements a user can compute (over the loose carrier sets) by invoking operations. Hence, in a first step, we can *restrict* to these elements. Since the observational Σ_{COL}-equality $\approx_{\Sigma_{COL},A}$ on A is a Σ-congruence on $\langle \mathcal{R}_{\Sigma_{COL}}(A) \rangle_\Sigma$, we can then construct the quotient $\langle \mathcal{R}_{\Sigma_{COL}}(A) \rangle_\Sigma / \approx_{\Sigma_{COL},A}$ which *identifies* all elements of $\langle \mathcal{R}_{\Sigma_{COL}}(A) \rangle_\Sigma$ which are indistinguishable "from the outside". $\langle \mathcal{R}_{\Sigma_{COL}}(A) \rangle_\Sigma / \approx_{\Sigma_{COL},A}$ can be considered as the *black box view* of A and represents the "observable behavior" of A. Note that $\langle \mathcal{R}_{\Sigma_{COL}}(A) \rangle_\Sigma / \approx_{\Sigma_{COL},A}$ is *fully abstract* since the observational equality (w.r.t. Σ_{COL}) on $\langle \mathcal{R}_{\Sigma_{COL}}(A) \rangle_\Sigma / \approx_{\Sigma_{COL},A}$ coincides with the set-theoretic equality. Moreover, since A satisfies by assumption the reachability constraint induced by Σ_{COL}, any element in $\langle \mathcal{R}_{\Sigma_{COL}}(A) \rangle_\Sigma$ is observationally equal to a reachable element (w.r.t. Σ_{COL}), and therefore $\langle \mathcal{R}_{\Sigma_{COL}}(A) \rangle_\Sigma / \approx_{\Sigma_{COL},A}$ is also a *reachable algebra*. By considering the Σ_{COL}-algebra $\langle \mathcal{R}_{\Sigma_{COL}}(A) \rangle_\Sigma / \approx_{\Sigma_{COL},A}$ just as a Σ-algebra, we obtain (for any signature Σ_{COL}) a functor from the category $Alg_{COL}(\Sigma_{COL})$ of Σ_{COL}-algebras into the category $Alg(\Sigma)$ of (standard) Σ-algebras.

Theorem 1 (Behavior functor). *For any COL-signature $\Sigma_{COL} = (\Sigma, OP_{Cons}, OP_{Obs})$, the following defines a full and faithful functor*
$\mathcal{RI}_{\Sigma_{COL}} : Alg_{COL}(\Sigma_{COL}) \to Alg(\Sigma)$. [4]

1. *For each $A \in Alg_{COL}(\Sigma_{COL})$, $\mathcal{RI}_{\Sigma_{COL}}(A) \stackrel{def}{=} \langle \mathcal{R}_{\Sigma_{COL}}(A) \rangle_\Sigma / \approx_{\Sigma_{COL},A}$ and is called the observational behavior of A.*
2. *For each COL-morphism $h : A \to B$,*
   $\mathcal{RI}_{\Sigma_{COL}}(h) : \langle \mathcal{R}_{\Sigma_{COL}}(A) \rangle_\Sigma / \approx_{\Sigma_{COL},A} \to \langle \mathcal{R}_{\Sigma_{COL}}(B) \rangle_\Sigma / \approx_{\Sigma_{COL},B}$ *is defined by $\mathcal{RI}_{\Sigma_{COL}}(h)([a]) = [b]$ if $a\,h\,b$.*

Definition 15 (Black box semantics). *Let SP_{COL} be a COL-specification with signature $Sig_{COL}(SP_{COL}) = \Sigma_{COL}$. Its black box semantics is defined by*
$[\![SP_{COL}]\!] \stackrel{def}{=} \mathcal{RI}_{\Sigma_{COL}}(Mod_{COL}(SP_{COL}))$.

Theorem 2 (Behavioral consequences). *Let $\Sigma_{COL} = (\Sigma, OP_{Cons}, OP_{Obs})$ be a COL-signature, let φ be a Σ-formula, let A be a Σ_{COL}-algebra, and let SP_{COL} be a COL-specification with signature Σ_{COL}.*
1. *$A \models_{\Sigma_{COL}} \varphi$ if and only if $\mathcal{RI}_{\Sigma_{COL}}(A) \models \varphi$.*
2. *$SP_{COL} \models_{\Sigma_{COL}} \varphi$ if and only if $[\![SP_{COL}]\!] \models \varphi$.*

---

[4] The notation $\mathcal{RI}_{\Sigma_{COL}}$ is chosen to emphasize the intuitive relationship to the "restrict-identify" steps used in various algebraic implementation concepts.

This theorem shows the adequacy of the black box semantics. The proof of the theorem is straightforward by induction on the structure of the formulas. The next theorem provides a characterization of the black box semantics of a COL-specification.

Theorem 3 (Black box semantics relies on reachable fully abstract models). *Let* $\text{SP}_{\text{COL}} = \langle \Sigma_{\text{COL}}, \text{Ax} \rangle$ *be a basic COL-specification with signature* $\Sigma_{\text{COL}} = (\Sigma, OP_{\text{Cons}}, OP_{\text{Obs}})$.
$[\![\text{SP}_{\text{COL}}]\!] = \{\Sigma - \text{algebra } A \mid A \models \text{Ax and } A \text{ is both reachable and fully abstract}$
w.r.t. $\Sigma_{\text{COL}}\}$.

For a proof see [4]. For instance, the black box semantics of the container specification given in Example 6 is (up to isomorphism) the algebra of finite sets of natural numbers.

4   Proof Systems
for Proving Consequences of Specifications

In the previous section we have shown how to relate the behavioral consequences of a COL-specification to the consequences in standard first-order logic of the black box semantics of the given specification. The next step is to find adequate axiomatizations of the black box semantics in order to be able to define sound and complete proof systems. According to Theorems 2 and 3, this amounts to find an axiomatic characterization of reachability and full abstractness. The next definitions provide the required axiomatizations which, in general, can only be stated by using *infinitary* first-order formulas.

Definition 16 (Reachability axiom). *Let* Σ_{COL} *be a COL-signature with underlying signature* Σ. *The* reachability axiom *associated to* Σ_{COL} *is the sentence* $\text{REACH}(\Sigma_{\text{COL}})$ *defined by:*
$$\text{REACH}(\Sigma_{\text{COL}}) \stackrel{\text{def}}{=} \bigwedge_{s \in S_{\text{Cons}}} \text{REACH}(\Sigma_{\text{COL}})_s$$
where for each constrained sort $s \in S_{\text{Cons}}$, $\text{REACH}(\Sigma_{\text{COL}})_s$ *is defined by:*
$$\text{REACH}(\Sigma_{\text{COL}})_s \stackrel{\text{def}}{=} \forall x{:}s. \bigvee_{t \in \mathcal{T}(\Sigma_{\text{COL}})_s} \exists \text{Var}(t).\ x = t\ .^{[5]}$$

Definition 17 (Fully abstract axiom). *Let* Σ_{COL} *be a COL-signature with underlying signature* Σ. *The* fully abstract axiom *associated to* Σ_{COL} *is the sentence* $\text{FA}(\Sigma_{\text{COL}})$ *defined by:*
$$\text{FA}(\Sigma_{\text{COL}}) \stackrel{\text{def}}{=} \bigwedge_{s \in S_{\text{State}}} \text{FA}(\Sigma_{\text{COL}})_s$$

---

[5] $\exists \text{Var}(t)$ is an abbreviation for $\exists x_1{:}s_1. \ldots . \exists x_n{:}s_n$ where $x_1, \ldots, x_n$ are the variables (of sort $s_1, \ldots, s_n$) of the constructor term t.

where for each state sort $s \in S_{\text{State}}$, $\mathrm{FA}(\Sigma_{\text{COL}})_s$ is defined by:

$$\mathrm{FA}(\Sigma_{\text{COL}})_s \stackrel{\text{def}}{=} \forall x, y{:}s. \left(\bigwedge_{s' \in S_{\text{Obs}}, c \in \mathcal{C}(\Sigma_{\text{COL}})_{s \to s'}} \forall \mathrm{Var}(c).\ c[x] = c[y] \right) \Rightarrow x = y\ .^{6}$$

Note that in special cases the above axioms may reduce to finitary ones. For instance, in the container example, the fully abstract axioms reads:
$\forall c1, c2{:}container.\ (\forall x{:}nat.\ isin(c1, x) = isin(c2, x)) \Rightarrow c1 = c2\ .$

Proposition 1. *Let Σ_{COL} be a COL-signature with underlying signature Σ. A Σ-algebra A is both reachable and fully abstract w.r.t. Σ_{COL} if and only if $A \models \mathrm{REACH}(\Sigma_{\text{COL}}) \wedge \mathrm{FA}(\Sigma_{\text{COL}})$.*

Now let Π_{IFOLEq} be a sound and complete proof system for infinitary first-order logic with equality (see [13]). We obtain a sound and complete proof system Π_{COL} for COL by adding to Π_{IFOLEq}, as an extra axiom, $\mathrm{REACH}(\Sigma_{\text{COL}}) \wedge \mathrm{FA}(\Sigma_{\text{COL}})$ (see [4] for details). The difficulty with the proof system Π_{COL} is that, in general, it uses infinitary formulas (and also infinitary proof rules of Π_{IFOLEq}). An alternative is to restrict to finitary formulas and to use only a particular set of infinitary proof rules (see the discussion in [2, Chapter 11]). The idea now is, instead of "capturing" reachability (full abstractness, respectively) by the infinitary axiom $\mathrm{REACH}(\Sigma_{\text{COL}})$ ($\mathrm{FA}(\Sigma_{\text{COL}})$, respectively), to "capture" it by specialized infinitary proof rules called infinitary induction (infinitary coinduction, respectively). These infinitary rules are necessary to ensure completeness.

Definition 18 (Infinitary induction). *Let Σ_{COL} be a COL-signature with underlying signature Σ. The infinitary induction rule $\mathrm{iI}(\Sigma_{\text{COL}})$ associated to Σ_{COL} is defined by:*
$\mathrm{iI}(\Sigma_{\text{COL}}) \stackrel{\text{def}}{=} \{\mathrm{iI}(\Sigma_{\text{COL}})_s \mid s \in S_{\text{Cons}}\}$
where for each constrained sort $s \in S_{\text{Cons}}$, $\mathrm{iI}(\Sigma_{\text{COL}})_s$ is defined by:

$$\mathrm{iI}(\Sigma_{\text{COL}})_s \qquad \frac{\varphi[t/x] \text{ for all constructor terms } t \in \mathcal{T}(\Sigma_{\text{COL}})_s}{\forall x{:}s.\ \varphi}$$

where φ denotes an arbitrary Σ-formula (with at least a free variable x of sort s).

Definition 19 (Infinitary coinduction). *Let Σ_{COL} be a COL-signature with underlying signature Σ. The infinitary coinduction rule $\mathrm{iCI}(\Sigma_{\text{COL}})$ associated to Σ_{COL} is defined by:*
$\mathrm{iCI}(\Sigma_{\text{COL}}) \stackrel{\text{def}}{=} \{\mathrm{iCI}(\Sigma_{\text{COL}})_s \mid s \in S_{\text{State}}\}$
where for each state sort $s \in S_{\text{State}}$, $\mathrm{iCI}(\Sigma_{\text{COL}})_s$ is defined by:

$$\mathrm{iCI}(\Sigma_{\text{COL}})_s \qquad \frac{\varphi \Rightarrow \forall \mathrm{Var}(c).\ c[x] = c[y] \quad \begin{array}{l} \textit{for all observable sorts } s' \in S_{\text{Obs}} \\ \textit{and all contexts } c \in \mathcal{C}(\Sigma_{\text{COL}})_{s \to s'}\ . \end{array}}{\varphi \Rightarrow x = y}$$

where φ denotes an arbitrary Σ-formula.

---

[6] $\forall \mathrm{Var}(c)$ is an abbreviation for $\forall x_1{:}s_1.\ldots.\forall x_n{:}s_n$ where $x_1, \ldots, x_n$ are the variables (of sort $s_1, \ldots, s_n$) of the context c, apart from its context variable z_s.

Now let Π_{FOLEq} be a sound and complete proof system for finitary first-order logic with equality. We obtain a sound and complete (semi-formal) proof system $\Pi^\star_{\mathrm{COL}}$ for COL by adding to the finitary proof system Π_{FOLEq} the extra infinitary proof rules $\mathrm{iI}(\Sigma_{\mathrm{COL}})$ and $\mathrm{iCI}(\Sigma_{\mathrm{COL}})$.

Theorem 4. *For any COL-signature Σ_{COL}, let*

$$\Pi^\star_{\mathrm{COL}} \stackrel{\mathrm{def}}{=} \Pi_{\mathrm{FOLEq}} \cup \mathrm{iI}(\Sigma_{\mathrm{COL}}) \cup \mathrm{iCI}(\Sigma_{\mathrm{COL}}).$$

Then for any basic COL-specification $\mathrm{SP}_{\mathrm{COL}} = \langle \Sigma_{\mathrm{COL}}, \mathrm{Ax} \rangle$ and any Σ-formula φ, we have:
$\mathrm{SP}_{\mathrm{COL}} \models_{\Sigma_{\mathrm{COL}}} \varphi$ *if and only if* $\mathrm{Ax} \vdash_{\Pi^\star_{\mathrm{COL}}} \varphi$.

In practice, for proving the infinitely many hypotheses $\varphi[t/x]$ of the rule $\mathrm{iI}(\Sigma_{\mathrm{COL}})_s$, one would use an induction scheme like structural induction with respect to the constructor terms $\mathcal{T}(\Sigma_{\mathrm{COL}})_s$. Similarly, to prove the infinitely many hypotheses $\varphi \Rightarrow \forall \mathrm{Var}(c).\ c[x] = c[y]$ of the rule $\mathrm{iCI}(\Sigma_{\mathrm{COL}})_s$, one would use a coinduction scheme according to the coinductive definition of the contexts $\mathcal{C}(\Sigma_{\mathrm{COL}})_{s \to s'}$ provided in Definition 5.

5   Conclusion

We have seen that the integration of the observational and the constructor-based logics presented in [11] and [5] leads to a powerful formalism which integrates observability and reachability concepts in a common institution. An important aspect, which has not been worked out here, concerns structuring mechanisms for specifications and structured proof systems which can be defined on top of the given institution by applying the institution-independent specification-building operators of [19] and the proof rules for structured specifications of [7]. Future research concerns the investigation of refinement notions for COL-specifications and corresponding proof methods.

References

[1] E. Astesiano, M. Bidoit, H. Kirchner, B. Krieg-Brückner, P.D. Mosses, D. Sannella, and A. Tarlecki. CASL: The Common Algebraic Specification Language. *Theoretical Computer Science*, 2002. To appear.

[2] E. Astesiano, H.-J. Kreowski, and B. Krieg-Brückner, editors. *Algebraic Foundations of Systems Specification*. Springer, 1999.

[3] M. Bidoit and R. Hennicker. Observer complete definitions are behaviourally coherent. In *Proc. OBJ/CafeOBJ/Maude Workshop at FM'99*, pages 83–94. THETA, 1999. http://www.lsv.ens-cachan.fr/Publis/PAPERS/CafeOBJ.ps.

[4] M. Bidoit and R. Hennicker. On the integration of observability and reachability concepts. Research Report LSV-02-2, 2002. Long version of this paper. http://www.lsv.ens-cachan.fr/Publis/RAPPORTS_LSV/rr-lsv-2002-2.rr.ps.

[5] M. Bidoit, R. Hennicker, and A. Kurz. On the duality between observability and reachability. In *Proc. FOSSACS'01, LNCS 2030*, pages 72–87. Springer, 2001. Long version: http://www.lsv.ens-cachan.fr/Publis/RAPPORTS_LSV/rr-lsv-2001-7.rr.ps.

[6] M. Bidoit, R. Hennicker, and M. Wirsing. Behavioural and abstractor specifications. *Science of Computer Programming*, 25:149–186, 1995.

[7] T. Borzyszkowski. Completeness of a logical system for structured specifications. In *Recent Trends in Algebraic Development Techniques, LNCS 1376*, pages 107–121. Springer, 1998.

[8] R. Diaconescu and K. Futatsugi. *CafeOBJ Report: The Language, Proof Techniques, and Methodologies for Object-Oriented Algebraic Specification*. AMAST Series in Computing 6. World Scientific, 1998.

[9] J. Goguen and R. Burstall. Institutions: abstract model theory for specification and programming. *Journal of the ACM*, 39 (1):95–146, 1992.

[10] J. Goguen and G. Roşu. Hiding more of hidden algebra. In *Proc. FM'99, LNCS 1709*, pages 1704–1719. Springer, 1999.

[11] R. Hennicker and M. Bidoit. Observational logic. In *Proc. AMAST'98, LNCS 1548*, pages 263–277. Springer, 1999.

[12] M. Hofmann and D. Sannella. On behavioural abstraction and behavioural satisfaction in higher-order logic. *Theoretical Computer Science*, 167:3–45, 1996.

[13] H. J. Keisler. *Model Theory for Infinitary Logic*. North-Holland, 1971.

[14] J. Loeckx, H.-D. Ehrich, and M. Wolf. *Specification of Abstract Data Types*. Wiley and Teubner, 1996.

[15] M.P. Nivela and F. Orejas. Initial behaviour semantics for algebraic specifications. In *Recent Trends in Data Type Specification, LNCS 332*, pages 184–207. Springer, 1988.

[16] P. Padawitz. Swinging data types: syntax, semantics, and theory. In *Recent Trends in Data Type Specification, LNCS 1130*, pages 409–435. Springer, 1996.

[17] Horst Reichel. *Initial computability, algebraic specifications, and partial algebras*. Oxford, Clarendon Press, 1987.

[18] D.T. Sannella and A. Tarlecki. On observational equivalence and algebraic specification. *Journal of Computer and System Sciences*, 34:150–178, 1987.

[19] D.T. Sannella and A. Tarlecki. Specifications in an arbitrary institution. *Information and Computation*, 76:165–210, 1988.

[20] M. Wirsing and M. Broy. A modular framework for specification and information. In *Proc. TAPSOFT'89, LNCS 351*, pages 42–73. Springer, 1989.

Proving Correctness
of Timed Concurrent Constraint Programs

Frank S. de Boer[1], Maurizio Gabbrielli[2], and Maria Chiara Meo[3]

[1] Universiteit Utrecht,
Department of Computer Science,
Padualaan 14, De Uithof, 3584 CH, Utrecht, The Netherlands
frankb@cs.ruu.nl
[2] Università di Bologna
Dipartimento di Scienze dell'Informazione
Mura A. Zamboni 7, 40127 Bologna, Italy
gabbri@dimi.uniud.it
[3] Università di Chieti
Dipartimento di Scienze
Viale Pindaro 42, 65127 Pescara, Italy
meo@univaq.it

Abstract. A temporal logic is presented for reasoning about the correctness of timed concurrent constraint programs. The logic is based on modalities which allow one to specify what a process produces as a reaction to what its environment inputs. These modalities provide an assumption/commitment style of specification which allows a sound and complete compositional axiomatization of the reactive behavior of timed concurrent constraint programs.

Keywords: Concurrency, constraints, real-time programming, temporal logic.

1 Introduction

Many "real-life" computer applications maintain some ongoing interaction with external physical processes and involve time-critical aspects. Characteristic of such applications, usually called real-time embedded systems, is the specification of timing constraints such as, for example, that an input is required within a bounded period of time. Typical examples of such systems are process controllers and signal processing systems.

In [5] *tccp*, a timed extension of the pure formalism of concurrent constraint programming([24]), is introduced. This extension is based on the hypothesis of *bounded asynchrony* (as introduced in [26]): Computation takes a bounded period of time rather than being instantaneous as in the concurrent synchronous languages ESTEREL [3], LUSTRE [15], SIGNAL [19] and Statecharts [16]. Time itself is measured by a discrete global clock, i.e, the internal clock of the *tccp* process. In [5] we also introduced *timed reactive sequences* which describe at each moment

M. Nielsen and U. Engberg (Eds.): Fossacs 2002, LNCS 2303, pp. 37–51, 2002.

in time the reaction of a tccp process to the input of the external environment. Formally, such a reaction is a pair of constraints $\langle c, d \rangle$, where c is the input given by the environment and d is the constraint produced by the process in response to the input c (such a response includes always the input because of the monotonicity of ccp computations).

In this paper we introduce a temporal logic for describing and reasoning about timed reactive sequences. The basic assertions of the temporal logic describe the reactions of such a sequence in terms of *modalities* which express either what a process *assumes* about the inputs of the environment and what a process *commits* to, i.e., has itself produced at one time-instant. These modalities thus provide a kind of assumption/commitment style of specification of the reactive behavior of a process. The main result of this paper is a sound and complete compositional proof system for reasoning about the correctness of *tccp* programs as specified by formulas in this temporal logic.

The remainder of this paper is organized as follows. In the next section we introduce the language *tccp* and its operational semantics. In Section 3 we introduce the temporal logic and the compositional proof system. in Section 4 we briefly discuss soundness and completeness of the proof system. Section 5 concludes by discussing related work and indicating future research.

2   The Programming Language

In this section we first define the *tccp* language and then we define formally its operational semantics by using a transition system.

Since the starting point is ccp, we introduce first some basic notions related to this programming paradigm. We refer to [25,27] for more details. The ccp languages are defined parametrically wrt to a given *constraint system*. The notion of constraint system has been formalized in [25] following Scott's treatment of information systems. Here we only consider the resulting structure.

Definition 1. *A constraint system is a complete algebraic lattice* $\langle \mathcal{C}, \leq, \sqcup, true, false \rangle$ *where* $\sqcup$ *is the lub operation, and true, false are the least and the greatest elements of* $\mathcal{C}$, *respectively.*

Following the standard terminology and notation, instead of $\leq$ we will refer to its inverse relation, denoted by $\vdash$ and called *entailment*. Formally, $\forall c, d \in \mathcal{C}.$ $c \vdash d \Leftrightarrow d \leq c$. In order to treat the hiding operator of the language a general notion of existential quantifier is introduced which is formalized in terms of cylindric algebras [17]. Moreover, in order to model parameter passing, *diagonal elements* [17] are added to the primitive constraints. This leads to the concept of a *cylindric constraint system*. In the following, we assume given a (denumerable) set of variables *Var* with typical elements $x, y, z, \dots$.

Definition 2. *Let* $\langle \mathcal{C}, \leq, \sqcup, true, false \rangle$ *be a constraint system. Assume that for each* $x \in Var$ *a function* $\exists_x : \mathcal{C} \to \mathcal{C}$ *is defined such that for any* $c, d \in \mathcal{C}$:

(i) $c \vdash \exists_x(c)$,   (ii) *if* $c \vdash d$ *then* $\exists_x(c) \vdash \exists_x(d)$,
(iii) $\exists_x(c \sqcup \exists_x(d)) = \exists_x(c) \sqcup \exists_x(d)$, (iv) $\exists_x(\exists_y(c)) = \exists_y(\exists_x(c))$.

Moreover assume that for x, y ranging in Var, $\mathcal{C}$ contains the constraints d_{xy} (so called diagonal elements) which satisfy the following axioms:

(v) *$true \vdash d_{xx}$,*   (vi) *if $z \neq x, y$ then $d_{xy} = \exists_z (d_{xz} \sqcup d_{zy})$,*
(vii) *if $x \neq y$ then $d_{xy} \sqcup \exists_x (c \sqcup d_{xy}) \vdash c$.*

Then $\mathbf{C} = \langle \mathcal{C}, \leq, \sqcup, true, false, Var, \exists_x, d_{xy} \rangle$ is a cylindric constraint system.

Note that if $\mathbf{C}$ models the equality theory, then the elements d_{xy} can be thought of as the formulas $x = y$. In the sequel we will identify a system $\mathbf{C}$ with its underlying set of constraints $\mathcal{C}$ and we will denote $\exists_x(c)$ by $\exists_x c$ with the convention that, in case of ambiguity, the scope of $\exists_x$ is limited to the first constraint sub-expression (so, for instance, $\exists_x c \sqcup d$ stands for $\exists_x(c) \sqcup d$).

The basic idea underlying ccp is that computation progresses via monotonic accumulation of information in a global store. Information is produced by the concurrent and asynchronous activity of several agents which can add (*tell*) a constraint to the store. Dually, agents can also check (*ask*) whether a constraint is entailed by the store, thus allowing synchronization among different agents. Parallel composition in ccp is modeled by the interleaving of the basic actions of its components.

When querying the store for some information which is not present (yet) a ccp agent will simply suspend until the required information has arrived. In timed applications however often one cannot wait indefinitely for an event. Consider for example the case of a bank teller machine. Once a card is accepted and its identification number has been checked, the machine asks the authorization of the bank to release the requested money. If the authorization does not arrive within a reasonable amount of time, then the card should be given back to the customer. A timed language should then allow us to specify that, in case a given time bound is exceeded (i.e. a *time-out* occurs), the wait is interrupted and an alternative action is taken. Moreover in some cases it is also necessary to abort an active process A and to start a process B when a specific event occurs (this is usually called *preemption* of A). For example, according to a typical pattern, A is the process controlling the normal activity of some physical device, the event indicates some abnormal situation and B is the exception handler.

In order to be able to specify these timing constraints in ccp we introduce a discrete global clock and assume that *ask* and *tell* actions take one time-unit. Computation evolves in steps of one time-unit, so called clock-cycles. We consider action prefixing as the syntactic marker which distinguishes a time instant from the next one. Furthermore we make the assumption that parallel processes are executed on different processors, which implies that at each moment every enabled agent of the system is activated. This assumption gives rise to what is called *maximal parallelism*. The time in between two successive moments of the global clock intuitively corresponds to the response time of the underlying constraint system. Thus essentially in our model all parallel agents are synchronized by the response time of the underlying constraint system.

Furthermore, on the basis of the above assumptions we introduce a timing construct of the form **now** c **then** A **else** B which can be interpreted as follows:

If the constraint c is entailed by the store at the current time t then the above agent behaves as A at time t, otherwise it behaves as B at time t. As shown in [5,26] this basic construct allows one to derive such timing mechanisms as time-out and preemption. Thus we end up with the following syntax of timed concurrent constraint programming.

Definition 3 (*tccp* **Language [5]**). *Assuming a given cylindric constraint system* $\mathbf{C}$ *the syntax of* agents *is given by the following grammar:*

$$A ::= \mathbf{tell}(c) \mid \textstyle\sum_{i=1}^{n} \mathbf{ask}(c_i) \rightarrow A_i \mid \mathbf{now}\ c\ \mathbf{then}\ A\ \mathbf{else}\ B \mid A \parallel B \mid \exists x A \mid p(x)$$

where the c, c_i *are supposed to be* finite *constraints (i.e. algebraic elements) in* $\mathcal{C}$. *A* tccp *process* P *is then an object of the form* $D.A$, *where* D *is a set of procedure declarations of the form* $p(x) :: A$ *and* A *is an agent.*

Action prefixing is denoted by $\rightarrow$, non-determinism is introduced via the guarded choice construct $\sum_{i=1}^{n} \mathbf{ask}(c_i) \rightarrow A_i$, parallel composition is denoted by $\parallel$, and a notion of locality is introduced by the agent $\exists x A$ which behaves like A with x considered local to A, thus hiding the information on x provided by the external environment. In the next subsection we describe formally the operational semantics of *tccp*. In order to simplify the notation, in the following we will omit the $\sum_{i=1}^{n}$ whenever $n = 1$ and we will use $tell(c) \rightarrow A$ as a shorthand for $tell(c) \parallel (\mathbf{ask}(true) \rightarrow A)$. In the following we also assume guarded recursion, that is we assume that each procedure call is in the scope of an **ask** construct. This assumption, which does not limit the expressive power of the language, is needed to ensure a proper definition of the operational semantics.

2.1   Operational Semantics

The operational model of *tccp* can be formally described by a transition system $T = (Conf, \longrightarrow)$ where we assume that each transition step takes exactly one time-unit. Configurations (in) $Conf$ are pairs consisting of a process and a constraint in $\mathcal{C}$ representing the common *store*. The transition relation $\longrightarrow \subseteq Conf \times Conf$ is the least relation satisfying the rules **R1-R11** in Table 1 and characterizes the (temporal) evolution of the system. So, $\langle A, c \rangle \longrightarrow \langle B, d \rangle$ means that if at time t we have the process A and the store c then at time $t + 1$ we have the process B and the store d. As usual, $\langle A, c \rangle \not\longrightarrow$ means that there exist no transitions for the configuration $\langle A, c \rangle$.

Let us now briefly discuss the rules in Table 1. In order to represent successful termination we introduce the auxiliary agent **stop**: it cannot make any transition. Rule **R1** shows that we are considering here the so called "eventual" tell: The agent **tell**(c) adds c to the store d without checking for consistency of $c \sqcup d$ and then stops. Note that the updated store $c \sqcup d$ will be visible only starting from the next time instant since each transition step involves exactly one time-unit. According to rule **R2** the guarded choice operator gives rise to global non-determinism: The external environment can affect the choice since $\mathbf{ask}(c_j)$ is enabled at time t (and A_j is started at time $t + 1$) iff the store d

Table 1. The transition system for *tccp*.

R1	$\langle \mathbf{tell}(c), d \rangle \longrightarrow \langle stop, c \sqcup d \rangle$
R2	$\langle \sum_{i=1}^{n} \mathbf{ask}(c_i) \to A_i, d \rangle \longrightarrow \langle A_j, d \rangle \qquad j \in [1, n] \; and \; d \vdash c_j$
R3	$\dfrac{\langle A, d \rangle \longrightarrow \langle A', d' \rangle}{\langle \mathbf{now}\ c\ \mathbf{then}\ A\ \mathbf{else}\ B, d \rangle \longrightarrow \langle A', d' \rangle} \quad d \vdash c$
R4	$\dfrac{\langle A, d \rangle \nrightarrow}{\langle \mathbf{now}\ c\ \mathbf{then}\ A\ \mathbf{else}\ B, d \rangle \longrightarrow \langle A, d \rangle} \quad d \vdash c$
R5	$\dfrac{\langle B, d \rangle \longrightarrow \langle B', d' \rangle}{\langle \mathbf{now}\ c\ \mathbf{then}\ A\ \mathbf{else}\ B, d \rangle \longrightarrow \langle B', d' \rangle} \quad d \nvdash c$
R6	$\dfrac{\langle B, d \rangle \nrightarrow}{\langle \mathbf{now}\ c\ \mathbf{then}\ A\ \mathbf{else}\ B, d \rangle \longrightarrow \langle B, d \rangle} \quad d \nvdash c$
R7	$\dfrac{\langle A, c \rangle \longrightarrow \langle A', c' \rangle \quad \langle B, c \rangle \longrightarrow \langle B', d' \rangle}{\langle A \parallel B, c \rangle \longrightarrow \langle A' \parallel B', c' \sqcup d' \rangle}$
R8	$\dfrac{\langle A, c \rangle \longrightarrow \langle A', c' \rangle \quad \langle B, c \rangle \nrightarrow}{\begin{array}{c} \langle A \parallel B, c \rangle \longrightarrow \langle A' \parallel B, c' \rangle \\ \langle B \parallel A, c \rangle \longrightarrow \langle B \parallel A', c' \rangle \end{array}}$
R9	$\dfrac{\langle A, d \sqcup \exists_x c \rangle \longrightarrow \langle B, d' \rangle}{\langle \exists^d x A, c \rangle \longrightarrow \langle \exists^{d'} x B, c \sqcup \exists_x d' \rangle}$
R10	$\dfrac{\langle A, c \rangle \longrightarrow \langle B, d \rangle}{\langle p(x), c \rangle \longrightarrow \langle B, d \rangle} \qquad p(x) : -A \in D$

entails c_j, and d can be modified by other agents. The rules **R3**-**R6** show that the agent **now** c **then** A **else** B behaves as A or B depending on the fact that c is or is not entailed by the store. Differently from the case of the ask, here the evaluation of the guard is instantaneous: If $\langle A, d \rangle$ $(\langle B, d \rangle)$ can make a transition at time t and c is (is not) entailed by the store d, then the agent **now** c **then** A **else** B can make the same transition at time t[1]. Moreover, observe that in any case the control is passed either to A (if c is entailed by the current store d) or to B (in case d does not entail c). Rules **R7** and **R8** model the parallel composition operator in terms of *maximal parallelism*: The agent $A \parallel B$ executes in one time-unit all the initial enabled actions of A and B. Thus, for example, the agent $A : (\mathbf{ask}(c) \to stop) \parallel (\mathbf{tell}(c) \to stop)$ evaluated in the store c will (successfully) terminate in one time-unit, while the same agent in the empty

---

[1] As discussed in [5], the evaluation of the guard needs to be instantaneous to be able to express in the *tccp* language such a construct as a time-out.

store will take two time-units to terminate. The agent $\exists x A$ behaves like A, with x considered *local* to A, i.e. the information on x provided by the external environment is hidden to A and, conversely, the information on x produced locally by A is hidden to the external world. To describe locality in rule **R9** the syntax has been extended by an agent $\exists^d x A$ where d is a local store of A containing information on x which is hidden in the external store. Initially the local store is empty, i.e. $\exists x A = \exists^{true} x A$.

Rule **R10** treats the case of a procedure call when the actual parameter equals the formal parameter. We do not need more rules since, for the sake of simplicity, here and in the following we assume that the set D of procedure declarations is closed wrt parameter names: That is, for every procedure call $p(y)$ appearing in a process $D.A$ we assume that if the original declaration for p in D is $p(x):- A$ then D contains also the declaration $p(y):- \exists^{d_{xy}} x A^2$.

Using the transition system described by (the rules in) Table 1 we can now define our notion of observables which associates with an agent a set of timed reactive sequences of the form $\langle c_1, d_1 \rangle \cdots \langle c_n, d_n \rangle \langle d, d \rangle$ where a pair of constraints $\langle c_i, d_i \rangle$ represents a reaction of the given agent at time i: Intuitively, the agent transforms the global store from c_i to d_i or, in other words, c_i is the assumption on the external environment while d_i is the contribution of the agent itself (which includes always the assumption). The last pair denotes a "stuttering step" in which no further information can be produced by the agent, thus indicating that a "resting point" has been reached.

Since the basic actions of *tccp* are monotonic and we can also model a new input of the external environment by a corresponding tell operation, it is natural to assume that reactive sequences are monotonically increasing. So in the following we will assume that each timed reactive sequence $\langle c_1, d_1 \rangle \cdots \langle c_{n-1}, d_{n-1} \rangle \langle c_n, c_n \rangle$ satisfies the following condition: $d_i \vdash c_i$ and $c_j \vdash d_{j-1}$, for any $i \in [1, n-1]$ and $j \in [2, n]$. Since the constraints arising from the reactions are finite, we also assume that a reactive sequence contains only finite constraints[3].

The set of all reactive sequences is denoted by $\mathcal{S}$ and its typical elements by $s, s_1 \ldots$, while sets of reactive sequences are denoted by $S, S_1 \ldots$ and ε indicates the empty reactive sequence. Furthermore, $\cdot$ denotes the operator which concatenates sequences. Operationally the reactive sequences of an agent are generated as follows.

Definition 4. *We define inductively the semantics* $R \in Agent \to \mathcal{P}(\mathcal{S})$ *by*

$$R(A) = \{\langle c, d \rangle \cdot w \in \mathcal{S} \mid \langle A, c \rangle \to \langle B, d \rangle \text{ and } w \in R(B)\}$$
$$\cup$$
$$\{\langle c, c \rangle \cdot w \in \mathcal{S} \mid \langle A, c \rangle \not\to \text{ and } w \in R(A) \cup \{\varepsilon\}\}.$$

---

[2] Here the (original) formal parameter is identified as a local alias of the actual parameter. Alternatively, we could have introduced a new rule treating explicitly this case, as it was in the original ccp papers.

[3] Note that here we implicitly assume that if c is a finite element then also $\exists_x c$ is finite.

Note that $R(A)$ is defined as the union of the set of all reactive sequences which start with a reaction of A and the set of all reactive sequences which start with a stuttering step of A. In fact, when an agent is blocked, i.e., it cannot react to the input of the environment, a stuttering step is generated. After such a stuttering step the computation can either continue with the further evaluation of A (possibly generating more stuttering steps) or it can terminate, as a "resting point" has been reached. These two case are reflected in the second part of the definition of $R(A)$ by the two conditions $w \in R(A)$ and $w \in \{\varepsilon\}$, respectively. Note also that, since the stop agent used in the transition system cannot make any move, an arbitrary (finite) sequence of stuttering steps is always appended to each reactive sequence.

Formally R is defined as the least fixed-point of the corresponding operator $\Phi \in (Agent \rightarrow \mathcal{P}(\mathcal{S})) \rightarrow Agent \rightarrow \mathcal{P}(\mathcal{S})$ defined by

$$\Phi(I)(A) = \{\langle c, d \rangle \cdot w \in \mathcal{S} \mid \langle A, c \rangle \rightarrow \langle B, d \rangle \text{ and } w \in I(B)\}$$
$$\cup$$
$$\{\langle c, c \rangle \cdot w \in \mathcal{S} \mid \langle A, c \rangle \not\rightarrow \text{ and } w \in I(A) \cup \{\varepsilon\}\}.$$

The ordering on $Agent \rightarrow \mathcal{P}(\mathcal{S})$ is that of (point-wise extended) set-inclusion (it is straightforward to check that Φ is continuous).

3   A Calculus for tccp

In this section we introduce a temporal logic for reasoning about the reactive behavior of *tccp* programs. We first define temporal formulas and the related notions of truth and validity in terms of timed reactive sequences. Then we introduce the correctness assertions that we consider and a corresponding proof system.

3.1   Temporal Logic

Given a set M, with typical elements $X, Y, \ldots$, of monadic constraint predicate variables, our temporal logic is based on atomic formulas of the form $X(c)$, where c is a constraint of the given underlying constraint system. The distinguished predicate I will be used to express the "assumptions" of a process about its inputs, that is, $I(c)$ holds if the process assumes the information represented by c is produced by its environment. On the other hand, the distinguished predicate O represents the output of a process, that is, $O(c)$ holds if the information represented by c is produced by the process itself (recall that the produced information includes always the input, as previously mentioned). More precisely, these formulas $I(c)$ and $O(c)$ will be interpreted with respect to a *reaction* which consists of a pair of constraints $\langle c, d \rangle$, where c represents the input of the external environment and d is the contribution of the process itself (as a reaction to the input c) which always contains c (i.e. such that $d \geq c$ holds).

An atomic formula in our temporal logic is a formula as described above or an atomic formula of the form $c \leq d$ which 'imports' information about the underlying constraint system, i.e., $c \leq d$ holds if $d \vdash c$. Compound formulas are constructed from these atomic formulas by using the (usual) logical operators of negation, conjunction and (existential) quantification and the temporal operators $\bigcirc$ (the next operator) and $\mathcal{U}$ (the until operator). We have the following three different kinds of quantification:

- quantification over the variables $x, y, \ldots$ of the underlying constraint system;
- quantification over the constraints $c, d, \ldots$ themselves;
- quantification over the monadic constraint predicate variables $X, Y, \ldots$.

Variables $p, q, \ldots$ will range over the constraints. We will use $V, W, \ldots$, to denote a variable x of the underlying constraint system, a constraint variable p or a constraint predicate X.

Definition 5 (Temporal formulas). *Given an underlying constraint system with set of constraints $\mathcal{C}$, formulas of the temporal logic are defined by*

$$\phi ::= p \leq q \mid X(c) \mid \neg \phi \mid \phi \wedge \psi \mid \exists V \phi \mid \bigcirc \phi \mid \phi \, \mathcal{U} \, \psi$$

In the sequel we assume that the temporal operators have binding priority over the propositional connectives. We introduce the following abbreviations: $\Diamond \phi$ for *true* $\mathcal{U} \, \phi$ and $\Box \phi$ for $\neg \Diamond \neg \phi$. We also use $\phi \vee \psi$ as a shorthand for $\neg(\neg \phi \wedge \neg \psi)$ and $\phi \to \psi$ as a shorthand for $\neg \phi \vee \psi$. Finally, $c = d$ stands for $c \leq d \wedge d \leq c$.

Definition 6. *Given an underlying constraint system with set of constraints $\mathcal{C}$, the truth of an atomic formula $X(c)$ is defined with respect to a predicate assignment $v \in M \to C$ which assigns to each monadic predicate X a constraint. We define*

$$v \models X(c) \text{ if } v(X) \vdash c.$$

Thus $X(c)$ holds if c is entailed by the constraint represented by X. In other words, a monadic constraint predicate X denotes a set $\{d \mid d \vdash c\}$ for some c. We restrict to constraint predicate assignments which are monotonic in the following sense: $v(O) \vdash v(I)$. In other words, the output of a process contains its input. The temporal operators are interpreted with respect to finite sequence $\rho = v_1, \ldots, v_n$ of constraint predicate assignments in the standard manner: $\bigcirc \phi$ holds if ϕ holds in the next time-instant and $\phi \, \mathcal{U} \, \psi$ holds if there exists a future moment (possibly the present) in which ψ holds and until then ϕ holds. We restrict to sequences $\rho = v_1, \ldots, v_n$ which are monotonic in the following sense: for $1 \leq i < n$, we have

- $v_{i+1}(X) \vdash v_i(X)$, for every predicate X;
- $v_{i+1}(I) \vdash v_i(O)$.

The latter condition requires that the input of a process contains its output at the previous time-instant. Note that these conditions corresponds with the monotonicity of reactive sequences as defined above. Moreover, we assume that time does not stop, so actually a finite sequence $v_1 \cdots v_n$ represents the infinite sequence $v_1 \cdots v_n v_n v_n \cdots$, with the last element repeated infinitely many times.

In order to define formally the truth of a temporal formula we introduce the following notions: $\rho < \rho'$ if ρ is a proper suffix of ρ' ($\rho \leq \rho'$ if $\rho < \rho'$ or $\rho = \rho'$). Furthermore, for $\rho = v_1 \cdots v_n$, we denote by $\bigcirc\rho = v_2 \cdots v_n$ (as a particular case, we have that $\bigcirc v = v$) and $\rho_i = v_i$, $1 \leq i \leq n$. Given a variable x of the underlying constraint systems and a predicate assignment v we define the predicate assignment $\exists x v$ by $\exists x v(X) = \exists_x d$, where $d = v(X)$. Given a sequence $\rho = v_1, \ldots, v_n$, we denote by $\exists x \rho$ the sequence $\exists x v_1, \ldots, \exists x v_n$. Moreover, given a monadic constraint predicate X and a predicate assignment v we denote by $\exists X v$ the *restriction* of v to $M \setminus \{X\}$. Given a sequence $\rho = v_1, \ldots, v_n$, we denote by $\exists X \rho$ the sequence $\exists X v_1, \ldots, \exists X v_n$. Furthermore, by γ we denote a constraint assignment which assigns to each constraint variable p a constraint $\gamma(p)$. Finally, $\gamma\{c/p\}$ denotes the result of assigning in γ the constraint c to the variable p.

Definition 7. *Given a sequence of predicate assignments ρ, a constraint assignment γ and ϕ a temporal formula, we define $\rho \models_\gamma \phi$ by:*

$$
\begin{aligned}
&\rho \models_\gamma p \leq q && \text{if } \gamma(q) \vdash \gamma(p) \\
&\rho \models_\gamma X(c) && \text{if } \rho_1 \models X(c) \\
&\rho \models_\gamma \neg\phi && \text{if } \rho \not\models_\gamma \phi \\
&\rho \models_\gamma \phi_1 \wedge \phi_2 && \text{if } \rho \models_\gamma \phi_1 \text{ and } \rho \models_\gamma \phi_2 \\
&\rho \models_\gamma \exists x \phi && \text{if } \rho' \models_\gamma \phi, \text{ for some } \rho' \text{ s.t. } \exists x \rho = \exists x \rho' \\
&\rho \models_\gamma \exists X \phi && \text{if } \rho' \models_\gamma \phi, \text{ for some } \rho' \text{ s.t. } \exists X \rho = \exists X \rho' \\
&\rho \models_\gamma \exists p \phi && \text{if } \rho \models_{\gamma'} \phi, \text{ for some } c \text{ s.t. } \gamma' = \gamma\{c/p\} \\
&\rho \models_\gamma \bigcirc\phi && \text{if } \bigcirc\rho \models_\gamma \phi \\
&\rho \models_\gamma \phi \,\mathcal{U}\, \psi && \text{if for some } \rho' \leq \rho, \rho' \models_\gamma \psi \text{ and for all } \rho' < \rho'' \leq \rho, \rho'' \models_\gamma \phi.
\end{aligned}
$$

Definition 8. *A formula ϕ is valid, notation $\models \phi$, iff $\rho \models_\gamma \phi$ for every sequence ρ of predicate assignments and constraint assignment γ.*

We have the validity of the usual temporal tautologies. Monotonicity of the constraint predicates wrt the entailment relation of the underlying constraint system is expressed by the formula

$$\forall p \forall q \forall X (p \leq q \rightarrow (X(q) \rightarrow X(p))).$$

Monotonicity of the constraint predicates wrt time implies the validity of the following formula

$$\forall p \forall X (X(p) \rightarrow \Box X(p)).$$

The relation between the distinguished constraint predicates I and O is logically described by the laws

$$\forall p (I(p) \rightarrow O(p)) \text{ and } \forall p (O(p) \rightarrow \bigcirc I(p)),$$

that is, the output of a process contains its input and is contained in the inputs of the next time-instant.

3.2   The Proof-System

We introduce now a proof-system for reasoning about the correctness of *tccp* programs. We first define formally the correctness assertions and their validity.

Definition 9. *Correctness assertions are of the form* A *sat* ϕ, *where* A *is a* tccp *process and* ϕ *is a temporal formula. The validity of an assertion* A *sat* ϕ, *denoted by* $\models A$ *sat* ϕ, *is defined as follows*

$$\models A \ sat \ \phi \ iff \ \rho \models_\gamma \phi, \ for \ all \ \gamma \ and \ \rho \in R'(A),$$

where $R'(A) = \{v_1, \ldots, v_n \mid \langle v_1(I), v_1(O)\rangle \cdots \langle v_n(I), v_n(O)\rangle \in R(A)\}.$

Roughly, the correctness assertion A *sat* ϕ states that every sequence ρ of predicate assignments such that its 'projection' onto the distinguished predicates I and O generates a reactive sequence of A, satisfies the temporal formula ϕ.

Table 2. The system TL for *tccp*.

T1 tell(c) *sat* $O(c) \wedge \forall p(O(p) \rightarrow \exists q(I(q) \wedge q \sqcup c = p)) \wedge \bigcirc \Box \, stut$
T2 $\dfrac{A_i \ sat \ \phi_i, \forall i \in [1,n]}{\sum_{i=1}^{n} \mathbf{ask}(c_i) \rightarrow A_i \ sat \ \bigvee_{i=1}^{n}\left(\left(\bigwedge_{j=1}^{n}\neg I_j \wedge stut\right) \mathcal{U} \ (I_i \wedge stut \wedge \bigcirc \phi_i)\right) \vee \Box\left(\bigwedge_{j=1}^{n} \neg I_j \wedge stut\right)}$
T3 $\dfrac{A \ sat \ \phi \quad B \ sat \ \psi}{\mathbf{now} \ c \ \mathbf{then} \ A \ \mathbf{else} \ B \ sat \ (I(c) \wedge \phi) \vee (\neg I(c) \wedge \psi)}$
T4 $\dfrac{A \ sat \ \phi}{\exists x A \ sat \ \exists x(\phi \wedge loc(x)) \wedge inv(x)}$
T5 $\dfrac{A \ sat \ \phi \quad B \ sat \ \psi}{A \parallel B \ sat \ \exists X, Y (\phi[X/O] \wedge \psi[Y/O] \wedge par(X,Y))}$
T6 $\dfrac{p(x) \ sat \ \phi \vdash_p A \ sat \ \phi}{p(x) \ sat \ \phi} \quad p(x)$ declared as A
T7 $\dfrac{A \ sat \ \phi \quad \models \phi \rightarrow \psi}{A \ sat \ \psi}$

Table 2 presents the proof-system. Axiom **T1** states that the execution of **tell**(c) consists of the output of c (as described by $O(c)$) together with any possible input (as described by $I(q)$). Moreover, at every time-instant in the future no further output is generated, which is expressed by the formula

$$\forall p(O(p) \leftrightarrow I(p)),$$

which we abbreviate by *stut* (since it represents stuttering steps). In rule **T2** I_i stands for $I(c_i)$. Given that A_i satisfies ϕ_i, rule **T2** allows the derivation of the specification for $\sum_{i=1}^{n} \mathbf{ask}(c_i) \to A_i$, which expresses that either eventually c_i is an input and, consequently, ϕ_i holds in the *next* time-instant (since the evaluation of the ask takes one time-unit), or none of the guards is ever satisfied. Rule **T3** simply states that if A satisfies ϕ and B satisfies ψ then every computation of **now** c **then** A **else** B satisfies either ϕ or ψ, depending on the fact that c is an input or not. Hiding of a local variable x is axiomatized in rule **T4** by first existentially quantifying x in $\phi \wedge loc(x)$, where $loc(x)$ denotes the following formula which expresses that x is local, i.e., the inputs of the environment do not contain new information on x:

$$\forall p (\exists_x p \neq p \to (\neg I(p) \wedge \Box(\bigcirc I(p) \to \exists r(O(r) \wedge \exists_x p \sqcup r = p))))).$$

This formula literally states that the initial input does not contain information on x and that everywhere in the computation if in the next state an input contains information on x then this information is already contained by the previous output. Finally, the following formula $inv(x)$

$$\forall p \Box(\exists_x p \neq p \to (O(p) \to \exists r(I(r) \wedge \exists_x p \sqcup r = p)))$$

states that the process does not provide new information on the *global* variable x. Rule **T5** gives a compositional axiomatization of parallel composition. The 'fresh' constraint predicates X and Y are used to represent the outputs of A and B, respectively ($\phi[X/O]$ and $\psi[Y/O]$ denote the result of replacing O by X and Y). Additionally, the formula

$$\forall p \Box(O(p) \leftrightarrow (\exists q_1, q_2 (X(q_1) \wedge Y(q_2) \wedge q_1 \sqcup q_2 = p))),$$

denoted by $par(X, Y)$, expresses that every output of $A \parallel B$ can be decomposed into outputs of A and B. Rule **T6**, where $\vdash_p$ denotes derivability within the proof system, describes recursion in the usual manner (see also [4]) and in this rule x is assumed to be both the formal and the actual parameter. We do not need more rules since, as previously mentioned, we may assume without loss of generality that the set D of procedure declarations is closed wrt parameter names. Rule **T7** allows to weaken the specification.

As an example of a sketch of a derivation consider the agent $\exists x A$ where

$$A :: \mathbf{ask}(x = a) \to \mathbf{tell}(true)$$
$$+$$
$$\mathbf{ask}(true) \to \mathbf{tell}(y = b).$$

(constraints are equations on the Herbrand universe). By **T1** and **T7** we derive

$$\mathbf{tell}(y = b) \; sat \; O(y = b) \quad and \quad \mathbf{tell}(true) \; sat \; O(true).$$

By **T2** and **T7** we subsequently derive $A \; sat \; I(x = a) \vee \bigcirc O(y = b)$ (note that $\neg I(true)$ is logically equivalent to *false* and *false* $\mathcal{U} \phi$ is equivalent to ϕ). Using rule **T4**, we derive the correctness assertion

$$\exists x A \; sat \; \exists x ((I(x = a) \vee \bigcirc O(y = b)) \wedge loc(x)).$$

It is easy to see that $I(x = a) \wedge loc(x)$ implies *false*. So we have that $\exists x((I(x = a) \vee \bigcirc O(y = b)) \wedge loc(x))$ implies $\exists x(loc(x) \wedge \bigcirc O(y = b))$. Clearly this latter formula implies $\bigcirc O(y = b)$. Summarizing the above, we obtain a derivation of the correctness assertion $\exists x A$ *sat* $\bigcirc O(y = b)$ which states that in every reactive sequence of $\exists x A$ the constraint $y = b$ is produced in the next (wrt the start of the sequence) time instant.

4   Soundness and Completeness

We denote by $\vdash_p A$ *sat* ϕ the derivability of the correctness assertion A *sat* ϕ in the proof system introduced in the previous section (assuming as additional axioms in rule **T7** all valid temporal formulas). The following theorem states the soundness and (relative) completeness of this proof system.

Theorem 1. *We have* $\vdash_p A$ *sat* ϕ *iff* $\models A$ *sat* ϕ, *for every correctness assertion* A *sat* ϕ.

At the heart of this theorem lies the compositionality of the semantics R' which follows from the compositionality of the underlying semantics R as described in [5]. Given the compositionality of the semantics R' soundness can be proved by induction on the length of the derivation. As for completeness, following the standard notion for Hoare-style proof systems as introduced by [12] we consider here a notion of relative completeness. We assume the existence of a property which describes exactly the denotation of a process, that is, we assume that for any process A there exists a formula $\psi(A)$, such that $\rho \in R'(A)$ iff, for any γ, $\rho \models_\gamma \psi(A)$ holds[4]. This is analogous to assume the expressibility of the strongest postcondition of a process P, as with standard Hoare-like proof systems. Furthermore, we assume as additional axioms all the valid temporal formulas, (for use in the consequence rule). Also this assumption, in general, is needed to obtain completeness of Hoare logics. Using these assumptions, the proof of completeness follows the lines of the analogous proof in [4].

5   Related Work

A simpler temporal logic for tccp has been defined in [7] by considering epistemic operators of "belief" and "knowledge" which corresponds to the operators I and O considered in the present paper. Even though the intuitive ideas of the two papers are similar, the technical treatment is different. In fact, the logic in [7] is

---

[4] In order to describe recursion, the syntax of the temporal formulas has to be extended with a fixpoint operator of the form $\mu p(x).\phi$, where $p(x)$ is supposed to occur positively in ϕ and the variable x denotes the formal parameter associated with the procedure p (see [4]). The meaning of $\mu p(x).\phi$ is given by a least fixpoint-construction which is defined in terms of the lattice of sets of sequences of predicate assignments ordered by set-inclusion.

less expressive than the present one, since it does not allow constraint (predicate) variables. As a consequence, the proof system defined in [7] was not complete.

Recently, a logic for a different timed extension of ccp, called ntcc, has been presented in [23]. The language ntcc [29,21] is a non deterministic extension of the timed ccp language defined in [26]. Its computational model, and therefore the underlying logic, are rather different from those that we considered. Analogously to the case of the ESTEREL language, computation in ntcc (and in the language defined in [26]) proceeds in "bursts of activity": in each phase a ccp process is executed to produce a response to an input provided by the environment. The process accumulates monotonically information in the store, according to the standard ccp computational model, until it reaches a "resting point", i.e. a terminal state in which no more information can be generated. When the resting point is reached, the absence of events can be checked and it can trigger actions in the next time interval. Thus, each time interval is identified with the time needed for a ccp process to terminate a computation. Clearly, in order to ensure that the next time instant is reached, the ccp program has to be always terminating, thus it is assumed that it does not contain recursion (a restricted form of recursion is allowed only across time boundaries). Furthermore, the programmer has to transfer explicitly the all information from a time instant to the next one by using special primitives, since at the end of a time interval all the constraints accumulated and all the processes suspended are discarded, unless they are argument to a specific primitive. These assumptions allow to obtain an elegant semantic model consisting of sequences of sets of resting points (each set describing the behavior at a time instant).

On the other hand, the tccp language that we consider has a different notion of time, since each time-unit is identified with the time needed for the underlying constraint system to accumulate the tell's and to answer the ask's issued at each computation step by the processes of the system. This assumption allows us to obtain a direct timed extension of ccp which maintain the essential features of ccp computations. No restriction on recursion is needed to ensure that the next time instant is reached, since at each time instant there are only a finite number of parallel agents which can perform a finite number of (ask and tell) actions. Also, no explicit transfer of information across time boundaries is needed in *tccp*, since the (monotonic) evolution of the store is the same as in ccp (these differences affects the expressive power of the language, see [5] for a detailed discussion). Since the store grows monotonically, some syntactic restrictions are needed also in tccp in order to obtain bounded response time, that is, to be able to statically determine the maximal length of each time-unit (see [5]).

From a logical point of view, as shown in [4] the set of resting points of a ccp program characterizes essentially the strongest post condition of the program (the characterization however is exact only for a certain class of programs). In [23] this logical view is integrated with (linear) temporal logic constructs which are interpreted in terms of sequences of sets of resting points, thus taking into account the temporal evolution of the system. A proof system for proving the resulting linear temporal properties is also defined in [23]. Since the resting points provide a compositional model (describing the final results of computations), in this approach there is no need for a semantic and logical representation of "assumptions". On the other hand such a need arises when one wants to describe the input/output behavior of a process, which for generic (non deterministic) processes cannot be obtained from the resting points. Since tccp maintains essentially the ccp computational model, at each time instant rather than a set of final results (i.e. a set of resting points) we have an input/ouput behavior corresponding to the interaction of the environment, which provides the input, with the process, which produces the output. This is reflected in the the logic we have defined.

Related to the present paper is also [13], where tcc specifications are represented in terms of graph structures in order to apply model checking techniques. A finite interval of time (introduced by the user) is considered in order to obtain a finite behavior of the tcc program, thus allowing the application of existing model checking algorithms.

6   Conclusions

We introduced a temporal logic for reasoning about the correctness of a timed extension of ccp and we proved the soundness and (relative) completeness of a related proof system. As discussed in the previous section, due to the need to characterize the input/output behaviour of processes (rather than the resting points) our logic is rather complex. Therefore it is important to investigate possible axiomatizations and decision procedures for this logic (for example considering a semantic tableaux method). We are currently investigating these issues, also in order to assess the practical usability of our proof-system (as the consequence rule requires a certain implication in the logic to be valid). Since *reactive sequences* have been used also in the semantics of several other languages, including dataflow and imperative ones [20,9,8,11,6], we plan also to consider extensions of our logic to deal with these different languages.

References

1. L. Aceto and D. Murphy. Timing and causality in process algebra. *Acta Informatica*, 33(4): 317-350, 1996.
2. J. Baeten and J. Bergstra. Real time process algebra. *Formal Aspects of Computing*, 3(2): 142-188, 1991.
3. G. Berry and G. Gonthier. The ESTEREL programming language: Design, semantics and implementation. *Science of Computer Programming*, 19(2):87-152, 1992.
4. F.S. de Boer, M. Gabbrielli, E. Marchiori and C. Palamidessi. Proving Concurrent Constraint Programs Correct. *TOPLAS*, 19(5): 685-725. ACM Press, 1997.
5. F.S. de Boer, M. Gabbrielli and M.C. Meo. A Timed CCP Language. *Information and Computation*, 161, 2000.
6. F. S. de Boer, M. Gabbrielli, and M. C. Meo. A Denotational Semantics for a Timed Linda Language. In *Proc. PPDP 2001*. ACM Press, 2001.

7. F.S. de Boer, M. Gabbrielli and M.C. Meo. A Temporal Logic for reasoning about Timed Concurrent Constraint Programs. In *Proc. TIME 01*. IEEE Press, 2001.

8. F.S. de Boer, J.N. Kok, C. Palamidessi, and J.J.M.M. Rutten. The failure of failures in a paradigm for asynchronous communication. In *Proc. of CONCUR'91*, vol. 527 of *LNCS*, pages 111–126. Springer-Verlag, 1991.

9. F.S. de Boer and C. Palamidessi. A Fully Abstract Model for Concurrent Constraint Programming. In S. Abramsky and T.S.E. Maibaum, editors, *Proc. of TAPSOFT/CAAP*, vol. 493 of *LNCS*, pages 296–319. Springer-Verlag, 1991.

10. P. Bremond-Gregoire and I. Lee. A Process Algebra of Communicating Shared Resources with Dense Time and Priorities. *Theoretical Computer Science* 189, 1997. Springer-Verlag, 1997.

11. S. Brookes. A fully abstract semantics of a shared variable parallel language. In *Proc. Eighth LICS*. IEEE Computer Society Press, 1993.

12. S. Cook. Soundness and completeness of an axiom system for program verification. *SIAM Journal of Computation 7*, 1, 70–90.

13. M. Falaschi, A. Policriti, A. Villanueva. Modeling Concurrent systems specified in a Temporal Concurrent Constraint language. in *Proc. AGP'2000*. 2000.

14. M. Fisher. An introduction to Executable Temporal Logics. *Knowledge Engineering Review*, 6(1): 43-56, 1996.

15. N. Halbwachs, P. Caspi, and D. Pilaud. The synchronous programming language LUSTRE. In *Special issue on Another Look at Real-time Systems*, Proceedings of the IEEE, 1991.

16. D. Harel. Statecharts: A Visual Formalism for Complex Systems. *Science of Computer Programming* 8, pages 231-274, 1987.

17. L. Henkin, J.D. Monk, and A. Tarski. *Cylindric Algebras (Part I)*. North-Holland, 1971.

18. M. Hennessy and T. Regan. A temporal process algebra. *Information and Computation*, 117: 221-239, 1995.

19. P. Le Guernic, M. Le Borgue, T. Gauthier, and C. Le Marie. Programming real time applications with SIGNAL. In *Special issue on Another Look at Real-time Systems*, Proceedings of the IEEE, 1991.

20. B. Jonsson. A model and a proof system for asynchronous processes. In *Proc. of the 4th ACM Symp. on Principles of Distributed Computing*, pages 49–58. ACM Press, 1985.

21. M. Nielsen and F.D. Valencia. The ntcc Calculus and its applications. Draft, 2001.

22. Z. Manna and A. Pnueli. *The temporal logic of reactive systems*. Springer-Verlag, 1991.

23. C. Palamidessi and F.D. Valencia. A Temporal Concurrent Constraint Programming Calculus. In *Proc. CP 01*, LNCS 2239, pag. 302-316. Springer-Verlag, 2001.

24. V.A. Saraswat. *Concurrent Constraint Programming Languages*. PhD thesis, Carnegie-Mellon University, January 1989. Published by The MIT Press, 1991.

25. V.A. Saraswat and M. Rinard. Concurrent constraint programming. In *Proc. of POPL*, pages 232–245. ACM Press, 1990.

26. V.A. Saraswat, R. Jagadeesan, and V. Gupta Timed Default Concurrent Constraint Programming. *Journal of Symbolic Computation*, 22(5-6):475–520, 1996.

27. V.A. Saraswat, M. Rinard, and P. Panangaden. Semantics foundations of Concurrent Constraint Programming. In *Proc. of POPL*. ACM Press, 1991.

28. G. Smolka. The Definition of Kernel Oz. In A. Podelski editor, *Constraints: Basics and Trends*, vol. 910 of *LNCS*, pages 251–292. Springer-Verlag, 1995.

29. F.D. Valencia. Reactive Constraint Programming. *Brics Progress Report*, June 2000.

Generalised Regular MSC Languages

Benedikt Bollig[1], Martin Leucker[2], and Thomas Noll[1]

[1] Lehrstuhl für Informatik II, Aachen University of Technology (RWTH), Germany
{bollig,noll}@informatik.rwth-aachen.de
[2] Dept. of Computer and Information Science*, University of Pennsylvania, USA
leucker@cis.upenn.edu

Abstract. We establish the concept of regularity for languages consisting of Message Sequence Charts (MSCs). To this aim, we formalise their behaviour by string languages and give a natural definition of regularity in terms of an appropriate Nerode right congruence. Moreover, we present a class of accepting automata and establish several decidability and closure properties of MSC languages. We also provide a logical characterisation by a monadic second-order logic interpreted over MSCs. In contrast to existing work on regular MSC languages, our approach is neither restricted to a certain class of MSCs nor tailored to a fixed communication medium (such as a FIFO channel). It explicitly allows MSCs with message overtaking and is thus applicable to a broad range of channel types like mixtures of stacks and FIFOs.

1 Introduction

Components of distributed systems usually communicate with each other via message passing: A sender process sends a message over a channel, from which it is taken by the receiver process. A prominent formalism to model this kind of systems is that of *Message Sequence Charts* (MSCs) [8,9]. They are standardised, can be denoted both textually and graphically, and are often employed in industry. Furthermore, they are quite similar to the notion of sequence charts of the Unified Modelling Language (UML) [2].

An MSC defines a set of processes and a set of communication actions between these processes. In the visual representation of an MSC, processes are drawn as vertical lines. A labelled arrow from one line to another corresponds to the communication event of sending the labelling value from the first process to the second. As the vertical lines are interpreted as time axes, there is the general rule that arrows must not go "upwards" because this would describe a situation that a message is received before it has been sent. Figure 1(a) gives an example of an MSC. Collections of MSCs are used to capture the scenarios that a designer might want the system to follow or to avoid.

When one considers the dynamic behaviour of an MSC, i.e., the sequences of actions that may be observed when the system is executed, one distinguishes between the so-called visual-order semantics and the causal-order semantics. The

---

* Most of the work was completed during the author's employment at Lehrstuhl für Informatik II, Aachen University of Technology, Germany.

M. Nielsen and U. Engberg (Eds.): Fossacs 2002, LNCS 2303, pp. 52–66, 2002.
© Springer-Verlag Berlin Heidelberg 2002

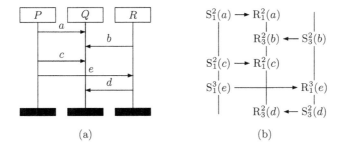

Fig. 1. An MSC and its formalisation

visual order assumes that the events are ordered as shown in the MSC. That is, the events on a single process line are linearly ordered, and sending events precede their corresponding receiving events. For example, Process Q in Figure 1(a) has to read the a symbol before it can read b. In the *causal order-based semantics*, a concrete communication medium between the processes is taken into account, e.g., a first-in-first-out (FIFO) channel. Furthermore, receiving events on the same process line are not ordered unless they are "causality dependent". For instance, reading event b may occur before reading a: As Process P might have sent a after R has sent b and assuming a single FIFO incoming channel for Q, Q will potentially receive b before a. Note that, under the same communication assumption, reading c must occur before reading d. To simplify our presentation, we adopt the visual-order point of view in the following. But we would like to stress that—with minor modifications—our very general approach also works wrt. the causal order.

Given the system specification in the form of a collection of MSCs, one is interested in doing formal analysis to discover errors at the early stages of system design. Of course, the first question arising is which kinds of collections of MSCs are amenable to formal methods. In a pioneering work by Henriksen et al. [7], a definition of *regularity* of MSC languages is proposed. A characterisation in terms of message-passing automata and in terms of monadic second-order logic is also given. The paper explains in a convincing way the benefits of these alternative descriptions, arguing that this is the "right" notion of regularity for MSCs. For example, a characterisation in terms of finite devices (automata) gives evidence for a collection of MSCs to be *realisable*.

However, this approach has a serious limitation. So-called "MSCs with message overtaking" cannot be considered. But these are explicitly defined in the official standard [8] and must be taken into account. The limitation stems from the fact that, for establishing a link between MSCs and classical language theory, the graphical representation of an MSC has somehow to be mapped to the domain of strings. The straightforward approach, enumerating the possible linearisations of the events that occur in an MSC, only works for simple types of MSCs where the correspondence between a sending event and its receiving counterpart can be derived from the order in which they occur in the string. Note that also [1] has to restrict the admissible class of MSCs in order to be able to relate MSCs and string languages.

Our solution to this problem is to associate with every communication event in the string representation of an MSC a natural number that explicitly establishes this correspondence. As it will become clear in the next section, this allows us to drop any restriction on the set of MSCs under consideration. The price to pay is that, for *arbitrary* collections of MSCs, we have to work with strings, automata, etc. over *infinite alphabets*. For practical applications though, the "simple" collections of MSCs are of interest. Therefore, within the domain of (MSC word) languages, we will spot the *regular* ones. These are defined in terms of a Nerode right congruence, which allows a straightforward generalisation to languages over infinite alphabets.

To support formal analysis, we introduce a new kind of automaton (MFA) accepting linearisations of MSCs. More precisely, our notion of MFAs guarantees that every accepted word is indeed a linearisation of an MSC. Moreover, we establish several closure properties and decidability results. In particular, we show that language inclusion is decidable, a crucial property for *model-checking* applications. Our concept of automata is similar to the one introduced by Kaminski and Francez [10]. Note, however, that in their setting the problem of language inclusion is undecidable [14]. Furthermore, our framework is well suited for extensions. In [6], compositional message sequence graphs (CMSGs) are introduced to describe larger classes of MSCs. Our automata model MFA is well prepared to accept languages of CMSGs, which can be characterised by MSC languages with *regular representative linearisations*, a concept defined and studied by Madhusudan and Meenakshi [12]. However, due to lack of space, this topic will be discussed elsewhere.

Subsequently, we follow the line of [7] and develop an alternative automata-theoretic characterisation based on message-passing automata as well as a description in terms of monadic second-order logic. Although the results are similar, the proofs are of a different nature because it is generally impossible to lift proofs directly from the setting of languages over finite alphabets to the infinite case.

Our main contribution is to develop a theory of regular collections of MSCs in terms of Nerode right congruences, finite automata, message-passing automata, and models of MSO formulas for the full class of MSCs. Thus, we provide the formal basis for subsequent verification questions. Our approach has already turned out to be useful in the setting of LTL model checking for MSCs [3].

Due to space constraints, we omit most proofs for the presented results. These can be found in the full version of the paper [4].

2   Message Sequence Charts and Their Linearisations

In this section, we present our formal model for MSCs and establish a string representation, which describes their behaviour in a linear way.

2.1 Message Sequence Charts

For $N \geq 2$, let $\mathcal{P}_N := \{1, \ldots, N\}$ be a set of *processes* and Λ a finite *message alphabet*. Let further $\Sigma_{\mathcal{S}} := \{S_p^q(\lambda) \mid p, q \in \mathcal{P}_N, \ p \neq q, \ \lambda \in \Lambda\}$ and $\Sigma_{\mathcal{R}} := \{R_p^q(\lambda) \mid p, q \in \mathcal{P}_N, \ p \neq q, \ \lambda \in \Lambda\}$ denote the sets of *send* and *receive actions*, respectively, and $\Sigma := \Sigma_{\mathcal{S}} \cup \Sigma_{\mathcal{R}}$ their union. An action $S_p^q(\lambda)$ stands for sending a message λ from Process p to Process q, and $R_p^q(\lambda)$ represents the corresponding receive action, which is then executed by Process q. In this sense, $Corr := \{(S_p^q(\lambda), R_p^q(\lambda)) \mid p, q \in \mathcal{P}_N, \ p \neq q, \ \lambda \in \Lambda\}$ relates those actions that belong together. From now on, all premises and definitions are made wrt. a fixed set $\mathcal{P}_N$ of processes and a fixed message alphabet Λ.

An MSC is a tuple of the form $M = (\{E_p\}_{p \in \mathcal{P}_N}, \{\preceq_p\}_{p \in \mathcal{P}_N}, f, L)$ where $\{E_p\}_{p \in \mathcal{P}_N}$ is a family of pairwise disjoint finite sets of *events*, each of which is totally ordered by a relation $\preceq_p \subseteq E_p \times E_p$. (For simplicity, we consider $\preceq_p$ as a relation over $E := \bigcup_{p \in \mathcal{P}_N} E_p$, the set of all events.) Let $P : E \cup \Sigma \to \mathcal{P}_N$ yield the process an event or an action belongs to, i.e., $P(e) = p$ for any $e \in E_p$, $P(S_p^q(\lambda)) = p$, and $P(R_p^q(\lambda)) = q$. M is required to induce a partition $E = S \cup R$ of the events into send (S) and receive events (R) such that $f : S \to R$ is a bijective mapping satisfying the following:

- The *visual order* $\preceq \subseteq E \times E$ of M, i.e., the reflexive and transitive closure of $\bigcup_{p \in \mathcal{P}_N} \preceq_p \cup \{(e, f(e)) \mid e \in S\}$, is a partial order; in particular, it is antisymmetric.
- $L : E \to \Sigma$ provides information about the messages being interchanged by communicating events whereby, for all $e \in S$, there is some $\lambda \in \Lambda$ such that
$$L(e) = S_{P(e)}^{P(f(e))}(\lambda) \text{ and } L(f(e)) = R_{P(e)}^{P(f(e))}(\lambda).$$

Figure 1(b) presents a formal version of the MSC shown in Figure 1(a).

A partial execution (configuration) of an MSC can be described by a downwards closed subset of events, containing those events that occurred so far. Formally, given an MSC $M = (\{E_p\}_{p \in \mathcal{P}_N}, \{\preceq_p\}_{p \in \mathcal{P}_N}, f, L)$, a *configuration* of M is a subset E' of E satisfying $E' = \downarrow E' := \{e \in E \mid \exists e' \in E' : e \preceq e'\}$. Let $Conf(M)$ denote the set of configurations of M. The execution of M can be described by a transition relation $\longrightarrow_M \subseteq Conf(M) \times \Sigma \times Conf(M)$ where $c \xrightarrow{\sigma}_M c'$ iff there exists $e \in E - c$ such that $L(e) = \sigma$ and $c' = c \cup \{e\}$.

2.2 MSC Words

A suitable notion of regularity for a class of objects should have similarities with existing notions for regular sets of objects. We will therefore reduce regularity of collections of MSCs to regularity of word languages. Thus, we have to identify an MSC with a set of words, which will be called *linearisations* or *MSC words*. A linearisation represents a possible execution sequence of the events occurring in an MSC. To justify this view, it is necessary to guarantee that—up to isomorphism—from a set of linearisations a corresponding MSC can be unambiguously inferred and vice versa. We are then able to define an equivalence on MSC words whose equivalence classes on their own determine exactly one MSC and, as a whole, stand for the set of all MSCs.

So one of the main problems is how to define an MSC word. For example, $w = S_1^2(a)S_1^2(a)R_1^2(a)R_1^2(a) \in \Sigma^*$ might define the MSC M_1 given in Figure 2. But as w is also a correct linearisation of the MSC aside, we could likewise imagine that w represents M_2, relating the first and the fourth position

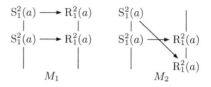

Fig. 2. MSCs generated by α_1 and α_2

of w. We therefore cannot unambiguously correlate a word in Σ^* with an MSC. Faced with causal-order semantics, the problem of relating events will be even more involved. In particular, if we make use of nondeterministic channels (which might allow MSCs to behave both in a FIFO manner and as a stack, for example), we need some information about which positions belong together. For this purpose, each position of a word $w \in \Sigma^*$ is equipped with a natural number indicating the matching positions (namely those showing the same number). The words $\alpha_1, \alpha_2 \in (\Sigma \times \mathbb{N})^*$ from Figure 3 are such MSC words. Notice that α_1 will determine the MSC M_1, whereas M_2 will emerge from α_2. To avoid these difficulties, [7] and [1] do not allow an MSC like M_2. However, M_2 is a perfect "MSC with message overtaking", which is explicitly allowed in the MSC standard [8,9].

Developing our theory step by step, we first call a word $\alpha \in (\Sigma \times \mathbb{N})^*$

- *proper* iff for all $(\sigma, \tau) \in Corr$, $\pi \in \mathbb{N}$, and prefixes α' of α, $|\alpha'|_{(\tau,\pi)} \leq |\alpha'|_{(\sigma,\pi)} \leq |\alpha'|_{(\tau,\pi)} + 1$, and
- *complete* iff it is proper and for all $(\sigma, \tau) \in Corr$ and $\pi \in \mathbb{N}$, $|\alpha|_{(\sigma,\pi)} = |\alpha|_{(\tau,\pi)}$.

Thus, in a proper word every receiving event (we sometimes refer to positions of MSC words as events) must be preceded by a sending counterpart, and, for each number π and each send action, at most one "open" sending event is admitted.

Definition 1 (MSC Word). *A word $\frac{\sigma_1}{\pi_1} \ldots \frac{\sigma_\ell}{\pi_\ell} \in (\Sigma \times \mathbb{N})^*$ is called an MSC word iff it is complete. Let* MW *denote the set of all MSC words and* PW *the set of proper words.*

To see some examples, look at the words $\alpha_1, \ldots, \alpha_4 \in (\Sigma \times \mathbb{N})^*$ given in Figure 3. As mentioned before, α_1 and α_2 are MSC words, whereas α_3 is certainly proper but not complete and α_4 is not even proper. We will refer to α_1 and α_2 as exemplary MSC words throughout the rest of the paper.

Given a proper word $\alpha = \frac{\sigma_1}{\pi_1} \ldots \frac{\sigma_\ell}{\pi_\ell} \in$ PW, we determine which positions are *matching*. For $i, j \in \{1, \ldots, \ell\}$, we write $i \searrow_\alpha j$ iff $i < j$, $(\sigma_i, \sigma_j) \in Corr$, and $j = \min\{k \mid k > i \text{ and } \pi_k = \pi_i \text{ and } (\sigma_i, \sigma_k) \in Corr\}$.

Referring to the previous example, $1 \searrow_{\alpha_1} 3$ and $2 \searrow_{\alpha_1} 4$ as well as $1 \searrow_{\alpha_2} 4$ and $2 \searrow_{\alpha_2} 3$.

$$\alpha_1 = \begin{matrix} S_1^2(a) & S_1^2(a) & R_1^2(a) & R_1^2(a) \\ 1 & 3 & 1 & 3 \end{matrix} \qquad \alpha_2 = \begin{matrix} S_1^2(a) & S_1^2(a) & R_1^2(a) & R_1^2(a) \\ 1 & 2 & 2 & 1 \end{matrix}$$

$$\alpha_3 = \begin{matrix} S_1^2(a) & S_2^1(b) & R_2^1(b) & S_2^1(b) & R_1^2(a) \\ 2 & 1 & 1 & 1 & 2 \end{matrix} \qquad \alpha_4 = \begin{matrix} S_1^2(a) & S_2^1(b) & R_2^1(b) & S_2^1(b) & S_1^2(a) \\ 2 & 1 & 1 & 1 & 2 \end{matrix}$$

Fig. 3. Exemplary words

2.3 From MSC Words to MSCs

Let us show that MSC words indeed represent MSCs. Falling back on the matching relation, a word $\alpha = \frac{\sigma_1}{\pi_1} \dots \frac{\sigma_\ell}{\pi_\ell} \in \text{MW}$ generates an MSC $M(\alpha) := (\{E_p\}_{p \in \mathcal{P}_N}, \{\preceq_p\}_{p \in \mathcal{P}_N}, f, L)$ where

- $E_p = \{n \in \{1, \dots, \ell\} \mid P(\sigma_n) = p\}$,
  $S = \{n \in \{1, \dots, \ell\} \mid \sigma_n \in \Sigma_S\}$,
  $R = \{n \in \{1, \dots, \ell\} \mid \sigma_n \in \Sigma_R\}$,
- $n \preceq_p m$ iff $n, m \in E_p$ and $n \leq m$,
- $f(n) = m$ iff $n \searrow_\alpha m$, and
- $L(n) = \sigma_n$.

For example, α_1 generates the MSC M_1 illustrated in Figure 2, whereas α_2 generates M_2.

Moreover, there is no problem in extending the above definition to proper words, which then determine prefixes of MSCs.

Note that two different proper words can stand—up to isomorphism—for one and the same MSC or configuration of an MSC, respectively: Since the naturals are only used for identifying matching positions, we have some freedom in choosing the actual value. Furthermore, we are free to choose the linearisation of independent events. Therefore, we define two equivalence relations $\approx \subseteq \text{PW} \times \text{PW}$ and $\sim \subseteq \text{MW} \times \text{MW}$. The first identifies words with equivalent projections onto the second component; the latter, as introduced further below, allows to permute the positions of an MSC word.

Thus, for $\alpha = \frac{\sigma_1}{\pi_1} \dots \frac{\sigma_\ell}{\pi_\ell} \in \text{PW}$ and $\beta = \frac{\tau_1}{\rho_1} \dots \frac{\tau_m}{\rho_m} \in \text{PW}$, let $\alpha \approx \beta$ iff $\sigma_1 \dots \sigma_\ell = \tau_1 \dots \tau_m$ and for all $i, j \in \{1, \dots, \ell\}$, $i \searrow_\alpha j$ iff $i \searrow_\beta j$.

For instance, let α_1^n emerge from α_1 by replacing 3 in the natural-number component with some $n \in \mathbb{N}$. Then, $\alpha_1^n \in \text{MW}$ iff $n \neq 1$, and $\alpha_1^n \in \text{MW}$ implies $\alpha_1 \approx \alpha_1^n$. But notice that $\alpha_1 \not\approx \alpha_2$ because the second condition in the definition of $\approx$ is violated.

For a proper word $\alpha = \frac{\sigma_1}{\pi_1} \dots \frac{\sigma_\ell}{\pi_\ell} \in \text{PW}$, let $open(\alpha) \subseteq \Sigma_S \times \mathbb{N}$ denote the set of those send events that are not followed by a matching receive event, i.e., $open(\alpha) := \{(\sigma_i, \pi_i) \mid \sigma_i \in \Sigma_S$ and there is no $j > i$ such that $i \searrow_\alpha j\}$. We call the elements of $open(\alpha)$ open events. A word $\alpha \in \text{PW}$ is called in normal form iff for all prefixes $\frac{\sigma_1}{\pi_1} \dots \frac{\sigma_k}{\pi_k}$ of α, $\sigma_k \in \Sigma_S$ implies $\pi_k = \min\{\pi \in \mathbb{N} \mid (\sigma_k, \pi) \notin open(\frac{\sigma_1}{\pi_1} \dots \frac{\sigma_{k-1}}{\pi_{k-1}})\}$. Thus, for every sending event, the lowest available number is chosen. Note that every equivalence class in $\text{PW}/_\approx$ contains exactly one word in normal form. For $\alpha \in PW$, let furthermore $nf(\alpha) = \beta$ iff $\alpha \approx \beta$ and β is in normal form. For instance, $nf(\alpha_1) = \alpha_1^2$, whereas α_2 is already in normal form so that $nf(\alpha_2) = \alpha_2$. nf is applied to sets of words in the expected manner.

In the following, we will not distinguish $\approx$-equivalent words.

Definition 2 (MSC Word Language). *A set $\mathcal{L} \subseteq MW$ is called an MSC word language iff $\mathcal{L} = \mathcal{L}^{\approx}$ where $\mathcal{L}^{\approx}$ denotes the $\approx$-closure of $\mathcal{L}$.*

Note that, for any MSC word language $\mathcal{L}$, it holds $\mathcal{L} = nf(\mathcal{L})^{\approx}$.

Characterising regular languages within the scope of MSCs, a certain restriction of words and MSCs will prove to be important. Given a natural number B, $\alpha \in MW$ is called B-*bounded* iff for all prefixes α' of α and actions $\sigma \in \Sigma_S$, $|open(\alpha') \cap \{(\sigma, \pi) \mid \pi \in \mathbb{N}\}| \leq B$. This means that, for every send action, the number of open events is bounded by B. Examples for 2-bounded MSC words are α_1 and α_2. Note that we could likewise call α B-bounded iff for all prefixes α' of α, $|open(\alpha')| \leq B$, i.e., the total number of open send events is bounded by B, or also iff for all prefixes α' of α and $p \in \mathcal{P}_N$, $|open(\alpha') \cap \{(\sigma, \pi) \mid \pi \in \mathbb{N}, P(\sigma) = p\}| \leq B$, which means that the number of open events per process is bounded by B.

The definitions differ in the concrete bound, and the appropriate definition taken may vary depending on an underlying channel type. However, all presented results hold for every of these definitions.

2.4   Linearisations of MSCs

To finally relate MSCs to the rich theories of languages and automata over words, the concept of linearisations of an MSC is essential. We call an MSC word $\alpha = \frac{\sigma_1 \cdots \sigma_{\ell}}{\pi_1 \cdots \pi_{\ell}} \in (\Sigma \times \mathbb{N})^*$ a *linearisation* of an MSC $M = (\{E_i\}_{i \in \mathcal{P}_N}, \{\preceq_i\}_{i \in \mathcal{P}_N}, f, L)$ with a set of events $E = \{e_1, \ldots, e_{\ell}\}$ iff there are $c_1, \ldots, c_{\ell} \in Conf(M)$ with $\emptyset \xrightarrow{\sigma_1}_M c_1 \xrightarrow{\sigma_2}_M \cdots \xrightarrow{\sigma_{\ell}}_M c_{\ell}$ and there is a bijective mapping $\chi : E \to \{1, \ldots, \ell\}$ such that for all $e \in E$, $L(e) = \sigma_{\chi(e)}$, and for all $e \in S$, $e' \in R$, $f(e) = e'$ implies $\chi(e) \searrow_\alpha \chi(e')$. $Lin(M)$ denotes the set of linearisations of M. For a set $\mathcal{M}$ of MSCs, we canonically define $Lin(\mathcal{M}) := \bigcup\{Lin(M) \mid M \in \mathcal{M}\}$. For instance, the exemplary word α_1 is a linearisation of the MSC M_1 shown in Figure 2, and α_2 is a linearisation of M_2. When, above, we spoke of isomorphism of two MSCs, we actually meant "inducing the same set of linearisations" instead.

An MSC is called B-bounded iff all of its linearisations are B-bounded. A collection of MSCs (a collection of MSC words, respectively) is B-bounded iff all members are B-bounded. Furthermore, we speak of *boundedness* in general iff we deal with B-boundedness for an arbitrary B.

We now turn towards $\sim \subseteq MW \times MW$, the second natural equivalence relation to study on linearisations of MSCs because it takes permutations of positions into account. For example, in Figure 1, it makes no real difference whether $S_3^2(b)$ occurs before $R_1^2(a)$ or after it. Given Σ, we define the *dependence relation* $D(\Sigma) \subseteq (\Sigma \times \mathbb{N})^2$ and write $(\sigma, \pi)D(\Sigma)(\sigma', \pi')$ iff $P(\sigma) = P(\sigma')$ or $[(\sigma, \sigma') \in Corr$ and $\pi = \pi']$ or $[(\sigma', \sigma) \in Corr$ and $\pi = \pi']$. It turns out that the pair $(\Sigma \times \{1, \ldots, B\}, D(\Sigma) \cap (\Sigma \times \{1, \ldots, B\})^2)$ is a Mazurkiewicz trace alphabet

[5] for every natural B—a fact which was already used in [11] providing a *direct* link between Mazurkiewicz traces and MSCs.

We then define the relation $\sim$ to be the least equivalence relation satisfying the following: If $\alpha = \beta_1(\sigma, \pi)(\sigma', \pi')\beta_2$ and $\alpha' = \beta_1(\sigma', \pi')(\sigma, \pi)\beta_2$ for suitable β_1, β_2 and not $(\sigma, \pi)D(\Sigma)(\sigma', \pi')$, then $\alpha \sim \alpha'$.

This section concludes with the following important properties of sets of linearisations that are induced by MSCs. In particular, they establish the expected connections between linearisations and the equivalence relations $\approx$ and $\sim$.

Theorem 1. *For an MSC M and $\alpha \in Lin(M)$, $Lin(M) = Lin(M(\alpha))$.*

Theorem 2. *For $\alpha \in \mathrm{MW}$, $Lin(M(\alpha)) = [\alpha]_{(\approx \cup \sim)^*}$.*

Theorems 1 and 2 can be shown by employing standard techniques taken, for example, from the Mazurkiewicz trace theory. The proofs are left to the reader.

3   Regular MSC Word Languages and Their Automata

We already mentioned that the regularity of collections of MSCs will be defined in terms of regular MSC word languages. But as MSC words are defined over the infinite alphabet $\Sigma \times \mathbb{N}$, we have to modify the usual notion of regularity. In [10], a definition of regular word languages over infinite alphabets is proposed by providing an extended automata model that employs a finite transition relation but generates a behaviour catering for the fact that we deal with an infinite alphabet. However, important questions for these automata are undecidable. Thus, we follow a different approach. We first constitute an algebraic characterisation of regularity by means of a slightly adapted version of the Nerode right congruence, which allows a straightforward extension to infinite alphabets. Then, we establish its equivalence to an automata model that has similarities with the one described in [10] but is better suited for MSCs and provides desired properties.

3.1   Regular MSC Word Languages

Given an MSC word language $\mathcal{L}$, recall the definition of the Nerode right congruence $\equiv_{\mathcal{L}} \subseteq \mathrm{PW} \times \mathrm{PW}$: $\alpha \equiv_{\mathcal{L}} \beta$ iff $\forall \gamma \in (\Sigma \times \mathbb{N})^*.(\alpha\gamma \in \mathcal{L}$ iff $\beta\gamma \in \mathcal{L})$. As we want to identify $\approx$-equivalent words, we define $\approx_{\mathcal{L}} \subseteq \mathrm{PW} \times \mathrm{PW}$ as an extension of the Nerode right congruence by $\alpha \approx_{\mathcal{L}} \beta$ iff $nf(\alpha) \equiv_{\mathcal{L}} nf(\beta)$.

Definition 3 (Regular MSC Word Language). *An MSC word language $\mathcal{L}$ is called* regular *iff $\approx_{\mathcal{L}}$ has finite index.*

The next characterisation of regular MSC word languages prepares for proving their correspondence with a certain class of finite automata, which we introduce further below.

Theorem 3. *Let $\mathcal{L}$ be an MSC word language. $\mathcal{L}$ is regular iff $nf(\mathcal{L})$ is a regular word language over $\Sigma \times Q$ for a finite subset Q of $\mathbb{N}$.*

Corollary 1. *Regular MSC word languages are bounded.*

The next theorem will be useful when, in Section 4, we consider $\sim$-closed MSC word languages.

Theorem 4. *Let $\mathcal{L}$ be a $\sim$-closed regular MSC word language. Then $nf(\mathcal{L})^{\sim}$ is a regular word language over a finite alphabet.*

The proof of Theorem 3 is technically involved while the one for Theorem 4 proceeds by establishing a link to Mazurkiewicz trace theory and borrows deeper results to show the claim. Cf. the long version of the paper for details.

3.2   MSC Finite-Memory Automata

We now present an automata model characterising the class of regular MSC word languages. Our definition is inspired by [10] but modified to suit the requirements for MSCs and to allow stronger decidability results. Our model can be described as a finite automaton that makes use of a finite window whose positions occur in the labellings of the transitions—as well as elements of Σ—and indicate where to store a symbol of the infinite alphabet $\Sigma \times \mathbb{N}$ (concerning send actions) and where to take it from (concerning receive actions), respectively. Normal forms of regular MSC word languages could also be accepted by "standard" finite automata and we can use this fact to establish certain closure properties. However, not every finite automaton accepts normal forms of MSC words so that we do not get a precise automata-theoretic characterisation of regular MSC word languages which is the basis for a powerful algorithmic support of the theory on MSCs.

Definition 4 (MSC Finite-Memory Automaton). *An* MSC finite-memory automaton *(MFA) is a quintuple of the form $\mathcal{A} = (S, r, \Delta, q_0, F)$ where*

- *S is a nonempty finite set of* states,
- *$r \geq 1$ is a natural number called* window length,
- *$\Delta \subseteq S \times (\Sigma \times \{1, \ldots, r\}) \times S$ is the* transition relation,
- *$q_0 \in S$ is the* initial state, *and*
- *$F \subseteq S$ is the set of* final states.

Figure 4 shows two MFAs, each with a window of length two. Let thereby S stand for $S_1^2(a)$ and R for $R_1^2(a)$.

Given an MFA $\mathcal{A}$ as above, a configuration of $\mathcal{A}$ lists the current state and the current window entries, which are either numbered send events or empty (denoted by #). Thus, let $Conf_{\mathcal{A}} := S \times ((\Sigma_{\mathcal{S}} \times \mathbb{N}) \cup \{\#\})^r$ denote the (infinite) set of *configurations* of $\mathcal{A}$. We define a transition relation $\Longrightarrow_{\mathcal{A}} \subseteq Conf_{\mathcal{A}} \times (\Sigma \times \mathbb{N}) \times Conf_{\mathcal{A}}$ as follows:

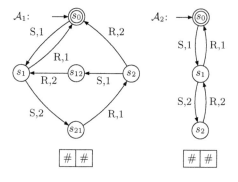

Fig. 4. Two MFAs

- For $\sigma \in \Sigma_\mathcal{S}$, $(s, \mathbf{w}) \xrightarrow{(\sigma, \pi)}_\mathcal{A} (t, \mathbf{v})$ iff (σ, π) does not occur in $\mathbf{w}$ and there is a transition $(s, (\sigma, k), t) \in \Delta$ such that $\mathbf{w}[k] = \#$, $\mathbf{v}[k] = (\sigma, \pi)$, and for each $l \neq k$, $\mathbf{w}[l] = \mathbf{v}[l]$.
- For $\sigma \in \Sigma_\mathcal{R}$, $(s, \mathbf{w}) \xrightarrow{(\sigma, \pi)}_\mathcal{A} (t, \mathbf{v})$ iff there is a transition $(s, (\sigma, k), t) \in \Delta$ such that $\mathbf{w}[k] = (\tau, \pi)$ where $(\tau, \sigma) \in Corr$, $\mathbf{v}[k] = \#$, and for each $l \neq k$, $\mathbf{w}[l] = \mathbf{v}[l]$.

Thus, the meaning of a transition $(s, (S_p^q(\lambda), k), t)$ is the following: If $\mathcal{A}$ is in state s, it is able to read an input symbol $(S_p^q(\lambda), \pi)$, $\pi \in \mathbb{N}$, iff the kth position of its window is currently free and, furthermore, $(S_p^q(\lambda), \pi)$ does not occur elsewhere in the window, i.e., there is no further open $(S_p^q(\lambda), \pi)$-labelled send event. Taking the transition, the automaton stores $(S_p^q(\lambda), \pi)$ in the kth position and enters state t. If, in contrast, the automaton reads an input symbol $(R_p^q(\lambda), \pi)$, there has to be a transition $(s, (R_p^q(\lambda), k), t)$ such that the kth position of the window currently shows the corresponding send symbol $(S_p^q(\lambda), \pi)$. Replacing this symbol with $\#$, the automaton enters state t.

A *run* of $\mathcal{A}$ on a word $\frac{\sigma_1}{\pi_1} \cdots \frac{\sigma_\ell}{\pi_\ell} \in (\Sigma \times \mathbb{N})^*$ is a corresponding sequence $(s_0, \mathbf{w}_0)(s_1, \mathbf{w}_1) \ldots (s_\ell, \mathbf{w}_\ell)$ of configurations such that $s_0 = q_0$, $\mathbf{w}_0 = \#^r$, and for each $i \in \{1, \ldots, \ell\}$, $(s_{i-1}, \mathbf{w}_{i-1}) \xrightarrow{(\sigma_i, \pi_i)}_\mathcal{A} (s_i, \mathbf{w}_i)$. The run is *accepting* iff $s_\ell \in F$ and $\mathbf{w}_\ell = \#^r$. $\mathcal{L}(\mathcal{A}) := \{\alpha \mid$ there is an accepting run of $\mathcal{A}$ on $\alpha\}$ forms the language defined by $\mathcal{A}$. We conclude that matching events in an accepted word use one and the same position of the window for their "agreement".

Due to the conditions we laid down for making transitions and accepting words, an MFA will accept MSC words only. A receive symbol has to be preceded by a corresponding send symbol, which, on its part, has to wait for the corresponding receive symbol before repeating the identical send symbol. Thus, we make sure that an accepted word is proper. Furthermore, as a run is accepting as soon as it ends in a final configuration featuring an empty window, completeness of accepted words is ensured. Moreover, the recognised language is $\approx$-closed because matching symbols can be read with—up to the MSC-word condition—arbitrary natural numbers. Notice that a regular MSC word language is not necessarily $\sim$-closed, a key feature allowing [12] to model CMSGs in terms of MSC word languages. We sum up these considerations as follows:

Proposition 1. *Given an MFA $\mathcal{A}$, $\mathcal{L}(\mathcal{A})$ is an MSC word language.*

For example, let us consider the MFAs $\mathcal{A}_1$ and $\mathcal{A}_2$ illustrated by Figure 4 and behaving in a FIFO manner and as a stack, respectively. For the sake of clarity, let S stand for $S_1^2(a)$ and R for $R_1^2(a)$. Note that our MFAs permit only Process 1 to send and only Process 2 to receive a message a.

Recall our exemplary words α_1 and α_2. In fact, $\alpha_1 \in \mathcal{L}(\mathcal{A}_1)$ and $\alpha_2 \in \mathcal{L}(\mathcal{A}_2)$, but $\alpha_1 \notin \mathcal{L}(\mathcal{A}_2)$ and $\alpha_2 \notin \mathcal{L}(\mathcal{A}_1)$. An accepting run of $\mathcal{A}_1$ on α_1 first writes $(S_1^2(a), 1)$ into the first position of the window and then $(S_1^2(a), 3)$ into the second, whereupon the window is cleared in the same order, reading first $(R_1^2(a), 1)$ and then $(R_1^2(a), 3)$.

Our notion of MFAs covers exactly the class of regular MSC word languages.

Theorem 5. *An MSC word language $\mathcal{L}$ is regular iff there is an MFA $\mathcal{A}$ such that $\mathcal{L} = \mathcal{L}(\mathcal{A})$.*

Proof. Exploiting Theorem 3, we specify respective automata.
($\Longrightarrow$) Let $\mathcal{A} = (S, \longrightarrow, q_0, F)$ be a finite automaton with $\longrightarrow \subseteq S \times (\Sigma \times Q) \times S$ for a finite set $Q \subseteq \mathbb{N}$ such that $\mathcal{L}(\mathcal{A}) = nf(\mathcal{L})$. The MFA $\mathcal{A}' = (S', r, \Delta, q_0', F')$ satisfying $\mathcal{L}(\mathcal{A}') = \mathcal{L}(\mathcal{A})^{\approx} = \mathcal{L}$ is given by $S' = S$, $r = |Q|$, $(s, (\sigma, k), t) \in \Delta$ iff $s \xrightarrow{(\sigma, k)} t$, $q_0' = q_0$, and $F' = F$.
($\Longleftarrow$) Given an MFA $\mathcal{A} = (S, r, \Delta, q_0, F)$, let first $Q = \{1, \ldots, r\}$ and let $\mathcal{A}' = (S', \longrightarrow, q_0', F')$ be the corresponding finite automaton satisfying $\mathcal{L}(\mathcal{A}') = nf(\mathcal{L}(\mathcal{A}))$, defined as follows: $S' = S \times ((\Sigma_{\mathcal{S}} \times Q) \cup \{\#\})^r$, $\longrightarrow \subseteq S' \times (\Sigma \times Q) \times S'$ where $(s, \mathbf{w}) \xrightarrow{(\sigma, \pi)} (t, \mathbf{v})$ iff both $(s, \mathbf{w}) \xRightarrow{(\sigma, \pi)}_{\mathcal{A}} (t, \mathbf{v})$ and $\sigma \in \Sigma_{\mathcal{S}}$ implies $\pi = \min\{\pi' \in \mathbb{N} \mid (\sigma, \pi')$ does not occur in $\mathbf{w}\}$, $q_0' = (q_0, \#^r)$, and $F' = F \times \{\#^r\}$. $\square$

Given an MSC word language in terms of an MFA, the first natural question is whether it defines the trivial language.

Theorem 6. *It is decidable whether a regular MSC word language given by an MFA is empty.*

We obtain this result applying the construction shown in the proof of Theorem 5.

Theorem 7. *The class of regular MSC word languages is closed under union, intersection, concatenation, and Kleene star.*

Theorem 7 follows from Theorem 3 and the fact that the concatenation of two MSC words in normal form is again in normal form.

To support the algorithmic handling of MFAs, one could alternatively provide automata-theoretic constructions that also establish the above closure properties. These are explained in the full version of the paper.

The class of regular MSC word languages is not closed under complement because the complement of a regular MSC word language is always unbounded. Thus, the standard way to show decidability of language inclusion does not work. However, in contrast to the general case of regular languages over infinite alphabets where this problem is undecidable (see [14]), we can show decidability in our setting, again applying the construction used for proving Theorem 5. This is of great importance for the development of model-checking algorithms.

Theorem 8. *Given MFAs $\mathcal{A}_1$ and $\mathcal{A}_2$, it is decidable whether $\mathcal{L}(\mathcal{A}_1) \subseteq \mathcal{L}(\mathcal{A}_2)$.*

4   Regular MSC Languages and Their Automata

4.1   Regular MSC Languages

We now extend our theory of regular MSC word languages to collections of MSCs. Regularity of such a collection is reduced to regularity of the set of corresponding linearisations.

Definition 5 (Regular MSC Language). *A collection $\mathcal{M}$ of MSCs is called a regular MSC language iff $Lin(\mathcal{M})$ is a regular MSC word language.*

According to this definition, the set of linearisations of a regular MSC language is necessarily $\sim$-closed by Theorem 2. Hence, regular MSC languages cannot be characterised by MFAs because these accept also non-$\sim$-closed languages. We therefore develop a generalisation of message-passing automata [7] that accepts exactly regular MSC word languages corresponding to regular MSC languages. Note that a regular MSC language is bounded.

One might ask at this stage for the reason considering regular MSC word languages as well as regular MSC languages because the latter seem to be the first choice studying linearisations of MSCs. This is true when we abstract from a communication medium between the processes of an MSC. Consider for example the MSC presented in Figure 1(b). In the visual-order approach, there is no difference whether $S_3^2(b)$ occurs before $R_1^2(a)$ or vice versa. However, turning towards more complex semantics of MSCs, this might not be true any longer. Suppose the two processes communicate via a one element buffer. Then the only linear execution we will see is that $R_1^2(a)$ occurs before $S_3^2(b)$. Thus, the set of linearisations of an MSC is no longer necessarily $\sim$-closed. It is indeed possible to model communication mediums by means of certain MFAs, which enrich a specification in form of MSCs [3].

4.2   Generalised Message-Passing Automata

The following automata model employs different automata components, each of which executes the actions of one single process. They communicate with each other over a window roughly as featured by an MFA. The length of this window is still bounded by a natural number r. The crucial point is that the window entries are no longer single send events (each paired with a natural number) but sequences of send events (each paired with a natural number and an additional message). To preserve $\sim$-closedness of the recognised languages, the components rather have to restrict themselves, whereas the window is a communication medium only. For example, we could imagine an automata component that has to keep a send action waiting until it executes a certain receive action, which, in turn, has to be preceded by a corresponding send action executed by another component. In fact, our view generalises the model proposed in [7], which has its origins in [15].

Definition 6 (Generalised Message-Passing Automaton). *A generalised message-passing automaton (GMPA) is a family $\mathcal{A} = (\{\mathcal{A}_p\}_{p \in \mathcal{P}_N}, r, \overline{q}_{in}, F, Mess)$ of local automata together with a natural number $r \geq 1$, a global initial state $\overline{q}_{in}$, a set of global final states F, and a nonempty finite set of messages Mess. A local automaton is of the form $\mathcal{A}_p = (S_p, \Delta_p)$ where S_p is a nonempty finite set of local states and $\Delta_p \subseteq S_p \times (\Sigma_p \times \{1, \ldots, r\} \times Mess) \times S_p$ is a set of local transitions (Σ_p contains the actions belonging to Process p). $\overline{q}_{in}$ is an element and F a subset of $S_{\mathcal{A}} := \times_{p \in \mathcal{P}_N} S_p$, the set of global states of $\mathcal{A}$.*

For a GMPA $\mathcal{A}$, the (infinite) set of its *configurations* is defined by $Conf_{\mathcal{A}} := S_{\mathcal{A}} \times \{\chi \mid \chi : \Sigma_{\mathcal{S}} \times \{1, \ldots, r\} \to (\mathbb{N} \times Mess)^*\}$. Let $\overline{s}[p]$ be the pth component of a global state $\bar{s} \in S_{\mathcal{A}}$. Furthermore, for $\mathtt{W} : \Sigma_{\mathcal{S}} \times \{1, \ldots, r\} \to (\mathbb{N} \times Mess)^*$, let $\mathtt{W}[(\sigma, k) \ / \ w]$ denote the function that coincides with $\mathtt{W}$ with the exception that, for (σ, k), it yields w. We define $\Longrightarrow_{\mathcal{A}} \subseteq Conf_{\mathcal{A}} \times (\Sigma \times \mathbb{N}) \times Conf_{\mathcal{A}}$ as follows:

- For $\sigma \in \Sigma_{\mathcal{S}}$ with $P(\sigma) = p$, $(\bar{s}, \mathtt{W}) \overset{(\sigma, \pi)}{\Longrightarrow}_{\mathcal{A}} (\bar{t}, \mathtt{V})$ iff for all $k' \in \{1, \ldots, r\}$ and $m' \in Mess$, (π, m') does not occur in $\mathtt{W}(\sigma, k')$, and there is a transition $(\bar{s}[p], (\sigma, k, m), \bar{t}[p]) \in \Delta_p$ such that $\mathtt{V} = \mathtt{W}[(\sigma, k) \ / \ \mathtt{W}(\sigma, k) \cdot (\pi, m)]$ and, for all $l \in \mathcal{P}_N - \{p\}$, $\bar{s}[l] = \bar{t}[l]$.

- For $\sigma \in \Sigma_{\mathcal{R}}$ with $P(\sigma) = p$ and $(\tau, \sigma) \in Corr$, $(\bar{s}, \mathtt{W}) \overset{(\sigma, \pi)}{\Longrightarrow}_{\mathcal{A}} (\bar{t}, \mathtt{V})$ iff there are a transition $(\bar{s}[p], (\sigma, k, m), \bar{t}[p]) \in \Delta_p$ and a word $w \in (\mathbb{N} \times Mess)^*$ such that $\mathtt{W}(\tau, k) = (\pi, m) \cdot w$, $\mathtt{V} = \mathtt{W}[(\tau, k) \ / \ w]$, and, for all $l \in \mathcal{P}_N - \{p\}$, $\bar{s}[l] = \bar{t}[l]$.

A *run* of $\mathcal{A}$ on a word $\frac{\sigma_1 \ldots \sigma_\ell}{\pi_1 \ldots \pi_\ell} \in (\Sigma \times \mathbb{N})^*$ is defined in analogy to the MFA case. That is, we are dealing with a sequence $(\bar{s}_0, \mathtt{W}_0)(\bar{s}_1, \mathtt{W}_1) \ldots (\bar{s}_\ell, \mathtt{W}_\ell)$ of configurations such that $\bar{s}_0 = \bar{q}_{in}$, $\mathtt{W}_0(\sigma, k) = \varepsilon$ for all $(\sigma, k) \in \Sigma_{\mathcal{S}} \times \{1, \ldots, r\}$, and $(\bar{s}_{i-1}, \mathtt{W}_{i-1}) \overset{(\sigma_i, \pi_i)}{\Longrightarrow}_{\mathcal{A}} (\bar{s}_i, \mathtt{W}_i)$ for each $i \in \{1, \ldots, \ell\}$. The run is *accepting* iff $\bar{s}_\ell \in F$ and $\mathtt{W}_\ell(\sigma, k) = \varepsilon$ for all $(\sigma, k) \in \Sigma_{\mathcal{S}} \times \{1, \ldots, r\}$. Finally, $\mathcal{L}(\mathcal{A}) := \{\alpha \mid$ there is an accepting run of $\mathcal{A}$ on $\alpha\}$ denotes the language defined by $\mathcal{A}$.

Let $Reach(\mathcal{A})$ denote the set of configurations reachable within a run of $\mathcal{A}$. For $B \in \mathbb{N}$, we call $\mathcal{A}$ *B-bounded* iff for all $(\bar{s}, \mathtt{W}) \in Reach(\mathcal{A})$ and $\sigma \in \Sigma_{\mathcal{S}}$, $\sum_{k \in \{1, \ldots, r\}} |\mathtt{W}(\sigma, k)| \leq B$. We call it *bounded* iff it is B-bounded for some B.

Let us formulate the fundamental result of this section.

Theorem 9. *Let $\mathcal{L} \subseteq$ MW be an MSC word language. The following statements are equivalent:*

1. *There is a regular MSC language $\mathcal{M}$ with $Lin(\mathcal{M}) = \mathcal{L}$.*
2. *$\mathcal{L}$ is a $\sim$-closed regular MSC word language.*
3. *There is a bounded GMPA $\mathcal{A}$ such that $\mathcal{L}(\mathcal{A}) = \mathcal{L}$.*

Proof. The equivalence of 1. and 2. immediately follows from the definitions. Given a bounded GMPA, it is an easy task to define an equivalent MFA which shows that 3. implies 2. The other direction, however, is more involved and requires some results on regular Mazurkiewicz trace languages and related automata due to Zielonka [15]. We give a sketch of the proof and refer to the full version for the details.

Given a $\sim$-closed regular MSC word language $\mathcal{L}$, we build a bounded GMPA $\mathcal{A}$ with $\mathcal{L}(\mathcal{A}) = \mathcal{L}$. The outline of this construction is as follows: We first observe that, for a certain B, $nf(\mathcal{L})^\sim$ can be considered to be a regular Mazurkiewicz trace language over $\Sigma \times \{1, \ldots, B\}$ with an appropriate dependence alphabet. Then we can find an asynchronous automaton recognising $nf(\mathcal{L})^\sim$. The underlying distributed alphabet will comprise, apart from alphabets for each process, some additional components, which guarantee that the induced dependence relation complies with $D(\Sigma)$ (see also the proof of Theorem 4). These additional components have to be factored into the process components and the transition relation, making the transformation of the asynchronous automaton into a GMPA complicated. Concretely, the transitions synchronously taken by several local automata have to be simulated by message passing. For example, consider Process P_1 sending a message to Process P_2 by executing (σ, k). Actually, an equally labelled transition would have to be taken on the part of an additional component, in which (σ, k) is involved. But as in the GMPA such a component is not at the disposal of P_1, P_1 guesses a corresponding move and writes it, along with the original message, into the message pool. The receiving process can take this message if the guessed move corresponds to the actual state of the additional component, which P_2 carries along. Our construction is similar to the one in [7] and uses the time-stamping protocol for non-FIFO computations described in [13] to ensure boundedness of the constructed GMPA   □

Thus, bounded GMPAs characterise exactly the $\sim$-closed regular MSC word languages and therewith exactly the regular MSC languages. For example, the 2-bounded GMPA $\mathcal{A}$ given in Figure 5 recognises the $(\approx \cup \sim)^*$-closure of

$$\left\{ \left(\begin{array}{cccccc} \mathrm{S}_1^2(a) & \mathrm{S}_1^2(a) & \mathrm{R}_1^2(a) & \mathrm{R}_1^2(a) & \mathrm{S}_2^1(b) & \mathrm{R}_2^1(b) \\ 1 & 2 & 1 & 2 & 1 & 1 \end{array} \right)^n \;\middle|\; n \geq 0 \right\}.$$

5   A Logical Characterisation

We formulate a monadic second-order logic that characterises exactly the class of regular MSC languages. Given supplies $\mathrm{Var} = \{x, y, \ldots\}$ of individual variables and $\mathrm{VAR} = \{X, Y, \ldots\}$ of set variables, the syntax of $\mathrm{MSO}(\mathcal{P}_N, \Lambda)$ is defined by

$$\varphi ::= L_\sigma(x) \mid x \in X \mid x \preceq y \mid \neg\varphi \mid \varphi_1 \vee \varphi_2 \mid \exists x\varphi \mid \exists X\varphi \in \mathrm{MSO}(\mathcal{P}_N, \Lambda)$$

where $\sigma \in \Sigma$, $x, y \in \mathrm{Var}$, and $X \in \mathrm{VAR}$. Given an MSC, individual variables are interpreted as events and set variables as sets of events. $L_\sigma(x)$ is satisfied if the event of x is labelled with σ, $\preceq$ is interpreted as the partial order of the MSC, and the remaining constructs are defined as usual. We only consider formulas without free variables. For $\varphi \in \mathrm{MSO}(\mathcal{P}_N, \Lambda)$ and $B \in \mathbb{N}$, let $\mathcal{M}_\varphi^B := \{M \mid M \text{ is } B\text{-bounded}, M \models \varphi\}$. We conclude with the fundamental result of this section.

Theorem 10. *Given a set $\mathcal{M}$ of MSCs, $\mathcal{M}$ is a regular MSC language iff there exist a formula $\varphi \in \mathrm{MSO}(\mathcal{P}_N, \Lambda)$ and $B \in \mathbb{N}$ such that $Lin(\mathcal{M}) = Lin(\mathcal{M}_\varphi^B)$.*

The proof follows the outline of [7] although the concrete steps are different.

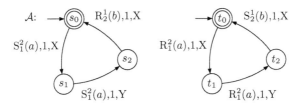

Fig. 5. A 2-bounded GMPA

References

1. R. Alur and M. Yannakakis. Model checking of message sequence charts. In *Proceedings of the 10th International Conference on Concurrency Theory*, volume 1664 of *Lecture Notes in Computer Science*, pages 114–129. Springer, 1999.
2. João Araújo. Formalizing sequence diagrams. In *Proceedings of the OOPSLA'98 Workshop on Formalizing UML. Why? How?*, volume 33, 10 of *ACM SIGPLAN Notices*, New York, 1998. ACM Press.
3. Benedikt Bollig and Martin Leucker. Modelling, Specifying, and Verifying Message Passing Systems. In Claudio Bettini and Angelo Montanari, editors, *Proceedings of the Symposium on Temporal Representation and Reasoning (TIME'01)*, pages 240–248. IEEE Computer Society Press, June 2001.
4. Benedikt Bollig, Martin Leucker, and Thomas Noll. Generalised Regular MSC Languages. Technical Report AIB-03-2002, RWTH Aachen, January 2002.
5. Volker Diekert and Yves Métivier. Partial commutation and traces. In G. Rozenberg and A. Salomaa, editors, *Handbook on Formal Languages*, volume III. Springer, Berlin-Heidelberg-New York, 1997.
6. Elsa Gunter, Anca Muscholl, and Doron Peled. Compositional message sequence charts. In Tiziana Margaria and Wang Yi, editors, *Proceedings of the 7th International Conference on Tools and Algorithms for the Construction and Analysis of Systems (TACAS'01)*, volume 2031 of *Lecture Notes in Computer Science*, pages 496–511. Springer, April 2001.
7. J. G. Henriksen, M. Mukund, K. Narayan Kumar, and P. S. Thiagarajan. Regular collections of message sequence charts. In *Proceedings of 25th International Symposium on Mathemtical Foundations of Computer Science (MFCS'2000)*, volume 1893 of *Lecture Notes in Computer Science*, pages 405–414. Springer, 2000.
8. ITU-TS. ITU-TS Recommendation Z.120anb: Formal Semantics of Message Sequence Charts. Technical report, ITU-TS, Geneva, 1998.
9. ITU-TS. ITU-TS Recommendation Z.120: Message Sequence Chart 1999 (MSC99). Technical report, ITU-TS, Geneva, 1999.
10. Michael Kaminski and Nissim Francez. Finite-memory automata. *Theoretical Computer Science*, 134(2):329–363, November 1994.
11. Dietrich Kuske. Another step towards a theory of regular MSC languages. In *Proceedings of the 19th International Symposium on Theoretical Aspects of Computer Science (STACS'02), 2002*, Lecture Notes in Computer Science. Springer, 2002.
12. P. Madhusudan and B. Meenakshi. Beyond message sequence graphs. In *Proceedings of the 21st Conference on Foundations of Software Technology and Theoretical Computer Science*, Lecture Notes in Computer Science. Springer, 2001.
13. M. Mukund, K. Narayan Kumar, and M. Sohoni. Keeping track of the latest gossip in message-passing systems. Technical Report TCS-95-3, School of Mathematics, SPIC Science Foundation, Madras, India, 1995.
14. Frank Neven, Thomas Schwentick, and Victor Vianu. Towards regular languages over infinite alphabets. In *Proceedings of 26th International Symposium on Mathematical Foundations of Computer Science (MFCS'01)*, Lecture Notes in Computer Science. Springer, 2001.
15. Wiesław Zielonka. Notes on finite asynchronous automata. *R.A.I.R.O. — Informatique Théorique et Applications*, 21:99–135, 1987.

On Compositional Reasoning in the Spi-calculus⋆

Michele Boreale and Daniele Gorla

Dipartimento di Sistemi e Informatica, Università di Firenze
boreale@dsi.unifi.it, gorla@gdn.dsi.unifi.it

Abstract. Observational equivalences can be used to reason about the
correctness of security protocols described in the spi-calculus. Unlike
in CCS or in π-calculus, these equivalences do not enjoy a simple
formulation in spi-calculus. The present paper aims at enriching the
set of tools for reasoning on processes by providing a few equational
laws for a sensible notion of spi-bisimilarity. We discuss the difficulties
underlying compositional reasoning in spi-calculus and show that, in
some cases and with some care, the proposed laws can be used to build
compositional proofs. A selection of these laws forms the basis of a proof
system that we show to be sound and complete for the strong version of
bisimilarity.

Keywords: process calculi, axiomatization, reasoning on security

1   Introduction

Observational equivalences can be used to reason about the correctness of security protocols described in the spi-calculus [2]. Unlike in CCS or in π-calculus,
these equivalences do not enjoy a simple formulation in spi-calculus. One reason is the interplay between cryptography and handling of private names, which
somehow forces a distinction between the knowledge of the observer and the interface of the observed process (i.e. the set of its free names). On the contrary, in
the simpler non-cryptographic setting, these two notions coincide. To illustrate
this point, let us consider two processes that send different, encrypted messages
along a public channel c: $P \stackrel{\triangle}{=} (\nu\,k\,)\,\overline{c}\{a\}_k.\mathbf{0}$ and $Q \stackrel{\triangle}{=} (\nu\,k\,)\,\overline{c}\{b\}_k.\mathbf{0}$. According
to π-like bisimulation, P and Q are not equivalent, because they give rise to
syntactically different transitions (names a and b are different). On the other
hand, messages $\{a\}_k$ and $\{b\}_k$ have the same effect upon an external observer:
in both cases, he/she simply cannot open the message because has no access to
the private key k. Thus, it would be reasonable to regard P and Q as equivalent.

   In [6], these considerations have led to the introduction of *environment sensitive (e.s.) bisimulation*, written $\sim$ below, where each process comes equipped
with an explicit representation of what its environment knows. The latter is
used to tell if two messages can be distinguished or not. Continuing with the

---

⋆ Research partially supported by the Italian MURST Project NAPOLI and by the
European FET project MIKADO (IST-2001-32222).

M. Nielsen and U. Engberg (Eds.): Fossacs 2002, LNCS 2303, pp. 67–81, 2002.

example above, P and Q are e.s. bisimilar under the environment $\epsilon_{(a,b,c)}$ that accounts for the knowledge of the free names a, b and c: this is written as $(\;\epsilon_{(a,b,c)}\;,\;\epsilon_{(a,b,c)}\;) \vdash P \sim Q$. Environmental knowledge grows after an output action is observed and two processes being compared may end up being placed in two different, though in some sense 'equivalent', environments. For instance, this is the case for P and Q above after the firing of the output actions. In [6], $\sim$ is shown to capture precisely barbed equivalence [12] in spi-calculus, which adds to the evidence that it is a sensible semantical notion.

The interplay between cryptography and private names makes compositional reasoning in spi-calculus difficult, when not impossible at all. A private name k can be extruded and hence become free, without this implying that k is learnt by the observer. Thus, we are sometimes confronted with equivalences like: $(\;\sigma_1\;,\;\sigma_2\;) \vdash \overline{c}\{a\}_k.P_1 \sim \overline{c}\{b\}_k.P_2$ where both σ_1 and σ_2 know a, b, c, but neither knows k. In general, this kind of equivalences are not preserved by parallel composition. For instance, when putting $\overline{c}k.\mathbf{0}$ in parallel to both sides of the previous relation, the equivalence breaks down. The reason is that $\overline{c}k.\mathbf{0}$ may provide the observer with the key k to open $\{a\}_k$ and $\{b\}_k$, thus enabling a distinction between these two messages. Similar problems arise from the non-deterministic choice and output prefix operators. (On the contrary, the congruence rules for restriction and input prefix appear to be somehow more liberal in spi-calculus than in π-calculus; this is further discussed in the paper).

In fact, one can devise congruence rules that work in some special cases and that are often sufficient to analyze concrete examples. In the paper, we show how to reason compositionally on a small security protocol like Wide Mouthed Frog [2]. However, special-case congruence rules appear to be not powerful enough to achieve completeness results in the same fashion as for CCS and π-calculus (see, e.g., [10,13]). Indeed, proving any process equivalent to, say, a head normal formal (hnf) requires a congruence law for parallel composition that, as seen above, is not sound in general for $\sim$. We get round this difficulty by noting that the set of equations needed to re-write every spi-process to a hnf *are* preserved by parallel composition. Starting from this consideration, we design a two-level proof system. The first level only contains these general, hnf-related equations. The second level contains those identities that are specific to spi-calculus, plus a law for importing equalities from the first level. The resulting proof system is perhaps not as elegant as a one-level proof system might be, but provides a reasonably informative axiomatization of $\sim$ over finite processes.

For the sake of presentation, in this paper we confine ourselves to shared-key cryptography, as presented e.g. in [6]. We believe that, with obvious modifications, the same arguments apply when the language is extended with other crypto-primitives, like public-key encryption (see [2,1]).

The rest of this paper is organized as follows. Sect. 2 provides a summary of the spi-calculus as presented in [6]. A set of equational laws that are meant to be useful in practice is presented in Sect. 3, together with some examples of their application. A more extensive example is in Sect. 4. Sect. 5 presents the proof system, and discuss its completeness. A few concluding remarks are in Sect. 6.

2   The Calculus and Its Semantics

In this section we only define the basics of the calculus. We refer to [6] for a comprehensive presentation. The syntax of the calculus is summarized in Table 1.[1]

Table 1. Syntax of the calculus

$a, b \ldots, h, k, \ldots, x, y, z \ldots$	*names* $\mathcal{N}$
$M, N ::= a \mid \{M\}_k \mid \langle M_1, M_2 \rangle$	*messages* $\mathcal{M}$
$\eta, \zeta \;\; ::= a \mid \{\eta\}_\zeta \mid \mathsf{dec}_\eta(\zeta)$ $\mid \langle \eta, \zeta \rangle \mid \pi_1(\zeta) \mid \pi_2(\zeta)$	*expressions* $\mathcal{Z}$
$\phi, \psi \;\; ::= t\!t \mid name(\zeta) \mid [\zeta = \eta]$ $\mid \mathtt{let}\ z = \zeta\ \mathtt{in}\ \phi \mid \phi \wedge \psi \mid \neg \phi$	*formulae* Φ
$P, Q \;\; ::= \mathbf{0} \mid \eta(x).P \mid \overline{\eta}\zeta.P \mid P + Q \mid P \mid Q$ $\mid\ !P \mid (\nu a)P \mid \phi P \mid \mathtt{let}\ z = \zeta\ \mathtt{in}\ P$	*processes* $\mathcal{P}$

It is assumed that $\mathsf{dec}.(\cdot)$ and $\pi_i(\cdot)$ do not occur in $name(\zeta)$, $[\zeta = \eta]$, $\eta(x)$ and $\overline{\eta}\zeta$. Operators $a(x).\cdot$, $(\nu a)\cdot$ and $\mathtt{let}\ z = \zeta\ \mathtt{in}\ \cdot$ are *binders*, with the obvious scope, for names x, a and z, respectively. In $\mathtt{let}\ z = \zeta\ \mathtt{in}\ \cdot$, it is assumed that $z \notin n(\zeta)$.

As usual, we use $\tilde{\cdot}$ to denote tuples of objects. Notions of alpha-equivalence, *free names* $(fn(P))$, *bound names* $(bn(P))$ and *names* $(n(P))$ of a process P arise as expected; in particular, we identify alpha-equivalent processes and formulae. We use two evaluation functions. The first one $(\hat{\cdot}: \mathcal{Z} \to \mathcal{M} \cup \{\bot\})$ transforms an expression into a message by properly evaluating decryptions and projections (e.g. $\widehat{\mathsf{dec}_k(\{M\}_k)} = M$ while $\widehat{\mathsf{dec}_h(\{M\}_k)} = \bot$ if $h \neq k$). The second function $(\ [\![\cdot]\!] : \Phi \to \{t\!t, f\!f\})$ takes a formula and gives its boolean value as expected.

Informally, an *environment* represents the knowledge of names and keys that an external observer has acquired about a certain process. We represent and use an environment as a substitution σ of names with messages. The domain and proper co-domain of σ are written as $dom(\sigma)$ and $range(\sigma)$, respectively; we let $n(\sigma) \stackrel{\triangle}{=} dom(\sigma) \cup (\cup_{M \in range(\sigma)} n(M))$. With ϵ_T we denote the substitution that acts like the identity on the set of names T. The extension of environment σ with the binding $[M/x]$, written $\sigma[M/x]$, and application σ to a term t, written $t\sigma$, are defined as usual.

A *configuration* is a pair $\sigma \vartriangleright P$ formed by an environment σ and a process P. Transitions between configurations take the form $\sigma \vartriangleright P \xmapsto[\delta]{\mu} \sigma' \vartriangleright P'$ and represent atomic interactions between P and σ. Here, μ is the *process action*

---

[1]   Compared to the spi-calculus in [2], we have the traditional process operators (i.e. input and output prefixes, non-deterministic choice, parallel composition, replication and restriction) plus a more general form of boolean guard and an operator for decryption and pair splitting.

(i.e. input, output or τ) and δ is the complementary, under σ, *environment action* (respectively output, input and 'no action'). The inference rules in Table 2 mention in the premises early-style transitions of the form $P \xrightarrow{\mu} P'$: the latter just account for actions that processes are willing to do, regardless of whether an external observer can react or not to them. Its definition is standard and can be found in [6].

Table 2. Rules for the environment-sensitive calculus

It is assumed that $n(\eta) \subseteq dom(\sigma)$ and that names in $\widetilde{b}$ are fresh for σ and P.

$$(\text{E-Out}) \quad \frac{P \xrightarrow{(\nu \widetilde{b})\overline{a}\,\langle M \rangle} P' \quad \widehat{\eta \sigma} = a}{\sigma \rhd P \xrightarrow[\eta(x)]{(\nu \widetilde{b})\overline{a}\,\langle M \rangle} \sigma[M/x] \rhd P'} \qquad (\text{E-Tau}) \quad \frac{P \xrightarrow{\tau} P'}{\sigma \rhd P \xrightarrow[-]{\tau} \sigma \rhd P'}$$

$$(\text{E-Inp}) \quad \frac{P \xrightarrow{a\,M} P' \quad \widehat{\eta \sigma} = a \quad M = \widehat{\zeta \sigma} \quad \widetilde{b} \triangleq (n(\zeta) - dom(\sigma))}{\sigma \rhd P \xrightarrow[(\nu \widetilde{b})\overline{\eta}\,\langle \zeta \rangle]{a\,M} \sigma[\widetilde{b}/\widetilde{b}] \rhd P'}$$

2.1 Environment-Sensitive Strong Bisimulation

Definition 1 (Equivalence on environments). *Two environments σ_1 and σ_2 are equivalent (written $\sigma_1 \sim \sigma_2$) if $dom(\sigma_1) = dom(\sigma_2)$ and $\forall \phi$ s.t. $fn(\phi) \subseteq dom(\sigma_1)$ it holds $[\![\, \phi\sigma_1 \,]\!] = [\![\, \phi\sigma_2 \,]\!]$.*

For example, $\sigma_1 \triangleq [a/x \,,\; b/y \,,\; \{a\}k/z]$ and $\sigma_2 \triangleq [a/x \,,\; b/y \,,\; \{b\}k/z]$ are equivalent. On the contrary, $\sigma_1' \triangleq \sigma_1[k/v]$ and $\sigma_2' \triangleq \sigma_2[k/v]$ are not (consider the formula let $w = dec_v(z)$ in $[x = w]$). A metatheory to reason on environment equivalence $\sim$ is presented in [6]; in particular, an equivalent definition is given there that leaves out universal quantifiers on ϕ and only works on the structure of the environments. However, the present definition suffices for our purposes.

If $\Re$ is a binary relation over configurations, we write $(\sigma_1 \rhd P, \sigma_2 \rhd Q) \in \Re$ as $(\,\sigma_1\,,\;\sigma_2\,) \vdash P \,\Re\, Q$; if $\sigma_1 \sim \sigma_2$ whenever $(\,\sigma_1\,,\;\sigma_2\,) \vdash P \,\Re\, Q$, we call $\Re$ *compatible*. We now give the strong version of e.s. bisimilarity from [6].

Definition 2 (Environment-sensitive strong bisimilarity). *Let $\Re$ be a binary and symmetric compatible relation of configurations. We say that $\Re$ is an environment-sensitive strong bisimulation if whenever $(\,\sigma_1\,,\;\sigma_2\,) \vdash P \,\Re\, Q$ and $\sigma_1 \rhd P \xrightarrow[\delta]{\mu} \sigma_1' \rhd P'$ then there are μ', σ_2' and Q' such that $\sigma_2 \rhd Q \xrightarrow[\delta]{\mu'} \sigma_2' \rhd Q'$ and $(\,\sigma_1'\,,\;\sigma_2'\,) \vdash P' \,\Re\, Q'$. Environment-sensitive bisimilarity, written $\sim$, is the largest environment-sensitive strong bisimulation.*

3   Laws for Compositional Reasoning

In this section we list and explain some laws that, in many cases, can be useful to prove bisimilarity of two processes in a simple and compositional way. As we shall see in Sect. 5, with some modifications, these laws form the basis of a complete proof system for $\sim$. In what follows, we discuss a little about significance of each law and provide explicative examples and countrexamples. Each law is a judgement of the form $(\,\sigma_1\,,\,\sigma_2\,)\vdash P \sim Q$, where $\sigma_1 \sim \sigma_2$.

Basic laws : The following laws are easily derived from the definition.

$$
\begin{array}{ll}
(\text{REFL}) \quad (\,\sigma\,,\,\sigma\,)\vdash P \sim P & (\text{SYM}) \quad \dfrac{(\,\sigma_1\,,\,\sigma_2\,)\vdash P \sim Q}{(\,\sigma_2\,,\,\sigma_1\,)\vdash Q \sim P}\\[2em]
(\text{TRANS}) \quad \dfrac{(\,\sigma_1\,,\,\sigma_2\,)\vdash P \sim Q \quad\wedge\quad (\,\sigma_2\,,\,\sigma_3\,)\vdash Q \sim R}{(\,\sigma_1\,,\,\sigma_3\,)\vdash P \sim R}
\end{array}
$$

We then have a form of 'weakening' which states that discarding some entries from the environments does preserve equivalence.

$$
(\text{WEAK}) \quad \dfrac{(\,\sigma_1[\widetilde{M_1/x}]\,,\,\sigma_2[\widetilde{M_2/x}]\,)\vdash P \sim Q}{(\,\sigma_1\,,\,\sigma_2\,)\vdash P \sim Q}
$$

The following law provides a basic step in compositional reasoning. Note that the more general formulation " $(\,\sigma_1\,,\,\sigma_2\,)\vdash P \sim P$ *if $\sigma_1 \sim \sigma_2$* " does not hold.

$$
(\text{NIL}) \quad (\,\sigma_1\,,\,\sigma_2\,)\vdash \mathbf{0} \sim \mathbf{0} \qquad \text{if } \sigma_1 \sim \sigma_2
$$

Example 1. In fact, let us consider $P \overset{\triangle}{=} p(x).\mathtt{let}\ y = \mathtt{dec}_k(x)\ \mathtt{in}\ [y = a]\overline{p}y.\mathbf{0}$ and the equivalent environments $\sigma_1 \overset{\triangle}{=} [p/p\,,\,\{a\}_k/y]$ and $\sigma_2 \overset{\triangle}{=} [p/p\,,\,\{b\}_k/y]$. A transition from $\sigma_1 \rhd P$ with $\delta = \overline{p}y$ leads to a process that is capable of a $\overline{p}a$-action, while the corresponding transition from $\sigma_2 \rhd P$ leads to a process that is stuck, because the matching $[b = a]$ is not satisfied. Thus $(\,\sigma_1\,,\,\sigma_2\,)\vdash P \not\sim P$. $\qquad\square$

The standard scope extrusion law can also be useful:

$$
(\text{EXTR}) \quad (\,\sigma_1\,,\,\sigma_2\,)\vdash (\nu\,k)\,(P\,|\,Q) \sim ((\nu\,k)\,P)\,|\,Q \qquad \text{if } k \notin fn(Q)
$$

The last basic law can be used to replace a decryption underneath a `let` with an equality test, under some conditions. Here and in the rest of this paper, we will use the abbreviation "$a(\{y\}_k).P$" for "$a(x).\mathtt{let}\ y = \mathtt{dec}_k(x)\ \mathtt{in}\ P$", where $x \notin fn(P,k)$. In the following law we also use the notion of *context* that is a generic process with a 'hole' that can be filled by any process.

(LET_1) $(\,\sigma\,,\,\sigma\,)\,\vdash\,(\nu\,\widetilde{h},k)\,(\,C[\,\overline{p}\{M\}_k.P\,]\mid D[\,p(\{y\}_k).Q\,])$ $\sim$
$\qquad\qquad\qquad (\nu\,\widetilde{h},k)\,(\,C[\,\overline{p}\{M\}_k.P\,]\mid D[\,p(x).[x=\{M\}_k]Q[M/y]\,])$

$k\notin n(P,C,D)$, contexts C and D do not bind names in $\overline{p}\{M\}_k$ and x is fresh

Example 2. In order to better understand the above law, consider the process $P\stackrel{\triangle}{=}(\nu\,k)\,(A\mid B)$ where $A\stackrel{\triangle}{=}\overline{p}\{M\}_k.R$, $B\stackrel{\triangle}{=}p(\{y\}_k).Q$ and $k\notin n(R)$. Intuitively, since k is initially not known by the environment, the only message B can read and then decrypt using k is the one written by A, i.e. $\{M\}_k$. In fact, the condition $k\notin n(R)$ prevents the environment from learning k, or anything encrypted with it, before Q evolves. Thus P is equivalent to $(\nu\,k)\,(A\mid p(x).[x=\{M\}_k]Q[M/y])$, where x is a fresh variable. $\square$

Output congruence :

(OUT) $\dfrac{(\,\sigma_1[M_1/x]\,,\,\sigma_2[M_2/x]\,)\vdash P\sim Q}{(\,\sigma_1[M_1/x]\,,\,\sigma_2[M_2/x]\,)\vdash \overline{a_1}M_1.P\sim\overline{a_2}M_2.Q}$

where $a_i\,=\,\widehat{\eta\sigma_i}$ for $i=1,2$ and for some η s.t. $n(\eta)\subseteq dom(\sigma_1)$

Notice that the two channels a_1 and a_2 may be different but are related via the two environments (e.g. a_1 and a_2 may be stored in the same entry of the two environments). Similarly, the messages M_1 and M_2 may well be different, but they must correspond to the same environment entry x. The use of (OUT) is tipically joined with the use of (WEAK), as shown below.

Example 3. We want to prove $(\,\sigma\,,\,\sigma\,)\vdash P\sim Q$, where $\sigma\stackrel{\triangle}{=}[p/p]$, $P\stackrel{\triangle}{=}\overline{p}\{a\}_k.\mathbf{0}$ and $Q\stackrel{\triangle}{=}\overline{p}\{b\}_k.\mathbf{0}$. Notice that $\sigma[\{a\}_k/x]\sim\sigma[\{b\}_k/x]$, since neither of $\{a\}_k$ and $\{b\}_k$ can be opened using the knowledge in σ. So, by (NIL), we get $(\,\sigma[\{a\}_k/x]\,,\,\sigma[\{b\}_k/x]\,)\vdash\mathbf{0}\sim\mathbf{0}$. Then, by (OUT) and (WEAK) (discarding the x entry), we conclude. $\square$

Input congruence : In the rest of the paper we shall use the following predicate:

$$\Gamma(\,\zeta,\,\widetilde{b},\,\sigma_1,\,\sigma_2,\,P,\,Q\,)\quad\stackrel{\triangle}{\Leftrightarrow}\quad\widehat{\zeta\sigma_1}\neq\bot\wedge\widetilde{b}=n(\zeta)-dom(\sigma_1)\wedge$$
$$\widetilde{b}\cap n(\sigma_1,\sigma_2,P,Q)=\emptyset$$

(notice that $\Gamma(\,\zeta,\,\widetilde{b},\,\sigma_1,\,\sigma_2,\,P,\,Q\,)\Leftrightarrow\Gamma(\,\zeta,\,\widetilde{b},\,\sigma_2,\,\sigma_1,\,P,\,Q\,)$, if $\sigma_1\sim\sigma_2$).

(IN) $\dfrac{\forall\,\zeta,\widetilde{b}\text{ s.t. } \Gamma(\,\zeta,\,\widetilde{b},\,\sigma_1,\,\sigma_2,\,P,\,Q\,)\,:\quad(\,\sigma_1[\widetilde{b/b}]\,,\,\sigma_2[\widetilde{b/b}]\,)\vdash P[\widehat{\zeta\sigma_1}/x]\sim Q[\widehat{\zeta\sigma_2}/x]}{(\,\sigma_1\,,\,\sigma_2\,)\vdash a_1(x).P\sim a_2(x).Q}$

where $a_i\,=\,\widehat{\eta\sigma_i}$ for $i=1,2$ and for some η s.t. $n(\eta)\subseteq dom(\sigma_1)$

The above formulation of the input rule is somehow more generous than the π-calculus style one. In fact, the premise does not require instantiating x to all possible messages, but only to those that can be built out of σ_1, σ_2 and some new names $\tilde{b}$, as specified by all ζ's that satisfies the predicate Γ. This is made clearer in the following example.

Example 4. Using (IN), we can prove an equivalence quite similar to (LET$_1$) (in the sense that a "let" is replaced with a test), that is

$$(\sigma , \sigma)\vdash a(x).\mathtt{let}\ x' = \mathsf{dec}_k(x)\ \mathtt{in}\ P \sim a(x).[x = \{b\}_k]P[^b\!/\!x']$$

where $\sigma \triangleq [^a\!/a , \{b\}_k/w]$. Indeed, it is easy to check that, whenever $\Gamma(\ \zeta,\ \tilde{c},\ \sigma,\ \sigma,\ \mathtt{let}\ldots,\ [x = \ldots\ )$ and $\widehat{\zeta\sigma} = \{M\}_k$, then $M = b$. This is a consequence of the fact that the environment does not know k and $k \notin \tilde{c}$. On the contrary, if the environment knew k, it could have created the message $\{a\}_k$, which, upon reception, would have stopped the second process and not the first one. Of course, the above two processes are not equivalent according to traditional bisimilarity. □

The formulation of the input rule given above fails to capture some equivalences: in fact, in the proof system, it will be replaced by a more general rule.

Example 5. Let us consider the following $\sigma \triangleq [^a\!/a]$, $P \triangleq a(x).\bar{a}\{x\}_k.\mathbf{0}$ and $Q \triangleq a(x).[x \neq b]\bar{a}\{x\}_k.\mathbf{0} + a(x).\bar{a}\{b\}_k.\mathbf{0}$. It is easy to see that $(\sigma , \sigma)\vdash P \sim Q$ but this equivalence is not an instance of (IN). □

Parallel composition :

$$\begin{array}{c} (\text{PAR}) \quad \dfrac{(\sigma_1 , \sigma_2)\vdash P \sim Q}{(\sigma_1 , \sigma_2)\vdash P\,|\,R\sigma_1 \sim Q\,|\,R\sigma_2}\ fn(R) \subseteq dom(\sigma_1) \end{array}$$

As pointed out in the introduction, congruence under parallel composition is a major problem in spi-calculus. In fact, a naive formulation like

$$\dfrac{(\sigma_1 , \sigma_2)\vdash P \sim Q \quad \wedge \quad (\sigma_1 , \sigma_2)\vdash R \sim S}{(\sigma_1 , \sigma_2)\vdash P\,|\,R \sim Q\,|\,S}$$

is not valid.

Example 6. To see this, let us consider $P \triangleq \bar{p}\{a\}_k.\mathbf{0}$, $Q \triangleq \bar{p}\{b\}_k.\mathbf{0}$, $R \triangleq \bar{p}k.\mathbf{0}$ and $\sigma \triangleq [^p\!/p , ^a\!/a , ^b\!/b]$. Following Example 3, we can prove $(\sigma , \sigma)\vdash P \sim Q$. However, $(\sigma , \sigma)\vdash\ P\,|\,R \not\sim Q\,|\,R$. In fact the output of the key k enables an external observer to distinguish $\{a\}_k$ from $\{b\}_k$, hence $P\,|\,R$ from $Q\,|\,R$. □

The side condition of (PAR) reduces the set of processes that can be composed with P and Q, by requiring that the composed processes are consistent with the knowledge available to the environment. In spite of this limitation, the rule allows for non trivial forms of compositional reasoning, as shown in Sect. 4.

Other Congruences :

$$
\begin{array}{ll}
\text{(SUM)} & \dfrac{(\,\sigma_1\,,\,\sigma_2\,)\vdash P_1 \sim P_2 \quad \wedge \quad (\,\sigma_1\,,\,\sigma_2\,)\vdash Q_1 \sim Q_2}{(\,\sigma_1\,,\,\sigma_2\,)\vdash P_1 + Q_1 \sim P_2 + Q_2}
\end{array}
$$

$$
\text{(RES)} \quad \dfrac{(\,\sigma_1\,,\,\sigma_2\,)\vdash P \sim Q}{(\,\sigma_1\,,\,\sigma_2\,)\vdash (\nu\,\widetilde{h}_1)\,P \sim (\nu\,\widetilde{h}_2)\,Q} \quad \widetilde{h}_i \cap n(\sigma_i)=\emptyset\ for\ i=1,2
$$

$$
\text{(GUARD)} \quad \dfrac{(\,\sigma_1\,,\,\sigma_2\,)\vdash P \sim Q}{(\,\sigma_1\,,\,\sigma_2\,)\vdash \phi P \sim \phi Q}
$$

$$
\text{(LET$_2$)} \quad \dfrac{\widehat{\zeta} \neq \bot \quad \wedge \quad (\,\sigma_1\,,\,\sigma_2\,)\vdash P[\widehat{\zeta}/z] \sim Q[\widehat{\zeta}/z]}{(\,\sigma_1\,,\,\sigma_2\,)\vdash \texttt{let } z = \zeta \texttt{ in } P \ \sim\ \texttt{let } z = \zeta \texttt{ in } Q}
$$

The only surprising aspect of these laws is in (RES): the tuples of restricted names $\widetilde{h}_1$ and $\widetilde{h}_2$ can be different even in length.

Example 7. Using (RES) one can prove $(\,\sigma\,,\,\sigma\,)\vdash P \sim (\nu\,k)\,P$, provided that $k \notin n(\sigma)$. □

4 A Compositional Secrecy Proof for WMF

In this section we verify a property of the *Wide Mouthed Frog* (WMF) protocol. Differently from [2,6], our proof is entirely compositional and syntactical, based on the simple equational laws introduced in the previous section.

Consider a system where two agents A and B share two secret keys, k_{AS} and k_{BS} respectively, with a server S. The purpose of the protocol is to establish a new secret key k between A and B, which A may use to pass some confidential information d to B. We suppose that the protocol is always started by A and that all communications occur on a public channel, say p. Informally, the protocol can be described as follows:

Message 1	$A \to S :$	$\{k\}_{k_{AS}}$
Message 2	$S \to B :$	$\{k\}_{k_{BS}}$
Message 3	$A \to B :$	$\{d\}_k$.

Our intent here is to verify a secrecy property for one run of the protocol. In our language, the above notation translates to a process $P(d)$ defined, like in [2], as follows (we use the notation $t(w)$ to emphasize that name w may occur free in t and, for any M, $t(M)$ abbreviates $t[M/w]$; bound names are all distinct):

$$
\begin{aligned}
A(d) &\stackrel{\triangle}{=} \overline{p}\{k\}_{k_{AS}}.\overline{p}\{d\}_k.G \\
S &\stackrel{\triangle}{=} p(\{x\}_{k_{AS}}).\overline{p}\{x\}_{k_{BS}}.\mathbf{0} \\
B &\stackrel{\triangle}{=} p(\{y\}_{k_{BS}}).p(\{z\}_y).F(z) \\
P(d) &\stackrel{\triangle}{=} (\nu\,k_{AS},\ k_{BS})\,(((\nu\,k)\,A(d))\,|\,S\,|\,B) .
\end{aligned}
$$

The processes G and $F(z)$ represent behaviuor of A and B respectively upon completion of the protocol. Below, we make the following assumptions:

1. the key k does not occur in G and F (that is, k is one-time);
2. k_{AS} and k_{BS} are used only to establish the new session key (in particular $k_{AS}, k_{BS} \notin n(F(z), G)$);
3. for each $M_1, M_2 \in \mathcal{M}$ and for each $\sigma_1(w)$ and $\sigma_2(w)$ s.t. $\sigma_1(M_1) \sim \sigma_2(M_2)$, it holds $(\sigma_1(M_1), \sigma_2(M_2)) \vdash F(M_1) \sim F(M_2)$.

Assumption 1 is necessary in order to apply (PAR), while assumtion 2 is necessary to apply (LET$_1$). At the moment we do not know how to discard these assumptions while preserving the compositionality of the proof. Assumption 3 seems reasonable because F should not leak the received datum itself. Following [2], the desired secrecy property is

$$\boxed{\begin{array}{c} \text{``}P(d) \text{ does not leak } d\text{''} : \forall\, M, M' \in \mathcal{M} \quad (\epsilon_V, \epsilon_V) \vdash P(M) \sim P(M') \\[4pt] \text{where} \quad V \triangleq fn(P(M), P(M')) \end{array}}$$

The proof of the above assertion takes these four steps (by alpha-equivalence, we assume $k_{AS}, k_{BS}, k \notin n(M, M')$):

(i) By (EXTR), $(\epsilon_V, \epsilon_V) \vdash P(M) \sim (\nu\, k_{AS}, k_{BS}, k)(A(M) | S | B)$. Then, by (LET$_1$) (applied to A and S) and (TRANS), $(\epsilon_V, \epsilon_V) \vdash P(M) \sim (\nu\, k_{AS}, k_{BS}, k)(A(M) | S' | B)$ where $S' \triangleq p(u).[u = \{k\}_{k_{AS}}]\overline{p}\{k\}_{k_{BS}}.0$. Again by (LET$_1$) (applied to S' and B) and (TRANS), we obtain

$$(\epsilon_V, \epsilon_V) \vdash P(M) \sim (\nu\, k_{AS}, k_{BS}, k)(A(M) | S' | B') \tag{1}$$

where $B' \triangleq p(v).[v = \{k\}_{k_{BS}}]p(w).\texttt{let } z = \texttt{dec}_k(w) \texttt{ in } F(z)$.

(ii) Similarly, replacing M with M', we obtain

$$(\epsilon_V, \epsilon_V) \vdash P(M') \sim (\nu\, k_{AS}, k_{BS}, k)(A(M') | S' | B') . \tag{2}$$

(iii) Let us define the environments $\sigma \triangleq \epsilon_V[\{k\}_{k_{AS}}/x_1, \{k\}_{k_{BS}}/x_2, \{M\}_k/x_3]$ and $\sigma' \triangleq \epsilon_V[\{k\}_{k_{AS}}/x_1, \{k\}_{k_{BS}}/x_2, \{M'\}_k/x_3]$, that are equivalent. Now suppose that we can prove

$$(\sigma, \sigma') \vdash B' \sim B' . \tag{3}$$

We let $S'' \triangleq p(u).[u = x_1]\overline{p}x_2.0$ and $A'' \triangleq \overline{p}x_1.\overline{p}x_3.G$. We trivially have $S' = S''\sigma = S''\sigma'$, $A(M) = A''\sigma$ and $A(M') = A''\sigma'$. Thus, by (PAR) and (3), we have $(\sigma, \sigma') \vdash (A'' | S'')\sigma | B' \sim (A'' | S'')\sigma' | B'$ which is the same as $(\sigma, \sigma') \vdash A(M) | S' | B' \sim A(M') | S' | B'$. By (WEAK), we obtain $(\epsilon_V, \epsilon_V) \vdash A(M) | S' | B' \sim A(M') | S' | B'$ and by (RES) we have $(\epsilon_V, \epsilon_V) \vdash (\nu\, k_{AS}, k_{BS}, k)(A(M) | S' | B') \sim (\nu\, k_{AS}, k_{BS}, k)(A(M') | S' | B')$. This equation, together with (TRANS), (1) and (2), allows us to conclude the desired $(\epsilon_V, \epsilon_V) \vdash P(M) \sim P(M')$.

(iv) We are now left with proving (3). The following steps prove our claim.

1. $(\sigma , \sigma') \vdash F(M) \sim F(M')$
2. $(\sigma , \sigma') \vdash \texttt{let } z = \texttt{dec}_k(\{M\}_k) \texttt{ in } F(z) \sim$
   $\texttt{let } z = \texttt{dec}_k(\{M'\}_k) \texttt{ in } F(z)$
3. $(\sigma , \sigma') \vdash p(w).\texttt{let } z = \texttt{dec}_k(w) \texttt{ in } F(z) \sim$
   $p(w).\texttt{let } z = \texttt{dec}_k(w) \texttt{ in } F(z)$
4. $(\sigma , \sigma') \vdash [v = \{k\}_{k_{BS}}]p(w).\texttt{let } z = \texttt{dec}_k(w) \texttt{ in } F(z) \sim$
   $[v = \{k\}_{k_{BS}}]p(w).\texttt{let } z = \texttt{dec}_k(w) \texttt{ in } F(z)$
5. $(\sigma , \sigma') \vdash p(v).[v = \{k\}_{k_{BS}}]p(w).\texttt{let } z = \texttt{dec}_k(w) \texttt{ in } F(z) \sim$
   $p(v).[v = \{k\}_{k_{BS}}]p(w).\texttt{let } z = \texttt{dec}_k(w) \texttt{ in } F(z)$
6. $(\sigma , \sigma') \vdash B' \sim B'$

where: step 1 follows by assumption, step 2 by (LET$_2$), step 3 by (IN),[2] step 4 by (GUARD), step 5 by (IN) (with considerations similar to 3) and finally step 6 by definition of B'.

Before leaving this example, we would like to stress that, in a similar way, we can prove other properties of the protocol, like integrity (*"if B accepts a message* $\{N\}_k$ *then* $N = d$*"*) and key authentication (*"B accepts only the key k generated by A"*). Moreover, following [7], we have also applied the same steps to a simplified Kerberos protocol, obtaining similar results; the work was only complicated by the presence of tuples of messages. We have presented WMF for its readability.

5   A Proof System

In this section we present a sound and complete proof system for $\sim$ over finite processes; we leave out from our language the replication operator ('!') which would lead to an undecidable theory (as shown in [11] for the π-calculus). The proof system has two levels. The first level is a proof system sound for ordinary strong bisimilarity (in the same vein as, e.g., the classical ones of the π-calculus [13]). The second level is tailored to the environment-sensitive semantics. Since ordinary bisimulation is finer than e.s. bisimulation, equivalences proven within the first proof system can be imported into the second one.

5.1   The Proof System *S1*

Definition 3. *A strong bisimulation is a symmetric relation between processes* $\Re$ *s.t. whenever* $P \Re Q$ *and* $P \xrightarrow{\mu} P'$ *then there is* Q' *s.t.* $Q \xrightarrow{\mu} Q'$ *and* $P' \Re Q'$*. We call* bisimilarity *(written* $\dot{\sim}$*) the largest strong bisimulation.*

---

[2] It is easy to check that for each ζ and $\widetilde{b}$ s.t. $\Gamma(\zeta, \widetilde{b}, \sigma, \sigma', \texttt{let}\dots, \texttt{let}\dots)$, if $\widehat{\zeta\sigma} = \{N\}_k$ and $\widehat{\zeta\sigma'} = \{N'\}_k$, then $N = M$ and $N' = M'$. In other words, the only readable message of the form $\{\cdot\}_k$ is that contained in x_3 and by assumption $(\sigma , \sigma') \vdash F(M) \sim F(M')$. If $\widehat{\zeta\sigma}$ is not of the form $\{\cdot\}_k$, then both processes are stuck, thus trivially equivalent to $\mathbf{0}$.

Table 3. The proof system *S1*

Axioms :

Monoid axioms for $+$ *and* $\mathbf{0}$

Monoid axioms for $\mid$ *and* $\mathbf{0}$

(Abs) $\quad P + P \doteq P$

(Exp) $\quad \sum_{i \in I} \alpha_i.P_i \mid \sum_{j \in J} \beta_j.Q_j \;\doteq\; \sum_{i \in I} \alpha_i.(P_i \mid \sum_{j \in J} \beta_j.Q_j) \;+$
$$\sum_{j \in J} \beta_j.(\sum_{i \in I} \alpha_i.P_i \mid Q_j) \;+$$
$$\sum_{\substack{\alpha_i \,=\, a_i(x) \\ \beta_j \,=\, (\nu\, \widetilde{b}_j\,)\,\overline{a_i}M_j}} \tau.(\nu\, \widetilde{b}_j\,)\,(P_i[M_j/x] \mid Q_j) \;+$$
$$\sum_{\substack{\beta_j \,=\, a_j(x) \\ \alpha_i \,=\, (\nu\, \widetilde{c}_i\,)\,\overline{a_j}N_i}} \tau.(\nu\, \widetilde{c}_i\,)\,(P_i \mid Q_j[N_i/x])$$

(Res$_1$) $\quad (\nu\, n\,)\, P \doteq P \qquad$ if $n \notin fn(P)$

(Res$_2$) $\quad (\nu\, n\,) \sum_{i \in I} \alpha_i.P_i \quad\doteq\quad \sum_{\substack{i \in I \\ n \notin n(\alpha_i)}} \alpha_i.(\nu\, n\,)\, P_i \;+$
$$\sum_{\substack{i \in I \\ \alpha_i \,=\, (\nu\, \widetilde{b}\,)\,\overline{a}M \,:\, n \,\neq a \,\wedge\, n \in n(M)}} ((\nu\, n\,)\,\alpha_i).P_i$$

(Phi) $\quad \phi P \;\doteq\; \begin{cases} \mathbf{0} & \text{if } [\![\,\phi\,]\!] = f\!f \\ P & \text{otherwise} \end{cases}$

(Let$_3$) $\quad \mathrm{let}\ z = \zeta\ \mathrm{in}\ P \;\doteq\; \begin{cases} \mathbf{0} & \text{if } \widehat{\zeta} = \bot \\ P[\widehat{\zeta}/z] & \text{otherwise} \end{cases}$

Congruence laws :

Congruence laws for $+$, $\mid$ *and* ν

(Phi$_0$) $\quad \dfrac{P \doteq Q}{\phi P \doteq \phi Q}$

(Let$_0$) $\quad \dfrac{P[\widehat{\zeta}/z] \doteq Q[\widehat{\zeta}/z]}{\mathrm{let}\ z = \zeta\ \mathrm{in}\ P \doteq \mathrm{let}\ z = \zeta\ \mathrm{in}\ Q} \quad \widehat{\zeta} \neq \bot$

Table 3 displays the axioms for $\doteq$. Essentially these are the axioms for bisimilarity in the π-calculus (see for example [13]) with some additional laws specific to the spi-calculus. Note that (Let$_0$) can be derived from (Let$_3$); we keep both for the sake of uniformity.

Proposition 1. *If* $P \doteq Q$ *then* $P \stackrel{.}{\sim} Q$.

In what follows, we use the notion of *bound output prefix*, that is an output prefix with some restrictions of the form $(\nu \tilde{b}) \bar{a} M$, where $a \notin \tilde{b}$ and $\tilde{b} \subseteq n(M)$.

Definition 4. *A process P is in* head normal form *(written hnf) if it is of the form $\sum_{i \in I} \alpha_i.P_i$ where α_i is a generic input-, (bound) output- or τ-prefix.*

Let us denote by $|P|$ the *depth* of a process P, inductively defined by

$$|P| \triangleq \begin{cases} 0 & \text{if } P = \mathbf{0} \\ 1 + |Q| & \text{if } P = \alpha.Q \\ max\{|Q|, |R|\} & \text{if } P = Q + R \\ |Q| + |R| & \text{if } P = Q \,|\, R \\ |Q| & \text{if } P = (\nu n)\, Q \,, \; P = \phi Q \text{ or } P = (\texttt{let } z = \zeta \texttt{ in } Q) \,. \end{cases}$$

Lemma 1. *For each process P there is a hnf P' s.t. $|P'| \leq |P|$ and $P \doteq P'$.*

The proof is by a standard induction over the number of operators in P. The inductive case for $P = P_1 \,|\, P_2$ relies on π-like congruence of $\sim$ for '$|$'.

5.2   The Proof System *S2*

The proof system is presented in Table 4. It consists of a selection (and modification) of laws presented in Sect. 3, plus the rule (IMPORT). The latter can be used to import equalities proved within *S1* into *S2*. Also notice the more general form of the input congruence, akin to those found in [9,5].

Theorem 1 (Soundness). *If $(\sigma_1, \sigma_2) \vdash P = Q$ then $(\sigma_1, \sigma_2) \vdash P \sim Q$.*

The main step of the completeness proof is that *S2* is complete for finite hnf (then, using (IMPORT), the proof for general finite processes is immediate). In order to obtain this first result we need a simple lemma:

Lemma 2. *For each $a \in \mathcal{N}$ let $a_{\sigma_1}^{-1} \triangleq \{\eta \in \mathcal{Z} : n(\eta) \subseteq dom(\sigma_1) \wedge \widehat{\eta \sigma_1} = a\}$. If $\sigma_1 \sim \sigma_2$, then there is a unique name b s.t. $\widehat{\eta \sigma_2} = b$ for each $\eta \in a_{\sigma_1}^{-1}$.*

Proposition 2 (Completeness for hnf). *Let P and Q be finite hnf. If $(\sigma_1, \sigma_2) \vdash P \sim Q$ then $(\sigma_1, \sigma_2) \vdash P = Q$.*

Proof. By induction on $|P| + |Q|$. The base case is trivial using (NIL). For the inductive step, we group the summands by the kind of their prefixes, obtaining $P \triangleq \sum_I \alpha_i.P_i = P_\tau + P_{out} + P_{in}$ and $Q \triangleq \sum_J \beta_j.Q_j = Q_\tau + Q_{out} + Q_{in}$. It is sufficient to prove that $(\sigma_1, \sigma_2) \vdash P_s = Q_s$ for $s \in \{\tau, out, in\}$.

$s = \tau$. We will prove that each summand of P_τ is provably equal to a summand of Q_τ. Consider $\sigma_1 \rhd P \overset{\tau}{\longmapsto} \sigma_1 \rhd P_i$. By hypothesis, there is $j \in J$ s.t. $\sigma_2 \rhd Q \overset{\tau}{\longmapsto} \sigma_2 \rhd Q_j$ and $(\sigma_1, \sigma_2) \vdash P_i \sim Q_j$. We cannot apply induction because P_i and Q_j are in general not hnf. However, by Lemma 1 and (IMPORT), we

Table 4. The proof system $S2$

Axioms :

(NIL) $(\sigma_1 , \sigma_2) \vdash \mathbf{0} = \mathbf{0}$ if $\sigma_1 \sim \sigma_2$ (REFL) $(\sigma_1 , \sigma_1) \vdash P = P$

(IMPORT) $\dfrac{P \doteq Q}{(\sigma , \sigma) \vdash P = Q}$ (SYM) $\dfrac{(\sigma_1 , \sigma_2) \vdash P = Q}{(\sigma_2 , \sigma_1) \vdash Q = P}$

(WEAK) $\dfrac{(\sigma_1[\widetilde{M_1/x}] , \sigma_2[\widetilde{M_2/x}]) \vdash P = Q}{(\sigma_1 , \sigma_2) \vdash P = Q}$ (TRANS) $\dfrac{\begin{array}{c}(\sigma_1 , \sigma_2) \vdash P = Q \; \wedge \\ (\sigma_2 , \sigma_3) \vdash Q = R\end{array}}{(\sigma_1 , \sigma_3) \vdash P = R}$

Congruence laws :

(TAU) $\dfrac{(\sigma_1 , \sigma_2) \vdash P = Q}{(\sigma_1 , \sigma_2) \vdash \tau.P = \tau.Q}$

(OUT) $\dfrac{(\sigma_1[M_1/x] , \sigma_2[M_2/x]) \vdash P = Q}{(\sigma_1[M_1/x] , \sigma_2[M_2/x]) \vdash \overline{a_1}M_1.P = \overline{a_2}M_2.Q}$

where $a_i = \widehat{\eta \sigma_i}$ for $i = 1, 2$ and for some η s.t. $n(\eta) \subseteq dom(\sigma_1)$

(INP) $\dfrac{\forall \zeta, \widetilde{b} \; s.t. \; \Gamma(\zeta, \widetilde{b}, \sigma_1, \sigma_2, \sum_{i \in I} P_i, \sum_{j \in J} Q_j) \quad : \\ (\sigma_1[\widetilde{b/b}] , \sigma_2[\widetilde{b/b}]) \vdash \sum_{i \in I} \tau.P_i[\widehat{\zeta \sigma_1}/x] = \sum_{j \in J} \tau.Q_j[\widehat{\zeta \sigma_2}/x]}{(\sigma_1 , \sigma_2) \vdash \sum_{i \in I} a_1(x).P_i = \sum_{j \in J} a_2(x).Q_j}$

where $a_i = \widehat{\eta \sigma_i}$ for $i = 1, 2$ and for some η s.t. $n(\eta) \subseteq dom(\sigma_1)$

(SUM) $\dfrac{(\sigma_1 , \sigma_2) \vdash P_1 = P_2 \quad \wedge \quad (\sigma_1 , \sigma_2) \vdash Q_1 = Q_2}{(\sigma_1 , \sigma_2) \vdash P_1 + Q_1 = P_2 + Q_2}$

(RES) $\dfrac{(\sigma_1 , \sigma_2) \vdash P = Q}{(\sigma_1 , \sigma_2) \vdash (\nu \widetilde{h_1}) P \sim (\nu \widetilde{h_2}) Q} \quad \widetilde{h_i} \cap n(\sigma_i) = \emptyset \; for \; i = 1, 2$

---

can find a hnf P' such that $(\sigma_1 , \sigma_1) \vdash P_i = P'$ and $|P'| \leq |P_i|$ (and similarly for Q_j and Q'). By Theorem 1 and (TRANS), we obtain $(\sigma_1 , \sigma_2) \vdash P' \sim Q'$. By induction and (TRANS), we obtain $(\sigma_1 , \sigma_2) \vdash P_i = Q_j$ and thus, by (TAU),

$(\sigma_1 , \sigma_2) \vdash \tau.P_i = \tau.Q_j$. Repeating this for each summand of P_τ, then for each summand of Q_τ and finally summing up (using (ABS) if necessary), we have the desired $(\sigma_1 , \sigma_2) \vdash P_\tau = Q_\tau$.

$s = out$. Similar to the previous case.

$s = in$. Let us partition the summands of P_{in} and Q_{in} according to their input channels, that is, let us write $P_{in} = P_{a_1} + \ldots + P_{a_m}$ and $Q_{in} = Q_{b_1} + \ldots + Q_{b_m}$. Let us consider now P_{a_1} and let us pick up any η s.t. $\widehat{\eta \sigma_1} = a_1$. By Lemma 2 we know that, indipendently from our choice of η, there is a unique $h \in \{1, \ldots, m\}$ s.t. $\widehat{\eta \sigma_2} = b_h$. We want to prove that $(\sigma_1 , \sigma_2) \vdash P_{a_1} = Q_{b_h}$. We define the sets $I' \triangleq \{i \in I : \alpha_i = a_1(x)\}$ and $J' \triangleq \{j \in J : \beta_j = b_h(x)\}$ and consider a generic ζ and $\tilde{c}$ such that $\Gamma(\zeta , \tilde{c} , \sigma_1, \sigma_2, \sum_{I'} P_i, \sum_{J'} Q_j)$; moreover, let $M_i \triangleq \widehat{\zeta \sigma_i}$, for $i = 1, 2$. By bisimilarity hypotesis and Lemma 2, for any $i \in I'$, there is a $j_i \in J'$ s.t. $(\sigma_1[\widetilde{c}/\widetilde{c}] , \sigma_2[\widetilde{c}/\widetilde{c}]) \vdash P_i[M_1/x] \sim Q_{j_i}[M_2/x]$. Similarly to τ-case, we can prove that $(\sigma_1[\widetilde{c}/\widetilde{c}] , \sigma_2[\widetilde{c}/\widetilde{c}]) \vdash \tau.P_i[M_1/x] = \tau.Q_{j_i}[M_2/x]$. Repeating this for each $i \in I'$ and finally summing up these equalities (using (ABS) if necessary) we have

$$(\sigma_1[\widetilde{c}/\widetilde{c}] , \sigma_2[\widetilde{c}/\widetilde{c}]) \vdash \sum_{i \in I'} \tau.P_i[M_1/x] = \sum_{i \in I'} \tau.Q_{j_i}[M_2/x] . \tag{4}$$

Similarly, for each $j \in J'$, we can find $i_j \in I'$ s.t.

$$(\sigma_1[\widetilde{c}/\widetilde{c}] , \sigma_2[\widetilde{c}/\widetilde{c}]) \vdash \sum_{j \in J'} \tau.P_{i_j}[M_1/x] = \sum_{j \in J'} \tau.Q_j[M_2/x] . \tag{5}$$

Now, notice that the left hand side of (5) is a sub-summatory of the left hand side of (4), and symmetrically for the right hand sides. Thus, by (SUM) and (ABS), we obtain $(\sigma_1[\widetilde{c}/\widetilde{c}] , \sigma_2[\widetilde{c}/\widetilde{c}]) \vdash \sum_{i \in I'} \tau.P_i[M_1/x] = \sum_{j \in J'} \tau.Q_j[M_2/x]$. We can apply (INP) and obtain $(\sigma_1 , \sigma_2) \vdash \sum_{i \in I'} a_1(x).P_i = \sum_{j \in J'} b_h(x).Q_j$, that is, $(\sigma_1 , \sigma_2) \vdash P_{a_1} = Q_{b_h}$. Repeating this for each summand of P_{in}, then for each summand of Q_{in} and finally summing up (using (ABS) if necessary), we obtain $(\sigma_1 , \sigma_2) \vdash P_{in} = Q_{in}$. □

Theorem 2 (Completeness). *Let P and Q be finite processes. If $(\sigma_1 , \sigma_2) \vdash P \sim Q$ then $(\sigma_1 , \sigma_2) \vdash P = Q$.*

6   Conclusions and Related Work

We have presented a set of equational laws for the spi-calculus that is useful to reason on concrete examples and forms the basis for a complete two-level proof system.

Our work can be extended in several directions. For example, one might consider the weak version of e.s. bisimilarity and/or a language extended with different crypto-primitives (in both cases, we do not foresee serious conceptual obstacles, though). Another direction is related to finding equational rules for the replication operator, which could be useful when, e.g., reasoning on protocols with an unbounded number of participants. A problem left open by our presentation is how to reduce to a finitary form the input congruence rule, which contains an infinitary premise. We think that, at least in the case of finite processes, bounds on the size of the ζ's can be statically determined. Symbolic techniques, in the same vein as [9,5,4], could be helpful (see also [8]).

The spi-calculus was introduced by Abadi and Gordon in [2]. Early work on spi-bisimilarity was presented in [3], where *framed* bisimulation was presented as a proof technique, though incomplete, for reasoning on contextual equivalences. In [6], e.s. bisimilarity was introduced and proved to be a (purely coinductive) characterization of barbed equivalence [12] in spi-calculus. Some of the congruence rules used in this paper were introduced there, but no proof system was defined.

References

1. M. Abadi, C. Fournet. Mobile Values, New Names and Secure Communication. POPL'01, Proceedings, 104-115.
2. M. Abadi, A.D. Gordon. A calculus for cryptographic protocols: The spi calculus. Information and Computation, 148(1):1-70, Academic Press, 1999.
3. M. Abadi, A.D. Gordon. A Bisimulation Method for Cryptographic Protocols. Nordic Journal of Computing, 5(4):267-303, 1998.
4. M. Boreale. Symbolic trace analysis of cryptographic protocols. ICALP'01, LNCS 2076, pp.667-681, Springer-Verlag, 2001.
5. M. Boreale, R. De Nicola. A Symbolic Semantics for the π-calculus. Information and Computation, vol.126, pp.34-52, 1996.
6. M. Boreale, R. De Nicola, R. Pugliese. Proof Techniques for Cryptographic Processes. LICS'99, Proceedings, IEEE Computer Society Press, pp.157-166, 1999. Full version to appear in SIAM Journal on Computing.
7. M. Boreale, R. De Nicola, R. Pugliese. Process Algebraic Analysis of Cryptographic Protocols. Proc. of 13th FORTE / 20th PSV, Kluiver, 2000.
8. A.S. Elkjaer, M. Höhle, H. Hüttel, K.O. Nielsen. Towards Automatic Bisimilarity Checking in the Spi Calculus, *Proc. of DMTCS'99+CATS'99*, 1999.
9. M. Hennessy, H. Lin. Symbolic Bisimulations. Theoretical Computers Science, 138, pp. 353-389, 1995.
10. R. Milner. Communication and Concurrency. Prentice Hall International, 1989.
11. R. Milner. The poliadic π-calculus: a tutorial. Logic and Algebra of Specification, ed. F.L.Bauer, W.Bauer and H.Schwichtenberg Springer-Verlag, 1993.
12. R. Milner, D. Sangiorgi. Barbed Bisimulation. ICALP'92, Proceedings (W. Kuich, Ed.), LNCS 623, pp.685-695, Springer-Verlag, 1992.
13. J. Parrow, D. Sangiorgi. Algebraic theories for name-passing calculi. Information and Computation, 120, pp.174-197, 1995.

On Specification Logics
for Algebra-Coalgebra Structures:
Reconciling Reachability and Observability

Corina Cîrstea*

Oxford University Computing Laboratory
Wolfson Building, Parks Road
Oxford OX1 3QD, UK
Corina.Cirstea@comlab.ox.ac.uk

Abstract. The paper builds on recent results regarding the expressiveness of modal logics for coalgebras in order to introduce a specification framework for coalgebraic structures which offers support for modular specification. An equational specification framework for algebraic structures is obtained in a similar way. The two frameworks are then integrated in order to account for structures comprising both a coalgebraic (observational) component and an algebraic (computational) component. The integration results in logics whose sentences are either coalgebraic (modal) or algebraic (equational) in nature, but whose associated notions of satisfaction take into account both the coalgebraic and the algebraic features of the structures being specified. Each of the logics thus obtained also supports modular specification.

1 Introduction

In studying structures that involve construction (e.g. data types), one typically uses algebras and their underlying equational logic for specification and reasoning. Such use is supported by the existence of characterisability results for classes of algebras, both in the concrete setting of many-sorted algebras [3] and in a more abstract, categorical setting [2,1], whereby equationally-specifiable classes of algebras coincide with *varieties* (that is, classes of algebras closed under subalgebras, homomorphic images and products[1]). In recent years, *coalgebras* (the categorical duals of algebras) have been used to study structures that involve observation (e.g. systems with state) [14,16], and various modal logics have been used to specify and reason about such structures [13,15,10,7]. Moreover, the results in [2] have been dualised in [9], where it was shown that modally-definable classes of coalgebras coincide with *covarieties* (the duals of varieties).

A framework which integrates algebraic and coalgebraic specification methods in order to specify structures comprising both computational and observational features was described in [5]. The approach taken there was to clearly

---

* Research supported by St. John's College, Oxford.
[1] In an abstract setting, the notions of subalgebra and homomorphic image are defined relatively to a factorisation system for the category of algebras in question.

M. Nielsen and U. Engberg (Eds.): Fossacs 2002, LNCS 2303, pp. 82–97, 2002.

separate the two categories of features, and to use algebra and respectively coalgebra for specifying them. Such an approach yielded an algebraically-defined notion of reachability under computations, as well as a coalgebraically-defined notion of indistinguishability by observations. Equational, either algebraic or coalgebraic sentences were then used to formalise correctness properties of combined structures, with both algebraic and coalgebraic features playing a rôle in defining the associated notions of satisfaction. Both notions of satisfaction were shown to give rise to *institutions* [6].

The equational sentences used in [5], although similar in their expressiveness to the equational formulae of [2] and the modal formulae of [9], have a strong semantic flavour, being indexed by classes of algebras and respectively coalgebras. This makes such sentences difficult to use for actual specification. In addition, the coalgebraic framework described in [5] only considers (coalgebras of) ω^{op}-continuous, pullback-preserving endofunctors, and thus does not account for endofunctors defined in terms of powersets. Similar ω-cocontinuity restrictions are imposed to the endofunctors used in [5] to specify algebraic structures. A first goal of this paper is to define individual frameworks for the specification of coalgebraic and respectively algebraic structures, which, on the one hand, have a more concrete notion of syntax associated to them, and, on the other hand, are more general than the ones in [5] w.r.t. the endofunctors considered. Then, a second goal of the paper is to integrate the resulting frameworks in order to account for structures having both a coalgebraic and an algebraic component.

In the first part of the paper, coalgebraic and respectively algebraic structures are considered independently of each other. In each case, an institution is shown to arise from suitable choices for the notions of signature, signature morphism, sentence and satisfaction (with the choices for the notion of sentence being driven by the results in [9] and respectively [2]). In the second part of the paper, structures comprising both observational and computational features are considered. As in [5], the choice of models incorporating both coalgebraic and algebraic structure, and of the syntax used to specify these models is based on the approach in [17], and results in a compatibility between the two categories of features, in that computations preserve observational indistinguishability whereas observations preserve reachability. The sentences used for specification are the ones employed by the individual frameworks, while the associated notions of satisfaction exploit the previously-mentioned compatibility in order to abstract away unwanted detail (in the form of unreachable and respectively observationally indistinguishable behaviours). This results in the availability of inductive and respectively coinductive techniques for correctness proofs. Suitably restricting the notions of signature morphism associated to the individual frameworks yields institutions w.r.t. each of the two notions of satisfaction.

2   Coalgebras and Modal Logic

This section builds on the approach in [9] in order to obtain notions of *cosignature*, *modal formula* and *satisfaction* of a modal formula by a coalgebra, and subsequently derives a specification logic for coalgebras based on these notions. The multi-modal logic described in [7] is used to exemplify the approach.

Definition 1. *A **cosignature** is a pair* (C, G), *with* C *a category and* G *an endofunctor on* C, *subject to the following constraints:*

1. C *is complete, cocomplete, regular[2], wellpowered and has enough injectives;*
2. G *preserves weak pullbacks[3];*
3. *the functor* $\mathsf{U}_\mathsf{G} : \mathsf{Coalg}(\mathsf{G}) \to \mathsf{C}$ *which takes* G*-coalgebras to their carrier has a right adjoint* R_G.

G-coalgebras are taken as models for a cosignature (C, G). A consequence of Def. 1 and of [8, Prop. 2.1] is that the functor U_G is comonadic, and hence $\mathsf{Coalg}(\mathsf{G}) \simeq \mathsf{Coalg}(\mathsf{D})$ for some comonad $(\mathsf{D}, \epsilon, \delta)$. Specifically, $\mathsf{D} : \mathsf{C} \to \mathsf{C}$ is given by $\mathsf{U}_\mathsf{G} \circ \mathsf{R}_\mathsf{G}$, $\epsilon : \mathsf{D} \Rightarrow \mathsf{Id}$ is given by the counit of the adjunction $\mathsf{U}_\mathsf{G} \dashv \mathsf{R}_\mathsf{G}$, while $\delta : \mathsf{D} \Rightarrow \mathsf{D} \circ \mathsf{D}$ is given by $\mathsf{U}_\mathsf{G} \eta_{\mathsf{R}_\mathsf{G}}$, with $\eta : \mathsf{Id} \Rightarrow \mathsf{R}_\mathsf{G} \circ \mathsf{U}_\mathsf{G}$ denoting the unit of $\mathsf{U}_\mathsf{G} \dashv \mathsf{R}_\mathsf{G}$.

Remark 1. The following hold for a cosignature (C, G):

1. U_G preserves and reflects monomorphisms. This is a consequence of Def. 1 (2).
2. The components of η are monomorphisms. This follows from $\mathsf{U}_\mathsf{G} \eta_\gamma$ being a split monomorphism (as $\epsilon_C \circ \mathsf{U}_\mathsf{G} \eta_\gamma = 1_C$) for any G-coalgebra $\langle C, \gamma \rangle$.
3. $\mathsf{Coalg}(\mathsf{G})$ has a final object, given by $\mathsf{R}_\mathsf{G} 1$. The final G-coalgebra incorporates all abstract G-behaviours. The homomorphisms into it abstract away the non-observable information contained in arbitrary coalgebras.
4. Largest bisimulations on G-coalgebras are constructed as kernel pairs of the C-arrows underlying the unique homomorphisms into the final G-coalgebra. Again, this is consequence of Def. 1 (2).

Definition 2. *Given a cosignature* (C, G), *a* G*-coalgebra is **observable**[4] if and only if its unique homomorphism into the final* G*-coalgebra is a monomorphism.*

Example 1. Finitely-branching transition systems are specified using the cosignature $(\mathsf{Set}, \mathsf{G}_{\mathsf{TS}})$, where $\mathsf{G}_{\mathsf{TS}} = \mathcal{P}_f(\mathsf{Id})$ (with the functor $\mathcal{P}_f : \mathsf{Set} \to \mathsf{Set}$ taking a set to the set of its finite subsets). Finitely-branching, A-labelled transition systems are specified using the cosignature $(\mathsf{Set}, \mathsf{G}_{\mathsf{LTS}})$, where $\mathsf{G}_{\mathsf{LTS}} = \mathcal{P}_f(A \times \mathsf{Id})$.

The following is a direct consequence of [8, Lemma 3.9].

Proposition 1. *For a cosignature* (C, G), *the category* $\mathsf{Coalg}(\mathsf{G})$ *is regular, and the functor* U_G *preserves regular-epi-mono factorisations.*

---

[2] Hence, C has regular-epi-mono factorisations. The existence of strong-epi-mono factorisations (which is a consequence of the completeness and wellpoweredness of C) is actually sufficient for the approach in this section. Regularity is only required here for consistency with the next two sections.

[3] Weak pullbacks are defined similarly to standard pullbacks, except that the mediating arrow is not required to be unique.

[4] Observable coalgebras are called *simple* in [16].

The existence of a factorisation system for $\mathsf{Coalg}(\mathsf{G})$ yields notions of G-*subcoalgebra* (given by a monomorphism in $\mathsf{Coalg}(\mathsf{G})$), G-*homomorphic image* (given by a regular epimorphism in $\mathsf{Coalg}(\mathsf{G})$), and G-*covariety* (given by a class of G-coalgebras which is closed under subcoalgebras, homomorphic images and coproducts[5]). A characterisability result for covarieties in terms of *modal formulae* is given in [9]. There, covarieties are defined in terms of factorisation systems $(\mathcal{E}, \mathcal{M})$ for categories of coalgebras, while modal formulae are defined as subcoalgebras with $\mathcal{M}$-injective codomains. However, as noted in [9, Thm. 2.5.4], in order to characterise covarieties it suffices to consider modal formulae given by subcoalgebras whose codomains belong to a subclass of $\mathcal{M}$-injective objects, namely a subclass which provides enough $\mathcal{M}$-injectives for the category of coalgebras in question. The notion of covariety considered here is obtained by instantiating the one in [9] with the factorisation system $(\mathsf{RegEpi}(\mathsf{Coalg}(\mathsf{G})), \mathsf{Mono}(\mathsf{Coalg}(\mathsf{G})))$. The following observations can be made relatively to this factorisation system:

1. If a C-object Z is injective (and hence $\mathsf{U_G}(\mathsf{Mono}(\mathsf{Coalg}(\mathsf{G})))$-injective), then the G-coalgebra $\mathsf{R_G}Z$ is injective (by [9, Prop. 2.2.10]).
2. If C has enough injectives, then $\mathsf{Coalg}(\mathsf{G})$ has enough injectives. Moreover, the cofree G-coalgebras over injective C-objects still provide enough injectives for $\mathsf{Coalg}(\mathsf{G})$. For, if $\langle C, \gamma \rangle$ is a G-coalgebra and $f : C \to Z$ is a $\mathsf{Mono}(\mathsf{C})$-arrow with an injective codomain, then $f^\flat = \mathsf{R_G}f \circ \eta_\gamma : \langle C, \gamma \rangle \to \mathsf{R_G}Z$ is a $\mathsf{Mono}(\mathsf{Coalg}(\mathsf{G}))$-arrow with an injective codomain. (Rem. 1 (2) and the preservation of monomorphisms by $\mathsf{R_G}$ are used here.)

These observations together with the previous remarks justify the following.

Definition 3. *A **modal formula** over a cosignature* (C, G) *is a G-subcoalgebra* $\iota : \langle D, \delta \rangle \to \mathsf{R_G}Z$ *with* Z *an injective C-object. A G-coalgebra* $\langle C, \gamma \rangle$ ***satisfies*** *a modal formula of this form (written* $\langle C, \gamma \rangle \models \iota$*) if and only if, for any C-arrow* $f : C \to Z$*, the G-coalgebra homomorphism* $f^\flat : \langle C, \gamma \rangle \to \mathsf{R_G}Z$ *factors through* ι.

$$
\begin{array}{ccc}
C & & \langle C, \gamma \rangle \\
\downarrow{\scriptstyle f} & & \quad\;\;\searrow^{\scriptstyle \kappa} \;\downarrow{\scriptstyle f^\flat} \\
Z & & \langle D, \delta \rangle \xrightarrow{\;\;\iota\;\;} \mathsf{R_G}Z
\end{array}
$$

Modal formulae $\iota : \langle D, \delta \rangle \to \mathsf{R_G}Z$ with Z final in C (and hence $\mathsf{R_G}Z$ final in $\mathsf{Coalg}(\mathsf{G})$) specify properties up to observational equivalence. Existing specification frameworks for coalgebras [13,15,10,7] only employ such modal formulae.

The satisfaction of modal formulae by coalgebras is preserved along homomorphic images and reflected along subcoalgebras. These are consequences of [9, Coroll. 2.4.6] and respectively [9, Prop. 2.4.8], but also follow directly from Def. 3 together with Prop. 1. Also, a consequence of [9, Coroll. 2.5.5] and of the dual of [1, Coroll. 20.29] is that, for a cosignature (C, G), modally definable[6] classes of G-coalgebras coincide with covarieties.

---

[5] Note that the cocompleteness of C results in the cocompleteness of $\mathsf{Coalg}(\mathsf{G})$, with colimits in $\mathsf{Coalg}(\mathsf{G})$ being created by $\mathsf{U_G}$.

[6] In the sense of Def. 3.

We now show that monomorphisms into the carriers of coalgebras induce largest subcoalgebras factoring through such monomorphisms.

Proposition 2. *Let* (C, G) *denote a cosignature, let* $\langle C, \gamma \rangle$ *denote a* G-*coalgebra, and let* $\iota : X \to C$ *denote a* C-*monomorphism. Then, the full subcategory of* $\mathsf{Coalg}(G)/\langle C, \gamma \rangle$ *whose objects* $\langle \langle D, \delta \rangle, d \rangle$ *are such that* $\mathsf{U_G}d$ *factors through* ι *has a final object* $\langle \langle E, \eta \rangle, m \rangle$. *Moreover, m defines a* G-*subcoalgebra of* $\langle C, \gamma \rangle$.

Proof (sketch). Since C is wellpowered, there is only a set $\mathcal{D}$ of G-coalgebra homomorphisms $d : \langle D, \delta \rangle \to \langle C, \gamma \rangle$ whose image under $\mathsf{U_G}$ is a monomorphism which factors through ι. If $c : \coprod_{d \in \mathcal{D}} \mathsf{dom}(d) \to \langle C, \gamma \rangle$ is the G-coalgebra homomorphism arising from the universality of $\coprod_{d \in \mathcal{D}} \mathsf{dom}(d)$, and if $c = m \circ e$ is a regular-epi-mono factorisation for c, then one can show that m defines a final object in the full subcategory of $\mathsf{Coalg}(G)/\langle C, \gamma \rangle$ whose objects $\langle \langle D, \delta \rangle, d \rangle$ are such that $\mathsf{U_G}d$ factors through ι. (The preservation of coproducts and of regular-epi-mono factorisations by $\mathsf{U_G}$ and the unique $(\mathsf{RegEpi}(C), \mathsf{Mono}(C))$-diagonalisation property of C are used.)

Similarly, modal formulae induce largest subcoalgebras of given coalgebras.

Proposition 3. *Let* (C, G) *denote a cosignature, let* $\langle C, \gamma \rangle$ *denote a* G-*coalgebra, and let* $\mathcal{F}$ *denote a set of modal formulae over* (C, G). *Then, the full subcategory of* $\mathsf{Coalg}(G)/\langle C, \gamma \rangle$ *whose objects satisfy the modal formulae in* $\mathcal{F}$ *has a final object, which at the same time defines a* G-*subcoalgebra of* $\langle C, \gamma \rangle$.

Proof. Similar to the proof of Prop. 2. The set $\mathcal{D}$ of G-coalgebra homomorphisms $d : \langle D, \delta \rangle \to \langle C, \gamma \rangle$ which are such that $\mathsf{U_G}d$ is a C-monomorphism and such that $f^\flat : \langle D, \delta \rangle \to \mathsf{R_G}Z$ factors through ι for any $\iota \in \mathcal{F}$ with codomain $\mathsf{R_G}Z$ and any $f : D \to Z$ is considered this time.

[7] (see also [15]) develops a modal logic for coalgebras of *(finite) Kripke polynomial endofunctors*, that is, endofunctors G on Set constructed from constant and identity endofunctors using products, coproducts, exponentials with constant exponent and (finite) powersets. Here we use finite Kripke polynomial endofunctors (which satisfy the conditions in Def. 1, and therefore give rise to cosignatures) to exemplify our approach. The modal formulae associated to such endofunctors, built from basic formulae of form a with $a \in A$ (where the set A appears covariantly in the definition of G) using propositional connectives and modal operators (whose form depends on G), induce predicates on the carriers of final G-coalgebras, and therefore, by Prop. 2, are an instance of the notion of modal formula given by Def. 3. Moreover, the fact that bisimulation coincides with logical equivalence (see [7, Coroll. 5.9], or [15, Prop. 4.8]) results in the notion of satisfaction used in [7] agreeing with the one given by Def. 3.

Example 2. Consider the cosignature $(\mathsf{Set}, \mathsf{G_{FTS}})$, with $\mathsf{G_{FTS}} = \mathcal{P}_f(\mathsf{Id}) \times \mathbb{N}$. Under the approach in [7], the modal language associated to $\mathsf{G_{FTS}}$ is given by:

$$\varphi ::= \bot \mid \varphi \to \psi \mid [\mathtt{succ}]\varphi \mid [\mathtt{depth}]\varphi_\mathbb{N} \quad \varphi_\mathbb{N} ::= \bot \mid \varphi_\mathbb{N} \to \psi_\mathbb{N} \mid n, \ n \in \mathbb{N}$$

while its associated notion of satisfaction is given by:

$$C, n' \models n \iff n' = n$$
$$C, c \models [\text{succ}]\varphi \iff (\forall s)\,(s \in \text{succ}(c) \Rightarrow C, s \models \varphi)$$
$$C, c \models [\text{depth}]\varphi_{\mathbb{N}} \iff (\forall n)\,(\text{depth}(c) = n \Rightarrow C, n \models \varphi_{\mathbb{N}})$$

for any $\mathsf{G}_{\mathsf{FTS}}$-coalgebra $C = \langle C, \langle \text{succ} : C \to \mathcal{P}_f(C), \text{depth} : C \to \mathbb{N} \rangle \rangle$, $n, n' \in \mathbb{N}$ and $c \in C$. One can also define modal operators $\langle \text{succ} \rangle$ and $\langle \text{depth} \rangle$, namely by $\langle \text{succ} \rangle \varphi ::= \neg [\text{succ}] \neg \varphi$ and $\langle \text{depth} \rangle \varphi_{\mathbb{N}} ::= \neg [\text{depth}] \neg \varphi_{\mathbb{N}}$. Thus:

$$C, c \models \langle \text{succ} \rangle \varphi \iff (\exists s)\,(s \in \text{succ}(c) \text{ and } C, s \models \varphi)$$
$$C, c \models \langle \text{depth} \rangle \varphi_{\mathbb{N}} \iff (\exists n)\,(\text{depth}(c) = n \text{ and } C, n \models \varphi_{\mathbb{N}})$$

(Note therefore that $\langle \text{depth} \rangle \varphi_{\mathbb{N}}$ and $[\text{depth}]\varphi_{\mathbb{N}}$ are semantically equivalent for any φ.) Finitely branching transition systems of finite depth can now be specified using the following modal formulae:

$$[\text{depth}]0 \leftrightarrow [\text{succ}]\bot$$
$$[\text{depth}](n+1) \leftrightarrow \langle \text{succ} \rangle [\text{depth}]n \wedge [\text{succ}][\text{depth}](0 \vee \ldots \vee n), \ n \in \mathbb{N}$$

formalising the statement that a rooted transition system has depth 0 precisely when its root has no successors, and has depth $n+1$ precisely when its root has a successor of depth n, and the depth of any of its successors does not exceed n. Alternatively, natural numbers can be regarded as *colours* used to decorate the states of an unlabelled transition system. The decorations of interest are those where the colour decreases by 1 in successor states, and where (only) states with no successor have colour 0. Such an approach, equivalent to the previous one, corresponds to specifying a subcoalgebra of the cofree $\mathcal{P}_f(\mathsf{Id})$-coalgebra over $\mathbb{N}$.

We now introduce a notion of *cosignature morphism*, capturing translations between different types of observational structures.

Definition 4. *A **cosignature morphism** between cosignatures* (C, G) *and* $(\mathsf{C}', \mathsf{G}')$ *consists of a pair* (U, τ) *with* $\mathsf{U} : \mathsf{C}' \to \mathsf{C}$ *a functor with right adjoint* R, *and with* $\tau : \mathsf{U} \circ \mathsf{G}' \Rightarrow \mathsf{G} \circ \mathsf{U}$ *a natural transformation.*

Cosignature morphisms $(\mathsf{U}, \tau) : (\mathsf{C}, \mathsf{G}) \to (\mathsf{C}', \mathsf{G}')$ induce reduct functors $\mathsf{U}_\tau : \mathsf{Coalg}(\mathsf{G}') \to \mathsf{Coalg}(\mathsf{G})$, with U_τ taking $\langle C', \gamma' \rangle \in |\mathsf{Coalg}(\mathsf{G}')|$ to $\langle \mathsf{U}C', \tau_{C'} \circ \mathsf{U}\gamma' \rangle \in |\mathsf{Coalg}(\mathsf{G})|$. Moreover, the existence of cofree coalgebras w.r.t. the functors U_G and $\mathsf{U}_{\mathsf{G}'}$, together with the existence of largest subcoalgebras induced by monomorphisms into the carriers of coalgebras (see Prop. 2) can be used to show that the reduct functors induced by cosignature morphisms have right adjoints.

Proposition 4. *Let* $(\mathsf{U}, \tau) : (\mathsf{C}, \mathsf{G}) \to (\mathsf{C}', \mathsf{G}')$ *denote a cosignature morphism. Then, the reduct functor* $\mathsf{U}_\tau : \mathsf{Coalg}(\mathsf{G}') \to \mathsf{Coalg}(\mathsf{G})$ *has a right adjoint.*

Proof (sketch). A cofree G'-coalgebra over a G-coalgebra $\langle C, \gamma \rangle$ w.r.t. U_τ is obtained as the largest G'-subcoalgebra of the cofree G'-coalgebra over $\mathsf{R}C$ w.r.t. $\mathsf{U}_{\mathsf{G}'}$ whose image under U_τ has a homomorphism into $\langle C, \gamma \rangle$.

The right adjoint to U_τ is denoted R_τ. The uniqueness up to isomorphism of right adjoints yields a natural isomorphism $i : R_\tau \circ R_G \Rightarrow R_{G'} \circ R$.

The existence of right adjoints to the reduct functors induced by cosignature morphisms yields translations of modal formulae over the sources of cosignature morphisms to modal formulae over their targets. Specifically, a modal formula $\iota : \langle D, \delta \rangle \to R_G Z$ translates along a cosignature morphism $(U, \tau) : (C, G) \to (C', G')$ to the modal formula $\tau(\iota) = i_Z \circ R_\tau \iota : R_\tau \langle D, \delta \rangle \to R_{G'} RZ$. (The fact that RZ is injective whenever Z is injective follows from the preservation of monomorphisms by U_G. Also, the fact that $U_{G'} R_\tau \iota$, and hence $i_Z \circ U_{G'} R_\tau \iota$, belongs to $\mathsf{Mono}(C')$ follows from $U_G \iota$ being a monomorphism together with the reflection of monomorphisms by U_G and their preservation by each of R_τ and $U_{G'}$.)

The translation of modal formulae along cosignature morphisms is such that the *satisfaction condition* of institutions (formalising the statement that *truth is invariant under changes of notation* [6]) holds for the resulting logic.

Theorem 1. *Let* $(U, \tau) : (C, G) \to (C', G')$ *denote a cosignature morphism, let* $\langle C', \gamma' \rangle$ *denote a* G'-*coalgebra, and let* $\iota : \langle D, \delta \rangle \to R_G Z$ *denote a modal formula over* (C, G)*. Then,* $U_\tau \langle C', \gamma' \rangle \models \iota$ *iff* $\langle C', \gamma' \rangle \models \tau(\iota)$.

Proof (sketch).

$$U_\tau \langle C', \gamma' \rangle \models \iota \ \Leftrightarrow \ \text{(defn. of} \models \text{)}$$

$$\text{for all } f : UC' \to Z, \ f^\flat \text{ factors through } \iota \ \Leftrightarrow \ (U \dashv R, \ U_\tau \dashv R_\tau, \ i\text{-iso})$$

$$\text{for all } f' : C' \to RZ, \ f'^\flat \text{ factors through } i_Z \circ R_\tau \iota \ \Leftrightarrow \ \text{(defn. of} \models \text{)}$$

$$\langle C', \gamma' \rangle \models \tau(\iota)$$

The second equivalence exploits the existence of isomorphisms $C(UC', Z) \simeq C'(C', RZ)$ and $\mathsf{Coalg}(G)(U_\tau \langle C', \gamma' \rangle, \langle D, \delta \rangle) \simeq \mathsf{Coalg}(G')(\langle C', \gamma' \rangle, R_\tau \langle D, \delta \rangle)$, and the relationship between the counits of the adjunctions $U \dashv R$, $U_\tau \dashv R_\tau$, $U_G \dashv R_G$ and $U_{G'} \dashv R_{G'}$, determined by the existence of the natural isomorphism i.

Example 3. Consider the cosignature $(\mathsf{Set}, G_{\mathsf{LFTS}})$, with $G_{\mathsf{LFTS}} = \mathcal{P}_f(A \times \mathsf{Id}) \times \mathbb{N}$. Then, (Id, τ) with $\tau = \mathcal{P}_f(\pi_2) \times 1_{\mathbb{N}} : \mathcal{P}_f(A \times \mathsf{Id}) \times \mathbb{N} \Rightarrow \mathcal{P}_f(\mathsf{Id}) \times \mathbb{N}$ defines a cosignature morphism from $(\mathsf{Set}, G_{\mathsf{FTS}})$ to $(\mathsf{Set}, G_{\mathsf{LFTS}})$. The induced reduct functor takes a G_{LFTS}-coalgebra $\langle C, \langle \mathtt{next}, \mathtt{depth} \rangle \rangle$ to the G_{FTS}-coalgebra $\langle C, \langle \mathcal{P}_f(\pi_2) \circ \mathtt{next}, \mathtt{depth} \rangle \rangle$. The modal language associated to G_{LFTS} is given by:

$$\varphi ::= \bot \mid \varphi \to \psi \mid [\mathtt{label}] \varphi_A \mid [\mathtt{succ}] \varphi \mid [\mathtt{depth}] \varphi_{\mathbb{N}} \quad \varphi_A ::= \bot \mid \varphi_A \to \psi_A \mid a, \ a \in A$$

while its associated notion of satisfaction is given by:

$$C, c \models [\mathtt{label}] \varphi_A \ \Leftrightarrow \ (\forall a) \, (a \in \mathcal{P}_f(\pi_1)(\mathtt{next}(c)) \Rightarrow C, a \models \varphi_A)$$
$$C, c \models [\mathtt{succ}] \varphi \ \Leftrightarrow \ (\forall s) \, (s \in \mathcal{P}_f(\pi_2)(\mathtt{next}(c)) \Rightarrow C, s \models \varphi)$$
$$C, c \models [\mathtt{depth}] \varphi_{\mathbb{N}} \ \Leftrightarrow \ (\forall n) \, (\mathtt{depth}(c) = n \Rightarrow C, n \models \varphi_{\mathbb{N}})$$

for any $\mathsf{G}_{\mathsf{LFTS}}$-coalgebra $C = \langle C, \langle \mathtt{next} : C \to \mathcal{P}_f(A \times C), \mathtt{depth} : C \to \mathbb{N} \rangle \rangle$ and $c \in C$. The translation along (Id, τ) of modal formulae over $\mathsf{G}_{\mathsf{FTS}}$ to modal formulae over $\mathsf{G}_{\mathsf{LFTS}}$ leaves $\mathsf{G}_{\mathsf{FTS}}$-formulae (including the ones in Ex. 2) unchanged.

Remark 2. Cosignature morphisms $(\mathsf{U}, \tau) : (\mathsf{C}, \mathsf{G}) \to (\mathsf{C}', \mathsf{G}')$ induce *comonad morphisms*[7] $(\mathsf{U}, \rho) : (\mathsf{D}, \epsilon, \delta) \Rightarrow (\mathsf{D}', \epsilon', \delta')$. Specifically, if $\overline{\delta} : \mathsf{D} \Rightarrow \mathsf{G} \circ \mathsf{D}$ and $\overline{\delta'} : \mathsf{D}' \Rightarrow \mathsf{G}' \circ \mathsf{D}'$ denote the G- and respectively G'-coalgebra structures on D and respectively D', then the natural transformation $\rho : \mathsf{U} \circ \mathsf{D}' \Rightarrow \mathsf{D} \circ \mathsf{U}$ arises from the cofreeness of $\langle \mathsf{D} \circ \mathsf{U}, \overline{\delta}_\mathsf{U} \rangle$ w.r.t. U_G: for $C' \in |\mathsf{C}'|$, $\rho_{C'}$ is the C-arrow underlying the G-coalgebra homomorphism $(\mathsf{U}\epsilon'_{C'})^\flat : \langle \mathsf{U}\mathsf{D}'C', \tau_{\mathsf{D}'C'} \circ \mathsf{U}\overline{\delta'}_{C'} \rangle \to \langle \mathsf{D}\mathsf{U}C', \overline{\delta}_{\mathsf{U}C'} \rangle$ (where $\mathsf{U}\epsilon'_{C'} : \mathsf{U}\mathsf{D}'C' \to \mathsf{U}C'$). The induced comonad morphism provides some information about the relationship between the notions of observability associated to G and G'. For, if $1'$ denotes a final C'-object, then the C-arrow $\rho_{1'} : \mathsf{U}\mathsf{D}'1' \to \mathsf{D}\mathsf{U}1'$ defines the unique homomorphism from the U_τ-reduct of the final G'-coalgebra to the final G-coalgebra. Hence, the fact that $\rho_{1'}$ belongs to $\mathsf{Mono}(\mathsf{C})$ reflects the fact that the target cosignature does not refine the notion of observability induced by the source cosignature.

Definition 5. *A cosignature morphism* (U, τ) *is* **horizontal** *if and only if* $\rho_{1'} \in \mathsf{Mono}(\mathsf{C})$, *with* (U, ρ) *denoting the induced comonad morphism.*

3   Algebras and Equational Logic

A framework for the specification of algebraic structures can be obtained using an approach similar to that of the previous section.

Definition 6. *A* **signature** *is a pair* (C, F), *with* C *a category and* F *an endofunctor on* C, *subject to the following constraints:*

1. C *is complete, cocomplete, regular,* $\mathsf{RegEpi}(\mathsf{C})$-*cowellpowered and has enough* $\mathsf{RegEpi}(\mathsf{C})$-*projectives;*
2. *all regular epimorphisms in* C *are split;*
3. *the functor taking* F-*algebras to their carrier has a left adjoint.*

It then follows by [1, Thm. 20.17][8] and respectively by [4, Thm. 4.3.5] that, for a signature (C, F), the functor taking F-algebras to their carrier is monadic and preserves regular epimorphisms[9]. Hence, by [1, Thm. 20.32], this functor is $\mathsf{RegEpi}(\mathsf{C})$-monadic. Thus, $\mathsf{Alg}(\mathsf{F}) \simeq \mathsf{Alg}(\mathsf{T})$, with the monad (T, η, μ) being defined similarly to the comonad $(\mathsf{D}, \epsilon, \delta)$ induced by a cosignature.

T-algebras are taken as models for a signature (C, F)[10]. The functor taking T-algebras to their carrier is denoted U_T, while its left adjoint (whose existence is guaranteed by Def. 6 (3)) is denoted L_T.

---

[7] The notion of (co)monad morphism considered here generalises the standard one, as defined e.g. in [1, Def. 20.55], being given by a pair (U, ρ) with $\mathsf{U} : \mathsf{C}' \to \mathsf{C}$ and $\rho : \mathsf{U} \circ \mathsf{D}' \Rightarrow \mathsf{D} \circ \mathsf{U}$, rather than by a natural transformation $\rho : \mathsf{D}' \Rightarrow \mathsf{D}$.

[8] See also [9, Thm. 1.1.8] for a proof in the dual case.

[9] Note that [4, Thm. 4.3.5] requires Def. 6 (2) to hold, and the category C to be regular.

[10] The choice of working with algebras of the induced monads rather than with algebras of endofunctors is driven by the approach in Section 4.

Remark 3. The following hold for a signature (C, F):

1. $\mathsf{Alg}(\mathsf{T})$ is cocomplete. This follows by [4, Thm. 4.3.5]. In particular, $\mathsf{Alg}(\mathsf{T})$ has an initial object, which incorporates all ground F-computations. The homomorphisms from it interpret ground computations in arbitrary algebras.
2. U_T preserves and reflects regular epimorphisms. Again, this follows by [4, Thm. 4.3.5].
3. The components of the counit ϵ of the adjunction $\mathsf{L}_\mathsf{T} \dashv \mathsf{U}_\mathsf{T}$ are regular epimorphisms (as the components of $\mathsf{U}_\mathsf{T}\epsilon$ are split, and hence regular epimorphisms).

Definition 7. *Given a signature* (C, F)*, a* T*-algebra is* **reachable** *if and only if the unique homomorphism from the initial* T*-algebra into it is a regular epimorphism.*

Example 4. Non-deterministic, sequential processes over an alphabet A are specified using the signature $(\mathsf{Set}, \mathsf{F}_\mathsf{NSP})$, with $\mathsf{F}_\mathsf{NSP} = 1 + A \times X + X \times X + X \times X$. An F_NSP-algebra is given by a Set-arrow $\alpha : \mathsf{F}_\mathsf{NSP}C \to C$, or equivalently, by four Set-arrows $\mathtt{nil} : 1 \to C$, $\_.\_ : A \times C \to C$, $\_+\_ : C \times C \to C$ and $\_;\_ : C \times C \to C$ (corresponding to the empty process, the prefixing operator, the non-deterministic choice operator and respectively sequential composition).

Proposition 5. *For a signature* (C, F)*, the category* $\mathsf{Alg}(\mathsf{T})$ *is regular, and the functor* U_T *preserves regular-epi-mono factorisations.*

The existence of a factorisation system for $\mathsf{Alg}(\mathsf{T})$ yields notions of T*-sub-algebra*, T*-homomorphic image* and T*-variety*.

Definition 8. *An* **equation** *over a signature* (C, F) *is a* T*-homomorphic image* $q : \mathsf{L}_\mathsf{T}X \to \langle B, \beta \rangle$ *with* X *a* $\mathsf{RegEpi}(\mathsf{C})$*-projective* C*-object. A* T*-algebra* $\langle A, \alpha \rangle$ **satisfies** *an equation of this form (written* $\langle A, \alpha \rangle \models q$*) if and only if, for any* C*-arrow* $f : X \to A$*, the* T*-algebra homomorphism* $f^\# : \mathsf{L}_\mathsf{T}X \to \langle A, \alpha \rangle$ *factors through* q*.*

$$
\begin{array}{ccc}
X & & \mathsf{L}_\mathsf{T}X \xrightarrow{\;q\;} \langle B, \beta \rangle \\
f\downarrow & & f^\#\downarrow \quad {}^{\kappa}\nearrow \\
A & & \langle A, \alpha \rangle
\end{array}
$$

Equations as defined above are an instance of the notion of equation defined in [2]. Moreover, equations over a signature are sufficient to characterise varieties. These are consequences of the following observations:

1. If a C-object X is $\mathsf{RegEpi}(\mathsf{C})$-projective (and hence $\mathsf{U}_\mathsf{T}(\mathsf{RegEpi}(\mathsf{Alg}(\mathsf{T})))$-projective), then the T-algebra $\mathsf{L}_\mathsf{T}X$ is $\mathsf{RegEpi}(\mathsf{Alg}(\mathsf{T}))$-projective.
2. If C has enough $\mathsf{RegEpi}(\mathsf{C})$-projectives, then $\mathsf{Alg}(\mathsf{T})$ has enough $\mathsf{RegEpi}(\mathsf{Alg}(\mathsf{T}))$-projectives. Moreover, the free T-algebras over $\mathsf{RegEpi}(\mathsf{C})$-projective C-objects still provide enough $\mathsf{RegEpi}(\mathsf{Alg}(\mathsf{T}))$-projectives for $\mathsf{Alg}(\mathsf{T})$.

Remark 4. Given a signature (C, F), equations $q : L_T X \to \langle B, \beta \rangle$ over (C, F) can be specified using pairs of C-arrows $l, r : K \to U_T L_T X$, with X a RegEpi(C)-projective C-object. For, such pairs induce pairs of T-algebra homomorphisms $l^\#, r^\# : L_T K \to L_T X$, whose coequaliser defines an equation over (C, F). (The preservation of regular epimorphisms by U_T is used to show this.)

$$
\begin{array}{c}
\mathsf{Alg}(\mathsf{T}) \\
{\scriptstyle U_T} \downarrow \uparrow {\scriptstyle L_T} \\
\mathsf{C}
\end{array}
\qquad
\begin{array}{ccc}
L_T K \overset{l^\#}{\underset{r^\#}{\rightrightarrows}} L_T X \overset{f^\#}{\underset{q}{\twoheadrightarrow}} \langle B, \beta \rangle \dashrightarrow \langle A, \alpha \rangle \\[2mm]
K \overset{l}{\underset{r}{\rightrightarrows}} U_T L_T X \xrightarrow{\ \ U_T f^\#\ \ } A
\end{array}
$$

Moreover, a T-algebra $\langle A, \alpha \rangle$ satisfies the induced equation if and only if $U_T f^\# \circ l = U_T f^\# \circ r$ for any $f : X \to A$. This follows from the definition of q using standard properties of adjunctions.

Equations $q : L_T X \to \langle B, \beta \rangle$ with X initial in C specify properties up to reachability under (ground) computations. Results dual to Props. 2 and 3 hold for algebras of signatures (with the proofs also dualising).

Example 5. The commutativity of the non-deterministic choice operator on processes is formalised by the equation: $(\forall X)(\forall Y)\ X + Y = Y + X$.

Definition 9. *A **signature morphism** between signatures (C, F) and (C', F') consists of a pair (U, ξ) with $U : C' \to C$ a functor with left adjoint L, and with $\xi : F \circ U \Rightarrow U \circ F'$ a natural transformation. (U, ξ) is **horizontal** if and only if $\nu_{0'} \in \mathsf{RegEpi}(C)$, with (U, ν) the induced monad morphism[11] and $0'$ initial in C'.*

Signature morphisms $(U, \xi) : (C, F) \to (C', F')$ induce reduct functors $U_\nu : \mathsf{Alg}(T') \to \mathsf{Alg}(T)$, with U_ν taking $\langle C', \alpha' \rangle \in |\mathsf{Alg}(T')|$ to $\langle UC', U\alpha' \circ \nu_{C'} \rangle \in |\mathsf{Alg}(T)|$. Horizontal signature morphisms capture situations where the target signature does not enrich the notion of reachability induced by the source signature. For, the C-arrow $\nu_{0'} : TU0' \Rightarrow UT'0'$ defines the unique homomorphism from the initial T-algebra to the U_ν-reduct of the initial T'-algebra.

Proposition 6. *Let $(U, \xi) : (C, F) \to (C', F')$ denote a signature morphism. Then, the reduct functor $U_\nu : \mathsf{Alg}(T') \to \mathsf{Alg}(T)$ has a left adjoint.*

Proof. The conclusion follows from $L \dashv U$, $L_T \dashv U_T$, $L_{T'} \dashv U_{T'}$ and $U_T \circ U_\nu = U \circ U_{T'}$ using the Adjoint Lifting Theorem (see e.g. [4, Thm. 4.5.6]), after noting that $\mathsf{Alg}(T')$ has coequalisers (by Rem. 3 (1)). $\qquad\square$

The left adjoint to U_ν is denoted L_ν. And, as in the coalgebraic case, there exists a natural isomorphism $j : L_{T'} \circ L \Rightarrow L_\nu \circ L_T$.

Signature morphisms also induce translations of equations over their source to equations over their target: an equation $q : L_T X \to \langle B, \beta \rangle$ translates along a signature morphism $(U, \xi) : (C, F) \to (C', F')$ to the equation $\nu(q) = L_\nu q \circ j_X$.

---

[11] The natural transformation $\nu : T \circ U \Rightarrow U \circ T'$ is obtained similarly to the natural transformation $\rho : U \circ D' \Rightarrow D \circ U$ in Rem. 2.

Remark 5. A signature morphism $(U, \xi) : (C, F) \to (C', F')$ also induces a mapping from pairs of C-arrows defining equations over (C, F) (see Rem. 4) to pairs of C'-arrows defining equations over (C', F'). The mapping takes a pair $l, r : K \to U_T L_T X$ to the pair $(UU_{T'} j_X^{-1} \circ U_T \eta_{\nu, L_T X} \circ l)^\#, (UU_{T'} j_X^{-1} \circ U_T \eta_{\nu, L_T X} \circ r)^\# : LK \to U_{T'} L_{T'} LX$, where $\eta_\nu : \mathsf{Id} \Rightarrow U_\nu \circ L_\nu$ denotes the unit of the adjunction $L_\nu \dashv U_\nu$.

$$
\begin{array}{ccc}
C' & LK \xrightarrow[\;(UU_{T'} j_X^{-1} \circ U_T \eta_{\nu, L_T X} \circ r)^\#\;]{\;(UU_{T'} j_X^{-1} \circ U_T \eta_{\nu, L_T X} \circ l)^\#\;} U_{T'} L_{T'} LX \\
U \big\uparrow\!\!\big\uparrow L & \\
C & K \xrightarrow[r]{l} U_T L_T X \xrightarrow{U_T \eta_{\nu, L_T X}} U_T U_\nu L_\nu L_T X \xrightarrow{UU_{T'} j_X^{-1}} UU_{T'} L_{T'} LX
\end{array}
$$

Moreover, the mapping thus defined agrees with the translation of equations over (C, F) to equations over (C', F'). That is, the translation along (U, ξ) of the equation induced by l, r coincides (up to isomorphism in $\mathsf{Alg}(T')$) with the equation induced by $(UU_{T'} j_X^{-1} \circ U_T \eta_{\nu, L_T X} \circ l)^\#, (UU_{T'} j_X^{-1} \circ U_T \eta_{\nu, L_T X} \circ r)^\#$. This follows using standard properties of adjunctions.

Theorem 2. *Let* $(U, \xi) : (C, F) \to (C', F')$ *denote a signature morphism, let* $\langle A', \alpha' \rangle$ *denote a* T'-*algebra, and let* $q : L_T X \to \langle B, \beta \rangle$ *denote an equation over* (C, F). *Then,* $U_\nu \langle A', \alpha' \rangle \models q$ *iff* $\langle A', \alpha' \rangle \models \nu(q)$.

4   Combined Structures and Their Logic

The frameworks described in Sections 2 and 3 are now integrated in order to account for structures incorporating both algebraic and coalgebraic features. Modal as well as equational formulae are used to formalise correctness properties of such structures, with the associated notions of satisfaction abstracting away unreachable and respectively observationally indistinguishable behaviours. Such an abstraction is possible due to a compatibility between computational and observational features in the structures considered. This compatibility, which amounts to computations preserving observational indistinguishability and to observations preserving reachability, is attained using an approach similar to that of [17], where liftings of monads to categories of coalgebras are used to define operational semantics which are well-behaved w.r.t. denotational ones.

Definition 10. *A **combined signature** is a tuple* (C, G, F, σ), *with* (C, G) *a cosignature,* (C, F) *a signature inducing a monad* (T, η, μ), *and* $\sigma : T \circ U_G \Rightarrow G \circ T \circ U_G$ *a natural transformation, such that the following diagram commutes:*

$$
\begin{array}{ccc}
U_G \xrightarrow{\eta U_G} T \circ U_G \xleftarrow{\mu U_G} T \circ T \circ U_G \\
\lambda \big\Downarrow \qquad \sigma \big\Downarrow \qquad \big\Downarrow \sigma T_\sigma \\
G \circ U_G \xrightarrow{G \eta U_G} G \circ T \circ U_G \xleftarrow{G \mu U_G} G \circ T \circ T \circ U_G
\end{array}
$$

where the natural transformation $\lambda : U_G \Rightarrow G \circ U_G$ *is given by* $\lambda_\gamma = \gamma$ *for* $\langle C, \gamma \rangle \in |\mathsf{Coalg}(G)|$, *while the functor* $T_\sigma : \mathsf{Coalg}(G) \to \mathsf{Coalg}(G)$ *is given by* $T_\sigma \langle C, \gamma \rangle = \langle TC, \sigma_\gamma \rangle$ *for* $\langle C, \gamma \rangle \in |\mathsf{Coalg}(G)|$ *(and consequently* $U_G \circ T_\sigma = T \circ U_G$*).*

*A **combined signature morphism** from* (C, G, F, σ) *to* (C', G', F', σ') *is a tuple* (U, τ, ξ), *with* $(U, \tau) : (C, G) \to (C', G')$ *a cosignature morphism and* $(U, \xi) : (C, F) \to (C', F')$ *a signature morphism inducing a monad morphism* $(U, \nu) : (T, \eta, \mu) \to (T', \eta', \mu')$, *such that the following diagram commutes:*

$$
\begin{array}{ccc}
\mathsf{T} \circ \mathsf{U} \circ \mathsf{U}_{\mathsf{G}'} = \mathsf{T} \circ \mathsf{U}_{\mathsf{G}} \circ \mathsf{U}_\tau \xRightarrow{\ \sigma_{\mathsf{U}_\tau}\ } \mathsf{G} \circ \mathsf{T} \circ \mathsf{U}_{\mathsf{G}} \circ \mathsf{U}_\tau = \mathsf{G} \circ \mathsf{T} \circ \mathsf{U} \circ \mathsf{U}_{\mathsf{G}'} \\
\Downarrow {\scriptstyle \nu_{\mathsf{U}_{\mathsf{G}'}}} \qquad\qquad\qquad\qquad\qquad\qquad\qquad\qquad \Downarrow {\scriptstyle \mathsf{G}\nu_{\mathsf{U}_{\mathsf{G}'}}} \\
\mathsf{U} \circ \mathsf{T}' \circ \mathsf{U}_{\mathsf{G}'} \xRightarrow{\ \mathsf{U}\sigma'\ } \mathsf{U} \circ \mathsf{G}' \circ \mathsf{T}' \circ \mathsf{U}_{\mathsf{G}'} \xRightarrow{\ \tau_{\mathsf{T}' \circ \mathsf{U}_{\mathsf{G}'}}\ } \mathsf{G} \circ \mathsf{U} \circ \mathsf{T}' \circ \mathsf{U}_{\mathsf{G}'}
\end{array}
$$

The natural transformation σ used in the definition of combined signatures specifies the relationship between the algebraic and coalgebraic substructures of combined structures. Its components define G-coalgebra structures on (the carriers of) the free T-algebras over (the carriers of) G-coalgebras[12]. The additional constraints on σ ensure that, for any G-coalgebra $\langle C, \gamma \rangle$, the C-arrows $\eta_C : C \to TC$ and $\mu_C : TTC \to C$ define G-coalgebra homomorphisms. This results in the tuple $(\mathsf{T}_\sigma, \eta, \mu)$ defining a monad on $\mathsf{Coalg}(\mathsf{G})$. The algebras of this monad are taken as models for a combined signature (C, G, F, σ). A T_σ-algebra is thus given by a C-object C carrying both a G-coalgebra structure $\langle C, \gamma \rangle$ and a T-algebra structure $\langle C, \alpha \rangle$, such that α defines a G-coalgebra homomorphism from $\langle TC, \sigma_\gamma \rangle$ to $\langle C, \gamma \rangle$. Then, the constraints defining a combined signature morphism (U, τ, ξ) ensure that, for a G'-coalgebra $\langle C', \gamma' \rangle$, the G'-coalgebra structure induced by σ' on $T'C'$ agrees with the G-coalgebra structure induced by σ on TUC'. This results in combined signature morphisms (U, τ, ξ) inducing reduct functors $\mathsf{U}_{(\tau,\nu)} : \mathsf{Alg}(\mathsf{T}'_{\sigma'}) \to \mathsf{Alg}(\mathsf{T}_\sigma)$, with $\mathsf{U}_{(\tau,\nu)}$ taking a $\mathsf{T}'_{\sigma'}$-algebra $\langle \langle C', \gamma' \rangle, \alpha' \rangle$ to the T_σ-algebra $\langle \langle UC', \tau_{C'} \circ U\gamma' \rangle, U\alpha' \circ \nu_{C'} \rangle$.

Remark 6. In [12,11], combined structures are captured using pairs consisting of an algebra and a coalgebra structure on the same carrier, with the additional requirement that bisimulation on the coalgebraic structure is a congruence w.r.t. the algebraic structure. Here, the presence of natural transformations σ in the definition of combined signatures ensures this, as well as the fact that reachable subalgebras carry coalgebraic structure. Another consequence of the use of such natural transformations is the existence of reduct functors induced by combined signature morphisms. An alternative approach to specifying combined structures would be to require the above-mentioned compatibility between the algebraic and coalgebraic structure directly, rather than ensuring it through the natural transformations σ. Formally, this would amount to requiring the reachable subalgebras of the underlying algebras to carry coalgebraic structure, and the observable homomorphic images of the underlying coalgebras to carry algebraic structure[13]. However, in this case, horizontality of the signature and cosignature morphisms used to define combined signature morphisms would be

---

[12] A dual approach would be to consider natural transformations of form $\mathsf{F} \circ \mathsf{D} \circ \mathsf{U}_\mathsf{F} \Rightarrow \mathsf{D} \circ \mathsf{U}_\mathsf{F}$, with D the comonad induced by G.

[13] The existence of factorisation systems for $\mathsf{Alg}(\mathsf{T})$ and $\mathsf{Coalg}(\mathsf{G})$ results in the *reachable subalgebra* of a T-algebra and the *observable homomorphic image* of a G-coalgebra being defined uniquely up to isomorphism in $\mathsf{Alg}(\mathsf{T})$ and respectively $\mathsf{Coalg}(\mathsf{G})$.

needed to ensure the well-definedness of reduct functors. ([11] also uses a condition which resembles horizontality to ensure that reduct functors preserve the compatibility between the algebraic operations and the bisimulation relation.)

Example 6. Non-deterministic, sequential processes are specified using the combined signature $(\mathsf{Set}, \mathsf{G_{LFTS}}, \mathsf{F_{NSP}}, \sigma)$, with $\sigma : \mathsf{T_{NSP}} \circ \mathsf{U} \Rightarrow \mathsf{G_{LFTS}} \circ \mathsf{T_{NSP}} \circ \mathsf{U}$ (where $\mathsf{T_{NSP}}$ denotes the monad induced by $\mathsf{F_{NSP}}$) being defined inductively by:

$$\sigma_\gamma(c) = \langle \mathtt{next}(c), \mathtt{depth}(c) \rangle$$
$$\sigma_\gamma(\mathtt{nil}) = \langle \emptyset, 0 \rangle$$
$$\sigma_\gamma(a.c) = \langle \{\langle a, c \rangle\}, 1 + \mathtt{depth}(c) \rangle$$
$$\sigma_\gamma(c + d) = \langle \mathtt{next}(c) \cup \mathtt{next}(d), \max(\mathtt{depth}(c), \mathtt{depth}(d)) \rangle$$
$$\sigma_\gamma(c; d) = \begin{cases} \langle \mathtt{next}(d), \mathtt{depth}(d) \rangle, & \text{if } \mathtt{depth}(c) = 0 \\ \langle \{\langle a, c'; d \rangle \mid \langle a, c' \rangle \in \mathtt{next}(c)\}, \mathtt{depth}(c) + \mathtt{depth}(d) \rangle, & \text{o/w} \end{cases}$$

for any $\mathsf{G_{LFTS}}$-coalgebra $\langle C, \langle \mathtt{next}, \mathtt{depth} \rangle \rangle$, $a \in A$ and $c, d \in C$.

It follows from [17] that, for a combined signature $(\mathsf{C}, \mathsf{G}, \mathsf{F}, \sigma)$, the category $\mathsf{Alg}(\mathsf{T}_\sigma)$ has both an initial and a final object. The initial T_σ-algebra provides an observational structure on ground computations, whereas the final T_σ-algebra provides a computational structure on abstract states. These T_σ-algebras will, from now on, be denoted $\langle \langle I, \gamma_I \rangle, \alpha_I \rangle$ and respectively $\langle \langle F, \gamma_F \rangle, \alpha_F \rangle$.

Proposition 7. *For a combined signature $(\mathsf{C}, \mathsf{G}, \mathsf{F}, \sigma)$, the factorisation system for $\mathsf{Coalg}(\mathsf{G})$ given by Prop. 1 lifts uniquely to a factorisation system for $\mathsf{Alg}(\mathsf{T}_\sigma)$. Moreover, the functor taking T_σ-algebras to their underlying T-algebras preserves factorisations.*

Proof. The first statement follows by [1, Prop. 20.28], after noting that T_σ preserves regular epimorphisms (as T preserves regular epimorphisms). For the second statement, let $\mathsf{U}_\sigma^\mathsf{G} : \mathsf{Alg}(\mathsf{T}_\sigma) \to \mathsf{Coalg}(\mathsf{G})$ and $\mathsf{U}_\sigma^\mathsf{T} : \mathsf{Alg}(\mathsf{T}_\sigma) \to \mathsf{Alg}(\mathsf{T})$ denote the functors taking T_σ-algebras to their underlying G-coalgebras and respectively T-algebras. Then, the statement follows from $\mathsf{U}_\mathsf{G} \circ \mathsf{U}_\sigma^\mathsf{G} = \mathsf{U}_\mathsf{T} \circ \mathsf{U}_\sigma^\mathsf{T}$, together with $\mathsf{U}_\mathsf{G} \circ \mathsf{U}_\sigma^\mathsf{G}$ preserving factorisations and U_T creating them.

As a consequence of Prop. 7, the observable homomorphic images of the G-coalgebras underlying T_σ-algebras carry T-algebra structure, whereas the reachable subalgebras of the T-algebras underlying T_σ-algebras carry G-coalgebra structure.

Definition 11. *Let $(\mathsf{C}, \mathsf{G}, \mathsf{F}, \sigma)$ denote a combined signature. A T_σ-algebra $\langle \langle C, \gamma \rangle, \alpha \rangle$ **satisfies** a modal formula $\iota : \langle D, \delta \rangle \to \mathsf{R_G} Z$ over (C, G) **up to reachability** (written $\langle \langle C, \gamma \rangle, \alpha \rangle \models^r \iota$) if and only if, for any C-arrow $f : C \to Z$, the G-coalgebra homomorphism $f^\flat \circ ! : \langle I, \gamma_I \rangle \to \mathsf{R_G} Z$, with $! : \langle I, \gamma_I \rangle \to \langle C, \gamma \rangle$ arising from the initiality of $\langle \langle I, \gamma_I \rangle, \alpha_I \rangle$, factors through ι.*

$$
\begin{array}{ccc}
C & \langle I, \gamma_I \rangle \xrightarrow{\;!\;} \langle C, \gamma \rangle \\
f \downarrow & \downarrow & \downarrow f^\flat \\
Z & \langle D, \delta \rangle \xrightarrow{\;\iota\;} \mathsf{R_G} Z
\end{array}
$$

Also, a T_σ*-algebra* $\langle\langle C,\gamma\rangle,\alpha\rangle$ **satisfies** *an equation* $q : L_T X \to \langle B,\beta\rangle$ *over* (C, F) **up to observability** *(written* $\langle\langle C,\gamma\rangle,\alpha\rangle \models^\circ q$*) if and only if, for any* C*-arrow* $f : X \to C$*, the* T*-algebra homomorphism* $!' \circ f^\# : L_T X \to \langle F,\alpha_F\rangle$*, with* $!' : \langle C,\alpha\rangle \to \langle F,\alpha_F\rangle$ *arising from the finality of* $\langle\langle F,\gamma_F\rangle,\alpha_F\rangle$*, factors through* q*.*

$$
\begin{array}{ccc}
X & L_T X \xrightarrow{\;q\;} \langle B,\beta\rangle \\
{\scriptstyle f}\downarrow & {\scriptstyle f^\#}\downarrow \qquad\quad \downarrow \\
C & \langle C,\alpha\rangle \xrightarrow[{!'}]{} \langle F,\alpha_F\rangle
\end{array}
$$

Remark 7. If the equation q in Def. 11 is given by a pair of C-arrows $l, r : K \to U_T L_T X$, then $\langle\langle C,\gamma\rangle,\alpha\rangle \models^\circ q$ translates to $U_T !' \circ U_T f^\# \circ l = U_T !' \circ U_T f^\# \circ r$ for any C-arrow $f : X \to C$. This follows similarly to Rem. 4.

Remark 8. The notions of satisfaction introduced in Def. 11 can also be defined in a more general setting, which does not assume the existence of initial/final T_σ-algebras. In particular, in a setting where combined structures are given by compatible algebra-coalgebra pairs (see Rem. 6), a notion of satisfaction of modal formulae up to reachability is obtained by replacing the G-coalgebra homomorphism $! : \langle I,\gamma_I\rangle \to \langle C,\gamma\rangle$ in Def. 11 with the G-coalgebra homomorphism $r : \langle R,\gamma_R\rangle \to \langle C,\gamma\rangle$ (with $\langle R,\gamma_R\rangle$ denoting the G-coalgebra structure on the carrier of the reachable T-subalgebra of $\langle C,\alpha\rangle$[14]). A notion of satisfaction of equations up to observability can be defined in a similar way.

The satisfaction of a modal formula by a T_σ-algebra only requires the formula to hold in reachable states. Also, as shown by the next result, the satisfaction of an equation by a T_σ-algebra only requires the equation to hold up to bisimilarity.

Proposition 8. *Let* (C, G, F, σ) *denote a combined signature. Then, a* T_σ*-algebra* $\langle\langle C,\gamma\rangle,\alpha\rangle$ *satisfies an equation* $l, r : K \to U_T L_T X$ *over* (C, F) *up to observability if and only if, for any* C*-arrow* $f : X \to C$*,* $\langle U_T f^\# \circ l, U_T f^\# \circ r\rangle$ *factors through* $\langle \pi_1,\pi_2\rangle$*, with* $\pi_1,\pi_2 : R \to C$ *defining the kernel pair of* $U_T !'$[15].

Proof (sketch). Rem. 7 is used.

The next result gives a necessary and sufficient condition for the satisfaction of modal formulae up to reachability by algebras of combined signatures.

Proposition 9. *Let* (C, G, F, σ) *denote a combined signature, let* $\langle\langle C,\gamma\rangle,\alpha\rangle$ *denote a* T_σ*-algebra with* $\langle\langle R,\gamma_R\rangle,\alpha_R\rangle$ *its reachable* T_σ*-subalgebra, and let* $\iota : \langle D,\delta\rangle \to R_G Z$ *denote a modal formula over* (C, G). *Then,* $\langle\langle C,\gamma\rangle,\alpha\rangle \models^r \iota$ *iff* $\langle R,\gamma_R\rangle \models \iota$.

Proof (sketch). The unique (RegEpi(Coalg(G)), Mono(Coalg(G)))-diagonalisation property of Coalg(G) and the injectivity of Z are used for the **only if** direction.

---

[14] The preservation of monomorphisms by G ensures the uniqueness of $\langle R,\gamma_R\rangle$.
[15] Hence, by Rem. 1 (4), $\langle R,\pi_1,\pi_2\rangle$ gives precisely the bisimilarity relation on $\langle C,\gamma\rangle$.

A similar result holds for the satisfaction of equations up to observability: a T_σ-algebra satisfies an equation up to observability if and only if the algebra underlying its observable homomorphic image satisfies that equation.

Initiality yields an inductive technique for proving the satisfaction of modal formulae up to reachability by algebras of combined signatures. Also, finality together with the existence of largest bisimulations yield a coinductive technique for proving the satisfaction of equations up to observability by algebras of combined signatures. These techniques are briefly illustrated in the following.

Example 7. Proving that the modal formulae defining finitely-branching, A-labelled transition systems of finite depth hold, up to reachability, in algebras of the combined signature for non-deterministic, sequential processes can be reduced to proving that they hold in `nil` and that their satisfaction is preserved by $\_.\_$, $\_+\_$ and $\_;\_$. But this follows directly from the constraints defining this combined signature. Also, proving that the equation in Ex. 5 holds, up to observability, in algebras of the same combined signature can be reduced to exhibiting a *generic bisimulation relation* (given by a functor $R : \mathsf{Coalg}(\mathsf{G_{LFTS}}) \to \mathsf{C}$ together with two natural transformations $\pi_1, \pi_2 : R \Rightarrow U_\mathsf{G}$, such that $\langle R\gamma, \pi_{1,\gamma}, \pi_{2,\gamma}\rangle$ is a bisimulation relation on $\langle C, \gamma\rangle$ for each $\mathsf{G_{LFTS}}$-coalgebra $\langle C, \gamma\rangle$), such that $R\gamma$ relates the interpretations in $\langle C, \alpha\rangle$ of the two sides of the equation, for any $(\mathsf{G_{LFTS}}, \mathsf{F_{NSP}}, \sigma)$-algebra $\langle\langle C, \gamma\rangle, \alpha\rangle$. Here, $R\gamma$ is taken to be the least reflexive relation on C such that $(c+d)\ R\gamma\ (d+c)$ for any $c, d \in C$ and any $(\mathsf{G_{LFTS}}, \mathsf{F_{NSP}}, \sigma)$-algebra $\langle\langle C, \gamma\rangle, \alpha\rangle$. The fourth constraint in the definition of this combined signature results in $R\gamma$ being a bisimulation relation on $\langle C, \gamma\rangle$.

Finally, we show that combined signature morphisms whose underlying signature and respectively cosignature morphisms are horizontal give rise to institutions w.r.t. the satisfaction of modal formulas up to reachability and respectively of equations up to observability by algebras of combined signatures.

Theorem 3. *Let $(\mathsf{U}, \tau, \xi) : (\mathsf{C}, \mathsf{G}, \mathsf{F}, \sigma) \to (\mathsf{C}', \mathsf{G}', \mathsf{F}', \sigma')$ denote a combined signature morphism, and let $\langle\langle C', \gamma'\rangle, \alpha'\rangle$ denote a $T'_{\sigma'}$-algebra. The following hold:*

1. *If (U, ξ) is horizontal and $\iota : \langle D, \delta\rangle \to \mathsf{R_G}Z$ denotes a modal formula over (C, G), then $\mathsf{U}_{\tau,\nu}\langle\langle C', \gamma'\rangle, \alpha'\rangle \models^r \iota$ iff $\langle\langle C', \gamma'\rangle, \alpha'\rangle \models^r \tau(\iota)$.*
2. *If (U, τ) is horizontal and $q : \mathsf{L_T}X \to \langle B, \beta\rangle$ denotes an equation over (C, F), then $\mathsf{U}_{\tau,\nu}\langle\langle C', \gamma'\rangle, \alpha'\rangle \models^o q$ iff $\langle\langle C', \gamma'\rangle, \alpha'\rangle \models^o \nu(q)$.*

Proof. $\mathsf{U}_{\tau,\nu}\langle\langle C', \gamma'\rangle, \alpha'\rangle \models^r \iota$ amounts to the existence, for any C-arrow $f : \mathsf{U}C' \to Z$, of a G-coalgebra homomorphism g making the outer left diagram below commute, whereas $\langle\langle C', \gamma'\rangle, \alpha'\rangle \models^r \tau(\iota)$ amounts to the existence, for any C'-arrow $f' : C' \to RZ$, of a G'-coalgebra homomorphism g' making the right diagram below commute. Also, since $\mathsf{U} \dashv R$, $\mathsf{C}(\mathsf{U}C', Z) \simeq \mathsf{C}'(C', RZ)$.

For the **if** direction, let $f : UC' \to Z$ denote a C-arrow, let $f' : C' \to RZ$ denote its corresponding C'-arrow, and let $g' : \langle I', \gamma_{I'} \rangle \to R_\tau \langle D, \delta \rangle$ denote the G'-coalgebra homomorphism which makes the right diagram commute. Then, g is taken to be $g'^{\#} \circ \tilde{\nu}_{0'}$. For the **only if** direction, let $f' : C' \to RZ$ denote a C'-arrow, and let $f : UC' \to Z$ denote its corresponding C-arrow. Since $U_G \tilde{\nu}_{0'} = \nu_{0'} \in \mathsf{RegEpi}(\mathsf{C})$ and $U_G \iota \in \mathsf{Mono}(\mathsf{C})$, the unique $(\mathsf{RegEpi}(\mathsf{Coalg}(\mathsf{G})), \mathsf{Mono}(\mathsf{Coalg}(\mathsf{G})))$-diagonalisation property of $\mathsf{Coalg}(\mathsf{G})$ yields a G-coalgebra homomorphism $h : U_\tau \langle I', \gamma_{I'} \rangle \to \langle D, \delta \rangle$ satisfying $h \circ \tilde{\nu}_{0'} = g$ and $\iota \circ h = f^\flat \circ U_\tau!'$. This, in turn, yields a G'-coalgebra homomorphism $g' : \langle I', \gamma_{I'} \rangle \to R_\tau \langle D, \delta \rangle$ (by $U_\tau \dashv R_\tau$).

The proof of the second statement is similar.

References

1. J. Adámek, H. Herrlich, and G.E. Strecker. *Abstract and Concrete Categories*. John Wiley and Sons, 1990.
2. B. Banaschewski and H. Herrlich. Subcategories defined by implications. *Houston Journal of Mathematics*, 2(2), 1976.
3. G. Birkhoff. On the structure of abstract algebras. In *Proceedings of the Cambridge Philosophical Society*, volume 31, 1935.
4. F. Borceux. *Handbook of Categorical Algebra*, volume 2. CUP, 1994.
5. C. Cîrstea. Integrating observational and computational features in the specification of state-based, dynamical systems. *Theoretical Informatics and Applications*, 35(1), 2001.
6. J. Goguen and R. Burstall. Institutions: Abstract model theory for specification and programming. *Journal of the ACM*, 39(1), 1992.
7. B. Jacobs. Many-sorted coalgebraic modal logic: A model-theoretic study. *Theoretical Informatics and Applications*, 35(1), 2001.
8. P. Johnstone, J. Power, T. Tsujishita, H. Watanabe, and J. Worrell. On the structure of categories of coalgebras. *TCS*, 260(1), 2001.
9. A. Kurz. *Logics for Coalgebras and Applications to Computer Science*. PhD thesis, Ludwig-Maximilians-Universität München, 2000.
10. A. Kurz. Specifying coalgebras with modal logic. *TCS*, 260(1), 2001.
11. A. Kurz and R. Hennicker. On institutions for modular coalgebraic specifications. To appear in Theoretical Computer Science.
12. G. Malcolm. Behavioural equivalence, bisimulation, and minimal realisation. In M. Haveraaen, O. Owe, and O.-J. Dahl, editors, *Proceedings, WADT*, volume 1130 of *LNCS*. Springer, 1996.
13. L.S. Moss. Coalgebraic logic. *Annals of Pure and Applied Logic*, 96, 1999.
14. H. Reichel. An approach to object semantics based on terminal coalgebras. *Mathematical Structures in Computer Science*, 5, 1995.
15. M. Rößiger. Coalgebras and modal logic. In H. Reichel, editor, *Coalgebraic Methods in Computer Science*, volume 33 of *ENTCS*. Elsevier Science, 2000.
16. J.J.M.M. Rutten. Universal coalgebra: a theory of systems. *TCS*, 249(1), 2000.
17. D. Turi and G. Plotkin. Towards a mathematical operational semantics. In *Proceedings, LICS*, 1997.

A First-Order One-Pass CPS Transformation

Olivier Danvy and Lasse R. Nielsen

BRICS*
Department of Computer Science, University of Aarhus
Ny Munkegade, Building 540, DK-8000 Aarhus C, Denmark
{danvy,lrn}@brics.dk
http://www.brics.dk/~{danvy,lrn}

Abstract. We present a new transformation of call-by-value lambda-terms into continuation-passing style (CPS). This transformation operates in one pass and is both compositional and first-order. Because it operates in one pass, it directly yields compact CPS programs that are comparable to what one would write by hand. Because it is compositional, it allows proofs by structural induction. Because it is first-order, reasoning about it does not require the use of a logical relation.
This new CPS transformation connects two separate lines of research. It has already been used to state a new and simpler correctness proof of a direct-style transformation, and to develop a new and simpler CPS transformation of control-flow information.

1   Introduction

The transformation into continuation-passing style (CPS) is an encoding of arbitrary λ-terms into an evaluation-order-independent subset of the λ-calculus [30,36]. As already reviewed by Reynolds [35], continuations and the CPS transformation share a long history. The CPS transformation was first formalized by Plotkin [30], and first used in practice by Steele, in the first compiler for the Scheme programming language [39]. Unfortunately, its direct implementation as a rewriting system yields extraneous redexes known as *administrative redexes*. These redexes interfere both with proving the correctness of a CPS transformation [30] and with using it in a compiler [22,39]. At the turn of the 1990's, two flavors of "one-pass" CPS transformations that contract administrative redexes at transformation time were developed. One flavor is compositional and higher-order, using a functional accumulator [1,10,41]. The other is non-compositional and first-order, using evaluation contexts [37]. They have both been proven correct and are used in compilers as well as to reason about CPS programs.

Because the existing one-pass CPS transformations are either higher-order or non-compositional, their correctness proofs are complicated, and so is reasoning about CPS-transformed programs. In this article, we present a one-pass CPS transformation that is both compositional and first-order and thus is simple to prove correct and to reason about. It is also more efficient in practice.

* Basic Research in Computer Science (www.brics.dk),
  funded by the Danish National Research Foundation.

M. Nielsen and U. Engberg (Eds.): Fossacs 2002, LNCS 2303, pp. 98–113, 2002.
© Springer-Verlag Berlin Heidelberg 2002

Overview: The rest of this article is structured as follows. We present three derivations of our first-order, one-pass, and compositional CPS transformation. We derive it from the higher-order one-pass CPS transformation (Section 2), from Sabry and Wadler's non-compositional CPS transformation (Section 3), and from Steele's two-pass CPS transformation (Section 4). We also prove its correctness with a simulation theorem à la Plotkin (Section 5).

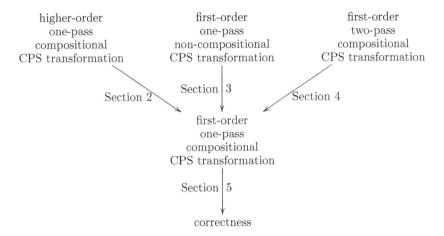

We then compare the process of reasoning about CPS-transformed programs, depending on which kind of CPS transformation is used (Section 6). Finally, we conclude (Section 7).

Prerequisites: The syntax of the λ-calculus is as follows. We follow the tradition of distinguishing between trivial and serious terms. (This distinction originates in Reynolds's work [36] and has been used by Moggi to distinguish between values and computations [25].)

$$
\begin{array}{lll}
e ::= t \mid s & e \in \text{Expr} & \text{(terms)} \\
t ::= x \mid \lambda x.e & t, K \in \text{Val} & \text{(trivial terms, i.e., values)} \\
s ::= e_0\, e_1 & s \in \text{Comp} & \text{(serious terms, i.e., computations)} \\
& x, k \in \text{Ide} & \text{(identifiers)}
\end{array}
$$

We distinguish terms up to α-equivalence, i.e., renaming of bound variables.

2   From Higher-Order to First-Order

2.1   A Higher-Order Specification

Figure 1 displays a higher-order, one-pass, compositional CPS transformation. $\mathcal{E}$ is applied to terms in tail position [3] and $\mathcal{E}'$ to terms appearing in non-tail position; they are otherwise similar. $\mathcal{S}$ is applied to serious terms in tail position

$$\mathcal{E} : \text{Expr} \to \text{Ide} \to \text{Comp}$$
$$\mathcal{E}[\![t]\!] = \overline{\lambda}k.k \,\underline{@}\, \mathcal{T}[\![t]\!]$$
$$\mathcal{E}[\![s]\!] = \overline{\lambda}k.\mathcal{S}[\![s]\!] \,\overline{@}\, k$$

$$\mathcal{S} : \text{Comp} \to \text{Ide} \to \text{Comp}$$
$$\mathcal{S}[\![e_0\ e_1]\!] = \overline{\lambda}k.\mathcal{E}'[\![e_0]\!] \,\overline{@}\, (\overline{\lambda}x_0.\mathcal{E}'[\![e_1]\!] \,\overline{@}\, (\overline{\lambda}x_1.x_0 \,\underline{@}\, x_1 \,\underline{@}\, k))$$

$$\mathcal{T} : \text{Val} \to \text{Val}$$
$$\mathcal{T}[\![x]\!] = x$$
$$\mathcal{T}[\![\lambda x.e]\!] = \underline{\lambda}x.\underline{\lambda}k.\mathcal{E}[\![e]\!] \,\overline{@}\, k$$

$$\mathcal{E}' : \text{Expr} \to (\text{Val} \to \text{Comp}) \to \text{Comp}$$
$$\mathcal{E}'[\![t]\!] = \overline{\lambda}\kappa.\kappa \,\overline{@}\, \mathcal{T}[\![t]\!]$$
$$\mathcal{E}'[\![s]\!] = \overline{\lambda}\kappa.\mathcal{S}'[\![s]\!] \,\overline{@}\, \kappa$$

$$\mathcal{S}' : \text{Comp} \to (\text{Val} \to \text{Comp}) \to \text{Comp}$$
$$\mathcal{S}'[\![e_0\ e_1]\!] = \overline{\lambda}\kappa.\mathcal{E}'[\![e_0]\!] \,\overline{@}\, (\overline{\lambda}x_0.\mathcal{E}'[\![e_1]\!] \,\overline{@}\, (\overline{\lambda}x_1.x_0 \,\underline{@}\, x_1 \,\underline{@}\, (\underline{\lambda}x_2.\kappa \,\overline{@}\, x_2)))$$

Fig. 1. Higher-order one-pass CPS transformation

and $\mathcal{S}'$ to terms appearing in non-tail position; they are otherwise similar. $\mathcal{T}$ is applied to trivial terms.

In Figure 1, transformation-time abstractions ($\overline{\lambda}$) and applications (infix $\overline{@}$) are overlined. Underlined abstractions ($\underline{\lambda}$) and applications (infix $\underline{@}$) are hygienic syntax constructors, i.e., they generate fresh variables.

An expression e is CPS-transformed into the result of $\underline{\lambda}k.\mathcal{E}[\![e]\!] \,\overline{@}\, k$.

2.2   Circumventing the Higher-Order Functions

Let us analyze the function spaces in Figure 1. All the calls to $\mathcal{E}$, $\mathcal{S}$, $\mathcal{E}'$, and $\mathcal{S}'$ are fully applied and thus these functions could as well be uncurried. The resulting CPS transformation is only higher order because of the function space $\text{Val} \to \text{Comp}$ used in $\mathcal{E}'$ and $\mathcal{S}'$. Let us try to circumvent this function space.

A simple control-flow analysis of the uncurried CPS transformation tells us that while both $\mathcal{E}$ and $\mathcal{E}'$ invoke $\mathcal{T}$, $\mathcal{T}$ only invokes $\mathcal{E}$, $\mathcal{E}$ only invokes $\mathcal{S}$, and $\mathcal{S}$ only invokes $\mathcal{E}'$ while $\mathcal{E}'$ and $\mathcal{S}'$ invoke each other. The following diagram illustrates these relationships.

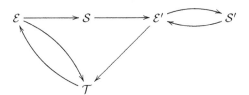

Therefore, if we could prevent $\mathcal{S}$ from calling $\mathcal{E}'$, both $\mathcal{E}'$ and $\mathcal{S}'$ would become dead code, and only $\mathcal{E}$, $\mathcal{S}$, and $\mathcal{T}$ would remain. We would then obtain a first-order one-pass CPS transformation.

Let us unfold the definition of $\mathcal{S}$ and reason by inversion. The four following cases occur. (We only detail the β-reductions in the first case.)

$$
\begin{aligned}
\mathcal{S}[\![t_0\, t_1]\!]\,\overline{@}\,k &=_{\mathrm{def}} \mathcal{E}'[\![t_0]\!]\,\overline{@}\,(\overline{\lambda}x_0.\mathcal{E}'[\![t_1]\!]\,\overline{@}\,(\overline{\lambda}x_1.x_0\,\underline{@}\,x_1\,\underline{@}\,k))\\
&=_{\mathrm{def}} (\overline{\lambda}x_0.\mathcal{E}'[\![t_1]\!]\,\overline{@}\,(\overline{\lambda}x_1.x_0\,\underline{@}\,x_1\,\underline{@}\,k))\,\overline{@}\,\mathcal{T}[\![t_0]\!]\\
&\to_\beta \mathcal{E}'[\![t_1]\!]\,\overline{@}\,(\overline{\lambda}x_1.\mathcal{T}[\![t_0]\!]\,\underline{@}\,x_1\,\underline{@}\,k)\\
&=_{\mathrm{def}} (\overline{\lambda}x_1.\mathcal{T}[\![t_0]\!]\,\underline{@}\,x_1\,\underline{@}\,k)\,\overline{@}\,\mathcal{T}[\![t_1]\!]\\
&\to_\beta \mathcal{T}[\![t_0]\!]\,\underline{@}\,\mathcal{T}[\![t_1]\!]\,\underline{@}\,k\\[4pt]
\mathcal{S}[\![t_0\, s_1]\!]\,\overline{@}\,k &=_\beta \mathcal{S}'[\![s_1]\!]\,\overline{@}\,(\overline{\lambda}x_1.\mathcal{T}[\![t_0]\!]\,\underline{@}\,x_1\,\underline{@}\,k)\\[4pt]
\mathcal{S}[\![s_0\, t_1]\!]\,\overline{@}\,k &=_\beta \mathcal{S}'[\![s_0]\!]\,\overline{@}\,(\overline{\lambda}x_0.x_0\,\underline{@}\,\mathcal{T}[\![t_1]\!]\,\underline{@}\,k)\\[4pt]
\mathcal{S}[\![s_0\, s_1]\!]\,\overline{@}\,k &=_\beta \mathcal{S}'[\![s_0]\!]\,\overline{@}\,(\overline{\lambda}x_0.\mathcal{S}'[\![s_1]\!]\,\overline{@}\,(\overline{\lambda}x_1.x_0\,\underline{@}\,x_1\,\underline{@}\,k))
\end{aligned}
$$

This analysis makes explicit all of the functions κ that $\mathcal{S}$ passes to $\mathcal{S}'$. By definition of $\mathcal{S}'$, we also know *where* these functions are applied: in the two-level eta-redex $\underline{\lambda}x_2.\kappa\,\overline{@}\,x_2$. We can take advantage of this knowledge by invoking $\mathcal{S}$ rather than $\mathcal{S}'$, extend its domain to $\mathrm{Comp} \to \mathrm{Expr} \to \mathrm{Comp}$, and pass it the result of eta-expanding κ. The result reads as follows.

$$
\begin{aligned}
\mathcal{S}[\![t_0\, t_1]\!]\,\overline{@}\,k &\equiv \mathcal{T}[\![t_0]\!]\,\underline{@}\,\mathcal{T}[\![t_1]\!]\,\underline{@}\,k\\
\mathcal{S}[\![t_0\, s_1]\!]\,\overline{@}\,k &\equiv \mathcal{S}[\![s_1]\!]\,\overline{@}\,(\underline{\lambda}x_1.\mathcal{T}[\![t_0]\!]\,\underline{@}\,x_1\,\underline{@}\,k)\\
\mathcal{S}[\![s_0\, t_1]\!]\,\overline{@}\,k &\equiv \mathcal{S}[\![s_0]\!]\,\overline{@}\,(\underline{\lambda}x_0.x_0\,\underline{@}\,\mathcal{T}[\![t_1]\!]\,\underline{@}\,k)\\
\mathcal{S}[\![s_0\, s_1]\!]\,\overline{@}\,k &\equiv \mathcal{S}[\![s_0]\!]\,\overline{@}\,(\underline{\lambda}x_0.\mathcal{S}[\![s_1]\!]\,\overline{@}\,(\underline{\lambda}x_1.x_0\,\underline{@}\,x_1\,\underline{@}\,k))
\end{aligned}
$$

In this derived transformation, $\mathcal{E}'$ and $\mathcal{S}'$ are no longer used. Since they are the only higher-order components of the uncurried CPS transformation, the derived transformation, while still one-pass and compositional, is first-order. Its control-flow graph can be depicted as follows.

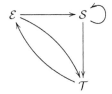

$$\mathcal{E} : \mathrm{Expr} \times \mathrm{Ide} \to \mathrm{Comp}$$
$$\mathcal{E}[\![t]\!]\, k \;=\; k\,\mathcal{T}[\![t]\!]$$
$$\mathcal{E}[\![s]\!]\, k \;=\; \mathcal{S}[\![s]\!]\, k$$

$$\mathcal{S} : \mathrm{Comp} \times \mathrm{Expr} \to \mathrm{Comp}$$
$$\mathcal{S}[\![t_0\, t_1]\!]\, K \;=\; \mathcal{T}[\![t_0]\!]\,\mathcal{T}[\![t_1]\!]\, K$$
$$\mathcal{S}[\![t_0\, s_1]\!]\, K \;=\; \mathcal{S}[\![s_1]\!]\,(\lambda x_1.\mathcal{T}[\![t_0]\!]\, x_1\, K)$$
$$\mathcal{S}[\![s_0\, t_1]\!]\, K \;=\; \mathcal{S}[\![s_0]\!]\,(\lambda x_0.x_0\,\mathcal{T}[\![t_1]\!]\, K)$$
$$\mathcal{S}[\![s_0\, s_1]\!]\, K \;=\; \mathcal{S}[\![s_0]\!]\,(\lambda x_0.\mathcal{S}[\![s_1]\!]\,(\lambda x_1.x_0\, x_1\, K))$$

$$\mathcal{T} : \mathrm{Val} \to \mathrm{Val}$$
$$\mathcal{T}[\![x]\!] \;=\; x$$
$$\mathcal{T}[\![\lambda x.e]\!] \;=\; \lambda x.\lambda k.\mathcal{E}[\![e]\!]\, k$$

Fig. 2. First-order one-pass CPS transformation

The resulting CPS transformation is displayed in Figure 2. Since it is first-order, there are no overlined abstractions and applications, and therefore we omit all underlines as well as the infix @. An expression e is CPS-transformed into the result of $\lambda k.\mathcal{E}[\![e]\!]\, k$.

This first-order CPS transformation is compositional (in the sense of denotational semantics) because on the right-hand side, all recursive calls are on proper sub-parts of the left-hand-side term [42, page 60]. One could say, however, that it is not purely defined by recursive descent, since $\mathcal{S}$ is defined by cases on immediate sub-expressions, using a sort of structural look-ahead. (A change of grammar would solve that problem, though.) The main cost incurred by the inversion step above is that it requires 2^n clauses for a source term with n sub-terms that need to be considered (e.g., a tuple).

3   From Non-compositional to Compositional

3.1   A Non-compositional Specification

The first edition of *Essentials of Programming Languages* [18] dedicated a chapter to the CPS transformation, with the goal to be as intuitive and pedagogical as possible and to produce CPS terms similar to what one would write by hand. This CPS transformation inspired Sabry and Felleisen to design a radically different CPS transformation based on evaluation contexts that produces a remarkably compact output due to an extra reduction rule, β_{lift} [11,37]. Sabry and Wadler then simplified this CPS transformation [38, Figure 18], e.g., omitting β_{lift}. This simplified CPS transformation now forms the basis of the chapter on the CPS transformation in the second edition of *Essentials of Programming Languages* [19].

Using the same notation as in Figure 2, Sabry and Wadler's CPS transformation reads as follows. An expression e is CPS-transformed into $\lambda k.\mathcal{E}[\![e]\!]$, where:

$$\mathcal{E}[\![e]\!] = \mathcal{S}[\![e]\!]\,k \qquad\qquad \mathcal{S}[\![t]\!]\,K = K\,\mathcal{T}[\![t]\!]$$
$$\mathcal{S}[\![t_0\,t_1]\!]\,K = \mathcal{T}[\![t_0]\!]\,\mathcal{T}[\![t_1]\!]\,K$$
$$\mathcal{T}[\![x]\!] = x \qquad\qquad \mathcal{S}[\![t_0\,s_1]\!]\,K = \mathcal{S}[\![s_1]\!]\,(\lambda x_1.\mathcal{S}[\![t_0\,x_1]\!]\,K)$$
$$\mathcal{T}[\![\lambda x.e]\!] = \lambda x.\lambda k.\mathcal{E}[\![e]\!] \qquad\qquad \mathcal{S}[\![s_0\,e_1]\!]\,K = \mathcal{S}[\![s_0]\!]\,(\lambda x_0.\mathcal{S}[\![x_0\,e_1]\!]\,K)$$

For each serious expression s with a serious immediate sub-expression s', $\mathcal{S}$ recursively traverses s' with a new continuation. In this new continuation, s' is replaced by a fresh variable (i.e., a trivial immediate sub-expression) in s. The result, now with one less serious immediate sub-expression, is transformed recursively. The idea was the same in Sabry and Felleisen's context-based CPS transformation [37, Definition 5], which we study elsewhere [12,15,27].

These CPS transformations hinge on a unique free variable k and also they are not compositional. For example, on the right-hand side of the definition of $\mathcal{S}$ just above, some recursive calls are on terms that are not proper sub-parts of the left-hand-side term. The input program changes dynamically during the transformation, and proving termination therefore requires a size argument. In contrast, a compositional transformation entails a simpler termination proof by structural induction.

3.2 Eliminating the Non-compositionality

Sabry and Wadler's CPS transformation can be made compositional through the following unfolding steps.

Unfolding $\mathcal{S}$ in $\mathcal{S}[\![t_0\,x_1]\!]\,K$: The result is $\mathcal{T}[\![t_0]\!]\,\mathcal{T}[\![x_1]\!]\,K$, which is equivalent to $\mathcal{T}[\![t_0]\!]\,x_1\,K$.

Unfolding $\mathcal{S}$ in $\mathcal{S}[\![x_0\,e_1]\!]\,K$: Two cases occur (thus splitting this clause for $\mathcal{S}$ into two).
- If e_1 is a value (call it t_1), the result is $\mathcal{T}[\![x_0]\!]\,\mathcal{T}[\![t_1]\!]\,K$, which is equivalent to $x_0\,\mathcal{T}[\![t_1]\!]\,K$.
- If e_1 is a computation (call it s_1), the result is $\mathcal{S}[\![s_1]\!]\,(\lambda x_1.\mathcal{S}[\![x_0\,x_1]\!]\,K)$. Unfolding the inner occurrence of $\mathcal{S}$ yields $\mathcal{S}[\![s_1]\!]\,(\lambda x_1.\mathcal{T}[\![x_0]\!]\,\mathcal{T}[\![x_1]\!]\,K)$, which is equivalent to $\mathcal{S}[\![s_1]\!]\,(\lambda x_1.x_0\,x_1\,K)$.

The resulting unfolded transformation is compositional. It also coincides with the definition of $\mathcal{S}$ in Figure 2 and thus connects the two separate lines of research.

4 From Two Passes to One Pass

4.1 A Two-Pass Specification

Plotkin's CPS transformation [30] can be phrased as follows.

$$\mathcal{C}[\![t]\!] = \lambda k.k\,\Phi(t) \qquad\qquad \Phi(x) = x$$
$$\mathcal{C}[\![e_0\,e_1]\!] = \lambda k.\mathcal{C}[\![e_0]\!]\,(\lambda x_0.\mathcal{C}[\![e_1]\!]\,(\lambda x_1.x_0\,x_1\,k)) \qquad\qquad \Phi(\lambda x.e) = \lambda x.\mathcal{C}[\![e]\!]$$

Directly implementing it yields CPS terms containing a mass of administrative redexes that need to be contracted in a second pass [39].

4.2   A Colon Translation for Proving Simulation

Plotkin's simulation theorem shows a correspondence between reductions in the source program and in the transformed program. To this end, he introduced the so-called "colon translation" to bypass the initial administrative reductions of a CPS-transformed term.

The colon translation makes it possible to focus on the reduction of the abstractions inherited from the source program. The simulation theorem is shown by relating each reduction step, as depicted by the following diagram.

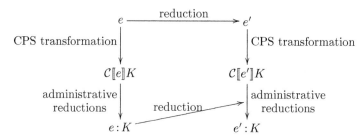

The colon translation is itself a CPS transformation. It transforms a source expression and a continuation into a CPS term; this CPS term is the one that appears after contracting the initial administrative redexes of the CPS-transformed expression applied to the continuation. In other words, if we write the colon translation of the expression e and the continuation K as $e : K$, then the following holds: $\mathcal{C}[\![e]\!]\, K \xrightarrow{*} e : K$.

The colon translation can be derived from the CPS transformation by predicting the result of the initial administrative reductions from the structure of the source term. For example, a serious term of the form $t_0\, e_1$ is CPS-transformed into $\lambda k.(\lambda k.k\ \Phi(v))\ (\lambda x_0.\mathcal{C}[\![e_1]\!]\ (\lambda x_1.x_0\ x_1\ k))$. Applying this CPS term to a continuation enables the following administrative reductions.

$$
\begin{aligned}
&(\lambda k.(\lambda k.k\ \Phi(t_0))\ (\lambda x_0.\mathcal{C}[\![e_1]\!]\ (\lambda x_1.x_0\ x_1\ k)))\ K \\
&\to_\beta (\lambda k.k\ \Phi(t_0))\ (\lambda x_0.\mathcal{C}[\![e_1]\!]\ (\lambda x_1.x_0\ x_1\ K)) \\
&\to_\beta (\lambda x_0.\mathcal{C}[\![e_1]\!]\ (\lambda x_1.x_0\ x_1\ K))\ \Phi(t_0) \\
&\to_\beta \mathcal{C}[\![e_1]\!]\ \lambda x_1.\Phi(t_0)\ x_1\ K
\end{aligned}
$$

The result is a smaller term that can be CPS-transformed recursively. This insight leads one to Plotkin's colon translation, as defined below.

$$
\begin{aligned}
t : K &= K\ \Phi(t) \\
t_0\ t_1 : K &= \Phi(t_0)\ \Phi(t_1)\ K \\
t_0\ s_1 : K &= s_1 : (\lambda x_1.\Phi(t_0)\ x_1\ K) \\
s_0\ e_1 : K &= s_0 : (\lambda x_0.\mathcal{C}[\![e_1]\!]\ (\lambda x_1.x_0\ x_1\ K))
\end{aligned}
$$

4.3   Merging CPS Transformation and Colon Translation

For Plotkin's purpose—reasoning about the output of the CPS transformation—contracting the initial administrative reductions in each step is sufficient. Our goal, however, is to remove all administrative redexes in one pass. Since the colon translation contracts some administrative redexes, and thus more than the CPS transformation, further administrative redexes can be contracted by using the colon translation in place of all occurrences of $\mathcal{C}$.

The CPS transformation is used once in the colon translation and once in the definition of Φ. For consistency, we distinguish two cases in the colon translation, depending on whether the expression is a value or not, and we use the colon translation if it is not a value. In the definition of Φ, we introduce the continuation identifier and then we use the colon translation. The resulting extended colon translation reads as follows.

$$t : K = K\ \Phi(t)$$
$$t_0\ t_1 : K = \Phi(t_0)\ \Phi(t_1)\ K$$
$$t_0\ s_1 : K = s_1 : (\lambda x_1.\Phi(t_0)\ x_1\ K)$$
$$s_0\ t_1 : K = s_0 : (\lambda x_0.x_0\ \Phi(t_1)\ K)$$
$$s_0\ s_1 : K = s_0 : (\lambda x_0.(s_1 : (\lambda x_1.x_0\ x_1\ K)))$$

$$\Phi(x) = x$$
$$\Phi(\lambda x.e) = \lambda x.\lambda k.(e : k)$$

With a change of notation, this extended colon translation coincides with the first-order one-pass CPS transformation from Figure 2. In other words, not only does the extended colon translation remove more administrative redexes than the original one, but it actually removes as many as the two-pass transformation.

5   Correctness
of the First-Order One-Pass CPS Transformation

Theorem 1 (Simulation). *A term e reduces to a value t if and only $\mathcal{E}[\![e]\!]\ \lambda x.x$ reduces to $\mathcal{T}[\![t]\!]$, where $\mathcal{E}$ and $\mathcal{T}$ are defined in Figure 2.*

The complete proof appears in the full version of this article [13]. It is more direct than Plotkin's [30] since we do not need a colon translation.

6   Reasoning about CPS-Transformed Programs

How to go about proving properties of CPS-transformed programs depends on which kind of CPS transformation was used. In this section, we review each of them in turn. As our running example, we prove that the CPS transformation preserves types. (The CPS transformation of types exists [24,40] and has a logical content [20,26].) We consider the simply typed λ-calculus, with a typing judgment of the form $\Gamma \vdash e : \tau$.

6.1   A Higher-Order One-Pass CPS Transformation

Danvy and Filinski used a typing argument to prove that their one-pass CPS transformation is well-defined [10, Theorem 1]. To prove the corresponding simulation theorem, they used a notion of schematic continuations. Since then, for the same purpose, we have developed a higher-order analogue of Plotkin's colon translation [14,27].

Proving structural properties of CPS programs is not completely trivial. Matching the higher-order nature of the one-pass CPS transformation, a logical relation is needed, e.g., to prove ordering properties of CPS terms [9,16,17]. (The analogy between these ordering properties and substitution properties of linear λ-calculi has prompted Polakow and Pfenning to develop an ordered logical framework [31,32,33].) A logical relation amounts to structural induction at higher types. Therefore, it is crucial that the higher-order one-pass CPS transformation be compositional.

The CPS transformation preserves types: To prove the well-typedness of a CPS-transformed term, we proceed by structural induction on the typing derivation of the source term (or by structural induction on the source expression), together with a logical relation on the functional accumulator.

6.2   A First-Order Two-Pass CPS Transformation

Sabry and Felleisen also considered a two-pass CPS transformation. They used developments [2, Section 11.2] to prove that it is total [37, Proposition 2].

To prove structural properties of simplified CPS programs, one can (1) characterize the property prior to simplification, and (2) prove that simplifications preserve the property. Danvy took these steps to prove occurrence conditions of continuation identifiers [8], and so did Damian and Danvy to characterize the effect of the CPS transformation on control flow and binding times [4,6]. It is Polakow's thesis that an ordered logical framework provides a good support for stating and proving such properties [31,34].

The CPS transformation preserves types: To prove the well-typedness of a CPS-transformed term, we first proceed by structural induction on the typing derivation of the source term. (It is thus crucial that the CPS transformation be compositional.) For the second pass, we need to show that the administrative contractions preserve the typeability and the type of the result. But this follows from the subject reduction property of the simply typed λ-calculus.

6.3   A First-Order One-Pass CPS Transformation

The proof in Section 5 follows the spirit of Plotkin's original proof [30] but is more direct since it does not require a colon translation.

A first-order CPS transformation makes it possible to prove structural properties of a CPS-transformed program by structural induction on the source program. We find these proofs noticeably simpler than the ones mentioned in Section 6.1. For another example, Damian and Danvy have used the present first-order CPS transformation to develop a CPS transformation of control-flow information [5] that is simpler than existing ones [4,6,29].

Again, for structural induction to go through, it is crucial that the CPS transformation be compositional.

The CPS transformation preserves types: To prove the well-typedness of a CPS-transformed term, we proceed by structural induction on the typing derivation of the source term.

6.4   Non-compositional CPS Transformations

Sabry and Felleisen's proofs are by induction on the size of the source program [37, Appendix A, page 337]. Proving type preservation would require a substitution lemma.

7   Conclusion and Issues

7.1   The Big Picture

Elsewhere [11,12,15], we have developed further connections between higher-order and context-based one-pass CPS transformations. The overall situation is summarized in the following diagram.

The following diagram is clearly in two parts: the left part stems from Plotkin's work and the right part from the first edition of *Essentials of Programming Languages*. The left-most part represents the CPS transformation with the colon translation. The vertical line in the middle represents the path of compositional CPS transformations. The vertical line on the right represents the path of non-compositional CPS transformations. The right arrow from the colon translation is our higher-order colon translation [14]. The upper arrows between the left part and the right part of the diagram correspond to our work on β-redexes [11], defunctionalization [12], and refocusing in syntactic theories [15]. The present work links the left part and the right part of the diagram further.

7.2   Scaling Up

Our derivation of a first-order, one-pass CPS transformation generalizes to other evaluation orders, e.g., call-by-name. (Indeed each evaluation order gives rise to a different CPS transformation [21].) The CPS transformation also scales up to the usual syntactic constructs of a programming language such as primitive operations, tuples, conditional expressions, and sequencing.

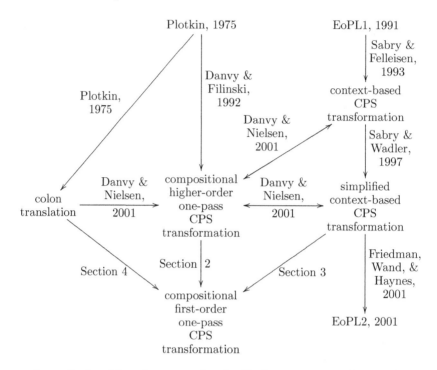

A practical problem, however, arises for block structure, i.e., let- and letrec-expressions. For example, a let-expression is CPS-transformed as follows (extending Figure 1).

$$\mathcal{S}[\![\text{let } x = e_1 \text{ in } e_2]\!] = \overline{\lambda}k.\mathcal{E}[\![e_1]\!]\,\overline{@}\,(\underline{\lambda}x.\mathcal{E}[\![e_2]\!]\,\overline{@}\,k)$$
$$\mathcal{S}'[\![\text{let } x = e_1 \text{ in } e_2]\!] = \overline{\lambda}\kappa.\mathcal{E}'[\![e_1]\!]\,\overline{@}\,(\underline{\lambda}x.\mathcal{E}'[\![e_2]\!]\,\overline{@}\,\kappa)$$

In contrast to Section 2.2, the call site of the functional accumulator (i.e., where it is applied) cannot be determined in one pass with finite look-ahead. This information is context sensitive because κ can be applied in arbitrarily deeply nested blocks. Therefore no first-order one-pass CPS transformation can flatten nested blocks in general if it is also to be compositional.

To flatten nested blocks, one can revert to a non-compositional CPS transformation, to a two-pass CPS transformation, or to a higher-order CPS transformation. (Elsewhere [11], we have shown that such a higher-order, compositional, and one-pass CPS transformation is dependently typed. Its type depends on the nesting depth.)

In the course of this work, and in the light of Section 3.2, we have conjectured that the problem of block structure should also apply to a first-order one-pass CPS transformation such as Sabry and Wadler's. This is the topic of the next section.

7.3   A Shortcoming

Sabry and Wadler's transformation [38] also handles let expressions (extending the CPS transformation of Section 3.1):

$$\mathcal{S}[\![\text{let } x = e_1 \text{ in } e_2]\!]\, K = \mathcal{S}[\![e_1]\!]\, (\lambda x.\mathcal{S}[\![e_2]\!]\, K)$$

If we view this equation as the result of circumventing a functional accumulator, we can see that it assumes this accumulator never to be applied. But it is easy to construct a source term where the accumulator would need to be applied—e.g., the following one.

$$
\begin{aligned}
\mathcal{S}[\![t_0 \ (\text{let } x = t_1 \text{ in } t_2)]\!]\, K &= \mathcal{S}[\![\text{let } x = t_1 \text{ in } t_2]\!]\, (\lambda x_1.\mathcal{T}[\![t_0]\!]\, x_1 \ K) \\
&= \mathcal{S}[\![t_1]\!]\, (\lambda x.\mathcal{S}[\![t_2]\!]\, (\lambda x_1.\mathcal{T}[\![t_0]\!]\, x_1 \ K)) \\
&= \mathcal{S}[\![t_1]\!]\, (\lambda x.(\lambda x_1.\mathcal{T}[\![t_0]\!]\, x_1 \ K) \ \mathcal{T}[\![t_2]\!]) \\
&= (\lambda x.(\lambda x_1.\mathcal{T}[\![t_0]\!]\, x_1 \ K) \ \mathcal{T}[\![t_2]\!]) \ \mathcal{T}[\![t_1]\!]
\end{aligned}
$$

The resulting term is semantically correct, but syntactically it contains an extraneous administrative redex.

   In contrast, a higher-order one-pass CPS transformation yields the following more compact term, corresponding to what one might write by hand (with the provision that one usually writes a let expression rather than a β-redex).

$$\mathcal{S}[\![t_0 \ (\text{let } x = t_1 \text{ in } t_2)]\!]\, k \equiv (\lambda x.\mathcal{T}[\![t_0]\!]\, \mathcal{T}[\![t_2]\!]\, k) \ \mathcal{T}[\![t_1]\!]$$

The CPS transformation of the second edition of *Essentials of Programming Languages* inherits this shortcoming for non-tail let expressions containing computations in their header (i.e., for non-simple let expressions that are not in tail position, to use the terminology of the book).

7.4   Summary and Conclusion

We have presented a one-pass CPS transformation that is both first-order and compositional. This CPS transformation makes it possible to reason about CPS-transformed programs by structural induction over source programs. Its correctness proof (i.e., the proof of its simulation theorem) is correspondingly very simple. The second author's PhD thesis [27,28] also contains a new and simpler correctness proof of the converse transformation, i.e., the direct-style transformation [7]. Finally, this new CPS transformation has enabled Damian and Danvy to define a one-pass CPS transformation of control-flow information [4,5].

Acknowledgments: Thanks are due to Dan Friedman for a substantial e-mail discussion with the first author about compositionality in the summer of 2000, and to Amr Sabry for a similar discussion at the Third ACM SIGPLAN Workshop on Continuations, in January 2001. This article results from an attempt at unifying our points of view, and has benefited from comments by Daniel Damian, Andrzej Filinski, Mayer Goldberg, Julia Lawall, David Toman, and the anonymous referees. Special thanks to Julia Lawall for a substantial round of proof-reading.

References

1. Andrew W. Appel. *Compiling with Continuations.* Cambridge University Press, New York, 1992.
2. Henk Barendregt. *The Lambda Calculus: Its Syntax and Semantics*, volume 103 of *Studies in Logic and the Foundation of Mathematics.* North-Holland, 1984. Revised edition.
3. William D. Clinger. Proper tail recursion and space efficiency. In Keith D. Cooper, editor, *Proceedings of the ACM SIGPLAN'98 Conference on Programming Languages Design and Implementation*, pages 174–185, Montréal, Canada, June 1998. ACM Press.
4. Daniel Damian. *On Static and Dynamic Control-Flow Information in Program Analysis and Transformation.* PhD thesis, BRICS PhD School, University of Aarhus, Aarhus, Denmark, July 2001. BRICS DS-01-5.
5. Daniel Damian and Olivier Danvy. A simple CPS transformation of control-flow information. Technical Report BRICS RS-01-55, DAIMI, Department of Computer Science, University of Aarhus, Aarhus, Denmark, December 2001.
6. Daniel Damian and Olivier Danvy. Syntactic accidents in program analysis: On the impact of the CPS transformation. *Journal of Functional Programming*, 2002. To appear. Extended version available as the technical report BRICS-RS-01-54.
7. Olivier Danvy. Back to direct style. *Science of Computer Programming*, 22(3):183–195, 1994.
8. Olivier Danvy. Formalizing implementation strategies for first-class continuations. In Gert Smolka, editor, *Proceedings of the Ninth European Symposium on Programming*, number 1782 in Lecture Notes in Computer Science, pages 88–103, Berlin, Germany, March 2000. Springer-Verlag.
9. Olivier Danvy, Belmina Dzafic, and Frank Pfenning. On proving syntactic properties of CPS programs. In *Third International Workshop on Higher-Order Operational Techniques in Semantics*, volume 26 of *Electronic Notes in Theoretical Computer Science*, pages 19–31, Paris, France, September 1999. Also available as the technical report BRICS RS-99-23.
10. Olivier Danvy and Andrzej Filinski. Representing control, a study of the CPS transformation. *Mathematical Structures in Computer Science*, 2(4):361–391, 1992.
11. Olivier Danvy and Lasse R. Nielsen. CPS transformation of beta-redexes. In Amr Sabry, editor, *Proceedings of the Third ACM SIGPLAN Workshop on Continuations*, Technical report 545, Computer Science Department, Indiana University, pages 35–39, London, England, January 2001. Also available as the technical report BRICS RS-00-35.
12. Olivier Danvy and Lasse R. Nielsen. Defunctionalization at work. In Harald Søndergaard, editor, *Proceedings of the Third International Conference on Principles and Practice of Declarative Programming*, pages 162–174, Firenze, Italy, September 2001. ACM Press. Extended version available as the technical report BRICS RS-01-23.
13. Olivier Danvy and Lasse R. Nielsen. A first-order one-pass CPS transformation. Technical Report BRICS RS-01-49, DAIMI, Department of Computer Science, University of Aarhus, Aarhus, Denmark, December 2001. Extended version of an article to appear in the proceedings of FOSSACS'02, Grenoble, France, April 2002.
14. Olivier Danvy and Lasse R. Nielsen. A higher-order colon translation. In Kuchen and Ueda [23], pages 78–91. Extended version available as the technical report BRICS RS-00-33.

15. Olivier Danvy and Lasse R. Nielsen. Syntactic theories in practice. In Mark van den Brand and Rakesh M. Verma, editors, *Informal proceedings of the Second International Workshop on Rule-Based Programming (RULE 2001)*, volume 59.4 of *Electronic Notes in Theoretical Computer Science*, Firenze, Italy, September 2001. Extended version available as the technical report BRICS RS-01-31.

16. Olivier Danvy and Frank Pfenning. The occurrence of continuation parameters in CPS terms. Technical report CMU-CS-95-121, School of Computer Science, Carnegie Mellon University, Pittsburgh, Pennsylvania, February 1995.

17. Belmina Dzafic. Formalizing program transformations. Master's thesis, DAIMI, Department of Computer Science, University of Aarhus, Aarhus, Denmark, December 1998.

18. Daniel P. Friedman, Mitchell Wand, and Christopher T. Haynes. *Essentials of Programming Languages*. The MIT Press and McGraw-Hill, 1991.

19. Daniel P. Friedman, Mitchell Wand, and Christopher T. Haynes. *Essentials of Programming Languages, second edition*. The MIT Press, 2001.

20. Timothy G. Griffin. A formulae-as-types notion of control. In Paul Hudak, editor, *Proceedings of the Seventeenth Annual ACM Symposium on Principles of Programming Languages*, pages 47–58, San Francisco, California, January 1990. ACM Press.

21. John Hatcliff and Olivier Danvy. A generic account of continuation-passing styles. In Hans-J. Boehm, editor, *Proceedings of the Twenty-First Annual ACM Symposium on Principles of Programming Languages*, pages 458–471, Portland, Oregon, January 1994. ACM Press.

22. David Kranz, Richard Kesley, Jonathan Rees, Paul Hudak, Jonathan Philbin, and Norman Adams. Orbit: An optimizing compiler for Scheme. In *Proceedings of the ACM SIGPLAN'86 Symposium on Compiler Construction*, pages 219–233, Palo Alto, California, June 1986. ACM Press.

23. Herbert Kuchen and Kazunori Ueda, editors. *Functional and Logic Programming, 5th International Symposium, FLOPS 2001*, number 2024 in Lecture Notes in Computer Science, Tokyo, Japan, March 2001. Springer-Verlag.

24. Albert R. Meyer and Mitchell Wand. Continuation semantics in typed lambda-calculi (summary). In Rohit Parikh, editor, *Logics of Programs – Proceedings*, number 193 in Lecture Notes in Computer Science, pages 219–224, Brooklyn, June 1985. Springer-Verlag.

25. Eugenio Moggi. Notions of computation and monads. *Information and Computation*, 93:55–92, 1991.

26. Chetan R. Murthy. *Extracting Constructive Content from Classical Proofs*. PhD thesis, Department of Computer Science, Cornell University, Ithaca, New York, 1990.

27. Lasse R. Nielsen. *A study of defunctionalization and continuation-passing style*. PhD thesis, BRICS PhD School, University of Aarhus, Aarhus, Denmark, July 2001. BRICS DS-01-7.

28. Lasse R. Nielsen. A simple correctness proof of the direct-style transformation. Technical Report BRICS RS-02-02, DAIMI, Department of Computer Science, University of Aarhus, Aarhus, Denmark, January 2002.

29. Jens Palsberg and Mitchell Wand. CPS transformation of flow information. Unpublished manuscript, available at `http://www.cs.purdue.edu/~palsberg/publications.html`, June 2001.

30. Gordon D. Plotkin. Call-by-name, call-by-value and the λ-calculus. *Theoretical Computer Science*, 1:125–159, 1975.

31. Jeff Polakow. *Ordered Linear Logic and Applications*. PhD thesis, School of Computer Science, Carnegie Mellon University, Pittsburgh, Pennsylvania, August 2001. Technical Report CMU-CS-01-152.
32. Jeff Polakow and Frank Pfenning. Natural deduction for intuitionistic noncommutative linear logic. In Jean-Yves Girard, editor, *Proceedings of the 4th International Conference on Typed Lambda Calculi and Applications*, number 1581 in Lecture Notes in Computer Science, pages 295–309, L'Aquila, Italy, April 1999. Springer-Verlag.
33. Jeff Polakow and Frank Pfenning. Properties of terms in continuation passing style in an ordered logical framework. In Joëlle Despeyroux, editor, *Workshop on Logical Frameworks and Meta-Languages (LFM 2000)*, Santa Barbara, California, June 2000. http://www-sop.inria.fr/certilab/LFM00/Proceedings/.
34. Jeff Polakow and Kwangkeun Yi. Proving syntactic properties of exceptions in an ordered logical framework. In Kuchen and Ueda [23], pages 61–77.
35. John C. Reynolds. The discoveries of continuations. *Lisp and Symbolic Computation*, 6(3/4):233–247, 1993.
36. John C. Reynolds. Definitional interpreters for higher-order programming languages. *Higher-Order and Symbolic Computation*, 11(4):363–397, 1998. Reprinted from the proceedings of the 25th ACM National Conference (1972).
37. Amr Sabry and Matthias Felleisen. Reasoning about programs in continuation-passing style. *Lisp and Symbolic Computation*, 6(3/4):289–360, 1993.
38. Amr Sabry and Philip Wadler. A reflection on call-by-value. *ACM Transactions on Programming Languages and Systems*, 19(6):916–941, 1997.
39. Guy L. Steele Jr. Rabbit: A compiler for Scheme. Technical Report AI-TR-474, Artificial Intelligence Laboratory, Massachusetts Institute of Technology, Cambridge, Massachusetts, May 1978.
40. Mitchell Wand. Embedding type structure in semantics. In Mary S. Van Deusen and Zvi Galil, editors, *Proceedings of the Twelfth Annual ACM Symposium on Principles of Programming Languages*, pages 1–6, New Orleans, Louisiana, January 1985. ACM Press.
41. Mitchell Wand. Correctness of procedure representations in higher-order assembly language. In Stephen Brookes, Michael Main, Austin Melton, Michael Mislove, and David Schmidt, editors, *Mathematical Foundations of Programming Semantics*, number 598 in Lecture Notes in Computer Science, pages 294–311, Pittsburgh, Pennsylvania, March 1991. Springer-Verlag. 7th International Conference.
42. Glynn Winskel. *The Formal Semantics of Programming Languages*. Foundation of Computing Series. The MIT Press, 1993.

A   An Example of Continuation-Passing Program

The following ML functions compute the map functional. One is in direct style, and the other one in CPS.

```
(*  map : ('a -> 'b) * 'a list -> 'b list *)
fun map (f, nil)
    = nil
  | map (f, x :: xs)
    = (f x) :: (map (f, xs))
```

```
(*  map_c : ('a * ('b -> 'c) -> 'c) * 'a list * ('b list -> 'c) -> 'c *)
fun map_c (f_c, nil, k)
   = k nil
 | map_c (f_c, x :: xs, k)
   = f_c (x, fn v => map_c (f_c, xs, fn vs => k (v :: vs)))
```

The direct-style function `map` takes a direct-style function and a list as arguments, and yields another list as result.

The continuation-passing function `map_c` takes a continuation-passing function, a list, and a continuation as arguments. It yields a result of type `'c`, which is also the type of the final result of any CPS program that uses `map_c`. Matching the result type `'b list` of `map`, the continuation of `map_c` has type `'b list -> 'c`. Matching the argument type `'a -> 'b` of `map`, the first argument of `map_c` is a continuation-passing function of type `'a * ('b -> 'c) -> 'c`.

In the base case, `map` returns `nil` whereas `map_c` sends `nil` to the continuation. For a non-empty list, `map` constructs a list with the result of its first argument on the head of the list and with the result of a recursive call on the rest of the list. In contrast, `map_c` calls its first argument on the head of the list with a new continuation that, when sent a result, recursively calls `map_c` on the rest of the list with a new continuation that, when sent a list of results, constructs a list and sends it to the continuation. In `map_c`, all calls are tail calls.

The Demonic Product of Probabilistic Relations

Ernst-Erich Doberkat

Chair for Software Technology
University of Dortmund
doberkat@acm.org

Abstract. The demonic product of two probabilistic relations is defined and investigated. It is shown that the product is stable under bisimulations when the mediating object is probabilistic, and that under some mild conditions the non-deterministic fringe of the probabilistic relations behaves properly: the fringe of the product equals the demonic product of the fringes.

Keywords: Probabilistic relations, bisimulation, demonic product, concurrency.

1 Introduction

Let $R \subseteq A \times B$ and $S \subseteq B \times C$ be set theoretic relations, then, interpreting R and S as filters which form the pipe $R \circ S$, input a may yield output c iff there exists an intermediate value b such that both $\langle a, b \rangle \in R$ and $\langle b, c \rangle \in S$ hold, hence input a produces output b via R which in turn is fed into S giving c. This is an angelic version of the composition of two relations. Demonic behavior, however, is worst case behavior: if something bad can happen, it happens. Thus if on input a relation R produces an output b which is not in the domain of relation S, then a will not be in the domain of the demonic product of R and S. This consideration leads [5, p. 169] to the definition of the demonic product $R \diamond S$ of R and S as $R \diamond S := R \circ S \cap \overline{R \circ \overline{S} \circ (C \times C)}$. Hence $\langle a, c \rangle \in R \diamond S$ iff $\langle a, c \rangle \in R \circ S$, and if for all $b \in B$ the following holds: if $\langle a, b \rangle \in R$, then there exists $c' \in C$ such that $\langle b, c' \rangle \in S$.

When systems are modelled as stochastic systems rather than non-deterministic ones, demonic behavior can still be described as worst case behavior. In the discrete case we would say that c is the possible output of the demonic product of two probabilistic relations K and L upon input a iff c may be produced by the usual product of K and L with positive probability, and if the following holds: whenever $K(a)(b) > 0$ through a terminating computation, we can always find $c' \in C$ such that $L(b)(c') > 0$, and the computation for L terminates upon input b. Widening the scope to probabilities on non-countable spaces, this description has to be adjusted somewhat, because positive probabilities may not necessarily be assigned to single outputs. This is what the present paper is about: we show how to carry over the definition of demonic product from set theoretic relations to probabilistic ones, and we investigate this product.

M. Nielsen and U. Engberg (Eds.): Fossacs 2002, LNCS 2303, pp. 114–128, 2002.
© Springer-Verlag Berlin Heidelberg 2002

Probabilistic relations are the stochastic counterparts to set based relations (see [1,16] or [7]). A probabilistic relation is a transition kernel between two measurable spaces, combining measurable maps with subprobability measures (a formal definition is given in Sect. 2). We employ subprobability measures here rather than their probabilistic step-twins because they permit modelling non-terminating computations: if $K(x)(B)$ is the probability that K with input $x \in X$ produces an output which lies in $B \subseteq Y$, then $K(x)(Y) < 1$ means that the computation does not produce an output with probability 1, i.e., that the computation does not necessarily terminate. The demon, however, forces us to continue only on inputs that guarantee termination, because only then the next computation L may start with an input that K has produced with certainty. This then leads to the probabilistic version $K \star L$ of the demonic product of K and L.

The analogy between set theoretic and probabilistic relations flows from two sources. First and informally, set theoretic relations may be used for non-deterministic processes, so that $\{y | \langle x, y \rangle \in R\}$ yields the set of all possible results of computation R after input x. Many applications, however, assign probabilities to possible outcomes (because some events carry more weight than others), and this leads to the notion of a transition probability which gives us the probability $K(x)(B)$ that upon input x the output will be an element of set B. The intuitive reasoning is supported formally, as e.g. [16] points out: the power set functor forms a monad in the category of sets and has set theoretic relations as the Kleisli construction; the functor assigning each measurable space its probability measures forms also a monad and has Markov kernels as its Kleisli construction, see [10]. In this way a categorical underpinning of the intuitive reasoning is provided.

This paper discusses the demonic product of two transition kernels, or probabilistic relations, as we will also call them, it proposes a definition for this product, and it investigates two properties, viz., stability under bisimulation and the behavior of an associated set theoretic relation. Two notions of bisimulations [4,18] are defined for transition kernels, and it is shown that they are very closely related. Then we show that bisimililarity is preserved through the ordinary, and through the demonic product: if the factors are bisimilar, and if the bisimulation is related through a probabilistic object, so are the respective products. For each probabilistic relation K we can find a set theoretic relation supp K that characterizes the unweighed outcome of K. This correspondence was investigated in depth in [6] with methods originating from stochastic dynamic programming, it is strengthened here to a relation supp$^*K$ (called the *non-deterministic fringe* of K) by taking termination into account. It is shown that under some mild conditions calculating the demonic product and forming the set theoretic relation may be interchanged, so that supp* $(K \star L) =$ supp$^*K \diamond$ supp$^*L$ holds.

Most of this is only possible under some topological assumptions that are satisfied e.g. when considering the real line. Some preparations are needed, they are provided in Sect. 2. Sect. 3 defines the demonic product and investigates some basic properties like associativity, Sect. 4 suggests two definitions of bisimilarity, relates them to each other, selects one for further work, and shows that bisimilarity and forming the product are compatible. Sect. 5 compares the set theoretic and the probabilistic demonic products, and Sect. 6 offers some conclusions together with some suggestions for further work. Most proofs had to be omitted for reasons of space; the reader is referred to the technical report [8] in which all proofs are provided.

Acknowledgements. Part of this work was done while I was visiting what is now the Dipartimento di Informatica at the University of L'Aquila. This research was in part supported through grants from the Exchange Programme for Scientists between Italy and Germany from the Italian Minstry of Foreign Affairs/Deutscher Akademischer Austauschdienst and from Progetto speciale I.N.D.A.M./GNIM "Nuovi paradigmi di calcolo: Linguaggi e Modelli". Professor Fabio Spizzichino made it possible for me to work in the impressive and exciting Mathematics Library of *La Sapienza* in Rome. I want to thank him, and Professor Eugenio Omodeo, my host in L'Aquila. The referees' comments are appreciated.

2   Preliminaries

This section provides for the reader's convenience some notions from measure theory and topology. We introduce transition kernels as, the probabilistic counterpart of set theoretic relations, as members of a suitably chosen comma category, remind the reader of Polish spaces, and give some basic definitions for relations.

Transition Kernels. Let $\mathcal{M}$ be the category of all measurable spaces with measurable maps as morphisms. Denote by $\boldsymbol{S}(X)$ the set of all subprobability measures on (the σ-algebra of) X; we usually omit the σ-algebra from the notation, when the context is clear, and talk about *measurable subsets* as the members of it. $\boldsymbol{S}(X)$ is endowed with the $* - \sigma$-algebra, i.e. the smallest σ-algebra that makes for each measurable subset A of X the map $\mu \mapsto \mu(A)$ measurable. $\boldsymbol{P}(X)$ consists of all probability measures on X.

Put for $f : X \to Y$ and $\mu \in \boldsymbol{S}(X)$ $\boldsymbol{S}(f)(\mu) : B \mapsto \mu(f^{-1}[B])$, (the *image of* μ under f; $\boldsymbol{P}(f)$ is defined through exactly the same expression, having $\boldsymbol{P}(X)$ and $\boldsymbol{P}(Y)$ as domain, and as range, resp.), then $\boldsymbol{S}(f) \in \boldsymbol{S}(Y)$. Consequently, $\boldsymbol{S}$ and $\boldsymbol{P}$ are functors $\mathcal{M} \to \mathcal{M}$, because $\boldsymbol{S}(f) : \boldsymbol{S}(X) \to \boldsymbol{S}(Y)$ and $\boldsymbol{P}(f) : \boldsymbol{P}(X) \to \boldsymbol{P}(Y)$ are $* - \sigma$-measurable whenever $f : X \to Y$ is measurable. The functor $\boldsymbol{P}$ has been investigated by Giry [10].

We will work in the comma category $\mathbb{1}_{\mathcal{M}} \downarrow \boldsymbol{S}$ [12, II.6] which has as objects triplets $\langle X, Y, K \rangle$ with objects X, Y from $\mathcal{M}$ and a morphism $K : X \to \boldsymbol{S}(Y)$ ($\mathbb{1}_{\mathcal{M}}$ is the identity functor on $\mathcal{M}$). Thus K has the following properties:

1. $x \mapsto K(x)(B)$ is a measurable map for each measurable subset B of Y,
2. $K(x) \in \boldsymbol{S}(Y)$ for each $x \in X$, thus $K(x)$ is a measure on the σ-algebra of Y such that $K(x)(Y) \leq 1$ holds.

Hence K is a *transition kernel from X to Y* in the parlance of probability theory. If $K(x)(Y) = 1$ holds for each $x \in X$, then K is called a *transition probability* or a *Markov kernel*, and the corresponding object $\langle X, Y, K \rangle$ a *probabilistic object*. In what follows, $K : X \overset{\bullet}{\hookrightarrow} Y$ indicates that K is a transition kernel from X to Y. These kernels are also called *probabilistic relations* [1,7,16].

Given $\mu_i \in S(X_i)$, the product measure $\mu_1 \otimes \mu_2$ assigns to measurable rectangles $A_1 \times A_2$ the product of the single measures: $(\mu_1 \otimes \mu_2)(A_1 \times A_2) := \mu_1(A_1) \cdot \mu_2(A_2)$. The product is uniquely determined by this property, since the set of all measurable rectangles generates the product σ-algebra and is closed under finite intersections; whenever we talk about the product of measurable spaces, we assume that the σ-algebra on the Cartesian product is the smallest σ-algebra that contains all rectangles. The product measure has the following property: if $f : X_1 \times X_2 \to R$ is measurable and bounded, then

$$\int_{X_1 \times X_2} f \, d\mu_1 \otimes \mu_2 = \int_{X_2} \int_{X_1} f(x_1, x_2) \, \mu_1(dx_1) \, \mu_2(dx_2)$$

$$= \int_{X_1} \int_{X_2} f(x_1, x_2) \, \mu_2(dx_2) \, \mu_1(dx_1)$$

by Fubini's Theorem. Now let $\mu \in S(X)$ and $K : X \overset{\bullet}{\hookrightarrow} Y$, then

$$(\mu \otimes K)(A) := \int_X K(x)(A_x) \, \mu(dx)$$

defines a measure on the product $X \times Y$ (where $A_x := \{y | \langle x, y \rangle \in A\}$). If $f : X \times Y \to R$ is measurable and bounded, then

$$\int_{X \times Y} f \, d\mu \otimes K = \int_X \int_Y f(x, y) \, K(x)(dy) \, \mu(dx).$$

A morphism between $\langle X, Y, K \rangle$ and $\langle X', Y', K' \rangle$ in $\mathbb{1}_\mathcal{M} \downarrow S$ is a pair $\langle f, g \rangle$ of measurable maps $f : X \to X'$, $g : Y \to Y'$ for which $K' \circ f = S(g) \circ K$ holds. Hence

$$K'(f(x))(B) = S(g)(K(x))(B) = K(x)(g^{-1}[B])$$

is true for $x \in X$ and the measurable set $B \subseteq Y'$.

Denote finally the indicator function χ_A of a set A by

$$\chi_A(x) := (x \in A ? 1 : 0).$$

Polish Spaces. A Polish space is a second countable topological space which is metrizable with a complete metric. Polish spaces have always their Borel sets as their measurable structure, hence we talk also about Borel sets when addressing measurable subsets of a topological space. The Polish space X induces a metric structure on $S(X)$ through the topology of weak convergence which is characterized through the famous Portmanteau Theorem [17]:

Proposition 1. *The following conditions are equivalent for a sequence $(\mu_n)_{n \geq 0}$ of finite measures and for the finite measure μ on the Polish space X:*

1. μ_n *converges weakly to* μ,
2. $\int_X f d\mu_n \to \int_X f d\mu$ *for each bounded and continuous* $f : X \to \mathbf{R}$,
3. $\liminf_{n\to\infty} \mu_n(F) \le \mu(F)$ *for each closed subset* $F \subseteq X$.   □

With this topology, $\mathbf{S}(X)$ becomes a Polish space with $\mathbf{P}(X)$ as a closed subspace. The $* - \sigma$-algebra are the Borel sets for the topology of weak convergence.

The Borel sets on a Polish space exhibit a certain flexibility because they do not uniquely determine the topology; in fact, the topology may be manipulated a bit without affecting the Borel structure. We will make use of this rather surprising fact, which is quoted from [19, Corollary 3.2.6]:

Proposition 2. *Suppose* $(X, \mathcal{T})$ *is a Polish space,* Y *a separable metric space, and* $f : X \to Y$ *a measurable map. Then there is a finer Polish topology* $\mathcal{T}'$ *on* X *generating the same Borel* σ-algebra such that $f : (X, \mathcal{T}') \to Y$ *is continuous.*   □

Define for $\mu \in \mathbf{S}(X)$ (X Polish) the support $\mathsf{supp}(\mu)$ of μ as the smallest closed subset $F \subseteq X$ such that $\mu(F) = \mu(X) > 0$, hence for positive $\mu(X)$

$$\mathsf{supp}(\mu) = \bigcap \{F | F \subseteq X \text{ is closed}, \mu(F) = \mu(X)\}$$

Because finite measures on Polish spaces are τ-additive, $\mu(\mathsf{supp}(\mu)) = \mu(X)$, and $x \in \mathsf{supp}(\mu)$ iff $\mu(U) > 0$ for each neighborhood U of x. The support for the null measure is defined as the empty set.

Relations. A relation R is, as usual, a subset of the Cartesian product $X \times Y$ of two sets X and Y. The universal relation on X is just $\mathbf{U}_X := \{\langle x, y \rangle | x, y \in X\}$, and sometimes we will need a part of the diagonal $\Delta_A := \{\langle x, x \rangle | x \in A\}$.

Assume that X carries a measurable structure, and that Y is a Polish space. If for each $x \in X$ the set valued map induced by R (and again denoted by R)

$$R(x) := \{y \in Y | \langle x, y \rangle \in R\}$$

takes closed and non-empty values, and if the weak inverse

$$(\exists R)(G) := \{x \in X | R(x) \cap G \ne \emptyset\}$$

is a measurable set, whenever $G \subseteq Y$ is open, then R is called a *measurable relation*. Since Y is Polish, R is a measurable relation iff the strong inverse

$$(\forall R)(F) := \{x \in X | F(x) \subseteq F\}$$

is measurable, whenever $F \subseteq Y$ is closed [11, Theorem 3.5].

Transition kernels yield measurable relations in a natural way: $K : X \overset{\bullet}{\to} Y$ with $K \ne 0$ induces a relation

$$\mathsf{supp}\, K := \{\langle x, y \rangle | x \in X, y \in \mathsf{supp}(K(x))\}$$

so that $\mathsf{supp}(K(x))$ takes closed values, and it is measurable, because for an open set $G \subseteq Y$ the weak inverse

$$(\exists \mathsf{supp}\ K)(G) = \{x \in X | K(x)(G) > 0\}$$

is measurable. Measurability is also easily established for the strong inverse $(\forall \mathsf{supp}\ K)(F)$ whenever $F \subseteq Y$ is closed, and, somewhat surprisingly, F may be replaced by an arbitrary measurable subset $A \subseteq Y$, as we will see in Prop. 3. This seems to be a peculiar property of set valued maps induced by the support of transition kernels; the general situation is that the weak inverse of a general measurable subset if analytic [11, Theorem 3.5].

3   The Demonic Product

For motivating the demonic product of probabilistic relations, we first have a look at the situation in the set based case. This then leads in quite a natural way to the definition for the probabilistic case. We need some preparations for the definition proper, mainly showing that sets interesting us here are measurable. As a byproduct we can establish the measurability of the strong inverse of a measurable set under a measurable relation, provided this relation is generated from a transition kernel. This is a rather surprising result when viewed from the theory of measurable relations. Some elementary properties for the demonic product are established, it is shown to be associative but not to posses the Dirac kernel as a neutral element.

Let $R \subseteq A \times B$, $S \subseteq B \times C$ be relations. The *demonic product* $R \diamond S$ of R and S is defined as

$$R \diamond S := R \circ S \cap \overline{R \circ \overline{S \circ U_C}}.$$

Thus $\langle a, c \rangle \in R \diamond S$ iff $\langle a, c \rangle \in R \circ S$, and if it is not possible from a by R to reach a b that is not in the domain of S [5, p. 169], hence $\langle a, c \rangle \in R \diamond S$ iff these conditions are satisfied:

1. $\langle a, c \rangle \in R \circ S$,
2. $\forall b \in B : [\langle a, b \rangle \in R \Rightarrow \exists c' \in C : \langle b, c' \rangle \in S]$

Call for the moment $a \in A$ *S-extendable* iff whenever $\langle a, b \rangle \in R$, then $\langle b, c' \rangle \in S$ for some $c' \in C$, hence $\langle a, c \rangle \in R \diamond S$ iff $\langle a, c \rangle \in R \circ S$, and a is S-extendable.

Example 1. Put $X := \{1, 2, 3\}, Y := \{a, b, c\}$ and $Z := \{\alpha, \beta, \gamma\}$, and let

$$R := \{\langle 2, a \rangle, \langle 2, b \rangle, \langle 2, c \rangle, \langle 3, a \rangle, \langle 3, c \rangle\},$$
$$S := \{\langle a, \alpha \rangle, \langle a, \beta \rangle, \langle a, \gamma \rangle, \langle b, \alpha \rangle, \langle b, \beta \rangle, \langle b, \gamma \rangle\}.$$

Then only 3 is S-extendable, and

$$R \diamond S = \{\langle 3, \alpha \rangle, \langle 3, \beta \rangle, \langle 3, \gamma \rangle\}. \qquad \square$$

Now suppose that we have stochastic relations $K : X \overset{\bullet}{\hookrightarrow} Y$ and $L : Y \overset{\bullet}{\hookrightarrow}$ Z for the Polish spaces X, Y and Z. We want to model computations with these kernels. Intuitively, the K-computation terminates on input x and yields output y iff both $K(x)(Y) = 1$ and $y \in \mathsf{supp}(K(x))$ are satisfied. Note that we usually cannot assign positive measure to any single point y, so $K(x)(\{y\})$ is not a suitable object for argumentation, which is the reason why we resort to $\mathsf{supp}(K(x))$ as manifesting the set of possible results. Termination of the computation for input x is thus described by membership of x in the set $\{x \in X | K(x)(Y) = 1\}$. The output of this K-computation is thus fed into L, and we postulate that then the L-computation terminates, too. Call by analogy $x \in X$ L-extendable iff the K-computation on input x terminates with an output for which the L-computation also terminates, hence, iff the conditions

1. $K(x)(Y) = 1$,
2. $\mathsf{supp}(K(x)) \subseteq \mathsf{Tr}(L)$

are both satisfied, where we have defined $\mathsf{Tr}(L) := \{y \in Y | L(y)(Z) = 1\}$.

Hence a *demon* will permit the combined (K, L)-computation to terminate, and to produce a result on input x iff the conditions above are satisfied for x. Then the result is produced in the usual manner.

Example 2. Continuing Example 1, define the transition kernels $K : X \overset{\bullet}{\hookrightarrow} Y$, and $L : Y \overset{\bullet}{\hookrightarrow} Z$ as follows:

K	a	b	c
1	0	.3	.4
2	.25	.25	.5
3	.5	0	.5

and

L	α	β	γ
a	.3	.3	.4
b	.6	.1	.1
c	.2	.3	.5

Then $\mathsf{Tr}(K) = \{2, 3\}, \mathsf{Tr}(L) = \{a, c\}$ and

$$K(x)(Y) = 1 \wedge \mathsf{supp}(K(x)) \subseteq \mathsf{Tr}(L) \Leftrightarrow x = 3.$$

The following equalities are straightforward:

$$\mathsf{supp}(K(1)) = \{b, c\}, \mathsf{supp}(K(2)) = \{a, b, c\}, \mathsf{supp}(K(3)) = \{a, c\}.$$

It is easy to see that 1 is not L-extendable, since $K(1)(Y) < 1$, and that 2 is not L-extendable, because $\mathsf{supp}(K(2)) \not\subseteq \mathsf{Tr}(L)$ holds; input 3, however, turns out to be L-extendable. □

The product $K ; L$ of the transition kernels K and L is defined as usual through $(K ; L)(x)(C) := \int_Y L(y)(C) \ K(x)(dy), \ (x \in X, \ C$ is a measurable subset of Z), and $K ; L : X \overset{\bullet}{\hookrightarrow} Z$ is easily established.

Before defining the demonic product for the probabilistic case, we need some technical preparations.

Proposition 3. *Let X be a measurable space, Y and Z Polish spaces with transition kernels $K : X \overset{\bullet}{\hookrightarrow} Y$ and $L : Y \overset{\bullet}{\hookrightarrow} Z$, then $\{x \in X | \mathsf{supp}(K(x)) \subseteq \mathsf{Tr}(L)\}$. is a measurable subset of X.* □

Note that the set $\mathsf{Tr}(L)$ introduced above is just the set of points on which L is a probability measure; modelling computations using transition kernels, $\mathsf{Tr}(L)$ represents the set of terminating computations.

Prop. 3 has a surprising consequence for the strong inverse of general measurable sets under the measurable relation $\mathsf{supp}\ K$:

Corollary 1. *Let under the assumptions of Proposition 3 $A \subseteq Y$ be a measurable subset. Then $(\forall\mathsf{supp}\ K)(A)$ is measurable.* □

Returning to the preparations for the definition of the demonic product, we observe that the expression $\mathsf{supp}(K(x)) \subseteq \mathsf{Tr}(L)$ is sometimes a little impractical to handle; it may be replaced by $K(x) \otimes L \in \mathbf{P}\,(Y \times Z)$, provided the input x to K makes K's computation terminate. Consequently, the former expression is equivalent for those inputs to $(K(x) \otimes L)\,(Y \times Z) = 1$. Note that this equivalence depends critically upon Prop. 3.

Corollary 2. *Define under the assumptions of Proposition 3 the measurable sets*

$$V(K, L) := \{x \in \mathsf{Tr}(K)|\mathsf{supp}(K(x)) \subseteq \mathsf{Tr}(L)\}$$
$$W(K, L) := \{x \in \mathsf{Tr}(K)|K(x) \otimes L \in \mathbf{P}\,(Y \times Z)\}$$

Then $V(K, L) = W(K, L)$ holds. □

Define the *L-relativization* $K_L^\natural$ of K by $K_L^\natural(x) := \chi_{W(K,L)}(x) \cdot K(x)$. Consequently, $K_L^\natural$ assumes the value of $K(x)$ on $W(K, L)$, and shrinks to the null measure on the complement. Corollary 2 makes sure that $K_L^\natural : X \overset{\bullet}{\hookrightarrow} Y$ holds.

Definition 1. *Let X, Y and Z be Polish spaces, and assume that $K : X \overset{\bullet}{\hookrightarrow} Y$ and $L : Y \overset{\bullet}{\hookrightarrow} Z$ are transition kernels. The demonic product $K \star L$ of K and L is defined as $K \star L := K_L^\natural\,;L$.*

The following is immediate:

Observation 1 *Under the assumptions of Definition 1 we have*

1. $K \star L : X \overset{\bullet}{\hookrightarrow} Z$,
2. for each bounded and measurable $f : Z \to \mathbf{R}$

$$\int_Z f\ d(K \star L)(x) = \chi_{W(K,L)}(x) \cdot \int_Y \left(\int_Z f(z)\ L(y)(dz) \right) K(x)(dy).\square$$

Example 3. Define K and L as in Example 2, then

$K\,;L$	α	β	γ
1	.26	.15	.23
2	.325	.25	.375
3	.25	.3	.45

and

$K \star L$	α	β	γ
1	0	0	0
2	0	0	0
3	.25	.3	.45

are easily established. □

Some elementary properties are collected in the next Proposition. Before stating and proving them, it will be helpful to calculate some W-sets. The next technical lemma states that termination of compound processes may be considered at different stages during their composition. The result for the entire process, however, is the same. We need this statement of course for establishing associativity of the demonic product in Prop. 4.

Lemma 1. $W(K \star L, M) = W(K, L \star M)$. □

Some elementary properties of the demonic product are collected for convenience, amplification and illustration. It turns out in particular that the demonic product $K \star L$ coincides with the usual one provided every input to K leads to a terminating computation.

Proposition 4. *Let I_X be the Dirac kernel on X, then*

1. $I_X \star K = \chi_{\mathsf{Tr}(K)} \cdot K$,
2. $K \star I_Y = K_{I_Y}^\natural$,
3. *if* $\mathsf{Tr}(K) = X$, *then* $K \star L = K ; L$,
4. *the demonic product is associative.* □

4   Bisimulations

The similarity in the behavior of transition kernels is captured through bisimulations, which are introduced as span of morphisms:

Definition 2. *Let O_1 and O_2 be objects in $\mathbb{1}_\mathcal{M} \downarrow S$ with $O_i = \langle X_i, Y_i, K_i \rangle$ $(i = 1, 2)$.*

1. *An object $P = \langle X, Y, K \rangle$ in $\mathbb{1}_\mathcal{M} \downarrow S$ together with morphisms $\sigma_1 = \langle s_1, t_1 \rangle : P \to O_1$ and $\sigma_2 = \langle s_2, t_2 \rangle : P \to O_2$ is called a 1-bisimulation for O_1 and O_2.*
2. *If X is a measurable subset of $X_1 \times X_2$, and if both σ and τ are constituted by the corresponding projections, then P is called a 2-bisimulation for O_1 and O_2. In this case P will be written as $\langle X, K \rangle$.*

P may be interpreted as an object *mediating* between O_1 and O_2. A 1-bisimulation makes the following diagram commutative:

$$
\begin{array}{ccccc}
X_1 & \xleftarrow{\ s_1\ } & X & \xrightarrow{\ s_2\ } & X_2 \\
{\scriptstyle K_1}\downarrow & & {\scriptstyle K}\downarrow & & \downarrow{\scriptstyle K_2} \\
S(Y_1) & \xleftarrow{\ S(t_1)\ } & S(Y) & \xrightarrow{\ S(t_2)\ } & S(Y_2)
\end{array}
$$

Suppose that $\mathcal{B}_i$ is the σ-algebra on Y_i $(i = 1, 2)$, then $\mathcal{B}_0 := g_1^{-1}[\mathcal{B}_1] \cap g_2^{-1}[\mathcal{B}_2]$ is the σ-algebra of all *shared events* on Y (via g_1, g_2), so that $B \in \mathcal{B}_0$ iff we can find $B_i \in \mathcal{B}_i$ with $g_1^{-1}[B_1] = B = g_2^{-1}[B_2]$. The transition kernels $K_1 \circ s_1$ and $K_2 \circ s_2$ coincide on $\mathcal{B}_0$:

$$
\begin{aligned}
K_1(s_1(x))(B_1) &= K(x)\left(g_1^{-1}[B_1]\right) \\
&= K(x)(B) \\
&= K(x)\left(g_2^{-1}[B_2]\right) \\
&= K_2(s_2(x))(B_2).
\end{aligned}
$$

In this sense, bisimilar objects display the same behavior on shared events. In particular, if one of them terminates, the other will, too, since $Y \in \mathcal{B}_0$.

It is plain that there exists always a 2-bisimulation between *probabilistic* objects $O_1 = \langle X_1, Y_1, K_1 \rangle$ and $O_2 = \langle X_2, Y_2, K_2 \rangle$: define the mediating object $P := \langle X_1 \times X_2, Y_1 \times Y_2, K \rangle$, where $K(x_1, x_2) := K_1(x_1) \otimes K_2(x_2)$ is the product of $K(x_1)$ and $K(x_2)$. Then both $K_1(x_1)(A_1) = K(x_1, x_2)(A_1 \times Y_2)$ and $K_2(x_2)(A_2) = K(x_1, x_2)(Y_1 \times A_2)$ hold, whenever $A_i \subseteq Y_i$ is a measurable subset $(i = 1, 2)$. Consequently, the projections

$$
\begin{aligned}
\langle \pi_{X_1}^{X_1 \times X_2}, \pi_{Y_1}^{Y_1 \times Y_2} \rangle &: P \to O_1 \\
\langle \pi_{X_2}^{X_1 \times X_2}, \pi_{Y_2}^{Y_1 \times Y_2} \rangle &: P \to O_2
\end{aligned}
$$

are the desired morphisms. Thus bisimulations are only non-trivial for the non-probabilistic objects in $\mathbb{1}_\mathcal{M} \downarrow \mathbf{S}$, i.e. for such objects the termination of which cannot always be guaranteed.

The following observation shows why we may and do restrict our attention to 2-bisimulations:

Proposition 5. *Let $O_i = \langle X_i, Y_i, K_i \rangle$ be objects in $\mathbb{1}_\mathcal{M} \downarrow \mathbf{S}$, then the following conditions are equivalent:*

1. *There exists a 1-bisimulation $\langle P, \langle s_1, t_1 \rangle, \langle s_2, t_2 \rangle \rangle$ with $P = \langle X, Y, K \rangle$ for O_1 and O_2 such that $\{\langle s_1(x), s_2(x) \rangle | x \in X\}$ is a measurable subset of $X_1 \times X_2$.*
2. *There exists a 2-bisimulation for O_1 and O_2.* □

Let us comment briefly on the condition that $\{\langle s_1(x), s_2(x) \rangle | x \in X\}$ is a measurable subset of $X_1 \times X_2$. This condition is in general not easy to handle, working in Polish spaces, however, a well-known Theorem attributed to Arsenin-Kunugui [19, 5.12.1] renders it somewhat more practical:

Observation 2 *Let X, X_1, X_2 be Polish spaces, and assume that $s_i : X \to X_i$ is measurable. Assume that $\{x \in X | \langle s_1(x), s_2(x) \rangle = \langle x_1, x_2 \rangle\}$ is σ-compact for each $x_i \in X_i$. Then $\{\langle s_1(x), s_2(x) \rangle | x \in X\}$ is a measurable subset of $X_1 \times X_2$.* □

Hence if s_i has compact or countable inverse point images, the condition is satisfied, in particular if s_i is one-to-one, generalizing the well-known fact that the image of the domain of a one-to-one Borel map on Polish spaces is a Borel set (this generalization is well known, too). If X_1 and X_2 are σ-compact, and both s_1 and s_2 are continuous, the condition also applies, thus real-valued functions on a Polish space are captured by Observation 2.

In what follows, bisimulation will mean 2-bisimulation; we write $O_1 \sim_{\langle A, K \rangle} O_2$ if $\langle A, K \rangle$ is a bisimulation for O_1 and O_2.

Remarks: **1.** Desharnais, Edalat and Panangaden [4] define bisimulations between labelled Markov processes as spans of zig-zag morphisms in the category $\mathcal{A}$ of analytic spaces. They work in the full subcategory of $\mathbb{1}_{\mathcal{A}} \downarrow \boldsymbol{S}$ that has objects of the diagonal form $\langle S, S, K \rangle$. Because the product of two analytic spaces is an analytic space again [17, Theorem I.3.2], two labelled Markov processes with probabilistic (rather than sub-probabilistic) transition kernels are always bisimilar.

2. Rutten [18] defines bisimulations through projections: let $\mathcal{S}$ be the category of sets, and $\boldsymbol{F} : \mathcal{S} \to \mathcal{S}$ a functor, then the pair $\langle S, \alpha \rangle$ with $\alpha : S \to \boldsymbol{F}(S)$ is a coalgebra, thus coalgebras are diagonal members of a full subcategory of $\mathbb{1}_{\mathcal{S}} \downarrow \boldsymbol{F}$. A bisimulation between the coalgebras $\langle S_1, \alpha_1 \rangle$ and $\langle S_2, \alpha_2 \rangle$ is a coalgebra $\langle R, \gamma \rangle$ with $R \subseteq S_1 \times S_2$ such that the projections $\pi_i : R \to S_i$ satisfy $\alpha_1 \circ \pi_i = \boldsymbol{F}(\pi_i) \circ \gamma$. In [3], de Rutten and Vink define probabilistic bisimulations through relations quite close to the definition for labelled transition systems given by Milner [14], and the definition given by Larsen and Skou [13]. They define also bisimulations for a functor similar to $\boldsymbol{P}$ on diagonal objects. They prove the equivalence on ultrametric spaces for what they call z-closed relations with a Borel decomposition ([3], Lemma 5.5, Theorem 5.8).

3. Moss [15, Sect. 3] defines a bisimulation *on* a coalgebra (rather than for two coalgebras), and he shows that the existence of a bisimulation can be established under rather weak conditions (Prop. 3.10, which he attributes to Aczel and Mendler). Moss works in the category of sets and classes, he bases coalgebras on a functor which is set based, and which preserves weak pullbacks, assumptions that are not met in the situation considered here.

We will show now that bisimulations respect the conventional and the demonic product and start out with a technical observation. It states that bisimilarity is maintained when we restrict the possible inputs (otherwise the similarity of behavior would depend on the chosen base set which would be irritating for a concept which exhibits local properties):

Observation 3 *Denote for $K : X \overset{\bullet}{\hookrightarrow} Y$ and the measurable subset $\emptyset \neq A \subseteq X$ the restriction of K to A by $K \downarrow A$. Then the following holds:*

1. $K \downarrow A : A \overset{\bullet}{\hookrightarrow} Y$, *and $\langle A, Y, K \downarrow A \rangle$ is a probabilistic object, if $\langle X, Y, K \rangle$ is one.*
2. *If $\langle X_1, Y_1, K_1 \rangle \sim_{\langle A, T \rangle} \langle X_2, Y_2, K_2 \rangle$, and if $\emptyset \neq A_i \subseteq X_i$ are measurable ($i = 1, 2$), then*
$$\langle A_1, Y_1, K_1 \downarrow A_1 \rangle \sim_{\langle B, R \rangle} \langle A_2, Y_2, K_2 \downarrow A_2 \rangle,$$
   where $B := A \cap (A_1 \times A_2)$, and $R := T \downarrow (A_1 \times A_2)$. $\qquad\square$

We show first that bisimilarity respects the conventional product. Suppose that $\langle A, T \rangle$ and $\langle B, S \rangle$ are the intermediate objects from which the respective spans are obtained. For maintaining bisimilarity, the composition of the mediating objects $\langle A, B, T \rangle$ should be a probabilistic one. This is intuitively clear: the mediating computation should terminate, otherwise similar behavior cannot be carried through the composition.

We will see subsequently that a mediating probabilistic object is also required for making bisimulation respect demonic products, too.

Proposition 6. *Let* $K_i : X_i \overset{\bullet}{\hookrightarrow} Y_i$, *and* $L_i : Y_i \overset{\bullet}{\hookrightarrow} Z_i$ $(i = 1, 2)$, *and assume that*

1. $\langle X_1, Y_1, K_1 \rangle \sim_{\langle A, T \rangle} \langle X_2, Y_2, K_2 \rangle$,
2. $\langle Y_1, Z_1, L_1 \rangle \sim_{\langle B, S \rangle} \langle Y_2, Z_2, L_2 \rangle$.

Then $\langle X_1, Z_1, K_1 \,;\, L_1 \rangle \sim_{\langle A, \ T \,;\, S \rangle} \langle X_2, Z_2, K_2 \,;\, L_2 \rangle$, *provided* $\langle A, B, T \rangle$ *is a probabilistic object.*   □

This carries readily over to the demonic product:

Corollary 3. *Put under the assumptions of Proposition 6*

$$C := A \cap (W(K_1, L_1) \times W(K_2, L_2)), \text{and } R := (T \,;\, S) \downarrow C,$$

and assume that $\langle C, B, R \rangle$ *is a probabilistic object. Then*

$$\langle X_1, Z_1, K_1 \star L_1 \rangle \sim_{\langle C, R \rangle} \langle X_2, Z_2, K_2 \star L_2 \rangle$$

holds.   □

5   Comparing Demonic Products

A transition kernel $K : X \overset{\bullet}{\hookrightarrow} Y$ induces a closed-valued relation via the support function, whenever Y is Polish (see Sect. 2). This correspondence was investigated in [6] with a view towards stochastic and non-deterministic automata, in particular it could be shown under which conditions a closed-valued relation in representable by a Markov kernel. The present line of investigation, however, requires a somewhat more discriminating instrument than the support function, because the set $\mathsf{supp}(K(x))$ does not tell us anything about termination upon input x — it merely states what outputs are produced.

Thus we work with the modified relation

Definition 3. *The* non-deterministic fringe *of the transition kernel K is defined as the relation* $\mathsf{supp}^* K := \Delta_{\mathsf{Tr}(K)} \circ \mathsf{supp}\ K$.

Hence the fringe captures exactly those inputs that contribute to termination, composition with relation $\Delta_{\mathsf{Tr}(K)}$ serving as a filter. Thus $\langle x, y \rangle \in \mathsf{supp}^* K$ holds iff $K(x)(Y) = 1$, and if y is a possible output to $K(x)$.

We will in this section investigate how the demonic product of transition kernels relates to the demonic product of the fringe as a modified support function, hence we will investigate the question under which conditions $\mathsf{supp}^*(K \star L) = \mathsf{supp}^* K \diamond \mathsf{supp}^* L$ (or possibly a weaker subset relation) holds, where $L : X \overset{\bullet}{\hookrightarrow} Y$ is the factor to K in this game. This will shed some light on the relationship between the set theoretic and the probabilistic version of the demonic product.

Since the latter is modelled after the former, it would intuitively be gratifying to see that they behave similar, provided they can be compared at all. The fringe relation serves exactly this purpose by converting a probabilistic relation into a set theoretic one.

Example 4. Let K and L be defined as in Example 2, then

$$\mathsf{supp}^* K = \{\langle 2, a \rangle, \langle 2, b \rangle, \langle 2, c \rangle, \langle 3, a \rangle, \langle 3, c \rangle\},$$
$$\mathsf{supp}^* L = \{\langle a, \alpha \rangle, \langle a, \beta \rangle, \langle a, \gamma \rangle, \langle b, \alpha \rangle, \langle b, \beta \rangle, \langle b, \gamma \rangle\},$$

with

$$\mathsf{supp}^* K \diamond \mathsf{supp}^* L = \{\langle 3, \alpha \rangle, \langle 3, \beta \rangle, \langle 3, \gamma \rangle\} = \mathsf{supp}^* (K \star L)$$

(cp. relations R and S from Example 1). □

We fix for the rest of this section the measurable space X and the Polish spaces Y, Z as well as the transition kernels $K : X \overset{\bullet}{\hookrightarrow} Y$ and $L : Y \overset{\bullet}{\hookrightarrow} Z$. L may be assumed to be (weakly) continuous in view of Prop. 2 . To avoid trivialities, we assume that both $\mathsf{Tr}(K) \neq \emptyset$ and $\mathsf{Tr}(L) \neq \emptyset$ holds.

It is known from [7, Obs. 4] that the support function has these properties when related to the product of transition kernels:

1. $\mathsf{supp}\, K \circ \mathsf{supp}\, L \subseteq \mathsf{supp}(K \,;\, L)$,
2. $\mathsf{supp}(K \,;\, L) \subseteq \mathsf{supp}\, K \circ \mathsf{supp}\, L$, provided $K(x)(G) > 0$ holds for each $x \in X$ and each open ball G in Y.

These properties have been established for Markov kernels, but the proofs carry over easily to the present situation.

We collect some readily established properties for the fringe relation:

Observation 4 *1.* $\mathsf{Tr}(K \star L) = W(K, L)$,
2. $\mathsf{supp}(K \star L) = \Delta_{W(K,L)} \circ \mathsf{supp}(K \,;\, L) = \mathsf{supp}^*(K \star L)$,
3. $W(K, L) \times Z = \overline{\mathsf{supp}^* K \circ \overline{\mathsf{supp}^* L \circ U_Z}}$,
4. $\Delta_{W(K,L)} \circ \mathsf{supp}\, K \circ \mathsf{supp}\, L \subseteq \mathsf{supp}^* K \circ \mathsf{supp}^* L$. □

With these preparations we are able to characterize the relationship between the demonic product of the fringes, and the fringe of the demonic product:

Proposition 7. *The non-deterministic fringe of the demonic product of probabilistic relations and the demonic product of their fringes are related in the following way:*

1. $\mathsf{supp}^* K \diamond \mathsf{supp}^* L \subseteq \mathsf{supp}^*(K \star L)$,
2. *if* $\mathsf{supp}\, (K \,;\, L) = \mathsf{supp}\, K \circ \mathsf{supp}\, L$ *can be established, then this implies* $\mathsf{supp}^* K \diamond \mathsf{supp}^* L = \mathsf{supp}^*\, (K \star L)$. □

Corollary 4. *Assume that* $K(x)(G) > 0$ *for each* $x \in X$ *and each open ball* G *in* Y, *then* $\mathsf{supp}^* K \diamond \mathsf{supp}^* L = \mathsf{supp}^*\, (K \star L)$ *holds.* □

Suppose that our probabilistic demon Π has a little brother Σ who is keen on set theoretic relations, and, being junior to Π, is handed always the fringe. Π performs two computations through the demonic product, and hands to Σ his share. In general, Σ is better off (in the sense of having obtained a larger relation) in not performing the demonic product himself (hence it pays for Σ to wait for Π doing the combined computation). If the first computation, however, is thrifty by never vanishing on non-empty open sets, then it is of no concern to Σ who combines the computations.

6   Conclusion

We make in this paper a proposal for the definition of the demonic product of two transition kernels. This product indicates how a probabilistic demon might act when composing two computations that are modelled through probabilistic relations. It turns out that the demonic product coincides with the ordinary product, provided Markov kernels are involved, i.e. computations that terminate with probability one. It could be shown that the demonic product is stable under bisimulations under the provision that the relating object is a Markov kernel. Bisimulations have been defined for the situation at hand, slightly generalizing the notion of bisimulation for stochastic systems given in [4], and relating it to the definition given in the context of coalgebras in [18]. The paper shows then that there is a close relationship between the demonic product of two probabilistic relations and the demonic product of their respective fringe relations, the latter product being the set theoretic product, as introduced and investigated in e.g. [5].

Further investigations in the area of probabilistic relations will deal with bisimulations along the lines suggested by Moss [15], cp. [4], in particular the characterization theorems for bisimulations that have been formulated for coalgebras should be transported to the comma category underlying the discussions here. Less abstract, we will see how bisimulation relates to the converse of a probabilistic relation, as defined and investigated in [7]. We still do not know under which conditions 2-bisimilarity is a transitive relation. In [9] a theory of hierarchical refinement of probabilistic relations is proposed in terms of the usual product. It would be interesting to see what happens when the demonic product is used instead.

References

1. S. Abramsky, R. Blute, and P. Panangaden. Nuclear and trace ideal in tensored *-categories. Technical report, School of Computer Science, McGill University, Montreal, June 1998.
2. C. Brink, W. Kahl, and G. Schmidt, editors. *Relational Methods in Computer Science.* Advances in Computing Science. Springer-Verlag, Wien, New York, 1997.
3. E. P. de Vink and J. J. M. M. Rutten. Bisimulation for probabilistic transition systems: a coalgebraic approach. Technical Report SEN-R9825, CWI, Amsterdam, 1998.

4. J. Desharnais, A. Edalat, and P. Panangaden. Bisimulation of labelled markov-processes. Technical report, School of Computer Science, McGill University, Montreal, 1998.

5. J. Desharnais, A. Mili, and T. T. Nguyen. Refinement and demonic semantics. In *[2]*, pages 166 – 184.

6. E.-E. Doberkat. *Stochastic Automata — Nondeterminism, Stability, and Prediction*, volume 113 of *Lecture Notes in Computer Science*. Springer-Verlag, Berlin, 1981.

7. E. E. Doberkat. The converse of a probabilistic relation. Technical Report 113, Chair for Software Technology, University of Dortmund, June 2001.

8. E.-E. Doberkat. The demonic product of probabilistic relations. Technical Report 116, Chair for Software Technology, University of Dortmund, September 2001. Available as `Technische-Berichte/Doberkat_SWT-Memo-116.ps.gz` in directory `ftp://ls10-www.cs.uni-dortmund.de/pub/`.

9. E.-E. Doberkat. The hierarchical refinement of probabilistic relations. Technical Report 118, Chair for Software Technology, University of Dortmund, November 2001.

10. M. Giry. A categorical approach to probability theory. In *Categorical Aspects of Topology and Analysis*, volume 915 of *Lecture Notes in Mathematics*, pages 68 – 85, Berlin, 1981. Springer-Verlag.

11. C. J. Himmelberg. Measurable relations. *Fund. Math.*, 87:53 – 72, 1975.

12. S. Mac Lane. *Categories for the Working Mathematician*. Number 5 in Graduate Texts in Mathematics. Springer-Verlag, Berlin, 2 edition, 1997.

13. K. G. Larsen and A. Skou. Bisimulation through probabilistic testing. *Information and Computation*, 94:1 – 28, 1991.

14. R. Milner. *A Calculus of Communicating Systems*. Number 92 in Lecture Notes in Computer Science. Springer-Verlag, Berlin, 1980.

15. L. S. Moss. Coalgebraic logic. *Annals of Pure and Applied Logic*, 96:277 – 317, 1999.

16. P. Panangaden. Probabilistic relations. In C. Baier, M. Huth, M. Kwiatkowska, and M. Ryan, editors, *Proc. PROBMIV*, pages 59 – 74, 1998. Also available from the School of Computer Science, McGill University, Montreal.

17. K. R. Parthasarathy. *Probability Measures on Metric Spaces*. Academic Press, New York, 1967.

18. J. J. M. M. Rutten. Universal coalgebra: a theory of systems. Technical Report CS-R9652, CWI, Amsterdam, 1996.

19. S. M. Srivastava. *A Course on Borel Sets*. Number 180 in Graduate Texts in Mathematics. Springer-Verlag, Berlin, 1998.

Minimizing Transition Systems for Name Passing Calculi: A Co-algebraic Formulation*

Gianluigi Ferrari[1], Ugo Montanari[1], and Marco Pistore[2]

[1] Dipartimento di Informatica, Università di Pisa
[2] ITC-IRST, Trento

Abstract. We address the problem of minimizing labelled transition systems for name passing calculi. We show how the co-algebraic formulation of automata with naming directly suggests an effective minimization algorithm which reduces the number of states to be analyzed in the verification of properties for name passing process calculi.

1 Introduction

Automatic methods for verifying finite state automata have been showed to be surprisingly effective [3]. Indeed, finite state verification techniques have enjoyed substantial and growing use over the last years. For instance several communication protocols and hardware systems of considerable complexity have been formalized and proved correct by exploiting finite state verification techniques. Since the state space is still very large for many designs, much research has been devoted to find techniques to combat state explosion. *Semantic minimization* [18,9] is a rather general technique which reduces the number of states to be analyzed by producing a minimal automaton that is equivalent to the original one. The minimal automaton is is indistinguishable from the original system with respect to the set of properties specified in many logical systems (e.g. μ-calculus) but easier to handle due to its possibly much smaller size [6]. The possibility of generating a minimal system provides further advantages. First, the minimal automaton can be exploited to verify different properties of the same system. Second, systems are usually obtained by composing components. Hence, minimizing components before combining them yields smaller state spaces.

The advent of world-wide networks and wireless communications are contributing to a growing interest in dynamic and reconfigurable systems. Unfortunately, finite state verification of these systems is much more difficult. Indeed, in this case, even simple systems can generate infinite state spaces. An illustrative example is provided by the π-calculus [11]. Its primitives are simple but expressive: channel names can be created, communicated (thus giving the possibility of dynamically reconfiguring process acquaintances) and they are subjected to sophisticated scoping rules. The π-calculus has greater expressive power than ordinary process calculi, but the possibility of dynamically generating new names leads also to models which are infinite-state and infinite branching.

---

* Work partially supported by FET Global Project PROFUNDIS and MURST Project COMETA

M. Nielsen and U. Engberg (Eds.): Fossacs 2002, LNCS 2303, pp. 129–143, 2002.
© Springer-Verlag Berlin Heidelberg 2002

Creation of new names is actually quite common also in practice. An example is provided by the creation of nonces to identify sessions in security protocols (see [10] for a critical review of the state-of-the-art on verification of security protocols). All these techniques are based on finite state verification, and typically can ensure error freedom only for a finite amount of the behaviour of protocols. Even if many protocols do not include iterations, however, an unbound number of principals may take part in the interleaved sessions of the protocol; moreover, many known attacks exploit the mixed interleaving of different sessions of the same protocol.

Hence, traditional finite state models of behaviour have important shortcomings to address the challenges of supporting verification of dynamic distributed systems via semantic equivalence. To support finite state verification of dynamic distributed systems two of the authors have introduced a novel foundational model called *History Dependent Automata (HD-automata)* [12,15]. HD-automata have been specifically designed to allocate and garbage collect names. The theory ensures that finite state, finite branching automata give a faithful representation of the behaviour of π-calculus processes. Furthermore, HD-automata are expressive enough to represent formalisms equipped with mobility, locality, and causality primitives [13,14]. The finite state representation of π-calculus processes given by the HD-automata has been exploited to check behavioral properties of the agents [8,7]. Few other approaches have been proposed for finite state verification of π-calculus processes [4,17]. The explicit management of names provided by HD-automata allows for an extremely compact representation of the behaviour of processes. HD-automata are not only a convenient format for representing the behaviour of π-calculus processes in a compact way, though. They may be considered the natural extension of automata to calculi with name passing and name generation also from a theoretical point of view. In particular, HD-automata can be defined as coalgebras on the top of permutation algebras of states [16]. The permutation algebra describes the acts of name permutations (i.e. renaming) on state transitions. This information is sufficient to describe in a semantically correct way the creation, communication, and deallocation of names: all the features needed to describe and reason about formalisms with operations over names.

General results concerning coalgebras [1,19,20,2,21] extend also to these kinds of coalgebras: they make sure that a final coalgebra exists and that it defines minimal realizations of HD-automata. Also, equivalent HD-automata, and hence equivalent π-calculus processes, have isomorphic minimal realizations.

Our aim in this paper is to tackle the problem of minimizing labelled transition systems for name passing calculi. Instead of presenting our construction in the abstract setting of category theory, namely the category of coalgebras for an endofunctor on some base category, we shall be working in the standard universe of sets and functions. The main point is to provide a concrete representation of the terminal coalgebra which directly suggests the data structures of a minimization module of a semantic-based verification environment. Indeed, a key goal of this paper is to provide a clear relationship between the structures of the semantic world and the data structures for the implementation. A main contribution of this paper is to show how the (theoretical) coalgebraic formulation of automata with naming directly suggests an effective minimization algorithm. The work reported in this paper is closely related to the theoretical development of coalgebras, and, at the same time, it formally specifies an effective procedure to perform finite state verification of distributed systems with dynamic name generation via semantic equivalence.

2   Transition Systems, Co-algebras and Minimization

A transition system T is a structure $(S, L, \rightarrow)$, where S is the set of *states*, L is the set of (action) *labels* and $\rightarrow \subseteq S \times L \times S$ is the *transition relation*. Usually, one writes $s \xrightarrow{\ell} s'$ to indicate $(s, \ell, s') \in \rightarrow$. In this section we provide a concrete representation of the terminal coalgebra (of an endofunctor over Set) which will yield the minimal transition system. Hereafter, we use the following notations:

- Set is the collection of all sets. By convention, Q : Set denotes a set and $q : Q$ denotes an element in the set Q;
- Fun is the collection of functions among sets. The function space over sets will have the following structure:

$$\text{Fun} = \{H \mid H = \langle S : \text{Set}, D : \text{Set}, h : S \rightarrow D\rangle\}.$$

By convention we use S_H, D_H and h_H to denote the components of an element of Fun.

Let H and K be functions (i.e. elements of Fun), then the *composition* of H and K ($H; K$) is defined provided that $S_K = D_H$ and it is the function given by $S_{H;K} = S_H$, $D_{H;K} = D_K$, and $h_{H;K} = h_K \circ h_H$.

Sometimes, we shall need to work with surjective functions. Let H be a function, then $\widehat{H}$ is the function given by:

- $S_{\widehat{H}} = S_H$, $D_{\widehat{H}} = \{q' : D_H \mid \exists q : S_H, h_H(q) = q'\}$ and $h_{\widehat{H}} = h_H$.

Transition systems are described co-algebraically employing two components: a set Q (the state space) together with a function $K : Q \rightarrow \wp(L \times Q)$ where $\wp(X)$ is the finite powerset of X. The idea is that function K determines the behaviour of the transition system: $K(q)$ is the set of pairs (ℓ, q') such that $q \xrightarrow{\ell} q'$. Functor $T(X) = \wp(L \times X)$ operates on both sets and functions, and characterizes a whole category of labelled transition systems, i.e. of coalgebras. In this paper, we aim at developing a concrete co-algebraic description of the minimization procedure, hence, we rephrase coalgebras in terms of certain structures called *bundles*.

Let L be the set of labels (ranged over by ℓ), then a *bundle* β over L is a structure $\langle D : \text{Set}, Step : \wp(L \times D)\rangle$. Given a fixed set of labels L, by convention, B denotes the collection of bundles and $\beta : B$ identifies the bundle β. Intuitively, the notion of bundle has to be understood as giving the data structure representing all the state transitions out of a given state. It details which states are reachable by performing certain actions.

The following clauses define functor T.

- $T(Q) = \{\beta : B \mid D_\beta = Q\}$, for each $Q :$ Set;
- For each $H :$ Fun, $T(H)$ is defined as follows:
  - $S_{T(H)} = T(S_H)$ and $D_{T(H)} = T(D_H)$;
  - $h_{T(H)}(\beta : T(S_H)) = \langle D_H, \{\langle \ell, h_H(q) \rangle \mid \langle \ell, q \rangle : Step_\beta \} \rangle$.

Definition 1. *Let L be a set of labels. Then a labelled transition system over L is a co-algebra for functor T, namely it is a function K such that $D_K = T(S_K)$.*

Aa already mentioned a co-algebra K for functor T represents a transition system where S_K is the set of states, and $h_K(q) = \beta$, with $D_\beta = S_K$ and $Step_\beta = \{(\ell, q') \mid q \xrightarrow{\ell} q'\}$. Figure 1 illustrates a labelled transition system and its coalgebraic formulation via the mapping h_K.

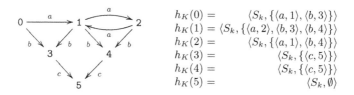

$$h_K(0) = \langle S_k, \{\langle a, 1 \rangle, \langle b, 3 \rangle\}\rangle$$
$$h_K(1) = \langle S_k, \{\langle a, 2 \rangle, \langle b, 3 \rangle, \langle b, 4 \rangle\}\rangle$$
$$h_K(2) = \langle S_k, \{\langle a, 1 \rangle, \langle b, 4 \rangle\}\rangle$$
$$h_K(3) = \langle S_k, \{\langle c, 5 \rangle\}\rangle$$
$$h_K(4) = \langle S_k, \{\langle c, 5 \rangle\}\rangle$$
$$h_K(5) = \langle S_k, \emptyset\rangle$$

Fig. 1. A labelled transition system and its coalgebraic specification

General results (e.g. [1]) ensure the existence of the final coalgebra for a large class of functors . These results apply to our formulation of transition systems. In particular, it is interesting to see the result of the iteration along the terminal sequence [21] of functor T.

Let K be a transition system, and let $H_0, H_1, \ldots, H_{n+1}, \ldots$ be the sequence of functions computed by $H_{n+1} = K; \widehat{T(H_n)}$, where H_0 is the unique function from S_K to the one-element set $\{*\}$ given by $S_{H_0} = S_K$; $D_{H_0} = \{*\}$; and $h_{H_0}(q : S_{H_0}) = *$. Finiteness of $\wp$ ensures convergence of the iteration along the terminal sequence. We can say much more if the transition system is finite state.

Theorem 1. *Let K be a finite-state transtion system. Then,*

- *The iteration along the terminal sequence converges in a finite number of steps, i.e. $D_{H_{n+1}} \equiv D_{H_n}$,*
- *The isomorphism mapping $F : D_{H_n} \to D_{H_{n+1}}$ yields the minimal realization of transition system K.*

Comparing the co-algebraic construction with the standard algorithm [9,6] which constructs the minimal labelled transition system we can observe:

- at each iteration i the elements of D_{H_i} are the blocks of the minimization algorithm (i.e. the i-th partition). Notice that the initial approximation D_{H_0} contains a single block: in fact H_0 maps all the states of the transition system into $\{*\}$.
- at each step the algorithm creates a new partition by identifying the *splitters* for states q and q'. This corresponds in our co-algebraic setting to the fact that $H_i(q) = H_i(q')$ but $H_{i+1}(q) \neq H_{i+1}(q')$.
- the iteration proceeds until a stable partition of blocks is reached: then the iteration along the terminal sequence converges.

We now apply the iteration along the terminal sequence to the coalgebraic formulation of the transition system of Figure 1. The initial approximation is the function H_0 defined as follows

$$H_0 = \langle S_{H_0} = S_K, D_{H_0} = \{*\}, h_{H_0}(q) = * \rangle$$

We now construct the first approximation H_1. We have that

$$h_{H_1}(q) = \langle D_{H_0}, \{\langle \ell, h_{H_0}(q') \rangle : q \xrightarrow{\ell} q'\} \rangle$$

$$T(H_0)\langle \{1, 2, 3, 4, 5\}, \{\langle a, 2 \rangle, \langle b, 3 \rangle, \langle b, 4 \rangle\} \rangle = \langle \{*\}, \{\langle a, * \rangle, \langle b, * \rangle\} \rangle$$

In our example we obtain the function h_{H_1} and the destination state $D_{H_1} = \{\beta_1, \beta_2, \beta_3\}$ as detailed below.

$$
\begin{array}{ll}
h_{H_1}(0) = \langle \{*\}, \{\langle a, * \rangle, \langle b, * \rangle\} \rangle & \\
h_{H_1}(1) = \langle \{*\}, \{\langle a, * \rangle, \langle b, * \rangle\} \rangle & \beta_1 = \langle \{*\}, \{\langle a, * \rangle, \langle b, * \rangle\} \rangle \\
h_{H_2}(2) = \langle \{*\}, \{\langle a, * \rangle, \langle b, * \rangle\} \rangle & \beta_2 = \langle \{*\}, \{\langle c, * \rangle\} \rangle \\
h_{H_1}(3) = \langle \{*\}, \{\langle c, * \rangle\} \rangle & \beta_3 = \emptyset \\
h_{H_1}(4) = \langle \{*\}, \{\langle c, * \rangle\} \rangle & \\
h_{H_1}(5) = \langle \{*\}, \emptyset \rangle &
\end{array}
$$

We continue to apply the iterative construction, we obtain:

$$
\begin{array}{l}
h_{H_2}(0) = \langle D_{H_1}, \{\langle a, \beta_1 \rangle, \langle b, \beta_2 \rangle\} \rangle \\
h_{H_2}(1) = \langle D_{H_1}, \{\langle a, \beta_1 \rangle, \langle b, \beta_2 \rangle\} \rangle \\
h_{H_2}(2) = \langle D_{H_1}, \{\langle a, \beta_1 \rangle, \langle b, \beta_2 \rangle\} \rangle \\
h_{H_2}(3) = \langle D_{H_1}, \{\langle c, \emptyset \rangle\} \rangle \\
h_{H_2}(4) = \langle D_{H_1}, \{\langle c, \emptyset \rangle\} \rangle \\
h_{H_2}(5) = \langle D_{H_1}, \emptyset \rangle
\end{array}
$$

Since $D_{H_2} \equiv D_{H_1}$ the iterative construction converges, thus providing the minimal labelled transition system illustrated in Figure 2, where $\bullet_1 = \{0, 1, 2\}$, $\bullet_2 = \{3, 4\}$ and $\bullet_3 = \{5\}$.

3 A Co-algebraic Formulation of HD-Automata

In this section we extend the co-algebraic minimization to *HD-automata*. HD-automata [15] are specifically designed to provide a compact representation of the

Fig. 2. Minimal labelled transition system

behavior of name passing process calculi. Names appear explicitly in the states of an HD-automaton: the idea is that the names associated to a state are the names which may play a role in the state evolution. A set $\{v_1, \ldots, v_{|q|}\}$ of local names is associated with each state q, and a permutation group G_q on $\{v_1, \ldots, v_{|q|}\}$ defines what renamings leave unchanged the behavior of q. Moreover, the identity of names is local to the state: states which differ only for the order of their names are identified. Due to the usage of local names, whenever a transition is performed a name correspondence between the name of the source state and the names of the target state is explicitly required.

3.1   Named Sets

Now we introduce the notion of *named sets*. Hereafter, we use $A \overset{bij}{\rightarrow} B$ ($A \overset{inj}{\rightarrow} B$) to denote a bijective (injective) function from A to B.

Definition 2. *A named set A is a structure*

$$A = \langle\, Q : Set, |\_| : Q \longrightarrow \omega, \leq : Q \times Q \longrightarrow Bool, G : \prod_{q:Q} \wp(\{v_1..v_{|q|}\}) \overset{bij}{\rightarrow} \{v_1..v_{|q|}\}) \,\rangle$$

where $\forall q : Q_A$, $G_A(q)$ is a permutation group and $\leq_A$ is a total ordering.

A named set is a set of states equipped with a mechanism to give local meaning to names occurring in each state. In particular, function $|\_|$ yields the number of local names of states. Moreover, the permutation group $G_A(q)$ allows one to describe directly the renamings that do not affect the behaviour of q, i.e., symmetries among the local names of q. Finally, we assume that states are totally ordered. By convention we write $\{q : Q_A\}_A$ to indicate the set $\{v_1..v_{|q|_A}\}$ and we use NSet to denote the universe of named sets. In the definition above, the general product $\prod$ is employed (as usual in type theory) to type functions f such that the type of $f(q)$ is dependent on q.

Definition 3. *A named function H is a structure*

$$H = \langle\, S : NSet, D : NSet, h : Q_S \longrightarrow Q_D, \Sigma : \prod_{q:Q_S} \wp(\{h(q)\}_D \overset{inj}{\rightarrow} \{q\}_S) \,\rangle$$

where $\forall q : Q_{S_H}, \forall \sigma : \Sigma_H(q)$, $G_{D_H}(h_H(q)); \sigma = \Sigma_H(q)$ and $\sigma; G_{S_H}(q) \subseteq \Sigma_H(q)$.

As in the case of standard transition systems, functions are used to determine the next state of transitions. As states are equipped with local names, a name correspondence (the mapping H_h) is needed to describe how names in the destination state are mapped into names of the source state. However, since names of corresponding states $(q, h_H(q))$ in h_H are defined up to permutation groups, we must equip H with a *set* $\Sigma_H(q)$ of injective functions. Since the name correspondence must be functional, the whole set $\Sigma_H(q)$ must be generated by saturating any of its elements by the permutation group of $h_H(q)$, and the result must be invariant with respect to the permutation group of q.

Named functions can be composed in the obvious way. Let H and K be named functions. Then $H; K$ is defined only if $D_H = S_K$, and

- $S_{H;K} = S_H,\ D_{H;K} = D_K,$
- $h_{H;K} : Q_{S_H} \longrightarrow Q_{D_K} = h_H; h_K,$
- $\Sigma_{H;K}(q : Q_{S_H}) = \Sigma_K(h_H(q)); \Sigma_H(q)$

Let H be a named function, $\widehat{H}$ denotes the surjective component of H:

- $S_{\widehat{H}} = S_H$ and $Q_{D_{\widehat{H}}} = \{q' : Q_{D_H} \mid \exists q : Q_{S_H}.h_H(q) = q'\},$
- $|q|_{D_{\widehat{H}}} = |q|_{D_H},$
- $G_{D_{\widehat{H}}}(q) = G_{D_H}(q),$
- $h_{\widehat{H}}(q) = h_H(q),$
- $\Sigma_{\widehat{H}}(q) = \Sigma_H(q)$

3.2   Bundles over π-Calculus Actions

To deal with HD-automata and named sets, the notion of bundle must be enriched. First we have to define the set of labels of transitions. Labels of transitions must distinguish among the different meanings of names occurring in π-calculus actions, namely synchronization, bound output (scope extrusion) free output, bound input, output where the subject and the object coincide, and so on. The set of π-calculus labels L_π is the set $\{TAU, BOUT, OUT, BIN, IN\}$. However, this is not enough. We still have to specify how many names are associated to labels. For instance, no name is associated to TAU (synchronization) labels, whereas one name, is associated to bound output $BOUT$ labels. Let $|\_|$ be the weight map associating to each π-label the set of indices of distinct names the label refers to. The weight map is defined as follows:

$$|TAU| = \emptyset \quad |BOUT| = |BIN| = \{1\} \quad |OUT| = |IN| = \{1, 2\}$$

Definition 4. *A bundle β consists of the structure*

$$\beta = \langle\, \mathcal{D} : \mathtt{NSet}, Step : \wp(qd\,\mathcal{D}) \,\rangle$$

where $qd\,\mathcal{D}$ is the set of quadruples of the form $\langle\, \ell, \pi, \sigma, q \,\rangle$ given by

$$qd\,\mathcal{D} = \{\langle\, \ell : L_\pi, \pi : |\ell| \xrightarrow{inj} \{v_1..\}, q : Q_\mathcal{D}, \sigma : \prod_{\ell \in L_\pi} \{q\}_\mathcal{D} \xrightarrow{inj} Q\ell \,\rangle\}.$$

and

$$Q\ell = \begin{cases} \{*, v_1..\} & \text{if } \ell \in \{BOUT, BIN\} \\ \{v_1..\} & \text{if } \ell \notin \{BOUT, BIN\} \end{cases}$$

under the constraint that $G_{\mathcal{D}_\beta}(q); S_q = S_q$, *where* $S_q = \{\langle \ell, \pi, q, \sigma \rangle \in Step_\beta\}$ *and* $\rho; \langle \ell, \pi, q, \sigma \rangle = \langle \ell, \pi, q, \rho; \sigma \rangle$.

The intuition is that a bundle provides the abstraction to describe the successor set of a state. More precisely, if $\langle \ell, \pi, q, \sigma \rangle \in qd\mathcal{D}$, then q is the destination state; ℓ is the label of the transition; π associates to the label the names observed in the transition; and σ states how names in the destination state are related with the names in the source state. Notice that the distinguished element $*$ belongs to the names of the source state when a new name is generated in the transition.

Some additional operations over bundles will be helpful. Given a function f, define f^* to be its $*$-extension as follows:

$$f^*(x) = \begin{cases} * & \text{if } x = * \\ f(x) & \text{otherwise} \end{cases}$$

Let $\{\!|\beta|\!\}$ be the function over bundles given by

$$\{\!|\beta|\!\} = \bigcup_{\langle \ell, \pi, q, \sigma \rangle \in Step_\beta} rng(\pi) \cup rng(\sigma) \setminus \{*\}$$

where rng yields the range of functions. Function $\{\!|\beta|\!\}$ gives the set of names which occur in the bundle β. Hereafter, we will only consider bundles β such that $\{\!|\beta|\!\}$ is finite. Moreover, we will use $\lfloor\beta\rfloor$ to indicate the number of names which occur in the bundle β (i.e. $\lfloor\beta\rfloor = |\{\!|\beta|\!\}|$).

The most important construction on bundles is the *normalization* operation. This operation is necessary for two different reasons. The first reason is that there are different equivalent ways for picking up the step components (i.e. quadruples $\langle \ell, \pi, q, \sigma \rangle$) of a bundle. We assume to have an ordering relation over the quadruples in $qd\,\mathcal{D}$, which yields an ordering $\sqsubseteq$ over the bundles on $\mathcal{D}$. This ordering relation will be used to define canonical representatives of bundles. The ordering on quadruples can be defined non ambiguously only assuming an ordering on $\mathcal{D}$. This is why we introduced an ordering relation on named sets in the first place.

The second, more important, reason for normalizing a bundle is for removing from the step component of a bundle all the input transitions which are *redundant*. Consider for instance the case of a state q having only one name v_1 and assume that the following two tuples appear in a bundle:

$$\langle IN, xy, q, \{v_1 \to y\} \rangle \qquad \text{and} \qquad \langle BIN, x, q, \{v_1 \to *\} \rangle.$$

Then, the first tuple is redundant, as it expresses exactly the same behavior of the second tuple, except that a "free" input transition is used rather than a "bound" one. Hence, the transformation removes the first tuple from the bundle. We have to remark that redundant transitions occur when building the HD-automaton for a π-calculus agent. Indeed, it is not possible to decide which free input transitions are required, and which transitions are covered by the bound input transition[1]. The solution to this problem consists of adding a superset of the required free input transitions when the HD-automaton is built, and to exploit a reduction function to remove the ones that are unnecessary. During the iterative execution of the minimization algorithm, bundles are split: this means that the set of redundant components of bundles decreases. Hence, when the iterative construction terminates, only those free inputs that are really redundant have been removed from the bundles.

The normalization of a bundle β is done in different steps. In the first step, the bundle is reduced by removing all the possibly redundant input transitions. Reduction function $red(\beta)$ on bundles is defined as follows:

- $\mathcal{D}_{red(\beta)} = \mathcal{D}_\beta$,
- $Step_{red(\beta)} = Step_\beta \setminus \{\langle\, IN, xy, q, \sigma\,\rangle \mid \langle\, BIN, x, q, \sigma'\,\rangle : Step_\beta \wedge \sigma' = (\sigma; \{y \to *\})\}$.

Once the redundant input transitions have been removed, it is possible to associate to bundle β the set of its "active names" $an_\beta = \{\!| \, red(\beta) \, |\!\}$. These are the names that appear either in a destination state or in a label of a non-redundant transition of the bundle. Finally, the *normalization* function $norm(\beta)$ is defined as follows:

- $\mathcal{D}_{norm(\beta)} = \mathcal{D}_\beta$
- $Step_{norm(\beta)} = min_\sqsubseteq (Step_\beta \setminus \{\langle\, IN, xy, q, \sigma\,\rangle \mid y \notin an_\beta\})$,

where $min_\sqsubseteq$ is the function that returns the minimal permutation of a given bundle with respect to order $\sqsubseteq$. More precisely, given a bundle β and a permutation $\theta : \{\!| \, \beta \, |\!\} \xrightarrow{bij} \{\!| \, \beta \, |\!\}$, bundle $\beta; \theta$ is defined as $\mathcal{D}_{\beta;\theta} = \mathcal{D}_\beta$, $step_{\beta;\theta} = \{(\ell, \pi; \theta, q, \sigma; \theta) \mid (\ell, \pi, q, \sigma) : \beta\}$. The bundle $min_\sqsubseteq \overline{\beta}$ is the minimal bundle in $\{\overline{\beta}; \theta \mid \theta : \{\!| \overline{\beta} |\!\} \xrightarrow{bij} \{\!| \overline{\beta} |\!\}\}$, with respect to the total ordering $\sqsubseteq$ of bundles over $\mathcal{D}$. In the following, we use $perm(\beta)$ to denote the canonical permutation that associates $Step_{norm(\beta)}$ and $Step_\beta \setminus \{\langle\, IN, xy, q, \sigma\,\rangle \mid y \notin an_\beta\}$.

We remark that, while *all* the IN transitions covered by BIN transitions are removed in the definition of $red(\beta)$, only those corresponding to the reception of non-active names are removed in the definition of $norm(\beta)$. In fact, even if an input transition is redundant, it might be the case that it corresponds to the reception of a name that is active due to some other transitions.

Finally, we need a construction which extracts in a canonical way a group of permutations out of a bundle. Let β be a bundle, define $Gr\ \beta$ to be the set $\{\rho \mid Step_\beta; \rho^* = Step_\beta\}$.

Proposition 1. $Gr\ \beta$ *is a group of permutations.*

3.3   The Minimization Algorithm

We are now ready to introduce the functor T that defines the co-algebras for HD-automata. The action of functor T over named sets is given by:

---

[1] In the general case, to decide whether a free input transition is required it is as difficult as to decide the bisimilarity of two π-calculus agents.

- $Q_{T(A)} = \{\beta : Bundle \mid \mathcal{D}_\beta = A, \beta \text{ normalized}\}$,
- $|\beta|_{T(A)} = \lfloor\beta\rfloor$,
- $G_{T(A)}(\beta) = Gr\ \beta$,
- $\beta_1 \leq_{T(A)} \beta_2$ iff $Step_{\beta_1} \sqsubseteq Step_{\beta_2}$,

while the action of functor T over named functions is given by:

- $S_{T(H)} = T(S_H)$, $D_{T(H)} = T(D_H)$,
- $h_{T(H)}(\beta : Q_{T(S_H)}) : Q_{T(D_H)} = norm(\beta')$,
- $\Sigma_{T(H)}(\beta : Q_{T(S_H)}) = Gr(norm(\beta')); (perm(\beta'))^{-1}; inj : \{\!|\, norm(\beta')\,|\!\} \longrightarrow \{\beta\}_{T(S_H)}$
  where $\beta' = \langle D_H, \{\langle\, \ell, \pi, h_H(q), \sigma'; \sigma\,\rangle \mid \langle\, \ell, \pi, q, \sigma\,\rangle : Step_\beta, \sigma' : \Sigma_H(q)\}\rangle$.

Notice that functor T maps every named set A into the named set $T(A)$ of its *normalized* bundles. Also a named function H is mapped into a named function $T(H)$ in such a way that every corresponding pair $(q, h_H(q))$ in h_H is mapped into a set of corresponding pairs $(\beta, norm(\beta'))$ of bundles in $h_{T(H)}$. The quadruples of bundle β' are obtained from those of β by replacing q with $h_H(q)$ and by saturating with respect to the set of name mappings in $\Sigma_H(q)$. The name mappings in $\Sigma_{T(H)}\beta$ are obtained by transforming the permutation group of bundle $norm(\beta')$ with the inverse of the canonical permutation of β' and with a fixed injective function inj mapping the set of names of $norm(\beta')$ into the set of names of β, defined as $i < j$, $inj(v_i) = v_{i'}$ and $inj(v_j) = v_{j'}$ implies $i' < j'$. Without bundle normalization, the choice of β' among those in $\beta'; \theta$ would have been arbitrary and not canonical with the consequence of mapping together fewer bundles than needed.

Definition 5. *A transition system over named sets and π-actions is a named function K such that $D_K = T(S_K)$.*

HD-automata are particular transition systems over named sets. Formally, an HD-automaton A is given by:

- the elements of the state Q_A are π-agents $p(v_1..v_n)$ ordered lexicographically: $p_1 \leq_A p_2$ iff $p_1 \leq_{lex} p_2$
- $|p(v_1..v_n)|_A = n$,
- $G_{Aq} = \{id : \{q\}_A \longrightarrow \{q\}_A\}$, where id denotes the identity function,
- $h : Q_A \longrightarrow \{\beta \mid \mathcal{D}_\beta = A\}$ is such that $\langle\, \ell, \pi, q', \sigma\,\rangle \in Step_{h(q)}$ represent the π-calculus transitions from agent q.

We remark that bundle $Step_{h(q)}$ should not contain all the transitions from q, but only a representative subset. For instance, it is not necessary to consider a free input transition where the received name is not active provided that there is a bound input transition which differs from it only for the bound name. Finally, by using renaming σ in the element of the bundles, it is possible to identify all those π-agents that differ only for an injective renaming. In the following, we represent as $q \xrightarrow[\pi]{\ell}_\sigma q'$ the "representative" transitions from agent q that are used in the construction of the HD-automaton.

We can now define the function K.

- $S_K = A$,
- $h_K(q) = norm(h(q))$,
- $\Sigma_K(q) = Gr(h_K(q)); (perm(h(q)))^{-1}; inj : \{\!| h(q) |\!\} \longrightarrow \{q\}_A$

We now construct the minimal HD-automata by an iterative procedure. We first need to define the initial approximation. Given a HD-automata K, the initial approximation H_0 is defined as follows:

- $S_{H_0} = S_K$, $D_{H_0} = unit$ where $Q_{unit} = \{*\}$, $|*|_{unit} = 0$ (and hence $\{*\} = \phi$), $G_{unit} * = \phi$, and $* \leq_{unit} *$,
- $h_{H_0}(q : Q_{s_{H_0}}) = *$,
- $\Sigma_{H_0} q = \{\phi\}$

The formula which details the iterative construction is given by

$$H_{n+1} = \widehat{K; T(H_n)}.$$

Two of the authors have developed in [16] a final coalgebra model for the π-calculus. In particular, the early transition system is modelled as a coalgebra on a suitable category of permutation algebras, and early bisimilarity is obtained as the final coalgebra of such a category. HD-automata are then proposed as a compact representation of these transition systems. It is possible to adapt the results of [16] to our framework, and hence, to prove convergence of the iteration along the terminal sequence. Furthermore, if we consider finite state HD-automata (i.e. finite state HD automata associated to finitary π-calculus processes) we can prove a stronger result.

Theorem 2. *Let K be a finite state HD-automaton. Then*

- *The iteration along the terminal sequence converges in a finite number of steps: n exists such that $D_{H_{n+1}} \equiv D_{H_n}$,*
- *The isomorphism mapping $F : D_{H_n} \to D_{H_{n+1}}$ yields the minimal realization of the transition system K up to strong early bisimilarity.*

Sketch of the proof. It is possible to see that at every iteration either a block is split (i.e. there are q and q' with $h_{H_n}(q) = h_{H_n}(q')$ but $h_{H_{n+1}}(q) \neq h_{H_{n+1}}(q')$); or, if no block is split, some block acquires additional names (i.e. there is q with $| h_{H_n}(q) | < | h_{H_{n+1}}(q)|$); or, if there are no additional names the group of permutations of some block decreases (i.e. there is q with $G_{h_{H_n}}(q) \supset G_{h_{H_{n+1}}}(q)$). Since blocks cannot be indefinitely split (there is a finite number of states), the number of names cannot indefinitely increase (each block cannot have a number of names larger than any state in it) and groups of permutations cannot indefinitely decrease (they are finite) every terminal sequence is well-founded.

The following functional expression (in a extended λ-calculus) makes the iteration step of the normalization algorithm explicit.

$h_{H_{n+1}} = (\lambda q.norm \langle A, \{\langle \ell, \pi, q', \sigma \rangle \mid q \xrightarrow[\pi]{\ell}_\sigma q'\}\rangle);$

$$\lambda\beta.norm \ \langle D_{H_n}, \{\langle\, \ell, \pi, h_{H_n}(q), \sigma'; \sigma\,\rangle \mid \langle\, \ell, \pi, q, \sigma\,\rangle : Step_\beta, \sigma' : \Sigma_{H_n}(q)\}\rangle$$

$$h_{H_{n+1}}(q) = norm \ \langle D_{H_n}, \{\langle\, \ell, \pi, h_{H_n}(q'), \sigma'; \sigma\,\rangle \mid q \xrightarrow[\pi]{\ell}_\sigma q', \sigma' : \Sigma_{H_n}(q')\}\rangle.$$

Notice that the normalization on the transition system is absorbed by the normalization on the resulting bundle.

4   Minimizing Behaviours of π-Calculus Processes

In this section we provide an example of minimization by considering a transition system which describes the behaviour of a π-calculus process. Let $S(x, y, z)$ be the π-calculus process

$$S(x, y, z) = x!y.R(x, y, z) + y!x.R(x, y, z)$$
$$R(x, y, z) = x?(w).S(x, y, w) + y?(w).S(y, x, z)$$

Here, we use $x!y$ (resp $x?(y)$) to denote output (resp. input) actions. Process $S(x, y, z)$ syntactically contains name z, however this name is not active in any system evolution. As we will see, name z disappears in the minimal realization for $S(x, y, z)$. The behaviour of the process $S(x, y, z)$ is illustrated by the labelled transition system displayed in the upper part of Figure 3.

The transition system has been automatically generated using the HAL environment [7,8]. The HAL environment is an integrated tool set for the specification, verification and analysis of mobile system specified in the π-calculus. HAL contains several modules to check bisimilarity; however, it does not include any module to minimize the state space of π-calculus processes under analysis. Notice that we extended labels of transitions. For instance, label $IN2$ is used to describe an input action where subject and object names coincide.

Hereafter, we adopt the following notations for name permutations. Term id_n denotes the identity permutation over n names and term $exch_2$ denotes the permutation that exchanges two names.

Let S_K be the set $\{q_0, q_1, q_2, q_3, q_4, q_5, q_6\}$, where $G_q = id_{|q|} \ \forall q : S_K$. The occurrences of names in the states are given by $|q_0| = |q_1| = |q_4| = 3$, $|q_2| = |q_3| = |q_5| = |q_6| = 2$, where $|q| = n$ means that state q contains names $\{v_1, v_2, \ldots, v_n\}$. The mapping h_K is displayed in the lower part of Figure 3.

Finally, let $\Sigma_K q$ be the injection of the names occurring in $h_k q$ into the corresponding names of q (i.e., either id_2 or id_3).

The initial approximation is the function H_0 defined as follows

$$H_0 = \langle S_{H_0} = S_K, D_{H_0} = unit, h_{H_0} = \lambda q : S_K.*, \Sigma_{H_0}q = \emptyset\rangle$$

Applying the definition of the iterative algorithm we have

$$q_0, q_2, q_3, q_4 \xrightarrow{h_{H_1}} \beta_1 \qquad q_1, q_5, q_6 \xrightarrow{h_{H_1}} \beta_2$$

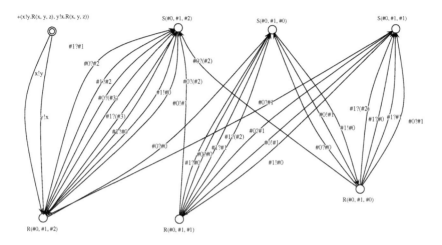

$$h_K(q_0) = \langle S_k, \{\ \langle OUT, v_1v_2, q_1, id_3\rangle,$$
$$\langle OUT, v_2v_1, q_1, id_3\rangle\}\rangle$$
$$h_K(q_1) = \langle S_k, \{\ \langle IN2, v_1, q_2, id_2\rangle,$$
$$\langle IN, v_1v_2, q_3, id_2\rangle,$$
$$\langle IN, v_1v_3, q_4, id_3\rangle,$$
$$\langle BIN, v_1, q_4, id_2 \cup (v_3, *)\rangle,$$
$$\langle IN, v_2v_1, q_4, exch_2 \cup (v_3, v_3)\rangle,$$
$$\langle IN2, v_2, q_4, exch_2 \cup (v_3, v_3)\rangle,$$
$$\langle IN, v_2v_3, q_4, exch_2 \cup (v_3, v_3)\rangle,$$
$$\langle BIN, v_2, q_4, exch_2 \cup (v_3, v_3)\rangle\}\rangle$$
$$h_K(q_2) = \langle S_k, \{\ \langle OUT, v_1v_2, q_6, id_2\rangle,$$
$$\langle OUT, v_2v_1, q_6, id_2\rangle\}\rangle$$
$$h_K(q_3) = \langle S_k, \{\ \langle OUT, v_1v_2, q_5, id_2\rangle,$$
$$\langle OUT, v_2v_1, q_5, id_2\rangle\}\rangle$$
$$h_K(q_4) = \langle S_k, \{\ \langle OUT, v_1v_2, q_1, id_3\rangle,$$
$$\langle OUT, v_2v_1, q_1, id_3\rangle\}\rangle$$
$$h_K(q_5) = \langle S_k, \{\ \langle IN2, v_1, q_2, id_2\rangle,$$
$$\langle IN, v_1v_2, q_3, id_2\rangle,$$
$$\langle BIN, v_1, q_4, id_2 \cup (v_3, *)\rangle,$$
$$\langle IN, v_2v_1, q_2, exch_2\rangle,$$
$$\langle IN2, v_2, q_2, exch_2\rangle,$$
$$\langle BIN, v_2, q_2, exch_2\rangle\}\rangle$$
$$h_K(q_6) = \langle S_k, \{\ \langle IN2, v_1, q_2, id_2\rangle,$$
$$\langle IN, v_1v_2, q_3, id_2\rangle,$$
$$\langle BIN, v_1, q_4, id_2 \cup (v_3, *)\rangle,$$
$$\langle IN, v_2v_1, q_3, exch_2\rangle,$$
$$\langle IN2, v_2, q_3, exch_2\rangle,$$
$$\langle BIN, v_2, q_3, exch_2\rangle\}\rangle$$

Fig. 3. An example of HD-automaton and its coalgebraic specification.

where bundles β_1 and β_2 and their associated permutation groups are defined as follows:

$$\beta_1 = \langle D_{H_0}, \{ \langle OUT, v_1v_2, *, \emptyset \rangle, \langle OUT, v_2v_1, *, \emptyset \rangle \} \rangle$$
$$\beta_2 = \langle D_{H_0}, \{ \langle IN2, v_1, *, \emptyset \rangle,$$
$$\langle IN, v_1v_2, *, \emptyset \rangle,$$
$$\langle BIN, v_1, *, \emptyset \rangle,$$
$$\langle IN, v_2v_1, *, \emptyset \rangle,$$
$$\langle IN2, v_2, *, \emptyset \rangle,$$
$$\langle BIN, v_2, *, \emptyset \rangle \} \rangle$$

$$\lfloor \beta_1 \rfloor = 2 \quad G\beta_1 = \{ id_2, exch_2 \}$$
$$\lfloor \beta_2 \rfloor = 2 \quad G\beta_2 = \{ id_2, exch_2 \}$$
$$\Sigma_{H_1} q = (id_2, exch_2) \quad \text{for all } q \in S_K.$$

Notice that the normalization construction has removed redundant transitions from bundles. Hence, the overall number of transitions decreases.

Applying again the definition of the iterative algorithm we have

$$q_0, q_2, q_3, q_4 \xrightarrow{h_{H_2}} \beta_1' \quad q_1, q_5, q_6 \xrightarrow{h_{H_2}} \beta_2'$$

where bundles β_1' and β_2' and their associated permutation groups are defined as follows:

$$\beta_1' = \langle D_{H_1}, \{ \langle OUT, v_1v_2, \beta_2, id_2 \rangle, \langle OUT, v_2v_1, \beta_2, id_2 \rangle,$$
$$\langle OUT, v_1v_2, \beta_2, exch_2 \rangle, \langle OUT, v_2v_1, \beta_2, exch_2 \rangle \} \rangle$$
$$\beta_2' = \langle D_{H_1}, \{ \langle IN2, v_1, \beta_1, id_2 \rangle,$$
$$\langle IN, v_1v_2, \beta_1, id_2 \rangle,$$
$$\langle BIN, v_1, \beta_1, id_2 \rangle,$$
$$\langle IN, v_2v_1, \beta_1, exch_2 \rangle,$$
$$\langle IN2, v_2, \beta_1, exch_2 \rangle,$$
$$\langle BIN, v_2, \beta_1, exch_2 \rangle \} \rangle$$

$$\lfloor \beta_1' \rfloor = 2 \quad G\beta_1' = \{ id_2, exch_2 \}$$
$$\lfloor \beta_2' \rfloor = 2 \quad G\beta_2' = \{ id_2, exch_2 \}$$
$$\Sigma_{H_2} q = (id_2, exch_2) \quad \text{for all } q \in S_K.$$

Since $D_{H_1} \equiv D_{H_2}$, the iterative algorithm terminates and H_2 defines the minimal HD-automaton. Notice that the minimal HD-automaton contains 2 states and 10 transitions rather than 7 states and 28 transitions of the original HD-automaton.

5   Concluding Remarks

In this paper we have developed a minimization procedure for finite state verification of name passing calculi. The minimization algorithm is automatically derived from the co-algebraic formulation. We plan to experiment with the minimization algorithm to evaluate its usefulness in practice by equipping the HAL verification environment with a module performing minimization of HD-automata. We are currently developing a prototype implementation of the minimization algorithm for HD-automata in O-Caml.

References

1. P. Aczel, N. Mendler, A Final Coalgebra Theorem, in *Category Theory and Computer Science*, LNCS 389, 1989.
2. A. Corradini, R. Heckel, U. Montanari, Compositional SOS and Beyond: A Coalgebraic View of Open Systems, Theoretical Computer Science, to appear.
3. E. Clarke and J. Wing Eds. Formal Methods: State of the Art and Future Directions. ACM Comp. Surv., December 1996.
4. M. Dam, On the decidability of process equivalences for the π-calculus. *Theoretical Computer Science*, 183(2):215–228, 1997.
5. B. Jacobs, J. Rutten A tutorial on (co)algebras and (co)induction. Bulletin of EATCS, 62, 222-259, 1997.
6. J.-C., Fernandez, An implementation of an efficient algorithm for bisimulation equivalence. Science of Computer Programming 13, 219-236, 1990.
7. G. Ferrari, G. Ferro, S. Gnesi, U. Montanari, M. Pistore, G. Ristori. An Automata-based Verification Environment for Mobile Processes In TACAS'97, LNCS 1217, 1997.
8. G. Ferrari, S. Gnesi, U. Montanari, M. Pistore, G. Ristori, Verifying Mobile Processes in the HAL Environment. CAV'98 , LNCS 1427, 1998.
9. P. Kannellakis, S. Smolka, CCS expressions, finite state processes, and three problems of equivalence. Information and Computation, 86, 43-68, 1990.
10. C. Meadows Open Issues in Formal Methods for Cryptographic Protocol Analysis, Proceedings of DISCEX 2000, IEEE Press, 237-250, 2000.
11. R. Milner, J. Parrow and D. Walker. A calculus of mobile processes, Part I and II. *Information and Computation*, 100(1):1–77, 1992.
12. U. Montanari and M. Pistore. Checking bisimilarity for finitary π-calculus. In *Proc. CONCUR'95*, LNCS 962. Springer Verlag, 1995.
13. U. Montanari and M. Pistore. History dependent verification for partial order systems. In *Partial Order Methods in Verification*, DIMACS Series, Vol. 29. American Mathematical Society, 1997.
14. U. Montanari, M. Pistore and D. Yankelevich. Efficient minimization up to location equivalence. In *Proc. ESOP'96*, LNCS 1058. Springer Verlag, 1996.
15. U. Montanari and M. Pistore. History-Dependent Automata. IRST Technical Report 0112-14, Istituto Trentino di Cultura, December 2001.
16. U. Montanari and M. Pistore. π-calculus, structured coalgebras and minimal HD-automata. In *Proc. MFCS'2000*, LNCS 1893, Springer Verlag, 2000.
17. M. Pistore and D. Sangiorgi, A partition refinement algorithm for the π-calculus. *Information and Computation* 164, 263-321, 2001.
18. R. Paige, R.E. Tarjan. Three partition refinement algorithms, SIAM Journal on Computing 16(6) 973–989, 1987.
19. J.J.M.M. Rutten. Universal coalgebra: a theory of systems. Technical Report CS-R9652, CWI, 1996. To appear in *Theoretical Computer Science*.
20. D. Turi, G.D. Plotkin, Towards a Mathematical Operational Semantics, In Proc. Logic in Computer Science 97, IEEE Press, 280-291, 1997.
21. J. Warell, Terminal Sequences for Accessible Endofunctors, In Proc. CMCS'99, ENCTS 19, 1999.

Varieties of Effects

Carsten Führmann

School of Computer Science, University of Birmingham
cxf@cs.bham.ac.uk

Abstract. We introduce the notion of *effectoid* as a way of axiomatising the notion of "computational effect". Guided by classical algebra, we define several effectoids equationally and explore their relationship with each other. We demonstrate their computational relevance by applying them to global exceptions, partiality, continuations, and global state.

1 Introduction

In this article, we shall introduce *effectoids* as sublanguages that stand for limitations of computational effects. The focus will be on call-by-value programming languages, and we shall use the computational lambda-calculus (λ_C-calculus) as the theoretical backbone.

Because the values of the λ_C-calculus are effect-free in any reasonable sense, one might think they should form the smallest effectoid. But this would be unsatisfactory, because values are not closed under equality. (For example, $(\lambda x.x)y$ is not a value, whereas its normal form y is.) In particular, the notion of value cannot be defined semantically. By contrast, effectoids will be closed under the equality in every denotational model, so we could treat them as sets of morphisms when required. In particular, we shall replace the notion of value by a notion of *algebraic value* which yields an effectoid.

Several sets of expressions (or morphisms) that received considerable attention in the recent literature turn out to be effectoids: Thielecke defined the sets of *central*, *copyable*, and *discardable* morphisms in models of continuations, capturing fundamental classes of program behaviour that correspond to different uses of control [12]. Selinger used these notions in his analysis of the duality between call-by-value and call-by-name in the presence of continuations [11]. Dealing with the same duality, Hasegawa and Kakutani pointed out a fundamental relationship between central expressions and rigid functionals [5], which play a key rôle in Filinski's recursion-from-iteration construction [2]. It was soon pointed out that those sets of expressions are interesting for arbitrary computational effects, not only continuations [3,4]. Recently, it was discovered that typical models of partiality (i.e. models where divergence is the only "effect") can be characterised by requiring every morphism to be central and "strongly copyable"[1], and also

---

[1] The notion of "strong copyability" was defined in the CTCS'99 conference version of [1], and we shall replace that terminology by "repeatable" in this article.

M. Nielsen and U. Engberg (Eds.): Fossacs 2002, LNCS 2303, pp. 144–159, 2002.

that discardable morphisms and algebraic values coincide for such models and yield the right notion of totality [1].

All sets of expressions mentioned above, except for the set of copyable expressions, will turn out to be effectoids. Also, all those sets are given as the solutions of equations. In algebraic geometric, sets given as solutions of (polynomial) equations are called *algebraic sets*. In analogy, we shall call effectoids that are given as solutions of equations *algebraic effectoids*.

The consideration of algebraic effectoids will lead us to notions that do not occur in the literature mentioned above: centralisers, stabilisers, and distributive expressions. Figure 1 presents an overview of most of the varieties that we shall discuss. (The numbers in the diagram are for later reference.)

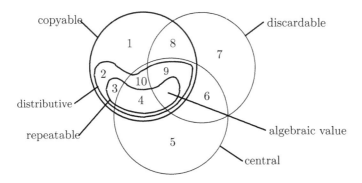

Fig. 1. Varieties introduced in this article

Remark 1. All effectoids presented in this article have interpretations in *premonoidal categories* with extra structure [10,4,3]. (In fact, several effectoids where introduced categorically.) However, the λ_C-calculus, which is the internal language of those premonoidal categories with extra structure, turned out to be the most efficient way of conveying these concepts in a computational context.

2   Preliminaries

The λ_C-calculus. The λ_C-calculus [7] has proved itself useful for reasoning about call-by-value programs. Its syntax, typing, and axioms on the well-typed terms are summarised in Figure 2, where b ranges over base types, and c^A ranges over constants of type A.

Following common practice, we write $\text{let } x^A \text{ be } M \text{ in } N$ for $(\lambda x^A.N)M$. We shall often omit type annotations of variables when the type is evident or does not matter.

A λ_C-*theory* over given base types and constants is a set $\mathcal{T}$ of equations $\Gamma \vdash M \equiv N : A$, where $\Gamma \vdash M : A$ and $\Gamma \vdash N : A$ are well-formed according to

$$\text{Types} \qquad A, B ::= b \mid A \to B \mid A \times B \mid 1$$

$$\text{Expressions} \qquad M, N ::= x \mid c^A \mid \lambda x^A.M \mid M\,N \mid (M, N) \mid \pi_i M \mid ()$$

$$\text{Values} \qquad V, U ::= x \mid c^A \mid \lambda x^A.M \mid (V, U) \mid \pi_i V \mid ()$$

$$\frac{}{\Gamma \vdash x : A}\, x^A \in \Gamma \qquad \Gamma \vdash c^A : A \qquad \frac{\Gamma, x^A \vdash M : B}{\Gamma \vdash \lambda x^A.M : A \to B} \qquad \frac{\Gamma \vdash M : A \to B \qquad \Gamma \vdash N : A}{\Gamma \vdash M\,N : B}$$

$$\frac{\Gamma \vdash M : A \qquad \Gamma \vdash N : B}{\Gamma \vdash (M, N) : A \times B} \qquad \frac{\Gamma \vdash M : A_1 \times A_2}{\Gamma \vdash \pi_i M : A_i} \qquad \Gamma \vdash () : 1$$

$$\texttt{let } x \texttt{ be } V \texttt{ in } M \equiv M[V/x]$$
$$\lambda x.V x \equiv V \qquad\qquad (x \notin \mathrm{FV}(V))$$
$$\pi_i(V_1, V_2) \equiv V_i$$
$$(\pi_1 V, \pi_2 V) \equiv V$$
$$V \equiv ()$$
$$\texttt{let } x \texttt{ be } M \texttt{ in } x \equiv M$$
$$\texttt{let } y \texttt{ be } (\texttt{let } x \texttt{ be } L \texttt{ in } M) \texttt{ in } N \equiv \texttt{let } x \texttt{ be } L \texttt{ in let } y \texttt{ be } M \texttt{ in } N \qquad (x \notin \mathrm{FV}(N))$$
$$M\,N \equiv \texttt{let } f \texttt{ be } M \texttt{ in let } x \texttt{ be } N \texttt{ in } f x$$
$$(M, N) \equiv \texttt{let } x \texttt{ be } M \texttt{ in let } y \texttt{ be } N \texttt{ in } (x, y)$$
$$\pi_1 M \equiv \texttt{let } x \texttt{ be } M \texttt{ in } \pi_i x$$

Fig. 2. The λ_C-calculus

the rules in Figure 2, that contains all equations presented in Figure 2 and is a congruence stable under weakening and permutation.

We write $N[M_1/x_1, \ldots, M_n/x_n]$ for the expression that results from substituting M_i for all free occurrences of x_i in N simultaneously for $i \in \{1, \ldots, n\}$ (avoiding the capture of free variables). We say that $y_1^{A_1}, \ldots, y_n^{A_n} \vdash N : B$ results from $x_1^{A_1}, \ldots, x_n^{A_n} \vdash M : B$ by *environment renaming* if $N = M[y_1/x_1, \ldots, y_n/x_n]$. We shall write $\lambda().M$ instead of $\lambda x^1.M$. If X is a set of occurrences of a variable x in M, we write $M[N/X]$ for the expression that results from replacing all those occurrences with N.

λ_C-*models and their internal language.* The semantics of the λ_C-calculus can be provided by λ_C-*models*. A λ_C-model is given by a strong monad T on a category C with finite products and T-exponentials—that is, exponentials of the form $(TA)^B$. (A strong monad is a monad T together with a *strength*, which is a natural transformation $t_{A,B} : A \times TB \longrightarrow T(A \times B)$ satisfying some equations due to Kock [6]. For a discussion of strong monads and a summary of those equations, see [8].)

It helps our calculations to work with the internal language of λ_C-models instead of their categorical presentation. That internal language is given by the simply-typed λ-calculus (with product types) together with a unary type constructor T, function types of the restricted form $A \to TB$ (instead of arbitrary function types), and typed-indexed families of constants $\eta_A : A \to TA$ and $*_{A,B} : TA \times (A \to TB) \to TB$ (written infix and without type annotations) satisfying the equations below (where L, M, and N range over open terms):

$$(L * M) * N \equiv L * \lambda l.((Ml) * N) \qquad \lambda x.((\eta x) * M) \equiv M \qquad M * \eta \equiv M$$

This internal language is essentially the "metalanguage" presented in [8].

Semantics of the λ_C-calculus. The categorical semantics of the λ_C-calculus can be presented by a transform $\overline{(-)}$ into the metalanguage. For every base type b, an *interpretation* must provide a type $\overline{b}$, and obey the laws

$$\overline{A \to B} = \overline{A} \to T\overline{B} \qquad \overline{A \times B} = \overline{A} \times \overline{B} \qquad \overline{1} = 1$$

For each constant c^A, an interpretation must provide a closed expression M_c of type $\overline{A}$, and transform every expression $x_1^{A_1}, \ldots, x_n^{A_n} \vdash M : B$ into an expression $x_1^{\overline{A_1}}, \ldots, x_n^{\overline{A_n}} \vdash \overline{M} : T\overline{B}$ as follows:

$$\overline{x} = \eta x \qquad \overline{\lambda x.M} = \eta(\lambda x.\overline{M}) \qquad \overline{MN} = \overline{M} * \lambda m.(\overline{N} * \lambda n.mn)$$

$$\overline{c^A} = \eta(M_c) \qquad \overline{\pi_i M} = \overline{M} * \lambda m.\eta(\pi_i m) \qquad \overline{(M,N)} = \overline{M} * \lambda m.(\overline{N} * \lambda n.\eta(m,n))$$

$$\overline{()} = \eta()$$

We call such a transform $\overline{(-)}$ a *monadic-style transform*. An interpretation of a λ_C-theory is called a *model* if it validates the theory's equations. This semantics is known to be sound and complete [7]. That is, the equations induced by an interpretation form a λ_C-theory (soundness), and when an equation holds in all models of a λ_C-theory, then it is a theorem (completeness).

3   Algebraic Effectoids

In this section, we shall define the notion of effectoid, introduce the varieties presented in Figure 1, show how they are related with each other, and apply them to some models (accumulation, powerset, global exceptions, partiality).

3.1   Algebraic Values

An *algebraic value* M is an expression that can be substituted for the occurrences of a formal parameter x in any procedure body N whenever M is passed as the actual parameter. Formally, an expression $\Gamma \vdash M : A$ is defined to be an algebraic value of a λ_C-theory $\mathcal{T}$ if every well-formed equation

$$\Gamma' \vdash \mathtt{let}\ x\ \mathtt{be}\ M\ \mathtt{in}\ N \equiv N[M/x] : B \tag{1}$$

is a theorem of $\mathcal{T}$ whenever Γ' contains Γ.

Every algebraic value M of function type is equivalent to a value, because $M \equiv \text{let } x \text{ be } M \text{ in } \lambda y.xy \equiv \lambda y.My$. At other types this can be false. For example, in λ_C-theories induced by computationally realistic interpretations, the algebraic value $x^{\text{int}} \vdash -x : \text{int}$ is not equivalent to a value. (This follows from a simple inductive argument, using only that the expression is not equivalent to a constant or a variable, and that its type is a base type different from 1.)

Importantly, if $\Gamma \vdash M : A$ and $\Gamma, x^A \vdash L : B$ are algebraic values, then so is $\Gamma \vdash \text{let } x \text{ be } M \text{ in } L : B$, because

$$\text{let } x \text{ be } (\text{let } y \text{ be } M \text{ in } L) \text{ in } N \equiv \text{let } y \text{ be } M \text{ in } \text{let } x \text{ be } L \text{ in } N$$
$$\equiv \text{let } y \text{ be } M \text{ in } N[L/x] \equiv N[L[M/y]/x] \equiv N[\text{let } y \text{ be } M \text{ in } L/x]$$

Definition 1. *An* effectoid *in a λ_C-theory is a set of expressions $\Gamma \vdash M : A$ which contains all algebraic values, and is closed under weakening, permutation, equality, and the let-construct.*

Evidently, effectoids are closed under arbitrary intersection, so they form a complete lattice, with the algebraic values as the smallest element.

Lemma 1. *An expression $\Gamma \vdash M : A$ is an algebraic value if and only if*

$$\Gamma \vdash \text{let } x \text{ be } M \text{ in } \lambda().x \equiv \lambda().M : 1 \to A \qquad (2)$$

To see the right-to-left implication, assume Equation 2, and consider

$$\text{let } x \text{ be } M \text{ in } N \equiv \text{let } y \text{ be } (\text{let } x \text{ be } M \text{ in } \lambda().x) \text{ in } N[y()/x]$$
$$\equiv \text{let } y \text{ be } \lambda().M \text{ in } N[y()/x] \equiv N[M/x]$$

Remark 2. Being an algebraic value is not well defined for expressions without environment. For example, for every $\Gamma \vdash M : A$, the weakened version $\Gamma, x^0 \vdash M : A$ is an algebraic value if $\overline{0}$ denotes the initial object. The same applies to all algebraic effectoids in this article.

3.2   Centralisers and Central Expressions

Just as we can state what it means for two group elements to commute, we can define a notion of commuting expressions for any λ_C-theory: expressions $\Gamma \vdash M : A$ and $\Delta \vdash N : B$ where Γ and Δ are disjoint are said to commute if the equation below is a theorem

$$\Gamma, \Delta \vdash \text{let } x \text{ be } M \text{ in } \text{let } y \text{ be } N \text{ in } (x, y)$$
$$\equiv \text{let } y \text{ be } N \text{ in } \text{let } x \text{ be } M \text{ in } (x, y) : A \times B \qquad (3)$$

If Γ and Δ have variables in common, then $\Gamma \vdash M : A$ and $\Delta \vdash N : B$ are said to commute if $\Gamma' \vdash M' : A$ and $\Delta' \vdash N' : B$ commute, where the latter two expressions result from environment-renaming the former such that Γ' and Δ' are disjoint. (Obviously, this definition does not depend on the choice of the renaming.)

Equation 3 holds if and only if for all expressions environments Γ' containing Γ and Δ, every well-formed equation of the form

$$\Gamma' \vdash \mathtt{let}\, x \,\mathtt{be}\, M \,\mathtt{in}\, \mathtt{let}\, y \,\mathtt{be}\, N \,\mathtt{in}\, L \equiv \mathtt{let}\, y \,\mathtt{be}\, N \,\mathtt{in}\, \mathtt{let}\, x \,\mathtt{be}\, M \,\mathtt{in}\, L : C \quad (4)$$

is a theorem. The right-to-left implication is trivial, and the left-to-right implication follows immediately from applying $\lambda(x, y).L$ to both sides of Equation 3.

In group theory, the *centraliser* $\mathrm{Cen}(S)$ of a set S of group elements is defined to be the set of group elements that commute with every element of S. We define the centraliser of a set S of λ_C-expressions in exactly the same way. Just as group-theoretic centralisers form a subgroup, centralisers in λ_C-theories form an effectoid. (The closure under $\mathtt{let}$ follows from the associativity of $\mathtt{let}$ and Equation 4.)

In analogy to group theory, we define the *centre* of a λ_C-theory to be the centraliser of the set of all expressions. (This notion of centre for computational models was first introduced, categorically and without defining centralisers, in [10], and used in [12,3,11,4,5].)

Example 1. The following model links centralisers in λ_C-theories with centralisers from classical algebra: for a monoid $(\mathcal{M}, \cdot, 1)$, consider the *accumulation monad* on **Set**:

$$TA = A \times \mathcal{M} \qquad \eta = \lambda x.(x, 1) \qquad (x, m) * f^{A \to B \times M} = (f_1 x, m \cdot f_2 x)$$

where $f_1 : A \to B$ and $f_2 : A \to \mathcal{M}$ are the evident components of f. Let $\mathcal{T}_{\mathcal{M}}$ be the λ_C-theory whose base types are sets, whose constants are of the form $f : A \to B$ where f is a function from A to TB, and whose equations are induced by the interpretation given by $\overline{A} = A$ and $\overline{f} = f$. Then two expressions $x^{A'} \vdash M : A$ and $y^{B'} \vdash N : B$ of $\mathcal{T}_{\mathcal{M}}$ commute if and only if $(\overline{M})_2 x$ and $(\overline{N})_2 y$ commute in $\mathcal{M}$ for all $x \in \overline{A'}$ and $y \in B'$.

3.3   Stabilisers and Discardable Expressions

For a group G acting on a set X, the stabiliser (a.k.a. isotropic group) $\mathrm{Stab}(x)$ of an element $x \in X$ is the set of group elements g that stabilise x—that is, for which $g(x) = x$. In particular, for the operation $g(h) = g \circ h$ of G on itself, the stabiliser of g is the set of all h such that $g \circ h = h$. In a λ_C-theory, an expression $\Gamma \vdash M : A$ is defined to stabilise an expression $\Delta \vdash N : B$ (with Δ disjoint from Γ) if the equation

$$\Gamma, \Delta \vdash M; N \equiv N : B \quad (5)$$

is a theorem where $M; N$ stands for $\mathtt{let}\, x \,\mathtt{be}\, M \,\mathtt{in}\, N$ where x is fresh. As in the previous section, we use environment-renaming to extend the definition to the case where Γ and Δ overlap. Just as group-theoretic stabilisers are subgroups, stabilisers in λ_C-theories are effectoids.

Of particular interest are the expressions that stabilise the empty tuple $\vdash$ $() : 1$. Such expressions are called *discardable*. (The notion of discardability was introduced categorically in [12] and consequently used in [3,11,4,1]. The notion of stabiliser is a contribution of this article.)

Lemma 2. *If an expression stabilises a value V, then it stabilises every expression N. (In particular, the discardable expressions are the smallest stabiliser.)*

This follows immediately from applying $\lambda x.N$ to both sides of the equation $M; V \equiv V$.

In our accumulation-monad example $\mathcal{T}_{\mathcal{M}}$, $x^{A'} \vdash M : A$ stabilises $y^{B'} \vdash N : B$ if and only if $(\overline{M})_2 x$ stabilises $(\overline{N})_2 y$ for all $x \in \overline{A'}$ and $y \in \overline{B'}$. Therefore, $x^{A'} \vdash M : A$ is discardable in $\mathcal{T}_{\mathcal{M}}$ if and only if $(\overline{M})_2 x \equiv 1$ for every $x \in \overline{A'}$. This already implies that $x^{A'} \vdash M : A$ is an algebraic value.

Example 2. Writing PA for the powerset of A, the *powerset monad* is given by

$$TA = PA \qquad \eta = \lambda x.\{x\} \qquad X * f^{A \to PB} = \bigcup_{x \in X} fx$$

Define $\mathcal{T}_{Pow}$ to be the evident λ_C-theory induced by the powerset monad. Essentially, expressions of $\mathcal{T}_{Pow}$ denote relations. While the algebraic values of $\mathcal{T}_{Pow}$ are the expressions that denote total functions, the discardable expressions are those that denote total relations—that is, relations R such that $\forall x \exists y : xRy$. All expressions are central.

3.4   Copyable Expressions

One notion that has found some attention in the literature is that of *copyable* expressions [12,11,3,4]. An expression $\Gamma \vdash M : A$ of a λ_C-theory $\mathcal{T}$ is called copyable if

$$\Gamma \vdash \mathtt{let}\ x\ \mathtt{be}\ M\ \mathtt{in}\ (x, x) \equiv (M, M) : A \times A \tag{6}$$

In our accumulation-monad example, an expression $x^{A'} \vdash M : A$ is copyable if and only if $(\overline{M})_2 x$ is an idempotent in $\mathcal{M}$ for every $x \in \overline{A'}$. In our powerset example, an expression is copyable if and only if the denoted relation is a partial function.

Among all varieties in this article, the copyable expressions form the only one which is not an effectoid. For the copyable expressions of $\mathcal{T}_{\mathcal{M}}$ where closed under **let**, then the idempotents of $\mathcal{M}$ would be closed under composition. But there are obviously counterexamples—for example, let $\mathcal{M}$ be the monoid of endofunctions on a set with at least three elements.

3.5   Distributive Expressions

Next we introduce a notion which has not been studied in the literature so far. An expression $\Gamma \vdash M : A$ is said to *distribute* over an expression $\Delta, x^A \vdash N : B$ with Δ disjoint from Γ if

$$\Gamma, \Delta \vdash \texttt{let } x \texttt{ be } M \texttt{ in let } y \texttt{ be } N \texttt{ in } (x, y)$$
$$\equiv \texttt{let } y \texttt{ be } (\texttt{let } x \texttt{ be } M \texttt{ in } N) \texttt{ in let } x \texttt{ be } M \texttt{ in } (x, y) : A \times B \qquad (7)$$

Using environment-renaming, we extend this definition to the case where Γ and Δ overlap. An expression $\Gamma \vdash M : A$ is called *distributive* if it distributes over all $\Delta, x^A \vdash N : B$.

In our accumulation-monad example, an expression $x^{A'} \vdash M : A$ distributes over $y^{B'}, x^{A'} \vdash N : B$ if and only if for all $x \in \overline{A'}$ and $y \in \overline{B'}$

$$(\overline{M})_2 x \cdot (\overline{N})_2 (y, x) \equiv (\overline{M})_2 x \cdot (\overline{N})_2 (y, x) \cdot (\overline{M})_2 x$$

Lemma 3. *An expression $\Gamma \vdash M : A$ is distributive if and only if every well-formed equation*

$$\Gamma' \vdash \texttt{let } x \texttt{ be } M \texttt{ in } N \equiv \texttt{let } x \texttt{ be } M \texttt{ in } N[M/X] : B$$

holds whenever Γ' contains Γ and X is any set of free occurrences of x in N which are outside the scope of any λ-binder.

The distributive expressions form an effectoid in every λ_C-theory. To see the closure under the let-construct, let $\Gamma \vdash M_1 : A$ and $\Gamma, y^A \vdash M_2 : B$ be distributive, let X be a set of free occurrences of x in N, and consider

$\texttt{let } x \texttt{ be } (\texttt{let } y \texttt{ be } M_1 \texttt{ in } M_2) \texttt{ in } N$
$\equiv \texttt{let } y \texttt{ be } M_1 \texttt{ in let } x \texttt{ be } M_2 \texttt{ in } N$
$\equiv \texttt{let } y \texttt{ be } M_1 \texttt{ in let } x \texttt{ be } M_2 \texttt{ in } N[M_2/X]$ (Lemma 3)
$\equiv \texttt{let } y \texttt{ be } M_1 \texttt{ in let } x \texttt{ be } M_2 \texttt{ in } N[\texttt{let } y' \texttt{ be } y \texttt{ in } M_2[y'/y]/X]$
$\equiv \texttt{let } y \texttt{ be } M_1 \texttt{ in let } x \texttt{ be } M_2 \texttt{ in } N[\texttt{let } y' \texttt{ be } M_1 \texttt{ in } M_2[y'/y]/X]$ (Lemma 3)
$\equiv \texttt{let } x \texttt{ be } (\texttt{let } y \texttt{ be } M_1 \texttt{ in } M_2) \texttt{ in } N[\texttt{let } y \texttt{ be } M_1 \texttt{ in } M_2/X]$

Proposition 1. *An expression $\Gamma \vdash M : A$ is copyable if and only if it distributes over $x^A \vdash x : A$.*

Proposition 2. *Expressions that are central and copyable are distributive.*

To see this, suppose that M is central and copyable, and consider

$\texttt{let } x \texttt{ be } M \texttt{ in let } y \texttt{ be } N \texttt{ in } (x, y)$
$\equiv \texttt{let } (x, x') \texttt{ be } (\texttt{let } z \texttt{ be } M \texttt{ in } (z, z)) \texttt{ in let } y \texttt{ be } N \texttt{ in } (x', y)$
$\equiv \texttt{let } (x, x') \texttt{ be } (M, M) \texttt{ in let } y \texttt{ be } N \texttt{ in } (x', y) \qquad (M \text{ copyable})$
$\equiv \texttt{let } x \texttt{ be } M \texttt{ in let } x' \texttt{ be } M \texttt{ in let } y \texttt{ be } N \texttt{ in } (x', y)$
$\equiv \texttt{let } x \texttt{ be } M \texttt{ in let } y \texttt{ be } N \texttt{ in let } x' \texttt{ be } M \texttt{ in } (x', y) \qquad (M \text{ central})$
$\equiv \texttt{let } y \texttt{ be } (\texttt{let } x \texttt{ be } M \texttt{ in } N) \texttt{ in let } x \texttt{ be } M \texttt{ in } (x, y)$

Proposition 3. *Expressions that are distributive and discardable are central.*

To see this, suppose that M is distributive and discardable and $x \notin \mathrm{FV}(N)$, and consider

$\texttt{let } x \texttt{ be } M \texttt{ in let } y \texttt{ be } N \texttt{ in } (x, y)$
$\equiv \texttt{let } y \texttt{ be } (M; N) \texttt{ in let } x \texttt{ be } M \texttt{ in } (x, y) \qquad (M \text{ distributive})$
$\equiv \texttt{let } y \texttt{ be } N \texttt{ in let } x \texttt{ be } M \texttt{ in } (x, y) \qquad (\text{Lemma 2})$

3.6   Repeatable Expressions

In this section, we introduce a very useful effectoid which has no evident counterparts in classical algebra. An expression $\Gamma \vdash M : A$ of a λ_C-theory is called *repeatable* if every well-formed equation

$$\Gamma' \vdash \texttt{let } x \texttt{ be } M \texttt{ in } N \equiv \texttt{let } x \texttt{ be } M \texttt{ in } N[M/X] : B \qquad (8)$$

is a theorem whenever Γ' contains Γ and X is any set of free occurrences of x in N. Lemma 3 immediately implies the following result:

Proposition 4. *Every repeatable expression is distributive.*

However, the converse is far from true: In our accumulation-monad example $\mathcal{T}_\mathcal{M}$, the repeatable expressions turn out to coincide with the algebraic values—that is, expressions that produce the unit of the monoid $\mathcal{M}$.

The repeatable expressions form an effectoid in every λ_C-theory. (Proving the closure under the let-construct works like for distributivity.)

Proposition 5. *An expression $\Gamma \vdash M : A$ is repeatable if and only if*

$$\Gamma \vdash \texttt{let } x \texttt{ be } M \texttt{ in } (x, \lambda().x) \equiv (M, \lambda().M) : A \times (1 \rightarrow A) \qquad (9)$$

To see the right-to-left implication, let S be the set of free occurrences of x in N, let $X \subseteq S$, and consider

$\texttt{let } x \texttt{ be } M \texttt{ in } N$
$\equiv \texttt{let } (y, f) \texttt{ be } (\texttt{let } x \texttt{ be } M \texttt{ in } (x, \lambda().x)) \texttt{ in } N[f()/X, y/S - X]$
$\equiv \texttt{let } (y, f) \texttt{ be } (M, \lambda().M) \texttt{ in } N[f()/X, y/S - X] \qquad (\text{Equation 9})$
$\equiv \texttt{let } x \texttt{ be } M \texttt{ in } N[M/X]$

Proposition 6. *An expression is an algebraic value if and only if it is discardable and repeatable.*

The left-to-right implication is trivial. For the other implication, suppose that M is discardable and repeatable, and consider

$$\text{let } x \text{ be } M \text{ in } N \equiv M; (N[M/x]) \qquad (M \text{ repeatable})$$
$$\equiv N[M/x] \qquad \text{(Lemma 2)}$$

Propositions 4 and 6 finish our validation of Figure 1. In our relations example, the repeatable expressions turn out to be the (expressions denoting) partial functions—that is, they coincide with the copyable expressions. The only non-empty areas in Figure 1 are area 4 (partial functions that are not total), area 6 (total relations that are not functions), algebraic values (total functions), and area 5 (relations that fit into none of the other categories). By contrast, in our accumulation-monad example $\mathcal{T}_\mathcal{M}$, we only have areas 1, 2, 5, 10, and the algebraic values. In fact, for each of those areas, there is a monoid $\mathcal{M}$ such for which $\mathcal{T}_\mathcal{M}$ has an inhabitant of the area. (The proof is left as a challenge to the reader.)

Repeatability and the lifting equation. In [1], *equational lifting monads* are defined as commutative monads that satisfy the *lifting equation*

$$T\langle \eta_A, \ id_A \rangle = t_{TA,A} \circ \langle id_{TA}, \ id_{TA} \rangle \qquad (10)$$

It is proved that a large class of models of partial computation, *dominical lifting monads*, are equational lifting monads[2]. Also, it is easy to check that *exceptions monads* (i.e. the well-known monads of the form $TA = A + E$) satisfy the lifting equation. (But in contrast to equational lifting monads, they are not generally commutative.) Due to this scope of the lifting equation, the following proposition is most useful:

Proposition 7. *Let $\mathcal{T}$ be a λ_C-theory induced by an interpretation $\overline{(-)}$ in a λ_C-model with monad T. If the λ_C-model satisfies the lifting equation, then every expression of $\mathcal{T}$ is repeatable. If $\overline{(-)}$ is full on types, the converse holds.*

Proof. In the metalanguage, the lifting equation is represented by

$$y^{TA} \vdash y * \lambda x.\eta(\eta x, x) \equiv y * \lambda x.\eta(y, x) : T(TA \times A) \qquad (11)$$

This implies, for all M,

$$\overline{M} * \lambda x.\eta(x, \eta x) \equiv \overline{M} * \lambda x.\eta(x, \overline{M}) \qquad (12)$$

which is Equation 9 sent through $\overline{(-)}$. So the lifting equation implies that every expression of $\mathcal{T}$ is repeatable. For the converse, suppose that $\overline{(-)}$ is full on objects, and that every expression of $\mathcal{T}$ is repeatable. Letting $M = f()$ for some variable $f : 1 \to A'$ with $\overline{A'} = A$, we have $\overline{M} \equiv f()$. Using this $\overline{M}$ in Equation 12 and substituting $\lambda().x$ for f implies Equation 11. □

---

[2] In fact, the point of [1] is to prove a more interesting statement in the opposite direction, which states that every equational lifting monad can in a certain sense be fully embedded into a dominical one.

4   Effectoids for Continuations

An analysis of algebraic values[3], centrality, copyability, and discardability for
continuations was undertaken by Hayo Thielecke [12]. The novelty in this section
is the analysis of distributivity and repeatability, as well as the consideration of
global state.

4.1   Continuations per Se

A *continuations* monad for response type R (for which exponentials of the form
$A \to R$ must exist) is given by the data below:

$$TA = (A \to R) \to R \qquad \eta = \lambda x.\lambda k.kx \qquad M * N = \lambda k.M(\lambda m.Nmk)$$

Instantiating the monadic-style transform with these data yields the "Plotkin
CPS-transform". This situation allows the definition of a unary type constructor
and operators for control flow manipulation:

$$A \text{ cont} \qquad \text{callcc} : (A \text{ cont} \to A) \to A \quad \text{throw} : A \text{ cont} \to A \to B$$
$$\overline{A \text{ cont}} = \overline{A} \to R \quad \overline{\text{callcc}} = \eta(\lambda f.\lambda k.f\,k\,k) \qquad \overline{\text{throw}} = \eta(\lambda l.\eta(\lambda x.\lambda k.l\,x))$$

(These operators are available in SML of New Jersey via the "SMLofNj.Cont"
module[4]). Before we prove the main results of this section (Propositions 8 and 9),
we gather some facts. We shall use the equation

$$\text{callcc}(\lambda k.\text{throw}\,k\,M) \equiv M : A \tag{13}$$

which can easily be checked with the CPS transform. Also, we define

$$\text{force} = \lambda x.\text{callcc}(\text{throw}\,x) : A \text{ cont cont} \to A$$
$$[M] = \text{callcc}(\lambda k.\text{throw}(\text{force}\,k)M) : A \text{ cont cont}$$

(where M is any expression of type A). We have $\overline{\text{force}\,h} \equiv \lambda k.hk$ in the case
where h is a variable, and $\overline{[M]} \equiv \lambda k.k\,\overline{M}$. With these CPS-transforms we can
easily check that $\text{force}[M] \equiv M$ and $[\text{force}\,h] \equiv h$. These two equations together and the fact that $[M]$ is an algebraic value imply immediately that the
following two maps are mutually inverse:

$$\varphi = \lambda h.\lambda().\text{force}\,h : A \text{ cont cont} \to (1 \to A)$$
$$\psi = \lambda f.[f()] : (1 \to A) \to A \text{ cont cont}$$

The following result is due to Hayo Thielecke (Remark 4.4.2 in [12]) and has
recently been used and restated several times (e.g. in [11] and [5]).

---

[3] under the name of "thunkable morphisms"
[4] Of course, the real implementation is not a simple CPS transform.

Proposition 8. *In the λ_C-theory of a continuations monad, central expressions are algebraic values.*

Proof. This is true because an expression that commutes with jumps must be effect free. Formally, if M is a central expression of type A, then it commutes with expressions of the form $\zeta\, h$, where h is a variable, and ζ is defined as $\lambda h.\texttt{throw}(\texttt{force}\, h)$. We have

$$\zeta\, hN \equiv \texttt{throw}\, h[N] \tag{14}$$

because the CPS transforms of both sides are equal to $\lambda k.h\overline{N}$. Now consider

$$
\begin{aligned}
&\texttt{let}\, x\, \texttt{be}\, M\, \texttt{in}\, [x] \\
&\equiv \texttt{callcc}(\lambda h.\texttt{throw}\, h(\texttt{let}\, x\, \texttt{be}\, M\, \texttt{in}\, [x])) &&\text{(Equation 13)} \\
&\equiv \texttt{callcc}(\lambda h.\texttt{let}\, x\, \texttt{be}\, M\, \texttt{in}\, \texttt{throw}\, h[x]) &&\text{(throw}\, h\, \text{is an alg. value)} \\
&\equiv \texttt{callcc}(\lambda h.\texttt{let}\, x\, \texttt{be}\, M\, \texttt{in}\, \zeta\, h\, x) &&\text{(Equation 14)} \\
&\equiv \texttt{callcc}(\lambda h.\zeta\, hM) &&\text{(M is central)} \\
&\equiv \texttt{callcc}(\lambda h.\texttt{throw}\, h[M]) &&\text{(Equation 14)} \\
&\equiv [M] &&\text{(Equation 13)}
\end{aligned}
$$

Applying φ to both sides yields Equation 2. $\qquad\square$

Proposition 9. *In the λ_C-theory of a continuations monad, distributive expressions are repeatable.*

Proof. Let $\zeta' = \lambda x.\lambda h.\texttt{throw}(\texttt{callcc}(\lambda l.\texttt{throw}\, h(x,l)))$. For every distributive expression M, we have

$$\zeta'\, h(x,N) \equiv \texttt{throw}\, h(x,[N]) \tag{15}$$

because the CPS transforms of both sides are $\lambda k.h(x,\overline{N})$. Now consider

$$
\begin{aligned}
&(M,[M]) \\
&\equiv \texttt{callcc}(\lambda h.\texttt{throw}\, h(\texttt{let}\, x\, \texttt{be}\, M\, \texttt{in}\, (x,[M]))) &&\text{(Equation 13)} \\
&\equiv \texttt{callcc}(\lambda h.\texttt{let}\, x\, \texttt{be}\, M\, \texttt{in}\, \texttt{throw}\, h(x,[M])) &&\text{(throw}\, h\, \text{is an alg. value)} \\
&\equiv \texttt{callcc}(\lambda h.\texttt{let}\, x\, \texttt{be}\, M\, \texttt{in}\, \zeta'\, x\, h(x,M)) &&\text{(Equation 15)} \\
&\equiv \texttt{callcc}(\lambda h.\texttt{let}\, x\, \texttt{be}\, M\, \texttt{in}\, \zeta'\, x\, h(x,x)) &&\text{(Lemma 3)} \\
&\equiv \texttt{callcc}(\lambda h.\texttt{let}\, x\, \texttt{be}\, M\, \texttt{in}\, \texttt{throw}\, h(x,[x])) &&\text{(Equation 15)} \\
&\equiv \texttt{callcc}(\lambda h.\texttt{throw}\, h(\texttt{let}\, x\, \texttt{be}\, M\, \texttt{in}\, (x,[x]))) &&\text{(throw}\, h\, \text{is an alg. value)} \\
&\equiv \texttt{let}\, x\, \texttt{be}\, M\, \texttt{in}\, (x,[x]) &&\text{(Equation 13)}
\end{aligned}
$$

Applying $\lambda(x,k).(x,\varphi k)$ to both sides yields Equation 9. $\qquad\square$

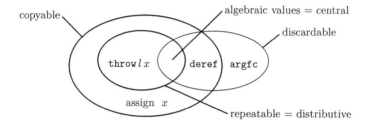

Fig. 3. Effectoids for continuations

Propositions 8 and 9 reduce Figure 1 to Figure 3. (The four expressions inhabiting the areas of Figure 3 will be discussed soon.)

To prove that an expression is inside an algebraic effectoid, we plug it into the effectoid's equations and check them with the CPS-transform. To prove that an expression is outside an algebraic effectoid, we plug it into one of the effectoid's equations and refute the equation using a *separator*. That is, letting M and N be the two sides of the equation, we find a context $C[-]$ such that $C[M]$ and $C[N]$ are programs of ground type that are reduced to different values[5]. While separators are computationally most convincing, they require a ground type with at least two elements (which we shall call **int**). So Figure 3 is to be interpreted as follows: whenever an expression is inside an area, it is in the corresponding effectoid for every continuations monad (or in the case of **assign** and **deref**, for every continuations monad with the required extra structure, which is introduced in the next section). Whenever an expression is outside an area, then it is outside the corresponding effectoid, provided that the model allows a realistic range of observations. (This includes all models for which there are at least two different expressions of type $\overline{\text{int}}$ and there exists a mono from $\overline{\text{int}}$ into R.)

That $M = \mathbf{throw}\, l\, x$ (where l and x are variables) is repeatable follows immediately from plugging $\overline{M} = \lambda k.l\, x$ into Equation 12. To see that $\mathbf{throw}\, l\, x$ is not discardable, it suffices to prove that $\mathbf{throw}\, l\, 42$ is not discardable. This can be checked by using the separator $C[-] = \mathbf{callcc}(\lambda l.\mathbf{let}\, x\, \mathbf{be}\, -\, \mathbf{in}\, 0)$ and observing that $C[\mathbf{let}\, y\, \mathbf{be}\, \mathbf{throw}\, l\, 42\, \mathbf{in}\, ()]$ evaluates to 42 whereas $C[()]$ evaluates to 0.

The expression **argfc** ("argument of first call"), and the following explanation why it is discardable but not copyable, are taken from [13]. We define

$$\mathbf{argfc} = \mathbf{callcc}(\lambda k.\lambda x.\mathbf{throw}\, k(\lambda y.x)) : A \to A$$

Roughly speaking, when **argfc** is called with an argument x, it turns into the constant function returning x. That **argfc** is discardable is easily checked by sending the equation $\mathbf{let}\, f\, \mathbf{be}\, \mathbf{argfc}\, \mathbf{in}\, () \equiv ()$ through the CPS transform. To see that **argfc** is not copyable, let $M_1 = \mathbf{let}\, f\, \mathbf{be}\, \mathbf{argfc}\, \mathbf{in}\, (f, f)$ and

---

[5] A separator is more than a distinguisher, because a distinguisher does not require both sides to terminate.

$M_2 = (\texttt{argfc}, \texttt{argfc})$. Then $C[-] = \texttt{let } (f_1, f_2) \texttt{ be } - \texttt{ in } (f_1 1; f_2 2)$ is a separator, because $C[M_1]$ evaluates to 1, whereas $C[M_2]$ evaluates to 2. Intuitively, during the evaluation of $C[M_1]$, evaluating $f_1 1$ causes backtracking to the binding of f, rebinding f (and therefore f_1 and f_2) to the constant function that returns 1. By contrast, during the evaluation of $C[M_2]$, evaluating $f_1 1$ causes backtracking to the binding of f_1, rebinding f_1 to the constant function that returns 1, and f_2 to $\texttt{argfc}$. Next, the evaluation of $f_2 2$ causes backtracking to the binding of f_2, rebinding f_2 to the constant function that returns 2. For a formal, operational discussion of these separators, please see [13].

4.2   Adding Global State

Next, we shall add a global reference of type S to the λ_C-theory of a continuations monad $TA = R^{R^{(-)}}$. Formally, we apply the "side-effect" monad transformer $\langle T \mapsto (T(- \times S))^S \rangle$ to the continuations monad, resulting in a monad $T_S A = (R^{R^{A \times S}})^S$. Because $(R^{R^{A \times S}})^S$ is isomorphic to $(R^S)^{(R^S)^B}$, we still have a continuations monad, with response object R^S rather than R. This means that $\texttt{callcc}$ and $\texttt{throw}$ can still be implemented by the CPS-transform (with the former response type R replaced by $S \to R$). Moreover, we can define operators $\texttt{assign} : S \to 1$ and $\texttt{deref} : S$ as follows:

$$\overline{\texttt{assign}} = \eta(\lambda x^S.\lambda k^{1 \to S \to R}.\lambda s^S.k()x) \qquad \overline{\texttt{deref}} = \lambda k^{S \to S \to R}.\lambda s^S.kss$$

From this definition, we can see that $\texttt{assign } x$ forgets the state s and replaces it by x, and $\texttt{deref}$ returns the state (the first s in kss) and also passes s on unchanged (the second s in kss).

   Amazingly, these two operators for state provide exactly the witnesses that we need to complete Figure 3. In particular, they drive a wedge between copyability and distributivity. That $\texttt{assign } x$ is copyable and that $\texttt{deref}$ is copyable and discardable can be easily checked with the CPS transform. To see that $\texttt{deref}$ is not repeatable, consider $\texttt{let } C[-] = \texttt{assign } 0; \texttt{let } f \texttt{ be } - \texttt{ in } (\texttt{assign } 1; f())$ and observe that $C[\lambda().\texttt{deref}]$ evaluates to 1 whereas $C[\texttt{let } x \texttt{ be deref in } \lambda().x]$ evaluates to 0. To see that $\texttt{assign } x$ is not repeatable, consider $\texttt{let } C[-] = \texttt{let } f \texttt{ be } - \texttt{ in } (\texttt{assign } 0; f(); \texttt{deref})$ and observe that $C[\lambda().\texttt{assign } 1]$ evaluates to 1 whereas $C[\texttt{let } x \texttt{ be assign } 1 \texttt{ in } \lambda().x]$ evaluates to 0. Showing that $\texttt{assign } x$ is not discardable is trivial. This completes the discussion of Figure 3.

5   Conclusions

Comparison with traditional effects. The notion of effectoid is definable in the λ_C-calculus *without extra structure* (i.e. without operators like $\texttt{assign}$, $\texttt{raise}$, etc.). The same is true for the specific effectoids we introduced in this article. By contrast, traditional effects depend on extra structure. For example, an effect can be a set of exceptions that might be raised, or—in "side-effect analysis"—a set of actions of the form $\texttt{deref } \pi$, $\texttt{assign } \pi$, or $\texttt{new } \pi$, where π is a "program point" [9]. So our effectoids apply to a wider range of models than traditional effects.

At a first glance, our effectoids seem to be less expressive than some traditional effects (e.g. those that involve program points). However, centralisers and stabilisers may turn out to be very expressive in their own way, because they allow to specify a set of expressions to commute with or stabilise. (E.g. if n is a global variable that cannot be aliased, then Cen(deref n) should exclude exactly those expressions that can change n *and return*.)

The *notion* of effectoids (as opposed to the specific effectoids defined in this article) covers *some* traditional effects: for example, the set of expressions that only raise exceptions in a given set is obviously an effectoid.

Algebraic effectoids turn the traditional approach to effects upside down: in the traditional approach, we define concrete effects first, and may study their equational aspects later. For algebraic effectoids, we define equational properties first and may study later how they constrain concrete effects. Crucially, the equational characterisation allows to use an algebraic effectoid without knowing its concrete meaning.

Acknowledgements

Many thanks to Hayo Thielecke, Uday Reddy, and Brian Dunphy for discussions, and to Peter Selinger and Masahito Hasegawa for helpful comments.

References

1. Anna Bucalo, Carsten Führmann, and Alex Simpson. An equational notion of lifting monad. *Theoretical Computer Science*, to appear.
2. Andrzej Filinski. Recursion from iteration. *Lisp and Symbolic Computation,*, 7(1):11–38, 1994.
3. Carsten Führmann. Direct models of the computational lambda-calculus. In *Proceedings MFPS XV*, volume 20 of *Electronic Notes in Theoretical Computer Science*, New Orleans, 1999. Elsevier.
4. Carsten Führmann. *The structure of call-by-value*. PhD thesis, Division of Informatics, University of Edinburgh, 2000.
5. Masahito Hasegawa and Yoshihiko Kakutani. Axioms for recursion in call-by-value. *Higher-Order and Symbolic Computation*, To appear.
6. A. Kock. Strong functors and monoidal monads. *Archive der Mathematik*, 23:113–120, 1972.
7. E. Moggi. Computational lambda-calculus and monads. Technical Report ECS-LFCS-88-66, Edinburgh Univ., Dept. of Comp. Sci., 1988.
8. E. Moggi. Notions of computation and monads. *Information and Computation*, 93(1), 1991.
9. Flemming Nielson, Hanne Riis Nielson, and Chris Hankin. *Principles of Program Analysis*. Springer-Verlag, 1999.
10. John Power and Edmund Robinson. Premonoidal categories and notions of computation. *Mathematical Structures in Computer Science*, 7(5):453–468, October 1997.

11. Peter Selinger. Control categories and duality: on the categorical semantics of the lambda-mu calculus. *Mathematical Structures in Computer Science*, 11:207–260, 2001.
12. Hayo Thielecke. *Categorical Structure of Continuation Passing Style*. PhD thesis, University of Edinburgh, 1997.
13. Hayo Thielecke. Using a continuation twice and its implications for the expressive power of `call/cc`. *Higher-Order and Symbolic Computation*, 12(1):47–74, 1999.

A Characterization of Families of Graphs in Which Election Is Possible

(Extended Abstract)

Emmanuel Godard and Yves Métivier

LaBRI, Université Bordeaux I, ENSEIRB,
351 cours de la Libération
33405 Talence, France
{godard,metivier}@labri.fr

1 Introduction

The Model. We consider networks of processors with arbitrary topology. A network is represented as a connected, undirected graph where vertices denote processors and edges denote direct communication links. Labels (or states) are attached to vertices and edges. Labels are modified locally, that is, on a subgraph of fixed radius 1 of the given graph, according to certain rules depending on the subgraph only (*local computations*). The relabelling is performed until no more transformation is possible, *i.e.*, until a normal form is obtained.

The Problem. The election problem is one of the paradigms of the theory of distributed computing. Considering a network of processors the election problem is to arrive at a configuration where exactly one process is in the state *elected* and all other processes are in the state *non-elected* see [Tel00]. The elected vertex is used to make decisions, to centralize or to broadcast some information.

Known Results. Graphs where election is possible were already studied but the algorithms usually involved some particular knowledge. Solving the problem for different knowledge has been investigated for some particular cases including (see [Tel00] for details): - the network is known to be a tree - the network is known to be complete - the network is known to be a grid - the nodes have different identification numbers - the network is known to be a ring and has a known prime number of vertices.

The classical proof techniques used for showing the non-existence of election algorithm are based on coverings [Ang80], which is a notion known from algebraic topology [Mas91]. A graph G is a covering of a graph H if there is a surjective morphism from G to H which is locally bijective. The general idea is as follows. If G and H are two graphs such that G covers H and $G \neq H$, then every local computation on H induces a local computation on G and every label which appears in H appears at least twice in G. Thus using H it is always possible to build a computation in G such that the label *elected* appears twice. By this way it is proved that there is no election algorithm for G and H [Ang80].

A graph G is called covering-minimal if every covering from G to some H is a bijection. Mazurkiewicz has proved that, knowing the size of graphs, there exists

M. Nielsen and U. Engberg (Eds.): Fossacs 2002, LNCS 2303, pp. 159–171, 2002.

an election algorithm for the class of covering-minimal graphs [Maz97]. This distributed algorithm, applied to a graph of size n, assigns bijectively numbers of $[1..n]$ to vertices of G.

In [MMW97] the notion of quasi-covering has been introduced to study the problem of termination detection. A graph G is a quasi-covering of a graph H if G is locally a covering of H (locally means that there is a vertex v of G and a positive integer k such that the ball centered on v of radius k is a covering of a ball of H).

The Main Result. In this paper, using some techniques of [MT00] developed for the termination detection problem, we characterize which knowledge is necessary and sufficient to have an election algorithm, or equivalently, what is the general condition for a class of graphs to admit an election algorithm. More precisely we prove the following theorem (Theorem 15):

There is an election algorithm for a family $\mathcal{I}$ of graphs if and only if graphs of $\mathcal{I}$ are minimal for the covering relation and every graph G of $\mathcal{I}$ has quasi-coverings of bounded radius in $\mathcal{I}$.

Sufficient conditions given below are just special cases of criteria of Theorem 15.

We explain new parts in this theorem. It is well known (see above) that the existence of an election algorithm needs graphs minimal for the covering relation. Analogously to [MMW97], we prove in this paper that if a graph is minimal for the covering relation and admits quasi-coverings of arbitrary large size in the family there is no election algorithm. This part can be illustrated by the family of prime rings. Indeed, prime rings are minimal for the covering relation nevertheless there is no election algorithm for this family: without the knowledge of the size, a ring admits quasi-covering prime rings of arbitrary large size.

These two results prove one direction of Theorem 15. To prove the converse:

- we extend the Mazurkiewicz algorithm to labelled graphs;
- we prove that the Mazurkiewicz algorithm applied in a graph G enables the reconstruction, on each node of G, of a graph K such that G is a quasi-covering of K; and when the computation is terminated G is a covering of K;
- we use an extension of an algorithm by Szymanski, Shi and Prywes [SSP85] which enables the distributed detection of stable properties in a graph;
- we prove that the bounded size of quasi-coverings of a given graph enables to each node v to detect the termination of the Mazurkiewicz algorithm and finally each node can decide if it has obtained the maximum number among numbers computed by the Mazurkiewicz algorithm.

Related Works. Among models related to our model there are local computation systems as defined by Rosenstiehl et al. [FHR72], Angluin [Ang80], Yamashita and Kameda [KY96] and Boldi and Vigna [BV99]. In [FHR72] a synchronous model is considered, where vertices represent (identical) deterministic finite automata. The basic computation step is to compute the next state of each processor according to its state and the states of its neighbours. In [Ang80] an asynchronous model is considered. A basic computation step means that two adjacent vertices exchange their labels and then compute new ones. In [KY96] an asynchronous model is studied where a basic computation step means that a processor either changes its state and sends a message or it receives a message. In [BV99] networks are directed graphs coloured on their arcs; each processor changes its state depending on its previous state and on the states of its in-neighbours. Activation of processors may be synchronous, asynchronous or interleaved.

2   Graphs, Labelled Graphs and Coverings

We only consider finite, undirected and connected graphs without multiple edges and self-loops. If G is a graph, $V(G)$ denotes the set of vertices and $E(G)$ denotes the set of edges. Let v be a vertex, we denote by $B_G(v, k)$, or briefly $B(v, k)$, the centered ball of radius k with center v. The set of neighbours of a vertex v in G is denoted by $N_G(v)$.

A homomorphism between two graphs G and H is a mapping $\gamma \colon V(G) \to V(H)$ such that if $\{u, v\}$ is an edge of G then $\{\gamma(u), \gamma(v)\}$ is an edge of H. Since we deal only with graphs without self-loops, this implies that $\gamma(u) \neq \gamma(v)$ if $\{u, v\}$ is an edge of G. Note also that $\gamma(N_G(u)) \subseteq N_H(\gamma(u))$. We say that γ is an isomorphism if γ is bijective and γ^{-1} is also a homomorphism. By $G \simeq G'$ we mean that G and G' are isomorphic. A class of graphs will be any class of graphs in the set-theoretical sense containing all graphs isomorphic to some of its members. The class of all graphs will be denoted $\mathcal{G}$.

Throughout the paper we will consider only connected graphs where vertices and edges are labelled with labels from a possibly infinite alphabet L. A graph labelled over L will be denoted by (G, λ), where G is a graph and $\lambda \colon V(G) \cup E(G) \to L$ is the labelling function The graph G is called the underlying graph and the mapping λ is a labelling of G. The class of labelled graphs over some fixed alphabet L will be denoted by $\mathcal{G}_L$.

Let (G, λ) and (G', λ') be two labelled graphs. Then (G, λ) is a subgraph of (G', λ'), denoted by $(G, \lambda) \subseteq (G', \lambda')$, if G is a subgraph of G' and λ is the restriction of the labelling λ' to $V(G) \cup E(G)$. A mapping φ is a homomorphism from (G, λ) to (G', λ') if φ is a graph homomorphism from G to G' which preserves the labelling, i.e. such that $\lambda'(\varphi(x)) = \lambda(x)$ holds for every $v \in V(G)$ and if $\{u, v\}$ is an edge of G then $\lambda(\{u, v\}) = \lambda(\{\varphi(u), \varphi(v)\})$. A labelled graph will be designed by a bold letter like $\mathbf{G}$, $\mathbf{H}$ etc ... If $\mathbf{G}$ is a labelled graph, G denotes the underlying graph. An *occurrence* of (G, λ) in (G', λ') is an isomorphism φ between (G, λ) and a subgraph (H, η) of (G', λ'). We say that a graph G is a *covering* of a graph H if there exists a surjective homomorphism γ from G onto H such that for every vertex v of $V(G)$ the restriction of γ to $B_G(v, 1)$ is a bijection onto $B_H(\gamma(v), 1)$. The covering is proper if G and H are not isomorphic. It is called connected if G (and thus also H) is connected. We extend the notion of covering to labelled graphs in an obvious way. The labelled graph (H, λ') is *covered* by (G, λ) via γ, if γ is a homomorphism from (G, λ) to (H, λ') whose restriction to $B_G(v, 1)$ is an isomorphism from $(B_G(v, 1), \lambda)$ to $(B_H(\gamma(v), 1), \lambda')$.

A graph G is called *covering-minimal* if every covering from G to some H is a bijection. Graphs with prime size (or with prime number of edges), trees, labelled graphs with a distinguished vertex, graphs with nodes having different identification numbers are examples of covering-minimal graphs.

Let H be a connected graph and let G be a covering of H via γ. Then there exists an integer q such that, for every $v \in V(H)$, we have $\mathrm{card}(\gamma^{-1}(v)) = q$. The integer q is called the number of *sheets* of the covering.

3   Local Computations in Graphs

Graph relabelling systems and more generally local computations satisfy the following constraints which seem to be natural when describing distributed computations with a decentralized control:

$(C1)$ they do not change the underlying graph but only the labelling of its components (edges and/or vertices), the final labelling being the result of the computation,

$(C2)$ they are *local*, that is, each relabelling step changes only a connected subgraph of a fixed size in the underlying graph,

$(C3)$ they are *locally generated*, that is, the application condition of the relabelling only depends on the *local context* of the relabelled subgraph.

3.1   Local Computations

Local computations as considered here can be described in the following general framework. Let $\mathcal{G}_L$ be the class of L-labelled graphs and let $\mathcal{R} \subseteq \mathcal{G}_L \times \mathcal{G}_L$ be a binary relation on $\mathcal{G}_L$. Then $\mathcal{R}$ will denote a graph rewriting relation. We assume that $\mathcal{R}$ is closed by isomorphism, i.e., whenever $\mathbf{G}\mathcal{R}\mathbf{G}'$ if $\mathbf{H} \simeq \mathbf{G}$ then $\mathbf{H}\mathcal{R}\mathbf{H}'$ for some labelled graph $\mathbf{H}' \simeq \mathbf{G}'$. In the remainder of this paper $\mathcal{R}^*$ stands for the reflexive and transitive closure of $\mathcal{R}$. The labelled graph $\mathbf{G}$ is $\mathcal{R}-irreducible$ if there is no $\mathbf{G}'$ such that $\mathbf{G}\mathcal{R}\mathbf{G}'$. Let $\mathbf{G} \in \mathcal{G}_L$, then $\mathrm{Irred}_{\mathcal{R}}(\mathbf{G})$ denotes the set of $\mathcal{R}-$irreducible graphs (or just irreducible if $\mathcal{R}$ is fixed) which can be obtained from $\mathbf{G}$ using $\mathcal{R}$. The relation $\mathcal{R}$ is noetherian if there is no infinite relabelling chain $\mathbf{G}_1\mathcal{R}\mathbf{G}_2\mathcal{R}\ldots$

Definition 1. *Let* $\mathcal{R} \subseteq \mathcal{G}_L \times \mathcal{G}_L$ *be a graph rewriting relation. 1.* $\mathcal{R}$ *is a relabelling relation if whenever two labelled graphs are in relation then the underlying graphs are equal i.e.:* $\mathbf{G}\mathcal{R}\mathbf{H} \implies G = H.$ *2.* $\mathcal{R}$ *is local if only labels of a ball of radius 1 may be changed by* $\mathcal{R}$, *i.e.,* $(G, \lambda)\mathcal{R}(G, \lambda')$ *implies that there exists a vertex* $v \in V(G)$ *such that* $\lambda(x) = \lambda'(x)$ *for every* $x \notin V(B_G(v, 1)) \cup E(B_G(v, 1)).$

The next definition states that a local relabelling relation $\mathcal{R}$ is *locally generated* if its restriction on centered balls of radius 1 determines its computation on any graph.

Definition 2. *Let $\mathcal{R}$ be a local relabelling relation. Then $\mathcal{R}$ is locally generated if the following is satisfied: For any labelled graphs (G, λ), (G, λ'), (H, η), (H, η') and any vertices $v \in V(G)$, $w \in V(H)$ such that the balls $B_G(v, 1)$ and $B_H(w, 1)$ are isomorphic via $\varphi \colon V(B_G(v, 1)) \longrightarrow V(B_H(w, 1))$ and $\varphi(v) = w$, the following three conditions*

1. *$\lambda(x) = \eta(\varphi(x))$ and $\lambda'(x) = \eta'(\varphi(x))$ for all $x \in V(B_G(v, 1)) \cup E(B_G(v, 1))$*
2. *$\lambda(x) = \lambda'(x)$, for all $x \notin V(B_G(v, 1)) \cup E(B_G(v, 1))$*
3. *$\eta(x) = \eta'(x)$, for all $x \notin V(B_H(w, 1)) \cup E(B_H(w, 1))$*

imply that $(G, \lambda)\mathcal{R}(G, \lambda')$ if and only if $(H, \eta)\mathcal{R}(H, \eta')$.

3.2   Local Computations and Coverings

The fundamental lemma which connects coverings and locally generated relabelling relations states that whenever **G** is a covering of **H**, every local computation in **H** can be lifted to a local computation in **G** which is compatible with the covering relation. This is expressed in the following diagram:

$$
\begin{array}{ccc}
\mathbf{G} & \xrightarrow{\;R^*\;} & \mathbf{G}' \\
\downarrow{\scriptstyle\text{covering}} & & \downarrow{\scriptstyle\text{covering}} \\
\mathbf{H} & \xrightarrow{\;R^*\;} & \mathbf{H}'
\end{array}
$$

Lemma 3 (Lifting Lemma). *Let $\mathcal{R}$ be a locally generated relabelling relation and let **G** be a covering of **H** via γ. Moreover, let $\mathbf{H}R^*\mathbf{H}'$. Then there exists **G**' such that $\mathbf{G}R^*\mathbf{G}'$ and **G**' is a covering of **H**'.*

3.3   Local Computations and Quasi-coverings

Definition 4. *Let $\mathbf{G}, \mathbf{H}$ be two labelled graphs and let γ be a partial function on $V(G)$ that assigns to each element of a subset of $V(G)$ exactly one element of $V(H)$. Then **G** is a quasi-covering of **H** via γ if there exists a finite or infinite covering $\mathbf{G}_0$ of **H** via δ, vertices $z_0 \in V(G_0)$, $z \in V(G)$, and an integer $r > 0$ such that:*

1. *$B_{\mathbf{G}}(z, r)$ is isomorphic via φ to $B_{\mathbf{G}_0}(z_0, r)$,*
2. *the domain of definition of γ contains $B_G(z, r)$, and*
3. *$\gamma = \delta \circ \varphi$ when restricted to $V(B_G(z, r))$.*

The integer r is called the radius of the quasi-covering, $\mathrm{card}(V(B_G(z, r)))$ is called the size of the quasi-covering, and z the center. The graph $\mathbf{G}_0$ is the associated covering of the quasi-covering.

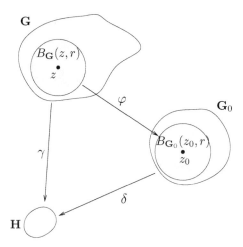

Fig. 1. **G** is a quasi-covering of **H** of radius r

The idea behind quasi-coverings is to enable the simulation of local computations on a given graph in a restricted area of a larger graph, such that the simulation can lead to false conclusions. The restricted area where we can perform the simulation will shrink while the number of simulated steps increases. They have been introduced to study the problem of the detection of the termination [MMW97]. The following lemma makes precise the shrinking of the radius when one step of simulation is performed :

Lemma 5 (Quasi-Lifting Lemma). *Let $\mathcal{R}$ be a locally generated relabelling relation and let **G** be a quasi-covering of **H** of radius r via γ. Moreover, let* **H**$\mathcal{R}$**H**$'$. *Then there exists* **G**$'$ *such that* **G**$\mathcal{R}^*$**G**$'$ *and* **G**$'$ *is a quasi-covering of radius $r - 2$ of* **H**$'$.

Definition 6. *We define the number of sheets q of a quasi-covering to be the minimal cardinality of the sets of preimages of vertices of **H** which are in the ball:* $q = \min_{v \in V(H)} |\{w \in \delta^{-1}(v)| B_\mathbf{G}(w, 1) \subset B_\mathbf{G}(z, r)\}|$.

Using the notation of the definition of a quasi-covering, we say that a quasi-covering is *strict* if $B_\mathbf{G}(z, r - 1)$ is not equal to G. Note that any non-strict quasi-covering is a covering. We have:

Lemma 7. *Let **G** be a strict quasi-covering of **H** of radius r via γ. Then, for any $q \in \mathbb{N}$, if $r \geq q|V(H)|$ then γ has at least q sheets.*

4 Two Fundamental Algorithms

4.1 The Mazurkiewicz Enumeration Algorithm

A distributed enumeration algorithm on a graph **G** is a distributed algorithm such that the result of any computation is a labelling of the vertices that is a bijection from $V(G)$ to $\{1, 2, \ldots, |V(G)|\}$. In particular, an enumeration of the vertices where vertices know whether the algorithm has terminated solves the election problem. In [Maz97] Mazurkiewicz presents a distributed enumeration algorithm for the class of graphs minimal for the covering relation. In [Maz97], the computation model consists exactly in relabelling balls of radius 1. The Mazurkiewicz algorithm will be denoted $\mathcal{M}$. In the following we give a description of the Mazurkiewicz algorithm including its extension to labelled graphs.

Description. We first give a general description of the algorithm $\mathcal{M}$ applied to the graph $\mathbf{G}$. Let $\mathbf{G} = (G, \lambda)$, let v_0 be a vertex of G, let $\{v_1, ..., v_d\}$ be the set of neighbours of v_0.

The label of the vertex v_0 used by $\mathcal{M}$ is the couple $(\lambda(v_0), c(v_0))$ where $c(v_0)$ is a triple $(n(v_0), N(v_0), M(v_0))$ representing the following information during the computation(formal definitions are given below) :

- $n(v_0) \in \mathbb{N}$ is the number of the vertex v_0 computed by the algorithm
- $N(v_0) \in \mathcal{N}$ is the local view of v_0, it is the set of triples defined by :

$$\{(n(v_i), \lambda(v_i), \lambda(\{v_0, v_i\}))|1 \leq i \leq d\}$$

- $M(v_0) \subset \mathbb{N} \times L \times \mathcal{N}$ is the mailbox of v_0 and contains all the information received by v_0 at this step of the computation.

Every vertex v attempts to get its own number $n(v)$, which shall be an integer between 1 and $|V(G)|$. A vertex chooses a number and broadcasts it together with its label and its labelled neighbourhood all over the network. If a vertex u discovers the existence of another vertex v with the same number, then it compares its label and its *local view*, i.e., its number-labelled ball, with the local view of its rival v. If the label of v or the local view of v is "stronger", then u chooses another number. Each new number, with its local view, is broadcasted again over the network. At the end of the computation it is not guaranteed that every node has a unique number, unless the graph is covering-minimal. However, all nodes with the same number will have the same label and the same *local view*.

The crucial property of the algorithm is based on a total order on local views such that the local view of any vertex cannot decrease during the computation. We assume that the set of labels L is equipped with a total order denoted $>$. Let v_0 be a vertex and let $\{v_1, ..., v_d\}$ the neighbours of v_0 we assume that: $n(v_1) \geq n(v_2) \geq ... \geq n(v_d)$, if $n(v_i) = n(v_{i+1})$ then $\lambda(v_i) \geq \lambda(v_{i+1})$, if $n(v_i) = n(v_{i+1})$ and $\lambda(v_i) = \lambda(v_{i+1})$ then $\lambda(\{v_0, v_i\}) \geq \lambda(\{v_0, v_{i+1}\})$. Then to $N(v)$, the local view, we associate the d-tuple $((n(v_1), \lambda(v_1), \lambda(\{v_0, v_1\})), \ldots, (n(v_d), \lambda(v_d), \lambda(\{v_0, v_d\})))$.

Let $\mathcal{N}_>$ be the set of such ordered tuples. We define a total order, $\prec$, on $\mathcal{N}_>$ by comparing the numbers, then the vertex labels and finally the edge labels. Formally, let $((n_1, l_1, e_1), ..., (n_d, l_d, e_d))$ and $((n'_1, l'_1, e'_1), ..., (n'_{d'}, l'_{d'}, e'_{d'}))$ be two elements of $\mathcal{N}_>$ then

$$((n'_1, l'_1, e'_1), ..., (n'_{d'}, l'_{d'}, e'_{d'})) \prec ((n_1, l_1, e_1), ..., (n_d, l_d, e_d))$$

if one of the following holds

1. $n_1 = n'_1, ..., n_{i-1} = n'_{i-1}$ and $n'_i < n_i$ for some i or
2. $d' < d$ and $n_1 = n'_1, ..., n_{d'} = n'_{d'}$ or
3. $d = d'$, $n_1 = n'_1, ..., n_d = n'_d$ and $l_1 = l'_1, ..., l_{i-1} = l'_{i-1}$ and $l'_i <_L l_i$ for some i or
4. $d = d'$ and $n_1 = n'_1, ..., n_d = n'_d$ and $l_1 = l'_1, ..., l_d = l'_d$ and $e_1 = e'_1, ..., e_{i-1} = e'_{i-1}$ and $e'_i <_L e_i$ for some i.

The initial labelling of the vertex v_0 is $(\lambda(v_0), (0, \emptyset, \emptyset))$. The rules are described below for a given centered ball $B = B(v_0, 1)$ with center v_0. The vertices v of B have labels $(\lambda(v), (n(v), N(v), M(v))$. The labels obtained after applying a rule are $(\lambda(v), (n'(v), N'(v), M'(v)))$. To make the rules easier to be read, we omit labels that are left unchanged.

$\mathcal{M}$–1 : **Diffusion rule**
> *Precondition :*
> - $\exists v \in B(v_0, 1), M(v) \neq M(v_0)$
> *Relabelling :*
> - For all $v \in B(v_0, 1), M'(v) := \bigcup_{w \in B} M(w)$

$\mathcal{M}$–2 : **Renaming rule**
> *Precondition :*
> - $\forall v, M(v) = M(v_0)$
> - 1. $n(v_0) = 0$
>   or
>   2. $(n(v_0) > 0$ and $\exists (n(v_0), l, N) \in M(v_0))$
>   such that $((\lambda(v_0) < l)$ or
> $((\lambda(v_0) = l)$ and $(N(v_0) \prec N)))$
> *Relabelling :*
> - $n'(v_0) = 1 + \max\{n \in \mathbb{N} \mid (n, l', N) \in M(v_0)\}$
> - $\forall v \in B(v_0, 1), N'(v)$ is obtained from $N(u)$ by replacing the value of $n(v_0)$ by $n'(v_0)$.
> - $\forall v \in B(v_0, 1)$, the mailbox contents $M(v)$ changes to
> $M'(v) = M(v) \cup \bigcup_{w \in B} \{(n'(w), \lambda(w), N'(w))\}$.

Let $\mathbf{G}$ be a labelled graph, if v is a vertex of G, the label of v after the run ρ of the Mazurkiewicz algorithm is denoted $(\lambda(v), c_\rho(v))$ with $c_\rho(v) = (n_\rho(v), N_\rho(v), M_\rho(v))$ and (λ, c_ρ) denotes the final labelling.

Similar to [Maz97], for covering-minimal graphs the algorithm computes a one-to-one correspondance n_ρ between the set of vertices of G and the set of integers $\{1, ..., |V(G)|\}$.

We interpret the final labelling as a graph that each vertex could compute. For a mailbox M, we define for each integer n in $\{1, ..., |V(G)|\}$ the maximal mail box element of the form (n, l, N) :

$$F(M) = \{(n, l, N) \in M \mid \text{ there is no } (n, l', N') \in M \text{ verifying}$$

$$l' > l \text{ or } (l = l' \text{ and } N \prec N')\}.$$

For a given M, we define the graph $\mathbf{G_M}$ as the following graph:

$$V(G_M) = \{n \mid \exists N, l, (n, l, N) \in F(M)\}$$
$$E(G_M) = \{\{n, n'\} \mid (n, l, N) \in F(M), \text{ and } N = (..., (n', l', l''), ...)\}$$

We also define a labelling on G_M as follows, $\lambda_M(n) = l$, such that there exists N, $(n, l, N) \in F(M)$. Note that uniqueness of l comes from the definition of $F(M)$. Let ρ be a run of $\mathcal{M}$, then $(G_{M_\rho(u)}, \lambda_{M_\rho(u)})$ does not depend on u. We then define $\rho(\mathbf{G}) = (G_{M_\rho(u)}, \lambda_{M_\rho(u)})$. As $F(M_\rho(u))$ represents the final numbers and neighbourhoods, we have the following.

Proposition 8. *For a given execution ρ of the Mazurkiewicz algorithm, we have* $V(\rho(\mathbf{G})) = \{n_\rho(v) \mid v \in V(G)\}$ *and* $E(\rho(\mathbf{G})) = \{\{n_\rho(v), n_\rho(w)\} \mid \{v, w\} \in E(G)\}$.

The proposition means that $\rho(\mathbf{G})$ is the quotient graph of $\mathbf{G}$ by n_ρ. Before we emphasize the role of $\rho(\mathbf{G})$, note that $\rho(\mathbf{G})$ can be locally computed by every vertex, and that the graph depends only on the label M_ρ.

If $\mathbf{G} = (G, \lambda)$ is a labelled graph $\rho(\mathbf{G})$ denotes the labelled graph defined on $(V(G_\rho), E(G_\rho))$ by the labelling such that the label of $n_\rho(v)$ is $\lambda(v)$.

The next proposition states that we can see a run of $\mathcal{M}$ as computing a graph such that:

Proposition 9. *Let $\mathbf{G}$ be a labelled graph. For all runs ρ of $\mathcal{M}$, $\mathbf{G}$ is a covering of $\rho(\mathbf{G})$. For all $\mathbf{H}$ such that $\mathbf{G}$ is a covering of $\mathbf{H}$, there exists a run ρ such that $\mathbf{H} \simeq \rho(\mathbf{G})$ (fairness).*

4.2   An Algorithm to Detect Stable Properties

In this section we describe in our framework the algorithm by Szymanski, Shi and Prywes (the SSP algorithm for short) [SSP85]. We consider a distributed algorithm which terminates when all processes reach their local termination conditions. Each process is able to determine only its own termination condition. The SSP algorithm detects an instant in which the entire computation is achieved. Let G be a graph, to each node v is associated a predicate $P(v)$ and an integer $a(v)$. Initially $P(v)$ is false and $a(v)$ is equal to -1. Transformations of the value of $a(v)$ are defined by the following rules. Each local computation acts on the integer $a(v_0)$ associated to the vertex v_0; the new value of $a(v_0)$ depends on values associated to vertices of $B_G(v_0, 1)$. More precisely, let v_0 be a vertex and let $\{v_1, ..., v_d\}$ be the set of vertices adjacent to v_0. If $P(v_0) = false$ then $a(v_0) = -1$; if $P(v_0) = true$ then $a(v_0) = 1 + Min\{a(v_k) \mid 0 \le k \le d\}$. In [SSP85] the following assumption is considered: for each node v the value of $P(v)$ eventually becomes true and remains true for ever.

In this paper we use a variant of the SSP algorithm presented in [MT00]. For each node v the value of $P(v)$ eventually becomes true and either remains true for ever or becomes false and remains false for ever. Thus the predicate $P(v)$ may change twice: initially $P(v)$ is false and $a(v)$ is equal to -1, $P(v)$ may become true and then $a(v)$ is equal to 0, if $P(v)$ is true it may become false, in this case it remains false for ever and $a(v)$ is equal to -1. We denote this variant by VSSP algorithm. We will use the following notation. Let $(\mathbf{G}_i)_{0 \leq i}$ be a relabelling chain associated to the VSSP algorithm. We denote by $a_i(v)$ (resp. $P_i(v)$) the integer (resp. the boolean) associated to the vertex v of $\mathbf{G}_i$. The fundamental property is:

Proposition 10. *Let $(\mathbf{G}_i)_{0 \leq i}$ be a relabelling chain associated to the VSSP algorithm. Let $v \in V(G)$, $i > 0$ such that $a_i(v) > 0$. Let $p > 0$, we suppose that for some integer $j > i : a_j(v) = a_i(v) + p$. Let $k < Min(a_i(v), \frac{p}{2})$. Then : $\forall w \in B(v,k)$ $a_i(w) \geq 0$.*

5   The Mazurkiewicz Algorithm + the VSSP Algorithm = Reconstruction Algorithm with Local Agreement

Following [MT00], the main idea develloped in this section is to use the VSSP algorithm for computing the radius of stability of $\mathcal{M}$ in a relabelling chain at a given step and at a given vertex. In other words, any vertex will know until which distance all vertices agree with its topology reconstruction.

Let $\mathbf{G} = (G, \lambda)$ be a labelled graph, let $(\mathbf{G}_i)_{0 \leq i}$ be a relabelling chain associated to a run of the Mazurkiewicz algorithm on the graph $\mathbf{G}$. To the node v of $\mathbf{G}_i$ is associated the label $(\lambda(v), (n_i(v), N_i(v), M_i(v)))$. Using the interpretation of Subsection 4.2 by defining $F(M_i)$, this label enables in some cases the reconstruction of a graph.

We introduce on the node v of the graph $\mathbf{G}_i$ the predicate $p_{\mathbf{H}}(v)$, that will be true if label of v in $\mathbf{G}_i$ enables the reconstruction of $\mathbf{H} = \mathbf{G}_{M_i}(v)$ and $(n_i(v), \lambda(v), N_i(v)) \in F(M_i(v))$. The associated value $a_{\mathbf{H}}(v)$ is computed by the VSSP algorithm. We note $\mathcal{Q}$ the merging of the two algorithms.

First, we formalize the output of $\mathcal{Q}$. We note

$$\mathbf{H}(v) = \begin{cases} \mathbf{G}_{M_i(v)} \text{if it is defined and } (n_i(v), \lambda(v), N_i(v)) \in F(M_i(v)) \\ \perp \text{ otherwise.} \end{cases} \quad (1)$$

$$a(v) = \begin{cases} -1 \text{ if } \mathbf{H}(v) = \perp \\ a_{\mathbf{H}(v)}(v) \text{ otherwise.} \end{cases} \quad (2)$$

Note that, while $\mathbf{H}(v) = \perp$, the node knows that it is in a non final state. The output of $\mathcal{Q}$ is now, on each vertex v, $< \mathbf{H}(v), a(v) >$.

For a run of the Mazurkiewicz algorithm on $\mathbf{G}$, we note $(\mathbf{G}^{(i)})_{(0 \leq i)}$ the labelled graph obtained by adding on each node v of $\mathbf{G}$ the number $n_i(v)$ computed by the Mazurkiewicz algorithm at step i on the vertex v. The main property of the computations is now:

Proposition 11 (quasi-covering progression). *At all step j, for all vertex v, the output of $\mathcal{Q}$ on v is a couple $< \mathbf{H}, a >$ such that if $\mathbf{H} \neq \perp$, then there exists a previous step $i < j$, such that $\mathbf{G}^{(i)}$ is a quasi-covering of $\mathbf{H}$ of center v and of radius $\lfloor \frac{a}{3} \rfloor$.*

6   Main Result: A Characterization of Families of Graphs in Which Election Is Possible

6.1   Impossibility

Considering a labelled graph, we say that a given vertex v has been elected when the graph is in a global state such that exactly one vertex has the label *elected* and all other vertices have the label *non-elected*.

Let $\mathcal{I}$ be a class of connected labelled graphs. Let $\mathcal{R}$ be a locally generated relabelling relation, we say that $\mathcal{R}$ is an election algorithm for the class $\mathcal{I}$ if $\mathcal{R}$ is noetherian and for any graph $\mathbf{G}$ of $\mathcal{I}$ and for any normal form $\mathbf{G}'$ obtained from $\mathbf{G}$, $\mathbf{G}\mathcal{R}^*\mathbf{G}'$, there exists exactly one vertex with the label *elected* all other vertices have the label *non-elected*.

Angluin showed that no election algorithm exists for a family of graphs containing a graph H and a proper covering of H [Ang80]. In fact there is no election algorithm for a not covering-minimal labelled graph. Furthermore if we consider a class $\mathcal{I}$ of labelled graphs containing a graph and quasi-coverings of arbitrary large size there is no election algorithm for this family. More precisely:

Proposition 12. *Let $\mathbf{G}$ be a labelled graph which is not covering-minimal. Then there is no election algorithm for $\mathbf{G}$.*

Proposition 13 (Necessary condition). *Let $\mathcal{I}$ be a class of connected covering-minimal labelled graphs such that there is an algorithm of election for this class. Then there exists a computable function $\tau : \mathcal{I} \to \mathbb{N}$ such that for all graph $\mathbf{H}$ of $\mathcal{I}$, there is no quasi-covering of $\mathbf{H}$, distinct of $\mathbf{H}$, of radius greater than $\tau(\mathbf{H})$ in $\mathcal{I}$.*

Proof. Let $\mathcal{R}$ denote an algorithm of election on $\mathcal{I}$. For a graph $\mathbf{H} \in \mathcal{I}$, define $\tau(\mathbf{H}) = 2|V(\mathbf{H})| + 2n$ where n is the number of steps of an entire execution of $\mathcal{R}$ on $\mathbf{H}$. Then τ has the desired property.

We prove this by contradiction. Let $\mathbf{H} \in \mathcal{I}$. Let $\mathcal{C}$ be the relabelling chain of length n on $\mathbf{H}$ used for the definition of $\tau(\mathbf{H})$. $\mathcal{C} = (\mathbf{H} = \mathbf{H}_0, \mathbf{H}_1, ..., \mathbf{H}_n)$ such that $\mathbf{H}_n$ is a normal form. By hypothesis the label *elected* appears exactly once in $\mathbf{H}_n$.

Let $\mathbf{G}$ be a quasi-covering of $\mathbf{H}$ of radius $\tau(\mathbf{H})$, distinct of H. By iteration of Lem. 5, we get $\mathbf{G}'$ such that $\mathbf{G}\mathcal{R}^*\mathbf{G}'$ and $\mathbf{G}'$ is a quasi-covering of $\mathbf{H}_n$ of radius $\tau(H) - 2n = 2|V(H)|$. The graph $\mathbf{G}$ being covering minimal and distinct of $\mathbf{H}$, the quasi-covering $\mathbf{G}'$ of $\mathbf{H}_n$ is strict. Hence, by Lem. 7, the label *elected* appears at least twice in $\mathbf{G}'$. A contradiction.

6.2   Possibility

Let $\mathcal{R}$ denote a locally generated relabelling relation and let $\mathbf{G}$ denote a labelled graph. Let $\mathcal{I}$ be a class of labelled graphs, terminal configurations obtained from $\mathcal{I}$ are said to be locally characterized if there exists a set F of labels such that for any $\mathbf{G} \in \mathcal{I}$ and for any $\mathbf{G}'$, with $\mathbf{G}\mathcal{R}^*\mathbf{G}'$, $\mathbf{G}'$ is a terminal configuration if and only if there exists a vertex v of $\mathbf{G}'$ having its label in F. In this case termination is said to be explicit. First we have the following theorem :

Proposition 14 (Graph reconstruction). *Let $\mathcal{I}$ be a class of connected covering-minimal labelled graphs. Suppose that there exists a computable function $\tau : \mathcal{I} \to \mathbb{N}$ such that for all graphs $\mathbf{G}$ of $\mathcal{I}$, there is no quasi-covering of $\mathbf{G}$ of radius greater than $\tau(\mathbf{G})$ in $\mathcal{I}$, except $\mathbf{G}$. Then there exists a locally generated relabelling relation with explicit termination which computes for any graph $\mathbf{G}$ in $\mathcal{I}$ and for any vertex v in $V(G)$ the graph $\mathbf{G}$.*

Proof. We use $\mathcal{Q}$ with the termination condition on the output $\mathbf{H} \in \mathcal{I}$ and $a \geq 3\tau(\mathbf{H})$. Termination is a corollary of the fact that $\mathcal{M}$ will eventually terminate and then the counter a will increase indefinitely. When this termination condition is fulfilled, by Prop. 11, we have that there exists a previous step n such that $\mathbf{G}^{(n)}$ is a quasi-covering of radius $\tau(\mathbf{H}(v))$ of $\mathbf{H}(v)$ and by hypothesis on τ, we deduce that $\mathbf{G}^{(n)} = \mathbf{H}(v)$.

The knowledge of this reconstructed graph implies that each node knows if its number is the maximal or not among numbers of the graph. Finally, each node can decide if it is elected or not. The result of this subsection and of the previous are summarized in the the following theorem.

Theorem 15. *Let $\mathcal{I}$ be a class of connected labelled graphs. There exists an election algorithm for $\mathcal{I}$ if and only if graphs of $\mathcal{I}$ are minimal for the covering relation, and there exists a computable function $\tau : \mathcal{I} \to \mathbb{N}$ such that for all graph $\mathbf{G}$ of $\mathcal{I}$, there is no quasi-covering of $\mathbf{G}$ of radius greater than $\tau(\mathbf{G})$ in $\mathcal{I}$, except $\mathbf{G}$ itself.*

6.3   Applications

Known results appears now as simple corollaries of Th. 15, for possibility:

– [Maz97] Covering minimal networks where the size is known ;
– Trees, complete graphs, grids, networks with identities: those families contains no q-sheeted quasi-covering of a given graph for $q \geq 2$, hence the τ function can be twice the size of the graph, see Lem. 7.

We also get some new possiblity results, in particular for covering-minimal graphs with at least 1 and at most k distinguished vertices or for covering-minimal graphs where a bound of the size is known (it is new and cannot be directly derived from [Maz97]). On the impossibility side, it is a corollary of Th. 15 that there is no election algorithm for the family of covering-minimal tori (prime rings are a particular case).

We also notice that the complexity of the algorithm of Mazurkievicz, computed in [Godar], is often worse than the optimal known bounds. That lack of optimality is the counterpart of the universality of the algorithm.

References

Ang80.   D. Angluin. Local and global properties in networks of processors. In *Proceedings of the 12th Symposium on theory of computing*, pages 82–93, 1980.

BV99.   P. Boldi and S. Vigna. Computing anonymously with arbitrary knowledge.
           In *Proceedings of the 18th ACM Symposium on principles of distributed com-
           puting*, pages 181–188. ACM Press, 1999.
FHR72.   J.-R. Fiksel, A. Holliger, and P. Rosenstiehl. Intelligent graphs. In R. Read,
           editor, *Graph theory and computing*, pages 219–265. Academic Press (New
           York), 1972.
Godar.   E. Godard. A self-stabilizing enumeration algorithm. *Inform. Proc. Letters*,
           to appear.
KY96.   T. Kameda and M. Yamashita. Computing on anonymous networks: Part
           i - characterizing the solvable cases. *IEEE Transactions on parallel and
           distributed systems*, 7(1):69–89, 1996.
Mas91.   W. S. Massey. *A basic course in algebraic topology*. Springer-Verlag, 1991.
           Graduate texts in mathematics.
Maz97.   A. Mazurkiewicz. Distributed enumeration. *Inf. Processing Letters*, 61:233–
           239, 1997.
MMW97.   Y. Métivier, A. Muscholl, and P.-A. Wacrenier. About the local detection of
           termination of local computations in graphs. In *International Colloquium on
           structural information and communication complexity*, pages 188–200, 1997.
MT00.   Y. Métivier and G. Tel. Termination detection and universal graph re-
           construction. In *International Colloquium on structural information and
           communication complexity*, pages 237–251, 2000.
SSP85.   B. Szymanski, Y. Shy, and N. Prywes. Terminating iterative solutions of
           simultaneous equations in distributed message passing systems. In *Proceed-
           ings of the 4th Symposium on Principles of Distributed computing*, pages
           287–292, 1985.
Tel00.   G. Tel. *Introduction to distributed algorithms*. Cambridge University Press,
           2000.

Equivalence-Checking with One-Counter Automata: A Generic Method for Proving Lower Bounds*

Petr Jančar[1], Antonín Kučera[2], Faron Moller[3], and Zdeněk Sawa[1]

[1] Dept. of Computer Science, FEI, Technical University of Ostrava
17. listopadu 15, CZ-708 33 Ostrava, Czech Republic
{Petr.Jancar,Zdenek.Sawa}@vsb.cz
[2] Faculty of Informatics, Masaryk University
Botanická 68a, CZ-602 00 Brno, Czech Republic
tony@fi.muni.cz
[3] Dept. of Computer Science, University of Wales Swansea
Singleton Park, Swansea SA2 8PP, Wales
F.G.Moller@swansea.ac.uk

Abstract. We present a general method for proving **DP**-hardness of equivalence-checking problems on one-counter automata. For this we show a reduction of the SAT-UNSAT problem to the truth problem for a fragment of (Presburger) arithmetic. The fragment contains only special formulas with one free variable, and is particularly apt for transforming to simulation-like equivalences on one-counter automata. In this way we show that the membership problem for any relation subsuming bisimilarity and subsumed by simulation preorder is **DP**-hard (even) for one-counter *nets* (where the counter cannot be tested for zero). We also show **DP**-hardness for deciding simulation between one-counter automata and finite-state systems (in both directions).

1 Introduction

In concurrency theory, a *process* is typically defined to be a state in a *transition system*, which is a triple $\mathcal{T} = (S, \Sigma, \rightarrow)$ where S is a set of *states*, Σ is a set of *actions* and $\rightarrow \subseteq S \times \Sigma \times S$ is a *transition relation*. We write $s \xrightarrow{a} t$ instead of $(s, a, t) \in \rightarrow$, and we extend this notation in the natural way to elements of Σ^*. A state t is *reachable* from a state s, written $s \rightarrow^* t$, iff $s \xrightarrow{w} t$ for some $w \in \Sigma^*$.

In this paper, we consider such processes generated by *one-counter automata*, non-deterministic finite-state automata operating on a single counter variable which takes values from the set $\mathbb{N} = \{0, 1, 2, \ldots\}$. Formally this is a tuple $\mathcal{A} = (Q, \Sigma, \delta^=, \delta^>, q_0)$ where Q is a finite set of *control states*, Σ is a finite set of *actions*,

$$\delta^= : Q \times \Sigma \rightarrow \mathcal{P}(Q \times \{0, 1\}) \quad \text{and}$$
$$\delta^> : Q \times \Sigma \rightarrow \mathcal{P}(Q \times \{-1, 0, 1\})$$

are *transition functions* (where $\mathcal{P}(M)$ denotes the power-set of M), and $q_0 \in Q$ is a distinguished *initial* control state. $\delta^=$ represents the transitions which are enabled when

---

* This work was supported by the Grant Agency of the Czech Republic, Grant No. 201/00/0400.

M. Nielsen and U. Engberg (Eds.): Fossacs 2002, LNCS 2303, pp. 172–186, 2002.

the counter value is zero, and $\delta^>$ represents the transitions which are enabled when the counter value is positive. $\mathcal{A}$ is a *one-counter net* if and only if for all pairs $(q, a) \in Q \times \Sigma$ we have that $\delta^=(q, a) \subseteq \delta^>(q, a)$.

To the one-counter automaton $\mathcal{A}$ we associate the transition system $\mathcal{T}_{\mathcal{A}} = (S, \Sigma, \to)$, where $S = \{p(n) : p \in Q, n \in \mathbb{N}\}$ and $\to$ is defined as follows:

$$p(n) \overset{a}{\to} q(n + i) \quad \text{iff} \quad \begin{cases} n = 0, \text{ and } (q, i) \in \delta^=(p, a); \ or \\ n > 0, \text{ and } (q, i) \in \delta^>(p, a). \end{cases}$$

Note that any transition increments, decrements, or leaves unchanged the counter value; and a decrementing transition is only possible if the counter value is positive. Also observe that when $n > 0$ the transitions of $p(n)$ do not depend on the actual value of n. Finally note that a one-counter *net* can in a sense test if its counter is nonzero (that is, it can perform some transitions only on the proviso that its counter is nonzero), but it cannot test in any sense if its counter is zero. For ease of presentation, we understand *finite-state* systems (corresponding to transition systems with finitely many states) to be one-counter nets where $\delta^= = \delta^>$ and the counter is never changed. Thus, the parts of $\mathcal{T}_{\mathcal{A}}$ reachable from $p(i)$ and $p(j)$ are isomorphic and finite for all $p \in Q$ and $i, j \in \mathbb{N}$.

Remark. Let us mention that the class of transition systems generated by one-counter nets is the same (up to isomorphism) as that generated by the class of labelled Petri nets with (at most) one unbounded place. The class of transition systems generated by one-counter automata is the same (up to isomorphism) as that generated by the class of realtime pushdown automata (i.e. pushdown automata without ε-transitions) with a single stack symbol (apart from a special bottom-of-stack marker).

The *equivalence-checking* approach to the formal verification of concurrent systems is based on the following scheme: the specification S (i.e., the intended behaviour) and the actual implementation I of a system are defined as states in transition systems, and then it is shown that S and I are *equivalent*. There are many ways to capture the notion of process equivalence (see, e.g., [15]); however, *simulation* and *bisimulation* equivalence [12, 14] are of special importance, as their accompanying theory has found its way into many practical applications.

Given a transition system $\mathcal{T} = (S, \Sigma, \to)$, a *simulation* is a binary relation $\mathcal{R} \subseteq S \times S$ satisfying the following property: whenever $(s, t) \in \mathcal{R}$,

$$\text{if } s \overset{a}{\to} s' \text{ then } t \overset{a}{\to} t' \text{ for some } t' \text{ with } (s', t') \in \mathcal{R}.$$

s *is simulated* by t, written $s \sqsubseteq t$, iff $(s, t) \in \mathcal{R}$ for some simulation $\mathcal{R}$; and s and t are *simulation equivalent*, written $s \simeq t$, iff $s \sqsubseteq t$ and $t \sqsubseteq s$. The union of a family of simulation relations is clearly itself a simulation relation; hence, the relation $\sqsubseteq$, being the union of all simulation relations, is in fact the maximal simulation relation, and is referred to as the *simulation preorder*. A characteristic property is that $s \sqsubseteq t$ iff the following holds: if $s \overset{a}{\to} s'$ then $t \overset{a}{\to} t'$ for some t' with $s' \sqsubseteq t'$.

A *bisimulation* is a symmetric simulation relation, and s and t are *bisimulation equivalent*, or *bisimilar*, written $s \sim t$, if they are related by a bisimulation.

Simulations and bisimulations can also be used to relate states of *different* transition systems; formally, we can consider two transition systems to be a single one by taking the disjoint union of their state sets.

Let A and B be classes of processes. The problem of deciding whether a given process s of A is simulated by a given process t of B is denoted by $A \sqsubseteq B$; similarly, the problem of deciding if s and t are simulation equivalent (or bisimilar) is denoted by $A \simeq B$ (or $A \sim B$, respectively). The classes of all one-counter automata, one-counter nets, and finite-state systems are denoted OC_A, OC_N, and FS, respectively.

The state of the art: The $OC_N \sqsubseteq OC_N$ problem was first considered in [1], where it was shown that if two OC_N processes are related by *some* simulation, then they are also related by a semilinear simulation (i.e. a simulation definable in Presburger arithmetic), which suffices for semidecidability (and thus decidability) of the positive subcase. (The negative subcase is semidecidable by standard arguments.) A simpler proof was given later in [7] by employing certain "geometric" techniques, which allow you to conclude that the simulation preorder (over a given one-counter net) is itself semilinear. Moreover, it was shown there that the $OC_A \sqsubseteq OC_A$ problem is undecidable. The decidability of the $OC_A \sim OC_A$ problem was demonstrated in [4] by showing that the greatest bisimulation relation over states of a given one-counter automaton is also semilinear. The relationship between simulation and bisimulation problems for processes of one-counter automata has been studied in [6] where it was shown that one can effectively reduce certain simulation problems to their bisimulation counterparts by applying a technique proposed in [10]. The complexity of bisimilarity-checking with one-counter automata was studied in [8], where the problem $OC_N \sim OC_N$ (as well as the problem of *weak* bisimilarity [12] between OC_N and FS processes) was shown to be **DP**-hard; however, the problem $OC_A \sim FS$ was shown to be solvable in polynomial time. Complexity bounds for simulation-checking were given in [9], where it was shown that the problems $OC_N \sqsubseteq FS$ and $FS \sqsubseteq OC_N$ (and thus also $OC_N \simeq FS$) are in **P**, while $OC_A \sqsubseteq FS$ and $OC_A \simeq FS$ are **coNP**-hard.

Our contribution: In this paper we generalize the techniques used in [8, 9] for establishing lower complexity bounds for certain equivalence-checking problems, and present a general method for showing **DP**-hardness of problems for one-counter automata. (The class **DP** [13] consists of those languages which are expressible as a difference of two languages from **NP**, and is generally believed to be larger than the union of **NP** and **coNP**. Section 2.2 contains further comments on **DP**.) The "generic part" of the method is presented in Section 2, where we define a simple fragment of Presburger arithmetic, denoted OCP, which is

- sufficiently powerful so that satisfiability and unsatisfiability of boolean formulas are both polynomially reducible to the problem of deciding the truth of formulas of OCP, which implies that this latter problem is **DP**-hard (Theorem 2); yet
- sufficiently simple so that the problem of deciding the truth of OCP formulas is polynomially reducible to various equivalence-checking problems (thus providing the "application part" of the proposed method). The reduction is typically constructed inductively on the structure of OCP formulas, thus making the proofs readable and easily verified.

In Section 3.1 we apply the method to the $OC_N \leftrightarrow OC_N$ problem where $\leftrightarrow$ is any relation which subsumes bisimilarity and is subsumed by simulation preorder (thus, besides bisimilarity and simulation equivalence also, e.g., ready simulation equivalence or 2-nested simulation equivalence), showing **DP**-hardness of these problems (Theorem 5). In Section 3.2 we concentrate on simulation problems between one-counter and finite-state automata, and prove that $OCA \sqsubseteq FS$, $FS \sqsubseteq OCA$, and $OCA \simeq FS$ are all **DP**-hard (Theorem 7), thus improving on the bounds presented in [8, 9]. Finally, in Section 4 we draw some conclusions and present a detailed summary of known results.

2   The OCP Fragment of Arithmetic

In this section, we introduce a fragment of (Presburger) arithmetic, denoted OCP (which can be read as "One-Counter Properties"). We then show how to encode the problems of satisfiability and unsatisfiability of boolean formulas in OCP, and thus deduce **DP**-hardness of the truth problem for (closed formulas of) OCP. (The name of the language is motivated by a relationship to one-counter automata which will be explored in the next section.)

2.1   Definition of OCP

OCP can be viewed as a certain set of first-order arithmetic formulas. We shall briefly give the syntax of these formulas; the semantics will be obvious. Since we only consider the interpretation of OCP formulas in the standard structure of natural numbers $\mathbb{N}$, the problem of deciding the truth of a closed OCP formula is well defined:

Problem: TRUTHOCP
INSTANCE: A closed formula $Q \in$ OCP.
QUESTION: Is Q true ?

Let x and y range over (first-order) *variables*. A formula $Q \in$ OCP can have at most one free variable x (i.e., outside the scope of quantifiers); we shall write $Q(x)$ to indicate the free variable (if there is one) of Q; that is, $Q(x)$ either has the one free variable x, or no free variables at all. For a number $k \in \mathbb{N}$, $\lceil k \rceil$ stands for a special term denoting k; we can think of $\lceil k \rceil$ as $SS \ldots S0$, i.e., the successor function S applied k times to 0. We stipulate that $size(\lceil k \rceil) = k+1$ (which corresponds to representing numbers in unary).

The formulas Q of OCP are defined inductively as follows; at the same time we inductively define their size (keeping in mind the unary representation of $\lceil k \rceil$):

(a) $x = 0$ $size(Q) = 1$

(b) $\lceil k \rceil \mid x$ ("k divides x"; $k > 0$) $size(Q) = k+1$

(c) $\lceil k \rceil \nmid x$ ("k does not divide x"; $k > 0$) $size(Q) = k+1$

(d) $Q_1(x) \wedge Q_2(x)$ $size(Q) = size(Q_1) + size(Q_2) + 1$

(e) $Q_1(x) \vee Q_2(x)$ $size(Q) = size(Q_1) + size(Q_2) + 1$

(f) $\exists y \leq x : Q'(y)$ (x and y distinct) $size(Q) = size(Q') + 1$

(g) $\forall x : Q'(x)$ $size(Q) = size(Q') + 1$

We shall need to consider the truth value of a formula $Q(x)$ in a valuation assigning a number $n \in \mathbb{N}$ to the (possibly) free variable x; this is given by the formula $Q[n/x]$

obtained by replacing each free occurrence of the variable x in Q by n. Slightly abusing notation, we shall denote this by $Q(n)$. (Symbols like i, j, k, n range over natural numbers, not variables.) For example, if $Q(x)$ is the formula $\exists y \leq x : ((3 \mid y) \wedge (2 \nmid y))$, then $Q(5)$ is true while $Q(2)$ is false; and if $Q(x)$ is a closed formula, then the truth value of $Q(n)$ is independent of n.

2.2 DP-hardness of TruthOCP

Recall the following problem:

Problem: SAT-UNSAT
INSTANCE: A pair (φ, ψ) of boolean formulas in conjunctive normal form (CNF).
QUESTION: Is it the case that φ is satisfiable and ψ is unsatisfiable ?

This problem is **DP**-complete, which corresponds to an intermediate level in the polynomial hierarchy, harder than both Σ_1^p and Π_1^p but still contained in Σ_2^p and Π_2^P (cf., e.g., [13]). Our aim here is to show that SAT-UNSAT is polynomial-time reducible to TRUTHOCP. In particular, we show how, given a boolean formula φ in CNF, we can in polynomial time construct a (closed) formula of OCP which claims that φ is satisfiable, and also a formula of OCP which claims that φ is unsatisfiable (Theorem 2).

First we introduce some notation. Let $Var(\varphi) = \{x_1, \ldots, x_m\}$ denote the set of (boolean) variables in φ. Further let π_j (for $j \geq 1$) denote the jth prime number. For every $n \in \mathbb{N}$ define the assignment $\nu_n : Var(\varphi) \to \{true, false\}$ by

$$\nu_n(x_j) = \begin{cases} true, & \text{if } \pi_j \mid n, \\ false, & \text{otherwise.} \end{cases}$$

Note that for an arbitrary assignment ν there is $n \in \mathbb{N}$ such that $\nu_n = \nu$; it suffices to take $n = \Pi\{\pi_j : 1 \leq j \leq m \text{ and } \nu(x_j)=true\}$. By $\|\varphi\|_\nu$ we denote the truth value of φ under the assignment ν.

Lemma 1. *There is a polynomial-time algorithm which, given a boolean formula φ in CNF, constructs OCP-formulas $Q_\varphi(x)$ and $\overline{Q}_\varphi(x)$ such that both $size(Q_\varphi)$ and $size(\overline{Q}_\varphi)$ are in $\mathcal{O}(|\varphi|^3)$, and such that for every $n \in \mathbb{N}$*

$$Q_\varphi(n) \text{ is true} \quad \textit{iff} \quad \overline{Q}_\varphi(n) \text{ is false} \quad \textit{iff} \quad \|\varphi\|_{\nu_n} = true.$$

Proof. Let $Var(\varphi) = \{x_1, \ldots, x_m\}$. Given a literal ℓ (that is, a variable x_j or its negation $\overline{x}_j$), define the OCP-formula $Q_\ell(x)$ as follows:

$$Q_{x_j}(x) = \lceil \pi_j \rceil \mid x \quad \text{and} \quad Q_{\overline{x}_j}(x) = \lceil \pi_j \rceil \nmid x.$$

Clearly, $Q_\ell(n)$ is true iff $Q_{\overline{\ell}}(n)$ is false iff $\|\ell\|_{\nu_n} = true$.

- Formula $Q_\varphi(x)$ is obtained from φ by replacing each literal ℓ with $Q_\ell(x)$. It is clear that $Q_\varphi(n)$ is true iff $\|\varphi\|_{\nu_n} = true$.
- Formula $\overline{Q}_\varphi(x)$ is obtained from φ by replacing each $\wedge$, $\vee$, and ℓ with $\vee$, $\wedge$, and $Q_{\overline{\ell}}(x)$, respectively. It is readily seen that $\overline{Q}_\varphi(n)$ is true iff $\|\varphi\|_{\nu_n} = false$.

It remains to evaluate the size of Q_φ and $\overline{Q}_\varphi$. Here we use a well-known fact from number theory (cf., e.g., [2]) which says that π_m is in $\mathcal{O}(m^2)$. Hence $size(Q_\ell)$ is in $\mathcal{O}(|\varphi|^2)$ for every literal ℓ of φ. As there are $\mathcal{O}(|\varphi|)$ literal occurrences and $\mathcal{O}(|\varphi|)$ boolean connectives in φ, we can see that $size(Q_\varphi)$ and $size(\overline{Q}_\varphi)$ are indeed in $\mathcal{O}(|\varphi|^3)$. □

We now come to the main result of the section.

Theorem 2. *Problem* SAT-UNSAT *is reducible in polynomial time to* TRUTHOCP. *Therefore,* TRUTHOCP *is* **DP**-*hard.*

Proof. We give a polynomial-time algorithm which, given an instance (φ, ψ) of SAT-UNSAT, constructs a closed OCP-formula Q, with $size(Q)$ in $\mathcal{O}(|\varphi|^3 + |\psi|^3)$, such that Q is true iff φ is satisfiable and ψ is unsatisfiable.

Expressing the unsatisfiability of ψ is straightforward: by Lemma 1, ψ is unsatisfiable iff the OCP-formula

$$\forall x : \overline{Q}_\psi(x)$$

is true. Thus, let Q_2 be this formula.

Expressing the satisfiability of φ is rather more involved. Let $g = \pi_1 \pi_2 \ldots \pi_m$, where $Var(\varphi) = \{x_1, \ldots, x_m\}$. Clearly φ is satisfiable iff there is some $n \leq g$ such that $\|\varphi\|_{\nu_n} = true$. Hence φ is satisfiable iff

the OCP-formula $\exists y \leq x : Q_\varphi(y)$ is true for any valuation assigning $i \geq g$ to x.

As it stands, it is unclear how this might be expressed; however, we can observe that the equivalence still holds if we replace the condition "$i \geq g$" with "i is a multiple of g". In other words, φ is satisfiable iff for every $i \in \mathbb{N}$ we have that either $i = 0$, or $g \nmid i$, or there is some $n \leq i$ such that $Q_\varphi(n)$ is true. This can be written as

$$\forall x \ : \ x = 0 \ \vee \ (\lceil \pi_1 \rceil \nmid x \ \vee \cdots \vee \ \lceil \pi_m \rceil \nmid x) \ \vee \ \exists y \leq x : Q_\varphi(y)$$

We thus let Q_1 be this formula.

Hence, (φ, ψ) is a positive instance of the SAT-UNSAT problem iff the formula

$$Q = Q_1 \wedge Q_2$$

is true. To finish the proof, we observe that $size(Q)$ is indeed in $\mathcal{O}(|\varphi|^3 + |\psi|^3)$. □

2.3 TruthOCP Is in Π_2^p

The conclusions we draw for our verification problems are that they are **DP**-hard, as we reduce the **DP**-hard problem TRUTHOCP to them. We cannot improve this lower bound by much using the reduction from TRUTHOCP, as TRUTHOCP is in Π_2^p. In this section we sketch the proof of this fact.

Proposition 3. TRUTHOCP *is in* Π_2^p.

Proof. We start by first proving that for every formula $Q(x)$ of OCP there is a d with $0 < d \leq 2^{size(Q)}$ such that $Q(i) = Q(i-d)$ for every $i > 2^{size(Q)}$. Hence, $\forall x : Q(x)$ holds iff $\forall x \leq 2^{size(Q)} : Q(x)$ holds. (Note that $\forall x \leq 2^{size(Q)} : Q(x)$ is not a formula of OCP.)

We prove the existence of d for every formula $Q(x)$ by induction on the structure of $Q(x)$. If $Q(x)$ is $x = 0$ then we can take $d = 1$; and if $Q(x)$ is $\lceil k \rceil \mid x$ or $\lceil k \rceil \nmid x$ then we can take $d = k$.

If $Q(x)$ is $Q_1(x) \wedge Q_2(x)$ or $Q_1(x) \vee Q_2(x)$, then we may assume by the induction hypothesis the existence of the relevant d_1 for Q_1 and d_2 for Q_2. We can then take $d = d_1 d_2$ to give the desired property that $Q(i) = Q(i-d)$ for every $i > 2^{size(Q)}$.

If $Q(x)$ is $\exists y \leq x : Q'(y)$ (x and y distinct) then by the induction hypothesis there is a d' with $0 < d' \leq 2^{size(Q')}$ such that $Q'(i) = Q'(i-d')$ for every $i > 2^{size(Q')}$. It follows that if $Q'(i)$ is true for some i, then it is true for some $i \leq 2^{size(Q')} < 2^{size(Q)}$. Furthermore, if $Q'(i)$ is true for some i then $Q(j)$ is true for every $j \geq i$; on the other hand, if $Q'(i)$ is false for every i, then $Q(j)$ is false for every j. Thus we can take $d = 1$.

If $Q(x)$ is $\forall y : Q'(y)$, then x is not free in $Q'(y)$, so the truth value of $Q(i)$ does not depend on i and we can take $d = 1$.

Next we note that every OCP-formula $Q(x)$ can be transformed into a formula $\widehat{Q}(x)$ (which need not be in OCP) in (pseudo-)prenex form

$$(\forall x_1 \leq 2^{size(Q_1)}) \cdots (\forall x_k \leq 2^{size(Q_k)})$$

$$(\exists y_1 \leq z_1) \cdots (\exists y_\ell \leq z_\ell) \, \mathcal{F}(x_1, \ldots, x_k, y_1, \ldots, y_\ell)$$

where

- $\forall x_i : Q_i(x_i)$ is a subformula of $Q(x)$;
- each $z_i \in \{x_1, \ldots, x_k, y_1, \ldots, y_{i-1}\}$; and
- $\mathcal{F}(x_1, \ldots, x_k, y_1, \ldots, y_\ell)$ is a $\wedge, \vee$-combination of atomic subformulas of $Q(x)$.

This can be proved by induction on the structure of $Q(x)$. The only case requiring some care is the case when $Q(x)$ is of the form $\exists y \leq x : Q'(y)$, because $\exists y \forall z : P(y,z)$ and $\forall z \exists y : P(y,z)$ are not equivalent in general, but they are in our case, as z never depends on y due to restrictions in OCP. Note that the size of $\widehat{Q}(x)$ is polynomial in $size(Q)$ (assuming that $2^{size(Q_1)}, \ldots, 2^{size(Q_k)}$ are encoded in binary).

We can construct an alternating Turing machine which first uses its universal states to assign all possible values (bounded as mentioned above) to $x_1, \ldots, x_k$, then uses its existential states to assign all possible values to $y_1, \ldots, y_\ell$, and finally evaluates (deterministically) the formula $\mathcal{F}(x_1, \ldots, x_k, y_1, \ldots, y_\ell)$. It is clear that this alternating Turing machine can be constructed so that it works in time which is polynomial in $size(Q)$. This implies the membership of TRUTHOCP in Π_2^p. □

3   Application to One-Counter Automata Problems

As we mentioned above, the language OCP was designed with one-counter automata in mind. The problem TRUTHOCP can be relatively smoothly reduced to various verification problems for such automata, by providing relevant constructions ("implementations") for the cases (a)-(g) of the OCP definition, and thus it constitutes a useful tool for proving lower complexity bounds (**DP**-hardness) for these problems. We shall demonstrate this for the $\text{OC}_\text{N} \leftrightarrow \text{OC}_\text{N}$ problem, where $\leftrightarrow$ is any relation satisfying that $\sim\ \subseteq\ \leftrightarrow\ \subseteq\ \sqsubseteq$, and then also for the $\text{OC}_\text{A} \sqsubseteq \text{FS}$, $\text{FS} \sqsubseteq \text{OC}_\text{A}$, and $\text{OC}_\text{A} \simeq \text{FS}$ problems.

For the purposes of our proofs, we adopt a "graphical" representation of one-counter automata as finite graphs with two kinds of edges (solid and dashed ones) which are labelled by pairs of the form $(a, i) \in \Sigma \times \{-1, 0, 1\}$; instead of $(a, -1)$, $(a, 1)$, and $(a, 0)$ we write simply $-a$, $+a$, and a, respectively. A *solid* edge from p to q labelled by (a, i) indicates that the represented one-counter automaton can make a transition $p(k) \xrightarrow{a} q(k + i)$ whenever $i \geq 0$ or $k > 0$. A *dashed* edge from p to q labelled by (a, i) (where i must not be -1) represents a zero-transition $p(0) \xrightarrow{a} q(i)$. Hence, graphs representing one-counter nets do not contain any dashed edges, and graphs corresponding to finite-state systems use only labels of the form $(a, 0)$ (remember that finite-state systems are formally understood as special one-counter nets). Also observe that the graphs cannot represent non-decrementing transitions which are enabled *only* for positive counter values; this does not matter since we do not need such transitions in our proofs. The distinguished initial control state(s) is (are) indicated by a black circle.

3.1   Results for One-Counter Nets

In this section we show that, for any relation $\leftrightarrow$ satisfying $\sim\ \subseteq\ \leftrightarrow\ \subseteq\ \sqsubseteq$, the problem of deciding whether two (states of) one-counter nets are in $\leftrightarrow$ is **DP**-hard. We first state an important technical result, but defer its proof until after we derive the desired theorem as a corollary.

Proposition 4. *There is an algorithm which, given a formula* $Q = Q(x) \in \text{OCP}$ *as input, halts after* $\mathcal{O}(size(Q))$ *steps and outputs a one-counter net with two distinguished control states* p *and* p' *such that for every* $k \in \mathbb{N}$ *we have:*

- *if* $Q(k)$ *is true   then* $p(k) \sim p'(k)$;
- *if* $Q(k)$ *is false   then* $p(k) \not\sqsubseteq p'(k)$.

(Note that if Q *is a closed formula, then this implies that* $p(0) \sim p'(0)$ *if* Q *is true, and* $p(0) \not\sqsubseteq p'(0)$ *if* Q *is false.)*

Theorem 5. *For any relation* $\leftrightarrow$ *such that* $\sim\ \subseteq\ \leftrightarrow\ \subseteq\ \sqsubseteq$, *the following problem is* **DP***-hard:*

   INSTANCE: *A one-counter net with two distinguished control states* p *and* p'.
   QUESTION: *Is* $p(0) \leftrightarrow p'(0)$?

Proof. Given an instance of TRUTHOCP, i.e., a *closed* formula $Q \in \text{OCP}$, we use the (polynomial) algorithm of Proposition 4 to construct a one-counter net with the two distinguished control states p and p'. If Q is true, then $p(0) \sim p'(0)$, and hence $p(0) \leftrightarrow p'(0)$; and if Q is false, then $p(0) \not\sqsubseteq p'(0)$, and hence $p(0) \not\leftrightarrow p'(0)$.   □

Proof of Proposition 4: We proceed by induction on the structure of Q. For each case, we show an *implementation*, i.e., the corresponding one-counter net $\mathcal{N}_Q$ with two distinguished control states p and p'. Constructions are sketched by figures which use our notational conventions; the distinguished control states are denoted by black dots (the left one p, the right one p'). It is worth noting that we only use two actions, a and b.

(a) $Q(x) = (x = 0)$: A suitable (and easily verifiable) implementation looks as follows:

(b,c) $Q(x) = \lceil k \rceil \mid x$ or $Q(x) = \lceil k \rceil \nmid x$, where $k > 0$: Given $J \subseteq \{0, 1, 2, \dots, k-1\}$, let $R_J(x) = (x \bmod k) \in J$. We shall show that this formula can be implemented in our sense; taking $J = \{0\}$ then gives us the construction for case (b), and taking $J = \{1, \dots, k-1\}$ gives us the construction for case (c).

An implementation of $R_J(x)$, where $1, 2 \in J$ but $0, 3, k-1 \notin J$, looks as follows:

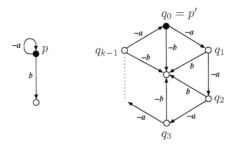

In this picture, each node q_i has an outgoing edge going to a "dead" state; this edge is labelled b if $i \in J$ and labelled $-b$ if $i \notin J$. It is straightforward to check that the proposed implementation of $R_J(x)$ is indeed correct.

(d) $Q(x) = Q_1(x) \wedge Q_2(x)$: We can assume (by induction) that implementations $\mathcal{N}_{Q_1}$ of $Q_1(x)$ and $\mathcal{N}_{Q_2}$ of $Q_2(x)$ have been constructed. $\mathcal{N}_Q$ is constructed, using $\mathcal{N}_{Q_1}$ and $\mathcal{N}_{Q_2}$, as follows:

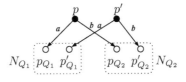

The dotted rectangles represent the graphs associated to $\mathcal{N}_{Q_1}$ and $\mathcal{N}_{Q_2}$ (where the only depicted control states are the distinguished ones). Verifying the correctness of this construction is straightforward.

(e) $Q(x) = Q_1(x) \vee Q_2(x)$: As in case (d), the construction uses the implementations of $Q_1(x)$ and $Q_2(x)$; but the situation is slightly more involved in this case:

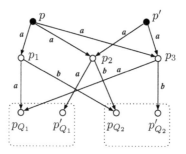

To verify correctness, we first consider the case when $Q(k)$ is true. By induction, either $p_{Q_1}(k) \sim p'_{Q_1}(k)$ or $p_{Q_2}(k) \sim p'_{Q_2}(k)$. In the first case, $p_{Q_1}(k) \sim p'_{Q_1}(k)$ implies that $p_1(k) \sim p_2(k)$, which in turn implies that $p(k) \sim p'(k)$; similarly, in the second case, $p_{Q_2}(k) \sim p'_{Q_2}(k)$ implies that $p_1(k) \sim p_3(k)$, which also implies that $p(k) \sim p'(k)$. Hence in either case $p(k) \sim p'(k)$.

Now consider the case when $Q(k)$ is false. By induction, $p_{Q_1}(k) \not\sqsubseteq p'_{Q_1}(k)$ and $p_{Q_2}(k) \not\sqsubseteq p'_{Q_2}(k)$. Obviously, $p_{Q_1}(k) \not\sqsubseteq p'_{Q_1}(k)$ implies that $p_1(k) \not\sqsubseteq p_2(k)$, and $p_{Q_2}(k) \not\sqsubseteq p'_{Q_2}(k)$ implies that $p_1(k) \not\sqsubseteq p_3(k)$. From this we have $p(k) \not\sqsubseteq p'(k)$.

(f) $Q(x) = \exists y \leq x : Q_1(y)$ (where x, y are distinct): We use the following construction:

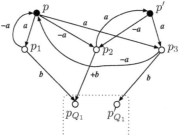

To verify correctness, we first consider the case when $Q(k)$ is true. This means that $Q_1(i)$ is true for some $i \leq k$, which by induction implies that $p_{Q_1}(i) \sim p'_{Q_1}(i)$ for this $i \leq k$. Our result, that $p(k) \sim p'(k)$, follows immediately from the following:

Claim: For all k, if $p_{Q_1}(i) \sim p'_{Q_1}(i)$ for some $i \leq k$, then $p(k) \sim p'(k)$.

Proof of Claim. By induction on k. For the base case ($k=0$), if $p_{Q_1}(i) \sim p'_{Q_1}(i)$ for some $i \leq 0$, then $p_{Q_1}(0) \sim p'_{Q_1}(0)$, which implies that $p_1(0) \sim p_3(0)$, and hence that $p(0) \sim p'(0)$. For the induction step ($k>0$), if $p_{Q_1}(i) \sim p'_{Q_1}(i)$ for some $i \leq k$, then either $p_{Q_1}(k) \sim p'_{Q_1}(k)$, which implies that $p_1(k) \sim p_3(k)$ which in turn implies that $p(k) \sim p'(k)$; or $p_{Q_1}(i) \sim p'_{Q_1}(i)$ for some $i \leq k-1$, which by induction implies that $p(k-1) \sim p'(k-1)$, which implies that $p_1(k) \sim p_2(k-1)$, which in turn implies that $p(k) \sim p'(k)$.

Next, we consider that case when $Q(k)$ is false. This means that $Q_1(i)$ is false for all $i \leq k$, which by induction implies that $p_{Q_1}(i) \not\sqsubseteq p'_{Q_1}(i)$ for all $i \leq k$. Our result, that $p(k) \not\sqsubseteq p'(k)$, follows immediately from the following:

Claim: For all k, if $p(k) \sqsubseteq p'(k)$ then $p_{Q_1}(i) \sqsubseteq p'_{Q_1}(i)$ for some $i \leq k$.

Proof of Claim. By induction on k. For the base case ($k=0$), if $p(0) \sqsubseteq p'(0)$ then $p_1(0) \sqsubseteq p_3(0)$, which in turn implies that $p_{Q_1}(0) \sqsubseteq p'_{Q_1}(0)$. For the induction step ($k>0$), if $p(k) \sqsubseteq p'(k)$ then either $p_1(k) \sqsubseteq p_2(k-1)$ or $p_1(k) \sqsubseteq p_3(k)$. In the first case, $p_1(k) \sqsubseteq p_2(k-1)$ implies that $p(k-1) \sqsubseteq p'(k-1)$, which by induction implies that $p_{Q_1}(i) \sqsubseteq p'_{Q_1}(i)$ for some $i \leq k-1$ and hence for some $i \leq k$; and in the second case, $p_1(k) \sqsubseteq p_3(k)$ implies that $p_{Q_1}(k) \sqsubseteq p'_{Q_1}(k)$.

(g) $Q = \forall x : Q_1(x)$: The implementation in the following figure can be easily verified.

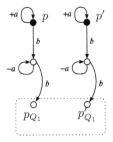

For any $Q \in$ OCP, the described construction terminates after $\mathcal{O}(size(Q))$ steps, because we add only a constant number of new nodes in each subcase except for (b) and (c), where we add $\mathcal{O}(k)$ new nodes (recall that the size of $\lceil k \rceil$ is $k+1$). □

3.2   Simulation Problems for One-Counter Automata and Finite-State Systems

Now we establish **DP**-hardness of the OCA $\sqsubseteq$ FS, FS $\sqsubseteq$ OCA, and OCA $\simeq$ FS problems. Again, we use the (inductively defined) reduction from TRUTHOCP; only the particular constructions are now slightly different.

By an *implementation* we now mean a 4-tuple $(\mathcal{A}, \mathcal{F}, \mathcal{F}', \mathcal{A}')$ where $\mathcal{A}, \mathcal{A}'$ are one-counter automata, and $\mathcal{F}, \mathcal{F}'$ are finite-state systems; the role of distinguished states is now played by the initial states, denoted q for $\mathcal{A}$, f for F, f' for F', and q' for $\mathcal{A}'$. We again first state an important technical result, and again defer its proof until after we derive the desired theorem as a corollary.

Proposition 6. *There is an algorithm which, given $Q = Q(x) \in$ OCP as input, halts after $\mathcal{O}(size(Q))$ steps and outputs an implementation $(\mathcal{A}, \mathcal{F}, \mathcal{F}', \mathcal{A}')$ (where q, f, f' and q' are the initial control states of $\mathcal{A}$, $\mathcal{F}$, $\mathcal{F}'$ and $\mathcal{A}'$, respectively) such that for every $k \in \mathbb{N}$ we have:*

$Q(k)$ *is true   iff $q(k) \sqsubseteq f$ iff $f' \sqsubseteq q'(k)$.*

(Note that if Q is a closed formula, then this implies that Q is true   iff $q(0) \sqsubseteq f$ iff $f' \sqsubseteq q'(0)$.)

Theorem 7. *Problems $\mathrm{OCA} \sqsubseteq \mathrm{FS}$, $\mathrm{FS} \sqsubseteq \mathrm{OCA}$, and $\mathrm{OCA} \simeq \mathrm{FS}$ are **DP**-hard.*

Proof. Recalling that TRUTHOCP is **DP**-hard, **DP**-hardness of the first two problems readily follows from Proposition 6.

DP-hardness of the third problem follows from a simple (general) reduction of $\mathrm{OCA} \sqsubseteq \mathrm{FS}$ to $\mathrm{OCA} \simeq \mathrm{FS}$: given a one-counter automaton $\mathcal{A}$ with initial state q, and a finite-state system $\mathcal{F}$ with initial state f, we first transform $\mathcal{F}$ to $\mathcal{F}_1$ by adding a new state f_1 and transition $f_1 \overset{a}{\to} f$, and then create $\mathcal{A}_1$ by taking (disjoint) union of $\mathcal{A}$, $\mathcal{F}_1$ and adding $\overline{f_1} \overset{a}{\to} q$, where $\overline{f_1}$ is the copy of f_1 in $\mathcal{A}_1$. Clearly $q(k) \sqsubseteq f$ iff $\overline{f_1}(k) \simeq f_1$. □

Proof of Proposition 6: We proceed by induction on the structure of Q. In the constructions we use only two actions, a and b; this also means that a state with non-decreasing a and b loops is *universal*, i.e, it can simulate "everything".

(a) $Q = (x = 0)$: A straightforward implementation looks as follows:

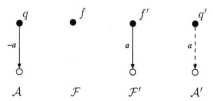

(b,c) $Q = \lceil k \rceil \,|\, x$ or $Q = \lceil k \rceil \!\!\restriction\! x$, where $k > 0$: Given $J \subseteq \{0, 1, 2, \ldots, k-1\}$, let $R_J(x) = (x \bmod k) \in J$. We shall show that this formula can be implemented in our sense; taking $J = \{0\}$ then gives us the construction for case (b), and taking $J = \{1, \ldots, k-1\}$ gives us the construction for case (c).

An implementation of $R_J(x)$, where $1, 2 \in J$ but $0, 3, k-1 \notin J$, looks as follows:

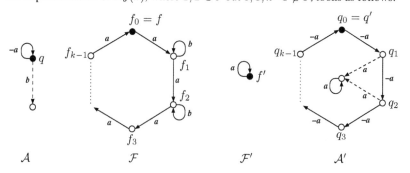

In this picture, node f_i has a b-loop in $\mathcal{F}$, and node q_i has an outgoing dashed a-edge in $\mathcal{A}'$, iff $i \in J$. It is straightforward to check that the proposed implementation of $R_J(x)$ is indeed correct.

(d) $Q(x) = Q_1(x) \wedge Q_2(x)$: The members of the implementation $(\mathcal{A}_Q, \mathcal{F}_Q, \mathcal{F}'_Q, \mathcal{A}'_Q)$ for Q can be constructed from the respective members of the implementations for Q_1, Q_2 (assumed by induction): $\mathcal{A}_Q$ from $\mathcal{A}_{Q_1}$ and $\mathcal{A}_{Q_2}$; $\mathcal{F}_Q$ from $\mathcal{F}_{Q_1}$ and $\mathcal{F}_{Q_2}$; $\mathcal{F}'_Q$ from $\mathcal{F}'_{Q_1}$ and $\mathcal{F}'_{Q_2}$; and $\mathcal{A}'_Q$ from $\mathcal{A}'_{Q_1}$ and $\mathcal{A}'_{Q_2}$. All these cases follow the schema depicted in the following figure:

Correctness is easily verifiable.

(e) $Q(x) = Q_1(x) \vee Q_2(x)$: We give constructions just for $\mathcal{A}$ and $\mathcal{F}$ (the constructions for $\mathcal{F}'$ and $\mathcal{A}'$ are almost identical):

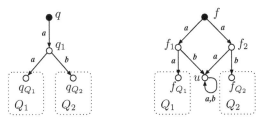

For any k, $Q(k)$ is true iff $Q_1(k)$ is true or $Q_2(k)$ is true, which by induction is true iff $q_{Q_1}(k) \sqsubseteq f_{Q_1}$ or $q_{Q_2}(k) \sqsubseteq f_{Q_2}$, which is true iff $q_1(k) \sqsubseteq f_1$ or $q_1(k) \sqsubseteq f_2$, which in turn is true iff $q(k) \sqsubseteq f$.

(f) $Q(x) = \exists y \leq x : Q_1(y)$ (where x, y are distinct): We use the following constructions:

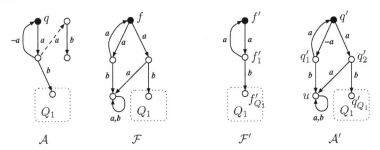

We prove that the construction is correct for $\mathcal{F}'$ and $\mathcal{A}'$ (the other case being similar). $Q(k)$ is true iff $Q_1(i)$ is true for some $i \leq k$, which by induction is true iff $f'_{Q_1} \sqsubseteq q'_{Q_1}(i)$ for some $i \leq k$, which in turn is true iff $f'_1 \sqsubseteq q'_2(i)$ for some $i \leq k$. Our result, that this is true iff $f' \sqsubseteq q'(k)$, follows immediately from the following:

Claim: For all k, $f' \sqsubseteq q'(k)$ iff $f'_1 \sqsubseteq q'_2(i)$ for some $i \leq k$.

Proof of Claim. By induction on k. For the base case ($k=0$), the result is immediate. For the induction step ($k>0$), first note that $f'_1 \sqsubseteq q'_1(k-1)$ iff $f' \sqsubseteq q'(k-1)$, which by induction is true iff $f'_1 \sqsubseteq q'_2(i)$ for some $i \leq k-1$. Thus $f' \sqsubseteq q'(k)$ iff $f'_1 \sqsubseteq q'_2(k)$ or $f'_1 \sqsubseteq q'_1(k-1)$, which is true iff $f'_1 \sqsubseteq q'_2(k)$ or $f'_1 \sqsubseteq q'_2(i)$ for some $i \leq k-1$, which in turn is true iff $f'_1 \sqsubseteq q'_2(i)$ for some $i \leq k$.

(g) $Q = \forall x : Q_1(x)$: It is easy to show the correctness of the implementation in the following figure.

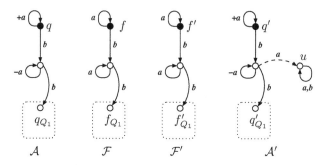

For any $Q \in \mathrm{OCP}$, the described construction terminates after $\mathcal{O}(size(Q))$ steps, because we add only a constant number of new nodes in each subcase except for (b) and (c), where we add $\mathcal{O}(k)$ new nodes.   □

4   Conclusions

Intuitively, the reason why we could not lift the **DP** lower bound to some higher complexity class (e.g., **PSPACE**) is that there is no apparent way to implement a "step-wise guessing" of assignments which would allow us to encode, e.g., the QBF problem. The difficulty is that if we modify the counter value, we were not able to find a way to check that the old and new values encode "compatible" assignments which agree on a certain subset of propositional constants. Each such attempt resulted in an exponential blow-up in the number of control states.

A summary of known results about equivalence-checking with one-counter automata is given below (where $\approx$ denotes weak bisimilarity).

- OCN $\approx$ OCN and OCA $\approx$ OCA remain open.
- OCA $\sqsubseteq$ OCA and OCA $\simeq$ OCA are undecidable.
- OCA $\sim$ OCA, OCN $\sim$ OCN, OCN $\sqsubseteq$ OCN and OCN $\simeq$ OCN are decidable and **DP**-hard, but without any known upper bound.
- OCA $\approx$ FS, OCN $\approx$ FS, OCA $\sqsubseteq$ FS, FS $\sqsubseteq$ OCA and OCA $\simeq$ FS are decidable, **DP**-hard, and in **EXPTIME**. The **EXPTIME** upper bound is due to the fact that all of the mentioned problems can be easily reduced to the model-checking problem with pushdown systems (see, e.g., [5, 10, 9]) and the modal μ-calculus which is **EXPTIME**-complete [16].

– $OC_A \sim FS$, $OC_N \sim FS$, $OC_N \sqsubseteq FS$, $FS \sqsubseteq OC_N$ and $OC_N \simeq FS$ are in **P**.

To complete the picture, let us also mention that the model-checking problem with a fixed formula $\Diamond[a]\Diamond[b]\mathtt{false}$ of a simple branching-time logic EF (which can be seen as a natural fragment of CTL [3]) is **NP**-hard for OC_N processes, which also means that model-checking with $\Box\langle a\rangle\Box\langle b\rangle\mathtt{true}$ (which is the negation of the above given formula) is **coNP**-hard [9]. From this one can readily see that model-checking with $[c]\Diamond[a]\Diamond[b]\mathtt{false}\wedge\langle d\rangle\Box\langle a\rangle\Box\langle b\rangle\mathtt{true}$ is in fact **DP**-hard for OC_N processes. It is quite interesting that model checking with Hennessy-Milner logic [12] is still polynomial even for OC_A processes (this problem is **PSPACE**-hard for related models like BPA or BPP [11]).

References

1. P. Abdulla and K. Čerāns. Simulation is decidable for one-counter nets. In *Proceedings of CONCUR'98*, volume 1466 of *LNCS*, pages 253–268. Springer, 1998.
2. E. Bach and J. Shallit. *Algorithmic Number Theory. Vol. 1, Efficient Algorithms*. The MIT Press, 1996.
3. E. Emerson. Temporal and modal logic. *Handbook of Theoretical Computer Science*, B, 1991.
4. P. Jančar. Decidability of bisimilarity for one-counter processes. *Information and Computation*, 158(1):1–17, 2000.
5. P. Jančar, A. Kučera, and R. Mayr. Deciding bisimulation-like equivalences with finite-state processes. *Theoretical Computer Science*, 258(1–2):409–433, 2001.
6. P. Jančar, A. Kučera, and F. Moller. Simulation and bisimulation over one-counter processes. In *Proceedings of STACS 2000*, volume 1770 of *LNCS*, pages 334–345. Springer, 2000.
7. P. Jančar, F. Moller, and Z. Sawa. Simulation problems for one-counter machines. In *Proceedings of SOFSEM'99*, volume 1725 of *LNCS*, pages 404–413. Springer, 1999.
8. A. Kučera. Efficient verification algorithms for one-counter processes. In *Proceedings of ICALP 2000*, volume 1853 of *LNCS*, pages 317–328. Springer, 2000.
9. A. Kučera. On simulation-checking with sequential systems. In *Proceedings of ASIAN 2000*, volume 1961 of *LNCS*, pages 133–148. Springer, 2000.
10. A. Kučera and R. Mayr. Simulation preorder on simple process algebras. In *Proceedings of ICALP'99*, volume 1644 of *LNCS*, pages 503–512. Springer, 1999.
11. R. Mayr. Strict lower bounds for model checking BPA. *Electronic Notes in Theoretical Computer Science*, 18, 1998.
12. R. Milner. *Communication and Concurrency*. Prentice-Hall, 1989.
13. C. Papadimitriou. *Computational Complexity*. Addison-Wesley, 1994.
14. D. Park. Concurrency and automata on infinite sequences. In *Proceedings 5th GI Conference*, volume 104 of *LNCS*, pages 167–183. Springer, 1981.
15. R. van Glabeek. The linear time - branching time spectrum I. In J. Bergstra, A. Ponse, and S. Smolka, editors, *Handbook of Process Algebra*, pages 3–99. Elsevier, 2001.
16. I. Walukiewicz. Pushdown processes: Games and model-checking. *Information and Computation*, 164(2):234–263, 2001.

Efficient Type Matching[*]

Somesh Jha[1], Jens Palsberg[2], and Tian Zhao[2]

[1] Computer Sciences Department,
University of Wisconsin, Madison, WI 53706,
jha@cs.wisc.edu.
[2] Department of Computer Science,
Purdue University, W. Lafayette, IN 47907,
{palsberg,tzhao}@cs.purdue.edu.

Abstract. Palsberg and Zhao [17] presented an $O(n^2)$ time algorithm for matching two recursive types. In this paper, we present an $O(n \log n)$ algorithm for the
same problem. Our algorithm works by reducing the type matching problem to the
well-understood problem of finding a size-stable partition of a graph. Our result
may help improve systems, such as Polyspin and Mockingbird, that are designed
to facilitate interoperability of software components. We also discuss possible applications of our algorithm to Java. Issues related to subtyping of recursive types
are also discussed.

1 Introduction

Interoperability is a fundamental problem in software engineering. Interoperability issues arise in various contexts, such as software reuse, distributed programming, use
of legacy components, and integration of software components developed by different
organizations. Interoperability of software components has to address two fundamental
problems: *matching* and *bridging*. Matching deals with determining whether two components A and B are compatible, and bridging allows one to use component B using
the interface defined for component A.

Matching: A common technique for facilitating matching is to associate signatures
with components. These signatures can then be used as keys to retrieve relevant components from an existing library of components. Use of finite types as signatures was first
proposed by Rittri [19]. Zaremski and Wing [23,24] used a similar approach for retrieving components from an ML-like functional library. Moreover, they also emphasized
flexibility and support for user-defined types.

Bridging: In a multi-lingual context, *bridge code* for "gluing" components written
in different languages (such as C, C++, and Java) has to be developed. CORBA [15],
PolySpin [4], and Mockingbird [2,3] allow composing components implemented in
different languages. Software components are considered to be of two kinds: *objects*,
which provide public interfaces, and *clients*, which invoke the methods of the objects
and thereby use the services provided by the objects.

---

[*] Palsberg was supported by an NSF CAREER award, CCR–9734265, and by IBM.

M. Nielsen and U. Engberg (Eds.): Fossacs 2002, LNCS 2303, pp. 187–204, 2002.
© Springer-Verlag Berlin Heidelberg 2002

The Problem: Assume that we use types as signatures for components. Thus, the type matching problem reduces to the problem of determining whether two types are equivalent. Much previous work on type matching focuses on non-recursive types [7,10,14,18], [19,20,21,23]. In this paper, we consider equivalence of recursive types. Equality and subtyping of recursive types have been studied in the 1990s by Amadio and Cardelli [1]; Kozen, Palsberg, and Schwartzbach [13]; Brandt and Henglein [6]; Jim and Palsberg [12]; and others. These papers concentrate on the case where two types are considered equal if their infinite unfoldings are identical. In this case, type equivalence can be decided in $O(n\alpha(n))$ time. If we allow a product-type constructor to be associative and commutative, then two recursive types may be considered equal *without* their infinite unfoldings being identical. Alternatively, think of a product type as a multiset, by which associativity and commutativity are obtained for free. Such flexibility has been advocated by Auerbach, Barton, and Raghavachari [2]. Palsberg and Zhao [17] presented a definition of type equivalence that supports this idea. They also presented an $O(n^2)$ time algorithm for deciding their notion of type equivalence.

A notion of subtyping defined by Amadio and Cardelli [1] can be decided in $O(n^2)$ time [13]. We also briefly discuss subtyping of recursive types in this paper.

Our result: We present an $O(n \log n)$ time algorithm for deciding the type equivalence of Palsberg and Zhao [17]. Our algorithm works by reducing the type matching problem to the well-understood problem of finding a size-stable partition of a graph [16].

The organization of the paper: A small example is described in Section 2. This example will be used throughout the paper for illustrative purposes. In Section 3 we recall the notions of terms and term automata [1,8,11,13], and we state the definitions of types and type equivalence from the paper by Palsberg and Zhao [17]. In Section 4 we prove our main result. An implementation of our algorithm is discussed Section 5. Subtyping of recursive types is discussed in Section 6. Concluding remarks appear in Section 7.

2   Example

In this section we provide a small example which will be used throughout the paper. It is straightforward to map a `Java` type to a recursive type of the form considered in this paper. A collection of method signatures can be mapped to a product type, a single method signature can be mapped to a function type, and in case a method has more than one argument, the list of arguments can be mapped to a product type. Recursion, direct or indirect, is expressed with the μ operator. This section provides an example of of `Java` interfaces and provides an illustration of our algorithm.

Suppose we are given the two sets of Java interfaces shown in Figures 1 and 2. We would like to find out whether interface I_1 is "structurally equal" to or "matches" with interface J_2. We want a notion of equality for which interface names and method names do not matter, and for which the order of the methods in an interface and the order of the arguments of a method do not matter.

Notice that interface I_1 is recursively defined. The method m_1 takes an argument of type I_1 and returns a floating point number. In the following, we use names of interfaces and methods to stand for their type structures. The type of method m_1 can be expressed

interface I_1 {   interface I_2 {
    float $m_1(I_1\ a)$; $I_1\ m_3(float\ a)$;
    int $m_2(I_2\ a)$; $I_2\ m_4(float\ a)$;
}   }

Fig. 1. Interfaces I_1 and I_2

interface J_1 {   interface J_2 {
    $J_1\ n_1(float\ a)$;   *int* $n_3(J_1\ a)$;
    $J_2\ n_2(float\ a)$;   *float* $n_4(J_2\ a)$;
}   }

Fig. 2. Interfaces J_1 and J_2

as $I_1 \rightarrow float$. The symbol $\rightarrow$ stands for the function type constructor. Similarly, the type of m_2 is $I_2 \rightarrow int$. We can then capture the structure of I_1 with conventional μ-notation for recursive types:

$$I_1 = \mu\alpha.(\alpha \rightarrow float) \times (I_2 \rightarrow int)$$

The symbol α is the type variable bound to the type I_1 by the symbol μ. The interface type I_1 is a product type with the symbol $\times$ as the type constructor. Since we think of the methods of interface I_1 as unordered, we could also write the structure of I_1 as

$$I_1 = \mu\alpha.(I_2 \rightarrow int) \times (\alpha \rightarrow float)\ ,$$
$$I_2 = \mu\delta.(float \rightarrow I_1) \times (float \rightarrow \delta)\ .$$

In the same way, the structures of the interfaces J_1, J_2 are:

$$J_1 = \mu\beta.(float \rightarrow \beta) \times (float \rightarrow J_2)$$
$$J_2 = \mu\eta.(J_1 \rightarrow int) \times (\eta \rightarrow float).$$

Trees corresponding to the two types are shown in Figures 3 and 4. The interface types I_1, J_2 are equivalent iff there exists a one-to-one mapping or a bijection from the methods in I_1 to the methods in J_2 such that each pair of methods in the bijection relation have the same type. The types of two methods are equal iff the types of the arguments and the return types are equal.

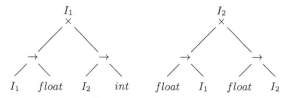

Fig. 3. Trees for interfaces I_1 and I_2

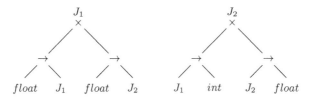

Fig. 4. Trees for interfaces J_1 and J_2

The equality of the interface types I_1 and J_2 can be determined by trying out all possible orderings of the methods in each interface and comparing the two types in the form of finite automata. In this case, there are only few possible orderings. However, if the number of methods is large and/or some methods take many arguments, the above approach becomes time consuming because the number of possible orderings grows exponentially. An efficient algorithm for determining equality of recursive types will be given later in the paper.

3   Definitions

A recursive type is a type described by a set of equations involving the μ operator. An example of a recursive type was provided in Section 2. This section provides representation of recursive types as terms and term automata.

Term automata and representation of types are described in Subsection 3.1. A definition of type equivalence for recursive types in terms of bisimulation is give in Subsection 3.2. An efficient algorithm for determining whether two types are equivalent is given in Section 4.

3.1   Terms and Term Automata

Here we give a general definition of (possibly infinite) terms over an arbitrary finite ranked alphabet Σ. Such terms are essentially labeled trees, which we represent as partial functions labeling strings over ω (the natural numbers) with elements of Σ.

Let Σ_n denote the set of elements of Σ of arity n. Let ω denote the set of natural numbers and let ω^* denote the set of finite-length strings over the alphabet ω.

A *term* over Σ is a partial function

$$t : \omega^* \to \Sigma$$

satisfying the following properties:

 – the domain of t is nonempty and prefix-closed;
 – if $t(\alpha) \in \Sigma_n$, then $\{\, i \mid \alpha i \in \text{ the domain of } t \,\} = \{0, 1, \ldots, n - 1\}$.

Let t be a term and $\alpha \in \omega^*$. Define the partial function $t {\downarrow} \alpha : \omega^* \to \Sigma$ by $t {\downarrow} \alpha(\beta) = t(\alpha\beta)$. If $t {\downarrow} \alpha$ has nonempty domain, then it is a term, and is called the *subterm of t at position α*.

A term t is said to be *regular* if it has only finitely many distinct subterms; that is, if $\{t{\downarrow}\alpha \mid \alpha \in \omega^*\}$ is a finite set.

Every regular term over a finite ranked alphabet Σ has a finite representation in terms of a special type of automaton called a *term automaton*. A term automaton over Σ is a tuple

$$A = (Q, \Sigma, q_0, \delta, \ell)$$

where:

- Q is a finite set of *states*,
- $q_0 \in Q$ is the *start state*,
- $\delta : Q \times \omega \to Q$ is a partial function called the *transition function*, and
- $\ell : Q \to \Sigma$ is a (total) *labeling function*,

such that for any state $q \in Q$, if $\ell(q) \in \Sigma_n$ then

$$\{i \mid \delta(q, i) \text{ is defined}\} = \{0, 1, \dots, n-1\} \,.$$

The partial function δ extends naturally to an inductively-defined partial function:

$$\hat{\delta} \; : \; Q \times \omega^* \to Q$$
$$\hat{\delta}(q, \epsilon) = q$$
$$\hat{\delta}(q, \alpha i) = \delta(\hat{\delta}(q, \alpha), i).$$

For any $q \in Q$, the domain of the partial function $\lambda\alpha.\hat{\delta}(q, \alpha)$ is nonempty (it always contains ϵ) and prefix-closed. Moreover, because of the condition on the existence of i-successors in the definition of term automata, the partial function

$$\lambda\alpha.\ell(\hat{\delta}(q, \alpha))$$

is a term.

Let A be a term automaton. The term *represented by* A is the term

$$t_A = \lambda\alpha.\ell(\hat{\delta}(q_0, \alpha)) \,.$$

A term t is said to be *representable* if $t = t_A$ for some A.

Intuitively, $t_A(\alpha)$ is determined by starting in the start state q_0 and scanning the input α, following transitions of A as far as possible. If it is not possible to scan all of α because some i-transition along the way does not exist, then $t_A(\alpha)$ is undefined. If on the other hand A scans the entire input α and ends up in state q, then $t_A(\alpha) = \ell(q)$.

It is straightforward to show that a term t is regular if and only if it is representable. Moreover, a term t is regular if and only if it can be described by a finite set of equations involving the μ operator.

3.2   Equivalence of Recursive Types

A recursive type is a regular term over the ranked alphabet

$$\Sigma = \Gamma \cup \{\rightarrow\} \cup \{\prod^{n}, n \geq 2\},$$

where Γ is a set of base types, $\rightarrow$ is binary, and $\prod^n$ is of arity n. Given a type σ, if $\sigma(\epsilon) = \rightarrow$, $\sigma(0) = \sigma_1$, and $\sigma(1) = \sigma_2$, then we write the type as $\sigma_1 \rightarrow \sigma_2$. If $\sigma(\epsilon) = \prod^n$ and $\sigma(i) = \sigma_i$, $\forall i \in \{0, 1, \ldots, n-1\}$, then we write the type σ as $\prod_{i=0}^{n-1} \sigma_i$.

Palsberg and Zhao [17] presented three equivalent definitions of type equivalence. Here we will work with the one which is based on the idea of bisimilarity. A relation R on types is called a *bisimulation* if it satisfies the following three conditions:

- if $(\sigma, \tau) \in R$, then $\sigma(\epsilon) = \tau(\epsilon)$
- if $(\sigma_1 \rightarrow \sigma_2, \tau_1 \rightarrow \tau_2) \in R$, then $(\sigma_1, \tau_1) \in R$ and $(\sigma_2, \tau_2) \in R$
- if $(\prod_{i=0}^{n-1} \sigma_i, \prod_{i=0}^{n-1} \tau_i) \in R$, then there exists a bijection $b : \{0..n-1\} \rightarrow \{0..n-1\}$ such that $\forall i \in \{0..n-1\}$, $(\sigma_i, \tau_{b(i)}) \in R$.

Bisimulations are closed under union, therefore, there exists a largest bisimulation

$$\mathcal{R} = \bigcup \{ R \mid R \text{ is a bisimulation} \}.$$

It is straightforward to show that $\mathcal{R}$ is an equivalence relation. Two types τ_1 and τ_2 are said to be *equivalent* (denoted by $\tau_1 \cong \tau_2$) iff $(\tau_1, \tau_2) \in \mathcal{R}$.

4   An Efficient Algorithm for Type Equivalence

Assume that we are given two types τ_1 and τ_2 that are represented as two term automata A_1 and A_2. Lemma 1 proves that $\tau_1 \cong \tau_2$ (or $(\tau_1, \tau_2) \in \mathcal{R}$) if and only if there is a reflexive bisimulation C between A_1 and A_2 such that the initial states of the term automata A_1 and A_2 are related by C. Lemma 3 essentially reduces the problem of finding a reflexive bisimulation C between A_1 and A_2 to finding a size-stable coarsest partition [16]. Theorem 1 uses the algorithm of Paige and Tarjan to determine in $O(n \log n)$ time (n is the sum of the sizes of the two term automata) whether there exists a reflexive bisimulation C between A_1 and A_2.

Throughout this section, we will use A_1, A_2 to denote two term automata over the alphabet Σ:

$$A_1 = (Q_1, \Sigma, q_{01}, \delta_1, \ell_1)$$
$$A_2 = (Q_2, \Sigma, q_{02}, \delta_2, \ell_2).$$

We assume that $Q_1 \cap Q_2 = \emptyset$. Define $Q = Q_1 \cup Q_2$, $\delta : Q \times \omega \rightarrow Q$ where $\delta = \delta_1 \oplus \delta_2$, and $\ell : Q \rightarrow \Sigma$, where $\ell = \ell_1 \oplus \ell_2$, where $\oplus$ denotes disjoint union of two functions. We say that A_1, A_2 are *bisimular* if and only if there exists a relation $C \subseteq Q \times Q$, called a bisimulation between A_1 and A_2, such that:

- if $(q, q') \in C$, then $\ell(q) = \ell(q')$
- if $(q, q') \in C$ and $\ell(q) = \rightarrow$, then $(\delta(q, 0), \delta(q', 0)) \in C$ and $(\delta(q, 1), \delta(q', 1)) \in C$
- if $(q, q') \in C$ and $\ell(q) = \prod^n$, then there exists a bijection $b : \{0..n-1\} \rightarrow \{0..n-1\}$ such that $\forall i \in \{0..n-1\}$: $(\delta(q, i), \delta(q', b(i))) \in C$.

Notice that the bisimulations between A_1 and A_2 are closed under union, therefore, there exists a largest bisimulation between A_1 and A_2. It is straightforward to show that the identity relation on Q is a bisimulation, and that any reflexive bisimulation is an equivalence relation. Hence, the largest bisimulation is an equivalence relation.

Lemma 1. *For types τ_1, τ_2 that are represented by the term automata A_1, A_2, respectively, we have $(\tau_1, \tau_2) \in \mathcal{R}$ if and only if there is a reflexive bisimulation C between A_1 and A_2 such that $(q_{01}, q_{02}) \in C$.*

Proof. Suppose $(\tau_1, \tau_2) \in \mathcal{R}$. Define:

$$C = \{ (q, q') \in Q \times Q \mid (\lambda\alpha.\ell(\hat{\delta}(q, \alpha)), \lambda\alpha.\ell(\hat{\delta}(q', \alpha))) \in \mathcal{R} \}.$$

It is straightforward to show that C is a bisimulation between A_1 and A_2, and that $(q_{01}, q_{02}) \in C$, we omit the details.

Conversely, let C be a reflexive bisimulation between A_1 and A_2 such that $(q_{01}, q_{02}) \in C$. Define:

$$R = \{ (\sigma_1, \sigma_2) \mid (q, q') \in C \wedge \sigma_1 = \lambda\alpha.\ell(\hat{\delta}(q, \alpha)) \wedge \sigma_2 = \lambda\alpha.\ell(\hat{\delta}(q', \alpha)) \}$$

From $(q_{01}, q_{02}) \in C$, we have $(\tau_1, \tau_2) \in R$. It is straightforward to prove that R is a bisimulation, we omit the details. From $(\tau_1, \tau_2) \in R$ and R being a bisimulation, we conclude that $(\tau_1, \tau_2) \in \mathcal{R}$. □

A *partitioned graph* is a 3-tuple (U, E, P), where U is a set of nodes, $E \subseteq U \times U$ is an edge relation, and P is a *partition* of U. A partition P of U is a set of pairwise disjoint subsets of U whose union is all of U. The elements of P are called its *blocks*. If P and S are partitions of U, then S is a *refinement* of P if and only if every block of S is contained in a block of P.

A partition S of a set U can be characterized by an equivalence relation K on U such that each block of S is an equivalence class of K. If U is a set and K is an equivalence relation on U, then we use U/K to denote the partition of U into equivalence classes for K.

A partition S is *size-stable* with respect to E if and only if for all blocks $B_1, B_2 \in S$, and for all $x, y \in B_1$, we have $|E(x) \cap B_2| = |E(y) \cap B_2|$, where $E(x)$ is the following set

$$\{y | (x, y) \in E\} .$$

If E is clear from the context, we will simply use size-stable. We will repeatedly use the following characterization of size-stable partitions.

Lemma 2. *For an equivalence relation K, we have that U/K is size-stable if and only if for all $(u, u') \in K$, there exists a bijection $\pi : E(u) \to E(u')$ such that for all $u_1 \in E(u)$, we have $(u_1, \pi(u_1)) \in K$.*

Proof. Suppose that U/K is size-stable. Let $(u, u') \in K$. Let B_1 be the block of U/K which contains u and u'. For each block B_2 of U/K, we have that $|E(u) \cap B_2| = |E(u') \cap B_2|$. So, for each block B_2 of U/K, we can construct a bijection from $E(u) \cap B_2$ to $E(u') \cap B_2$, such that for all $u_1 \in E(u) \cap B_2$, we have $(u_1, \pi(u_1)) \in K$. These bijections can then be merged to single bijection $\pi : E(u) \to E(u')$ with the desired property.

Conversely, suppose that for all $(u, u') \in K$, there exists a bijection $\pi : E(u) \to E(u')$ such that for all $u_1 \in E(u)$, we have $(u_1, \pi(u_1)) \in K$. Let $B_1, B_2 \in U/K$, and let $x, y \in B_1$. We have that $(x, y) \in K$, so there exists a bijection $\pi : E(x) \to E(y)$ such that for all $u_1 \in E(x)$, we have $(u_1, \pi(u_1)) \in K$. Each element of $E(x) \cap B_2$ is mapped by π to an element of $E(y) \cap B_2$. Moreover, each element of $E(y) \cap B_2$ must be the image under π of an element of $E(x) \cap B_2$. We conclude that π restricted to $E(x) \cap B_2$ is a bijection to $E(y) \cap B_2$, so $|E(x) \cap B_2| = |E(y) \cap B_2|$.   □

Given two term automata A_1, A_2, we define a partitioned graph (U, E, P):

$$U = Q \cup \{ \langle q, i \rangle \mid q \in Q \wedge \delta(q, i) \text{ is defined } \}$$
$$E = \{ (q, \langle q, i \rangle) \mid \delta(q, i) \text{ is defined } \}$$
$$\cup \{ (\langle q, i \rangle, \delta(q, i)) \mid \delta(q, i) \text{ is defined } \}$$
$$L = \{ (q, q') \in Q \times Q \mid \ell(q) = \ell(q') \}$$
$$\cup \{ (\langle q, i \rangle, \langle q', i' \rangle) \mid \ell(q) = \ell(q') \text{ and if } \ell(q) =\to, \text{ then } i = i' \}$$
$$P = U/L.$$

The graph contains one node for each state and transition in A_1, A_2. Each transition in A_1, A_2 is mapped to two edges in the graph. This construction ensures that if a node in the graph corresponds to a state labeled $\prod^n$, then that node will have n distinct successors in the graph. This is convenient when establishing a bijection between the successors of two nodes labeled $\prod^n$.

The equivalence relation L creates a distinction between the two successors of a node that corresponds to a state labeled $\to$. This is done by ensuring that if $(\langle q, i \rangle, \langle q, i' \rangle) \in L$ and $\ell(q) =\to$, then $i = i'$. This is convenient when establishing a bijection between the successors of two nodes labeled $\to$.

Lemma 3. *There exists a reflexive bisimulation C between A_1 and A_2 such that $(q_{01}, q_{02}) \in C$ if and only if there exists a size-stable refinement S of P such that q_{01} and q_{02} belong to the same block of S.*

Proof. Let $C \subseteq Q \times Q$ be a reflexive bisimulation between A_1 and A_2 such that $(q_{01}, q_{02}) \in C$. Define an equivalence relation $K \subseteq U \times U$ such that:

$$K = C$$
$$\cup \{ (\langle q, i \rangle, \langle q', i \rangle) \mid (q, q') \in C \wedge \ell(q) = \ell(q') =\to \}$$
$$\cup \{ (\langle q, i \rangle, \langle q', i' \rangle) \mid (q, q') \in C \wedge (\delta(q, i), \delta(q', i')) \in C$$
$$\wedge \ell(q) = \ell(q') \wedge \ell(q) \neq\to \}$$
$$S = U/K.$$

From $(q_{01}, q_{02}) \in C$, we have $(q_{01}, q_{02}) \in K$, so q_{01} and q_{02} belong to the same block of S. We will now show that S is a size-stable refinement of P.

Let $(u, u') \in K$. From Lemma 2 we have that it is sufficient to show that there exists a bijection $\pi : E(u) \to E(u')$, such that for all $u_1 \in E(u)$, we have $(u_1, \pi(u_1)) \in K$. There are three cases.

First, suppose $(u, u') \in C$. We have

$$E(u) = \{ \langle u, i \rangle \mid \delta(u, i) \text{ is defined } \}$$
$$E(u') = \{ \langle u', i' \rangle \mid \delta(u', i') \text{ is defined } \}.$$

Let us consider each of the possible cases of u and u'. If $\ell(u) = \ell(u') \in \Gamma$, then $E(u) = E(u') = \emptyset$, and the desired bijection exists trivially. Next, if $\ell(u) = \ell(u') =\rightarrow$, then

$$E(u) = \{ \langle u, 0 \rangle, \langle u, 1 \rangle \}$$
$$E(u') = \{ \langle u', 0 \rangle, \langle u', 1 \rangle \},$$

so the desired bijection is $\pi : E(u) \rightarrow E(u')$, where $\pi(\langle u, 0 \rangle) = \langle u', 0 \rangle$ and $\pi(\langle u, 1 \rangle) = \langle u', 1 \rangle$, because $(\langle u, 0 \rangle, \langle u', 0 \rangle) \in K$ and $(\langle u, 1 \rangle, \langle u', 1 \rangle) \in K$. Finally, if $\ell(u) = \ell(u') = \prod^n$, then

$$E(u) = \{ \langle u, i \rangle \mid \delta(u, i) \text{ is defined } \}$$
$$E(u') = \{ \langle u', i' \rangle \mid \delta(u', i') \text{ is defined } \}.$$

From $(u, u') \in C$, we have a bijection $b : \{0..n-1\} \rightarrow \{0..n-1\}$ such that $\forall i \in \{0..n-1\} : (\delta(u, i), \delta(u', b(i))) \in C$. From that, the desired bijection can be constructed.

Second, suppose $u = \langle q, i \rangle$ and $u' = \langle q', i \rangle$, where $(q, q') \in C$, and $\ell(q) = \ell(q') =\rightarrow$. We have

$$E(u) = \{ \delta(q, i) \}$$
$$E(u') = \{ \delta(q', i) \},$$

and from $(q, q') \in C$ we have $(\delta(q, i), \delta(q', i)) \in C \subseteq K$, so the desired bijection exists.

Third, suppose $u = \langle q, i \rangle$ and $u' = \langle q', i' \rangle$, where $(q, q') \in C$, $(\delta(q, i), \delta(q', i')) \in C$, $\ell(q) = \ell(q')$, and $\ell(q) \neq \rightarrow$. We have

$$E(u) = \{ \delta(q, i) \}$$
$$E(u') = \{ \delta(q', i') \},$$

and $(\delta(q, i), \delta(q', i')) \in C \subseteq K$, so the desired bijection exists.

Conversely, let S be a size-stable refinement of P such that q_{01} and q_{02} belong to the same block of S. Define:

$$K = \{ (u, u') \in U \times U \mid u, u' \text{ belong to the same block of } S \}$$
$$C = K \cap (Q \times Q).$$

Notice that $(q_{01}, q_{02}) \in C$ and that C is reflexive. We will now show that C is a bisimulation between A and A'.

First, suppose $(q, q') \in C$. From S being a refinement of P we have $(q, q') \in L$, so $\ell(q) = \ell(q')$.

Second, suppose $(q, q') \in C$ and $\ell(q) =\rightarrow$. From the definition of E we have

$$E(q) = \{ \langle q, 0 \rangle, \langle q, 1 \rangle \}$$
$$E(q') = \{ \langle q', 0 \rangle, \langle q', 1 \rangle \}.$$

From S being size-stable, $(q, q') \in C \subseteq K$, and Lemma 2 we have that there exists a bijection $\pi : E(q) \to E(q')$ such that for all $u \in E(q)$ we have that $(u, \pi(u)) \in K$. From $K \subseteq L$ and $\ell(q) = \to$ we have that there is only one possible bijection π:

$$\pi(\langle q, 0 \rangle) = \langle q', 0 \rangle$$
$$\pi(\langle q, 1 \rangle) = \langle q', 1 \rangle,$$

so $(\langle q, 0 \rangle, \langle q', 0 \rangle) \in K$ and $(\langle q, 1 \rangle, \langle q', 1 \rangle) \in K$. From the definition of E we have, for $i \in \{0, 1\}$,

$$E(\langle q, i \rangle) = \delta(q, i)$$
$$E(\langle q', i \rangle) = \delta(q', i),$$

and since S is size-stable, we have, for $i \in \{0, 1\}$, $(\delta(q, i), \delta(q', i)) \in K$. Moreover, for $i \in \{0, 1\}$, $(\delta(q, i), \delta(q', i)) \in Q \times Q$, so we conclude, $(\delta(q, i), \delta(q', i)) \in C$.

Third, suppose $(q, q') \in C$ and $\ell(q) = \prod^n$. From the definition of E we have

$$E(q) = \{ \langle q, i \rangle \mid \delta(q, i) \text{ is defined } \}$$
$$E(q') = \{ \langle q', i \rangle \mid \delta(q', i) \text{ is defined } \}.$$

Notice that $|E(q)| = |E(q')| = n$. From S being size-stable, $(q, q') \in C \subseteq K$, and Lemma 2, we have that there exists a bijection $\pi : E(q) \to E(q')$ such that for all $u \in E(q)$ we have that $(u, \pi(u)) \in K$. From π we can derive a bijection $b : \{0..n-1\} \to \{0..n-1\}$ such that $\forall i \in \{0..n-1\}: (\langle q, i \rangle, \langle q', b(i) \rangle) \in K$. From the definitions of E and E' we have that for $i \in \{0..n-1\}$,

$$E(\langle q, i \rangle) = \{ \delta(q, i) \}$$
$$E(\langle q', i \rangle) = \{ \delta(q', i) \},$$

and since S is size-stable, and, for all $i \in \{0..n-1\}$, $(\langle q, i \rangle, \langle q', b(i) \rangle) \in K$, we have $(\delta(q, i), \delta(q', b(i))) \in K$. Moreover, $(\delta(q, i), \delta(q', b(i))) \in Q \times Q$, so we conclude $(\delta(q, i), \delta(q', b(i))) \in C$. □

The *size* of a term automata $A = (Q, \Sigma, q_0, \delta, l)$ is $|Q| + |\delta|$, i.e., the sum of the number of states and transitions in the automata.

Theorem 1. *For types τ_1, τ_2 that can be represented by term automata A_1, A_2 of size at most n, we can decide $(\tau_1, \tau_2) \in \mathcal{R}$ in $O(n \log n)$ time.*

Proof. From Lemma 1 we have that $(\tau_1, \tau_2) \in \mathcal{R}$ if and only if there is a reflexive bisimulation C between A_1 and A_2 such that $(q_{01}, q_{02}) \in C$. From Lemma 3 we have that there exists a reflexive bisimulation C between A_1 and A_2 such that $(q_{01}, q_{02}) \in C$ if and only if there exists a size-stable refinement S of P such that q_{01} and q_{02} belong to the same block of S.

Paige and Tarjan [16] give an $O(m \log p)$ algorithm to find the coarsest size-stable refinement of P, where m is the size of E and p is the size of the universe U.

Our algorithm first constructs (U, E, P) from A_1 and A_2, then runs the Paige-Tarjan algorithm to find the coarsest size-stable refinement S of P, and finally checks whether q_{01} and q_{02} belong to the same block of S.

If A_1 and A_2 are of size at most n, then the size of E is at most $2n$, and the size of U is at most $2n$, so the total running time of our algorithm is $O(2n \log(2n)) = O(n \log n)$. □

Next, we illustrate how our algorithm determines that equivalence between the types. Details of the algorithm can be found in [16]. Consider two types I_1 and J_1 defined in Section 2. The set of types corresponding to the two interfaces are:

$$\{I_1, I_2, m_1, m_2, m_3, m_4, int, float\}$$
$$\{J_1, J_2, n_1, n_2, n_3, n_4, int, float\}$$

Figure 5 shows various steps of our algorithm. For simplicity, the figure only shows the blocks of actual types, but not the blocks of the extra nodes of the form $\langle q, i \rangle$. The blocks in the first row are based on labels, e.g., states labeled with $\times$ are in the same block. In the next step, the block containing the methods are split based on the type of the result of the method, e.g.. methods m_1 and n_4 both return *float*, so they are in the same block. In the next step (corresponding to the third row) the block $\{I_1, I_2, J_1, J_2\}$ are split. The final partition, where block $\{m_3, m_4, n_1, n_2\}$ is split, is shown in the fourth row.

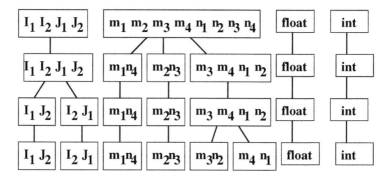

Fig. 5. Blocks of types

Our algorithm can be tuned to take a specific user needs into account. This is done simply by modifying the definition of the equivalence relation L. For example, suppose a user cares about the order of the arguments to a method. This means that the components of the product type that models the argument list should not be allowed to be shuffled during type matching. We can prevent shuffling by employing the same technique that the current definition of L uses for function types. The idea is to insist that two component types may only be matched when they have the same component index.

Another example of the tunability of our algorithm involves the modifiers in `Java`. Suppose a programmer is developing a product that is multi-threaded. In this case the programmer may only want to match `synchronized` methods with other `synchro-nized` methods. This can be handled easily in our framework by changing L such that two method types may only be matched when they are both synchronized. On the other hand if the user is working on a single-threaded product, the keyword `synchronized` can be ignored. The same observation applies to other modifiers such as `static`.

5   Our Implementation

We have implemented our algorithm in `Java` and the current version is based on the code written by Wanjun Wang. The implementation and documentation are freely available at

> `http://www.cs.purdue.edu/homes/tzhao/matching/matching.htm.`

The current version has a graphical user interface so that users may input type definitions written in a file and also may specify restrictions on type isomorphism.

Suppose we are given the following file with four `Java` interfaces.

interface I_1 {   interface I_2 {
    $float$ m_1 $(I_1\ a, int\ b)$; J_2 m_3 $(float\ a)$;
    int m_2 $(I_2\ a)$; I_1 m_4 $(float\ a)$;
}   }

interface J_1 {   interface J_2 {
    I_1 n_1 $(float\ a)$; int n_3 $(J_1\ a)$;
    J_2 n_2 $(float\ a)$; $float$ n_4 $(int\ a, J_2\ b)$;
}   }

The implementation, as illustrated in the Figure 6, will read and parse the input file and then transform the type definitions into partitions of numbers with each type definition and dummy type assigned a unique number. The partitions will be refined by Paige-Tarjan algorithm until it is *size-stable* as defined in this paper. Finally, we will be

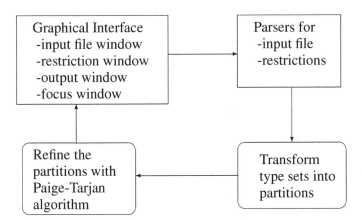

Fig. 6. Schematic diagram for the implementation

able to read the results from the final partitions. Two types are isomorphic if the numbers assigned to them are in the same partition.

The implementation will give the following output:

$$I_1 = J_2$$
$$I_2 = J_1$$

$$I_1.m_1 = J_2.n_4$$
$$I_2.m_3 = I_2.m_4 = J_1.n_1 = J_1.n_2$$
$$I_1.m_2 = J_2.n_3 \; .$$

We can see that the types of interfaces I_2 and J_1 are isomorphic and moreover, all method types of I_2, J_1 match. Suppose that we have additional information about the method types such that only method m_3 and n_1 should have isomorphic types. We can restrict the type matching by adding $I_2.m_3 = J_1.n_1$ to the *restrictions* window of the user interface. The new matching result is illustrated by the screen shot in figure 7.

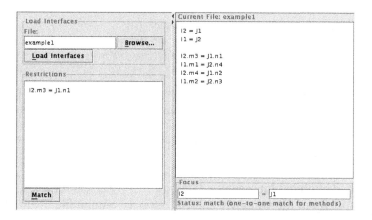

Fig. 7. Screen shot

Note that we are able to focus on the matching of two interface types such as I_2, J_1 as in the *focus* windows of Figure 7, where I_2, J_1 are matched and their methods are matched one to one.

6   Subtyping of Recursive Types

In this section we discuss subtyping and formalize it using a simulation relation. We also discuss reasons why the algorithm given in Section 4 is not applicable to subtyping of of recursive types. Consider the interfaces I_1 and I_2 shown in Figure 8, and suppose a

```
interface I₁ {                          interface I₂ {
        I₁  m  (float a, boolean b);          I₂  m  (int i, boolean b);
    boolean  p  (I₁ j);                   }
}
```

Fig. 8. Interfaces I_1 and I_2

user is looking for I_2. The interfaces I_1 and I_2 can be mapped to the following recursive types:

$$\tau_1 = \mu\alpha.((float \times boolean) \to \alpha) \times (\alpha \to boolean)$$
$$\tau_2 = \mu\beta.(int \times boolean) \to \beta$$

Assuming that int is a subtype of $float$ (we can always coerce integers into floats) we have that τ_1 is a subtype of τ_2. Therefore, the user can use the interface I_1. There are several points to notice from this example. In the context of subtyping, we need two kinds of products: one that models a collection of methods and another that models sequence of parameters. In our example, the user only specified a type corresponding to method m. Therefore, during the subtyping algorithm method p should be ignored. However, the parameters of method m are also modeled using products and none of these can be ignored. Therefore, we consider two types of product type constructors in our type systems and the subtyping rule for these two types of products are different.

As stated before, a type is a regular term, in this case over the ranked alphabet

$$\Sigma = \Gamma \cup \{\to\} \cup \{\prod^n, n \geq 2\} \cup \{\times^n, n \geq 2\}.$$

Roughly speaking, $\prod^n$ and $\times^n$ will model collection of parameters and methods respectively. Also assume that we are given a subtyping relation on the base types Γ. If τ_1 is a subtype of τ_2, we will write it as $\tau_1 \preceq \tau_2$. A relation S is called a *simulation* on types if it satisfies the following conditions:

- if $(\sigma, \tau) \in S$ and $\sigma(\epsilon) \in \Gamma$, then $\tau(\epsilon) \in \Gamma$ and $\sigma(\epsilon) \preceq \tau(\epsilon)$.
- if $(\sigma, \tau) \in S$ and $\sigma(\epsilon) \in (\{\to\} \cup \{\prod^n, n \geq 2\})$, then $\sigma(\epsilon) = \tau(\epsilon)$.
- if $(\sigma_1 \to \sigma_2, \tau_1 \to \tau_2) \in S$, then $(\tau_1, \sigma_1) \in S$ and $(\sigma_2, \tau_2) \in S$.
- if $(\prod_{i=0}^{n-1} \sigma_i, \prod_{i=0}^{n-1} \tau_i) \in S$, then there exists a bijection $b : \{0 \cdots n - 1\} \to \{0 \cdots n - 1\}$ such that for all $i \in \{0 \cdots n - 1\}$, we have $(\sigma_i, \tau_{b(i)}) \in S$.
- Suppose $(\sigma, \tau) \in S$, $\sigma(\epsilon) = \times^n$, and $\sigma = \times_{i=0}^{n-1} \sigma_i$. If $\tau(\epsilon) \notin \{\times^m, m \geq 2\}$, then there exists a $j \in \{0 \cdots n-1\}$ such that $(\sigma_j, \tau) \in S$. Otherwise, assume that $\tau(\epsilon) = \times^m$, where $m \leq n$ and $\tau = \times_{i=0}^{m-1} \tau_i$. In this case, then there exists an injective function $c : \{0 \cdots m - 1\} \to \{0 \cdots n - 1\}$ such that for all $i \in \{0 \cdots m - 1\}$, we have $(\sigma_{c(i)}, \tau_i) \in S$. Notice that this rule allows ignoring certain components of σ.

As is the case with bisimulations, simulations are closed under union, therefore there exists a largest simulation (denoted by $\mathcal{S}$).

Let A_1, A_2 denote two term automata over Σ:

$$A_1 = (Q_1, \Sigma, q_{01}, \delta_1, \ell_1)$$
$$A_2 = (Q_2, \Sigma, q_{02}, \delta_2, \ell_2).$$

We assume that $Q_1 \cap Q_2 = \emptyset$. Define $Q = Q_1 \cup Q_2$, $\delta : Q \times \omega \to Q$ where $\delta = \delta_1 \oplus \delta_2$, and $\ell : Q \to \Sigma$, where $\ell = \ell_1 \oplus \ell_2$, where $\oplus$ denotes disjoint union of two functions. We say that A_2 *simulates* A_1 (denoted by $A_1 \preceq A_2$) if and only if there exists a relation $D \subseteq Q \times Q$, called a *simulation relation* between A_1 and A_2, such that:

- if $(q, q') \in D$ and $\ell(q) \in \Gamma$, then $\ell(q') \in \Gamma$ and $\ell(q) \preceq \ell(q')$).
- if $(q, q') \in D$ and $\ell(q) \in (\{\to\} \cup \{\prod^n, n \geq 2\})$, then $\ell(q) = \ell(q')$.
- if $(q, q'), \in D$ and $\ell(q) = \to$, then $(\delta(q, 0), \delta(q', 0)) \in D$ and $(\delta(q, 1), \delta(q', 1)) \in D$.
- if $(q, q'), \in D$ and $\ell(q) = \prod^n$, then there exists a bijection $b : \{0 \cdots n - 1\} \to \{0 \cdots n - 1\}$ such that for all $i \in \{0 \cdots n - 1\}$, we have $(\delta(q, i), \delta(q'i)) \in D$.
- Suppose $(q, q') \in D$ and $\ell(q) = \times^n$. If $\ell(q') \notin \{\times^m, m \geq 2\}$, then there exists a $j \in \{0 \cdots n - 1\}$ such that $(\delta(q, j), q') \in D$. Otherwise, assume that $\ell(q') = \times^m$, where $m \leq n$ and in this case, there exists an injective function $c : \{0 \cdots m - 1\} \to \{0 \cdots n - 1\}$ such that for all $i \in \{0 \cdots m - 1\}$, we have $(\delta(q, c(i)), \delta(q', i)) \in D$.

Notice that the simulations between A_1 and A_2 are closed under union, therefore, there exists a largest simulation between A_1 and A_2. The proof of Lemma 4 is similar to the proof of Lemma 1 and is omitted.

Lemma 4. *For types τ_1, τ_2 that are represented by the term automata A_1, A_2, respectively, we have $(\tau_1, \tau_2) \in S$ if and if only there is a reflexive simulation D between A_1 and A_2 such that $(q_{01}, q_{02}) \in D$.*

The largest simulation between the term automata A_1 and A_2 is given by the following greatest fixed point

$$\nu D.sim(q, q', D).$$

where $D \subseteq Q_1 \times Q_2$ and the predicate $sim(q, q', D)$ is the conjunction of the five conditions which appear in the definition of the simulation relation between two automata. Let n and m be the size of the term automata A_1 and A_2 respectively. Since nm is a bound on the size of D, the number of iterations in computing the greatest fixed point is bounded by nm. In general, the relation D (or for that matter the simulation relation) is not symmetric. On the other hand, the bisimulation relation was an equivalence relation, and so could be represented as a partition on the set $Q_1 \cup Q_2$, or in other words, partitions give us a representation of an equivalence relation that is linear in the sum of the sizes of the set of states Q_1 and Q_2. The Paige-Tarjan algorithm uses the partition representation of the equivalence relation. Since D is not symmetric (and thus not an equivalence relation), it cannot be represented by a partition. This is the crucial reason why our previous algorithm cannot be used for subtyping.

7 Conclusion

In this paper we addressed the problem of matching recursive types. We presented an algorithm with $O(n \log n)$ time complexity that determines whether two types are equivalent. To our knowledge, this is the most efficient algorithm for this problem. Our results are applicable to the problem of matching signatures of software components. Applications to Java were also discussed. Issues related to subtyping of recursive types were also addressed. Next we discuss potential applications of our algorithm.

CORBA: The CORBA approach utilizes a separate definition language called IDL. Objects are associated with language-independent interfaces defined in IDL. These interfaces are then translated into the language being used by the client. The translated interface then enables the clients to call the objects. Since the IDL interfaces have to be translated into several languages, their type system is very restrictive. Therefore, IDL interfaces lack expressive power because, intuitively speaking, the type system used in IDL has to be the intersection of the type system for each language it supports. The drawback of for CORBA-style approaches to interoperability are well articulated in [3,4].

Polyspin and Mockingbird: The Polyspin and Mockingbird approaches do not require a common interface language, such as IDL. In both these approaches, clients and objects are written in languages with separate type systems, and an operation that crosses the language boundary is supported by bridge code that is automatically generated. Therefore, systems such as Polyspin and Mockingbird support seamless interoperability since the programmer is not burdened with writing interfaces in a second language, such as IDL in CORBA. Polyspin supports only finite types. Mockingbird on the other hand supports recursive types, including records, linked lists, and arrays. The type system used in Mockingbird is called the *Mockingbird Signature Language* or *MockSL*. The problem of deciding type equivalence for MockSL remains open [2]. In this paper we considered a type system which is related to the one used in Mockingbird. However, we are investigating a translation from *MockSL* to recursive types.

Megaprogramming: Techniques suitable for very large software systems have been a major goal of software engineering. The term *megaprogramming* was introduced by DARPA to motivate this goal [5]. Roughly speaking, in megaprogramming, *megamodules* provide a higher level of abstraction than modules or components. For example, a megamodule can encapsulate the entire logistics of ground transportation in a major city. Megaprogramming is explained in detail in [22]. Interoperability issues arise when megaprograms are constructed using megamodules (see [22, Section 4.2]). We believe that the framework presented in this paper can be used to address mismatch between interfaces of megamodules.

Future work includes investigating type inference. Coppo's recent paper [9] on type inference with recursive type equations may contain techniques that are applicable.

References

1. Roberto M. Amadio and Luca Cardelli. Subtyping recursive types. *ACM Transactions on Programming Languages and Systems*, 15(4):575–631, 1993. Also in Proceedings of POPL'91.
2. Joshua Auerbach, Charles Barton, and Mukund Raghavachari. Type isomorphisms with recursive types. Research report RC 21247, IBM Research Division, T. J. Watson Research Center, Yorktown Heights, NY, August 1998.
3. Joshua Auerbach and Mark C. Chu-Carroll. The mockingbird system: A compiler-based approach to maximally interoperable distributed programming. Research report RC 20718,

IBM Research Division, T. J. Watson Research Center, Yorktown Heights, NY, February 1997.

4. Daniel J. Barrett, Alan Kaplan, and Jack C. Wileden. Automated support for seamless interoperability in polylingual software systems. In *ACM SIGSOFT'96, Fourth Symposium on the Foundations of Software Engineering*, San Francisco, California, October 1996.

5. B. Boehm and B. Scherlis. Megaprogramming. In *Proceedings of DARPA Software Technology Conference*, April 28-30, Meridien Corporation, Arlington, VA 1992.

6. Michael Brandt and Fritz Henglein. Coinductive axiomatization of recursive type equality and subtyping. In *Proceedings of TLCA'97, 3rd International Conference on Typed Lambda Calculus and Applications*, 1997.

7. Kim B. Bruce, Roberto Di Cosmo, and Giuseppe Longo. Provable isomorphisms of types. *Mathematical Structures in Computer Science*, 2(2):231–247, 1992.

8. Luca Cardelli and Peter Wegner. On understanding types, data abstraction, and polymorphism. *ACM Computing Surveys*, 17(4):471–522, December 1985.

9. Mario Coppo. Type inference with recursive type equations. In *Proceedings of FOSSACS'01, Foundations of Software Science and Computation Structures*, pages 184–198. Springer-Verlag (*LNCS* 2030), 2001.

10. Roberto Di Cosmo. *Isomorphisms of Types: from λ-calculus to information retrieval and language design*. Birkhäuser, 1995.

11. Bruno Courcelle. Fundamental properties of infinite trees. *Theoretical Computer Science*, 25(1):95–169, 1983.

12. Trevor Jim and Jens Palsberg. Type inference in systems of recursive types with subtyping. Manuscript, 1997.

13. Dexter Kozen, Jens Palsberg, and Michael I. Schwartzbach. Efficient recursive subtyping. *Mathematical Structures in Computer Science*, 5(1):113–125, 1995. Preliminary version in Proceedings of POPL'93, Twentieth Annual SIGPLAN–SIGACT Symposium on Principles of Programming Languages, pages 419–428, Charleston, South Carolina, January 1993.

14. Paliath Narendran, Frank Pfenning, and Richard Statman. On the unification problem for Cartesian closed categories. In *Proceedings, Eighth Annual IEEE Symposium on Logic in Computer Science*, pages 57–63. IEEE Computer Society Press, 1993.

15. OMG. The common object request broker: Architecture and specification. Technical report, Object Management Group, 1999. Version 2.3.1.

16. Robert Paige and Robert Tarjan. Three partition refinement algorithms. *SIAM Journal on Computing*, 16(6):973–989, December 1987.

17. Jens Palsberg and Tian Zhao. Efficient and flexible matching of recursive types. *Information and Computation*, to appear. Preliminary version in Proceedings of LICS'00, Fifteenth Annual IEEE Symposium on Logic in Computer Science, pages 388–398, Santa Barbara, California, June 2000.

18. Mikael Rittri. Retrieving library identifiers via equational matching of types. In M. E. Stickel, editor, *Proceedings of the 10th International Conference on Automated Deduction*, volume 449 of *LNAI*, pages 603–617, Kaiserslautern, FRG, July 1990. Springer Verlag.

19. Mikael Rittri. Using types as search keys in function libraries. *Journal of Functional Programming*, 1(1):71–89, 1991.

20. Mikael Rittri. Retrieving library functions by unifying types modulo linear isomorphism. *RAIRO Theoretical Informatics and Applications*, 27(6):523–540, 1993.

21. Sergei V. Soloviev. The category of finite sets and cartesian closed categories. *Journal of Soviet Mathematics*, 22:1387–1400, 1983.

22. G. Wiederhold, P. Wegner, and S. Ceri. Towards Megaprogramming: A paradigm for component-based programming. *Communications of the ACM*, 35(11):89–99, November 1992.

23. A. M. Zaremski and J. M. Wing. Signature matching: a tool for using software libraries. *ACM Transactions on Software Engineering Methodology*, 4(2):146–170, April 1995.
24. A. M. Zaremski and J. M. Wing. Specification matching of software components. In *Proceedings of 3rd ACM SIGSOFT Symposium on the Foundation of Software Engineering*, pages 6–17, 1995.

Higher-Order Pushdown Trees Are Easy

Teodor Knapik[1], Damian Niwiński[2*], and Paweł Urzyczyn[2**]

[1] Université de la Réunion, BP 7151,
97715 Saint Denis Messageries Cedex 9, Réunion
`knapik@univ--reunion.fr`
[2] Institute of Informatics, Warsaw University
ul. Banacha 2, 02–097 Warszawa, Poland
`{niwinski,urzy}@mimuw.edu.pl`

Abstract. We show that the monadic second-order theory of an infinite tree recognized by a higher-order pushdown automaton of any level is decidable. We also show that trees recognized by pushdown automata of level n coincide with trees generated by safe higher-order grammars of level n. Our decidability result extends the result of Courcelle on algebraic (pushdown of level 1) trees and our own result on trees of level 2.

Introduction

The Rabin Tree Theorem, stating the decidability of the monadic second-order (MSO) theory of the full n-ary tree (SnS), is among the most widely applied decidability results. Rabin himself [15] inferred a number of decidability results for various mathematical structures interpretable in SnS (e.g., countable linear orders). Muller and Schupp [14] gave rise to the study of graphs definable in SnS, by showing decidability of the MSO theory of any graph generated by a pushdown automaton; this result was further extended by Courcelle [2] to equational graphs, and by Caucal [1] to prefix–recognizable graphs.

However, a more sophisticated use of the Rabin Tree Theorem allows to go beyond the structures directly interpretable in SnS. Indeed, Courcelle [2] established the decidability of the MSO theory of any algebraic tree, i.e., a tree generated by a context–free (algebraic) tree grammar. Such a tree can be also presented as a computation tree of a pushdown automaton. The interest in this kind of structures (and their theories) arose in recent years in the verification community, in the context of verification of infinite state systems (see [13] and references therein, and [18] particularly for the model-checking problem on pushdown trees).

Context-free grammars and pushdown automata can be viewed as the first level of an infinite hierarchy of higher-order grammars and higher-order pushdown automata. These hierarchies, introduced in the early eighties by Engelfriet [6], have been subsequently extensively studied, in particular by Damm [4],

---

* Partly supported by KBN Grant 7 T11C 027 20.
** Partly supported by KBN Grant 7 T11C 028 20.

M. Nielsen and U. Engberg (Eds.): Fossacs 2002, LNCS 2303, pp. 205–222, 2002.

and Damm and Goerdt [5]. We find it natural to examine the computation trees of higher-order pushdown automata, as well as trees generated by higher-order grammars, from the point of view of the decidability of their MSO theories. Indeed, we would like to push the frontier of decidability in order to capture more complex trees.

In [11], we have made the first step in this direction by showing decidability of the MSO theory of trees generated by grammars of level two subject to an additional restriction on grammars which we called *safety*. This constraint is similar to the restriction to "derived types" in [4, 5]. It is still an open problem if this restriction is essential for decidability, or whether it really reduces the generating power of grammars. However, in the present paper we are able to state two results.

(1) After a natural generalization of the concept of safety, a tree generated by a safe grammar of any level enjoys a decidable MSO theory.
(2) A tree is generated by a safe grammar of level n if and only if it can be recognized by a pushdown automaton of level n.

Consequently (by (1) and the "if" part of (2)), the monadic second order theory of a tree recognized by a pushdown automaton of any level is decidable.

The "only if" part of (2) is of independent interest: it can be understood as an implementation of higher-order recursion by higher-order stack. This implementation is simpler than that of [5] for the following reasons: because we are using a simpler notion of a higher-order pushdown store, and because it works essentially for arbitrary safe grammars, without any specific normal form restrictions. (The few syntactic conditions we assume are merely for convenience.)

The question of decidability of MSO theories of higher-level trees has been recently investigated also by Courcelle and Knapik [3]. Following ideas of Damm [4], the authors study an operation of *evaluation* which, when applied to a tree (generated by a grammar) of level n, produces a tree of level $n + 1$. They show that this evaluation operation preserves MSO decidability, and that any algebraic (level 1) tree can be obtained by evaluation of a regular tree. While multiple application of evaluation leads to trees of arbitrary high level, it is not clear if all trees generated by safe grammars can be obtained in this way.

Problems related to ours were addressed by H. Hungar, who studied graphs generated by some specific higher-order graph grammars. He showed [7] decidability of the monadic second-order theory (S1S) of *paths* of such graphs (not the full MSO theory of graphs).

1   Preliminaries

Throughout the paper, the set of natural numbers is denoted ω and, for $n \in \omega$, the symbol $[n]$ abbreviates $\{1, \ldots, n\}$.

Types. We consider a set of types $\mathcal{T}$ constructed from a unique *basic* type **0**: **0** is a type and, if τ_1, τ_2 are types, so is $(\tau_1 \to \tau_2) \in \mathcal{T}$. The operator $\to$ is assumed to associate to the right. Note that each type is of the form $\tau_1 \rightarrow \cdots \rightarrow \tau_n \rightarrow \mathbf{0}$, for some $n \geq 0$. A type $\mathbf{0} \rightarrow \cdots \rightarrow \mathbf{0}$ with $n + 1$ occurrences of $\mathbf{0}$ is also written $\mathbf{0}^n \rightarrow \mathbf{0}$.

The level $\ell(\tau)$ of a type τ is defined by $\ell(\mathbf{0}) = 0$, and $\ell(\tau_1 \rightarrow \tau_2) = \max(1 + \ell(\tau_1), \ell(\tau_2))$. Thus $\mathbf{0}$ is the only type of level 0 and each type of level 1 is of the form $\mathbf{0}^n \rightarrow \mathbf{0}$ for some $n > 0$. A type $\tau_1 \rightarrow \cdots \rightarrow \tau_n \rightarrow \mathbf{0}$ is *homogeneous* (where $n \geq 0$) if each τ_i is homogeneous and $\ell(\tau_1) \geq \ell(\tau_2) \geq \ldots \geq \ell(\tau_n)$. For example a type $((\mathbf{0} \rightarrow \mathbf{0}) \rightarrow \mathbf{0}) \rightarrow (\mathbf{0} \rightarrow \mathbf{0}) \rightarrow (\mathbf{0} \rightarrow \mathbf{0} \rightarrow \mathbf{0}) \rightarrow \mathbf{0} \rightarrow \mathbf{0}$ is homogeneous, but a type $\mathbf{0} \rightarrow (\mathbf{0} \rightarrow \mathbf{0}) \rightarrow \mathbf{0}$ is not.

Higher–order terms. A *typed alphabet* is a set Γ of symbols with types in $\mathcal{T}$. Thus Γ can be also presented as a $\mathcal{T}$-indexed family $\{\Gamma_\tau\}_{\tau \in \mathcal{T}}$, where Γ_τ is the set of all symbols of Γ of type τ. We let the *type level* $\ell(\Gamma)$ of Γ be the supremum of $\ell(\tau)$, such that Γ_τ is nonempty.

Given a typed alphabet Γ, the set $T(\Gamma) = \{T(\Gamma)_\tau\}_{\tau \in \mathcal{T}}$ of *applicative terms* is defined inductively, by

(1) $\Gamma_\tau \subseteq T(\Gamma)_\tau$;
(2) if $t \in T(\Gamma)_{\tau_1 \rightarrow \tau_2}$ and $s \in T(\Gamma)_{\tau_1}$ then $(ts) \in T(\Gamma)_{\tau_2}$.

Note that each applicative term can be presented in a form $Zt_1 \ldots t_n$, where $n \geq 0$, $Z \in \Gamma$, and $t_1, \ldots, t_n$ are applicative terms. We say that a term $t \in T(\Gamma)_\tau$ is of type τ, which we also write $t : \tau$. A term $t : \tau$ is said to be of *level k* iff τ is of level k. We adopt the usual notational convention that application associates to the left, i.e. we write $t_0 t_1 \ldots t_n$ instead of $(\cdots((t_0 t_1)t_2)\cdots)t_n$. For applicative terms $t, t_1, \ldots, t_m$, and symbols $z_1, \ldots, z_m$, of appropriate types, the term $t[z_1 := t_1, \ldots, z_k := t_k]$ is defined as the result of simultaneous replacement in t of z_i by t_i, for $i = 1, \ldots, m$.

Trees. The free monoid generated by a set X is written X^* and the empty word is written ε. The length of word $w \in X^*$ is denoted by $|w|$.

A *tree* is any nonempty prefix–closed subset T of X^* (with ε considered as the *root*). If $u \in T$, $x \in X$, and $ux \in T$ then ux is an *immediate successor* of u in T. For $w \in T$, the set $T.w = \{v \in X^* : wv \in T\}$ is the *subtree* of T induced by w. Note that $T.w$ is also a tree, and $T.\varepsilon = T$.

Now let Σ be a typed alphabet of level 1. A symbol f in Σ is of type $\mathbf{0}^n \rightarrow \mathbf{0}$, for $n \geq 0$, and can be viewed as a (first–order) function symbol of *arity* n. Let $T \subseteq \omega^*$ be a tree. A mapping $t : T \rightarrow \Sigma$ is called a Σ-*tree* provided that if $t(w) : \mathbf{0}^k \rightarrow \mathbf{0}$ then w has exactly k immediate successors which are $w1, \ldots, wk$ (hence w is a leaf whenever $t(w) : \mathbf{0}$). The set of Σ-trees is written $T^\infty(\Sigma)$.

If $t : T \rightarrow \Sigma$ is a Σ-tree, then T is called the *domain* of t and denoted by $T = \mathrm{Dom}\, t$. For $v \in \mathrm{Dom}\, t$, the *subtree* of t induced by v is a Σ-tree $t.v$ such that $\mathrm{Dom}\, t.v = (\mathrm{Dom}\, t).v$, and $t.v(w) = t(vw)$, for $w \in \mathrm{Dom}\, t.v$. It is convenient to organize the set $T^\infty(\Sigma)$ into an algebra over the signature Σ, where for each $f \in \Sigma_{\mathbf{0}^n \rightarrow \mathbf{0}}$, the operation associated with f sends an n–tuple of trees $t_1, \ldots, t_n$

onto the unique tree t such that $t(\varepsilon) = f$ and $t.i = t_i$, for $i \in [n]$. Finite trees in $T^\infty(\Sigma)$ can be also identified with applicative terms of type $\mathbf{0}$ over the alphabet Σ in the usual manner.

We also introduce a concept of limit. For a Σ-tree t, let $t{\restriction}n$ be its truncation to the level n, i.e., the restriction of the function t to the set $\{w \in \mathcal{D}om\, t \mid |w| \leq n\}$. Suppose $t_0, t_1, \ldots$ is a sequence of Σ-trees such that, for all k, there is an m, say $m(k)$, such that, for all $n, n' \geq m(k)$, $t_n{\restriction}k = t_{n'}{\restriction}k$. (This is a Cauchy condition in a suitable metric space of trees.) Then the *limit* of the sequence t_n, in symbols $\lim t_n$, is a Σ-tree t which is the set-theoretical union of the functions $t_n{\restriction}m(n)$ (understanding a function as a set of pairs).

Monadic second–order logic. Let R be a *relational vocabulary*, i.e., a set of relational symbols, each r in R given with an arity $\rho(r) > 0$. The formulas of *monadic second order (MSO) logic* over vocabulary R use two kinds of variables : *individual variables* $x_0, x_1, \ldots$, and *set variables* $X_0, X_1, \ldots$. Atomic formulas are $x_i = x_j$, $r(x_{i_1}, \ldots, x_{i_{\rho(r)}})$, and $X_i(x_j)$. The other formulas are built using propositional connectives $\vee, \neg$, and the quantifier $\exists$ ranging over both kinds of variables. (The connectives $\wedge, \Rightarrow$, etc., as well as the quantifier $\forall$ are introduced in the usual way as abbreviations.) A formula without free variables is called a *sentence*. Formulas are interpreted in relational structures over the vocabulary R, which we usually present by $\mathbf{A} = \langle A, \{r^{\mathbf{A}} : r \in R\}\rangle$, where A is the *universe* of $\mathbf{A}$, and $r^{\mathbf{A}} \subseteq A^{\rho(r)}$ is a $\rho(r)$-ary relation on A. A *valuation* is a mapping v from the set of variables (of both kinds), such that $v(x_i) \in A$, and $v(X_i) \subseteq A$. The *satisfaction* of a formula φ in $\mathbf{A}$ under the valuation v, in symbols $\mathbf{A}, v \models \varphi$ is defined by induction on φ in the usual manner.

Clearly, the satisfaction of a formula depends only on the valuation of its free variables. The *monadic second–order theory* of $\mathbf{A}$ is the set of all MSO sentences satisfied in $\mathbf{A}$, in symbols $MSO(\mathbf{A}) = \{\varphi : \mathbf{A} \models \varphi\}$.

Let Σ be a typed alphabet of level 1, and suppose that the maximum of the arities of symbols in Σ exists and equals m_Σ. A tree $t \in T^\infty(\Sigma)$ can be viewed as a logical structure $\mathbf{t}$, over the vocabulary $R_\Sigma = \{p_f : f \in \Sigma\} \cup \{d_i : 1 \leq i \leq m_\Sigma\}$, with $\rho(p_f) = 1$, and $\rho(d_i) = 2$:

$$\mathbf{t} = \langle \mathcal{D}om\, t, \{p_f^{\mathbf{t}} : f \in \Sigma\} \cup \{d_i^{\mathbf{t}} : 1 \leq i \leq m_\Sigma\}\rangle.$$

The universe of $\mathbf{t}$ is the domain of t, and the predicate symbols are interpreted by $p_f^{\mathbf{t}} = \{w \in \mathcal{D}om\, t : t(w) = f\}$, for $f \in \Sigma$, and $d_i^{\mathbf{t}} = \{(w, wi) : wi \in \mathcal{D}om\, t\}$, for $1 \leq i \leq m_\Sigma$. We refer the reader to [16] for a survey of the results on monadic second-order theory of trees.

Grammars. We now fix two disjoint typed alphabets, $N = \{N_\tau\}_{\tau \in \mathcal{T}}$ and $\mathcal{X} = \{\mathcal{X}_\tau\}_{\tau \in \mathcal{T}}$ of *nonterminals* and *variables* (or *parameters*), respectively. A *grammar* is a tuple $\mathcal{G} = (\Sigma, V, \mathcal{S}, E)$, where Σ is a *signature* (i.e., a finite alphabet of level 1), $V \subseteq N$ is a finite set of nonterminals, $\mathcal{S} \in V$ is a *start symbol* of type $\mathbf{0}$, and E is a set of productions of the form

$$\mathcal{F}z_1 \ldots z_m \Rightarrow w$$

where $\mathcal{F} : \tau_1 \to \tau_2 \cdots \to \tau_m \to \mathbf{0}$ is a nonterminal in V, z_i is a variable of type τ_i, and w is an applicative term in $T(\Sigma \cup V \cup \{z_1 \ldots z_m\})$.

We assume that for each $\mathcal{F}$ in V, there is exactly one production in E with $\mathcal{F}$ occurring on the left hand side. Furthermore, we make a *proviso* that each nonterminal in a grammar has a homogeneous type, and that if $m \geq 1$ then $\tau_m = \mathbf{0}$. This implies that each nonterminal of level > 0 has at least one parameter of level 0 (which needs not, of course, occur at the right-hand side). The *level* of a grammar is the highest level of its nonterminals.

In this paper, we are interested in grammars as generators of Σ-trees. Let, as before, $\Sigma^\perp = \Sigma \cup \{\perp\}$, with $\perp : \mathbf{0}$. First, with any applicative term t over $\Sigma \cup V$, we associate an expression $t^\perp$ over signature $\Sigma^\perp$ inductively as follows.

- If $t = f$, $f \in \Sigma$, then $t^\perp = f$.
- If $t = X$, $X \in V$, then $t^\perp = \perp$.
- If $t = (sr)$ then if $s^\perp \neq \perp$ then $t^\perp = (s^\perp r^\perp)$, otherwise $t^\perp = \perp$.

Informally speaking, the operation $t \mapsto t^\perp$ replaces in t each nonterminal, together with its arguments, by $\perp$. It is easy to see that if t is an applicative term (over $\Sigma \cup V$) of type $\mathbf{0}$ then $t^\perp$ is an applicative term over $\Sigma^\perp$ of type $\mathbf{0}$. Recall that applicative terms over $\Sigma^\perp$ of type $\mathbf{0}$ can be identified with finite trees.

We will now define the single-step rewriting relation $\to_g$ among the terms over $\Sigma \cup V$. Informally speaking, $t \to_g t'$ whenever t' is obtained from t by replacing some occurrence of a nonterminal F by the right–hand side of the appropriate production in which all parameters are in turn replaced by the actual arguments of F. Such a replacement is allowed only if F occurs as a head of a subterm of type $\mathbf{0}$. More precisely, the relation $\to_g \subseteq T(\Sigma \cup V) \times T(\Sigma \cup V)$ is defined inductively by the following clauses.

- $\mathcal{F} t_1 \ldots t_k \to_g t[z_1 := t_1, \ldots, z_k := t_k]$ if there is a production $\mathcal{F} z_1 \ldots z_k \Rightarrow t$ (with $z_i : \rho_i$, $i = 1, \ldots, k$), and $t_i \in T(\Sigma \cup V)_{\rho_i}$, for $i = 1, \ldots, k$.
- If $t \to_g t'$ then $(st) \to_g (st')$ and $(tq) \to_g (t'q)$, whenever the expressions in question are applicative terms.

A *reduction* is a finite or infinite sequence of terms in $T(\Sigma \cup V)$, $t_0 \to_g t_1 \to_g \ldots$. As usual, the symbol $\twoheadrightarrow_g$ stands for the reflexive transitive closure of $\to_g$. We also define the relation $t \twoheadrightarrow_g^\infty t'$, where t is an applicative term in $T(\Sigma \cup V)$ and t' is a tree in $T^\infty(\Sigma^\perp)$, by

- t' is a finite tree, and there is a finite reduction sequence $t = t_0 \to_g \ldots \to_g t_n = t'$, or
- t' is infinite, and there is an infinite reduction sequence $t = t_0 \to_g t_1 \to_g \ldots$ such that $t' = \lim t_n^\perp$.

To define a unique tree produced by the grammar, we recall a standard *approximation ordering* on $T^\infty(\Sigma^\perp)$: $t' \sqsubseteq t$ if $\mathrm{Dom}\ t' \subseteq \mathrm{Dom}\ t$ and, for each $w \in \mathrm{Dom}\ t'$, $t'(w) = t(w)$ or $t'(w) = \perp$. (In other words, t' is obtained from t by replacing some of its subtrees by $\perp$.) Then we let

$$[\![\mathcal{G}]\!] = \sup\{t \in T^\infty(\Sigma^\perp) : S \twoheadrightarrow_g^\infty t\}$$

It is easy to see that, by the Church–Rosser property of our grammar, the above set is directed, and hence $[\![\mathcal{G}]\!]$ is well defined since $T^\infty(\Sigma^\perp)$ with the approximation ordering is a cpo. Furthermore, it is routine to show that if an infinite reduction $S = t_0 \to_{\mathcal{G}} t_1 \to_{\mathcal{G}} \dots$ is *fair*, i.e., any occurrence of a nonterminal symbol is eventually rewritten, then its result $t' = \lim t_n^\perp$ is $[\![\mathcal{G}]\!]$.

If a tree t is generated by a grammar of level n, we will sometimes say that t is of level n.

2   Infinitary Lambda Calculus

In this section we recall some concepts and results from [11]. Our motivation for introducing infinite lambda terms comes from the strategy of our proof. Basically, we wish to reduce the MSO theory of a tree t of level n to the MSO theory of some tree t' of level $n - 1$. However, like in [11], it will be useful to view the latter tree as an infinite lambda term (intuitively, evaluating to t).

Infinitary lambda calculus is an extension of the ordinary lambda calculus, which allows the use of infinite lambda terms. We will identify infinite lambda terms with certain infinite trees. More specifically, we fix a *finite* alphabet Σ of level 1 called *signature*, and let $\Sigma^\perp = \Sigma \cup \{\perp\}$, where $\perp$ is a fresh symbol of type **0**. All our finite and infinite terms, called *lambda trees* are simply typed and may involve constants from $\Sigma^\perp$, and variables from a fixed countably infinite set. In fact, we only consider lambda trees of types of level at most 1.

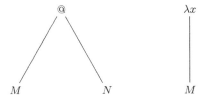

Fig. 1. Application and abstraction

Definition 2.1. Let Σ° be an infinite alphabet of level 1, consisting of

- A binary function symbol @;
- All symbols from $\Sigma^\perp$, as individual constants, regardless of their actual types;
- Infinitely many individual variables, as individual constants;
- Unary function symbols λx for all variables x.

The set of all *lambda trees* (over a signature Σ) is the greatest set of Σ°-trees, given together with their *types*, such that the following conditions hold.

- Each variable x is a lambda tree of type **0**.
- Each function symbol $f \in \Sigma^\perp$ of type τ is a lambda tree of type τ.

- Otherwise each lambda tree is of type of level at most 1 and is either an *application* (MN) or an *abstraction* $(\lambda x.M)$ (see Figure 1).
- If a lambda tree P of type τ is an application (MN) then M is a lambda tree of type $\mathbf{0} \to \tau$, and N is a lambda tree of type $\mathbf{0}$.
- If a lambda tree P of type τ has the form $(\lambda x.M)$, then $\tau = \mathbf{0} \to \sigma$, and M is a lambda tree of type σ.

Strictly speaking, the above is a co-inductive definition of the two-argument relation "M is a lambda tree of type τ". Formally, a lambda tree can be presented as a pair (M, τ), where M is a Σ°-tree (as defined in section 1), and τ is its type satisfying the conditions above. Whenever we talk about a "lambda tree" we actually mean a lambda tree together with its type. We warn the reader about a possible confusion: The types associated with lambda trees by the above definition are *not* the types of these trees viewed as terms over Σ° (but rather as terms over Σ).

Let M be a lambda tree and let x be a variable. Each node of M labeled x is called an *occurrence* of x in M. An occurrence of x is *bound*, iff it has an ancestor labeled λx. The *binder* of this occurrence of x is the closest of all such ancestors λx (i.e., one occurring at the largest depth). An occurrence of x which is not bound is called *free*. We say that a variable x is *free* in a lambda tree M iff it has a free occurrence in M. The (possibly infinite) set of all free variables of M will be denoted by $FV(M)$. A lambda tree M with $FV(M) = \varnothing$ is called *closed*.

Clearly, ordinary lambda terms can be seen as a special case of lambda trees, and the notion of a free variable in a lambda tree generalizes the notion of a free variable in a lambda term. The *n-th approximant* of a lambda tree M, denoted $M{\upharpoonright}n$ is defined by induction as follows:

- $M{\upharpoonright}0 = \bot$, for all M;
- $(MN){\upharpoonright}n+1 = (M{\upharpoonright}n)(N{\upharpoonright}n)$;
- $(\lambda x.M){\upharpoonright}n+1 = \lambda x(M{\upharpoonright}n)$.

That is, the n-th approximant is obtained by replacing all subtrees rooted at depth n by the constant $\bot$.

Let $P(z/x)$ denote the result of replacing in P all free occurrences of a variable x by another variable z.

Definition 2.2. A *bisimulation* on lambda trees is a binary relation $\sim$ satisfying the following conditions:

(1) If $M \sim N$ then M and N are of the same type.
(2) If $M \sim N$ then the root labels of M and N are either the same or both M and N are abstractions.
(3) If $\lambda x.M \sim \lambda y.N$, then $M(z/x) \sim N(z/y)$, whenever z is a fresh variable (neither free nor bound in $\lambda x.M$ and $\lambda y.N$).
(4) If $(MN) \sim (M'N')$ then $M \sim M'$ and $N \sim N'$.

Lemma 2.3. (1) *The union $\approx$ of all bisimulations is a bisimulation itself.*

(2) *On ordinary lambda-terms, the relation $\approx$ coincides with the α-equivalence $=_\alpha$.*
(3) *$M \approx N$ holds if and only if $M{\upharpoonright}n =_\alpha N{\upharpoonright}n$ holds for all n.*
(4) *If $M \approx N$ then $FV(M) = FV(N)$.*

The above lemma provides evidence that the greatest bisimulation is a correct generalization of the notion of α-equivalence. That is, $M \approx N$ holds iff M and N are identical up to names of bound variables. Following a common practice in lambda calculus, alpha-equivalent lambda trees will be identified. In consequence, all three statements $M \approx N$, $M =_\alpha N$ and $M = N$ will be understood as expressing the same property.

Lemma 2.4 (Principle of co-induction [8]). *In order to prove that $M =_\alpha N$, it is enough to find a bisimulation $\sim$ such that $M \sim N$.*

2.1   From Grammar Terms to Lambda Trees

Given a grammar $\mathcal{G}$, we define co-inductively a relation $\beth_\mathcal{G}$ as the greatest relation between terms in $T(\Sigma \cup V \cup \mathcal{X})$ and lambda trees (over Σ) such that, for all $(t, M) \in \beth_\mathcal{G}$,

(1) if t is a function symbol f then $M = f$,
(2) if t is a variable $x \in \mathcal{X}_0$ then $M = x$,
(3) if $t = \mathcal{F}t_1, \ldots t_m$, where $\mathcal{F}$ is a nonterminal whose production in $\mathcal{G}$ is
    $\mathcal{F}\phi_1 \ldots \phi_m x_1 \ldots x_n \Rightarrow r$, with variables $\phi_1, \ldots, \phi_m$ of level ≥ 1 and variables $x_1, \ldots, x_n$ of level 0, $t_1 \ldots t_m$ are terms such that $\text{type}(\phi_i) = \text{type}(t_i)$, for $i \in [m]$ then

$$M \in \{\lambda x'_1 \ldots x'_n.N \mid (r[\phi_1{:=}t_1, \ldots, \phi_m{:=}t_m, x_1{:=}x'_1, \ldots, x_n{:=}x'_n], N) \in \beth_\mathcal{G}\},$$

where the variables $x'_1, \ldots, x'_n$ are chosen so that no x'_i occurs free in any of t_j,
(4) if $t = (t_1 t_2)$ where $t_1 : \mathbf{0} \to \tau$ and $t_2 : \mathbf{0}$ then $M \in \{(M_1 M_2) \mid (t_1, M_1), (t_2, M_2) \in \beth_\mathcal{G}\}$.

It is easy to see that any term t of level ≤ 1 using variables only from $\mathcal{X}_0$ is in the form (1)–(4).

Lemma 2.5. *$\beth_\mathcal{G}$ is a partial function defined for all terms in $T(\Sigma \cup V \cup \mathcal{X}_0)$ of level ≤ 1. That is, for any such t, there exists a unique M (up to α-equivalence) such that $(t, M) \in \beth_\mathcal{G}$.*

From now on $\beth_\mathcal{G}$ is considered as a function. The conditions (1)–(4) of the above definition can now be stated as follows.

(1) $\beth_\mathcal{G}(t) = f$, if t is a function symbol $f \in \Sigma$,
(2) $\beth_\mathcal{G}(t) = x$, if t is a variable $x \in \mathcal{X}_0$,
(3) $\beth_\mathcal{G}(t) = \lambda x'_1 \ldots x'_n.\beth_\mathcal{G}(r[\phi_1{:=}t_1, \ldots, \phi_m{:=}t_m, x_1{:=}x'_1, \ldots, x_n{:=}x'_n])$, if $t = \mathcal{F}t_1 \ldots t_m$, for some nonterminal $\mathcal{F}$, such that $\mathcal{F}\phi_1 \ldots \phi_m x_1 \ldots x_n = r$ is a production of $\mathcal{G}$. The variables $x'_1, \ldots, x'_n$ are chosen so that no x'_i occurs free in any of t_j,

(4) $\beth_{\mathcal{G}}(t) = (\beth_{\mathcal{G}}(t_1)\beth_{\mathcal{G}}(t_2))$, if $t = (t_1t_2)$ where $t_1 : \mathbf{0} \to \tau$ and $t_2 : \mathbf{0}$.

We will be mainly interested in $\beth_{\mathcal{G}}(S)$, where S is the start symbol of the grammar. It can be viewed as a lambda term obtained by a usually infinite process of expansion, according to the rules of the grammar. (Intuitively, it is a lambda term "evaluating" to the tree $[\![\mathcal{G}]\!]$.)

3   Safe Grammars

The following is an extension of the definition from [11] to higher types.

Definition 3.1. A term of level $k > 0$ is *unsafe* if it contains an occurrence of a parameter of level strictly less than k, otherwise the term is *safe*. An *occurrence* of an unsafe term t as a subexpression of a term t' is *safe* if it is in the context $\ldots(ts)\ldots$, otherwise the occurrence is *unsafe*. A grammar is *safe* if no unsafe term has an unsafe occurrence at a right-hand side of any production.

Example: Let f, g, h, a, b be signature symbols of arity 2,1,1,0,0, respectively. Consider a grammar of level 2 with nonterminals $S : \mathbf{0}$, and $\mathcal{F} : (\mathbf{0} \to \mathbf{0}) \to \mathbf{0} \to \mathbf{0} \to \mathbf{0}$, and productions

$$S \Rightarrow \mathcal{F}gab$$

$$\mathcal{F}\varphi xy \Rightarrow f(\mathcal{F}(\mathcal{F}\varphi x)y(hy))(f(\varphi x)y)$$

This grammar is not safe, because of the unsafe subterm $\mathcal{F}\varphi x$, which is not applied to an argument. However, it is equivalent to an algebraic grammar with the following productions:

$$S \Rightarrow \mathcal{G}(ga)b$$

$$\mathcal{G}zy \Rightarrow f(\mathcal{G}(\mathcal{G}zy)(hy))(fzy)$$

But life is not always so easy. If we replace the above production for $\mathcal{F}$ by a slightly different one:

$$\mathcal{F}\varphi xy \Rightarrow f(\mathcal{F}(\mathcal{F}\varphi x)y(hy))(f(\varphi y)x)$$

we obtain a grammar which is conjectured not to be equivalent to a safe grammar of any level.

The crucial observation is the following.

Lemma 3.2. *If a grammar $\mathcal{G}$ is safe then the lambda tree $\beth_{\mathcal{G}}(S)$ can be constructed using only the original variables of the grammar. That is, whenever clause (3) is applied, the variables $x'_1, \ldots, x'_n$ can be chosen just $x_1, \ldots, x_n$.*

Proof. We use safety only with respect to parameters of level $\mathbf{0}$. Observe that substitution preserves safety and a subterm of a safe term is again safe. This follows that whenever clause (3) is applied, the terms $t_1, \ldots, t_m$ are safe. Formally, we modify the definition of $\beth_{\mathcal{G}}$ to $\beth'_{\mathcal{G}}$, such that the clause (3) applies only if the terms $t_1, \ldots, t_m$ are safe (otherwise, say, $\beth'_{\mathcal{G}}(t) = \bot$), and show that $\beth'_{\mathcal{G}}(S)$ and $\beth_{\mathcal{G}}(S)$ are bisimilar using the condition (3) of Lemma 2.3. $\square$

In [11], we have essentially established the result which, by combining Theorem 2 and Proposition 4 from there with Lemma 3.2 above, can be rephrased as follows.[1]

Theorem 3.3 ([11]). *If a grammar $\mathcal{G}$ is safe then the MSO theory of the tree $[\![\mathcal{G}]\!]$ is reducible to the MSO theory of $\mathbf{J}_\mathcal{G}(S)$, that is, there exists a recursive mapping of sentences $\varphi \mapsto \varphi'$ such that $[\![\mathcal{G}]\!] \models \varphi$ iff $\mathbf{J}_\mathcal{G}(S) \models \varphi'$.*

By this, MSO theory of a tree generated by a safe grammar $\mathcal{G}$ reduces to the MSO theory of $\mathbf{J}_\mathcal{G}(S)$. Our induction argument will consist in showing that the latter can be generated by a grammar of level $n-1$.

Definition 3.4. Let $\mathcal{G} = (\Sigma, V, S, E)$ be a safe grammar of level $n \geq 2$. We may assume that the parameters of type $\mathbf{0}$ occurring in distinct productions are different. Let $\mathcal{X}^{\mathcal{G}_0} = \{x_1, \ldots, x_L\}$ be the set of all parameters of type $\mathbf{0}$ occurring in grammar $\mathcal{G}$. We define a grammar of level $n-1$ $\mathcal{G}^\alpha = (\Sigma^\alpha, V^\alpha, S^\alpha, E^\alpha)$ as follows.

It is convenient first to define a transformation α of (homogeneous) types, that maps $\mathbf{0}$ to $\mathbf{0}$, $\mathbf{0}^\ell \to \mathbf{0}$ to $\mathbf{0}$ and maps a type $\tau_1 \to \cdots \to \tau_n$ with $\ell(\tau_n) \leq 1$ and $\ell(\tau_{n-1}) > 1$, inductively, to $\alpha(\tau_1) \to \cdots \to \alpha(\tau_n)$. Note that, in particular, α maps $(\mathbf{0}^{k_1} \to \mathbf{0}) \to \cdots \to (\mathbf{0}^{k_m} \to \mathbf{0}) \to \mathbf{0}^\ell \to \mathbf{0}$ to $\mathbf{0}^m \to \mathbf{0}$. We will denote $\alpha(\tau)$ by τ^α. Let $\Sigma^\alpha = \Sigma \cup \{@, \lambda x_1, \ldots, \lambda x_L, x_1, \ldots, x_L\}$, where all symbols from Σ as well as (former) parameters $x_1, \ldots, x_L$ are of arity 0, the symbol $@$ is binary, and the symbols λx_i are unary. The set $V^\alpha = \{\mathcal{F}^\alpha : \mathcal{F} \in V\}$ is a copy of V, with $\mathcal{F}^\alpha : \tau^\alpha$, whenever $\mathcal{F} : \tau$. Finally, whenever there is a production $\mathcal{F}\phi_1 \ldots \phi_m y_1 \ldots y_n \Rightarrow r$ in E, where $y_1, \ldots, y_n$ are the parameters of level 0, there is a production $\mathcal{F}^\alpha \phi_1 \ldots \phi_m \Rightarrow \lambda y_1 \ldots \lambda y_n.r^\alpha$ in E^α, where the transformation of typed terms $r : \tau \mapsto r^\alpha : \tau^\alpha$ is defined inductively by

- $\alpha : \mathcal{F} \mapsto \mathcal{F}^\alpha$,
- $\alpha : z \mapsto z$, for any parameter z,
- $\alpha : (ts) \mapsto (t^\alpha s^\alpha)$, whenever $s : \tau$ with $\ell(\tau) \geq 1$,
- $\alpha : (ts) \mapsto ((@t^\alpha)s^\alpha)$, whenever $s : \mathbf{0}$ (hence consequently $t^\alpha, s^\alpha : \mathbf{0}$).

Note that all parameters of $\mathcal{G}$ of type τ become parameters of $\mathcal{G}^\alpha$ of type τ^α except for the parameters of type $\mathbf{0}$ which become constants.

The following is an immediate consequence of the definition.

Lemma 3.5. *If $\mathcal{G}$ is safe then $\mathcal{G}^\alpha$ is safe, too.*

Lemma 3.6. *The trees $\mathbf{J}_\mathcal{G}(S)$ and $[\![\mathcal{G}^\alpha]\!]$ coincide.*

Proof. By Principle of co-induction 2.4, we check that these trees are bisimilar using the condition (3) of Lemma 2.3. □

---

[1] The main step in [11] is a reduction of the MSO theory of $[\![\mathcal{G}]\!]$ to the MSO theory of a certain graph associated with $\mathbf{J}_\mathcal{G}(S)$ (Theorem 2 and Proposition 4 there). Lemma 3.2 allows to interpret that graph in the MSO theory of $\mathbf{J}_\mathcal{G}(S)$.

Theorem 3.7. *Let $\mathcal{G}$ be a safe grammar of level n. Then the monadic theory of $[\![\mathcal{G}]\!]$ is decidable.*

Proof. For $n = 0$ the claim amounts to the decidability of the MSO theory of a regular tree that was essentially established already by Rabin [15]. For grammars of level 1 (algebraic), the result was proved by Courcelle [2]. (Clearly, for level $n \leq 1$, the safety assumption holds trivially.)

Now let $t = [\![\mathcal{G}]\!]$ be a tree generated by a grammar of level $n \geq 2$ and let $t^\alpha = [\![\mathcal{G}^\alpha]\!]$. By induction hypothesis, the MSO theory of t^α is decidable. The claim follows from Lemma 3.6 and Theorem 3.3.   □

4   Pushdown Automata

We use the abbreviation "pds" for the expression "pushdown store". A *level* 1 *pds* (or a 1-*pds*) over an alphabet A is an arbitrary sequence $[a_1, \ldots, a_l]$ of elements of A, with $l \geq 1$. A *level* n *pds* (or a n-*pds*), for $n \geq 2$, is a sequence $[s_1, \ldots, s_l]$ of $(n-1)$-pds's, where $l \geq 1$. (That is, we assume that a pds is never empty.) For a given symbol $\bot \in A$, we define $\bot_k$ as follows: $\bot_1 = [\bot]$ and $\bot_{k+1} = [\bot_k]$. Thus $\bot_k$ is the level k pds which contains only $\bot$ at the bottom.

Let s be an n-pds and let s' be a k-pds, for some $k \leq n$. We write $s' \subset s$ iff one of the following cases holds:

- $s = [s_1, \ldots, s_l]$ and $s' = s_i$, for some $i = 1, \ldots, l-1$.
- $s = [s_1, \ldots, s_l]$ and $s' \subset s_i$, for some $i = 1, \ldots, l$.

The following operations are possible on pushdown stores

- $push_1^a([a_1, \ldots, a_{l-1}, a_l]) = [a_1, \ldots, a_l, a]$, where $a \in A$;
- $pop_1([a_1, \ldots, a_{l-1}, a_l]) = [a_1, \ldots, a_{l-1}]$;
- $top_1([a_1, \ldots, a_{l-1}, a_l]) = a_l$.

On pushdown stores of level $n > 1$ one can perform the following operations:

- $push_n([s_1, \ldots, s_{l-1}, s_l]) = [s_1, \ldots, s_l, s_l]$;
- $pop_n([s_1, \ldots, s_{l-1}, s_l]) = [s_1, \ldots, s_{l-1}]$;
- $push_k([s_1, \ldots, s_{l-1}, s_l]) = [s_1, \ldots, s_{l-1}, push_k(s_l)]$, where $2 \leq k < n$;
- $push_1^a([s_1, \ldots, s_{l-1}, s_l]) = [s_1, \ldots, s_{l-1}, push_1^a(s_l)]$, where $a \in A$;
- $pop_k([s_1, \ldots, s_{l-1}, s_l]) = [s_1, \ldots, s_{l-1}, pop_k(s_l)]$, where $1 \leq k < n$;
- $top_n([s_1, \ldots, s_{l-1}, s_l]) = s_l$;
- $top_k([s_1, \ldots, s_{l-1}, s_l]) = top_k(s_l)$, for $1 \leq k < n$.

The operation pop_k is undefined on a push down store, whose top pds of level k consists of only one element.

Let Σ be a signature, and let Q and A be finite sets. Let $\bot \in A$ be a distinguished element of A. The set $\mathcal{I}_n$ of *instructions* of level n (parameterized by Σ, Q and A) consists of all tuples of the following forms:

(1) $(push_k, p)$, where $p \in Q$ and $1 < k \leq n$;

(2) $(push_1^a, p)$, where $p \in Q$, and $a \in A$, $a \neq \perp$.
(3) (pop_k, p), where $p \in Q$ and $1 \leq k \leq n$.
(4) $(f, p_1, \ldots, p_r)$, where $f \in \Sigma_r$ and $p_1, \ldots, p_r \in Q$;

A *pushdown automaton of level n* is defined as a tuple

$$\mathcal{A} = \langle Q, \Sigma, A, q_0, \delta, \perp \rangle,$$

where Q is a finite set of *states*, with an *initial state* q_0, Σ is a signature, A is a pds alphabet, with a distinguished *bottom symbol* $\perp$, and

$$\delta : Q \times A \to \mathcal{I}_n$$

is a *transition function*.

A *configuration* of an automaton $\mathcal{A}$ as above is a pair $\langle q, s \rangle$, where $q \in Q$ and s is an n-pds over A. The *initial configuration* is $\langle q_0, \perp_n \rangle$. The set of all configurations is denoted by $\mathcal{C}$.

We define a relation $\to_\mathcal{A}$ on configurations as follows:

(1) If $top_1(s) = a$ and $\delta(q, a) = (push_k, p)$, with $k > 1$, then $\langle q, s \rangle \to_\mathcal{A}$ $\langle p, push_k(s) \rangle$.
(2) If $top_1(s) = a$ and $\delta(q, a) = (push_1^b, p)$, then $\langle q, s \rangle \to_\mathcal{A} \langle p, push_1^b(s) \rangle$.
(3) If $top_1(s) = a$ and $\delta(q, a) = (pop_k, p)$, then $\langle q, s \rangle \to_\mathcal{A} \langle p, pop_k(s) \rangle$, provided $pop_k(s)$ is defined.

The symbol $\twoheadrightarrow_\mathcal{A}$ stands for the reflexive and transitive closure of $\to_\mathcal{A}$.

Now let $t : T \to \Sigma$ be a Σ-tree. A partial function $\varrho : T \to \mathcal{C}$ defined on an initial fragment of T is called a *partial run* of $\mathcal{A}$ on t iff the following conditions hold:

- $\langle q_0, \perp_n \rangle \twoheadrightarrow_\mathcal{A} \varrho(\varepsilon)$.
- If $w \in T$ and $\varrho(w) = \langle q, s \rangle$ then $\delta(\langle q, top_1(s) \rangle) = (f, p_1, \ldots, p_r)$, where $t(w) = f \in \Sigma_r$ and $p_1, \ldots, p_r \in Q$. In addition, $\langle p_i, s \rangle \twoheadrightarrow_\mathcal{A} \varrho(wi)$, for each $i = 1, \ldots, r$ when $\varrho(wi)$ is defined.

If a partial run is total, it is called a *run*. If $\mathcal{A}$ has a run on t, then we say that t is *accepted* by $\mathcal{A}$. It should be clear that any given automaton $\mathcal{A}$ can accept at most one tree.

Remark: The above definition of a pushdown automaton is based on the definitions from [12, 17, 9] rather than the original definition of Engelfriet, used in [6, 5]. The latter differs from ours in that a pushdown store of level k, for $k > 1$, is defined as a sequence of pairs $[(s_1, a_1), \ldots, (s_l, a_l)]$, where the s_i are pds's of level $k - 1$, and the a_i are symbols from the alphabet. An automaton has access to the symbol a_l, as well as to the top symbol of s_l, the top symbol of the top pds of s_l, etc. However, it is not difficult to see that these two models are equivalent. Indeed, the additional label of a k-pds can be stored on the top of its top 1-pds. (Note that a 1-pds on top of a k-pds is also on top of pds's of level $2, 3, \ldots, k - 1$, and thus must carry up to k additional labels.) Each move of an Engelfriet style automaton is then simulated by a sequence of moves of our automaton.

It should also be clear that our higher-order pushdown trees generalize to higher levels the pushdown trees considered by Walukiewicz in [18]. In the context of verification, pushdown automata (in general, nondeterministic) are considered as processes rather than acceptors, i.e., the input alphabet is omitted. The interest is focused on the graph of all possible configurations of a process. However, by suitable choice of a signature, it is easy to identify the tree of configurations of a higher-order pushdown process with the tree recognized by an automaton in our sense. The branching nodes in the tree correspond to the points of nondeterministic choice of the process.

5   Automata and Grammars

Theorem 5.1. *Let t be accepted by a pushdown automaton of level n. Then it is generated by a safe grammar of level n.*

Corollary 5.2. *The MSO theory of every tree recognized by a higher-order pushdown automaton is decidable.*

Theorem 5.3. *A tree generated by a safe grammar of level n is accepted by a pushdown automaton of level n.*

5.1   Proof of Theorem 5.1

Assume that our automaton $\mathcal{A} = \langle Q, \Sigma, A, q_0, \delta, \perp \rangle$ has m states $0, \ldots, m-1$. (It is convenient to simply identify the states with their numbers.) We use the following abbreviations: $\mathbf{1} = \mathbf{0}^m \to \mathbf{0}$, $\mathbf{2} = \mathbf{1}^m \to \mathbf{1}$, and so on: $\mathbf{k} = (\mathbf{k\text{-}1})^m \to \mathbf{k}$, up to $\mathbf{n} = (\mathbf{n\text{-}1})^m \to \mathbf{n\text{-}1}$. Observe that $\mathbf{k} = (\mathbf{k\text{-}1})^m \to (\mathbf{k\text{-}2})^m \to \cdots \to \mathbf{1}^m \to \mathbf{0}^m \to \mathbf{0}$, for each $k = 0, \ldots, n$.

We construct a grammar which generates the tree t, with the following nonterminals:

- For each $q \in Q$ and each $a \in A$, there is a nonterminal $\mathcal{F}_q^a$ of type $\mathbf{n}$.
- For each $k = 1, \ldots, n$ there is a nonterminal $Void_k$ of type $\mathbf{n\text{-}k}$.
- And there is an initial nonterminal $\mathcal{S}$ of type $\mathbf{0}$.

The initial production of our grammar is:

$$\mathcal{S} \Rightarrow \mathcal{F}_{q_0}^{\perp} \ \overrightarrow{Void}_1 \ \overrightarrow{Void}_2 \ \ldots \ \overrightarrow{Void}_n,$$

where $\overrightarrow{Void}_k$ stands for m repetitions of $Void_k$. Other productions apply to the nonterminals $\mathcal{F}_i^a$ and depend on $\delta(q_i, a)$. In order to understand the productions below, one should interpret an expression of the form

$$\mathcal{F}_q^a \ \overrightarrow{x}_1 \overrightarrow{x}_2 \ldots \overrightarrow{x}_n$$

as a representation of a configuration $\langle q, s \rangle$, where $top_1(s) = a$, and each vector $\overrightarrow{x}_k = x_k^0 \ldots x_k^{m-1}$ refers to the possible configurations to which the automaton may return after executing pop_k. There is always m such possible configurations, corresponding to the m internal states. (A call to $Void_k$ corresponds to an attempt to pop an "empty" stack.) Observe that the types of variables in $\vec{x}_k$ are more complex for lower level pds's. We think of it as follows: the information contained in a parameter $x_k^i : \mathbf{n\text{-}k}$ occurring in the sequence $\vec{x}_k$ represents directly the contents of $top_k(s)$. The actual state of the n-pds should then be seen as a function depending on the contents of $pop_k(s)$, understood as a sequence of pds's of levels $k+1, k+2, \ldots, n$. Here are the productions:

- $\mathcal{F}_q^a \ \vec{x}_1 \vec{x}_2 \ldots \vec{x}_n \Rightarrow \mathcal{F}_p^a \ \vec{x}_1 \ldots \vec{x}_{k-1} \ (\mathcal{F}_0^a \ \vec{x}_1 \ldots \vec{x}_k) \ldots (\mathcal{F}_{m-1}^a \ \vec{x}_1 \ldots \vec{x}_k)$
  $\vec{x}_{k+1} \ldots \vec{x}_n,$
  if $\delta(q,a) = (push_k, p)$, with $k > 1$.
- $\mathcal{F}_q^a \ \vec{x}_1 \vec{x}_2 \ldots \vec{x}_n \Rightarrow \mathcal{F}_p^b (\mathcal{F}_0^a \ \vec{x}_1) \ldots (\mathcal{F}_{m-1}^a \ \vec{x}_1) \ \vec{x}_2 \ldots \vec{x}_n,$
  if $\delta(q,a) = (push_1^b, p)$.
- $\mathcal{F}_q^a \ \vec{x}_1 \vec{x}_2 \ldots \vec{x}_n \Rightarrow x_k^p \ \vec{x}_{k+1} \ldots \vec{x}_n,$
  if $\delta(q,a) = (pop_k, p)$.
- $\mathcal{F}_q^a \ \vec{x} \Rightarrow f(\mathcal{F}_{p_1}^a \ \vec{x}) \ldots (\mathcal{F}_{p_r}^a \ \vec{x}),$
  if $\delta(q,a) = (f, p_1, \ldots, p_r)$, where $\vec{x}$ stands for $\vec{x}_1 \vec{x}_2 \ldots \vec{x}_n$.

Note that, in particular, the production corresponding to a pop_n is simply $\mathcal{F}_q^a \ldots \Rightarrow x_n^p$. Also note that the maximal incomplete applications of level k at the right hand side do not contain variables of level less than k. It follows that our grammar is safe.

In order to show the correctness of the simulation we must make precise how an expression of type $\mathbf{n\text{-}k}$ should represent a k-pds. More precisely, we define terms $Code_{q,s}$ meant to represent the contents of s in state q. If s is an n-pds then $Code_{q,s}$ represents the whole configuration. The definition is by induction with respect to the length of the pds.

We begin with $k = 1$. If $s = [\bot]$, then $Code_{q,s} = \mathcal{F}_q^\bot \ \overrightarrow{Void}_1$, and if $s = push_1^a(s')$ then $Code_{q,s} = \mathcal{F}_q^a \ Code_{1,s'} \ldots Code_{m,s'}$.

For $k > 1$, and $s = [s_1]$ we define $Code_{q,s} = Code_{q,s_1} \ \overrightarrow{Void}_k$. If $s = [s_1, \ldots, s_l]$, with $l > 1$, then $Code_{q,s} = Code_{q,s_l} \ Code_{1,s'} \ldots Code_{m,s'}$, where $s' = [s_1, \ldots, s_{l-1}]$.

Lemma 5.4. Let $\langle q, s \rangle \to_{\mathcal{A}} \langle p, s' \rangle$. Then $Code_{q,s} \to_{\mathcal{G}} Code_{p,s'}$.

Proof. By inspection of the possible cases. □

Theorem 5.1 now follows from the following fact:

Lemma 5.5. Let ϱ be the run of $\mathcal{A}$ on $t : T \to \Sigma$ and let $w \in T$. Let $\varrho(w) = \langle q, s \rangle$, with $top_1(s) = a$, and let $\delta(\langle q, a \rangle) = (f, p_1, \ldots, p_r)$. Then $\mathcal{S} \twoheadrightarrow_{\mathcal{G}} t'$, for some finite tree t' with $t'(w) = Code_{q,s}$.

Proof. Induction with respect to the length of w. □

5.2   Proof of Theorem 5.3

The proof is based on an idea from [10], where it was shown how to implement recursive programs with level 2 procedures with help of a 2-pds. The simulation of [10] was possible at level 2 because the individual parameters were passed *by value*. Thus, a nonlocal access to an individual meant an immediate access to a register value and did not require any additional evaluation. Under the safety restriction, one can generalize the construction in [10] to all levels.

Suppose a safe grammar $\mathcal{G}$ of level n generates $t : T \to \Sigma$. With no loss of generality we may assume the following:

- Whenever a right hand side of a production in $\mathcal{G}$ is of the form $fu_1 \ldots u_r$, where $f \in \Sigma_r$, then each of the terms $u_1, \ldots, u_r$ begins with a nonterminal or a variable (but not with a signature constant).
- The initial nonterminal $\mathcal{S}$ does not occur at the right hand sides of productions.

In addition, we assume that the formal parameters of any m-ary nonterminal $\mathcal{F}$ are always $x_1, \ldots, x_m$.

For each expression u we define *formal parameters of u*, not to be confused with variables actually occurring in u.

- If u begins with a nonterminal $\mathcal{F} : \sigma$, then the formal parameters of u are the formal parameters of $\mathcal{F}$.
- If u begins with a variable or a signature constant of type $\sigma = \tau_1 \to \cdots \to \tau_d \to \mathbf{0}$ then the formal parameters of u are $x_i : \tau_i$, for $i \leq d$.

In addition, with every expression $u = F \ldots$, we associate a *formal operator*, which is a variable *head* of the same type as F.

We construct a level n automaton $\mathcal{A}$ accepting t. The pushdown alphabet of $\mathcal{A}$ consists of all safe subexpressions of all the right hand sides of the productions of G. Every element of $\mathcal{A}$ represents a possible call to a nonterminal, or to a variable, together with a (possibly incomplete) list of actual parameters. In order to distinguish between identifiers of $\mathcal{G}$ and pds symbols, the latter will be called *items*.

The bottom pds symbol is $\mathcal{S}$, the initial nonterminal. The set of states includes $q_0, q_1, \ldots q_g$, where g is the maximal arity of an identifier[2] occurring in the grammar. The intended meaning of these states is as follows: in a configuration $\langle q_0, s \rangle$ the automaton attempts to evaluate the expression $top_1(s)$, while in a configuration $\langle q_i, s \rangle$ with $i > 0$ and $top_1(s) = Fu_1u_2 \ldots$ the goal is to evaluate the i-th argument of F. The automaton works in phases beginning and ending in the distinguished states q_i, using some auxiliary states in between.

We now describe the possible behaviour in each phase, assuming the following induction hypothesis to hold for every configuration $\langle q_i, s \rangle$.

- All the "internal" items (not on top of 1-pds's) begin with nonterminals.

---

[2] Variables, signature constants and nonterminals are all called *identifiers*. An identifier of type $\tau_1 \to \tau_2 \to \cdots \to \tau_n \to \mathbf{0}$ is said to be of *arity* n.

- If an item t occurs on a 1-pds directly atop of another item of the form $\mathcal{F}\ldots$ then all variables occurring in t are formal parameters of $\mathcal{F}$.
- If $i \neq 0$ then $top_1(s)$ has at least i formal parameters.
- Let $s' \subset s$ be a pds of level $n-k$, and let s'' be a $(n-k)$-pds occurring directly atop s' on the same $(n-k+1)$-pds. Then
  - $top_1(s')$ is an expression beginning with a variable $\varphi : \tau$ of level k.
  - If $i \neq 0$ and $s'' = top_{n-k+1}(s)$ and the i-th formal parameter x_i of $top_1(s)$ is of level k then x_i has type τ.
  - Otherwise, the topmost incomplete application on s'' of level k has type τ.

Assume that the current configuration of the automaton is $\langle q_0, s \rangle$.

Case 1: Let $top_1(s) = \mathcal{F}u_1\ldots u_d$ where $\mathcal{F}$ is a nonterminal and $\mathcal{F}x_1\ldots x_n \Rightarrow t$ is the corresponding production. Then the automaton executes the instruction $push_1^t$, and remains in state q_0.

Case 2: If $top_1(s) = f$ or $top_1(s) = ft_1\ldots t_r$ with $f \in \Sigma_r$ then the next instruction is $(f, q_1, \ldots q_r)$.

Case 3: If $top_1(s) = x : \mathbf{0}$ then x must be a formal parameter of the previous item $top_1(pop_1(s))$, say the j-th one. The automaton executes (pop_1, q_j).

Case 4: Let $top_1(s) = \varphi t_1\ldots t_d$, where φ is a variable of level $k > 0$ and arity at least d. Assume that φ is an r-th formal parameter of $top_1(pop_1(s))$. The actions to be executed are $push_{n-k+1}$ followed by pop_1, and the next state is q_r.

That is, a call to a variable of level $1, 2, \ldots, n-1$ results in a "push" operation respectively of level $n, n-1, \ldots, 2$. The higher is the level of the variable, the lower is the level of the corresponding pds operation.

Now consider a current configuration of the automaton of the form $\langle q_i, s \rangle$, with $i > 0$.

Case 5: If $top_1(s) = Ft_1\ldots t_r$ and $i \leq r$ then the top item is simply replaced by t_i and the next state is q_0.

Case 6: Let $top_1(s) = Ft_1\ldots t_r$, but $i > r$. Assume that $top_1(s) : \tau$ is of level k. The action to be performed is (pop_{n-k+1}, q_{i-r}).

Now we prove the correctness of this construction. First we define the *meaning* of an expression u at s, written as $[\![u]\!]_s$.

- If F is a signature constant or a nonterminal, then $[\![F]\!]_s = F$.
- If u is an application $t_1 t_2$ then $[\![u]\!]_s = [\![t_1]\!]_s [\![t_2]\!]_s$.
- If $top_1(s) = Ft_1\ldots t_r$, then $[\![head]\!]_s = [\![F]\!]_{pop_1(s)}$. An exception is when $top_1(s) = \mathcal{S}$, in which case we set $[\![head]\!]_s = \mathcal{S}$.
- Let $top_1(s) = Ft_1\ldots t_r$, and let x_d be the d-th formal parameter at $top_1(s)$. If $d \leq r$ then $[\![x_d]\!]_s = [\![t_d]\!]_{pop_1(s)}$.
- Otherwise, $[\![x_d]\!]_s = [\![x_{d-r}]\!]_{pop_{n-k+1}(s)}$, where k is the level of $Ft_1\ldots t_r$.

If $top_1(s) = Ft_1\ldots t_r$, where F is an identifier of arity $m \geq r$, then we define $[\![s]\!] = [\![head\, x_1\ldots x_r]\!]_s$.

Lemma 5.6. *For an arbitrary identifier x of level $k = 1, \ldots, n-1$, we have*
$$[\![x]\!]_s = [\![x]\!]_{top_{n-k+1}(s)}$$
In other words, the meaning of x is determined by the top pds of level $n-k$.

Proof. Induction with respect to s. Note that to define $[\![x]\!]_s$ one never has to consider variables of levels less than k. This is because the grammar $\mathcal{G}$ is assumed to be safe. $\qquad\square$

Lemma 5.7. *Assume that the configuration $\langle q_i, s \rangle$ with $i > 0$ satisfies our induction hypothesis. Then $\langle q_i, s \rangle \twoheadrightarrow_\mathcal{A} \langle q_0, s' \rangle$, for some s' with $[\![s']\!] = [\![x_i]\!]_s$.*

Proof. The proof is by induction with respect to s. If the automaton moves according to Case 5, the hypothesis is immediate. Otherwise we have $[\![x_r]\!]_s = [\![x_{i-r}]\!]_{pop_{n-k+1}(s)}$ and we apply induction. $\qquad\square$

Lemma 5.8. *Assume that the configuration $\langle q_0, s \rangle$ satisfies our induction hypothesis, and let the top item $top_1(s)$ begin with a variable. Then $\langle q_0, s \rangle \twoheadrightarrow_\mathcal{A} \langle q_0, s' \rangle$, where $[\![s']\!] = [\![s]\!]$ and $top_1(s)$ begins with a nonterminal or a signature constant.*

Proof. If the head variable φ is of level k then we have $[\![\varphi]\!]_{pop_1(s)} = [\![\varphi]\!]_{pop_1(push_{n-k+1}(s))}$, by Lemma 5.6. Thus the actions performed according to Case 4 do not change the meaning of the pds. Termination follows by induction on $n - k$ and the size of $top_{n-k+1}(s)$. $\qquad\square$

Lemma 5.9. *Assume that the configuration $\langle q_0, s \rangle$ satisfies our induction hypothesis, and that $[\![s]\!] = t$. Suppose that $t \to_G t_1 \to_G \cdots \to_G t_m$ and let $t_m = g u_1 \ldots u_r$ be the first term in the reduction sequence which begins with a signature constant. Then $\langle q_0, s \rangle \twoheadrightarrow_\mathcal{A} \langle q_0, s' \rangle$, where $[\![s']\!] = g u_1 \ldots u_r$.*

Proof. The proof is by induction with respect to the number of steps in the reduction sequence $t \twoheadrightarrow_G g u_1 \ldots u_r$. There are cases depending on the first reduction step $t \to_G t_1$. The nontrivial case is when $top_1(s)$ begins with a variable φ, i.e., not with the same symbol as t. This corresponds to Case 4 in the definition of the automaton. But it follows from Lemma 5.8 that the meaning $[\![s]\!]$ remains unchanged until a head nonterminal or terminal is exposed. $\qquad\square$

Lemma 5.10. *Suppose that $S \to_G t_1 \to_G \cdots \to_G t_m$ is an outermost reduction sequence and that t_m is the first in the sequence term with $t_m(w) = f$, where f is a signature constant. Let the subterm of t_m occurring at w be $f u_1 \ldots u_k$. Then $\mathcal{A}$ has a partial run ϱ on t such that $\varrho(w) = \langle q_0, s \rangle$, with $top_1(s) = f v_1 \ldots v_k$ and $[\![s]\!] = f u_1 \ldots u_k$.*

Proof. Induction with respect to the length of w. Assuming induction hypothesis for the immediate predecessor of w, the automaton then simulates grammar reductions. First, a "split" action is executed without changing the pds, and we apply Lemma 5.7. Then we evaluate the expression on top of the pds and the correctness of this evaluation follows from Lemma 5.9. $\qquad\square$

The conclusion is that for every $w \in \mathcal{D}om\, t$ there is a partial run that reaches w. Thus the unique tree accepted by $\mathcal{A}$ coincides with t.

References

1. D. Caucal. On infinite transition graphs having a decidable monadic second–order theory. In F. Meyer auf der Heide and B. Monien, editors, *23th International Colloquium on Automata Languages and Programming*, LNCS 1099, pages 194–205, 1996. A long version will appear in TCS.
2. B. Courcelle. The monadic second–order theory of graphs IX: Machines and their behaviours. *Theoretical Comput. Sci.*, 151:125–162, 1995.
3. B. Courcelle and T. Knapik. The evaluation of first-order substitution is monadic second–order compatible. *Theoretical Comput. Sci.*, 2002. To appear.
4. W. Damm. The IO– and OI–hierarchies. *Theoretical Comput. Sci.*, 20(2):95–208, 1982.
5. W. Damm and A. Goerdt. An automata-theoretic characterization of the OI-hierarchy. *Information and Control*, 71:1–32, 1986.
6. J. Engelfriet. Iterated push-down automata and complexity classes. In *Proc. 15th STOC*, pages 365–373, 1983.
7. H. Hungar. Model checking and higher-order recursion. In L. Pacholski, M. Kutyłowski and T. Wierzbicki, editors, *Mathematical Foundations of Computer Science 1999*, LNCS 1672, pages 149–159, 1999.
8. B. Jacobs and J. Rutten. A tutorial on (co)algebras and (co)induction. *Bulletin of EATCS*, 1997(62):222–259.
9. A.J. Kfoury, J. Tiuryn and P. Urzyczyn. On the expressive power of finitely typed and universally polymorphic recursive procedures. *Theoretical Comput. Sci.*, 93:1–41, 1992.
10. A. Kfoury and P. Urzyczyn. Finitely typed functional programs, part II: comparisons to imperative languages. Report, Boston University, 1988.
11. T. Knapik, D. Niwiński, and P. Urzyczyn. Deciding monadic theories of hyperalgebraic trees. In *Typed Lambda Calculi and Applications, 5th International Conference*, LNCS 2044, pages 253–267. Springer-Verlag, 2001.
12. W. Kowalczyk, D. Niwiński, and J. Tiuryn. A generalization of of Cook's auxiliary-pushdown-automata theorem. *Fundamenta Informaticae*, 12:497–506, 1989.
13. O. Kupferman and M. Vardi. An automata-theoretic approach to reasoning about infinite-state systems. In *Computer Aided Verification, Proc. 12th Int. Conference*, Lecture Notes in Computer Science. Springer-Verlag, 2000.
14. D. Muller and P. Schupp. The theory of ends, pushdown automata, and second-order logic. *Theoretical Comput. Sci.*, 37:51–75, 1985.
15. M. O. Rabin. Decidability of second-order theories and automata on infinite trees. *Trans. Amer. Soc*, 141:1–35, 1969.
16. W. Thomas. Languages, automata, and logic. In G. Rozenberg and A. Salomaa, editors, *Handbook of Formal Languages*, volume 3, pages 389–455. Springer-Verlag, 1997.
17. J. Tiuryn. Higher-order arrays and stacks in programming: An application of complexity theory to logics of programs. In *Proc. 12th MFCS*, LNCS 233, pages 177–198. Springer-Verlag, 1986.
18. I. Walukiewicz. Pushdown processes: Games and model checking. *Information and Computation*, 164(2):234–263, 2001.

Conflict Detection and Resolution in Access Control Policy Specifications*

Manuel Koch[1], Luigi V. Mancini[2], and Francesco Parisi-Presicce[2,3]

[1] Freie Universität Berlin, Berlin (DE)
mkoch@inf.fu-berlin.de
[2] Univ. di Roma La Sapienza, Rome (IT)
lv.mancini@dsi.uniroma1.it
[3] George Mason University, Fairfax VA (USA)
parisi@dsi.uniroma1.it, fparisi@ise.gmu.edu

Abstract. Graph-based specification formalisms for Access Control (AC) policies combine the advantages of an intuitive visual framework with a rigorous semantical foundation. A security policy framework specifies a set of (constructive) rules to build the system states and sets of positive and negative (declarative) constraints to specify wanted and unwanted substates. Models for AC (e.g. role-based, lattice-based or an access control list) have been specified in this framework elsewhere. Here we address the problem of inconsistent policies within this framework. Using formal properties of graph transformations, we can systematically detect inconsistencies between constraints, between rules and between a rule and a constraint and lay the foundation for their resolutions.

1 Introduction

Access Control (AC) deals with decisions involving the legitimacy of requests to access files and resources on the part of users and processes. One of the main advantages of separating the logical structure from the implementation of a system is the possibility to reason about its properties. In [KMPP00,KMPP01a] we have proposed a formalism based on graphs and graph transformations for the specification of AC policies. This conceptual framework, that we have used in [KMPP00,KMPP01a] to specify well-known security models such as role-based policies [San98], lattice-based access control (LBAC) policies (examples of mandatory policies) [San93] and access control lists (ACL) (examples of discretionary policies) [SS94], allows for the uniform comparison of these different models, often specified in ad hoc languages and requiring ad hoc conversions to compare their relative strength and weakness.

Our graph-based specification formalism for AC policies combines the advantages of an intuitive visual framework with a rigor and precision of a semantics

---

* partially supported by the EC under TMR Network GETGRATS and under Esprit WG APPLIGRAPH, and by the Italian MURST.

M. Nielsen and U. Engberg (Eds.): Fossacs 2002, LNCS 2303, pp. 223–238, 2002.

founded on category theory. In addition, tools developed for generic graph transformation engines can be adapted to or can form the basis for applications that can assist in the development of a specific policy.

We use in this paper examples from the LBAC and the ACL models to illustrate the different concepts, with no pretense of giving complete or unique solutions by these examples.

The main goal of this paper is to present some basic properties of a formal model for AC policies based on graphs and graph transformations and to address the problem of detecting and resolving conflicts in a categorical setting. A system state is represented by a graph and graph transformation rules describe how a system state evolves. The specification ("framework") of an AC policy contains also declarative information ("invariants") on what a system graph must contain (positive) and what it cannot contain (negative). A crucial property of a framework is that it specifies a coherent policy, that is one without internal contradictions. Formal results are presented to help in recognizing when the positive and the negative constraints of a framework cannot be simultaneously satisfied, when two rules, possibly coming from previously distinct subframeworks, do (partly) the same things but under different conditions, and when the application of a rule produces a system graph that violates one of the constraints (after one or the other has been added to a framework during the evolution of a policy). The solutions proposed on a formal level can be made part of a methodology and incorporated into an Access Control Policy Assistant.

The paper is organized as follows: the next section reviews the basic notations of graph transformations and recalls the formal framework to specify AC policies [KMPP01a]; Sect.3 discusses the notion of a conflict of constraints, Sect.4 introduces conflicts between rules and mentions strategies to resolve conflicts; Sect.5 discusses how to modify a rule so that its application does not contradict one of the constraints; the last section mentions related and future work.

2   Graph-Based Security Policy Frameworks

We assume that the reader is familiar with the basic notation for graph transformations as in [Roz97] and in [KMPP01a]. Parts of a LBAC model are used throughout the section to illustrate the explanations by examples.

Graphs $G = (G_V, G_E, s_G, t_G, l_G)$ carry labels taken from a set X of *variables* and a set C of *constants*. A path of unspecified length between nodes a and b is indicated by an edge $a \xrightarrow{*} b$ as an abbreviation for a set containing all possible paths from a to b through the graph.

A *total morphism* $f : G \to H$ is a pair $(f_V : G_V \to H_V, f_E : G_E \to H_E)$ of total mappings that respect the graph structure and may replace a variable with other variables or constants. A *partial graph morphism* $f : G \rightharpoonup H$ is a total graph morphism $\bar{f} : dom(f) \to H$ from a subgraph $dom(f) \subseteq G$ to H.

Graphs can be typed by defining a total morphism $t_G : G \to TG$ to a fixed *type graph* TG that represents the type information in a graph transformation system [CELP96] and specifies the node and edge types which may occur in the

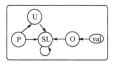

Fig. 1. *The type graph for the LBAC model.*

instance graphs modeling system states. For example, the type graph in Figure 1 shows the possible types for the LBAC graph model. The node U is the type of nodes representing users, the node O the objects, the node val the actual information of objects and the node P the processes that run on behalf of users. The node SL with its loop represents a whole security lattice, and there is an edge from security level SL_1 to SL_2 if $SL_1 > SL_2$. The attachment of security levels to objects, users and processes is modeled by an edge to a security level of the security lattice. The typing morphism t_G maps a node with label Tx to the type T, and morphisms must preserve the typing.

A *rule* $p : r$ consists of a name p, and a label preserving injective morphism $r : L \rightharpoonup R$. The *left-hand side* L describes the elements a graph must contain for p to be applicable. The partial morphism r is undefined on nodes/edges that are intended to be deleted, defined on nodes/edges that are intended to be preserved. Nodes and edges of R, *right-hand side*, without a pre-image are newly created. Note that the actual deletions/additions are performed on the graphs to which the rule is applied. The application of a rule $p : r$ to a graph G requires a total graph morphism $m : L \rightarrow G$, called *match*, and the direct derivation $G \overset{p,m}{\Rightarrow} H$ is given by the pushout of r and m in the category of graphs typed over TG [EHK$^+$97].

Example 1 (LBAC graph rules). Figure 2 shows the rules for the LBAC policy. The labels for the nodes $(Ux, Px, SLx, SLy, ...)$ of the rules are variables.

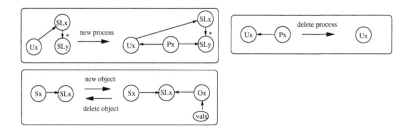

Fig. 2. *Graph rules for the LBAC policy.*

The rule **new object** creates a new object Ox connected to a node $valx$ (the initial value of the object) and assigned to the security level SLx. The label SLx is generic and is substituted by the actual security level of the process when the rule is applied. The rule `delete object` for the deletion of objects is represented by reversing the partial morphism of the rule `new object`. The rule `new process` creates a process Px on behalf of a user Ux. The new process is attached to a security level SLy that is no higher in the security lattice graph than the security level SLx of the user Ux. This requirement is specified by the path from SLx to SLy. Processes are removed by the rule `delete process`.

For the specification of AC policies by graph transformations, *negative application conditions* for rules are needed. A negative application condition (NAC) for a rule $p : L \xrightarrow{r} R$ consists of a set $A(p)$ of pairs (L, N), where the graph L is a subgraph of N. The part $N \setminus L$ represents a structure that must not occur in a graph G for the rule to be applicable. In the figures, we represent (L, N) with N, where the subgraph L is drawn with solid and $N \setminus L$ with dashed lines. A rule $p : L \xrightarrow{r} R$ with a NAC $A(p)$ is applicable to G if L occurs in G via m and it is not possible to extend m to N for each (L, N) in $A(p)$.

Example 2 (NAC). Figure 3 shows the rules for modifying the security lattice. New security levels can be inserted above an existing security level (rule `new level 1`), below (`new level 2`) or between existing levels (`new level 3`). (Notice that the lattice structure is not preserved by these rules.) The rule `delete level` removes a security level. Since users, processes and objects need a security level, security levels cannot be removed if a user, process or object possesses this level. Thus, the NAC of the rule `delete level`, whose left-hand side contains the node SLx, has three pairs (L, N): the first one prevents the deletion of security levels that are assigned to a process, the second one concerns users and the last one objects. Only if the NAC is satisfied, a security level can be removed.

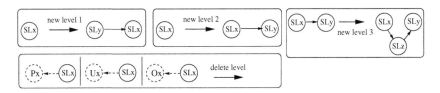

Fig. 3. *LBAC rules for modifying the security lattice.*

Negative application conditions are a form of constraint on the applicability of a rule. Constraints can be defined independently of rules.

Definition 1 (Constraints). *A constraint (positive or negative) is given by a total morphism $c : X \to Y$. A total morphism $p : X \to G$ satisfies a positive (negative) constraint c if there exists (does not exist) a total morphism $q : Y \to G$ such that $X \xrightarrow{c} Y \xrightarrow{q} G = X \xrightarrow{p} G$.*
A graph G satisfies a constraint c if each total morphism $p : X \to G$ satisfies c. A graph G vacuously satisfies c if there is no total morphism $p : X \to G$; G properly satisfies c otherwise.

Example 3 (Constraints for LBAC). Figure 4 shows a positive and a negative constraint for the LBAC model. The morphism for the negative constraint is the identity on the graph shown (to simplify the presentation, we depict only the graph). The constraints require that objects always have one (the positive constraint) and only one (negative constraint) security level.

positive constraint: negative constraint:

Fig. 4. *Positive and negative constraints for LBAC.*

We now review the specification of AC policies based on graph transformations [KMPP00]. The framework is called *security policy framework* and consists of a type graph that provides the type information of the AC policy, a set of rules (specifying the policy rules) that generate the graphs representing the states accepted by the AC policy, a set of *negative constraints* to specify graphs that shall not be contained in any system graph and a set of *positive constraints* to specify graphs that must be explicitly constructed as parts of a system graph.

Definition 2 (Security Policy Framework). *A security policy framework, or just* framework, *is a tuple* $SP = (TG, (P, rules_P), Pos, Neg)$, *where* TG *is a type graph,* P *a set of rule names,* $rules_P : P \to \mathbf{Rule}(TG)$ *a total mapping from names to* TG*–typed rules, Pos is a set of positive constraints, and Neg is a set of negative constraints.*

The graphs constructed by the rules of a framework represent the system states possible within the policy model. These graphs are called *system graphs.*

Definition 3 (Coherence). *A security policy framework is coherent if all system graphs satisfy the constraints in Pos and Neg.*

Integration is concerned with the merging of AC policies and consists of two levels, a syntactical level, i.e. a merge of the security policy frameworks, and a semantical level, i.e. the merge of the system graphs representing the state at merge time. The integration of two AC policies on the syntactical level is a pushout of the frameworks in the category **SP**. It has been shown in [KMPP01b] that the category **SP** of frameworks and framework morphisms is closed under finite colimit constructions. An important aspect of integration is the preservation of coherence: if two frameworks are coherent, is their gluing also coherent? Generally, this is not the case. Conflicts also arise when modifying a framework by adding/removing a rule or by adding/removing a positive/negative constraint. In the next three sections, the problems of conflicting constraints, conflicting rules and conflicts between a rule and a constraint are addressed.

3   Constraint-Constraint Conflict

One way to determine whether a framework is contradictory is to analyze constraints in pairs.

Definition 4 (Conflict of Constraints). *Given constraints $c_i : X_i \to Y_i$ for $i = 1, 2$, c_1 is in conflict with c_2 iff there exist morphisms $f_X : X_1 \to X_2$ and $f_Y : Y_1 \to Y_2$ such that $f_Y \circ c_1 = c_2 \circ f_X$ and f_X does not satisfy c_1. The conflict is* strict *if the diagram is a pushout.*

$$
\begin{array}{ccc}
X_1 & \xrightarrow{c_1} & Y_1 \\
{\scriptstyle f_X}\downarrow & & \downarrow{\scriptstyle f_Y} \\
X_2 & \xrightarrow{c_2} & Y_2
\end{array}
$$

When two constraints contain redundant restrictions, the conflict is *harmless*.

Proposition 1 (Harmless Conflicts). *Let c_1 be in conflict with c_2 and G satisfy c_1. Then G satisfies c_2 whenever either $c_1, c_2 \in Neg$ or $c_1, c_2 \in Pos$ and c_1 is in strict conflict with c_2.*

When the two constraints in conflict are one positive and one negative, then any graph satisfying one cannot properly satisfy the other one.

Proposition 2 (Critical Conflicts). *Let c_1 be in conflict with c_2 and G properly satisfy c_2. If either $c_1 \in Pos$, $c_2 \in Neg$ and the conflict is strict, or $c_1 \in Neg$, then G does not properly satisfy c_1.*

Critical conflicts between constraints can be resolved by removing or weakening one of the constraints by adding a condition.

Definition 5 (Conditional Constraint). *A* positive (negative) conditional constraint (x, c) *consists of a negative constraint $x : X \to N$, called* constraint condition, *and a positive (negative) constraint $c : X \to Y$. A total morphism $p : X \to G$ satisfies (x, c) iff whenever p satisfies x, p satisfies c. A graph G satisfies (x, c) iff each total morphism $p : X \to G$ satisfies (x, c).*

A conditional constraint solves the conflict of c_1 with c_2 (via f_X and f_Y) by introducing a constraint condition for c_1 that requires the satisfaction of c_1 if and only if c_2 is vacuously satisfied.

Proposition 3. *Let $c_1 : X_1 \to Y_1$ be in conflict with $c_2 : X_2 \to Y_2$ via f_X and f_Y, then G satisfies f_X if and only if G vacuously satisfies c_2.*

Definition 6 (Weak Constraint). *If c_1 is in conflict with c_2 via f_X and f_Y, then the* weak constraint $c_1(c_2)$ *for c_1 with respect to c_2 is the conditional constraint $c_1(c_2) = (f_X, c_1)$.*

Proposition 4. *If c_1 is in conflict with c_2, then the weak constraint $c_1(c_2)$ is not in conflict with c_2.*

Weakening a constraint is one strategy to solve conflicts. A general discussion of strategies is outlined in [KMPP01b]. It is worth stressing that determining a conflict between constraints can be performed statically and automatically.

4 Rule-Rule Conflicts

Two rules are in a *potential-conflict (p-conflict)* if they do (partly) the same things but under different conditions. A *conflict* occurs if p-conflicting rules can be applied to a common graph. If the choice for one rule in a conflict may prevent the applicability of the other rule, the conflict is called *critical*, otherwise it is a *choice conflict*. The LBAC rule **new object** and the access control list (ACL) rule **create object** in Figure 5 are in p-conflict, since both rules create a new object node Ox. An ACL (such as the one in UNIX) is a structure that stores the access rights to an object with the object itself. The rule **create object** specifies the creation of an object by a process that runs on behalf of a user. Initially, there are no access rights to the new object and the user becomes the owner of the new object[1].

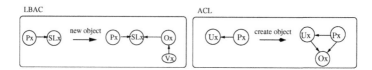

Fig. 5. *The LBAC rule* **new object** *and the ACL rule* **create object**.

The rule **new object** creates an object with a security level, the rule **create object** an object without one. Which rule shall be applied to introduce a new object in the system? A static analysis of the rules can detect the critical and the choice conflicts before run-time so that rules can be changed to avoid conflicts.

Definition 7 (p-Conflict, Conflict Pair, Conflict). *Rules $p_i : L_i \xrightarrow{r_i} R_i$, $i = 1,2$, with NAC $A(p_i)$ are in p-conflict if there is a common non-empty subrule[2] for p_1 and p_2. Each pair of matches $(m_1 : L_1 \to G, m_2 : L_2 \to G)$ is a conflict pair for p_1 and p_2. The rules p_1 and p_2 are in conflict, if they are in p-conflict and there is a conflict pair for p_1 and p_2. Otherwise, they are called conflict-free.*

Generally, there exist an infinite number of matches for one rule, so the set of matches must be reduced for a static analysis. To detect a rule conflict, it is sufficient to consider the left-hand sides of the rules.

---

[1] The complete specification of the framework for the ACL is given in [KMPP01a].

[2] A rule $p_0 : L_0 \xrightarrow{r_0} R_0$ is a subrule of rule $p : L \xrightarrow{r} R$ if there are total morphisms $f_L : L_0 \to L$ and $f_R : R_0 \to R$ with $r \circ f_L = f_R \circ r_0$.

Definition 8 (Set of Conflict Pairs). *The set $CP(p_1, p_2)$ of conflict pairs for rules $(p_i : L_i \xrightarrow{r_i} R_i, A(p_i))$, $i = 1, 2$, consists of all pairs of matches $(m_1 : L_1 \to G, m_2 : L_2 \to G)$, where m_1 and m_2 are jointly surjective.*

The set of conflict pairs for two rules in a p-conflict consists of a finite number of pairs since the left-hand side of a rule is a finite graph.

Proposition 5 (Conflict Freeness). *Let $CP(p_1, p_2)$ be the set of conflict pairs for the p-conflicting rules $(p_1 : L_1 \xrightarrow{r_1} R_1, A(p_1))$ and $(p_2 : L_2 \xrightarrow{r_2} R_2, A(p_2))$. Then, the rules p_1 and p_2 are conflict-free if and only if $CP(p_1, p_2)$ is empty.*

The set of conflict pairs for rules may be split into *choice* and *conflict* critical pairs: in the latter, after applying p_1 at match m_1, the rule p_2 is no longer applicable at m_2 or vice versa, while in the former, the order does not matter and after applying p_1 at m_1, p_2 is still applicable and vice versa. Critical and choice conflict pairs are detected by the concept of *parallel independence* [EHK+97].

Definition 9 (Parallel Independence). *Given rules $(p_i : L_i \xrightarrow{r_i} R_i, A(p_i))$, $i = 1, 2$, the derivations $G \overset{p_1}{\Rightarrow} H_1$ and $G \overset{p_2}{\Rightarrow} H_2$ are parallel independent if $r_2^* \circ m_1$ is total and satisfies $A(p_1)$ and $r_1^* \circ m_2$ is total and satisfies $A(p_2)$. Otherwise, the derivations are called parallel dependent.*

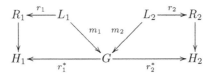

In the case of parallel independence, the application of p_1 at m_1 and the delayed application of p_2 at $r_1^* \circ m_2$ results in the same graph (up to isomorphism) as the application of p_2 at m_2 and the delayed application of p_1 at $r_2^* \circ m_1$.

Definition 10 (Choice and Critical Conflict Pair). *A conflict pair (m_1, m_2) for rules p_1 and p_2 is a choice conflict if the derivations $G \overset{p_1, m_1}{\Rightarrow} H_1$ and $G \overset{p_2, m_2}{\Rightarrow} H_2$ are parallel independent. It is a critical conflict otherwise.*

We propose two strategies to solve rule conflicts. In the first strategy, we take one rule p_1 as *major rule*, and one p_2 as *minor rule*. For a conflict pair (m_1, m_2), p_2 is changed by adding a NAC that forbids its application at match m_2 if p_1 can be applied at m_1. The second strategy integrates the rules into one rule.

Definition 11 (Weak Condition, Weak Rule). *Given a conflict pair (m_1, m_2) for rules $(p_i : L_i \xrightarrow{r_i} R_i, A(p_i))$, $i = 1, 2$, the weak condition for p_2 w.r.t. (m_1, m_2), denoted by $WC(p_1, p_2, (m_1, m_2))$, is given by the NAC (L_2, N),* *where the outer diagram is a pullback and the diagram (1) is a pushout diagram.*

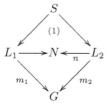

The rule p_2 with this added NAC is called weak rule.

The weak condition for the minor rule ensures that the major and the minor rule cannot be both applied to a common system graph at match m_1 and m_2.

Example 4 (weak rule). The top of Figure 6 shows the p-conflicting ACL rule `create object` and the LBAC rule `new object`. Conflict pairs for these rules are the inclusions $(in_1 : L_1 \rightarrow L_1 \oplus L_2, in_2 : L_2 \rightarrow L_1 \oplus L_2)$ of the left-hand sides into their disjoint union, and the inclusions $(in'_1 : L_1 \rightarrow G, in'_2 : L_2 \rightarrow G)$ of the left-hand sides into the graph G (the gluing of the left-hand sides over the node Px). Figure 6 shows the weak rules with respect to the second conflict pair. The weak rule for `create object` w.r.t. `new object` has a NAC that forbids the application when there is a security level for the process. Therefore, the weak rule for `create object` is only applicable to processes created with the ACL rule and without a counterpart in the LBAC model. The weak rule for `new object` w.r.t. `create object` has a NAC that forbids the presence of a user connected to the process. Since each user is connected to a process, the rule is not applicable to processes created by ACL rules.

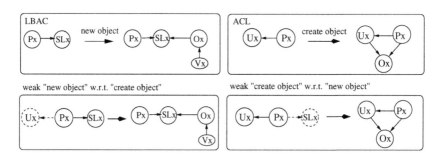

Fig. 6. *The weak rules for* `new object` *and* `create object`.

Theorem 1 (Weak Rule is Conflict-free). *Given the set of conflict pairs $CP(p_1, p_2)$ for p_1 and p_2, the rule p_1 and the rule p_2, extended by $WC(p_1, p_2, (m_1, m_2))$ for each $(m_1, m_2) \in CP(p_1, p_2)$, are conflict-free.*

The second solution for solving conflicts between rules is the *amalgamation* of the p-conflicting rules over their common subrule.

Definition 12 (Integrated Rule). *Let* $(p_i : L_i \xrightarrow{r_i} R_i, A(p_i))$ *for* $i = 1, 2$ *be p-conflicting rules and* $p_0 : L_0 \xrightarrow{r_0} R_0$ *with* $f_{L_i} : L_0 \to L_i$ *and* $f_{R_i} : R_0 \to R_i$ *their common subrule (cf. Figure 7).*

The integrated rule *is given by* $(p : L \xrightarrow{r} R, A(p))$, *where diagram (1) is the pushout of* f_{L_1} *and* f_{L_2}, *diagram (2) is the pushout of* f_{R_1} *and* f_{R_2} *and* r *is the universal pushout morphism.*

The set $A(p)$ *contains a NAC* $n : L \to N$ *for each pair of NACs* $n_1 : L_1 \to N_1 \in A(p_1)$ *and* $n_2 : L_2 \to N_2 \in A(p_2)$, *where* N *is the pushout of* $n_1 \circ f_{L_1}$ *and* $n_2 \circ f_{L_2}$ *and* n *is the universal pushout morphism.*

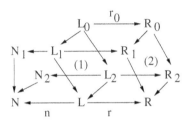

Fig. 7. *Amalgamation of p-conflicting rules.*

Example 5. Figure 8 shows the integrated rule for the rules `create object` and `new object`. Their common subrule is marked in the rules and contains the process node Px in the left-hand side and the nodes Px and Ox in the right-hand side. The integrated rule creates an object that belongs to a user, as well as a process, and that carries a security level.

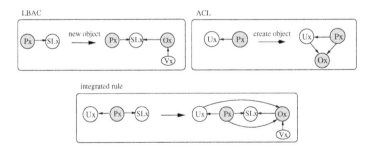

Fig. 8. *Amalgamation of p-conflicting rules* `create object` *and* `new object`.

5   Rule-Constraint Conflict

Rules can be classified into *deleting rules* that only delete graph elements, without adding anything (i.e., $dom(r) = R \subset L$) and *expanding rules* that only add graph elements, but do not delete anything (i.e., $dom(r) = L \subseteq R$).

A *conflict* between a rule and a constraint occurs when the application of the rule produces a graph which does not satisfy the constraint. The potential for conflict can be checked statically directly with the rule and the constraint without knowledge of specific graphs and derivations. A deleting rule p and a positive constraint c are in conflict if the added part required by c (i.e., $Y \backslash c(X)$) overlaps with what p removes (i.e., $L \backslash dom(r)$). Similarly, an expanding rule p conflicts with a negative constraint c if what is added by p (i.e., $R \backslash r(L)$) overlaps with something forbidden by c (i.e., $Y \backslash c(X)$).

Definition 13 (Rule-Constraint Conflicts). *Let $p : L \xrightarrow{r} R$ be an expanding rule and $c : X \to Y$ a constraint, then p and c are in* conflict *if there exists a nonempty graph S and injective total morphisms $s_1 : S \to R$ and $s_2 : S \to X$ so that $s_1(S) \cap (R \backslash r(L)) \neq \emptyset$.*

Let $p : L \xrightarrow{r} R$ be a deleting rule and $c : X \to Y$ a positive constraint, then p and c are in conflict *if there exists a nonempty graph S and injective total morphisms $s_1 : S \to L$ and $s_2 : S \to Y$ so that $s_1(S) \cap (L \backslash dom(r)) \neq \emptyset$ and $s_2(S) \cap (Y \backslash c(X)) \neq \emptyset$.*

Conflicts between rules p and constraints $c : X \to Y$ can be resolved (in favor of the constraint) by adding NACs to the rules p. For the conflict between expanding rules and negative constraints, the NACs prevent the rule from completing the conclusion of the constraint. For the conflict between expanding rules and positive constraints, the NACs prevent the rule from completing the condition X, and for the conflict between deleting rules and positive constraints, the NACs prevent the rule from destroying the conclusion Y.

Definition 14 (Reduction). *Given a rule $p : L \xrightarrow{r} R$ and a nonempty overlap S of R and the condition X of the constraint $c : X \to Y$.*

$$
\begin{array}{ccccccc}
L & \xrightarrow{r} & R & \xleftarrow{s_1} & S & \xrightarrow{s_2} & X \\
\downarrow & & \downarrow{\scriptstyle h} & & & & \downarrow{\scriptstyle c} \\
N & \xrightarrow{r^*} & C & \xleftarrow{\hspace{2cm}} & & & Y
\end{array}
$$

*Let C be the pushout object of $s_1 : S \to R$ and $c \circ s_2 : S \to Y$ in **Graph**, and let $C \xRightarrow{r^{-1}, h} N$ be the derivation with the inverse rule $p^{-1} : R \xrightarrow{r^{-1}} L$ at match h. The reduction $p(c)$ of p by c consists of the partial morphism $L \xrightarrow{r} R$ and the set $A(p, c) = \{(L, N) | C \xRightarrow{(r^{-1}, h)} N, C = R +_S Y \text{ for some overlap } S \}$ of NACs.*

The construction considers arbitrary rules and constraints, i.e., it is not restricted to deleting or expanding rules, respectively. This construction reduces to the one in [HW95] if the constraint $c : X \to Y$ is the identity morphism.

Theorem 2 (Reduction preserves Satisfaction). *Let* $p : L \xrightarrow{r} R$ *be a rule and* G *a graph that satisfies the constraint* $c : X \rightarrow Y$.

1. *If* c *is negative,* p *is expanding,* $p(c)$ *the reduction of* p *by* c *and* $G \xRightarrow{p(c)} H$ *is a derivation with* $p(c)$, *then* H *satisfies* c.
2. *If* c *is positive,* p *is expanding,* $p(id_X)$ *the reduction of* p *by* $id_X : X \rightarrow X$, *and* $G \xRightarrow{p(id_X)} H$ *a derivation with* $p(id_X)$, *then* H *satisfies* c.
3. *If* c *is positive,* p *is deleting,* $p(c) = (r, A(id_L, c))$, *and* $G \xRightarrow{p(c)} H$, *then* H *satisfies* c.

Consider the negative constraint $c(succ)$ in Figure 9 forbidding two (or more) successor levels, and the (expanding) rule **new level 2** in Figure 3 that may produce an inconsistent state by adding a successor level. We describe now, in algorithmic form, the construction of the reduction of **new level 2** by $c(succ)$:

Fig. 9. *Negative constraint $c(succ)$ forbidding more than two successor security levels.*

Step 1: Construction of all possible nonempty overlaps of R of the rule **new level 2** and the graph of $c(succ)$. Figure 10 shows the nonempty overlaps $S1$, $S2$ and $S3$ with morphisms s_1 and s_2. The remaining overlaps of R and X use the same subgraphs $S1, S2, S3$, but different morphisms s_1 and s_2.

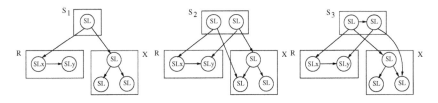

Fig. 10. *Nonempty overlaps between **new level 2** and $c(succ)$.*

Step 2: For each overlap S in step 1, the pushout C of the morphisms $S \rightarrow R$ and $S \rightarrow X$ is constructed. The application condition (L, N) is constructed by applying the inverse rule of **new level 2** at match $R \rightarrow C$ resulting in graph N. The inverse rule of **new level 2** deletes a security level. Figure 11 shows the pairs (L, N) for the three overlaps in Figure 10.

The construction in Definition 14 may generate redundant application conditions. In fact, if we assume that G already satisfies the constraint c, some application conditions are automatically satisfied. This corresponds to the case

Fig. 11. *NACs constructed from the overlaps.*

where the overlap $S \to R$ can be decomposed into $S \to L \to R$. The graph N generated from such overlap can be eliminated directly from Definition 14 by requiring only overlaps S for which $s_1(S) \cap (R \setminus r(L)) \neq \emptyset$. In this manner, the application condition NAC_1 of Figure 11 can be removed.

Another form of redundancy stems from the fact that, if S_1 with morphisms s_1^1 and s_2^1 and S_2 with morphisms s_1^2 and s_2^2 are overlaps and, say, $S_1 \subseteq S_2$, $s_1^1|_{S_1} = s_1^2$, $s_2^1|_{S_1} = s_2^2$ then $C_2 = R +_{S_2} Y \subseteq C_1 = R +_{S_1} Y$ and thus $N_2 \subseteq N_1$. Hence, if a match $L \to G$ satisfies (L, N_2), then it also satisfies (L, N_1) and the application condition (L, N_1) can be removed from $A(p, c)$. For example, the overlap S_1 is included into the overlap S_3 (cf. Figure 10). Therefore, $NAC3 \subseteq NAC1$ (cf. Figure 11) and we can remove $NAC1$.

The solution of conflicts between expanding rules and negative constraints and of conflicts between deleting rules and positive constraints is a reasonable reduction of the number of system graphs which the rules can produce. The solution for conflicts between expanding rules and positive constraints, however, is not very satisfactory, since it reduces more than necessary the number of system graphs that can be generated. Another solution is a construction which extends the right-hand side of a rule so that the rule creates the entire conclusion Y of a constraint $c : X \to Y$ and not only parts of it.

Definition 15 (Completing Rule). *The* completing rule *for an expanding rule* $p : L \xrightarrow{r} R$ *and a positive constraint* c *is defined by* $p^c(c) = v_i \circ h_i \circ r$, *where*

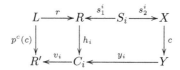

- $\Omega = \{R \xleftarrow{s_1^i} S_i \xrightarrow{s_2^i} X\}$ *is the set of all nonempty overlaps of R and X so that* $s_1^i(S_i) \cap (R \setminus r(L)) \neq \emptyset$,
- *for each* $S_i \in \Omega$, (C_i, h_i, y_i) *is the pushout of* s_1^i *and* $c \circ s_2^i$ *in* **Graph**,
- $(R', v_i : C_i \to R')$ *is the pushout of the morphisms* $h_i : R \to C_i$ *in* **Graph**.

The completing rule for the ACL rule `create object` and the positive constraint requiring a value for each object is shown in Figure 12.

Lemma 1. *If* $p^c(c) : L \to R'$ *is the completing rule for* p, c, *then* R' *satisfies* c.

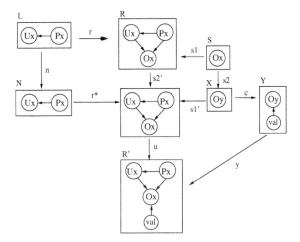

Fig. 12. *Construction of the completing rule.*

The completing rule, however, does not preserve consistency for each positive constraint. If we restrict positive constraints to *single* (X contains at most one node) or *edge-retricted* (for each edge $s \xrightarrow{e} t \in (Y \setminus c(X))$, $s, t \in (Y \setminus c(X))$), the construction results always in a consistence preserving rule.

Proposition 6. *If c is a single or edge-retricted positive constraint, the completing rule $p^c(c)$ for a rule p is consistent with respect to c.*

The construction of the completing rule could be generalized to arbitrary constraints by using *set nodes*: a set node in the left-hand side of a rule matches all occurrences of this node in a graph and the rule is applied to all the occurrences.

Another possibility to solve conflicts between positive constraints and expanding rules p is to transform the constraint $X \to Y$ into a rule and require that this rule is applied (after the application of p) as long as there are occurrences of X not "visited" in H. The new rule is just the constraint $X \to Y$ with negative application condition (X, Y) to avoid its application repeatedly on the same part of H. It is neccessary to add "control" on the framework to ensure that this new rule is applied 'as long as possible'. Control can be introduced either by using rule expressions [GRPPS00] or transformation units [EKMR99] as an encapsulation mechanism used in a way similar to procedure calls.

6   Concluding Remarks

In a graph-based approach to the specification of AC policies, states are represented by graphs and their evolution by graph transformations. A policy is formalized by four components: a type graph, positive and negative constraints (a declarative way of describing what is wanted and what is forbidden) and a set of rules (an operational way of describing what can be constructed). An important problem addressed here is how to deal with inconsistencies caused by conflicts between two of the constraints, two of the rules or between a rule and a constraint. Often such problems arise when trying to predict the behavior of an AC policy obtained by integrating two separate coherent policies [KMPP01a]. The conflict between a rule of one policy and a simple constraint of the other policy has been addressed in part elsewhere [KMPP00], where it is also shown the adequacy of this framework to represent a Role-based Access Control policy. Here we have tackled the problem of conflicts by making effective use of the graph based formalism. Conflicts are detected and resolved statically by using standard formal tools typical of this graph based formalism. In the process, we have introduced the notions of conditional constraint and of weakening of a rule.

A tool, based on a generic graph transformation engine, is under development to assist in the systematic detection and resolution of conflicts and in the stepwise modification of an evolving policy while maintaining its coherence.

References

CELP96.   A. Corradini, H. Ehrig, M. Löwe, and J. Padberg. The category of typed graph grammars and their adjunction with categories of derivations. In *5th Int. Workshop on Graph Grammars and their Application to Computer Science*, number 1073 in LNCS, pages 56–74. Springer, 1996.

EHK⁺97.   H. Ehrig, R. Heckel, M. Korff, M. Löwe, L. Ribeiro, A. Wagner, and A. Corradini. *Handbook of Graph Grammars and Computing by Graph Transformations. Vol. I: Foundations*, chapter Algebraic Approaches to Graph Transformation Part II: Single Pushout Approach and Comparison with Double Pushout Approach. In Rozenberg [Roz97], 1997.

EKMR99.   H. Ehrig, H.-J. Kreowski, U. Montanari, and G. Rozenberg, editors. *Handbook of Graph Grammars and Computing by Graph Transformations. Vol. III: Concurrency, Parallelism, and Distribution*. World Scientific, 1999.

GRPPS00.   M. Große-Rhode, F. Parisi-Presicce, and M. Simeoni. Refinements of Graph Transformation Systems via Rule Expressions. In H. Ehrig, G. Engels, H.-J. Kreowski, and G. Rozenberg, editors, *Proc. of TAGT'98*, number 1764 in Lect. Notes in Comp. Sci., pages 368–382. Springer, 2000.

HW95.   R. Heckel and A. Wagner. Ensuring consistency of conditional graph grammars - a constructive approach. In *Proc. SEGRAGRA'95 Graph Rewriting and Computation*, number 2. Electronic Notes of TCS, 1995.

KMPP00.   M. Koch, L.V. Mancini, and F. Parisi-Presicce. A Formal Model for Role-Based Access Control using Graph Transformation. In F.Cuppens, Y.Deswarte, D.Gollmann, and M.Waidner, editors, *Proc. of the 6th European Symposium on Research in Computer Security (ESORICS 2000)*, number 1895 in Lect. Notes in Comp. Sci., pages 122–139. Springer, 2000.

KMPP01a.   M. Koch, L. V. Mancini, and F. Parisi-Presicce. On the Specification and Evolution of Access Control Policies. In S. Osborne, editor, *Proc. 6th ACM Symp. on Access Control Models and Technologies*, pages 121–130. ACM, May 2001.

KMPP01b.   M. Koch, L.V. Mancini, and F. Parisi-Presicce.   Foundations for a
           graph-based approach to the Specification of Access Control Policies.
           In F.Honsell and M.Miculan, editors, *Proc. of Foundations of Software
           Science and Computation Structures (FoSSaCS 2001)*, number 2030 in
           Lect. Notes in Comp. Sci., pages 287–302. Springer, 2001.
Roz97.   G. Rozenberg, editor. *Handbook of Graph Grammars and Computing by
           Graph Transformations. Vol. I: Foundations.* World Scientific, 1997.
San93.   R. S. Sandhu. Lattice-based access control models. *IEEE Computer*,
           26(11):9–19, 1993.
San98.   R. S. Sandhu. Role-Based Access Control. In *Advances in Computers*,
           volume 46. Academic Press, 1998.
SS94.   R.S. Sandhu and P. Samarati. Access Control: Principles and Practice.
           IEEE Communication Magazine, pages 40–48, 1994.

Logics Admitting Final Semantics

Alexander Kurz

CWI, P.O. Box 94079, 1090 GB Amsterdam, The Netherlands
kurz@cwi.nl

Abstract. A logic for coalgebras is said to admit final semantics iff—
up to some technical requirements—all definable classes contain a fully
abstract final coalgebra. It is shown that a logic admits final semantics iff
the formulas of the logic are preserved under coproducts (disjoint unions)
and quotients (homomorphic images).

Introduction

In the last few years it became clear that a great variety of state-based dynamical
systems, like transition systems, automata, process calculi can be captured uniformly as coalgebras, see [24,7] for an introduction to coalgebras and [6,8,20,3] for
recent developments. One of the important features of coalgebras is that under
rather weak conditions, categories of coalgebras have final (or cofree) coalgebras.
This allows to give final semantics to systems and to use coinduction as a proof
and definition principle.

In the view of coalgebras as systems, logics for coalgebras are specification
languages for systems. Examples of different approaches to logics for coalgebras
include [17,14,22,10,4,18]. These examples show that—due to the generality provided by functors as signatures—there is no uniform syntax for specification
languages for coalgebras.

The purpose of this paper is not to develop a new logical syntax for coalgebras (although we make the proposal to use modal logics with a global diamond).
Rather, we want to take an abstract approach. To this end, we consider as a logic
for coalgebras any pair $(\mathcal{L}, \models)$ consisting of a class of formulas $\mathcal{L}$ and a satisfaction relation $\models$ between coalgebras and formulas, subject to the condition
that definable classes are closed under isomorphism. We then ask the question
whether we can characterise those logics for coalgebras which admit final semantics.

The definition of a logic admitting final semantics as well as the proof of
our characterisation theorem follow the work of Mahr and Makowsky [15] and
Tarlecki [26] who characterised logics for algebras admitting initial semantics.

The first section covers preliminaries, the second gives a characterisation of
logics admitting final semantics. The third section points out that logics admitting final semantics may be quite stronger than those cited as examples above
and makes two suggestions that can be used to strengthen (these and others)
logics in a way that they still admit final semantics.

M. Nielsen and U. Engberg (Eds.): Fossacs 2002, LNCS 2303, pp. 238–249, 2002.
© Springer-Verlag Berlin Heidelberg 2002

1   Preliminaries

We first review coalgebras and final semantics and then briefly discuss logics for coalgebras. For more details on coalgebras and modal logic we refer to [24] and [2], respectively.

1.1   Coalgebras and Final Semantics

A *coalgebra* is given wrt. a base category $\mathcal{X}$ and an endofunctor (also called *signature*) $\Sigma : \mathcal{X} \rightarrow \mathcal{X}$. A Σ-coalgebra (X, ξ) consists of a carrier $X \in \mathcal{X}$ and an arrow $\xi : X \rightarrow \Sigma X$. Σ-coalgebras form a category $\mathsf{Coalg}(\Sigma)$ where a coalgebra morphism $f : (X, \xi) \rightarrow (X', \xi')$ is an arrow $f : X \rightarrow X'$ in $\mathcal{X}$ such that $\Sigma f \circ \xi = \xi' \circ f$. In the following we assume $\mathcal{X} = \mathsf{Set}$, the category of sets and functions. Given a coalgebra (X, ξ), we call the elements of X *states* and ξ the *(transition) structure*. We sometimes denote a coalgebra (X, ξ) by its structure ξ.

We mention only the following paradigmatic example in which coalgebras appear as transition systems (or as Kripke frames, in the terminology of modal logic).

Example 1 (Kripke frames). Consider the functor $\Sigma X = \mathcal{P}_\omega X$ where $\mathcal{P}_\omega$ denotes the finite powerset.[1] Then $\mathcal{P}_\omega$-coalgebras $\xi : X \rightarrow \mathcal{P}X$ are image-finite (ie., finitely branching) *Kripke frames*: For $x \in X$, $\xi(x)$ is the set of successors of x. Morphisms are functional bisimulations, also known as *p*-morphisms or bounded morphisms.

A Σ-coalgebra Z is *final* iff for all $\mathsf{X} \in \mathsf{Coalg}(\Sigma)$ there is a unique morphism $!_\mathsf{X} : \mathsf{X} \rightarrow \mathsf{Z}$. The interest in the final coalgebra comes from the following definition of behavioural equivalence. Given two coalgebras $\mathsf{X} = (X, \xi)$, $\mathsf{Y} = (Y, \nu)$ one says that $x \in X$ and $y \in Y$ are behaviourally equivalent, written $(\mathsf{X}, x) \sim (\mathsf{Y}, y)$, iff $!_\mathsf{X}(x) = !_\mathsf{Y}(y)$.

We call a pair (X, x) a **process** and x its initial state. Every element of the final coalgebra represents a class of behaviourally equivalent processes. We call the elements of the final coalgebra **behaviours** and $!_\mathsf{X}(x)$ the behaviour of (X, x). The **final semantics** of a coalgebra X is given by the unique morphism $!_\mathsf{X} : \mathsf{X} \rightarrow \mathsf{Z}$ (assigning to each process in X its behaviour).

Example 2 (Kripke frames, cont'd). Given two image-finite Kripke frames $\mathsf{X} = (X, \xi)$, $\mathsf{Y} = (Y, \nu)$, and $x \in X$, $y \in Y$ then $(\mathsf{X}, x) \sim (\mathsf{Y}, y)$ iff (X, x) and (Y, y) are bisimilar, that is, iff there is a relation $R \subseteq X \times Y$ with $x \, R \, y$ and

$$x \, R \, y \, \& \, x' \in \xi(x) \; \Rightarrow \; \exists y' \in \nu(y) \, \& \, x' \, R \, y',$$
$$x \, R \, y \, \& \, y' \in \nu(y) \; \Rightarrow \; \exists x' \in \xi(x) \, \& \, x' \, R \, y'.$$

The notion of a final coalgebra can be extended to incorporate additional observations of the states as follows. Let C be a set, called a set of colours, and

---

[1] That is, $\mathcal{P}_\omega(X) = \{A \subseteq X : A \text{ finite}\}$. On functions $\mathcal{P}$ is defined as follows: given $f : X \rightarrow Y$, $\mathcal{P}_\omega f = \lambda A \in \mathcal{P}X.\{f(a) : a \in A\}$.

$\mathsf{X} = (X, \xi)$ be a coalgebra. A mapping $v : X \to C$ is called a colouring of the states. X together with v gives rise to a $(\Sigma \times C)$-coalgebra $\langle \xi, v \rangle : X \to \Sigma X \times C$. We write (X, v), or $\langle \xi, v \rangle$, for a $(\Sigma \times C)$-coalgebra consisting of a Σ-coalgebra $\mathsf{X} = (X, \xi)$ and a colouring v. Triples $((\mathsf{X}, v), x)$ for $x \in X$ are called **coloured processes** and abbreviated as (X, v, x).

Example 3 (Kripke models). Let $\Sigma = \mathcal{P}_\omega$ and $C = \mathcal{P}\mathbf{P}$ where $\mathbf{P}$ is a set of propositional variables. Then $(\Sigma \times C)$-coalgebras $\langle \xi, v \rangle : X \to \mathcal{P}_\omega X \times \mathcal{P}\mathbf{P}$ are *Kripke models*: For $x \in X$, $\xi(x)$ is the set of successors of x and $v(x)$ is the set of propositions holding in x. As for Kripke frames, $(\Sigma \times C)$-morphism are functional bisimulations (respecting, this time, the valuations of propositional variables).

We can think of the colouring v as allowing additional observations. Accordingly, a notion of behavioural equivalence is of interest that takes into account these additional observations. This is provided by the final $(\Sigma \times C)$-coalgebra $\langle \zeta_C, \varepsilon_C \rangle : Z_C \to \Sigma Z_C \times C$. We call ζ_C the **cofree Σ-coalgebra over C**.

Definition 1 (having cofree coalgebras). *We say that $\mathsf{Coalg}(\Sigma)$ has cofree coalgebras iff for all $C \in \mathsf{Set}$ a final coalgebra exists in $\mathsf{Coalg}(\Sigma \times C)$.*

Remark 1. The standard way to establish that for a given functor Σ the category $\mathsf{Coalg}(\Sigma)$ has a final coalgebra is to show that Σ is bounded (see [24]). In that case $\Sigma \times C$ is also bounded and $\mathsf{Coalg}(\Sigma)$ has cofree coalgebras as well. Since the class of bounded functors seems to include the signatures which are important in specifying systems,[2] requiring cofree coalgebras is not much stronger than requiring only a final coalgebra.

Nevertheless, there are examples of categories $\mathsf{Coalg}(\Sigma)$ which don't have all cofree coalgebras but still a final one. The use of the functor $\mathcal{P}_{ne}$ in the following example was suggested to the author by Falk Bartels.

Example. Let $\mathcal{P}_{ne}$ be the functor mapping a set to the set of its non-empty subsets. $\mathsf{Coalg}(\mathcal{P}_{ne})$ has $(\{*\}, \mathrm{id})$ as a final coalgebra. But $\mathsf{Coalg}(\mathcal{P}_{ne})$ does not have a coalgebra cofree over a two element set 2. This follows from the fact that a final $(\mathcal{P}_{ne} \times 2)$-coalgebra can not exist due to cardinality reasons (same argument as the one showing that $\mathsf{Coalg}(\mathcal{P})$ has no final coalgebra).

We conclude this subsection with two more definitions needed later. First, we note that coalgebras for signatures $\Sigma \times C$ and $\Sigma \times D$ are related as follows.

Definition 2 (the functor $\bar{\lambda}$). *Given a mapping $\lambda : C \to D$ we write $\bar{\lambda}$ for the functor*

$$\bar{\lambda} : \mathsf{Coalg}(\Sigma \times C) \to \mathsf{Coalg}(\Sigma \times D)$$
$$\langle \xi, v \rangle \mapsto \langle \xi, \lambda \circ v \rangle$$

where $\xi : X \to \Sigma X$ and $v : X \to C$. On morphisms, $\bar{\lambda}$ is given by $\bar{\lambda}(f) = f$.

---

[2] $\mathsf{Coalg}(\mathcal{P})$, the category of coalgebras for the powerset functor, does not have a final coalgebra. But $\mathsf{Coalg}(\mathcal{P}_\kappa)$, where the cardinality of the subsets is restricted to be smaller than some cardinal κ, has cofree coalgebras.

Finally, a coalgebra is said to be fully abstract iff it has no proper quotient. In case that a final coalgebra exists, this is equivalent to being a subcoalgebra of the final coalgebra.

Definition 3 (fully abstract final coalgebras). X *is a final coalgebra in* $\mathcal{B} \subseteq \mathsf{Coalg}(\Sigma)$ *iff* $X \in \mathcal{B}$ *and for all* $Y \in \mathcal{B}$ *there is a unique morphism* $Y \to X$. *Assuming that* $\mathsf{Coalg}(\Sigma)$ *has a final coalgebra, we call* X *fully abstract iff* X *is a subcoalgebra of the final* Σ*-coalgebra.*

1.2 Logics for Coalgebras

Recalling Definition 2, we begin with

Definition 4 (logic for coalgebras). *Let* $\Sigma : \mathsf{Set} \to \mathsf{Set}$ *be a functor. A logic for* Σ*-coalgebras* $\mathcal{L} = (\mathcal{L}_C, \models_C)_{C \in \mathsf{Set}}$ *consists of classes* $\mathcal{L}_C$ *and satisfaction relations* $\models_C \subseteq \mathsf{Coalg}(\Sigma \times C) \times \mathcal{L}_C$ *for all* $C \in \mathsf{Set}$ *and translations of formulas* $\lambda^* : \mathcal{L}_D \to \mathcal{L}_C$ *for all mappings* $\lambda : C \to D$. *This data has to satisfy for all* $X \in \mathsf{Coalg}(\Sigma \times C)$ *and* $\varphi \in \mathcal{L}_D$

$$X \models \lambda^*(\varphi) \quad \Longleftrightarrow \quad \bar{\lambda}(X) \models \varphi. \tag{1}$$

Moreover, we require $(\lambda_2 \circ \lambda_1)^* = \lambda_1^* \circ \lambda_2^*$, $(\mathrm{id}_C)^* = \mathrm{id}_{\mathcal{L}_C}$, *and* $\forall \varphi \in \mathcal{L}_C : X \models \varphi \Leftrightarrow X' \models \varphi$ *for isomorphic* $(\Sigma \times C)$*-coalgebras* $X \cong X'$.

A class $\mathcal{B} \subseteq \mathsf{Coalg}(\Sigma \times C)$ *is called* $\mathcal{L}$*-definable, or also* $\mathcal{L}_C$*-definable, iff there is* $\Phi \subseteq \mathcal{L}_C$ *such that* $\mathcal{B} = \{X \in \mathsf{Coalg}(\Sigma \times C) : X \models_C \varphi \text{ for all } \varphi \in \Phi\}$.

Remark 2.   1. The simpler notion of a logic for Σ-coalgebras as a pair $(\mathcal{L}, \models)$ where $\mathcal{L}$ is a class and $\models$ is a relation $\models \subseteq \mathsf{Coalg}(\Sigma) \times \mathcal{L}$ is a special case. Indeed, $(\mathcal{L}, \models)$ can be considered as a logic $(\mathcal{L}_C, \models_C)_{C \in \mathsf{Set}}$ as follows. Let $\mathcal{L}_C = \mathcal{L}$, $\langle \xi, v \rangle \models_C \varphi \Leftrightarrow \xi \models \varphi$, and $\lambda^*(\varphi) = \varphi$ for all $C, D \in \mathsf{Set}$, $\xi : X \to \Sigma X$, $v : X \to C$, $\lambda : C \to D$, $\varphi \in \mathcal{L}$. Conversely, any logic for Σ-coalgebras $(\mathcal{L}_C, \models_C)_{C \in \mathsf{Set}}$ gives rise to the pair $(\mathcal{L}, \models)$ defined as $\mathcal{L} = \mathcal{L}_1$, $\models = \models_1$ where 1 is some one-element set.

2. Condition (1) ensures that if a class $\mathcal{B} \subseteq \mathsf{Coalg}(\Sigma \times C)$ is $\mathcal{L}$-definable then $\bar{\lambda}^{-1}(\mathcal{B})$ is $\mathcal{L}$-definable as well.

3. The condition that $(-)^*$ be functorial ensures that $C \cong D$ implies that $\mathcal{L}_C \cong \mathcal{L}_D$ and that $(\mathcal{L}_C, \models_C)$ and $(\mathcal{L}_D, \models_D)$ are equivalent logics. It plays no role in the sequel.

Example 4 (Hennessy-Milner logic). Hennessy-Milner logic is a typical example of a logic for $\mathcal{P}_\omega$-coalgebras $(\mathcal{L}, \models)$ (in the sense of Remark 2.1). Formulas in $\mathcal{L}$ are built from the propositional constant $\bot$ (falsum), boolean operators, and a modal operator $\Box$. Given a formula φ and a process (X, ξ, x), one has $(X, \xi, x) \models \Box \varphi \Leftrightarrow (X, \xi, x') \models \varphi$ for all $x' \in \xi(x)$. And $(X, \xi) \models \varphi$ iff $(X, \xi, x) \models \varphi$ for all $x \in X$.

Example 5. We extend Hennessy-Milner logic to a logic $(\mathcal{L}_C, \models_C)_{C \in \mathsf{Set}}$ whose formulas involve colours. For each $C \in \mathsf{Set}$, let $\mathcal{L}_C$ be the logic with formulas built from propositional constants $c \in C$, infinitary disjunctions, boolean operators, and a modal operator $\square$. Define the semantics as in Example 4 with the additional clause $(X, \xi, x) \models c \Leftrightarrow \pi_2(\xi(x)) = c$ where (X, ξ) is a $(\mathcal{P}_\omega \times C)$-coalgebra and π_2 is the projection $\mathcal{P}_\omega X \times C \to C$. For all $\lambda : C \to D$, let $\lambda^* : \mathcal{L}_D \to \mathcal{L}_C$ be the map replacing each occurrence of $d \in D$ by $\bigvee \{\lambda^{-1}(d)\}$. Note that the disjunction may be infinitary.

The notions of a formula being *preserved under subcoalgebras, quotients, coproducts,* respectively, are defined as usual.[3] Similarly, we say that a class $\mathcal{B} \subseteq \mathsf{Coalg}(\Sigma)$ is *closed under domains of quotients* iff for $B \in \mathcal{B}$ and $A \to B$ a surjective coalgebra morphism we have $A \in \mathcal{B}$. Note that the formulas of a logic are preserved under ... iff every definable class of coalgebras is closed under ....

Formulas of Hennessy-Milner logic are preserved under subcoalgebras, quotients, coproducts, and domains of quotients. The same holds for the logics of the above cited papers [17,14,22,10,4,18].

Of interest for us are also the notions of covariety and quasi-covariety which dualise the corresponding notions from algebra. Behavioural covarieties[4] dualise ground varieties.

Definition 5 ((quasi-)covariety, behavioural covariety). *A quasi-covariety is a class of coalgebras closed under coproducts and quotients. A covariety is a quasi-covariety closed under subcoalgebras. A behavioural covariety is a covariety closed under domains of quotients.*

We will use the following fact about quasi-covarieties.

Proposition 1. *Let* $\mathsf{Coalg}(\Sigma)$ *have cofree coalgebras. Then each quasi-covariety in* $\mathsf{Coalg}(\Sigma \times C)$ *has a fully abstract final coalgebra.*

Proof. This follows from the fact (see eg. [13], Proposition 2.3) that each quasi-covariety $\mathcal{B}$ is an injective-coreflective subcategory, that is, for all $\mathsf{X} \in \mathsf{Coalg}(\Sigma \times C)$ there is $\mathsf{X}' \in \mathcal{B}$ and an injective morphism $r : \mathsf{X}' \hookrightarrow \mathsf{X}$ such that for all $\mathsf{Y} \in \mathcal{B}$ and all $f : \mathsf{Y} \to \mathsf{X}$ there is a unique $g : \mathsf{Y} \to \mathsf{X}'$ such that $r \circ g = f$. Since, by assumption, $\mathsf{Coalg}(\Sigma \times C)$ has a final coalgebra Z, the fully abstract final coalgebra in $\mathcal{B}$ is given by the coreflection $r : \mathsf{Z}' \hookrightarrow \mathsf{Z}$.

In contrast to algebra where already a weak logic as equational logic allows to define any variety, finitary logics for coalgebras are in general not even expressive

---

[3] In modal logic terminology one would rather speak of preservation under generated subframes, bounded images, and disjoint unions, respectively.

[4] The name 'behavioural' covariety is due to the fact that a behavioural covariety $\mathcal{B} \subseteq \mathsf{Coalg}(\Sigma)$ is closed under behavioural equivalence in the sense that, given $\mathsf{X} \in \mathcal{B}$ and $\mathsf{Y} \in \mathsf{Coalg}(\Sigma)$ such that $!_\mathsf{X}(X) = !_\mathsf{Y}(Y)$, then $\mathsf{Y} \in \mathcal{B}$ (where X, Y are the carriers of X, Y respectively). Behavioural covarieties are studied eg. in [5,21,1].

enough to define all behavioural covarieties. Nevertheless, and this will be used in the proof of our main theorem, any logic for coalgebras is the fragment of an expressive logic, as explained below.

Definition 6 (fragment/extension of a logic). *We say that $\mathcal{L}'$ extends the logic for Σ-coalgebras $\mathcal{L}$ and that $\mathcal{L}$ is a fragment of $\mathcal{L}'$ iff $\mathcal{L}'$ is a logic for Σ-coalgebras with $\mathcal{L}_C \subseteq \mathcal{L}'_C$ and $\varphi \in \mathcal{L}_C \Rightarrow (\forall X \in \mathsf{Coalg}(\Sigma \times C) : X \models_C \varphi \Leftrightarrow X \models'_C \varphi)$ for all $C \in \mathsf{Set}$.*

Definition 7 (expressive logic). *A logic for Σ-coalgebras $\mathcal{L}$ is expressive iff, for all $C \in \mathsf{Set}$, every behavioural covariety in $\mathsf{Coalg}(\Sigma \times C)$ is $\mathcal{L}$-definable.*

Remark 3. If $\mathsf{Coalg}(\Sigma)$ has cofree coalgebras then any logic $\mathcal{L}$ for Σ-coalgebras has a smallest expressive extension $\mathcal{L}'$. The idea of the construction is simply to add, for each behavioural covariety $\mathcal{B}$, a formula defining $\mathcal{B}$. That this results indeed in a logic in the sense of Definition 4 follows from [11], Theorem 4.12. The extension $\mathcal{L}'$ is the smallest expressive extension in the sense that $\mathcal{L}'$-definable classes are also definable in any other expressive extension of $\mathcal{L}$.

2   Logics Admitting Final Semantics

The notion of a logic admitting final semantics is adapted from Mahr and Makowsky [15] and Tarlecki [26] who characterised logics for algebras admitting initial semantics. For the notion of a class having a fully abstract final coalgebra see Definition 3.

Definition 8 (logic admitting final semantics). *A logic for Σ-coalgebras $\mathcal{L}$ admits final semantics iff $\mathcal{L}$ is a fragment of an expressive logic $\mathcal{L}'$ such that every $\mathcal{L}'$-definable class has a fully abstract final coalgebra.*

Remark 4.   1. Comparing with [15,26] the analogous requirement would be to demand that $\mathcal{L}$ itself is expressive. This is too strong in our setting since many logics for coalgebras are not expressive. On the other hand all the logics for coalgebras considered in the papers mentioned in the introduction satisfy our weakened requirement.

2. The requirement of full abstractness means that any definable class $\mathcal{B} \subseteq \mathsf{Coalg}(\Sigma)$ not only has a final semantics but that the final semantics of $\mathcal{B}$ is 'inherited' from the final semantics of $\mathsf{Coalg}(\Sigma)$, that is, if two processes of $\mathcal{B}$ are identified in the final semantics of $\mathsf{Coalg}(\Sigma)$, then they are also identified in the final semantics of $\mathcal{B}$.

   The following gives an example—based on a similar one due to Tobias Schröder [25]—of a category $\mathcal{B}$ which has a final coalgebra which is not fully abstract.

Example. Consider $\mathsf{Coalg}(\mathcal{P}_\omega)$ consisting of the finitely branching transition systems. $\mathsf{Coalg}(\mathcal{P}_\omega)$ has cofree coalgebras. Consider the class $\mathcal{B} \subseteq \mathsf{Coalg}(\mathcal{P}_\omega)$ consisting only of the following transition system X

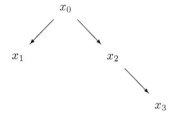

It is not difficult to see that X has only one endomorphism, the identity (recall that morphisms are bisimulations). It follows that X is the final coalgebra of $\mathcal{B} = \{\mathsf{X}\}$. But X is not fully abstract: It distinguishes the states x_1 and x_3 which are identified in the final semantics of $\mathsf{Coalg}(\mathcal{P}_\omega)$ (corresponding to the fact that both states are terminating).

We now formulate our main result.

Theorem 1. *Let* $\mathsf{Coalg}(\Sigma)$ *have cofree coalgebras and let* $\mathcal{L}$ *be a logic for* Σ-*coalgebras. Then* $\mathcal{L}$ *admits final semantics iff the formulas of* $\mathcal{L}$ *are preserved under coproducts and quotients.*

As in the results on logics admitting initial semantics [15,26], the proof is based on a theorem by Mal'cev [16] which we state and prove in the following dualised form (cf. [26] Theorem 4.2).

Theorem 2. *Let* $\mathsf{Coalg}(\Sigma)$ *have cofree coalgebras. Then for a class of coalgebras* $\mathcal{B} \subseteq \mathsf{Coalg}(\Sigma \times C)$ *the following are equivalent.*

1. *For all mappings* $\lambda : D \to C$ *and all behavioural covarieties* $\mathcal{V} \subseteq \mathsf{Coalg}(\Sigma \times D)$ *it holds that* $\bar{\lambda}^{-1}(\mathcal{B}) \cap \mathcal{V}$ *has a fully abstract final* $(\Sigma \times D)$-*coalgebra.*

2. $\mathcal{B}$ *is closed under coproducts and quotients.*

Proof (of Theorem 2). ' $\Leftarrow$ ': If $\mathcal{B}$ is a quasi-covariety then $\bar{\lambda}^{-1}(\mathcal{B})$ is a quasi-covariety. The intersection of a quasi-covariety with a behavioural covariety is a quasi-covariety. And quasi-covarieties have fully abstract final coalgebras, see Proposition 1.

' $\Rightarrow$ ': We use that $\mathcal{B}$ is a quasi-covariety if it is an injective-coreflective subcategory (see eg. [13] Proposition 2.3), that is, if for any $(X, \xi) \in \mathsf{Coalg}(\Sigma \times C)$ there is $(X', \xi') \in \mathcal{B}$ and an injective morphism $r : (X', \xi') \hookrightarrow (X, \xi)$ such that for all $(Y, \nu) \in \mathcal{B}$ and all $f : (Y, \nu) \to (X, \xi)$ there is $g : (Y, \nu) \to (X', \xi')$ such that $r \circ g = f$.

Given (X, ξ) we let $D = C \times X$ and $\lambda : C \times X \to C$ the projection. In the following we denote $(\Sigma \times C)$-coalgebras by their structure and $(\Sigma \times C \times X)$-coalgebras by pairs $\langle \nu, v \rangle$ where ν is a $(\Sigma \times C)$-coalgebra and v is a colouring. Let

$\mathcal{V} \subseteq \mathsf{Coalg}(\Sigma \times D)$ be the behavioural covariety $\{\langle \nu, v \rangle \mid \exists f : \langle \nu, v \rangle \to \langle \xi, \mathrm{id}_X \rangle\}$ and note that (ξ, id_X) is a fully abstract final coalgebra in $\mathcal{V}$. It follows from our assumption on $\mathcal{B}$ that $\bar{\lambda}^{-1}(\mathcal{B}) \cap \mathcal{V}$ has a final coalgebra $\langle \xi', v' \rangle$ and (by full abstractness) that there is an injective morphism $r : \langle \xi', v' \rangle \to \langle \xi, \mathrm{id}_X \rangle$. To show that $r : \xi' \to \xi$ is the required 'coreflection'-morphism, let $\nu \in \mathcal{B}$ and consider a $(\Sigma \times C)$-coalgebra morphism $f : \nu \to \xi$. Then $f : \langle \nu, f \rangle \to \langle \xi, \mathrm{id}_X \rangle$ is a $(\Sigma \times D)$-coalgebra morphism. Since $\langle \nu, f \rangle \in \bar{\lambda}^{-1}(\mathcal{B}) \cap \mathcal{V}$, there is $g : \langle \nu, f \rangle \to \langle \xi', v' \rangle$ by the finality of $\langle \xi', v' \rangle$. Hence $f = r \circ g$ as required.

Proof (of Theorem 1). ' $\Rightarrow$ ': Let $\mathcal{B} \subseteq \mathsf{Coalg}(\Sigma \times C)$ be $\mathcal{L}$-definable and $\mathcal{L}'$ be an expressive extension of $\mathcal{L}$. It follows that for all $\lambda : D \to C$ and all behavioural covarieties $\mathcal{V} \subseteq \mathsf{Coalg}(\Sigma \times D)$ the class $\bar{\lambda}^{-1}(\mathcal{B}) \cap \mathcal{V}$ is $\mathcal{L}'$-definable and, therefore, has a fully abstract final coalgebra. Now apply Theorem 2.

' $\Leftarrow$ ': Let $\mathcal{L}''$ be a logic having precisely the behavioural covarieties as definable classes. That $\mathcal{L}''$ is a logic in the sense of Definition 4 follows from Theorem 4.12 in [11]. Define, for all $C \in \mathsf{Set}$, $\mathcal{L}'_C$ as the disjoint union $\mathcal{L}_C + \mathcal{L}''_C$ and $\models'_C = (\models_C \cup \models''_C)$. Then $\mathcal{L}$ is a fragment of the expressive logic $\mathcal{L}'$. Since $\mathcal{L}$-definable classes are quasi-covarieties and $\mathcal{L}''$-definable classes are behavioural covarieties, $\mathcal{L}'$-definable classes are quasi-covarieties. And quasi-covarieties have fully abstract final coalgebras, see Proposition 1.

Remark 5. 1. In ' $\Rightarrow$ ' of the proof of Theorem 1 we see why we need to require that definable classes of an *expressive* extension of $\mathcal{L}$ have fully abstract final coalgebras. For an example showing that it does not suffice to require that $\mathcal{L}$-definable classes have fully abstract final coalgebras, recall Remark 2.1 and consider a logic $(\mathcal{L}, \models)$ that has as the only definable class $\mathcal{B} \subset \mathsf{Coalg}(\Sigma)$ the class consisting of precisely the cofree coalgebras (for, say, $\Sigma = \mathcal{P}_\omega$). Then every $\mathcal{L}_C$-definable class $\subseteq \mathsf{Coalg}(\Sigma \times C)$ has a fully abstract final coalgebra but $\mathcal{B}$ is not closed under quotients.

2. The corresponding result in Tarlecki [26], Theorem 4.4, is proved more generally not only for algebras but for 'abstract algebraic institutions'. Our result can be generalised along the same lines. In fact, a logic for coalgebras as in Definition 4 is a co-institution (see [11]). It suffices therefore to extract the additional requirements needed to prove the theorems above in order to reach a corresponding notion of 'abstract coalgebraic co-institution'. But in contrast to abstract algebraic institutions which subsume not only (standard) algebras but also other structures as eg. partial algebras and continuous algebras, we are not aware of analogous examples in the coalgebraic world that would justify the generalisation of our result to 'abstract coalgebraic co-institutions'.

3   Examples of Logics Admitting Final Semantics

As mentioned already, most logics for coalgebras studied so far, only allow for definable classes closed under coproducts, quotients, subcoalgebras, and domains of quotients. On the other hand, as our theorem shows, stronger specification languages with formulas not necessarily preserved under subcoalgebras and domains of quotients may be of interest. In this section we show some ways of how to extend known logics for coalgebras to such stronger ones. Since the ideas from modal logic used in this section are completely standard, we avoid providing full details. They can be found, eg., in [2].

Let us first go back to the example of Hennessy-Milner logic. We can extend the expressive power of Hennessy-Milner logic by *adding propositional variables*.

Example 6 (adding propositional variables). Let us extend the logic of Example 4 by adding propositional variables from a set $\mathbf{P}$. The satisfaction relation is now defined by referring to coloured processes (X, v, x) where $v : X \to \mathcal{P}\mathbf{P}$. For propositional variables $p \in \mathbf{P}$ we have $(\mathsf{X}, v, x) \models p \Leftrightarrow p \in v(x)$. Boolean and modal operators are defined as usual. And $\mathsf{X} \models \varphi$ iff $(\mathsf{X}, v, x) \models \varphi$ for all $v : X \to \mathcal{P}\mathbf{P}$ and all $x \in X$.

Note that the definition of $\mathsf{X} \models \varphi$ involves a quantification over all valuations of propositional variables $v : X \to \mathcal{P}\mathbf{P}$. Since the extension of a propositional variable can be any subset of the carrier of X, adding propositional variables can be described as *allowing a prefix of universally quantified monadic second-order variables* in the formulas (cf. [2], Definition 2.45 and Proposition 3.12).

Typical examples of how adding propositional variables increases expressiveness are the following. Referring to Example 6, the formulas $\Box p \to p$ and $\Box p \to \Box\Box p$ with $p \in \mathbf{P}$ define, respectively, the class of reflexive Kripke frames and the class of transitive Kripke frames. Both classes are not closed under domains of quotients, showing that propositional variables add indeed expressiveness. On the other hand, formulas with propositional variables are still preserved under subcoalgebras, that is, definable classes are covarieties. Conversely, every covariety is definable by an (infinitary) modal logic with propositional variables (see [12]).

We show now how to build logics whose formulas are not necessarily preserved under subcoalgebras. A logic for coalgebras, possibly with propositional variables, can be strengthened by *adding rules*. Given two formulas φ, ψ we call φ/ψ a rule and extend the satisfaction relation via

$$\mathsf{X} \models \varphi/\psi \quad \text{iff} \quad (\mathsf{X}, v) \models \varphi \Rightarrow (\mathsf{X}, v) \models \psi \quad \text{for all valuations } v : X \to \mathcal{P}\mathbf{P}.$$

This definition dualises the definition of implications for algebras and was studied in [13] where it was shown that—allowing infinitary conjunctions—any quasi-covariety is definable by a logic for coalgebras with rules.

Since rules can be rather unintuitive in writing specifications, *adding a global diamond* instead (suggested to the author by Alexandru Baltag) may be preferable. A global diamond $\mathbf{E}$ (cf. [2], Section 7.1) is a unary modal operator defined via

$$(\mathsf{X}, v, x) \models \mathbf{E}\varphi \quad \text{iff} \quad (\mathsf{X}, v, y) \models \varphi \text{ for some } y \in X.$$

E is called global because the range of quantification is not confined by the transition structure. Of course, adding a global diamond, we have to restrict occurrences of **E** to appear only positively in the formulas (otherwise we would also add the defining power of a global box[5]).

Concerning expressiveness, adding the global diamond is equivalent to adding rules. To sketch the argument: On the one hand, every rule φ/ψ is equivalent to the formula $\neg\psi \to \mathbf{E}\neg\varphi$; on the other hand, formulas containing a global diamond are still preserved under coproducts and quotients and therefore can not be more expressive than rules.

Conclusion

We have shown that a logic for coalgebras admits final semantics iff its formulas are preserved under coproducts and quotients.

On the one hand, this result allows to design specifications languages admitting final semantics, since it is usually not difficult to check whether formulas are preserved under coproducts and quotients. This can be of interest for specification languages for coalgebras like CCSL [23]. CCSL allows the coalgebraic specification of classes of object-oriented programs. A question in this context is to determine the largest fragment of CCSL that ensures that specified classes of objects have a final semantics (final semantics for objects was proposed by Reichel [19] and Jacobs [9]). The value of our result in such a concrete setting needs further exploration.

On the other hand we have pointed out possibilities to extend weaker logics in a way that they still admit final semantics. Possible strengthenings may allow formulas with (1) prefixes of universally quantified monadic second-variables (propositional variables) and (2) positive occurrences of a first-order existential quantifier (global diamond).

Acknowledgements

I am indebted to Alexandru Baltag for suggesting to consider logics with a global diamond, to Tobias Schröder for his example showing that a Kripke model admitting no non-trivial endomorphisms still can have distinct bisimilar points, and to Falk Bartels for suggesting $\mathcal{P}_{ne}$ when looking for a category of coalgebras with a final but not all cofree coalgebras. I want to thank Till Mossakowski and Hendrik Tews for asking me the question answered in this paper. Finally, I want to thank the anonymous referees for their helpful and interesting comments. The diagram was drawn with Paul Taylor's macro package.

---

[5] A global box **A** (defined as $\neg\mathbf{E}\neg$) would allow to define classes that do not have final coalgebras. Eg., for a propositional variable p, $p \to \mathbf{A}p$ defines the class of $\mathcal{P}_\omega$-coalgebras with at most one element (and this class contains exactly three coalgebras none of which is final).

References

1. S. Awodey and J. Hughes. The coalgebraic dual of Birkhoff's variety theorem. Technical Report CMU-PHIL-109, Carnegie Mellon University, Pittsburgh, PA, 15213, November 2000.
2. P. Blackburn, M. de Rijke, and Y. Venema. *Modal Logic*. Cambridge University Press, 2001. See also http://www.mlbook.org.
3. A. Corradini, M. Lenisa, and U. Montanari, editors. *Coalgebraic Methods in Computer Science (CMCS'01)*, volume 44-1 of *Electronic Notes in Theoretical Computer Science*, 2001.
4. Robert Goldblatt. A calculus of terms for coalgebras of polynomial functors. In A. Corradini, M. Lenisa, and U. Montanari, editors, *Coalgebraic Methods in Computer Science (CMCS'01)*, volume 44.1 of *ENTCS*. Elsevier, 2001.
5. H. P. Gumm and T. Schröder. Covarieties and complete covarieties. *Theoretical Computer Science*, 260:71–86, 2001.
6. B. Jacobs, L. Moss, H. Reichel, and J. Rutten, editors. *Coalgebraic Methods in Computer Science (CMCS'98)*, volume 11. Electronic Notes in Theoretical Computer Science, 1998.
7. B. Jacobs and J. Rutten. A tutorial on (co)algebras and (co)induction. *EATCS Bulletin*, 62, 1997.
8. B. Jacobs and J. Rutten, editors. *Coalgebraic Methods in Computer Science*, volume 19. Electronic Notes in Theoretical Computer Science, 1999.
9. Bart Jacobs. Objects and classes, co-algebraically. In B. Freitag, C. B. Jones, C. Lengauer, and H.-J. Schek, editors, *Object-Orientation with Parallelism and Persistence*, pages 83–103. Kluwer Acad. Publ., 1996.
10. Bart Jacobs. Many-sorted coalgebraic modal logic: a model-theoretic study. *Theoretical Informatics and Applications*, 35(1):31–59, 2001.
11. A. Kurz and D. Pattinson. Coalgebras and modal logics for parameterised endofunctors. Technical Report SEN-R0040, CWI, 2000. http:www.cwi.nl/~kurz.
12. Alexander Kurz. A co-variety-theorem for modal logic. In *Advances in Modal Logic 2*. Center for the Study of Language and Information, Stanford University, 2001.
13. Alexander Kurz. Modal rules are co-implications. In A. Corradini, M. Lenisa, and U. Montanari, editors, *Coalgebraic Methods in Computer Science (CMCS'01)*, volume 44.1 of *ENTCS*. Elsevier, 2001.
14. Alexander Kurz. Specifying coalgebras with modal logic. *Theoretical Computer Science*, 260:119–138, 2001.
15. B. Mahr and J. A. Makowsky. Characterizing specification language which admit initial semantics. *Theoretical Computer Science*, 31(1+2):59–60, 1984.
16. A. I. Mal'cev. Quasiprimitive classes of abstract algebras. In *The Metamathematics of Algebraic Systems, Collected Papers: 1936–1967*. North-Holland, 1971. Originally published in Dokl. Akad. Nauk SSSR 108, 187–189, 1956.
17. Lawrence Moss. Coalgebraic logic. *Annals of Pure and Applied Logic*, 96:277–317, 1999.
18. Dirk Pattinson. Semantical principles in the modal logic of coalgebras. In *Proceedings 18th International Symposium on Theoretical Aspects of Computer Science (STACS 2001)*, volume 2010 of *LNCS*, Berlin, 2001. Springer. Also available as technical report at http://www.informatik.uni-muenchen.de/~pattinso/.
19. Horst Reichel. An approach to object semantics based on terminal co-algebras. *Mathematical Structures in Computer Science*, 5(2):129–152, June 1995.

20. Horst Reichel, editor. *Coalgebraic Methods in Computer Science (CMCS'00)*, volume 33 of *Electronic Notes in Theoretical Computer Science*, 2000.
21. Grigore Roşu. Equational axiomatizability for coalgebra. *Theoretical Computer Science*, 260:229–247, 2001.
22. Martin Rößiger. Coalgebras and modal logic. In Horst Reichel, editor, *Coalgebraic Methods in Computer Science (CMCS'00)*, volume 33 of *Electronic Notes in Theoretical Computer Science*, pages 299–320, 2000.
23. J. Rothe, H. Tews, and B. Jacobs. The coalgebraic class specification language CCSL. *Journal of Universal Computer Science*, 7(2):175–193, 2001.
24. J.J.M.M. Rutten. Universal coalgebra: A theory of systems. *Theoretical Computer Science*, 249:3–80, 2000. First appeared as technical report CS R 9652, CWI, Amsterdam, 1996.
25. Tobias Schröder, January 2001. Personal Communication.
26. Andrzej Tarlecki. On the existence of free models in abstract algebraic institutions. *Theoretical Computer Science*, 37:269–304, 1986. Preliminary version, University of Edinburgh, Computer Science Department, Report CSR-165-84, 1984.

Model Checking Fixed Point Logic with Chop

Martin Lange and Colin Stirling

Laboratory for Foundations of Computer Science
Division of Informatics
University of Edinburgh
{martin,cps}@dcs.ed.ac.uk

Abstract. This paper examines FLC,
which is the modal μ-calculus enriched with a sequential composition operator. Bisimulation invariance and the tree model property are proved. Its succinctness is compared to the modal μ-calculus. The main focus lies on FLC's model checking problem over finite transition systems. It is proved to be PSPACE-hard. A tableau model checker is given and an upper EXPTIME bound is derived from it. For a fixed alternation depth FLC's model checking problem turns out to be PSPACE-complete.

1 Introduction

Modal and temporal logics are well established research areas in computer science, artificial intelligence, philosophy, etc. [2, 4, 10]. An important temporal logic is Kozen's modal μ-calculus $\mathcal{L}_\mu$ [7] because it contains almost all other propositional temporal logics. In fact, it is equi-expressive to the bisimulation invariant fragment of monadic second-order logic over transition graphs [6]. Therefore, properties expressed by $\mathcal{L}_\mu$ formulas are essentially "regular".

In [9], Müller-Olm introduced FLC, fixed point logic with chop, that extends $\mathcal{L}_\mu$ with sequential composition. He showed that the expressive power of FLC is strictly greater than $\mathcal{L}_\mu$ because FLC can define non-regular properties. Whereas the semantics of a modal μ-calculus formula is a subset of states of a transition system, the semantics of an FLC formula is a predicate transformer, a function from sets of states to sets of states. This makes it easy to introduce a composition operator in the logic.

Müller-Olm proved that the satisfiability problem for FLC is undecidable because of its rich expressiveness. However, he notes that model checking finite transition systems is decidable. There are only finitely many (monotonic) functions from subsets to subsets of a finite set. Using the Tarski-Knaster Theorem [11], he shows that model checking can be done in the function lattice using fixed point approximants.

In this paper we examine FLC in more detail. We show that FLC retains some features of $\mathcal{L}_\mu$ such as the tree model property. However, most of the paper is devoted to FLC model checking over finite transition systems. We provide a tableau based model checker that avoids explicit calculation of functions and approximants. We also give lower, PSPACE, and upper, EXPTIME, complexity

M. Nielsen and U. Engberg (Eds.): Fossacs 2002, LNCS 2303, pp. 250–263, 2002.
© Springer-Verlag Berlin Heidelberg 2002

bounds on model checking. The upper bound is derived directly from the tableau model checker. An interesting open question is whether there is a suitable notion of automaton that captures FLC model checking.

In Section 2 we recall the syntax and semantics of FLC, example formulas that express non-regular properties and a proof of the tree model property. The tableau based model checker is defined and shown to be sound and complete in Section 3. In Section 4 we examine the complexity of model checking FLC in the general case and for fixed alternation depth, and we give upper and lower bounds. The paper concludes with some remarks on possible further research.

2   Preliminaries

Let $\mathcal{P} = \{\mathtt{tt}, \mathtt{ff}, q, \overline{q}, \ldots\}$ be a set of propositional constants that is closed under complementation, $\mathcal{V} = \{Z, Y, \ldots\}$ a set of propositional variables, and $\mathcal{A} = \{a, b, \ldots\}$ a set of action names. A labelled *transition system* is a graph $\mathcal{T} = (\mathcal{S}, \{\overset{a}{\to} \mid a \in \mathcal{A}\}, L)$ where $\mathcal{S}$ is a set of states, $\overset{a}{\to}$ for each $a \in \mathcal{A}$ is a binary relation on states and $L : \mathcal{S} \to 2^{\mathcal{P}}$ labels the states such that, for all $s \in \mathcal{S} : q \in L(s)$ iff $\overline{q} \notin L(s)$, $\mathtt{tt} \in L(s)$, and $\mathtt{ff} \notin L(s)$. We will use infix notation $s \overset{a}{\to} t$ for transition relations.

Formulas of FLC are given by

$$\varphi \quad ::= \quad q \mid Z \mid \tau \mid \langle a \rangle \mid [a] \mid \varphi \vee \varphi \mid \varphi \wedge \varphi \mid \mu Z.\varphi \mid \nu Z.\varphi \mid \varphi; \varphi$$

where $q \in \mathcal{P}$, $Z \in \mathcal{V}$, and $a \in \mathcal{A}$.[1] We will write σ for μ or ν. To save brackets we introduce the convention that ; binds stronger than $\wedge$ which binds stronger than $\vee$. Formulas are assumed to be well named in the sense that each binder variable is distinct. Our main interest is with closed formulas, that do not have free variables. In which case there is a function $fp : \mathcal{V} \to$ FLC that maps each variable to its defining fixed point formula (that may contain free variables).

The set $Sub(\varphi)$ of subformulas of φ is defined as usual, with $Sub(\sigma Z.\psi) = \{\sigma Z.\psi\} \cup Sub(\psi)$. We say that Z depends on Y in φ, written $Z \prec_{\varphi} Y$, if Y occurs free in $fp(Z)$. We write $Z <_{\varphi} Y$ iff (Z, Y) is in the transitive closure of $\prec_{\varphi}$. The *alternation depth* of φ, $ad(\varphi)$, is the maximum number of variables of φ in a chain $Z_0 <_{\varphi} Z_1 <_{\varphi} \ldots <_{\varphi} Z_k$ where Z_{i-1} and Z_i are of different fixed point types for $0 < i \leq k$. FLC$^k = \{\varphi \in$ FLC $\mid ad(\varphi) \leq k\}$.

An *environment* $\rho : \mathcal{V} \to (2^{\mathcal{S}} \to 2^{\mathcal{S}})$ maps variables to monotone functions of sets to sets. $\rho[Z \mapsto f]$ is the function that maps Z to f and agrees with ρ on all other arguments. The semantics $[\![\cdot]\!]_{\rho}^{\mathcal{T}} : 2^{\mathcal{S}} \to 2^{\mathcal{S}}$ of an FLC formula, relative to $\mathcal{T}$ and ρ, is a monotone function on subsets of states with respect to the inclusion ordering on $2^{\mathcal{S}}$. These functions together with the partial order given by

$$f \sqsubseteq g \text{ iff } \forall X \subseteq \mathcal{S} : f(X) \subseteq g(X)$$

form a complete lattice with joins $\sqcup$ and meets $\sqcap$. By the Tarski-Knaster Theorem [11] the least and greatest fixed points of functionals $F : (2^{\mathcal{S}} \to 2^{\mathcal{S}}) \to (2^{\mathcal{S}} \to 2^{\mathcal{S}})$ exist. They are used to interpret fixed point formulas of FLC.

---

[1] In [9], τ is called `term`.

To simplify the notation we assume a transition system $\mathcal{T}$ to be fixed for the remainder of the paper, and drop it from the semantic brackets.

$$\llbracket q \rrbracket_\rho = \lambda X.\{s \in \mathcal{S} \mid q \in L(s)\}$$
$$\llbracket Z \rrbracket_\rho = \rho(Z)$$
$$\llbracket \tau \rrbracket_\rho = \lambda X.X$$
$$\llbracket \varphi \vee \psi \rrbracket_\rho = \lambda X.\llbracket \varphi \rrbracket_\rho(X) \cup \llbracket \psi \rrbracket_\rho(X)$$
$$\llbracket \varphi \wedge \psi \rrbracket_\rho = \lambda X.\llbracket \varphi \rrbracket_\rho(X) \cap \llbracket \psi \rrbracket_\rho(X)$$
$$\llbracket \langle a \rangle \rrbracket_\rho = \lambda X.\{s \in \mathcal{S} \mid \exists t \in X, \text{ s.t. } s \overset{a}{\to} t\}$$
$$\llbracket [a] \rrbracket_\rho = \lambda X.\{s \in \mathcal{S} \mid \forall t \in \mathcal{S}, s \overset{a}{\to} t \Rightarrow t \in X\}$$
$$\llbracket \mu Z.\varphi \rrbracket_\rho = \bigsqcap\{f : 2^{\mathcal{S}} \to 2^{\mathcal{S}} \mid f \text{ monotone}, \llbracket \varphi \rrbracket_{\rho[Z \mapsto f]} \sqsubseteq f\}$$
$$\llbracket \nu Z.\varphi \rrbracket_\rho = \bigsqcup\{f : 2^{\mathcal{S}} \to 2^{\mathcal{S}} \mid f \text{ monotone}, f \sqsubseteq \llbracket \varphi \rrbracket_{\rho[Z \mapsto f]}\}$$
$$\llbracket \varphi; \psi \rrbracket_\rho = \llbracket \varphi \rrbracket_\rho \circ \llbracket \psi \rrbracket_\rho$$

A state s satisfies a formula φ, written $s \models_\rho \varphi$, iff $s \in \llbracket \varphi \rrbracket_\rho(\mathcal{S})$ for some ρ. If φ is a closed formula then ρ can be omitted and we write $s \models \varphi$.

Two formulas φ and ψ are *equivalent*, written $\varphi \equiv \psi$, iff their semantics are the same, i.e. for every $\mathcal{T}$ and every ρ: $\llbracket \varphi \rrbracket_\rho^{\mathcal{T}} = \llbracket \psi \rrbracket_\rho^{\mathcal{T}}$. This equivalence is a congruence and thus allows substituitivity. It is easy to see that there is no FLC formula φ that does not contain τ as a subformula, s.t. $\varphi \equiv \tau$.

For model checking purposes it is useful to consider a weaker equivalence. φ and ψ are called *weakly equivalent*, written $\varphi \approx \psi$, iff they are satisfied by the same states, i.e. $s \models_\rho \varphi$ iff $s \models_\rho \psi$ for any state s of any transition system $\mathcal{T}$ and every ρ. Note that weak equivalence is not a congruence.

Lemma 1. *(Equivalences)*
a) If $\varphi \equiv \psi$ then $\varphi \approx \psi$.
b) If $\varphi \approx \psi$ then $\varphi; \mathtt{tt} \equiv \psi; \mathtt{tt}$.
c) $\varphi \approx \varphi; \mathtt{tt}$.
d) $(\varphi \vee \psi); \chi \equiv \varphi; \chi \vee \psi; \chi$ *and* $(\varphi \wedge \psi); \chi \equiv \varphi; \chi \wedge \psi; \chi$
e) $\tau; \varphi \equiv \varphi \equiv \varphi; \tau$.
f) $q; \varphi \equiv q$ *for* $q \in \mathcal{P}$.

Proof. a) If $\varphi \equiv \psi$ then $\llbracket \varphi \rrbracket_\rho(\mathcal{S}) = \llbracket \psi \rrbracket_\rho(\mathcal{S})$ for every set of states $\mathcal{S}$ and every ρ, and therefore $\varphi \approx \psi$. b) $\llbracket \varphi; \mathtt{tt} \rrbracket_\rho = \llbracket \varphi \rrbracket_\rho \circ \llbracket \mathtt{tt} \rrbracket_\rho = \lambda X.\llbracket \varphi \rrbracket_\rho(\mathcal{S})$ for any transition system with state set $\mathcal{S}$ and any ρ. But $\varphi \approx \psi$ implies $\llbracket \varphi \rrbracket_\rho(\mathcal{S}) = \llbracket \psi \rrbracket_\rho(\mathcal{S})$ and therefore $\varphi; \mathtt{tt} \equiv \psi; \mathtt{tt}$. c) Trivial. d) $\llbracket (\varphi \vee \psi); \chi \rrbracket_\rho = (\lambda X.\llbracket \varphi \rrbracket_\rho(X) \cup \llbracket \psi \rrbracket_\rho(X)) \circ \llbracket \chi \rrbracket_\rho = \lambda X.\llbracket \varphi \rrbracket_\rho(\llbracket \chi \rrbracket_\rho(X)) \cup \llbracket \psi \rrbracket_\rho(\llbracket \chi \rrbracket_\rho(X)) = \llbracket \varphi; \chi \vee \psi; \chi \rrbracket_\rho$ and similar for $\wedge$. e)–f) Trivial. $\qquad\square$

In [9] it is shown how to embed $\mathcal{L}_\mu$ into FLC by using sequential composition: for instance, $\langle a \rangle \varphi$ becomes $\langle a \rangle; \varphi$. Therefore, we will sometimes omit the semicolon to maintain a strong resemblance to the syntax of $\mathcal{L}_\mu$. For example, $\langle a \rangle Z \langle a \rangle$ abbreviates $\langle a \rangle; Z; \langle a \rangle$.

In order to prove correctness of the tableau construction in Section 3 we introduce *approximants* of fixed point formulas. Let $fp(Z) = \mu Z.\varphi$ for some φ and let $\alpha, \lambda \in \mathbb{O}\text{rd}$, the ordinals, where λ is a limit ordinal. Then $Z^0 := \mathtt{ff}$,

$Z^{\alpha+1} = \varphi[Z^{\alpha}/Z]$, $Z^{\lambda} = \bigvee_{\alpha<\lambda} Z^{\alpha}$. If $fp(Z) = \nu Z.\varphi$ then $Z^0 := \mathtt{tt}$, $Z^{\alpha+1} = \varphi[Z^{\alpha}/Z]$, $Z^{\lambda} = \bigwedge_{\alpha<\lambda} Z^{\alpha}$. Note that $\mu Z.\varphi \equiv \bigvee_{\alpha\in\mathbb{O}\mathrm{rd}} Z^{\alpha}$ and $\nu Z.\varphi \equiv \bigwedge_{\alpha\in\mathbb{O}\mathrm{rd}} Z^{\alpha}$. If only finite transition systems are considered $\mathbb{O}\mathrm{rd}$ can be replaced by $\mathbb{N}$.

First we recall some properties of FLC shown by Müller-Olm.

Theorem 1. [9]
a) Satisfiability for FLC is undecidable.
b) FLC does not have the finite model property.

The proof of part a) uses a reduction from the simulation equivalence problem for Basic Process Algebra which is undecidable [5]. For every BPA process P one can construct two characteristic FLC formulas ϕ_{P-} that is satisfied by all processes that simulate P, and ϕ_{P+} that is satisfied by all processes that are simulated by P. Hence the formula $\phi_{P-} \wedge \phi_{P+} \wedge \phi_{Q-} \wedge \phi_{Q+}$ is satisfiable iff P is simulation equivalent to Q. Part b) also follows from the existence of such characteristic formulas: however, also see example 2 later.

Example 1. Let $\mathcal{A} = \{a,b\}$ and $\varphi = \nu Y.[b]\mathtt{ff} \wedge [a](\nu Z.[b] \wedge [a](Z;Z)); (([a]\mathtt{ff} \wedge [b]\mathtt{ff}) \vee Y)$. Formula φ expresses "the number of bs never exceeds the number of as" which is non-regular and, therefore, is not expressible in $\mathcal{L}_\mu$. This is an interesting property of protocols when a and b are the actions *send* and *receive*.

The subformula $\psi = \nu Z.[b] \wedge [a](Z;Z)$ expresses "there can be at most one b more than there are as". This can be understood best by unfolding the fixed point formula and thus obtaining sequences of modalities and variables. It is easy to see that replacing a Z with a $[b]$ reduces the number of Zs whereas replacing it with the other conjunct adds a new Z to the sequence.

Then, $[b]\mathtt{ff} \wedge [a]\psi$ postulates that at the beginning no b is possible and for every n as there can be at most n bs. Finally, the Y in φ allows such sequences to be composed or finished in a deadlock state.

We now establish that FLC has the tree model property, by showing that each closed formula defines a bisimulation invariant property[2].

Theorem 2. (Bisimulation invariance) *Let $\mathcal{T} = (\mathcal{S}, \{\xrightarrow{a} \mid a \in \mathcal{A}\}, L)$ and $s, t \in \mathcal{S}$. If s and t are bisimilar, $s \sim t$, then for all closed $\varphi \in FLC$: $s \models \varphi$ iff $t \models \varphi$.*

Proof. Let $\varphi \in FLC$ be closed. φ is equivalent to an infinitary formula of FLC without fixed point operators and variables, using $\mu Z.\varphi \equiv \bigvee_{i\in\mathbb{N}} Z^i$ and $\nu Z.\varphi \equiv \bigwedge_{i\in\mathbb{N}} Z^i$ since $\mathcal{T}$ is assumed to be finite. Lemma 1 c) says that the resulting φ' is weakly equivalent to $\varphi'; \mathtt{tt}$. Using parts d)–f) of Lemma 1 one can transform $\varphi'; \mathtt{tt}$ into a formula that does not contain τ, and which is a (possibly infinitary) boolean combination of sequences of the form q or $\langle a \rangle; \psi$ or $[a]; \psi$ where ψ again is of the described form. Every α, obtained in such a way, is equivalent to an infinitary modal formula q or $\langle a \rangle \psi$ or $[a]\psi$, where equivalence

---

[2] The definition of bisimulation here includes the condition that states also preserve atomic properties in $\mathcal{P}$.

means being satisfied by the same states. But a formula of infinitary modal logic cannot distinguish between bisimilar states and weak equivalence preserves this property.   □

An immediate corollary of Theorem 2 is the tree model property.

Corollary 1. *FLC has the tree model property.*

Example 2. Let $\mathcal{A} = \{a, b\}$. An FLC formula that is satisfiable but does not have any finite model is $\varphi = (\nu Z.\langle a \rangle(Z \wedge \tau); ([b] \wedge \langle b \rangle)); ([a]\mathbf{ff} \wedge [b]\mathbf{ff})$. The formula postulates the existence of an infinite a-path, s.t. after every prefix of n as exactly n bs are possible. The body of the fixed point formula can be rewritten as $\langle a \rangle(([b] \wedge \langle b \rangle) \wedge Z; ([b] \wedge \langle b \rangle))$. This expresses that there must be a path labelled ab and all such bs lead to states that have similar properties. Moreover, after the a there is another path of the same style with one more b at its end.

Clearly, φ has an infinite model. Suppose φ has a finite model, too. This could be regarded as a finite automaton $\mathfrak{A}$ with final states being the deadlock states. But $\mathfrak{A}$ would accept the context-free and non-regular language $L = \{a^n b^n \mid n \in \mathbb{N}\}$.

The proof of Theorem 2 is similar to showing bisimulation invariance of $\mathcal{L}_\mu$ formulas. If the transition system is image-finite, i.e. $|\{t \in \mathcal{S} \mid s \xrightarrow{a} t\}| < \infty$ for every $s \in \mathcal{S}$, $a \in \mathcal{A}$, the converse implication in Theorem 2 holds, too. It is well-known that, if the transition system is finite and fixed, $\mathcal{L}_\mu$ formulas become equivalent to formulas of finitary modal logic. In particular, $\mu Z.\varphi \equiv \bigvee_{i \leq n} Z^i$ and $\nu Z.\varphi \equiv \bigwedge_{i \leq n} Z^i$ where $n = |\mathcal{S}|$. In the case of an FLC formula, $|\mathcal{S}| \cdot 2^{|\mathcal{S}|}$ is an upper bound for n according to Tarski-Knaster since this is the maximal length of a chain $f_0 \sqsubseteq f_1 \sqsubseteq \ldots \sqsubseteq f_n$. From Theorem 2 follows that, in fact, there is a linear upper bound for the number of approximants needed to eliminate fixed points in FLC.

Theorem 3. *(Approximants) Let* $\mathcal{T} = (\mathcal{S}, \{\xrightarrow{a} \mid a \in \mathcal{A}\}, L)$ *be finite with* $s \in \mathcal{S}, S \subseteq \mathcal{S}$.
a) $s \in [\![\mu Z.\varphi]\!]_\rho^{\mathcal{T}}(S)$ *iff* $\exists k \leq |\mathcal{S}|$, *s.t.* $s \in [\![Z^k]\!]_\rho^{\mathcal{T}}(S)$.
b) $s \in [\![\nu Z.\varphi]\!]_\rho^{\mathcal{T}}(S)$ *iff* $\forall k \leq |\mathcal{S}|: s \in [\![Z^k]\!]_\rho^{\mathcal{T}}(S)$.

Proof. a) The "if" part is trivial. For the "only if" part consider the general approximant characterisation of fixed point formulas. It implies the existence of a $k \in \mathbb{N}$ that makes $s \in [\![Z^k]\!]_\rho^{\mathcal{T}}(S)$ true. To show that it is bounded we introduce a new proposition q_S s.t. $[\![q_S]\!]^{\mathcal{T}} = \lambda X.S$. Then $s \in [\![\mu Z.\varphi]\!]_\rho^{\mathcal{T}}(S)$ iff $s \models (\mu Z.\varphi); q_S$. According to Theorem 2 $(\mu Z.\varphi); q_S$ can be translated into a sequence $\{\alpha_i \mid i \in \mathbb{N}\}$ of formulas of infinitary modal logic. We show by induction on the fixed point depth of φ that finitary modal logic suffices.

Suppose φ does not contain any $\sigma Y.\psi$. Clearly, in this case every α_i is a formula of finitary modal logic. Consider now the function $f : \alpha_i \mapsto \alpha_{i+1}$ for every $i \in \mathbb{N}$. f is monotone since α_{i+1} arises from α_i by variable substitution and transformations that preserve equivalence. This means that $s \models (\mu Z.\varphi); q_S$ implies the existence of a $k \leq |\mathcal{S}|$ s.t. $s \models \alpha_k$. But then $s \in [\![Z^k]\!]_\rho^T(S)$.

Suppose now that φ has fixed point depth $n + 1$ and every $\sigma Y.\psi \in Sub(\varphi)$ has fixed point depth at most n and can therefore be translated into a formula of finitary modal logic. Replacing every such $\mu Y.\psi$ in φ by $\bigvee_{k=0}^{|\mathcal{S}|} Z^k$, and every $\nu Y.\psi$ with $\bigwedge_{k=0}^{|\mathcal{S}|} Z^k$, yields a formula φ' of fixed point depth 0 that is equivalent to φ. The latter substitution uses part b) of the Lemma on a smaller formula. The same argument as above holds now for translating $\mu Z.\varphi'$ into a sequence $\{\alpha_i \mid i \leq |\mathcal{S}|\}$.

b) Here, the "only if" part is trivial. The "if" part is dual to the "only if" part of a). $\qquad\square$

Theorem 4. *FLC is exponentially more succinct than $\mathcal{L}_\mu$.*

Proof. Let $\mathcal{A} = \{a_0, b_0, \ldots, a_n, b_n\}$. Consider the binary, finite tree of depth $n+1$ whose nodes at level i have two transitions labelled a_i and b_i. It is easy to see that the minimal characteristic $\mathcal{L}_\mu$ formula χ_n for this tree is exponential in n. Consider now the infinite tree that arises from the finite one by pasting itself iteratively to its leaves. Again, every $\mathcal{L}_\mu$ formula describing this tree must be exponentially long in n. However, $\nu Z.(\langle a_0 \rangle \wedge \langle b_0 \rangle); \ldots; (\langle a_n \rangle \wedge \langle b_n \rangle); Z$ describes this tree too and has linear length in n. $\qquad\square$

For each $a \in \mathcal{A}$ one can regard *converse modalities* $\langle a^- \rangle, [a^-]$. Their semantics is

$$[\![\langle a^- \rangle]\!] = \lambda X.\{s \in \mathcal{S} \mid \exists t \in X, \text{ s.t. } t \xrightarrow{a} s\}$$
$$[\![[a^-]]\!] = \lambda X.\{s \in \mathcal{S} \mid \forall t \in \mathcal{S}, t \xrightarrow{a} s \Rightarrow t \in X\}$$

The tableaux of section 3 can easily be extended to handle these formulas as well. Indeed, all the complexity results of section 4 also hold for the extended logic.

Example 3. This extension of FLC is capable of defining *uniform inevitability*, ψ holds in all paths of a transition system at the same moment. Let $\mathcal{A} = \{a\}$ and $\varphi = \mu Y.\langle a \rangle Y \vee (\psi \wedge (\nu Z.[a^-]; (Z \wedge \tau); [a]); \psi)$. φ is an instance of an *eventually* formula of $\mathcal{L}_\mu$, i.e. $\mu Y.\langle a \rangle Y \vee \psi'$ says that there is a path on which ψ' eventually holds. $(\nu Z.[a^-]; (Z \wedge \tau); [a]); \psi$ says that at every state that can be reached by a sequence of n as backwards and then n as forwards ψ holds. Composing these two formulas achieves uniform inevitability. In [3] it is shown that φ has no equivalent in $\mathcal{L}_\mu$.

3   A Tableau Based Model Checker for FLC

For the remainder of the paper we restrict ourselves to finite transition systems only. In this section we present a tableau based model checker for FLC that is

$$(\vee)\ \frac{(T,S)\vdash\varphi_0\vee\varphi_1}{(T_0,S)\vdash\varphi_0\quad(T_1,S)\vdash\varphi_1}\quad T=T_0\cup T_1$$

$$(\wedge)\ \frac{(T,S)\vdash\varphi_0\wedge\varphi_1}{(T_0,S)\vdash\varphi_0\quad(T_1,S)\vdash\varphi_1}\quad T=T_0\cap T_1$$

$$(;)\ \frac{(T,S)\vdash\varphi_0;\varphi_1}{(T,T')\vdash\varphi_0\quad(T',S)\vdash\varphi_1}$$

$$\text{FP}\ \frac{(T,S)\vdash\sigma Z.\varphi}{(T,S)\vdash Z}\qquad\qquad\text{VAR}\ \frac{(T,S)\vdash Z}{(T,S)\vdash\varphi}\quad\text{if } fp(Z)=\sigma Z.\varphi$$

Fig. 1. The tableau rules for FLC.

sound and complete and that avoids explicit calculation of functions and approx-imants. The extra expressiveness of FLC and its succinctness suggest that the complexity of model checking FLC is higher than $\mathcal{L}_\mu$: exact bounds are presented in the next section.

Let $\mathcal{T}=(\mathcal{S},\{\xrightarrow{a}\mid a\in\mathcal{A}\},L)$ and assume that $T,S\subseteq\mathcal{S}$. A *tableau* for T,S and $\varphi\in$ FLC is a finite tree whose nodes are labelled $(T',S')\vdash\psi$, where $T',S'\subseteq\mathcal{S}$, and $\psi\in Sub(\varphi)$. The intended meaning of such a configuration is $T'\subseteq[\![\psi]\!](S')$, i.e. all the states in T' satisfy ψ relative to S'.

The tableau rules for the boolean connectives and the sequential composition operator are justified by the semantics of FLC. Fixed point formulas are replaced by their corresponding variables. A variable itself is replaced by the body of its fixed point definition. The rules are shown in figure 1.

Let $C_0=(T_0,S_0)\vdash\varphi$. A branch $C_0,C_1,\ldots,C_n$ of a tableau for T_0,S_0 and φ is *successful* iff

- $C_n=(\emptyset,S)\vdash\psi$ for some S and ψ, or
- $C_n=(T,S)\vdash\psi$, $\psi\in\{\tau,q,\langle a\rangle,[a]\}$, and $T\subseteq[\![\psi]\!](S)$, or
- $C_n=(T_n,S_n)\vdash Z$ with $fp(Z)=\nu Z.\varphi$ for some φ, and
  - $\exists i<n$, s.t. $C_i=(T_i,S_i)\vdash Z$, and
  - $T_n\subseteq T_i$ and $S_n\supseteq S_i$, and
  - $\nexists j$, s.t. $i<j<n$ and $C_j=(T,S)\vdash Y$ and $Z<_\varphi Y$.

It is *unsuccessful* iff

- $C_n=(T,S)\vdash\psi$, $\psi\in\{\tau,q,\langle a\rangle,[a]\}$, and $T\not\subseteq[\![\psi]\!](S)$, or
- $C_n=(T_n,S_n)\vdash Z$ with $fp(Z)=\mu Z.\varphi$ for some φ, and
  - $\exists i<n$, s.t. $C_i=(T_i,S_i)\vdash Z$, and
  - $T_n\supseteq T_i$ and $S_n\subseteq S_i$, and
  - $\nexists j$, s.t. $i<j<n$ and $C_j=(T,S)\vdash Y$ and $Z<_\varphi Y$.

In all cases, C_n is called a *leaf*. A tableau is successful if all its branches are successful.

$$\frac{\dfrac{\dfrac{\dfrac{(\{s\},\mathcal{S}) \vdash \nu Z.\mu Y.\langle a\rangle Z \wedge ([b];(Y \vee \tau);\langle b\rangle)}{(\{s\},\mathcal{S}) \vdash Z}}{\dfrac{(\{s\},\mathcal{S}) \vdash \mu Y.\langle a\rangle Z \wedge ([b];(Y \vee \tau);\langle b\rangle)}{(\{s\},\mathcal{S}) \vdash Y}}}{(\{s\},\mathcal{S}) \vdash \langle a\rangle Z \wedge ([b];(Y \vee \tau);\langle b\rangle)}}{}$$

$(\{s\},\mathcal{S}) \vdash \langle a\rangle Z$	$(\mathcal{S},\mathcal{S}) \vdash [b];(Y \vee \tau);\langle b\rangle$
$(\{s\},\{s\}) \vdash \langle a\rangle \quad (\{s\},\mathcal{S}) \vdash Z$	$(\mathcal{S},\mathcal{S}) \vdash [b] \quad (\mathcal{S},\mathcal{S}) \vdash Y \vee \tau \quad (\mathcal{S},\mathcal{S}) \vdash \langle b\rangle$
	$(\emptyset,\mathcal{S}) \vdash Y \quad (\mathcal{S},\mathcal{S}) \vdash \tau$

Fig. 2. The tableau for example 4.

Example 4. Let $\varphi = \nu Z.\mu Y.\langle a\rangle Z \wedge ([b];(Y \vee \tau);\langle b\rangle)$ and $\mathcal{T}$ be the transition system consisting of states $\mathcal{S} = \{s,t\}$ and transitions $s \xrightarrow{a} s$, $s \xrightarrow{b} t$, and $t \xrightarrow{b} s$. Φ says "there exists an infinite a-path from which every sequence of n b-actions can be repeated by another n b-actions.". The tableau of figure 2 shows that state s satisfies φ. To save space, rule $(;)$ has been extended to

$$\frac{(T,S) \vdash \varphi_0;\ldots;\varphi_k}{(T,T_0) \vdash \varphi_0 \quad (T_0,T_1) \vdash \varphi_1 \quad \cdots \quad (T_{k-1},S) \vdash \varphi_k}$$

3.1   Correctness

Theorem 5. *(Soundness) Let $\mathcal{T} = (\mathcal{S}, \{\xrightarrow{a} \mid a \in \mathcal{A}\}, L)$ be a finite transition system, $T_0, S_0 \subseteq \mathcal{S}$, and $\varphi \in FLC$. If there is a successful tableau with root $(T_0, S_0) \vdash \varphi$, then $T_0 \subseteq \llbracket \varphi \rrbracket (S_0)$.*

Proof. Let $C = (T,S) \vdash \psi$ be a configuration with a $t \in T$ s.t. $t \notin \llbracket \psi \rrbracket (S)$. C will be called *false* in this case. The tableau rules are backwards sound, i.e. if all the successors of a configuration C are not false then C is not false. This holds for rule VAR because a fixed point is equivalent to its unfolding, and for rule FP when variables are interpreted as approximants. We show that rule $(\vee)$ is backwards sound. Suppose there is a $t \in T$, s.t. $t \notin \llbracket \varphi_0 \vee \varphi_1 \rrbracket (S)$. Then $t \in T_i$ for some $i \in \{0,1\}$ because $T = T_0 \cup T_1$. But $\llbracket \varphi_0 \vee \varphi_1 \rrbracket (S) = \llbracket \varphi_0 \rrbracket (S) \cup \llbracket \varphi_1 \rrbracket (S)$ and therefore $t \notin \llbracket \varphi_i \rrbracket (S)$ which means that $(T_i,S) \vdash \varphi_i$ is false. Backwards soundness of rules $(\wedge)$ and $(;)$ is established similarly.

Suppose now that the tableau for $C_0 = (T_0,S_0) \vdash \varphi$ is successful but $T_0 \not\subseteq \llbracket \varphi \rrbracket (S_0)$, i.e. C_0 is false. From backwards soundness follows that at least one leaf $(T,S) \vdash \psi$ of the tableau must be false. $\psi \in \{\tau,q,\langle a\rangle,[a]\}$ is impossible because the branch to this leaf would be unsuccessful and, hence, the tableau itself cannot be successful.

Suppose therefore it is a configuration $C = (T,S) \vdash Z_0$ with Z_0 denoting a greatest fixed point. Then Z_0 is interpreted as the least approximant $Z_0^{k_0}$, s.t.

$T \not\subseteq [\![Z_0^{k_0}]\!](S)$ but $T \subseteq [\![Z_0^{k_0-1}]\!](S)$. Note that $k_0 > 0$ because it is impossible to have a false configuration $(T, S) \vdash Z$ where Z is interpreted as Z^0. Starting from C one can continue to build a tableau and using backwards soundness again, falsity of a configuration can be pushed through this tableau towards a leaf $C' = (T', S') \vdash Z_1$. Note that the false successor of a configuration may depend on the index of an approximant and therefore Z_1 need not equal Z_0. However, Z_1 is interpreted as the least approximant $Z_1^{k_1}$ in the same way as above and the argument can be iterated. Since φ contains only a finite number of variables and the transition system at hand is finite too, the tableau must contain a branch $C_0, \ldots, C_j, \ldots, C'_j$ s.t. $C_j = (T, S) \vdash Z_j$, $C'_j = (T', S') \vdash Z_j$, $T' \subseteq T$, $S' \supseteq S$ and C'_j is false. But if there is a t s.t. $t \notin T$ then $t \notin T'$, and $[\![Z_j]\!](S) \subseteq [\![Z_j]\!](S')$. By monotonicity C_j must be false too. Note that in C_j Z_j was interpreted as the least approximant $Z_j^{k_j}$ in the described sense. Since between C_j and C'_j rule VAR must have been applied at least once and no greater variable occurs, C'_j contradicts the assumption that k_j was the least approximant index for which C_j is false. $\square$

Theorem 6. (Completeness) *Let* $\mathcal{T} = (\mathcal{S}, \{\overset{a}{\to} \mid a \in \mathcal{A}\}, L)$ *be a finite transition system,* $T_0, S_0 \subseteq \mathcal{S}$, *and* $\varphi \in FLC$. *If* $T_0 \subseteq [\![\varphi]\!](S_0)$ *then there is a successful tableau rooted* $(T_0, S_0) \vdash \varphi$.

Proof. Let $C = (T, S) \vdash \psi$ be a configuration s.t. $T \subseteq [\![\psi]\!](S)$. In this case C will be called *true*. Note that the tableau rules can always be applied so that they preserve truth: if the antecedent of a rule is true then so are the consequents. This remains true when variables are interpreted by their approximants. The proof proceeds by constructing a tableau such that each node is true, and then stopping a branch whenever there is a leaf. However, if the application of the rule is FP and $fp(Z) = \mu Z.\psi$ then the formula in the consequent is interpreted as the least approximant Z^k s.t. $T \subseteq [\![Z^k]\!](S)$ but $T \not\subseteq [\![Z^{k-1}]\!](S)$. Note that $k > 0$ since $T \subseteq [\![Z^0]\!](S)$ only if $T = \emptyset$ and so a leaf is already reached.

Continuing from this configuration $(T, S) \vdash Z$ a tableau is built preserving truth. Suppose this tableau is unsuccessful, i.e. it has an unsuccessful branch. This branch cannot end on a configuration $(T', S') \vdash \psi$ where ψ is atomic because this configuration would be false. As in the proof of Theorem 5 a configuration $(T', S') \vdash Z$ with $T' \subseteq T$ and $S' \supseteq S$ must eventually be reached. But this contradicts the assumption that Z^k is the least approximant. We conclude that there is no least approximant and therefore that $T \not\subseteq [\![\mu Z.\psi]\!](S)$ which means the configuration $(T, S) \vdash \mu Z.\psi$ could not have been true. $\square$

Corollary 2. *If there is a successful tableau for* $(T, S) \vdash \varphi$ *then there are successful tableaux* $(T', S') \vdash \varphi$ *for every* $T' \subseteq T$ *and every* $S' \supseteq S$.

4   Complexity of Model Checking

In this section we provide upper and lower bounds on the complexity of model checking FLC over finite transition systems.

Theorem 7. (*General upper bound*) *FLC model checking is in EXPTIME.*

Proof. We describe an alternating algorithm that, given a finite transition system $\mathcal{T} = (\mathcal{S}, \{\overset{a}{\to} \mid a \in \mathcal{A}\}, L)$, a set $S_0 \subseteq \mathcal{S}$, and an FLC formula φ, finds a successful tableau for $(S_0, \mathcal{S}) \vdash \varphi$ if one exists. Alternating algorithms allow both nondeterministic and co-nondeterministic choices. They are taken by players $\exists$ and $\forall$. $\exists$ wants to show that a successful tableau exists. $\forall$ wants to show the opposite. Therefore he will choose which branch of the tableau is inspected, whereas $\exists$ is in charge of choosing the correct elements of the next configuration on this branch. She wins the play if the branch is successful. $\forall$ wins if they exhibit an unsuccessful branch of the tableau. It is easy to see that $\exists$ has a winning strategy iff there is a successful tableau for $(S_0, \mathcal{S}) \vdash \varphi$.

During the play each player is allowed to store one configuration $C_i = (T, S) \vdash Z$. If the play visits another configuration $C' = (T', S') \vdash Y$ with $Z <_\varphi Y$ then C_i will be deleted or overwritten by C'. Note that only an actual configuration can be stored. If the actual configuration is $(T, S) \vdash \psi$ and $\psi = \psi_0 \vee \psi_1$ or $\psi = \psi_0 \wedge \psi_1$ player $\exists$ chooses two sets T_0 and T_1 s.t. $T = T_0 \cup T_1$, resp. $T = T_0 \cap T_1$, and player $\forall$ chooses an $i \in \{0, 1\}$. The next configuration will be $(T_i, S) \vdash \psi_i$. If $\psi = \psi_0; \psi_1$ player $\exists$ chooses a $T' \subseteq \mathcal{S}$. Again, $\forall$ determines which branch of rule (;) to follow. The rules for fixed points and variables are deterministic. The stored configurations are used to determine whether a branch is successful or unsuccessful.

A play can be implemented using polynomial space since three configurations only need to be kept in memory, namely the actual one and a C_i for each player in the sense of the condition for success and unsuccess. Their sizes are polynomial in both the size of the transition system and the size of the formula. Therefore, FLC model checking can be done in alternating PSPACE. This is the same as EXPTIME [1]. □

Theorem 8. (*Upper bounds*) FLC^k *model checking is in PSPACE for every* $k \in \mathbb{N}$.

Proof. Let $\mathcal{T} = (\mathcal{S}, \{\overset{a}{\to} \mid a \in \mathcal{A}\}, L)$ be finite and $\varphi \in$ FLC. Using Theorems 2 and 3 one can translate a fixed point formula $\sigma Z.\varphi$ into a series $\{\alpha_i \mid 0 \leq i \leq |\mathcal{S}|\}$ of modal formulas, where α_i is allowed to contain the subformula Z^{i-1}. Every such α_i can be stored as a directed acyclic graph with atomic formulas as nodes and the connectives $\vee$, $\wedge$ and ; as labelled edges. In fact, the entire sequence can be represented as one directed acyclic graph with a counter for the approximant. Evaluating a formula in a state corresponds to tracing the paths of this graph. This avoids a possible exponential blow-up in the size of α_i which could occur if the technique described in the proofs of Theorems 2 and 3 was explicitly used.

To establish whether for some $s \in \mathcal{S}$, $s \models \sigma Z.\varphi$ holds, it is enough to check $s \models \alpha_i$ for $0 \leq i \leq |\mathcal{S}|$. This might involve checking whether $t \models Z^{i-1}$ for some $t \in \mathcal{S}$. It is possible to store this information in a table of size $|\mathcal{S}| \cdot O(\varphi)^{ad(\varphi)}$, which is polynomial in the size of the input if the alternation depth of φ is fixed. □

Theorem 9. (Lower bound) *FLC model checking is PSPACE-hard.*

Proof. It is known that QBF (quantified boolean logic) is PSPACE-hard [8]. We show a reduction from QBF to the model checking problem for FLC. Let $\Phi = Q_1 x_1 \ldots Q_k x_k (C_1 \wedge \ldots \wedge C_n)$ with each $C_i = l_{i,1} \vee l_{i,2} \vee l_{i,3}$ and each $l_{i,j} \in \{x_h, \overline{x}_h \mid 1 \le h \le k\}$. We construct a finite transition system $\mathcal{T}$ and a formula φ, s.t. $\mathcal{T} \models \varphi$ iff Φ is valid. The actions of $\mathcal{T}$ will be $\mathcal{A} = \{c, 0, 1, x_1, \ldots, x_k, \overline{x}_1, \ldots, \overline{x}_k\}$.

For each clause C_i construct a tree of depth $k + 1$ in the following way. Beginning with $j = k$ introduce a node that has two transitions labelled x_j and $\overline{x}_j$ to two different subtrees if x_j appears in clause C_i, and to the same subtree if it does not. Continue with $j - 1$ at the successor(s) until $j = 1$. Every path π in this tree induces a valuation function $\eta_\pi : \{x_1, \ldots, x_k\} \to \{0, 1\}$ by $\eta_\pi(x_i) = 1$ if x_i occurs on π. The leaves at the end of each path π are now extended with one further transition which is labelled 1, resp. 0, if η_π makes the clause evaluate to true, resp. false.

The second part of the transition system consists of states $\{0, 1, \overline{1}, \ldots, k, \overline{k}\}$. The transitions are $0 \xrightarrow{x_1} 1, 0 \xrightarrow{\overline{x}_1} \overline{1}, z \xrightarrow{x_i} i, z \xrightarrow{\overline{x}_i} \overline{i}$ for $z \in \{i - 1, \overline{i - 1}\}$ and $2 \le i \le k$.

Finally, there are transitions labelled c from nodes $k, \overline{k}$ to every root of the trees representing the clauses. As an example the corresponding transition system for $\Phi = \exists x_1 \forall x_2 \forall x_3 \exists x_4 (x_1 \vee \overline{x}_2 \vee \overline{x}_4) \wedge (\overline{x}_2 \vee x_3 \vee x_4)$ is given in figure 3.

The formula φ is constructed in the following way.

$$\psi_i = \begin{cases} \langle x_i \rangle Z \langle x_i \rangle \vee \langle \overline{x}_i \rangle Z \langle \overline{x}_i \rangle & \text{if } Q_i = \exists \\ \langle x_i \rangle Z \langle x_i \rangle \wedge \langle \overline{x}_i \rangle Z \langle \overline{x}_i \rangle & \text{if } Q_i = \forall \end{cases} \quad \text{for } 1 \le i < k$$

$$\psi_k = \begin{cases} \langle x_k \rangle [c] \langle x_k \rangle \vee \langle \overline{x}_k \rangle [c] \langle \overline{x}_k \rangle & \text{if } Q_i = \exists \\ \langle x_k \rangle [c] \langle x_k \rangle \wedge \langle \overline{x}_k \rangle [c] \langle \overline{x}_k \rangle & \text{if } Q_i = \forall \end{cases}$$

$$\varphi = (\mu Z. \bigvee_{i=1}^{k} \psi_i); \langle 1 \rangle$$

Intuitively for a Φ that has existential quantification only φ says: There exists a path labelled with a $w \in \mathcal{A}^*$ s.t. after every c action there is a path labelled with $\overleftarrow{w}$ and after that a 1 action is possible. If Φ contains universal quantification the path becomes a tree.

The resulting transition system has $O(|\Phi|^2)$ transitions, and $|\varphi| = O(|\Phi|)$. Therefore the reduction can be computed in polynomial time. Since only counters for the clauses and variables are needed it can even be computed in logarithmic space. It remains to show that the reduction is correct.

Suppose $\mathcal{T}, 0 \models \varphi$. Since $\mathcal{T}$ is acyclic and an action 1 only occurs at the end of a path through $\mathcal{T}$ this is only possible if $0 \models Z^k; \langle 1 \rangle$. Then $Z^k; \langle 1 \rangle$ describes a tree through $\mathcal{T}$ starting with node 0 s.t. every path of the tree ends on an action 1. Furthermore, every universally quantified variable x_i corresponds to a genuine branching $\bullet \xrightarrow{x_i} \bullet$ and $\bullet \xrightarrow{\overline{x}_i} \bullet$ whereas every existentially quantified variable corresponds to either of these transitions. It is now easy to see that this tree is a witness for the validity of Φ.

Suppose now that Φ is valid. Let $\Phi = Q_1 x_1 \Phi'$. Case $Q_1 = \exists$. Φ is valid if there exists $v \in \{0,1\}$ s.t. $\Phi'[v/x_1]$ is valid. By hypothesis there exists a tree through $\mathcal{T}$, starting with node 1 if $v = 1$ or with node $\overline{1}$ if $v = 0$, that witnesses the validity of $\Phi'[v/x_1]$. Extend this tree at its root with a transition $\bullet \xrightarrow{x_1} \bullet$ if $v = 1$, and $\bullet \xrightarrow{\overline{x_1}} \bullet$ if $v = 0$. In the case of $Q_1 = \forall$ there are two trees through $\mathcal{T}$ that witness the validity of $\Phi'[0/x_1]$ and $\Phi'[1/x_1]$. It remains to show that this tree witnesses that $\mathcal{T}, 0 \models \varphi$.

Again, let $\Phi = \exists x_1 \Phi'$ and $\Phi'[v/x_1]$ be valid, and assume w.l.o.g. that $v = 1$. Then $0 \models \varphi$ iff $1 \models (\mu Z. \bigvee_{i=2}^{k} \psi_i); \langle x_1 \rangle; \langle 1 \rangle$. Suppose $\Phi = \forall x_1 \Phi'$. Then $0 \models \varphi$ iff $1 \models (\mu Z. \bigvee_{i=2}^{k} \psi_i); \langle x_1 \rangle; \langle 1 \rangle$ and $\overline{1} \models (\mu Z. \bigvee_{i=2}^{k} \psi_i); \langle \overline{x_1} \rangle; \langle 1 \rangle$. The fixed point formula can be unfolded further, ruling out those disjuncts that can obviously not be satisfied by the current state. Finally, after $(k-1)$ unfoldings one obtains a formula that implies $Z^k; \langle 1 \rangle$ by propositional reasoning already. $\square$

Müller-Olm has found a simpler proof of PSPACE-hardness but not published it. He uses a reduction from the universal acceptance problem for non-deterministic finite automata. Given an NFA $\mathfrak{A}$ over the alphabet Σ, does $\mathfrak{A}$

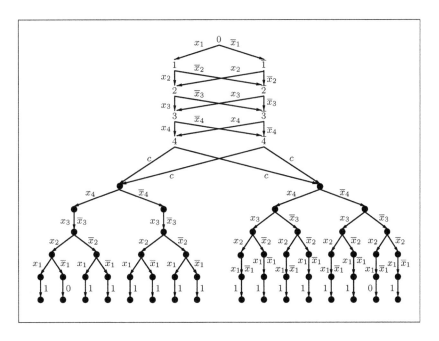

Fig. 3. The transition system for Φ.

accept Σ^*? For the reduction, $\mathfrak{A}$ is regarded as a transition system that satisfies $(\nu Z.\tau \wedge \bigwedge_{a \in \Sigma} Z; \langle a \rangle); q_{fin}$ iff $\mathfrak{A}$ accepts Σ^* where q_{fin} is true in all final states of $\mathfrak{A}$.

This proves the even stronger result that model checking FLC is PSPACE-hard for fixed formulas already. The reduction does not work for $\mathcal{L}_\mu$ since fixed point formulas in $\mathcal{L}_\mu$ are right-linear. But the automaton at hand is nondeterministic and a left-linear formula is needed to allow prefixes of a word w to be accepted along paths that are not prefixes of the one accepting w.

Corollary 3. *FLC^k model checking is PSPACE-complete for every $k \geq 0$.*

5 Conclusion

FLC is a very interesting general temporal logic. Its expressive power goes beyond regular properties: indeed it can express both context-free and context-sensitive features (such as, "every path has the label sequence $a^n b^n c^n$", see [9]). Although satisfiability is undecidable, model checking finite transition systems is decidable. In the paper we have provided a reasonably simple tableau based model checker that does not explicitly calculate functions and approximants. This model checker yields an EXPTIME complexity upper bound. We also showed a PSPACE lower bound and PSPACE-completeness when alternation depth is fixed. There is a similarity with the model checking $\mathcal{L}_\mu$ problem. It is P-complete for fixed alternation depth and is in NP∩co-NP for the general case.

An interesting open question is whether there is a suitable notion of (alternating) automaton or graph game that is equivalent to model checking FLC.

Acknowledgments We would like to thank Markus Müller-Olm and the people of the Concurrency Workshop at BRICS for helpful comments on this topic.

References

1. A. K. Chandra, D. C. Kozen, and L. J. Stockmeyer. Alternation. *Journal of the ACM*, 28(1):114–133, January 1981.
2. E. A. Emerson. Temporal and modal logic. In J. van Leeuwen, editor, *Handbook of Theoretical Computer Science*, volume B: Formal Models and Semantics, chapter 14, pages 996–1072. Elsevier Science Publishers B.V.: Amsterdam, The Netherlands, New York, N.Y., 1990.
3. E. Allen Emerson. Uniform inevitability is tree automaton ineffable. *Information Processing Letters*, 24(2):77–79, January 1987.
4. R. Goré. Tableau methods for modal and temporal logics. In M. D'Agostino, D. Gabbay, R. Hähnle, and J. Posegga, editors, *Handbook of Tableau Methods*. Kluwer, Dordrecht, 1999.
5. J. F. Groote and H. Hüttel. Undecidable equivalences for basic process algebra. *Information and Computation*, 115(2):354–371, December 1994.

6. D. Janin and I. Walukiewicz. On the expressive completeness of the propositional μ-calculus with respect to monadic second order logic. In U. Montanari and V. Sassone, editors, *CONCUR '96: Concurrency Theory, 7th Int. Conf.*, volume 1119 of *LNCS*, pages 263–277, Pisa, Italy, 26–29 August 1996. Springer.

7. D. Kozen. Results on the propositional mu-calculus. *TCS*, 27:333–354, December 1983.

8. A. R. Meyer and L. J. Stockmeyer. Word problems requiring exponential time. In *ACM Symp. on Theory of Computing (STOC '73)*, pages 1–9, New York, April 1973. ACM Press.

9. M. Müller-Olm. A modal fixpoint logic with chop. In C. Meinel and S. Tison, editors, *Proc. 16th Annual Symp. on Theoretical Aspects of Computer Science, STACS'99*, volume 1563 of *LNCS*, pages 510–520, Trier, Germany, 1999. Springer.

10. C. Stirling. Modal and temporal logics. In *Handbook of Logic in Computer Science*, volume 2 (Background: Computational Structures), pages 477–563. Clarendon Press, Oxford, 1992.

11. A. Tarski. A lattice-theoretical fixpoint theorem and its application. *Pacific J.Math.*, 5:285–309, 1955.

On Model Checking
Durational Kripke Structures
(Extended Abstract)

François Laroussinie, Nicolas Markey, and Philippe Schnoebelen

Lab. Spécification & Vérification
ENS de Cachan & CNRS UMR 8643
61, av. Pdt. Wilson, 94235 Cachan Cedex France
{fl,markey,phs}@lsv.ens-cachan.fr

Abstract. We consider quantitative model checking in *durational Kripke structures* (Kripke structures where transitions have integer durations) with timed temporal logics where subscripts put quantitative constraints on the time it takes before a property is satisfied.

We investigate the conditions that allow polynomial-time model checking algorithms for timed versions of *CTL* and exhibit an important gap between logics where subscripts of the form "$= c$" (exact duration) are allowed, and simpler logics that only allow subscripts of the form "$\leq c$" or "$\geq c$" (bounded duration).

A surprising outcome of this study is that it provides the second example of a Δ_2^p-complete model checking problem.

1 Introduction

Model checking (the automatic verification that a model fulfills temporal logic specifications) is widely used when designing and debugging critical reactive systems [Eme90,CGP99]. During the last decade, model checking has been extended to *real-time systems*, where quantitative information about timings is required.

Real-time model checking has been mostly studied and developed in the framework of Alur and Dill's *Timed Automata* [ACD93]. There now exists a large body of theoretical knowledge and practical experience for this class of systems, and it is agreed that their main drawback is the complexity blowup induced by timing constraints: all model checking problems are at least PSPACE-hard over Timed Automata [Alu91,CY92,ACD93,AL99].

However, there exist simpler families of timed models, for which polynomial-time model checking is possible. Usually, these are based on classical, discrete, Kripke structures (KS). Here there is no inherent concept of time (contrary to clocks in Timed Automata) and the elapsing of time is encoded by events. For example, in [EMSS92] each transition of a KS is viewed as taking exactly one time unit, and in [LST00] a "tick" proposition labels states where the clock is incremented. This framework is less expressive than Timed Automata, but it is conceptually simpler, it allows efficient model checking algorithms, and is convenient in many situations.

M. Nielsen and U. Engberg (Eds.): Fossacs 2002, LNCS 2303, pp. 264–279, 2002.
© Springer-Verlag Berlin Heidelberg 2002

There are two main popular approaches for extending temporal logics with the ability to express timing aspects of computations (see [AH92] for a survey).

First, the use of *freeze variables* (also *formula clocks*) in temporal formulae allows the comparison of delays between events. The resulting logics are very expressive but often have hard model checking problems (because they make it possible to combine the timings of several different events in arbitrary ways).

A simpler approach is the use of timing constraints tagging temporal modalities. For example, the formula $\mathsf{EF}_{<10}\ A$ states that it is possible to reach a state verifying A ("$\mathsf{EF}\ A$") in less than 10 time units. These constraints are less expressive than freeze variables but they lead to more readable formulae, and sometimes allow easier model checking.

Timing constraints can have three main forms: "$\leq c$" and "$\geq c$" set a lower or upper bound for durations, while "$= c$" requires a precise value. $TCTL$ is the extension of CTL with all three types of constraints, while $TCTL_{\leq,\geq}$ is the fragment of $TCTL$ where the "$=c$" constraints are forbidden. Other classical temporal logics can be extended in the same way, and we call $TCTL^*$, $TLTL_{\leq,\geq}$, etc. the resulting formalisms.

Model checking $TCTL$ over Kripke structures can be done in time[1] $O(|S|^3 \cdot |\varphi|)$ [EMSS92]. This is in sharp contrast with model checking over Timed Automata (PSPACE-complete [ACD93]) and with model checking CTL extended by freeze variables (PSPACE-complete over KSs [LST00]).

Thus it appears that polynomial-time model checking of timed properties is possible if one picks the right logic (e.g. $TCTL$) and the right models (e.g. KSs).

Our contribution. In this paper, we propose and study *durational Kripke structures* (DKSs), a very natural extension of KSs. As illustrated in Fig. 1, a DKS is a KS where transitions have possible durations specified by an interval of integers. Such structures generalize the models of [EMSS92] or [LST00] and provide a higher-level viewpoint. For example, steps having long durations can be modeled without long sequences of transitions. Also, the size of a DKS is mostly insensitive to a change of time scale. Still, the model does not allow anything like the synchronization of several clocks in Timed Automata: the main limitation of DKSs is that there is no simple way to combine several components.

We show that model checking DKSs can be done in polynomial time when $TCTL_{\leq,\geq}$ is considered, i.e. when exact durations are not allowed as subscripts of modalities. This extends the positive results from [EMSS92,LST00] to a more expressive class of models.

Allowing exact duration constraints increases the complexity of model checking: we show that model checking $TCTL$ over DKSs is Δ_2^p-complete. This last result is technically involved, and it is also quite surprising since Δ_2^p, the class $\mathrm{P^{NP}}$ of problems that can be solved by a deterministic polynomial-time Turing machine that has access to an NP oracle [Sto76,Pap94], does not contain many natural complete problems [Pap84,Wag87,Kre88]. Indeed, the only known

---

[1]   In such statements, $|S|$ denotes the size of the structure, and $|\varphi|$ the length of the temporal formula.

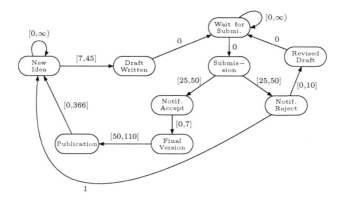

Fig. 1. A DKS modeling publications by one author (time in days)

Δ_2^p-complete problem from the field of temporal model checking has only been recently identified [LMS01].

Finally, we show that exact duration constraints induce a similar complexity blowup when model checking DKSs with other logics like *TLTL* and *TCTL**.

Related work. Quantitative logics *for Timed Automata* are now well-known and many results are available regarding their expressive power, or the complexity of satisfiability and model checking [AH94,ACD93,AH93,AFH96,Hen98]. That exact durations may induce harder model checking complexity was already observed in the case of *TLTL* and Timed Automata [AFH96].

The literature contains several models that are close to DKSs but mostly linear-time logics were considered [Ost90,AH94] and this makes model checking at least PSPACE-hard.

Emerson *et al.* give polynomial time algorithms for model checking *TCTL* over discrete KSs in [EMSS92] and *TCTL$_\le$* over "tight DKS" (all intervals are singletons) in [ET99, section 4]. They also study model checking for quantitative logics with more complex constraints in [ET97,ET99]. Model checking *TCTL* over "small-step DKS" (see section 2) is considered in [LST00] where the expressive power of constraints is investigated. [Lew90] describes a quantitative *CTL* over discrete timed structures but does not investigate complexity of model checking.

2   Durational Kripke Structures

We write $\mathbb{N}$ for the set of natural numbers, and $\mathcal{I}_\mathbb{N}$ (or just $\mathcal{I}$) for the set of intervals over $\mathbb{N}$. An interval $\rho \in \mathcal{I}$ is either finite (of the form "$[n, m]$") or right-open and infinite (of the form "$[n, \infty)$").

Assume a countable set $AP = \{P_1, P_2, \ldots\}$ of *atomic propositions*.

Definition 2.1. *A durational Kripke structure (DKS) is a 3-tuple $S = \langle Q, R, l \rangle$ where Q is a set of* states, $R \subseteq Q \times \mathcal{I} \times Q$ *is a* total *transition relation with duration and $l : Q \to 2^{AP}$ labels every state with a subset of AP.*

Below we only consider finite DKSs, such that Q, R and all $l(q)$ are finite sets.

Graphically, a DKS is just a directed graph where a triple $(q, \rho, q') \in R$ is depicted as a ρ-labeled edge from q to q'.

Semantics. The intended meaning of an edge (q, ρ, q') is that it is possible to move from q to q' with any *integer* duration d belonging to the interval ρ. We write $q \xrightarrow{d} q'$ when $d \in \rho$ for some $(q, \rho, q') \in R$. A sequence $\pi = q_0 \xrightarrow{d_0} q_1 \xrightarrow{d_1} q_2 \ldots$ with $q_i \xrightarrow{d_i} q_{i+1} \in R$ for all i is called a *path* if it is finite and a *run* if it is infinite. A *simple* path is a path where no state is visited twice (a loop-free path). For a run π, $\pi_{|n}$ is the path obtained by only considering the first n steps in π. For $q \in Q$, we let $\mathrm{Exec}(q)$ denote the set of runs starting from q: because R is total, any state is the start of at least one run.

The *size* (or *length*) of a path $\pi = q_0 \xrightarrow{d_0} q_1 \xrightarrow{d_1} q_2 \cdots q_n$ is n (the number of steps), and its *duration*, denoted $\mathsf{Time}(\pi)$, is $d_0 + \cdots + d_{n-1}$.

Example 2.2. The DKS of Fig. 1 models the publication process of one busy researcher, assuming time in counted in days. (This example does not distinguish between the name of the states and their labeling by propositions. Also, singleton intervals $[n, n]$ are written simply n.) A property we would like to express (and model-check) is *"whenever a notification is received, either publication or submission occurs in less than 150 days"*.

Restricted DKSs. There are several natural restrictions one can put on the general model of DKS:

- A *tight DKS* is a DKS where all intervals are singletons. The Timed Kripke structures of [ET99, section 4] are tight DKSs and the Timed State Graphs considered in [AH94] are equivalent to tight DKS. Below we show that, in general, restricting to tight DKSs does not make model checking easier.
- A *small-step DKS* (a ssDKS) is a tight DKS where all steps have duration 0 or 1. The model used in [LST00] is very close to small-step DKSs, but the duration information, "0 or 1 time unit?", is carried by the nodes.
- A KS is a small-step DKS where all steps have duration 1. This is the model assumed in [EMSS92].

There are fundamental differences between ssDKSs and DKSs. First, if there is a path connecting some q to some q', then the shortest such path has duration at most $|Q| - 1$ in a ssDKS, while it can have exponential duration in DKSs.

Moreover, in ssDKSs time progresses smoothly along paths: a path π of duration c can always be decomposed into two subpaths $\pi = \pi'.\pi''$ with $\mathsf{Time}(\pi') = \lfloor \frac{c}{2} \rfloor$ and $\mathsf{Time}(\pi'') = \lceil \frac{c}{2} \rceil$. This property plays a crucial rôle in efficient *TCTL* model checking algorithms over ssDKSs [EMSS92,LST00].

3   Quantitative Temporal Logic

$TCTL$ is the quantitative extension of CTL where temporal modalities are subscripted with constraints on duration [ACD93]. Here it is interpreted over DKSs states.

Definition 3.1 (Syntax of $TCTL$). *TCTL formulae are given by the following grammar:*

$$\varphi, \psi ::= P_1 \mid P_2 \mid \ldots \mid \neg\varphi \mid \varphi \wedge \psi \mid \mathsf{EX}\varphi \mid \mathsf{E}\varphi\mathsf{U}_{\sim c}\,\psi \mid \mathsf{A}\varphi\mathsf{U}_{\sim c}\,\psi$$

where $\sim$ can be any comparator in $\{<, \leq, =, \geq, >\}$ and c any natural number.

Standard abbreviations include $\top, \bot, \varphi \vee \psi, \varphi \Rightarrow \psi, \ldots$ as well as $\mathsf{AX}\varphi$ (for $\neg\mathsf{EX}\neg\varphi$), $\mathsf{EF}_{\sim c}\,\varphi$ (for $\mathsf{E}\top\mathsf{U}_{\sim c}\,\varphi$), $\mathsf{AF}_{\sim c}\,\varphi$ (for $\mathsf{A}\top\mathsf{U}_{\sim c}\,\varphi$), $\mathsf{EG}_{\sim c}\,\varphi$ (for $\neg\mathsf{AF}_{\sim c}\,\neg\varphi$) and $\mathsf{AG}_{\sim c}\,\varphi$ (for $\neg\mathsf{EF}_{\sim c}\,\neg\varphi$). Further, the modalities U, F and G without subscripts are shorthand for $\mathsf{U}_{\geq 0}$, etc. The size $|\varphi|$ of a formula φ is defined in the standard way, with constants written in binary notation.

Definition 3.2 (Semantics). *The following clauses define when a state q of some DKS S, satisfies a TCTL formula φ, written $q \models \varphi$, by induction over the structure of φ (semantics of boolean operators is omitted).*

$q \models \mathsf{EX}\varphi \qquad$ *iff there is a $q \overset{d}{\to} q'$ s.t. $q' \models \varphi$,*

$q \models \mathsf{E}\varphi\mathsf{U}_{\sim c}\,\psi$ *iff there is a run π of the form $q = q_0 \overset{d_0}{\to} q_1 \overset{d_1}{\to} q_2 \cdots$ and a n s.t. $\mathsf{Time}(\pi_{|n}) \sim c$, $q_n \models \psi$, and $q_i \models \varphi$ for all $0 \leq i < n$,*

$q \models \mathsf{A}\varphi\mathsf{U}_{\sim c}\,\psi$ *iff for all runs π of the form $q = q_0 \overset{d_0}{\to} q_1 \overset{d_1}{\to} q_2 \cdots$ there is a n s.t. $\mathsf{Time}(\pi_{|n}) \sim c$, $q_n \models \psi$, and $q_i \models \varphi$ for all $0 \leq i < n$.*

Thus, in $\mathsf{E}\varphi\mathsf{U}_{\sim c}\,\psi$, the classical until is extended by requiring that ψ be satisfied within a duration (from the current state) verifying the constraint "$\sim c$".

Here are some examples of $TCTL$ formulae stating expected properties for the DKS from Figure 1:

$$\mathsf{AG}(\texttt{New\_Idea} \Rightarrow \neg\mathsf{EF}_{<100}\,\texttt{Publication})$$
$$\mathsf{AG}(\texttt{Submission} \Rightarrow \mathsf{AF}_{<40}\,(\texttt{Publication} \vee \texttt{Revised\_Draft} \vee \texttt{New\_Idea}))$$

The first formula states that a new idea is never followed by a publication in less than 100 days. The second formula states that any submission is inevitably followed by a notification of acceptance, a revised draft, or a new idea, in less than 40 days.

Equivalent formulae. We write $\varphi \equiv \psi$ when φ and ψ are *equivalent* (every state of every DKS satisfies $\varphi \Leftrightarrow \psi$) and $\varphi \equiv_{ss} \psi$ when the equivalence only holds in states of small-step DKSs.

The following equivalences hold:

$$\mathsf{A}\,\varphi\,\mathsf{U}_{\leq c}\,\psi \equiv \mathsf{AF}_{\leq c}\,\psi \,\wedge\, \neg\mathsf{E}(\neg\psi)\mathsf{U}(\neg\varphi \wedge \neg\psi) \tag{1}$$

$$\mathsf{A}\,\varphi\,\mathsf{U}_{\geq c}\,\psi \equiv \mathsf{AG}_{<c}\left(\varphi \,\wedge\, \mathsf{A}\,\varphi\,\mathsf{U}_{>0}\,\psi\right) \tag{2}$$

Some seemingly natural equivalences only hold for small-step DKSs (but do not hold for DKSs in general). For example:

$$\mathsf{E}\,\varphi\,\mathsf{U}_{\leq c}\,\psi \equiv_{ss} \mathsf{E}\,\varphi\,\mathsf{U}_{\leq 1}\,(\psi \vee \mathsf{E}\,\varphi\,\mathsf{U}_{\leq c-1}\,\psi) \tag{3}$$

$$\mathsf{E}\,\varphi\,\mathsf{U}_{=c}\,\psi \equiv_{ss} \mathsf{E}\,\varphi\,\mathsf{U}_{=1}\,(\mathsf{E}\,\varphi\,\mathsf{U}_{=c-1}\,\psi) \tag{4}$$

$$\mathsf{E}\,\varphi\,\mathsf{U}_{\geq c}\,\psi \equiv_{ss} \mathsf{E}\,\varphi\,\mathsf{U}_{=c}\,(\mathsf{E}\,\varphi\,\mathsf{U}\,\psi) \tag{5}$$

4 Model Checking *TCTL* over DKSs

The model checking problem we consider in this section is, given some DKS S, some state q, and some *TCTL* formula φ, to decide whether $q \models \varphi$.

Model checking algorithms for *TCTL* have to deal with the timing constraints carried by the modalities. Constraints of the form "$= c$" (exact durations) are usually more difficult than inequality constraints. Furthermore, when dealing with DKSs, the durations associated with the transitions make the problem even harder. Indeed NP-hard problems appear for simple formulae:

Proposition 4.1 (Hardness of reachability with exact duration).
Model checking formulae of the form $\mathsf{EF}_{=c}\,P$ *over DKS is NP-hard.*

Proof. By reduction from SUBSET-SUM [GJ79, p. 223]: an instance is a finite set $A = \{a_1, \ldots, a_n\}$ of natural numbers and some number D. One asks whether there exists a subset A' of A such that $D = \sum_{a \in A'} a$. This is the case iff $q_0 \models \mathsf{EF}_{=D}\,P$ in the following DKS:

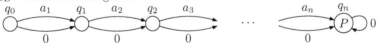

Therefore model checking *TCTL* over DKSs is NP-hard and coNP-hard. Now, the problem is clearly in PSPACE: one can easily adapt algorithms for model checking *TCTL* over Timed Automata (a PSPACE-complete problem [ACD93]) to handle DKSs.

4.1 Polynomial-Time Model Checking for Restricted Cases

It turns out that polynomial-time model checking remains possible as long as equality constraints *or* durations on transitions are forbidden, as we now show.

Let $TCTL_{\leq, \geq}$ denote the fragment of *TCTL* where equality constraints on modalities are not allowed:

Theorem 4.2.
Model checking $TCTL_{\leq, \geq}$ *over DKSs can be done in time* $O(|S|^2 \cdot |\varphi|)$.

Proof. It is enough to extend the classical *CTL* algorithm with labeling procedures running in time $|S|^2 \cdot \lceil \log c \rceil$ for each modality $\mathsf{E}\,P_1\,\mathsf{U}_{\sim c}\,P_2$ and $\mathsf{A}\,P_1\,\mathsf{U}_{\sim c}\,P_2$.

φ **is** $\mathsf{E} P_1 \mathsf{U}_{\leq c} P_2$**:** We restrict to the subgraph where only states satisfying
$\mathsf{E} P_1 \mathsf{U} P_2$ have been kept, and where we only consider the left extremity
of intervals ρ on edges. Then for every state q we compute the smallest du-
ration (call it c_q) such that $q \models \mathsf{E} P_1 \mathsf{U}_{\leq c_q} P_2$. This can be done in time $O(|S^2|)$
using a classical *single-source shortest paths* algorithm [CLR90]. Then $q \models \varphi$
iff $c_q \leq c$.

φ **is** $\mathsf{E} P_1 \mathsf{U}_{\geq c} P_2$**:** We start with some preprocessing of S: let us introduce a new
proposition $P_{\mathsf{SCC}^+(\psi)}$ and use it to label every node belonging to a strongly
connected set of nodes satisfying ψ and where at least one edge allows a
strictly positive duration. That is, $q \models P_{\mathsf{SCC}^+(\psi)}$ iff it is possible to loop on
ψ-states around q with ever increasing durations. Labeling states for $P_{\mathsf{SCC}^+(\psi)}$
can be done in time $O(|S|)$ once they are labeled for ψ.

We can now solve the original problem. There are two ways a state can satisfy
φ. Either a simple path is enough, or a path with loops is required so that a
long enough duration is reached. We check the existence of a path of the first
kind with a variant of the earlier shortest paths method, this times geared
towards *longest acyclic paths*. We check for the existence of a path of the
second kind by model checking the *CTL* formula $\mathsf{E} P_1 \mathsf{U}(P_{\mathsf{SCC}^+(P_1)} \wedge \mathsf{E} P_1 \mathsf{U} P_2)$.

φ **is** $\mathsf{A} P_1 \mathsf{U}_{\leq c} P_2$**:** We reduce to the previous cases using equivalence (1) and
$\mathsf{AF}_{\leq c}\, \psi \equiv \neg \mathsf{E} \neg \psi\, \mathsf{U}_{>c}\top \wedge \neg \mathsf{E} \neg \psi \mathsf{U}\, P_{\mathsf{SCC}^0(\neg \psi)}$. Here $P_{\mathsf{SCC}^0(\neg \psi)}$ labels strongly
connected components where one can loop on $\neg \psi$-states using only transi-
tions allowing for zero durations.

φ **is** $\mathsf{A} P_1 \mathsf{U}_{\geq c} P_2$**:** We reduce to the previous cases using equivalence (2) and
$\mathsf{AG}_{<c}\, \varphi \equiv \neg \mathsf{EF}_{<c}\, \neg \varphi$. □

Note that this result extends Theorems 3 and 4 of [ET99] on model checking
$\mathsf{E} P_1 \mathsf{U}_{\leq c} P_2$ and $\mathsf{EG}_{\leq c} P$ over tight DKSs.

When equality constraints are allowed but arbitrary large durations in DKSs
are forbidden, we rely on the following result:

Theorem 4.3 ([EMSS92,LST00]).
Model checking TCTL over small-step DKSs can be done in polynomial-time.

Now, since model checking is already P-hard for *CTL* over KSs, model checking
$TCTL_{\leq,\geq}$ over DKSs, or *TCTL* over ssDKSs, is PTIME-complete.

4.2 Δ_2^p Model Checking for *TCTL* over DKSs

Allowing both exact durations *and* general DKSs makes model checking harder
(Prop. 4.1) but this is not enough to make the problem PSPACE-complete[2]. In
fact, we have:

Proposition 4.4. *Model checking TCTL over DKSs is in Δ_2^p.*

Proof. A natural Δ_2^p algorithm is to use the natural *CTL*-like labeling algorithm,
accessing an NP oracle for the basic modalities. Theorem 4.2 provides deterministic polynomial-time solutions for modalities where exact duration is not used.

---
[2] This sentence assumes there is no collapse in the polynomial-time hierarchy.

Therefore it remains to provide NP routines for modalities of the form $\mathsf{E} P_1 \mathsf{U}_{=c} P_2$ and $\mathsf{A} P_1 \mathsf{U}_{=c} P_2$. We deal with the $\mathsf{E} P_1 \mathsf{U}_{=c} P_2$ modalities in Lemma 4.5, and with the $\mathsf{A} P_1 \mathsf{U}_{=c} P_2$ modalities in Lemma 4.6.   □

Lemma 4.5. *Model checking the formula* $\mathsf{E} P_1 \mathsf{U}_{=c} P_2$ *over DKSs is in* NP.

Proof. Let $S = \langle Q, R, l \rangle$ be a DKS. We first deal with the simpler case where S is tight (all intervals labeling R are singletons).

Assume there exists a path $\pi = q_0 \overset{d_0}{\to} q_1 \overset{d_1}{\to} q_2 \cdots q_n$ in S witnessing $q_0 \models \mathsf{E} P_1 \mathsf{U}_{=c} P_2$. We can assume $n < c \cdot |Q|$ since any null duration loop can be removed from π, but this is not enough to guarantee that π has size polynomial in $|S| + \lceil \log c \rceil$.

With π we associate the Parikh image of its transitions, that is, the map $\Phi_\pi : R \mapsto \mathbb{N}$ that counts the number of times each transition appears in π. Such a Φ also counts the number of times each node is entered and left: $\Phi^i(q) = \sum \{\Phi(t) \mid t \text{ enters } q\}$ and $\Phi^o(q) = \sum \{\Phi(t) \mid t \text{ leaves } q\}$.

Obviously, Φ_π satisfies the following properties:

1. $\Phi_\pi^i(q) = \Phi_\pi^o(q)$ for any q different from q_0 and q_n. Furthermore, if $q_0 = q_n$, then $\Phi_\pi^i(q_0) = \Phi_\pi^o(q_0)$, otherwise $\Phi_\pi^o(q_0) - \Phi_\pi^i(q_0) = 1 = \Phi_\pi^i(q_n) - \Phi_\pi^o(q_n)$.
2. The subgraph of S induced by the transitions $t \in R$ with $\Phi_\pi(t) > 0$ is connected.
3. Φ_π has duration c, i.e. $c = \sum \{d \cdot \Phi(t) \mid t = (q, [d, d], q') \in R\}$.
4. $q_n \models P_2$ and $q \models P_1$ for any state q such that $\Phi_\pi^o(q) > 0$.

Conversely, if some Φ (with q_0, q_n) fulfills conditions 1. and 2., then by Euler circuit theorem, Φ is Φ_π for some path π from q_0 to q_n in S. If conditions 3. and 4. also hold, then π proves that $q_0 \models \mathsf{E} P_1 \mathsf{U}_{=c} P_2$. If we assume $n < c \cdot |Q|$, then Φ can be encoded in polynomial-size, conditions 1 to 4 can be checked in polynomial-time, and Φ (with q_n) can be used as the polynomial-size witness we need for an NP algorithm.

Now, if we remove the assumption that S is tight, it is enough to replace condition 3. by

$$\sum_{t=(q,\rho,q')} \min(\rho) \cdot \Phi(t) \;\le\; c \;\le\; \sum_{t=(q,\rho,q')} \max(\rho) \cdot \Phi(t)$$

□

Lemma 4.6. *Model checking the formula* $\mathsf{A} P_1 \mathsf{U}_{=c} P_2$ *over DKSs is in* coNP.

Proof (Sketch). Since $\mathsf{A} P_1 \mathsf{U}_{=c} P_2 \equiv \mathsf{A} P_1 \mathsf{U}_{\ge c} P_2 \wedge \neg \mathsf{EG}_{=c} \neg P_2$, it is enough to show that model checking formulae of the form $\mathsf{EG}_{=c} P$ can be done in NP. This is done using techniques similar to the previous Lemma. (One difference is that we have to consider two cases: the path visits duration c, or it avoids it.)   □

4.3 Δ_2^p-Hardness of $TCTL$ Model Checking

We now show that model checking $TCTL$ over DKSs is Δ_2^p-hard, and hence Δ_2^p-complete. This means that there is no essentially better way for model checking $TCTL$ over DKS than the labeling algorithm used in Prop. 4.4.

Proving Δ_2^p-hardness is difficult in part because there exist very few natural problems that are Δ_2^p-complete and that could be used in reductions to $TCTL$ model checking. Here we capitalize on our recent proof that model-checking $FCTL$ is Δ_2^p-complete [LMS01] and follow its pattern. However, this pattern must be altered and we have to encode boolean problems in numerical problems. Since model-checking $TCTL$ becomes polynomial-time when the numerical constants are written in unary, the Δ_2^p-hardness proof has to encode information in the bits of the numbers used in the DKS and the $TCTL$ formula.

A Δ_2^p-complete problem. We start by briefly recalling SNSAT (for *sequentially nested* satisfiability), the Δ_2^p-complete satisfiability problem we reduce from. An instance $\mathcal{I}$ of SNSAT has the form

$$
\mathcal{I} \;=\; \begin{bmatrix} x_1 := \exists Z_1 \; F_1(Z_1), \\ x_2 := \exists Z_2 \; F_2(x_1, Z_2), \\ \vdots \\ x_n := \exists Z_n \; F_n(x_1, \ldots, x_{n-1}, Z_n) \end{bmatrix}
$$

where each F_i is a boolean expression, each Z_i is a set of (auxiliary) boolean variables, and the x_i are the main variables. We write X for $\{x_1, \ldots, x_n\}$, Z for $Z_1 \cup \cdots \cup Z_n$, and assume the sets $X, Z_1, \ldots, Z_n$ are pairwise disjoint. *Var* denotes $X \cup Z$ and $p = |Z|$.

W.l.o.g., we assume every F_i is a 3-CNF of the form $\bigwedge_l \bigvee_{m=1}^3 \alpha_{i,l,m}$ where the $\alpha_{i,l,m}$ are literals. With every disjunct $\bigvee_m \alpha_{i,l,m}$ we associate a clause $C_{i,l}$ of the form $\overline{x_i} \vee \bigvee_m \alpha_{i,l,m}$ and write $Cl = \{C_1, \ldots, C_r\}$ for the resulting set of clauses.

$\mathcal{I}$ defines a unique valuation $v_{\mathcal{I}}$ of the variables in X where $v_{\mathcal{I}}(x_i) = \top$ iff $F_i(v_{\mathcal{I}}(x_1), \ldots, v_{\mathcal{I}}(x_{i-1}), Z_i)$ is satisfiable. The computational problem called SNSAT is, given an instance $\mathcal{I}$ as above, to decide whether $v_{\mathcal{I}}(x_n) = \top$. Therefore $\mathcal{I}$ can be seen as a sequence of n satisfiability problems where the ith problem depends on the answers of the earlier problems.

With this in mind, we say a valuation w of *Var* is:

safe: if, for all $i = 1, \ldots, n$, $w(x_i)$ implies $F_i(w(x_1), \ldots, w(x_{i-1}), w(Z_i))$,

correct: if, for all $i = 1, \ldots, n$, $w(x_i) = F_i(w(x_1), \ldots, w(x_{i-1}), w(Z_i))$,

admissible: if w is correct and coincide with $v_{\mathcal{I}}$ over X.

A correct valuation is safe and is also consistent for negative values assigned to some x_i. Still, this does not guarantee that the values of variables in Z are best possible, i.e. that w is admissible. An arbitrary valuation over Z extends into a correct valuation in a unique way, and checking that a given w is correct can be done in polynomial-time.

An admissible valuation is just a valuation for Z that yields $v_{\mathcal{I}}$ for X. Hence it is optimal over Z. Clearly, admissible valuations exist for any SNSAT instance, positive ($v_\mathcal{I}(x_n) = \top$) or negative, but checking that a given w is admissible is Δ_2^p-complete.

Reducing SNSAT to TCTL model checking. Fix some $K \in \mathbb{N}$. To variables $u \in Var$ and clauses $C \in Cl$ we assign weights $s(u)$ and $s(C)$ given by:

$$s(x_i) = K^i \qquad s(z_i) = K^{n+i} \qquad s(C_i) = K^{n+p+i}$$

A multiset $\mathcal{M}$ of variables and clauses ($\mathcal{M} \in \mathbb{N}^{Var \cup Cl}$) has weight $s(\mathcal{M}) = \sum_x s(x) \times \mathcal{M}(x)$. Now if $\mathcal{M}(x) < K$ and $\mathcal{M}'(x) < K$ for all $x \in Var \cup Cl$, then $s(\mathcal{M}) = s(\mathcal{M}')$ iff $\mathcal{M} = \mathcal{M}'$. Therefore, by picking K large enough, we can reduce the equality of small multisets to the equality of their weights.

We now build $\mathcal{S}_\mathcal{I}$, a DKS associated with $\mathcal{I}$. See Fig. 2. Nodes in $\mathcal{S}_\mathcal{I}$ are of two kinds: literal nodes (in the upper part of the figure) and filling nodes (in the lower part). With a path through the literal nodes that avoids the vertical "$\overline{x_i} \to x_i$" edges one associates a valuation of Var in the obvious way. The filling nodes are there for accounting purposes (see below).

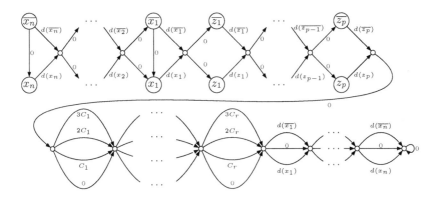

Fig. 2. Kripke structure $\mathcal{S}_\mathcal{I}$ associated with SNSAT instance $\mathcal{I}$

For a literal α of the form $\pm u$, the duration $d(\alpha)$ is defined as $s(u) + \sum\{s(C) \mid C \in Cl, \alpha \Rightarrow C\}$. Therefore a path through the literal nodes will collect in its duration the weight of all the variables it visits plus the weight of all the clauses these literals satisfy (each clause being counted up to four times since it may be satisfied thanks to four different literals). Then the path visits the filling nodes where it can gather further clause or literal weights.

Now define

$$K' \stackrel{\text{def}}{=} \sum_{u \in Var} s(u) + 4 \times \sum_{C \in Cl} s(C)$$

and assume K is large enough (here $K > 11$ suffices). Then, for any $u \in Var$, a path π of weight K' must collect $d(u)$ or $d(\overline{u})$ once and only once. Thus π

defines a valuation of Var. Furthermore π has to gather 4 times the weight of all clauses from Cl. Since, for $C \in Cl$, we can only collect $3s(C)$ via filling nodes, π must visit at least one literal that satisfies C.

Hence paths of length K' correspond to valuations that satisfy all the clauses. We rely on this and introduce the following $TCTL$ formulae:

$$\varphi_0 \overset{\text{def}}{=} \top,$$

$$\text{and, for } k > 0, \quad \varphi_k \overset{\text{def}}{=} \mathsf{E}\Big[P_{\overline{x}} \Rightarrow \mathsf{EX}\big(P_x \wedge \neg\varphi_{k-1}\big)\Big]\mathsf{U}_{=K'}\top,$$

where P_x (resp. $P_{\overline{x}}$) is an atomic proposition that labels the n positive x_i nodes (resp. the $\overline{x_i}$ nodes).

We can now link $v_{\mathcal{I}}$ and the φ_k by:

Lemma 4.7. *For $k \in \mathbb{N}$ and $r = 1, \ldots, n$:*
(a) if $k \geq 2r - 1$ then $(v_{\mathcal{I}}(x_r) = \top$ iff $\mathcal{S}_{\mathcal{I}}, x_r \models \varphi_k)$,
(b) if $k \geq 2r$ then $(v_{\mathcal{I}}(x_r) = \bot$ iff $\mathcal{S}_{\mathcal{I}}, \overline{x_r} \models \varphi_k)$.

Proof. By induction on k. The case $k = 0$ holds vacuously. We now assume that $k > 0$ and that the Lemma holds for $k - 1$.
i. We prove the "$\Rightarrow$" direction of both "iff"s.

Let w be an admissible valuation. We use w to build a path π that starts at x_r (or $\overline{x_r}$ if $w(x_r) = \bot$), has total duration K', and only visit literals true under w (such a π exists because w is admissible). We claim π proves $x_r \models \varphi_k$ (or $\overline{x_r} \models \varphi_k$). This only requires that all nodes visited by π satisfy $P_{\overline{x}} \Rightarrow \mathsf{EX}(P_x \wedge \neg\varphi_{k-1})$ but on $\mathcal{S}_{\mathcal{I}}$ this translates into "$w(x_i) = \bot$ for $i \leq r$ implies $x_i \models \neg\varphi_{k-1}$" and is given by the induction hypothesis.
ii. We now prove the "$\Leftarrow$" direction of both "iff"s.

Assume $k \geq 2r - 1$ and $x_r \models \varphi_k$ (or $k \geq 2r$ and $\overline{x_r} \models \varphi_k$). Thus there is a path π starting from x_r (or $\overline{x_r}$), with duration K', and only visiting states satisfying $P_{\overline{x}} \Rightarrow \mathsf{EX}(P_x \wedge \neg\varphi_{k-1})$. Since $\mathsf{Time}(\pi) = K'$ the valuation w induced by π satisfies all $C \in Cl$. We further claim that $w(x_i) = v_{\mathcal{I}}(x_i)$ for $i = 1, \ldots, r$ and prove this by induction over i:
iia. If $w(x_i) = \top$ then $\bigwedge_l \bigvee_m w(\alpha_{i,l,m}) = \top$, so that $F_i(w(x_1), \ldots, w(x_{i-1}), Z_i)$ is satisfiable. By ind. hyp. we get that $F_i(v_{\mathcal{I}}(x_1), \ldots, v_{\mathcal{I}}(x_{i-1}), Z_i)$ is satisfiable, so that $v_{\mathcal{I}}(x_i) = \top$.
iib. If $w(x_i) = \bot$ then $\overline{x_i} \models \mathsf{EX}(P_x \wedge \neg\varphi_{k-1})$, implying $x_i \models \neg\varphi_{k-1}$. If $i < r$ we have $k - 1 \geq 2i - 1$ and, by ind. hyp., $v_{\mathcal{I}}(x_i) = \bot$. If $i = r$ then we are dealing with the case $k \geq 2r$ and $\overline{x_k} \models \varphi_k$, so that $k - 1 \geq 2i - 1$ and again $v_{\mathcal{I}}(x_i) = \bot$ by ind. hyp. □

Proposition 4.8. *Model checking $TCTL$ over DKSs is Δ_2^p-hard.*

Proof. By Lemma 4.7, $\mathcal{I}$ is a positive instance iff $\mathcal{S}_{\mathcal{I}}, x_n \models \varphi_{2n-1}$. Observe that $\mathcal{S}_{\mathcal{I}}$ and φ_{2n-1} can be built in logspace from $\mathcal{I}$. Thus SNSAT, a Δ_2^p-complete [LMS01], reduces to $TCTL$ model checking. □

Theorem 4.9. *Model checking TCTL over DKSs is Δ_2^p-complete.*

Proof. Combine Props 4.4 and 4.8.   □

Remark 4.10. Theorem 4.9 can be strengthened in various ways. E.g. note that S_I is a *tight DKS*. Further, we used the EX modality in φ_k but this is not necessary (and could be replaced by $EF_{\leq 0}$). Moreover S_I contains transitions with null duration but it is easy to adapt the construction and show that Theorem 4.9 still holds over tight DKSs with strictly positive durations.

5   When Are Exact Durations Harder over DKSs?

Comparing Theorems 4.2 and 4.9 shows that allowing subscripts "$= c$" makes model checking *TCTL* over DKSs significantly harder. There exist other situations where exact duration subscripts make problems harder. For example:

- In small-step DKSs, model checking *TCTL* and $TCTL_{\leq,\geq}$ are both PTIME-complete[3] but satisfiability is harder for *TCTL* than for $TCTL_{\leq,\geq}$ [EMSS92].
- Over Timed Automata, exact duration subscripts do not make model checking harder for *TCTL* (PSPACE-complete for *TCTL* [ACD93]), but they do for the linear time temporal logic *MITL* [AFH96].

In this section we consider how exact duration subscripts do or do not increase the cost of model checking when the models are DKSs and the logic is a timed variant of classic temporal logics like *LTL* or CTL^*.

We will write *TLTL*, $TCTL^*$ and $TCTL^+$ for the timed variants of the logics *LTL*, CTL^* and CTL^+ (definitions omitted, see [Eme90]) and will let $TLTL_{\leq,\geq}$, etc., denote the fragments where exact duration is not allowed.

5.1   Model Checking *TLTL* over DKSs

TLTL formulae are *path* formulae and are interpreted over runs in a DKS. As usual in this case, we consider *existential model checking*, that is the problem of deciding for a DKS S, a state q and a formula φ, whether there exists a path from q verifying φ.

Theorem 5.1.
1. Model checking TLTL over DKSs (and ssDKSs) is EXPSPACE-complete.
2. Model checking $TLTL_{\leq,\geq}$ over DKSs (and ssDKSs) is PSPACE-complete.

Proof. 1. EXPSPACE-hardness: it is possible to describe with a *TLTL* formula the accepting runs of a Turing Machine that runs in space 2^n. As usual, a run of the TM is seen as a sequence of instantaneous descriptions (i.d.). Here each

---

[3]   More precisely, model checking full *TCTL* can be done in time $O(|S|^3 \cdot |\varphi|)$ while model checking $TCTL_{\leq,\geq}$ can be done in time $O(|S| \cdot |\varphi|)$ [LST00].

i.d. has length 2^n. One easily writes that any two consecutive i.d.'s agree with the TM rules by means of the $F_{=2^n}$ modality, a modality of size $O(n)$.

Membership in EXPSPACE: this can be seen as a special case of the EXPSPACE upper bound for TPTL [AH94], a logic more expressive than $TLTL$ interpreted over "timed state graphs" (a model in which one can encode DKSs).

2. PSPACE-hardness: comes from PSPACE-hardness of LTL model checking.

Membership in PSPACE: [AFH96] shows that model checking $MITL_{<,>}$ (a logic equivalent to $TLTL_{\leq,\geq}$) over Timed Automata can be done in PSPACE. Since Timed Automata easily encode DKSs, the upper bound follows.   □

5.2   Model Checking $TCTL^*$ over DKSs

Theorem 5.2.
1. Model checking $TCTL^*$ over DKSs (and ssDKSs) is EXPSPACE-complete.
2. Model checking $TCTL^*_{\leq,\geq}$ over DKSs (and ssDKSs) is PSPACE-complete.

Proof. A direct consequence of Theorem 5.1: the techniques from [EL87] produce an algorithm for $TCTL^*$ under the form of a simple polynomial-time labeling algorithm that calls an oracle for $TLTL$ model checking. Hence model checking belongs to $P^{EXPSPACE}$, that is EXPSPACE. The same reasoning applies to $TCTL^*_{\leq,\geq}$ and yields a a P^{PSPACE}, that is a PSPACE algorithm.   □

5.3   Model Checking $TCTL^+$ over DKSs

CTL^+ is the extension of CTL in which *boolean combinations* of path formulae are allowed to appear under a path quantifier [Eme90]. For example, $A(F_{<3} \text{ req}_1 \Rightarrow F_{<5} \text{ req}_2)$ is a $TCTL^+$ formula.

Theorem 5.3.
Model checking $TCTL^+$ and $TCTL^+_{\leq,\geq}$ over DKSs (and ssDKSs) is Δ^p_2-complete.

Proof. Δ^p_2-hardness comes from Δ^p_2-hardness of (untimed) CTL^+ model checking [LMS01]. Membership in Δ^p_2 is a consequence on Lemma 5.4, an extension of Lemma 4.5.   □

Lemma 5.4. *Model checking formulae of the form $E\left(\bigwedge_i P_i \ U_{\sim c_i} \ P'_i \ \wedge \bigwedge_j \neg(P_j \ U_{\sim c_j} P'_j)\right)$ over DKSs is NP-complete.*

Proof (Idea). Only membership in NP needs be proved. This is done by combining ideas from Lemmas 4.5 and 4.6, where we show how it is possible to witness the existence of a path through its Parikh image (and a few additional bits of information), and ideas from CTL^+ model checking, where a witness simply indicates in what order the different $P_i U P'_i$ modalities are eventually satisfied along the path, with the choice of nodes that appear at these satisfaction points.   □

Therefore, unlike the classical untimed case where model checking is harder for CTL^+ than for CTL, there is essentially no complexity cost for using $TCTL^+$ instead of $TCTL$ over DKSs.

6   Conclusion

Figure 3 summarizes our results on the complexity of model checking quantitative temporal logics over DKSs. A general pattern is that exact durations make model checking harder. Polynomial-time model checking is possible if one considers $TCTL$ and forbids exact durations or restricts to small-step DKSs.

We see two main directions for future work. First, it appears that DKSs can be seen as Timed Automata where *only one clock is used* and *this clock is reset with every transition*. It would be interesting to see if our results generalize to Timed Automata with one clock but without the reset restriction.

	ssDKSs ($\xrightarrow{0/1}$)	tight DKSs ($\xrightarrow{n}$), DKSs ($\xrightarrow{\rho}$)
$TCTL$ $\quad \leq, \geq$	PTIME-complete	PTIME-complete (Th. 4.2)
$\quad\quad\quad \leq, \geq, =$		Δ_2^p-complete (Th. 4.9)
$TLTL$ $\quad \leq, \geq$	PSPACE-complete (Th. 5.1.2)	
$\quad\quad\quad \leq, \geq, =$	EXPSPACE-complete (Th. 5.1.1)	
$TCTL^*$ $\;\; \leq, \geq$	PSPACE-complete (Th. 5.2.2)	
$\quad\quad\quad \leq, \geq, =$	EXPSPACE-complete (Th. 5.2.1)	
$TCTL^+$ $\;\; \leq, \geq$	Δ_2^p-complete (Th. 4.9)	
$\quad\quad\quad \leq, \geq, =$		

Fig. 3. The complexity of model checking over DKSs

The second direction is to investigate alternate semantics for DKSs. Our assumption that steps in a DKS are all $q \xrightarrow{d} q'$ for $d \in \rho$ has practical, not philosophical, motivations: it makes technicalities and notations simpler. But DKSs could be given alternate semantics.

For example, one could assume that an edge $q \xrightarrow{d} q'$ is a succinct description of d edges between q and q', visiting $d - 1$ intermediary states. Here time flows more smoothly. The behavior is the same but the temporal logic can refer to more observation points (so that its meaning is modified). Another possibility is to consider that an interval $\rho = [n, n']$ in a transition $(q, \rho, q') \in R$ states that the system must wait at least n time units and at most n' *before making the choice to move from q to q'*. This impacts the branching behavior of S.

These two variant semantics may or may not be preferable. The complexity of model checking remains PTIME-complete for $TCTL_{\leq,\geq}$, but becomes PSPACE-complete for $TCTL$ (proofs will appear in a full version of this paper).

References

ACD93.   R. Alur, C. Courcoubetis, and D. Dill. Model-checking in dense real-time. *Information and Computation*, 104(1):2–34, 1993.

AFH96.   R. Alur, T. Feder, and T. A. Henzinger. The benefits of relaxing punctuality. *Journal of the ACM*, 43(1):116–146, 1996.

AH92.   R. Alur and T. A. Henzinger. Logics and models of real time: A survey. In *Real-Time: Theory in Practice, Proc. REX Workshop, Mook, NL, June 1991*, volume 600 of *Lecture Notes in Computer Science*, pages 74–106. Springer, 1992.

AH93.   R. Alur and T. A. Henzinger. Real-time logics: Complexity and expressiveness. *Information and Computation*, 104(1):35–77, 1993.

AH94.   R. Alur and T. A. Henzinger. A really temporal logic. *Journal of the ACM*, 41(1):181–203, 1994.

AL99.   L. Aceto and F. Laroussinie. Is your model checker on time? In *Proc. 24th Int. Symp. Math. Found. Comp. Sci. (MFCS'99), Szklarska Poreba, Poland, Sep. 1999*, volume 1672 of *Lecture Notes in Computer Science*, pages 125–136. Springer, 1999.

Alu91.   R. Alur. *Techniques for Automatic Verification of Real-Time Systems*. PhD thesis, Stanford Univ., August 1991. Available as Tech. Report STAN-CS-91-1378.

CGP99.   E. M. Clarke, O. Grumberg, and D. A. Peled. *Model Checking*. MIT Press, 1999.

CLR90.   T. H. Cormen, C. E. Leiserson, and R. L. Rivest. *Introduction to algorithms*. MIT Press, 1990.

CY92.   C. Courcoubetis and M. Yannakakis. Minimum and maximum delay problems in real-time systems. *Formal Methods in System Design*, 1(4):385–415, 1992.

EL87.   E. A. Emerson and Chin-Laung Lei. Modalities for model checking: Branching time logic strikes back. *Science of Computer Programming*, 8(3):275–306, 1987.

Eme90.   E. A. Emerson. Temporal and modal logic. In J. van Leeuwen, editor, *Handbook of Theoretical Computer Science, vol. B*, chapter 16, pages 995–1072. Elsevier Science, 1990.

EMSS92.   E. A. Emerson, A. K. Mok, A. P. Sistla, and J. Srinivasan. Quantitative temporal reasoning. *Real-Time Systems*, 4(4):331–352, 1992.

ET97.   E. A. Emerson and R. J. Trefler. Generalized quantitative temporal reasoning: An automata-theoretic approach. In *Proc. 7th Int. Joint Conf. Theory and Practice of Software Development (TAPSOFT'97), Lille, France, Apr. 1997*, volume 1214 of *Lecture Notes in Computer Science*, pages 189–200. Springer, 1997.

ET99.   E. A. Emerson and R. J. Trefler. Parametric quantitative temporal reasoning. In *Proc. 14th IEEE Symp. Logic in Computer Science (LICS'99), Trento, Italy, July 1999*, pages 336–343. IEEE Comp. Soc. Press, 1999.

GJ79.   M. R. Garey and D. S. Johnson. *Computers and Intractability. A Guide to the Theory of NP-Completeness*. Freeman, 1979.

Hen98.   T. A. Henzinger. It's about time: real-time logics reviewed. In *Proc. 9th Int. Conf. Concurrency Theory (CONCUR'98), Nice, France, Sep. 1998*, volume 1466 of *Lecture Notes in Computer Science*, pages 439–454. Springer, 1998.

Kre88.   M. W. Krentel. The complexity of optimization problems. *Journal of Computer and System Sciences*, 36(3):490–509, 1988.

Lew90.   H. R. Lewis. A logic of concrete time intervals (extended abstract). In *Proc. 5th IEEE Symp. Logic in Computer Science (LICS'90), Philadelphia, PA, USA, June 1990*, pages 380–389. IEEE Comp. Soc. Press, 1990.

LMS01.   F. Laroussinie, N. Markey, and Ph. Schnoebelen. Model checking CTL^+ and $FCTL$ is hard. In *Proc. 4th Int. Conf. Foundations of Software Science and Computation Structures (FOSSACS'2001), Genova, Italy, Apr. 2001*, volume 2030 of *Lecture Notes in Computer Science*, pages 318–331. Springer, 2001.

LST00.   F. Laroussinie, Ph. Schnoebelen, and M. Turuani. On the expressivity and complexity of quantitative branching-time temporal logics. In *Proc. 4th Latin American Symposium on Theoretical Informatics (LATIN'2000), Punta del Este, Uruguay, Apr. 2000*, volume 1776 of *Lecture Notes in Computer Science*, pages 437–446. Springer, 2000.

Ost90.   J. S. Ostroff. Deciding properties of timed transition models. *IEEE Transactions on Parallel and Distributed Systems*, 1(2):170–183, 1990.

Pap84.   C. H. Papadimitriou. On the complexity of unique solutions. *Journal of the ACM*, 31(2):392–400, 1984.

Pap94.   C. H. Papadimitriou. *Computational Complexity*. Addison-Wesley, 1994.

Sto76.   L. J. Stockmeyer. The polynomial-time hierarchy. *Theoretical Computer Science*, 3(1):1–22, 1976.

Wag87.   K. W. Wagner. More complicated questions about maxima and minima, and some closures of NP. *Theoretical Computer Science*, 51(1–2):53–80, 1987.

Model-Checking Infinite Systems
Generated by Ground Tree Rewriting

Christof Löding

RWTH Aachen, Lehrstuhl Informatik VII, 52056 Aachen, Germany
loeding@informatik.rwth-aachen.de

Abstract. We consider infinite graphs that are generated by ground tree (or term) rewriting systems. The vertices of these graphs are trees. Thus, with a finite tree automaton one can represent a regular set of vertices. It is shown that for a regular set T of vertices the set of vertices from where one can reach (respectively, infinitely often reach) the set T is again regular. Furthermore it is shown that the problems, given a tree t and a regular set T, whether all paths starting in t eventually (respectively, infinitely often) reach T, are undecidable. We then define a logic which is in some sense a maximal fragment of temporal logic with a decidable model-checking problem for the class of ground tree rewriting graphs.

1 Introduction

Graphs play an important role in the behavioral description of programs or processes. The use of theoretically unbounded data structures (such as stacks, queues, etc.) in these programs requires the use of infinite (transition-)graphs. In order to allow algorithmic applications like verification of infinite-state systems, these systems have to be given effectively, i.e., by some finite object. In recent years many classes of finitely representable infinite graphs have been studied. A starting point for this research on infinite graphs was an analysis of the configuration graphs of pushdown automata by Muller and Schupp in [13]. The vertices of pushdown graphs are words (the control state followed by the stack content) and the edges are defined via the transitions which are prefix rewriting rules on these words. In [13] it is shown that pushdown graphs have a decidable monadic second-order (MSO) theory. Later, more efficient algorithms have been developed for solving reachability problems, model-checking temporal logics [8], and synthezising strategies for games [10,14] on pushdown graphs.

Using rewriting as the basic process for generation of infinite graphs, a variety of possibilities arises to define classes of graphs different from pushdown graphs. Let us briefly review some of the approaches. The result on the decidability of the MSO theory generalizes from pushdown graphs to prefix recognizable graphs [3], which are also generated by prefix rewriting on words; but the rewriting rules refer to to regular languages instead of single words. Even more general classes of graphs can be obtained when using finite word transducers to define the edge relations of graphs. This leads to automatic graphs in case of synchronous

M. Nielsen and U. Engberg (Eds.): Fossacs 2002, LNCS 2303, pp. 280–294, 2002.
© Springer-Verlag Berlin Heidelberg 2002

transducers (see e.g. [1]) and to rational graphs [12] in case of asynchronous transducers. The formalisms to generate automatic and rational graphs are very strong and even simple reachability problems on these graphs are undecidable. In [11] model-checking problems for process rewriting graphs are studied (in process rewriting parallel composition of words is allowed in addition to the usual sequential composition).

In the present paper we use another generalization of word rewriting, namely tree rewriting, as already considered in [2]. In tree (or term) rewriting the basic objects in the rewriting systems are trees. For ground tree rewrite systems (GTRS) confluence [6], the first-order theory [7], and several reachability problems [5] have been shown to be decidable. As the example of the infinite grid (see Section 2 below) shows, the MSO theory of a GTRS graph can be undecidable. Our goal is to develop an expressive fragment of temporal logic with a decidable model-checking problem on GTRS graphs. Since reachability analysis of systems constitutes an important part of verification, we analyze different reachability problems. As a means of specification we will use finite tree automata to represent sets of vertices. Given such a regular set T represented by a tree automaton we address the following problems for GTRS graphs.

(1) Compute the set of all vertices from where one can reach T.
(2) Compute the set of all vertices from where one can infinitely often visit T.
(3) Given a single tree t, do all paths starting in t eventually (respectively, infinitely often) visit T?

We give algorithms to solve the Problems (1) and (2). The first problem was already solved in the context of term rewriting (see e.g. [4]), so the solution of the second problem is the main contribution of the present paper. The problems in (3) are shown to be undecidable and hence mark a boundary in the design of a fragment of temporal logic with decidable model-checking problem for GTRS graphs.

The paper is organized as follows. In Section 2 we introduce GTRS and tree automata. In Section 3 we give an algorithm to solve the reachability problem (1), in Section 4 we solve the recurrence problem (2), and in Section 5 we show the undecidability of the problems of universal reachability and universal recurrence from (3). Finally, in Section 6, we use the results of the former sections and present a logic with a decidable model-checking problem for GTRS graphs.

I would like to thank Wolfgang Thomas and the anonymous referees for many helpful comments.

2   Ground Tree Rewriting Systems and Tree Automata

A ranked alphabet A is a family of sets $(A_i)_{i \in [k]}$, where $[k] = \{0, \ldots, k\}$. For simplicity we identify A with the set $\bigcup_{i=0}^{k} A_i$. A ranked tree t over A is a mapping $t : D_t \to A$ with $D_t \subseteq [k-1]^*$ such that $D_t \neq \emptyset$ is prefix closed, for each $ui \in D_t$ we have $uj \in D_t$ for all $j \leq i$, and if $u0, \ldots, u(i-1) \in D_t$, $ui \notin D_t$, then $t(u) \in A_i$. D_t is called the domain of t. We will mainly be interested in finite trees, except for Section 4 where we also use infinite trees. The set of all finite trees over A is called T_A. By $\sqsubseteq$ we denote the prefix ordering on $\mathbb{N}^*$.

For $u \in \mathbb{N}^*$ we define $uD_t = \{uv \in \mathbb{N}^* \mid v \in D_t\}$ and $u^{-1}D_t = \{v \in \mathbb{N}^* \mid uv \in D_t\}$. For $u \in D_t$ the subtree t^u of t at u is the tree with domain $D_{t^u} = u^{-1}D_t$ and $t^u(v) = t(uv)$. For trees $t, t' \in T_A$ and $u \in D_t$ we define $t(u \leftarrow t')$ to be the tree s with domain $D_s = uD_{t'} \cup (D_t \setminus u(u^{-1}D_t))$ and $s(v) = t'(u^{-1}v)$ for $v \in uD_{t'}$ and $s(v) = t(v)$ for $v \in D_t \setminus u(u^{-1}D_t)$. This means we replace the subtree t^u in t by t'.

To denote trees we will use the usual graphical notation (as e.g. in Figure 1) and the term notation, where $a(t_0, \ldots, t_{i-1})$ denotes the tree with a at the root and $t_0, \ldots, t_{i-1}$ as subtrees.

A ground tree rewriting system (GTRS) is a tuple $S = (A, \Sigma, P, t_I)$, where $A = (A_i)_{i \in [k]}$ is a ranked alphabet, Σ is an alphabet, P is a finite set of rules $t_1 \to^\sigma t_2$ with $t_1, t_2 \in T_A$, $\sigma \in \Sigma$, and $t_I \in T_A$ is the initial tree. For two trees $t, t' \in T_A$ we write $t \to_S^\sigma t'$ iff there exists a rule $t_1 \to^\sigma t_2$ in P and $u \in D_t$ such that $t^u = t_1$ and $t' = t(u \leftarrow t_2)$. We write $t \to_S t'$ iff there is a $\sigma \in \Sigma$ with $t \to_S^\sigma t'$. By $\to_S^+$ we denote the transitive closure of $\to_S$ and by $\to_S^*$ we denote the transitive and reflexive closure of $\to_S$.

The tree language generated by S is $T(S) = \{t \in T_A \mid t_I \to_S^* t\}$. The edge labeled graph $G_S = (V_S, E_S, \Sigma)$ generated by S is defined by $V_S = T(S)$, and $(t, \sigma, t') \in E_S$ iff $t \to_S^\sigma t'$.

Example 1. The GTRS $S = (A, \Sigma, P, t_I)$ given by $\Sigma = \{0, 1\}$, $A = (A_i)_{i \in [2]}$ with $A_0 = \{a, b\}$, $A_1 = \{c\}$, and $A_2 = \{d\}$, $P = \{b \to^0 c(b), a \to^1 c(a)\}$, and $t_I = d(a, b)$ generates the infinite grid as shown in Figure 1.   □

As usual a path π through a graph $G = (V, E)$ is a (possibly infinite) sequence of vertices such that two successive vertices on this path form an edge. If we consider a path π through a graph G_S for a GTRS S, then the edges are generated by rewriting rules. We will sometimes refer to these rewritings as the

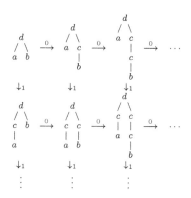

Fig. 1. The infinite grid generated by a GTRS.

rewritings on π. Given a path π and $i \in \mathbb{N}$ we denote the ith element on π by $\pi(i)$ and the suffix of π starting at $\pi(i)$ by π^i.

If $T \subseteq T_A$, then $t \to_S^\omega T$ means that there is a path through G_S starting in t that infinitely often visits the set T and if π is a path through G_S, then $\pi : t \to_S^\omega T$ means that π is a path starting in t that infinitely often visits T. Furthermore we use similar notations as, e.g., $t \to_S^* T_1 \to_S^* T_2$ if there is a path that starts in t and first visits T_1 and then T_2.

For a set $T \subseteq T_A$ of trees let $\mathrm{sub}(T) = \{t' \in T_A \mid \exists t \in T \text{ and } u \in D_t \text{ with } t^u = t'\}$ be the set of all subtrees of trees in T. For later use we define the sets $P_L = \{t \in T_A \mid \exists t' \in T_A \text{ with } t \to t' \in P\}$, $P_R = \{t \in T_A \mid \exists t' \in T_A \text{ with } t \to t' \in P\}$, and $\mathrm{sub}(P) = \mathrm{sub}(P_L) \cup \mathrm{sub}(P_R)$.

A nondeterministic tree automaton (NTA) is a tuple $\mathcal{A} = (Q, A, \Delta, F)$, where Q is a finite set of states, $A = (A_i)_{i \in [k]}$ is a ranked alphabet, $F \subseteq Q$ is a set of final states and $\Delta \subseteq (\bigcup_{i=0}^k Q^i \times A_i) \times Q$ is the transition relation. Given a tree $t \in T_A$, a tree $\rho \in T_Q$ is a run of $\mathcal{A}$ on t iff $D_\rho = D_t$, and for each $u \in D_t$ with $t(u) \in A_i$ we have $(\rho(u0), \ldots, \rho(u(i-1)), t(u), \rho(u)) \in \Delta$. We extend Δ to trees in the natural way: $(t, q) \in \Delta$ iff $\rho(\varepsilon) = q$ for a run ρ of $\mathcal{A}$ on t. A tree t is accepted by $\mathcal{A}$ iff $(t, q) \in \Delta$ for some $q \in F$ and the language $T(\mathcal{A})$ accepted by $\mathcal{A}$ is $T(\mathcal{A}) = \{t \in T_A \mid (t, q) \in \Delta(t) \text{ for some } q \in F\}$. A language of trees is called regular iff it can be recognized by an NTA.

For $t \in T_A$, a run ρ of an NTA on t, and a vertex $u \in D_t$ it is clear that the subtree ρ^u of ρ is a run of the NTA on t^u.

The notion of a run can also be applied to infinite trees. This will be used in Section 4.

In the next section we also consider a more general type of automata, namely nondeterministic tree automata with ε-transitions (ε-NTA). An ε-NTA is a tuple $\mathcal{A} = (Q, A, \Delta, F)$, where Q, A, and F are as in NTA and $\Delta \subseteq ((\bigcup_{i=0}^k Q^i \times A_i) \cup Q) \times Q$ is the transition relation. The transitions of Δ from the set $Q \times Q$ are called ε-transitions because in a run these ε-transitions do not depend on the input tree. For an ε-NTA $\mathcal{A} = (Q, A, \Delta, F)$ one can easily define an equivalent ε-free NTA $\mathcal{A}^- = (Q, A, \Delta^-, F)$ by $(q_1, \ldots, q_i, a, q) \in \Delta^-$ if there are $p_0, \ldots, p_j \in Q$ with $p_j = q$, $(q_1, \ldots, q_i, a, p_0) \in \Delta$, and $(p_l, p_{l+1}) \in \Delta$ for all $l \in \{0, \ldots, j-1\}$. Then we can define $(t, q) \in \Delta$ iff $(t, q) \in \Delta^-$.

3 Reachability

In this section we give an algorithm to solve the following reachability problem:

(Reachability): Given a GTRS $S = (A, \Sigma, P, t_I)$ and a regular set of trees $T \subseteq T_A$, compute the set of all trees in T_A from which one can reach a tree of T in the graph G_S associated to S.

This problem was already solved in [5] and an algorithm similar to the one presented here can be found in [4] for more general rewrite systems. Thus, we only provide the algorithm for the sake of completeness and without correctness proof.

The main idea of the algorithm is to simulate the rewriting rules within the tree automaton $\mathcal{A} = (Q, A, \Delta, F)$ that accepts the regular set $T = T(\mathcal{A})$. If the automaton contains for each rewriting rule $t_1 \to t_2$ a unique state q_{t_1} that identifies t_1, i.e., $(t, q_{t_1}) \in \Delta$ iff $t = t_1$, then such the rule $t_1 \to t_2$ can be simulated by adding an ε-transition (q_{t_1}, q) to Δ, where q is a state with $(t_2, q) \in \Delta$. So the algorithm adds a new part to $\mathcal{A}$ such that subtrees from P_L can be uniquely identified and then starts adding ε-transitions as described above.

First we define the new part that is added to $\mathcal{A}$. Given a set P of rewriting rules over a ranked alphabet $A = (A_i)_{i \in [k]}$, let

- $Q^P = \{q_t \mid t \in \text{sub}(P_L)\}$, and
- $\Delta^P = \{(q_{t_1}, \ldots, q_{t_i}, a, q_{a(t_1, \ldots, t_i)}) \mid a(t_1, \ldots, t_i) \in \text{sub}(P_L)\}$.

If these new states and transitions are added to $\mathcal{A}$, then the accepted language does not change and for each $t \in P_L$ the state q_t can only be reached via t.

Figure 2 shows an algorithm solving the reachability problem. Note that the algorithm always terminates since only finitely many transitions can be added to the automaton $\mathcal{A}_0$.

INPUT: GTRS $S = (A, \Sigma, P, t_I)$, ε-NTA $\mathcal{A} = (Q, A, \Delta, F)$
$Q_0 = Q \dot\cup Q^P$, $\Delta_0 = \Delta \dot\cup \Delta^P$, $F_0 = F$
$\mathcal{A}_0 := (Q_0, A, \Delta_0, F_0)$
$i := 0$
while $\exists t_1 \to t_2 \in P, q \in Q_0$ with $(t_2, q) \in \Delta_i$ and $(t_1, q) \notin \Delta_i$ **do**
$\quad i := i + 1$
$\quad \Delta_i := \Delta_{i-1} \cup \{(q_{t_1}, q)\}$
$\quad \mathcal{A}_i := (Q_0, A, \Delta_i, F_0)$
end
$m := i$
OUTPUT: ε-NTA $\mathcal{A}_m$

Fig. 2. Algorithm to solve the reachability problem.

For a proof of the following theorem see e.g. [4] (or [8] for the special case of pushdown systems).

Theorem 1. *Given a GTRS $S = (A, \Sigma, P, t_I)$ and an ε-NTA $\mathcal{A}$, the algorithm from Figure 2 computes an ε-NTA with $|Q| + |\text{sub}(P_L)|$ states accepting the set $\{t \in T_A \mid t \to_S^* T\}$.*

4   Recurrence

After having solved the reachability problem from the former section the next step is to deal with repeated reachability or recurrence.

(Recurrence): Given a GTRS $S = (A, \Sigma, P, t_I)$ and a regular set of trees $T \subseteq T_A$, compute the set $\{t \in T_A \mid t \to_S^\omega T\}$.

For this section we fix a GTRS $S = (A, \Sigma, P, t_I)$ and an NTA $\mathcal{A} = (Q, A, \Delta, F)$. By $\mathcal{A}_q$ we denote the automaton $\mathcal{A}_q = (Q, A, \Delta, \{q\})$.

There are two main steps in the construction of an NTA for the set $\{t \in T_A \mid t \to_S^\omega T(\mathcal{A})\}$.

Step 1. We reduce the recurrence problem for $T(\mathcal{A})$ to the reachability problem for a set $R(\mathcal{A})$ (defined below) by showing $\{t \in T_A \mid t \to_S^\omega T(\mathcal{A})\} = \{t \in T_A \mid t \to_S^* R(\mathcal{A})\}$. The set $R(\mathcal{A})$ is regular and can be constructed if we can decide for all trees $t \in P_L$ and all states $q \in Q$ whether $t \to_S^\omega T(\mathcal{A}_q)$.

Step 2. We give a procedure for deciding for $t \in P_L$ and $q \in Q$ if $t \to_S^\omega T(\mathcal{A}_q)$.

Step 1. Informally speaking, the set $R(\mathcal{A})$ (for a fixed GTRS S) contains all the trees t such that there is a state $q \in Q$ and vertex $u \in D_t$ with $t^u \in P_L$, $t^u \to_S^\omega T(\mathcal{A}_q)$, and if we assume that there is a run of $\mathcal{A}$ on t that labels u with q, then there is an accepting run of $\mathcal{A}$ on t. The last condition ensures that $t(u \leftarrow t') \in T(\mathcal{A})$ for each $t' \in T(\mathcal{A}_q)$. Since the second requirement says that from t^u we can infinitely often reach a tree from $T(\mathcal{A}_q)$, it is clear that from t we can infinitely often reach $T(\mathcal{A})$. On the other hand, if we are given a tree t with $t \to_S^\omega T(\mathcal{A})$, then we can also reach $R(\mathcal{A})$ from t. Before we prove this in Lemma 1 we give a formal definition of $R(\mathcal{A})$.

Given $t \in T_A$, $u \in D_t$, and $q \in Q$, we say that $t(u \leftarrow q)$ is in $T(\mathcal{A})$ if there is a tree $t_1 \in T_A$ such that there is an accepting run ρ of $\mathcal{A}$ on $t(u \leftarrow t_1)$ with $\rho(u) = q$. For this definition we assume that all states of $\mathcal{A}$ are reachable, i.e., for each $q \in Q$ there is a $t \in T_A$ with $(t, q) \in \Delta$. We define the set

$$R(\mathcal{A}) = \left\{ t \in T_A \mid \exists u \in D_t, q \in Q : \begin{array}{c} t^u \in P_L, t^u \to_S^\omega T(\mathcal{A}_q), \\ \text{and } t(u \leftarrow q) \in T(\mathcal{A}) \end{array} \right\}.$$

Lemma 1. *Let $t \in T_A$. Then $t \to_S^\omega T(\mathcal{A})$ iff $t \to_S^* R(\mathcal{A})$.*

Proof. "$\Rightarrow$": Assume that $t \to_S^\omega T(\mathcal{A})$ and let $\pi = t_0 \to_S t_1 \to_S t_2 \to_S t_3 \to_S \cdots$ be a path starting at $t = t_0$ that infinitely often visits $T(\mathcal{A})$. For $i \in \mathbb{N}$ let $u_i \in D_{t_i}$ and $t_i' \in T_A$ such that $t_{i+1} = t_i(u_i \leftarrow t_i')$ (i.e. the rewriting rules are applied to the $t_i^{u_i}$). There is a $j \in \mathbb{N}$ such that no u_i is a proper prefix of u_j for all $i > j$, and there is an infinite number of $i > j$ such that u_j is a prefix of u_i. In particular, this means $u_j \in D_{t_i}$ for all $i > j$. Let $t_L = t_j^{u_j}$. We know that $t_L \in P_L$. Since π infinitely often visits $T(\mathcal{A})$, there must be $q \in Q$ that is infinitely often at u_j in accepting runs on trees from $T(\mathcal{A})$ on π. We get $t_L \to_S^\omega T(\mathcal{A}_q)$ since u_i is not a proper prefix of u_j for $i > j$ and because there are infinitely many substitutions "below" u_j (u_j is a prefix of u_i for infinitely many $i > j$).

Let $k > j$ be such that there is an accepting run of $\mathcal{A}$ on t_k that labels u_j with q. Define $t' = t_k(u_j \leftarrow t_L)$ and $u = u_j$. Then $(t')^u = t_L$. From the accepting run on t_k that labels u with q we get $t'(u \leftarrow q) \in T(\mathcal{A})$. Thus, $t' \in R(\mathcal{A})$.

For all $i > j$ we have that u_i is not a proper prefix of u_j. Therefore we get $t_j \to_S^* t'$ and as a consequence $t \to_S^* t'$.

"$\Leftarrow$": Let $t' \in R(\mathcal{A})$ such that $t \to_S^* t'$. It is sufficient to show that $t' \to_S^\omega T(\mathcal{A})$. Let $q \in Q$ and $u \in D_{t'}$ be such that $(t')^u \in P_L$ and $(t')^u \to_S^\omega T(\mathcal{A}_q)$. Let $t_0 = (t')^u$ and let $t_0 \to_S t_1 \to_S t_2 \to_S t_3 \to_S \cdots$ be a path starting at t_0 that infinitely often visits $T(\mathcal{A}_q)$. Then $t \to_S t(u \leftarrow t_1) \to_S t(u \leftarrow t_2) \to_S t(u \leftarrow t_3) \to_S \cdots$ is a path starting in t that infinitely often visits $T(\mathcal{A})$.   □

Since the set P_L is finite, it is not difficult to verify that the defining properties of trees in $R(\mathcal{A})$ can be checked by a finite tree automaton. But to construct such an automaton we have to decide for each $t \in P_L$ and $q \in Q$ whether $t \to_S^\omega T(\mathcal{A}_q)$. This is the second step mentioned above and will be done in the remainder of this section.

Step 2. There are two possibilities on how to visit the set $T(\mathcal{A})$ infinitely often along a path π.

(a) There is a single tree $t \in T(\mathcal{A})$ that is visited infinitely often along π.
(b) There are infinitely many different trees from $T(\mathcal{A})$ on π.

To distinguish the two cases we analyze how the trees evolve along a path π by defining the limit of π. This is the tree consisting of all the vertices of trees on π that are eventually not involved in the rewriting steps any more (i.e. the vertices that are fixed from a certain point onwards). In case (a) this limit will be a finite tree. If the limit of π is infinite, then we have to deal with case (b). In both cases we can find a normal form for paths infinitely often visiting $T(\mathcal{A})$. That is, if there is a path $\pi' : t \to_S^\omega T(\mathcal{A})$ for $t \in P_L$, then there is also a path π in normal form with $\pi : t \to_S^\omega T(\mathcal{A})$. Then we describe a procedure to decide for $t \in P_L$ and $q \in Q$ if there exists a path π in normal form with $\pi : t \to_S^\omega T(\mathcal{A}_q)$.

The normal form for case (a) is based on the same ideas as in Step 1 from above and is stated without proof in Lemma 2. The normal form for case (b) (Lemma 3) is more complicated and will be described in more detail after the formal definition of the limit of a path.

A branch β of a tree t is a maximal prefix closed subset of D_t such that for each $u \in \beta$ there is at most one $i \in \mathbb{N}$ with $ui \in \beta$ (in other words: a maximal subset of D_t that is linearly ordered by $\sqsubseteq$). Given a branch β of a tree t and a vertex $v \in D_t$ we define $\beta(v)$ to be the maximal prefix u of v with $u \in \beta$.

Let π be an infinite path through G_S. We say that $u \in \mathbb{N}^*$ is stable on π if $u \in D_{\pi(i)}$ for each $i \in \mathbb{N}$ and none of the vertices used in the rewritings on π is a prefix of u. This simply means that u is never involved in any of the substitutions on the path π (note that u is a prefix of itself). The limit $\lim(\pi)$ of π is a (possibly infinite) tree with domain

$$D_{\lim(\pi)} = \{u \in \mathbb{N}^* \mid \exists j \in \mathbb{N} : u \text{ stable on } \pi^j\}.$$

If a vertex u is eventually stable on π then it eventually has a fixed label a. We take this label to be the label of u in $\lim(\pi)$, i.e., $\lim(\pi)(u) = a$.

The path π is called stable iff for all $u \notin D_{\lim(\pi)}$ there is a $j \in \mathbb{N}$ such that $u \notin D_{\pi(i)}$ for all $i \geq j$.

If $\lim(\pi)$ is finite for a path $\pi : t \to T(\mathcal{A})$, then it is not difficult to see that it is possible to visit $T(\mathcal{A})$ infinitely often in the following way. From t one can reach a tree t'' which has a subtree $t' = (t'')^u \in P_L$. From t' we can reach a tree r and from r one can reach t' again such that $t''(u \leftarrow r) \in T(\mathcal{A})$. This is formalized in the next lemma. The proof is similar to the construction in the proof of Lemma 1.

Lemma 2. *If there exists a path* $\pi : t \to_S^\omega T(\mathcal{A})$ *with* $\lim(\pi)$ *finite, then there are* $t' \in P_L$, $t'' \in T_A$, $u \in D_{t''}$, *and* $q \in Q$ *such that* $t \to_S^* t''$, $(t'')^u = t'$, $t' \to_S^* T(\mathcal{A}_q) \to_S^+ t'$, *and* $t''(u \leftarrow q) \in T(\mathcal{A})$. $\quad\square$

The normal form for paths π' with $\lim(\pi')$ infinite is obtained by removing unnecessary rewritings. By unnecessary we mean that these rewritings are not essential for visiting $T(\mathcal{A})$ infinitely often. This results in a new path π that is stable such that $\lim(\pi)$ only has one infinite branch. Furthermore we can ensure that there are infinitely many trees on π that are accepted by $\mathcal{A}$ such that the accepting runs agree on growing initial segments of the infinite branch of $\lim(\pi)$.

Lemma 3. *If there exists a path* $\pi' : t \to_S^\omega T(\mathcal{A})$ *with* $\lim(\pi')$ *infinite, then there is a path* $\pi : t \to_S^\omega T(\mathcal{A})$ *with*

(i) π *is stable,*
(ii) $\lim(\pi)$ *has exactly one infinite branch* β, *and*
(iii) *there is a run* $\rho_{\lim}$ *of* $\mathcal{A}$ *on* $\lim(\pi)$ *with the following property. For each* $u \in \beta$ *there are infinitely many* $i \in \mathbb{N}$ *such that there is an accepting run* ρ_i *of* $\mathcal{A}$ *on* $\pi(i)$ *that agrees with* $\rho_{\lim}$ *on* $\{v \mid \beta(v) \sqsubseteq u\}$.

Proof. For simplicity we will only speak of runs instead of runs of $\mathcal{A}$.

Let β be an infinite branch of $\lim(\pi')$. We first define a mapping ρ_β on β that will be extended to the run $\rho_{\lim}$. In the definition of ρ_β we make use of König's Lemma to be able to satisfy property (iii).

For $u \in \beta$ let $\beta_u = \{v \in \beta \mid v \sqsubseteq u\}$ be the initial segment of β up to u and $V_u = \{\rho : \beta_u \to Q \mid \exists^\omega i : \pi'(i)$ is accepted by a run that agrees with ρ on $\beta_u\}$ ($\exists^\omega$ means "there are infinitely many"). Define a graph $G = (V, E)$ with $V = (\bigcup_{u \in \beta} V_u) \cup \{\emptyset\}$. The edge relation E is defined as follows.

 – $(\rho, \rho') \in E$ if there are $u, u' \in \beta$ with $u' = ui$ for some $i \in \mathbb{N}$ such that $\rho : \beta_u \to Q$, $\rho' : \beta_{u'} \to Q$, and ρ, ρ' agree on β_u.
 – $(\emptyset, \rho) \in E$ if $\rho : \beta_\varepsilon \to Q$.

Then G is an infinite tree (in the graph theoretic sense) of finite degree. Therefore, by König's Lemma, there is an infinite path in G. On this path growing initial segments of β are labelled consistently. This gives us our mapping ρ_β.

Now we will modify the path π' to obtain the path π. For each $u \in \beta$ let $i_u \in \mathbb{N}$ be minimal such that the successor $s(u)$ of u on β is stable on $(\pi')^{i_u}$ and $\pi'(i_u)$ is accepted by a run ρ_u that agrees with ρ_β on $\beta_{s(u)}$. To obtain π remove for each $u \in \beta$ all substitutions on $(\pi')^{i_u}$ at a vertex v with $\beta(v) = u$. Then π is still an infinite path and π is stable. Furthermore $\lim(\pi)$ only contains the infinite branch β. It remains to define $\rho_{\lim}$ and verify (iii). For each $u \in D_{\lim(\pi)}$ let $\rho_{\lim}(u) = \rho_{\beta(u)}(u)$. Then one can verify that $\rho_{\lim}$ is indeed a run of $\mathcal{A}$ on $\lim(\pi)$. Since π is obtained from π' by removing rewritings we get a natural mapping $\varphi : \mathbb{N} \to \mathbb{N}$ associating $\pi'(i)$ with $\pi(\varphi(i))$. This mapping is inductively defined as $\varphi(0) = 0$ and

$$\varphi(i+1) = \begin{cases} \varphi(i) & \text{if the rewriting generating the edge from } \pi'(i) \text{ to} \\ & \pi'(i+1) \text{ was removed from } \pi', \\ \varphi(i) + 1 & \text{otherwise.} \end{cases}$$

By the definition of π the tree $\pi(\varphi(i_u))$ is accepted for each $u \in \beta$ by a run that agrees with $\rho_{\lim}$ on $\{v \mid \beta(v) \sqsubseteq u\}$.   □

Lemmas 2 and 3 provide us with normal forms for paths infinitely often visiting $T(\mathcal{A})$ (or any other regular set of trees). To decide for $t \in P_L$ and $q \in Q$ whether $t \to_S^\omega T(\mathcal{A}_q)$ we construct a finite graph G with vertex set $\mathrm{sub}(P) \times Q \times Q$ and edges labelled with 0 or 1 such that there is a path π in normal form with $\pi : t \to_S^\omega T(\mathcal{A}_q)$ iff there is a path through G with infinitely many edges labelled 1. We will motivate the construction of G by the normal form obtained in Lemma 3 but it is not difficult to see that we can also use G to find paths with finite limit.

In the first component of the vertices of G the rewriting steps at vertices on the infinite branch β (according to Lemma 3) will be simulated (usually more than one at a time). The second component will keep track of the state labelling $\rho_{\lim}$ of β. As we have seen in Lemma 3, there are accepting runs for trees on the infinite path π that agree with $\rho_{\lim}$ on growing initial segments of $\lim(\pi)$. But it is not guaranteed that these runs completely agree with $\rho_{\lim}$. So, in the third component of the vertices we will simulate the actual accepting runs on trees that are on π. The property that we will find runs that agree with $\rho_{\lim}$ on growing initial segments allow us to reset the third component to the second one whenever we find an accepting run.

Traversing one edge in G corresponds to going one vertex along the branch β. If we are at vertex u on β and ui is the successor of u on β, then going from (t, q, p) to (t', q', p') in G means that t is the tree at u before the first substitution takes place at u and t' is the tree at ui after the last substitution at u. Thus, one edge of G corresponds to the sequence of substitutions starting at the first substitution at a certain vertex on β and ending after the last substitution at this vertex. The edge of G is labelled with 1 if during this sequence of substitutions a tree from $T(\mathcal{A}_q)$ occurs. This is checked using the states in the second and third component of the vertices of G.

Formally we define $G = (V, E)$, where $V = \mathrm{sub}(P) \times Q \times Q$ and E contains the following edges.

(1) $(t, q, p) \xrightarrow{0} (t', q', p') \in E$ if there exist $t_1, \ldots, t_l \in T_A$, $q_1, \ldots, q_l, p_1, \ldots, p_l \in Q$, $i \in \{1, \ldots, l\}$ such that

  - $a(t_1, \ldots, t_l) \in \mathrm{sub}(P)$ and $t \to_S^* a(t_1, \ldots, t_l)$,
  - $t' = t_i$, $q' = q_i$, $p' = p_i$,
  - $(q_1, \ldots, q_l, a, q), (p_1, \ldots, p_l, a, p) \in \Delta$, and
  - $t_j \to_S^* T(\mathcal{A}_{p_j}) \to_S^* T(\mathcal{A}_{q_j})$ for all $j \in \{1, \ldots, l\}$ with $j \neq i$.

(2) $(t, q, p) \xrightarrow{1} (t', q', p') \in E$ if there exist $t_1, \ldots, t_l \in T_A$, $q_1, \ldots, q_l, p_1, \ldots, p_l \in Q$, $i \in \{1, \ldots, l\}$ such that
  - $a(t_1, \ldots, t_l) \in \mathrm{sub}(P)$ and $t \to_S^* T(\mathcal{A}_p) \to_S^* a(t_1, \ldots, t_l)$,
  - $t' = t_i$, $q' = q_i$, $p' = p_i$,
  - $(q_1, \ldots, q_l, a, q), (p_1, \ldots, p_l, a, q) \in \Delta$, and
  - $t_j \to_S^* T(\mathcal{A}_{p_j}) \to_S^* T(\mathcal{A}_{q_j})$ for all $j \in \{1, \ldots, l\}$ with $j \neq i$.

The only differences between (1) and (2) are that in (2) we require $a(t_1, \ldots, t_l)$ to be reachable from t via a tree from $T(\mathcal{A}_p)$ and that we reset the simulation of a run in the third component.

Lemma 4. *Let $t \in P_L$ and $q \in Q$.*

  (i) *There is a path π in G_S with $\pi : t \to_S^\omega T(\mathcal{A}_q)$ and $\lim(\pi)$ infinite iff there is an infinite path in G with infinitely many edges labelled 1 starting from (t, q, q).*
  (ii) *There is a path π in G_S with $\pi : t \to_S^\omega T(\mathcal{A}_q)$ and $\lim(\pi)$ finite iff there is a path in G from (t, q, q) to (t', q', q') such that $t' \to_S^* T(\mathcal{A}_{q'}) \to_S^+ t'$.*

Proof. The proof for (ii) is rather simple with the use of Lemma 2. The idea for the proof of (i) is as follows.

"$\Leftarrow$": By induction on n one can show that if there is a path from (t, q, p) to (t', q', p') in G starting with n 0-edges and ending with one 1-edge, then there is a tree t'' and $u \in D_{t''}$ such that $t \to_S^* T(\mathcal{A}_p) \to_S^* t''$, $(t'')^u = t'$, and $t''(u \leftarrow q') \in T(\mathcal{A}_q)$. So, from an infinite path in G starting in (t, q, q) and having infinitely many 1-edges one can construct a path in G_S that infinitely often visits $T(\mathcal{A}_q)$.

"$\Rightarrow$": For this direction the normal form of Lemma 3 is used. The first component in the vertices of G is used to simulate the rewritings on the branch β at the point where the vertices on β become stable. The second component guesses the labelling of β by $\rho_{\lim}$ and the third component is used to simulate the labelling of β by accepting runs on trees that are on π. Property (iii) from Lemma 3 ensures that there are accepting runs that agree with $\rho_{\lim}$ on growing initial segments of $\lim(\pi)$. $\qquad\square$

The graph G can be constructed effectively since the only nontrivial conditions in the construction of the edges are instances of the reachability problem. Furthermore condition (i) of the previous lemma is decidable by standard algorithms on finite graphs. Condition (ii) of the previous lemma is decidable because the condition $t' \to_S^* T(\mathcal{A}_{q'}) \to_S^+ t'$ can also be formulated as an instance of the reachability problem. Therefore we get the following lemma.

Lemma 5. *For $t \in P_L$ and $q \in Q$ it is decidable whether $t \to_S^\omega T(\mathcal{A}_q)$.*

Summarizing the results from this section we get the following theorem.

Theorem 2. *Given a GTRS $S = (A, \Sigma, P, t_I)$ and an NTA $\mathcal{A} = (Q, A, \Delta, F)$, one can construct an ε-NTA with $\mathcal{O}(|Q| + |\mathrm{sub}(P_L)|)$ states accepting the set $\{t \in T_A \mid t \to_S^\omega T(\mathcal{A})\}$.*

Proof. An automaton for $R(\mathcal{A})$ on an input $t \in T_A$ has to guess a subtree $t^u \in P_L$ and $q \in Q$ with $t^u \to_S^\omega T(\mathcal{A}_q)$ and then verify that $t(u \leftarrow q)$ is in $T(\mathcal{A})$. This can be done by an automaton with $\mathcal{O}(|Q| + |\mathrm{sub}(P_L)|)$ states (and by Lemma 5 we can also construct this automaton). Then we apply Theorem 1 and obtain an automaton for $\{t \in T_A \mid t \to_S^\omega T(\mathcal{A})\}$ with $\mathcal{O}(|Q| + |\mathrm{sub}(P_L)|)$ states.   □

5   Universal Reachability and Universal Recurrence

In the previous sections we asked for the existence of a path with a certain property. In this section we address the dual problems.

(**Universal Reachability**): Given a GTRS $S = (A, \Sigma, P, t_I)$ and a regular set of trees $T \subseteq T_A$, does every maximal path in G_S starting in t_I visit T?

(**Universal Recurrence**): Given a GTRS $S = (A, \Sigma, P, t_I)$ and a regular set of trees $T \subseteq T_A$, does every infinite path in G_S starting in t_I visit T infinitely often?

We will show the undecidability of these two problems using the same ideas as in [9] where the undecidability of a similar property for Basic Parallel Processes is shown. The general idea is to use reductions from undecidable problems for Turing machines (TM) by defining for a given TM M a GTRS S_M that can simulate computations of M. A TM configuration $a_1 \cdots a_k q b_l \cdots b_1$, where the word $a_1 \cdots a_k b_l \cdots b_1$ is on the tape and the TM is in state q with the reading head on b_l, will be represented by a tree with two branches with $X, a_1, \ldots, a_k$ on the left branch and $X, b_1, \ldots, b_l, q$ on the right branch. The X symbols are used to model the infinite blank parts of the tape to the left and to the right. For example the first tree in Figure 3 represents the configuration qa. For a configuration κ of M we will denote the corresponding tree as $t(\kappa)$.

With this coding of configurations it is not possible to exactly simulate the transitions of M by S_M. The GTRS S_M can simulate the correct behavior of M as well as incorrect behavior (i.e., in S_M one can reach $t(\kappa')$ from $t(\kappa)$ although M cannot reach κ' when started in κ). But S_M will be constructed in such a way that for every path π through G_{S_M} that leads from $t(\kappa)$ to $t(\kappa')$ there is a tree from a regular set T_{err} on π iff M cannot reach κ' when started κ. This property is obtained by adding auxiliary symbols to the tree alphabet and simulating a transition of M in more than one rewriting step with intermediate trees that do not code configurations.

Let $M = (Q, B, \Gamma, q_0, q_s, \delta)$ be a deterministic TM with state set Q, input alphabet B, tape alphabet Γ, starting state q_0, stop state q_s, and transition function $\delta : Q \times \Gamma \to Q \times \Gamma \times \{L, R\}$. Furthermore let $Q \cap \Gamma = \emptyset$, and $\sqcup$ be the blank symbol. If κ and κ' are configurations of M, then we write as usual $\kappa \vdash_M \kappa'$

if κ' is the successor configuration of κ, and $\kappa \vdash^*_M \kappa'$ if κ' is a configuration that is reachable from κ. The initial configuration of M on the empty tape is denoted by κ_ε.

The GTRS $S_M = (A, \Sigma, P, t_I)$ is defined as follows. The tree alphabet is $A = A_0 \cup A_1 \cup A_2$ with $A_2 = \{\bullet\}$, $A_1 = Q \cup \Gamma \cup \{X\}$, and $A_0 = A_1 \cup \{add_1, add_2, add_3, rem_1, rem_2, err\}$. We do not need the transition labels Σ, thus we assume that Σ contains one symbol and omit this symbol in the rest of the proof.

The initial tree is $t_I = t(\kappa_\varepsilon) = $
```
     •
    ╱ ╲
   X   X
   │
   q0
```

The set P contains the following rewriting rules.

1. For $\delta(q, a) = (p, b, L)$, $c \in \Gamma$:
```
   a        b
   │        │
   q   →    p
            │
            c
            │
          add1
```
and if $a = \sqcup$, then
```
   X        X
   │        │
   q   →    b
            │
            p
            │
            c
            │
          add1
```
.

2. For $\delta(q, a) = (p, b, R)$:
```
   a        p
   │        │
   q   →    b
            │
          rem1
```
and if $a = \sqcup$, then
```
   X        X
   │        │
   q   →    p
            │
            b
            │
          rem1
```
.

3. For all $a \in \Gamma \cup \{X\}$, $b \in \Gamma$:
```
   a        a          b            X
   │   →    │  ,  b →  │  ,  X →    │
            b        rem1           ⊔
            │                       │
          add1                    rem1
```
.

4. $add_1 \to add_2$, $add_2 \to add_3$, $rem_1 \to rem_2$.

5. For all $a \in \Gamma \cup \{X\}$, $b \in \Gamma$, $q \in Q$:
```
   q        a          a        a
   │        │          │        │
   b   →    │  ,       b   →    │
   │        q          │        b
 add3                add3
```
.

6. For all $a \in \Gamma \cup \{X\}$, $b \in \Gamma$, $q \in Q$:
```
   a                   q
   │                   │
   b   →  a,           b   →  q.
   │                   │
 rem2                rem2
```

7. For all $a \in \Gamma \cup \{X\}$, $b \in \Gamma$, $p, q \in Q$:
```
   a                   q
   │                   │
   q   →  p,           │   →  q.
   │                  err
  err
```

Figure 3 shows the correct simulation of the transition $\delta(q, a) = (p, b, L)$ (the TM is in the configuration qa). The symbols a and q are replaced by b and p. Since the TM moves the head to the left, it has to guess which symbol is on the left hand side of the head. Here it is the blank symbol. The symbol add_1 indicates that the blank symbol should be added to the right branch of the tree. Now the left branch has to confirm with rem_1. Then the two branches alternatingly increase their add and rem symbols until they reach add_3 and rem_2. Now the blank symbol can be removed from the left branch and then it is added to the right branch.

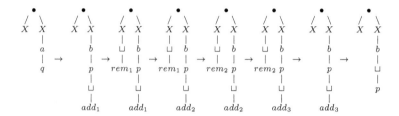

Fig. 3. Example for the simulation of a TM-transition by a GTRS.

The set T_{err} contains all trees that result from a violation of the protocol and all the trees that encode a stop configuration of the TM. From the description below it is easy to see that T_{err} can be defined by an NTA. A tree t is in T_{err} iff

1. t contains the *err* symbol,
2. t contains more than one *add* or more than one *rem* symbol,
3. t contains a rem_i symbol and no add_i or add_{i+1} symbol,
4. t contains an add_2 symbol and no *rem* symbol, or
5. t contains subtrees of the form $\genfrac{}{}{0pt}{}{a}{|}{rem_i}$ and $\genfrac{}{}{0pt}{}{b}{|}{add_j}$ with $a \neq b$.

By a tedious distinction of cases one can check the following lemma.

Lemma 6.   (i) For each configuration κ of M: $t(\kappa_\varepsilon) \to_S^* t(\kappa)$.
(ii) For all configurations κ, κ' of M there is a path from $t(\kappa)$ to $t(\kappa')$ in G_{S_M} not visiting T_{err} iff $\kappa \vdash_M^* \kappa'$.

Theorem 3. The problem (Universal Reachability) is undecidable.

Proof. Let T_{stop} be the set of all trees encoding a stop or deadlocking configuration. Then, by Lemma 6 (ii), it is clear that a TM M does not stop on the empty tape iff there is a path through G_{S_M} starting in t_I that never visits $T_{err} \cup T_{stop}$. □

Theorem 4. The problem (Universal Recurrence) is undecidable.

Proof. We use a reduction from a problem similar to the halting problem which can easily be shown to be undecidable:

Given a Turing machine M, does there exist a configuration κ of M such that M does not stop when started in κ?

Suppose that such a configuration of M exists. then $t(\kappa_\varepsilon) \to_S^* t(\kappa)$ by Lemma 6 (i), and by Lemma 6 (ii) there is an infinite path starting in $t(\kappa)$ not visiting T_{err}.

If there is an infinite path π that visits T_{err} only finitely often, then one can pick a tree of the form $t(\kappa)$ on π such that there is no tree from T_{err} on the suffix of π starting in $t(\kappa)$ (it is not difficult to see that such a tree exists). Then the suffix of π starting in $t(\kappa)$ corresponds to an infinite computation of M starting in κ, again by Lemma 6 (ii). □

6   A Logic for Model-Checking over GTRS Graphs

For a fixed ranked alphabet A and an alphabet Σ formulas of our logic are defined by the grammar (in CTL-like syntax)

$$\phi := \top \mid \bot \mid T \mid \neg\phi \mid \phi \vee \phi \mid \langle \sigma \rangle \phi \mid EF\phi \mid EGF\phi$$

where $\sigma \in \Sigma$ and $T \subseteq T_A$ regular. Given a GTRS $S = (A, \Sigma, P, t_I)$ define the semantics $\|\phi\|_S$ (or simply $\|\phi\|$) of a formula ϕ as follows.

- $\|\top\| = T_A$, $\|\bot\| = \emptyset$, $\|T\| = T$, $\|\neg\phi\| = T_A \setminus \|\phi\|$, $\|\phi_1 \vee \phi_2\| = \|\phi_1\| \cup \|\phi_2\|$,
- $\|\langle \sigma \rangle \phi\| = \{t \in T_A \mid t \to_S^\sigma \|\phi\|\}$,
- $\|EF\phi\| = \{t \in T_A \mid t \to_S^* \|\phi\|\}$, and
- $\|EGF\phi\| = \{t \in T_A \mid t \to_S^\omega \|\phi\|\}$.

Then S is a model of ϕ, denoted by $S \models \phi$, iff $t_I \in \|\phi\|$. With the results from the previous sections we get the following theorem.

Theorem 5. *For a GTRS $S = (A, \Sigma, P, t_I)$ and a formula ϕ one can decide whether $S \models \phi$.*

Proof. We can construct automata for $\|\top\|$, $\|\bot\|$, $\|T\|$, $\|\neg\phi\|$, $\|\phi_1 \vee \phi\|$ with standard tree automaton constructions. Given an automaton for $\|\phi\|$, the automata for $\|EF\phi\|$ and $\|EGF\phi\|$ can be constructed according to Theorems 1 and 2. An automaton for $\|\langle \sigma \rangle \phi\|$ has to guess a subtree and a rewriting rule such that rewriting this subtree with this rule yields a tree from $\|\phi\|$. We do not give the details of this straightforward construction here. Thus, to decide if $S \models \phi$ we construct the automaton for $\|\phi\|$ and then check if $t_I \in \|\phi\|$. $\square$

The fragment of temporal logic presented here is maximal in the sense that including the operators EG or EFG leads to an undecidable model-checking problem as shown by the results from the previous section. Furthermore, until-operators (as known from temporal logic) also lead to undecidability, because in the GTRS constructed in the proof of Theorem 3 the fact that the TM stops on the empty tape can easily expressed by the until formula $E(\neg T_{\mathrm{err}})UT_{\mathrm{stop}}$ because the existence of a path starting in the initial tree and remaining in the complement of T_{err} until it eventually reaches T_{stop} is equivalent to the existence of a halting computation of the TM on the empty tape.

Conclusion

In the present paper we have analyzed various decision problems for infinite graphs generated by ground tree rewriting. The problems of reachability and recurrence as stated in Sections 3 and 4 were solved whereas the problems of universal reachability and universal recurrence from Section 5 were shown to be undecidable. These considerations lead to a rather expressive and in some sense maximal fragment of temporal logic with a decidable model-checking problem for GTRS graphs.

A drawback of the decision algorithm is that the size of the constructed automaton is non-elementary in the number of nested negations in the formula since complementing NTA gives an exponential blow-up. Note that we cannot simply push the negations inwards to the atomic formulas because this would lead to universal path quantifiers (A instead of E) which are difficult to handle with nondeterministic tree automata. The use of alternating tree automata may help to obtain a better complexity.

References

1. Achim Blumensath and Erich Grädel. Automatic structures. In *Proceedings of LICS '00*, pages 51–62. IEEE Computer Society Press, 2000.
2. Walter S. Brainerd. Tree generating regular systems. *Information and Control*, 14:217–231, 1969.
3. Didier Caucal. On infinite transition graphs having a decidable monadic theory. In *Proceedings ICALP '96*, volume 1099 of *LNCS*. Springer-Verlag, 1996.
4. J.L. Coquidé, M. Dauchet, R. Gilleron, and S. Vágvölgyi. Bottom-up tree pushdown automata: Classification and connection with rewrite systems. *Theoretical Computer Science*, 127(1):69–98, 1994.
5. J.L. Coquidé and R. Gilleron. Proofs and reachability problem for ground rewrite systems. In *Aspects and Prospects of Theoretical Computer Science*, volume 464 of *LNCS*, pages 120–129. Springer, 1990.
6. Max Dauchet, Thierry Heuillard, Pierre Lescanne, and Sophie Tison. Decidability of the confluence of finite ground term rewrite systems and of other related term rewrite systems. *Information and Computation*, 88(2):187–201, October 1990.
7. Max Dauchet and Sophie Tison. The theory of ground rewrite systems is decidable. In *Proceedings LICS '90*, pages 242–248. IEEE Computer Society Press, 1990.
8. Javier Esparza, David Hansel, Peter Rossmanith, and Stefan Schwoon. Efficient algorithms for model checking pushdown systems. In *Proceedings of CAV 2000*, volume 1855 of *LNCS*, pages 232–247. Springer-Verlag, 2000.
9. Javier Esparza and Astrid Kiehn. On the model checking problem for branching time logics and Basic Parallel Processes. In *Proceedings of CAV '95*, volume 939 of *LNCS*, pages 353–366, 1995.
10. Orna Kupferman and Moshe Y. Vardi. An automata-theoretic approach to reasoning about infinite-state systems. In E. A. Emerson and A. P. Sistla, editors, *Proceedings of CAV 2000*, volume 1855 of *LNCS*. Springer-Verlag, 2000.
11. Richard Mayr. Process rewrite systems. *Information and Computation*, 156(1–2):264–286, 2000.
12. Christophe Morvan. On rational graphs. In *Proceedings of FoSSaCS '99*, volume 1784 of *LNCS*, pages 252–266. Springer, 1999.
13. David E. Muller and Paul E. Schupp. The theory of ends, pushdown automata, and second-order logic. *Theoretical Computer Science*, 37:51–75, 1985.
14. Igor Walukiewicz. Pushdown processes: Games and model checking. In Rajeev Alur and Thomas A. Henzinger, editors, *Proceedings of CAV '96*, volume 1102 of *LNCS*, pages 62–74. Springer-Verlag, July-August 1996.

Bounded MSC Communication[*]

Markus Lohrey[**] and Anca Muscholl

LIAFA, Université Paris VII
2, place Jussieu, case 7014
75251 Paris cedex 05, France
{lohrey,muscholl}@liafa.jussieu.fr

Abstract. Message sequence charts (MSCs) and high-level message sequence charts (HMSCs) are popular formalisms for the specification of communication protocols between asynchronous processes. An important concept in this context is the size of the communication buffers used between processes. Since real systems impose limitations on the capacity (or speed) of communication links, we ask whether a given HMSC can be implemented with respect to a given buffer size imposed by the environment. We introduce four different measures for buffer sizes and investigate for each of these measures the complexity of deciding whether a given MSC (or HMSC, or hierarchical MSC) satisfies a given bound on the buffer size. The complexity of these problems varies between the classes P, NP, and coNP.

1 Introduction

Message sequence charts (MSC) and high-level message sequence charts (HMSC) are popular visual formalisms for the specification of communication of asynchronous processes, where most of the details (variables, timing constraints, etc) are abstracted away. An important aspect for implementing such specifications is the size of the channel buffers used by the communicating processes. Since real systems impose limitations on the capacity (or speed) of communication links, it is natural to ask whether an HMSC can be implemented with respect to a given buffer size imposed by the environment.

In this paper we introduce four different measures for buffer sizes of (H)MSCs. These measures result from two orthogonal dimensions: In the first dimension we distinguish whether *all* linearizations of an MSC M satisfy a certain buffer bound ($\forall$-boundedness), respectively whether *at least one* linearization of M respects the bound ($\exists$-boundedness). Universal boundedness is a kind of safety requirement, expressing that any interleaving of the MSC execution is possible within the constraints imposed by the environment. Existential boundedness is important for instance when we want to simulate a given specification, e.g. for determining the reachable nodes of an HMSC. In this case it suffices to consider one interleaving for each MSC execution.

---

[*] Research supported by the INRIA cooperative research action FISC.
[**] Current address: IRISA, Campus de Beaulieu, F-35042 Rennes Cedex, France.

M. Nielsen and U. Engberg (Eds.): Fossacs 2002, LNCS 2303, pp. 295–309, 2002.

In the second dimension we distinguish between measuring the channel size as the number of undelivered messages over all channels (*global* boundedness), respectively as the maximum of the number of undelivered messages in a given communication channel, where the maximum is taken over all channels (*local* boundedness). The local notion of boundedness is important for implementing an MSC specification in a distributed process environment. Global boundedness arises naturally when one simulates MSC executions on a single-processor environment, for instance for test purposes.

By combining both dimensions we say for instance that an MSC M is $\exists^b_{glob}$-bounded (existentially, globally) for some $b \in \mathbb{N}$, if there exists a linearization of M such that for each prefix of this linearization the total number of undelivered messages is at most b. The notions of $\forall^b_{glob}$-boundedness (universally, globally), $\exists^b_{loc}$-boundedness (existentially, locally), and $\forall^b_{loc}$-boundedness (universally, locally) for MSCs are defined similarly. All these notions can be extended to HMSCs, by referring to all executions of an HMSC. We also consider the channel boundedness problem for MSCs using references, i.e., already defined MSCs (*nested MSCs*, [1]).

We note that the notion of universal-local-boundedness corresponds to the notion of channel-boundedness used in [2,3,5,6] in the context of regular MSC-languages. For each of our four measures we investigate the complexity of deciding whether a given (H)MSC or nMSC satisfies a given bound on the buffer size. The complexity of these problems varies between the classes P, NP, and coNP, see Table 1 in Section 7 for a summary of our results.

2   Preliminaries

For complexity results we will use standard classes like non-deterministic logarithmic space (NL), polynomial time (P), non-deterministic polynomial time (NP) and co-NP (complements of NP-problems), see [8] for definitions.

A *linearization* of a partially ordered set $(A, \prec)$ is a total order on A that extends the partial order $\prec$. The transitive closure of a binary relation E is the least transitive relation E^+ containing E. The transitive reduction of E is a minimal relation $F \subseteq E$ such that $E^+ = F^+$. For any alphabets $A \subseteq B$ and any word $w \in B^*$ we define $|w|_A$ as the number of symbols from A in w.

2.1   Message Sequence Charts

Following the ITU norm Z.120 a *message sequence chart (MSC)* M is a tuple $(\mathcal{E}, P, \lambda, t, m, \prec)$, where:

- $\mathcal{E}$ is a finite set of *events*.
- P is a finite set of *processes*.
- $\lambda : \mathcal{E} \to P$ associates with each event e a process $\lambda(e)$ on which e is located.
- $t : \mathcal{E} \to \{S, R\}$ associates with each event a type. Events in $t^{-1}(S)$ (resp. $t^{-1}(R)$) are called *send* (resp. *receive*) events.

- $m : t^{-1}(S) \to t^{-1}(R)$ is a bijection. A pair $(s, m(s))$ with s a send event is also called a *message* from process $p = \lambda(s)$ to process $q = \lambda(m(s))$. The *channel type* of s (resp. $m(s)$) is defined as $S(p, q)$ (resp. $R(p, q)$). The channel type of $e \in \mathcal{E}$ is denoted $\mathrm{ch}(e)$.
- $\prec$ is a partial order on $\mathcal{E}$, also called the *visual order of M*. We require that the set of events $\lambda^{-1}(p)$ is totally ordered by $\prec$, for every $p \in P$, and that $\prec$ equals the transitive closure of the *acyclic* relation

$$\bigcup_{p \in P} \prec|_{\lambda^{-1}(p)} \cup \{(s, m(s)) \mid t(s) = S\}.$$

The size of the MSC M is the number of events in M. Often MSCs are further restricted to satisfy the FIFO-condition, which means that whenever there are two send events s_1 and s_2 with $\mathrm{ch}(s_1) = \mathrm{ch}(s_2)$ and $s_1 \prec s_2$ then also $m(s_1) \prec m(s_2)$, i.e, message overtaking on any channel is disallowed. A *channel* is a pair (p, q) of distinct processes. The MSC definition may also include message contents or local actions, however this is not important in the present setting. The complexity results in this paper mostly hold independently of the FIFO-restriction (respectively whether message names are allowed or not). This is due to the fact that all lower bound proofs in this paper hold under the FIFO-restriction, whereas all upper bound proofs (excepting those for nMSCs) hold without the FIFO-restriction.

Let $M = (\mathcal{E}, P, \lambda, t, m, \prec)$ be an MSC. A *linearization* of M is a linearization of the visual order $(\mathcal{E}, \prec)$. Let L be a linearization of M and let $b \in \mathbb{N}$. We say that L is *globally-bounded* by b if $|K|_{t^{-1}(S)} - |K|_{t^{-1}(R)} \leq b$ for every prefix K of L. We say that L is *locally-bounded* by b if for all channels (p, q) and every prefix K of L it holds $|K|_{\mathrm{ch}^{-1}(S(p,q))} - |K|_{\mathrm{ch}^{-1}(R(p,q))} \leq b$. We say that M is $\exists^b_{\mathrm{glob}}$-bounded (resp. $\exists^b_{\mathrm{loc}}$-bounded) if there exists a linearization of M which is globally-bounded (resp. locally-bounded) by b. We say that M is $\forall^b_{\mathrm{glob}}$-bounded (resp. $\forall^b_{\mathrm{loc}}$-bounded) if every linearization of M is globally-bounded (resp. locally-bounded) by b. Of course for $Q \in \{\exists, \forall\}$, if M is Q^b_{glob}-bounded, then M is also Q^b_{loc}-bounded. Vice versa, if M is Q^b_{loc}-bounded, then M is Q^c_{glob}-bounded, where $c = |P|^2 \cdot b$.

For $Q \in \{\exists, \forall\}$ and $Y \in \{\mathrm{loc}, \mathrm{glob}\}$, we define Q_Y-MSC-BOUNDED as the following decision problem.

INPUT: MSC M and positive integer b.

QUESTION: Is M Q^b_Y-bounded?

Instead of speaking about prefixes of linearizations of MSCs, it is sometimes more convenient to consider configurations of MSCs. A *configuration* C of M is a downward-closed subset $C \subseteq \mathcal{E}$, i.e., if $e \prec f \in C$ then also $e \in C$. A prefix of a linearization of M defines in the obvious way a unique configuration of M. Vice versa, for every configuration C of M there exists at least one prefix K of a linearization of M such that K defines C. Let C be a configuration of M. The number of messages (s, r) in M with $s \in C$ and $r \notin C$ is denote by $\mathrm{gs}(C, M)$ (**g**lobally unmatched sends). The maximum over all channels (p, q) of the number of messages (s, r) in M with $\mathrm{ch}(s) = S(p, q)$, $\mathrm{ch}(r) = R(p, q)$, $s \in C$, and $r \notin C$ is denote by $\mathrm{ls}(C, M)$ (locally unmatched sends). Note that M is $\forall_{\mathrm{glob}}^b$-bounded (resp. $\forall_{\mathrm{loc}}^b$-bounded) if and only if for every configuration C of M it holds $\mathrm{gs}(C, M) \leq b$ (resp. $\mathrm{ls}(C, M) \leq b$).

Let $M_i = (\mathcal{E}_i, P, \lambda_i, t_i, m_i, \prec_i)$, $i = 1, 2$, be two MSCs over the same set P of processes, where furthermore $\mathcal{E}_1 \cap \mathcal{E}_2 = \emptyset$. Then the concatenation of M_1 and M_2 is the MSC $M_1 M_2 = (\mathcal{E}_1 \cup \mathcal{E}_2, P, \lambda_1 \cup \lambda_2, t_1 \cup t_2, m_1 \cup m_2, \prec)$, where

$$\prec = (\prec_1 \cup \prec_2 \cup \{(e_1, e_2) \mid e_1 \in \mathcal{E}_1, e_2 \in \mathcal{E}_2 : \lambda_1(e_1) = \lambda_2(e_2)\})^+.$$

The standard ITU definition Z.120 defines also a *high-level message sequence chart (HMSC)* as a finite transition system with nodes labeled by finite MSCs. Formally, let an HMSC H be given as $H = (V, \rightarrow, P, \mu, v)$, where $(V, \rightarrow)$ is a finite transition system with initial node v, P is the set of processes and μ maps every node $u \in V$ to a finite MSC $\mu(u)$ over the set of processes P. The MSC-language $L(H)$ defined by H is the set of all MSCs $\mu(u_1)\mu(u_2)\cdots$, where $u_1 = v$ and $u_1 \rightarrow u_2 \rightarrow \cdots$ is a (finite or infinite) maximal path in $(V, \rightarrow)$. (Formally, for infinite paths we have to define the limit of $(\mu(u_1 \cdots u_k)_{k \geq 1})$. We impose the restriction that every node u is accessible from the initial node v. Let $Q \in \{\exists, \forall\}$ and $Y \in \{\mathrm{loc}, \mathrm{glob}\}$. We say that an HMSC H is Q_Y^b-bounded, where $b \in \mathbb{N}$, if all $M \in L(H)$ are Q_Y^b-bounded. Finally, we define Q_Y-HMSC-BOUNDED as the following decision problem.

INPUT: HMSC H and positive integer b.
QUESTION: Is H Q_Y^b-bounded?

2.2 Pebble Games

As we will see in Section 3 there is a tight connection between the existential-global boundedness problem and pebble games on directed graphs. In this section we recall the definition of pebble games and related results.

Let $G = (V, E)$ be a finite *directed acyclic graph* (dag) with node set V and edges $E \subseteq V \times V$. A *game-configuration* is a subset of V. For two game-configurations $C_1, C_2 \subseteq V$ and a node $v \in V$ we write $C_2 = C_1 \dot\cup \{v\}$ whenever $C_2 = C_1 \cup \{v\}$ and $v \notin C_1$, i.e., C_2 is the disjoint union of C_1 and v. A *move* in G is a pair (C_1, C_2) of game-configurations such that one of the following three cases holds:

(1) There exists a node $w \in C_1$ with $C_2 = C_1 \backslash \{w\}$.
(2) There exists a node $v \in C_2$ such that $C_2 = C_1 \dot\cup \{v\}$ and for all $u \in V$ with $(u, v) \in E$ it holds $u \in C_1$.
(3) There exist nodes $w \in C_1, v \in C_2$ such that $(w, v) \in E$, $C_2 = (C_1 \backslash \{w\}) \dot\cup \{v\}$, and for all $u \in V$ with $(u, v) \in E$ it holds $u \in C_1$.

More precisely we say that (C_1, C_2) is an *i-move*, $i \in \{1, 2, 3\}$, if case (i) in the enumeration above holds. Let $b \in \mathbb{N}$. We say that the graph G can be *b-pebbled* if there exists a sequence $C_1, C_2, \ldots, C_n \subseteq V$ of game-configurations such that the following holds:

(a) $C_1 = C_n = \emptyset$, $|C_i| \leq b$ for $1 \leq i \leq n$,

(b) For every node $v \in V$ there exists exactly one $i \in \{1, \ldots, n-1\}$ such that $v \notin C_i$ and $v \in C_{i+1}$.

(c) (C_i, C_{i+1}) is a move for $1 \leq i < n$.

If instead of (c) we require that (C_i, C_{i+1}) is a 1-move or a 2-move for $1 \leq i < n$, then we say that the graph G can be b-pebbled without the move rule.

Theorem 1 ([9]). *The following problem is NP-complete:*
INPUT: Finite dag G with only one node of outdegree 0, positive integer b.
QUESTION: Can G be b-pebbled?

It is not hard to see that a dag with exactly one node of outdegree 0 can be b-pebbled if and only if it can be $(b+1)$-pebbled without the move rule. Hence we obtain

Corollary 1. *The following problem is NP-complete:*
INPUT: Finite dag G, positive integer b.
QUESTION: Can G be b-pebbled without the move rule?

For a finite dag (V, E) let $\overline{V} = \{\overline{v} \mid v \in V\}$ be a disjoint copy of the node set V and let $\tilde{E} = \{(u, v), (v, \overline{u}) \mid (u, v) \in E\} \cup \{(u, \overline{u}) \mid u \in V\}$. Note that the graph $(V \cup \overline{V}, \tilde{E})$ is again a finite dag. The following lemma is easy to prove.

Lemma 1. *A finite dag (V, E) can be b-pebbled without the move rule if and only if there exists a linearization ℓ of the partial order $(V \cup \overline{V}, \tilde{E}^+)$ such that for every prefix k of ℓ we have $|k|_V - |k|_{\overline{V}} \leq b$.*

3 Bounded Communication in Finite MSCs

For the local boundedness problems we can argue by considering some additional ordering on events. Let us fix a bound b and an MSC $M = (\mathcal{E}, P, \lambda, t, m, \prec)$. We define a binary relation $\rightsquigarrow$ on $\mathcal{E}$ as follows. We let $r \rightsquigarrow s$ whenever for some channel (p, q) and some $i \geq 1$ we have that s is the $(i+b)$-th send of channel type $S(p, q)$, whereas r is the i-th receive of channel type $R(p, q)$. The following lemma is easy to prove.

Lemma 2. *An MSC is $\exists^b_{\mathrm{loc}}$-bounded if and only if the relation $\prec \cup \rightsquigarrow$ is acyclic, where $\prec$ is the visual order of M and $\rightsquigarrow$ is the relation associated with M, b.*

Since it can be checked in linear time whether a directed graph is acyclic, the previous lemma immediately yields the following result:

Proposition 1. $\exists_{\mathrm{loc}}$-MSC-BOUNDED *can be solved in linear time.*

Surprisingly, if we consider the *global* boundedness instead of the local one, the existential variant of the problem becomes more difficult, more exactly it is NP-complete:

Theorem 2. $\exists_{\mathrm{glob}}$-MSC-BOUNDED *is NP-complete.*

Proof. Membership in NP is obvious. In order to prove NP-hardness, we will construct for a finite dag $G = (V, E)$ a finite MSC $M(G) = (\mathcal{E}, P, \lambda, t, m, \prec)$ such that G can be b-pebbled without the move rule if and only if $M(G)$ is $\exists_{\text{glob}}^{(b+1)}$-bounded. With each node $v \in V$ we associate the set of processes $P_v = \{p_{in}(v), p(v), p_{out}(v)\} \cup \{p(v, w) \mid (v, w) \in E\}$, the set of all processes is then $P = \bigcup_{v \in V} P_v$. The set $\mathcal{E}$ of events consists of $V \cup \overline{V}$ plus some additional events (see Figure 1). We have $\lambda(v) = p_{in}(v)$ and $\lambda(\overline{v}) = p_{out}(v)$. For each node v there is a message $(v, \overline{v})$ from process $p_{in}(v)$ to process $p_{out}(v)$. This messages crosses the chain of the two messages from $p_{in}(v)$ to $p(v)$ and from $p(v)$ to $p_{out}(v)$. Furthermore for each edge $(u, v) \in E$ we have exactly one message from process $p(u, v)$ to $p_{in}(v)$ and back from $p_{in}(v)$ to $p(u, v)$. Finally if $(v, w_1), \ldots, (v, w_n)$ are all outgoing edges of node v (listed in an arbitrary order) then there is exactly one message from process $p_{out}(v)$ to $p(v, w_1)$ and back and exactly one message from process $p(v, w_i)$ to $p(v, w_{i+1})$ and back ($1 \leq i \leq n - 1$). The order of the events on the processes in P_v is shown in Figure 1, where we show an example where $(u_1, v), (u_2, v), (v, w_1), (v, w_2)$, and (v, w_3) are the adjacent edges of v. The process names labeling message arrows specify the source, resp. target process of the message. Note that $\prec$ is indeed acyclic, for instance the sends of the messages from process $p(u, v)$ to $p_{in}(v)$ must precede the sends of the messages from process $p(v, w)$ to $p_{in}(w)$, with $(u, v), (v, w)$ edges of the dag. Moreover, it is easy to check that $M(G)$ respects the FIFO-restriction, in fact this was the only reason for introducing process $p(v)$. The crucial point of our construction is that the restriction $\prec|_{V \cup \overline{V}}$ of the visual order $\prec$ of $M(G)$ to the set $V \cup \overline{V} \subseteq \mathcal{E}$ is precisely the transitive closure of the relation $\tilde{E}$ from Lemma 1.

Claim 1: If G can be b-pebbled without the move rule then $M(G)$ is $\exists_{\text{glob}}^{(b+1)}$-bounded.

Assume that G can be b-pebbled without the move rule by a sequence of moves. We translate each move into a sequence of events, such that the resulting sequence of events is a linearization of M which is globally-bounded by $b + 1$. Consider a move $(\mathcal{C}_1, \mathcal{C}_2)$. If $\mathcal{C}_2 = \mathcal{C}_1 \dot\cup \{v\}$, i.e., node v is pebbled in the move, then we execute the following sequence of events:

(1) Send and immediately receive the message from process $p(u_i, v)$ to $p_{in}(v)$ for $1 \leq i \leq k$, where $(u_1, v), \ldots, (u_k, v)$ are all incoming edges of node v.
(2) Execute send event v on process $p_{in}(v)$.
(3) Send and immediately receive the message from process $p_{in}(v)$ to $p(u_i, v)$ for $1 \leq i \leq k$.
(4) Send and immediately receive the message from process $p_{in}(v)$ to $p(v)$, followed by the message from $p(v)$ to $p_{out}(v)$.
(5) Send and immediately receive the message from process $p_{out}(v)$ to $p(v, w_1)$ followed by the messages from $p(v, w_i)$ to $p(v, w_{i+1})$ for $1 \leq i < n$, where $(v, w_1), \ldots, (v, w_n)$ are all outgoing edges of node v.

Of course if v has indegree 0 (resp. outdegree 0) then (1) and (3) (resp. (5)) disappear. On the other hand if $\mathcal{C}_2 = \mathcal{C}_1 \setminus \{v\}$, i.e., a pebble is taken from node v in the move, then we execute the following sequence of events:

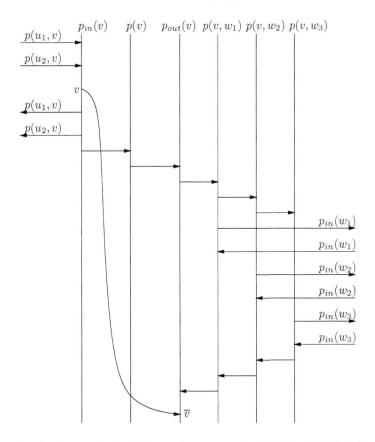

Fig. 1. Communication between the processes in P_v in the MSC $M(G)$

(1) Send and immediately receive the message from process $p(v, w_{i+1})$ to $p(v, w_i)$ for $n > i \geq 1$, where $(v, w_1), \ldots, (v, w_n)$ are all outgoing edges of node v.
(2) Send and immediately receive the message from process $p(v, w_1)$ to $p_{out}(v)$.
(3) Execute the receive event $\overline{v}$ on process $p_{out}(v)$.

Claim 2: If $M(G)$ is $\exists_{\text{glob}}^{(b+1)}$-bounded then G can be b-pebbled without the move rule.

Let L be a linearization of $M(G)$, which is globally-bounded by $b+1$, such that furthermore the number of prefixes K of L that satisfy $|K|_{t^{-1}(S)} - |K|_{t^{-1}(R)} = b + 1$ is minimal among all linearizations of $M(G)$ that are globally-bounded by $b + 1$. Clearly such an L exists. Let $\pi(L)$ be the projection of the word L onto $V \cup \overline{V} \subseteq \mathcal{E}$. Since of course $\pi(L)$ is a linearization of $\prec|_{V \cup \overline{V}}$, by Lemma 1 it suffices to prove the following claim:

Claim 3: For every prefix k of $\pi(L)$ it holds $|k|_V - |k|_{\overline{V}} \leq b$.

Clearly we have $|k|_V - |k|_{\overline{V}} \le b+1$ for every prefix k of $\pi(L)$. In order to prove the claim let us assume that $|\pi(L_1 v)|_V - |\pi(L_1 v)|_{\overline{V}} = b+1$, where $v \in V$ and $L = L_1 v L_2$. Let $L_2 = e L_3$, where $e \in \mathcal{E}$ (note that we must have $L_2 \neq \epsilon$). If e would be a send event then $|L_1 v e|_{t^{-1}(S)} - |L_1 v e|_{t^{-1}(R)} \ge b+2$, a contradiction. Thus e must be a receive event. If $e \notin \overline{V}$ then we would have $|L_1 v|_{t^{-1}(S)} - |L_1 v|_{t^{-1}(R)} \ge b+2$ (note that already $|\pi(L_1 v)|_{t^{-1}(S)} - |\pi(L_1 v)|_{t^{-1}(R)} = b+1$). Thus $e = \overline{u}$ for some $u \in V$. We cannot have $v \prec \overline{u}$, since if by the construction of $M(G)$ this implies that several events occur between v and $\overline{u}$. It follows that $L' = L_1 \overline{u} v L_3$ is also a linearization of $M(G)$ that is globally-bounded by $b+1$. Since furthermore the number of prefixes K of L' such that $|K|_{t^{-1}(S)} - |K|_{t^{-1}(R)} = b+1$ is smaller then for L, we have a contradiction. This proves claim 3 and the theorem. $\square$

If we consider universal-boundedness instead of the existential one, then by the following simple lemma we will obtain again a polynomial algorithm in the local setting of the problem.

Lemma 3. *An MSC is $\forall_{\text{loc}}^b$-bounded if and only if $\rightsquigarrow$ is contained in $\prec$.*

Proposition 2. $\forall_{\text{loc}}$-MSC-BOUNDED *can be solved in time $O(|M|^2)$.*

For universal-global-boundedness we can also obtain a polynomial time solution using flow theory:

Theorem 3. $\forall_{\text{glob}}$-MSC-BOUNDED *can be solved in time $O(|M|^2 \log(|M|))$.*

Proof. In order to check universal-global-boundedness we consider the complementary problem, namely whether given a finite MSC M and $b \in \mathbb{N}$ there exists a configuration C of M such that $\text{gs}(C, M) > b$. This question can be answered in polynomial time using the min-flow max-cut theorem, see e.g. [4]. More precisely we construct from M a dag as follows: View M as a dag, where the nodes are the events of M, and the edges are the messages of M plus pairs of events (e, f) such that e immediately precedes f on some process. To this dag we add two nodes σ and τ. We add an edge from σ to each minimal event of M, and similarly we add an edge from each maximal event of M to τ. Let us call the resulting dag $G(M)$. To each edge (v, w) of $G(M)$ we assign an *upper capacity* $c_{v,w}$ and a *lower capacity* $\ell_{v,w}$ as follows: All edges receive the upper capacity ∞. For all messages $(s, m(s))$ of M we let $\ell_{s,m(s)} = 1$, whereas for all other edges (v, w) of $G(M)$ we let $\ell_{v,w} = 0$. By the min-flow max-cut theorem the minimum value of a (σ, τ)-flow of $G(M)$ is equal to the maximum of $\sum_{v \in S, w \in T} \ell_{v,w} - \sum_{v \in S, w \in T} c_{w,v}$, where the maximum is taken over all partitions $\{S, T\}$ of the nodes of $G(M)$ with $\sigma \in S$ and $\tau \in T$. By the choice of the capacities this is precisely the maximum over all configurations C of M of $\text{gs}(C, M)$. We note also that before computing the minimal flow we may reduce the graph $G(M)$ as follows: If two nodes v and w are such that v immediately precedes w on some process and either v has outdegree one, or w has indegree one (initially this holds for all immediate successors on some process), then the edge (v, w) can be contracted to a single node. This reduction step can be iterated as long as possible. Call the resulting graph $G(M)_{\mathrm{red}}$. Note that $G(M)_{\mathrm{red}}$ may be considerably smaller than $G(M)$. Finally, since all upper capacities are ∞, we can use [10] in order to compute $\max(\sum_{v\in S,w\in T}\ell_{v,w} - \sum_{v\in S,w\in T}c_{w,v})$ in time $O(n\log(n)r)$, where n is the number of nodes of $G(M)_{\mathrm{red}}$ and $r \in O(n)$ is the number of edges in a transitive reduction of $G(M)_{\mathrm{red}}$. $\square$

4   Bounded Communication in HMSCs

The following result follows easily from Theorem 4.

Theorem 4. $\exists_{\mathrm{glob}}$-HMSC-BOUNDED *is NP-complete.*

Proof. The lower bound follows directly from Theorem 2. For the upper bound note that an HMSC $H = (V, \to, P, \mu, v)$ is $\exists_{\mathrm{glob}}^{b}$-bounded if for every node $u \in V$ the MSC $\mu(u)$ is $\exists_{\mathrm{glob}}^{b}$-bounded. $\square$

Analogously to Theorem 4 it follows that $\exists_{\mathrm{loc}}$-HMSC-BOUNDED can be solved in linear time.

For the universal-boundedness question for HMSCs we need the concept of the communication graph $G(M)$ of a finite MSC $M = (\mathcal{E}, P, \lambda, t, m, \prec)$. It is defined as $G(M) = (P, \mapsto)$, where $p_1 \mapsto p_2$ if and only if there exists a message $(s, m(s))$ in M with $\lambda(s) = p_1$ and $\lambda(m(s)) = p_2$. We say that $G(M)$ is *locally strongly connected* if every connected component of $G(M)$ is strongly connected. We say that M is *locally strongly connected* if $G(M)$ is locally strongly connected. Finally an HMSC $H = (V, \to, P, \mu, v)$ is locally strongly connected if for every cycle $v_1 \to v_2 \to \cdots \to v_n \to v_1$ of $(V, \to)$ the MSC $\mu(v_1)\mu(v_2)\cdots\mu(v_n)$ is locally strongly connected. It is easy to see that H is locally strongly connected if and only if for all simple cycles $v_1 \to v_2 \to \cdots \to v_n \to v_1$ (i.e, $v_i \neq v_j$ for $i \neq j$) the MSC $\mu(v_1)\mu(v_2)\cdots\mu(v_n)$ is locally strongly connected. For this just note that if we have some cycle $v_1 \to \cdots \to v_i = w_1 \to \cdots \to w_m \to v_i \to \cdots \to v_n \to v_1$ then $G = G(\mu(v_1)\cdots\mu(v_i)\mu(w_2)\cdots\mu(w_m)\mu(v_i)\cdots\mu(v_n))$ is the union of the two communication graphs $G(\mu(v_1)\cdots\mu(v_n))$ and $G(\mu(w_1)\cdots\mu(w_m))$. Thus if both of them are locally strongly connected then the same holds for G. Recently it was shown in [5] that an HMSC H is $\forall_{\mathrm{loc}}^{b}$-bounded for some b if and only if H is locally strongly connected. The fact that H is locally strongly connected if H is $\forall_{\mathrm{loc}}^{b}$-bounded by some b is quite easy to see. Lemma 4 below will allow us to present a simpler proof of the other direction of the result of [5], together with a sharper bound on the buffer size, which we need later.

Lemma 4. *Let the HMSC $H = (V, \to, P, \mu, v)$ be locally strongly connected. Let $u_1 \to u_2 \to \cdots \to u_m$ be a path in $(V, \to)$ with $m > |P| \cdot |V|$ and let C be a configuration of the MSC $M = \mu(u_1)\cdots\mu(u_m)$. Then there exists a path $v_1 \to v_2 \to \cdots \to v_n$ in $(V, \to)$ and a configuration D of the MSC $N = \mu(v_1)\cdots\mu(v_n)$ such that $n < m$, $\mathrm{gs}(C, M) = \mathrm{gs}(D, N)$, and $\mathrm{ls}(C, M) = \mathrm{ls}(D, N)$.*

Proof (sketch). The basic idea is the following: Mark on each process line the cut-point, where C cuts this line. Since $m > |P| \cdot |V|$ we can find a loop $u_i \to$

$u_{i+1} \to \cdots \to u_j = u_i$ inside our path $u_1 \to \cdots \to u_m$ such that none of the resulting $|P|$ cut-points is located in the factor $M' = \mu(u_i) \cdots \mu(u_j)$ of M. Since H is locally strongly connected, none of the messages of M' can go from C to its complement, and we may omit the loop $u_i \to \cdots \to u_j$ from the original path. $\square$

For a finite MSC $M = (\mathcal{E}, P, \lambda, t, m, \prec)$ let $S(M) = |t^{-1}(S)|$. For an HMSC $H = (V, \to, P, \mu, v)$ let $S(H) = \max\{S(\mu(u)) \mid u \in V\}$.

Lemma 5. *Let the HMSC $H = (V, \to, P, \mu, v)$ be locally strongly connected. Then H is $\forall^b_{\mathrm{glob}}$-bounded (and hence also $\forall^b_{\mathrm{loc}}$-bounded) for some $b \leq |P| \cdot |V| \cdot S(H)$. Furthermore if $b \in \mathbb{N}$ is minimal such that H is $\forall^b_{\mathrm{glob}}$-bounded (resp. $\forall^b_{\mathrm{loc}}$-bounded) then there exists a path $v_1 \to v_2 \to \cdots \to v_n$ in $(V, \to)$ and a configuration C of the MSC $M = \mu(v_1) \cdots \mu(v_n)$ such that $n \leq |P| \cdot |V|$ and $\mathrm{gs}(C, M) = b$ (resp. $\mathrm{ls}(C, M) = b$).*

We should remark that Theorem 2.8 of [5], which corresponds to the first statement of Lemma 5, is formulated in terms of regular MSC-expressions instead of HMSCs. Using the notation of [5], we can prove the following statement in the same fashion as Lemma 5.

Lemma 6. *Let L be a set of finite MSCs over some fixed set of processes P. Assume that each $M \in L$ is locally strongly connected and $\forall^b_{\mathrm{glob}}$-bounded (resp. $\forall^b_{\mathrm{loc}}$-bounded). Then every MSC in L^* is $\forall^{|P| \cdot b}_{\mathrm{glob}}$-bounded (resp. $\forall^{|P| \cdot b}_{\mathrm{loc}}$-bounded).*

Theorem 5. $\forall_{\mathrm{glob}}$-HMSC-BOUNDED *is coNP-complete.*

Proof. We show that the complementary problem is NP-complete:
    INPUT: HMSC H and positive integer b.
    QUESTION: Is there an MSC $M \in L(H)$ which is not $\forall^b_{\mathrm{glob}}$-bounded?
An NP-algorithm that solves this problem proceeds as follows: Fix an HMSC $H = (V, \to, P, \mu, v)$. First we guess in $(V, \to)$ a simple cycle $u_1 \to u_2 \to \cdots \to u_m \to u_1$ and a path $v_1 \to v_2 \to \cdots \to v_n$ with $n \leq |P| \cdot |V|$ together with a configuration C in the MSC $M = \mu(v_1) \cdots \mu(v_n)$. Then the algorithm outputs "yes" if and only if either the communication graph of the MSC $\mu(u_1)\mu(u_2) \cdots \mu(u_m)$ is not locally strongly connected or $\mathrm{gs}(C, M) \geq b + 1$. We claim that this NP-algorithm is correct. Clearly if the algorithm outputs "yes" then there exists an MSC in $L(H)$ which is not $\forall^b_{\mathrm{glob}}$-bounded. On the other hand assume that there exists an MSC in $L(H)$ which is not $\forall^b_{\mathrm{glob}}$-bounded. Either H is not locally strongly connected, which can be detected by the algorithm, or there exists some b' such that H is $\forall^{b'}_{\mathrm{glob}}$-bounded. Let b' be minimal with this property. Then $b < b'$ and by Lemma 5 there exists a path $v_1 \to v_2 \to \cdots \to v_n$ with $n \leq |P| \cdot |V|$ together with a configuration C in the MSC $M = \mu(v_1) \cdots \mu(v_n)$ such that $\mathrm{gs}(C, M) = b' \geq b + 1$. Again both this path and the configuration can be detected by the algorithm.

    In order to prove NP-hardness, we reduce SAT to our problem. A construction similar to the following one was also used in [7]. Let $\{x_1, \ldots, x_n\}$ be a set of propositional variables, and let $C = \{C_1, \ldots, C_m\}$ be a set of clauses, where each clause C_i consists of variables and negated variables. We construct an HMSC $H = (V, \rightarrow, P, \mu, v)$ such that C is satisfiable if and only if there exists $M \in L(H)$ which is not $\forall_{\text{glob}}^{m-1}$-bounded. Let $V = \{v, v_1, \overline{v}_1, \ldots, v_n, \overline{v}_n\}$ and $\rightarrow = \{(v, v_1), (v, \overline{v}_1)\} \cup \{(v_i, v_{i+1}), (v_i, \overline{v}_{i+1}), (\overline{v}_i, v_{i+1}), (\overline{v}_i, \overline{v}_{i+1}) \mid 1 \leq i < n\}$. The set of processes is $P = \{c_i, c_i' \mid 1 \leq i \leq m\}$. It remains to define the MSCs $\mu(u)$ for $u \in V$. The MSC $\mu(v)$ is empty. The MSC $\mu(v_i)$ contains a message from process c_j to process c_j' and back from c_j' to c_j if $x_i \in C_j$. Similarly the MSC $\mu(\overline{v}_i)$ contains a message from process c_j to process c_j' and back from c_j' to c_j if $\overline{x}_i \in C_j$. No other messages are present. It follows that C is satisfiable if and only if there exists an MSC $M \in L(H)$ such that for every $1 \leq j \leq m$ the projection of M onto the processes c_j and c_j' is a non-empty iteration of the MSC that sends a message from c_j to c_j' and back. This holds if and only if there exists an MSC $M \in L(H)$ that is not $\forall_{\text{glob}}^{m-1}$-bounded.   □

It should be noted that Theorem 5 holds no matter whether the buffer bound $b \in \mathbb{N}$ is represented unary or binary. Our lower bound proof holds also for the unary representation, whereas the upper bound proof holds for the binary representation. Furthermore note that the HMSC H used for the lower-bound proof is based on an acyclic graph $(V, \rightarrow)$, thus H defines a finite set of MSCs.

Theorem 6. $\forall_{\text{loc}}$-HMSC-BOUNDED *is coNP-complete. Furthermore this problem is coNP-complete even if the input parameter b is fixed to $b = 2$.*

Proof. Membership in coNP follows in exactly the same way as in Theorem 5. In order to show coNP-hardness we will reduce NAE-SAT (not-all-equal-SAT) to the complement of our problem. We consider a collection of m clauses $C = \{C_1, \ldots, C_m\}$ each of length three, over variables $\{x_1, \ldots, x_n\}$ and we want to find out whether there is a variable assignment such that for each clause C_i, the literals of C_i do not have the same value. We will construct an HMSC H such that for a given channel (A, B) of H there is an execution with more than 2 sends in the corresponding buffer if and only if there is an assignment as above for C. For every channel different from (A, B) each execution of H will contain at most one message for that buffer, so channels different from (A, B) will be universally bounded by 1.

The graph underlying H is similar to the one from Theorem 5. The node set is $V = \{v, v_1, \overline{v}_1, \ldots, v_n, \overline{v}_n, v'\}$, and $\rightarrow = \{(v, v_1), (v, \overline{v}_1), (v_n, v'), (\overline{v}_n, v')\} \cup \{(v_i, v_{i+1}), (v_i, \overline{v}_{i+1}), (\overline{v}_i, v_{i+1}), (\overline{v}_i, \overline{v}_{i+1}) \mid 1 \leq i < n\}$. Again, vertex v_i stands for x_i true, whereas $\overline{v}_i$ stands for x_i false. The HMSC H uses processes A, B and processes $P_{j,1}, P_{j,2}, P_{j,3}, P_{j,4}, N_{j,1}, N_{j,2}, N_{j,3}, N_{j,4}$ for $j \in \{1, \ldots, m\}$ ranging over the clauses. We denote as P_j-group the processes in $P_{j,1}, P_{j,2}, P_{j,3}, P_{j,4}$, and as N_j-group the processes in $N_{j,1}, N_{j,2}, N_{j,3}, N_{j,4}$. The initial node v contains two messages from A to B, followed by one message from B to each of $P_{j,1}$ and $N_{j,1}$. Each node v_i contains a message in the P_j-group for every clause C_j where x_i occurs positively, and a message in the N_j-group for every clause C_j where x_i occurs negatively. Precisely, v_i contains a message from $P_{j,k}$ to $P_{j,k+1}$, if x_i is the k-th literal of C_j, $k \in \{1, 2, 3\}$. Here, the ordering of the literals in each clause has to respect the order $x_1, \ldots, x_n$ of the variables. We define analogously the messages from $N_{j,\ell}$ to $N_{j,\ell+1}$ in v_i, for each C_j containing $\overline{x}_i$. Finally for the messages in $\overline{v}_i$ we switch the roles of P_j and N_j. The final node v' is labeled by messages from each of $P_{j,4}$, $N_{j,4}$ to A, followed by a message from A to B.

Note that paths from v to v' correspond precisely to variable assignments. Moreover, for a given path, the second receive of type $R(A, B)$ precedes in the visual order the third send of type $S(A, B)$ if and only if there is some j and a $\prec$-path either from $P_{j,1}$ to $P_{j,4}$, or from $N_{j,1}$ to $N_{j,4}$. But this holds if and only if there is a clause C_j in which all literals have the same value under the variable assignment corresponding to the chosen path from v to v'. But this is exactly the case where C is not satisfied as an NAE-SAT instance.   □

Let us remark that a simple extension of the construction from the previous proof also shows that it is coNP-complete, whether a given HMSC is $\forall_{\mathrm{loc}}^b$-bounded for some b, i.e., whether it is locally strongly connected. For this we have to add an edge from the final node v' back to the initial node v. Furthermore we have to add confirm messages that ensure that only the buffer (A, B) may contain an arbitrary number of undelivered messages. For this we simply confirm each message from a process p to q where $(p, q) \neq (A, B)$ directly by a message from q back to p.

5   Local Boundedness and Nested MSCs

A *nested MSC (nMSC)* is a sequence $M = (M_k)_{1 \leq k \leq m}$ of modules M_k. Each module M_k is defined as an MSC to which we add references to modules M_i with $k < i \leq m$, by specifying the start and end of each reference to M_i on the process lines belonging to M_i. We use the definition of [1], where messages are restricted to be matched on the same hierarchy level (in particular, we don't consider ports), but they can cross submodules, see the following figure.

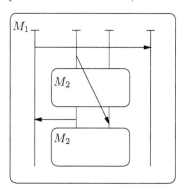

The definition above is analogous to the notion of straight-line expressions, where any expression may use in its definition sub-expressions that were previously defined. Each module M_k of M can be expanded to a finite MSC flat(M_k) by replacing inductively in M_k each reference to a module M_j $(j > k)$ by the MSC flat(M_j). Finally we define flat$(M) = $ flat(M_1). Let $P(M_k)$ be the set of processes of flat(M_k). Note that if an occurrence of flat(M_i) appears within flat(M_k) then $P(M_i) \subseteq P(M_k)$. Thus, if M_k contains a message (s, r) from p to q that crosses a reference M_i, $i > k$, (i.e., p, q are processes of M_i and s precedes the beginning of M_i on p, whereas r succeeds the end of M_i on q), then M_i cannot contain any message from p to q, unless the FIFO-restriction is violated. We show in this section that both versions (existential and universal) of the local-boundedness problem for nMSCs can be solved in polynomial time, provided that the nMSC M satisfies the FIFO-restriction, i.e., flat(M) satisfies the FIFO-restriction. Of course, the algorithms must exploit the hierarchy, since nMSCs can be exponentially more succinct than the MSCs they define (i.e., a module M_k of M may have exponentially many copies in the MSC flat(M)).

For the further consideration let us fix an nMSC $M = (M_k)_{1 \leq k \leq m}$. For $1 \leq k \leq m$ let $\leadsto_k$ (resp. $\prec_k$) be the $\leadsto$-relation (resp. visual order) associated with flat(M_k) (recall the definition of $\leadsto$ in Section 3). Furthermore let $\prec = \prec_1$, $\leadsto = \leadsto_1$, and $P = P(M_1)$.

Lemma 7. *Let M satisfy the FIFO-restriction. Let $\mathcal{E}$ be the set of events of some occurrence of* flat(M_k) *in* flat(M), $1 \leq k \leq m$. *Then $\leadsto \cap (\mathcal{E} \times \mathcal{E}) = \leadsto_k$.*

Note that Lemma 7 does not hold for the case where the nMSC violates the FIFO-restriction. In this case different occurrences of the MSC flat(M_k) in flat(M) may have different local $\leadsto$-relations depending on their context.

Lemma 8. *Suppose that the relation $\leadsto \cup \prec$ contains a cycle. Then for some $k \leq |P|$ there exists a cycle of the form $r_1 \leadsto s_1 \prec r_2 \leadsto s_2 \prec \cdots \prec r_k \leadsto s_k \prec r_1$.*

In the following we call an event e of the MSC flat(M) a *top level event* if it belongs to the events of the module M_1 (but not to the events of some module M_k with $k > 1$).

Theorem 7. *Let $Q \in \{\forall, \exists\}$. The following problem can be solved in polynomial time:*

INPUT: nMSC M satisfying the FIFO-restriction and positive integer b.
QUESTION: Is flat(M) Q_{loc}^b*-bounded?*

Proof. We will only consider existential-local boundedness. For universal-local boundedness we can argue similarly. By Lemma 2 it suffices to verify that the transitive closure of the relation $\prec \cup \leadsto$ associated with the MSC flat(M) is acyclic. Of course, we cannot explicitly generate the $\leadsto$-edges, since there can be exponentially many $\leadsto$-edges leading out of a copy of M_i within M_k, or vice versa. By Lemma 8 it suffices to look for a cycle containing at most $|P|$ new $\leadsto$-edges.

Let us first describe how we can compute the set $\mathrm{Succ}_\prec(e) = \{f \mid e \prec f\}$ of $\prec$-successors of e for any given event e of flat(M), described by the position on its process. Since this set may be of exponential size, we describe it by a tuple $(k_p)_{p \in P}$ of positions, one for each process p. The position k_p corresponds to the first event $f \in \lambda^{-1}(p)$ with $e \prec f$. Note that if $e \prec f$ then there exists a chain $e = e_1 \preceq f_1 \prec e_2 \prec f_2 \prec \cdots \prec f_t \prec e_{t+1} \preceq f_{t+1} = f$ with $\lambda(e_i) = \lambda(f_i)$, $m(f_i) = e_{i+1}$, and $t < |P|$. Here $\preceq$ denotes the reflexive closure of the visual order $\prec$. The computation of $\mathrm{Succ}_{\prec}(e)$ can be performed by induction on t. We start by setting $k_{\lambda(e)}$ to the direct successor of e on process $\lambda(e)$ and $k_{\lambda(m(e))} = m(e)$ if e is a send, all k_p that are not defined in this way are set to ∞ For the inductive step we determine for all $k_p < \infty$ and all processes $q \neq p$ the first send s of type $S(p, q)$ with $s \succeq k_p$, and we compute the minimum between its matching receive and k_q. This step can be performed in time $O(|P|^3 |M|)$.

A similar argument applies when we want to determine whether there is a cycle in $\rightsquigarrow \cup \prec$. Of course we cannot check for every event e of $\mathrm{flat}(M)$ whether $e \in \mathrm{Succ}_{(\prec \cup \rightsquigarrow)^+}(e)$, since there might be exponentially many such events. But in fact it suffices to show that it can be checked in polynomial time whether $\rightsquigarrow \cup \prec$ contains a cycle that visits some top level event of $\mathrm{flat}(M)$, because then we may apply this polynomial time algorithm to each of the nMSCs $(M_k)_{i \le k \le n}$ for $1 \le i \le n$. For the correctness of the resulting algorithm we have to use Lemma 7 which ensures that $\prec \cup \rightsquigarrow$ contains a cycle which is completely contained in some occurrence of $\mathrm{flat}(M_k)$ within $\mathrm{flat}(M)$ if and only if $\prec_k \cup \rightsquigarrow_k$ contains a cycle.

Thus, let e be some top level event of $\mathrm{flat}(M)$. We will compute $\mathrm{Succ}_{(\prec \cup \rightsquigarrow)^+}(e)$ and test whether $e \in \mathrm{Succ}_{(\prec \cup \rightsquigarrow)^+}(e)$. We start with $\mathrm{Succ}_{(\prec \cup \rightsquigarrow)^+}(e) = \mathrm{Succ}_{\prec}(e)$, represented by the tuple of positions $(k_p)_{p \in P}$. For the inductive step we determine for all $k_q < \infty$ and all processes $p \neq q$ the first receive r of type $R(p, q)$ with $r \succeq k_q$, and we compute the send s of type $S(p, q)$ with $r \rightsquigarrow s$. Then we compute for each such s the set $\mathrm{Succ}_{\prec}(s)$ and we build the minima with $(k_p)_{p \in P}$ on every process. The overall running time is of order $O(|P|^4 |M|^2)$. $\square$

6   Fixed Number of Processes

In practice, the set of processes of an MSC can be much smaller than the number of messages. Hence we are interested in the complexity of our problem when the number of processes is fixed. The main result of this section states that for a fixed number of processes all the variants of the channel boundedness problem can be solved in polynomial time (more precisely in nondeterministic logspace).

Theorem 8. *Let $Q \in \{\forall, \exists\}$ and $Y \in \{\mathrm{glob}, \mathrm{loc}\}$. Let P be a fixed set of processes. The following problem is solvable in polynomial time (precisely, it is NL-complete):*

INPUT: HMSC M over the set of processes P and positive integer b.
QUESTION: Is M Q_Y^b-bounded?

7   Summary and Open Problems

Table 1 summarizes our results for boundedness problems for finite MSCs and HMSCs, for which we precisely determined the tractable boundedness problems. Concerning nMSCs we have shown that the two local-boundedness problems can be decided in polynomial time. The precise complexity of the two global-boundedness problems remains open for nMSCs. An NP-lower bound for existential-global-boundedness follows trivially from the NP-lower bound for finite MSCs. Concerning the upper bound we can only prove membership in PSPACE. For universal-global-boundedness we can prove membership in coNP for nMSCs, but the existence of a polynomial time algorithm remains open. Another interesting problem might be to investigate the complexity of boundedness problems for a fixed buffer-bound b, which means that b does not contribute to the input size. One might expect that the complexity of boundedness problems decreases under this restriction.

Table 1. Complexity results for finite MSCs and HMSCs

finite MSCs	$\exists$	$\forall$
global	NP-complete	P
local	P	P
local (nMSC)	P	P

HMSCs	$\exists$	$\forall$
global	NP-complete	coNP-complete
local	P	coNP-complete

References

1. B. Genest, and A. Muscholl. Pattern Matching and Membership for Hierarchical Message Sequence Charts. To appear in *Proc. of LATIN 2002*.
2. J. G. Henriksen, M. Mukund, K. N. Kumar, and P. Thiagarajan. On message sequence graphs and finitely generated regular MSC languages. In *Proc. of ICALP'00*, LNCS 1853, pp. 675–686, 2000.
3. J. G. Henriksen, M. Mukund, K. N. Kumar, and P. Thiagarajan. Regular collections of message sequence charts. In *Proc. of MFCS'00*, LNCS 1893, pp. 675–686, 2000.
4. E. L. Lawler. *Combinatorial Optimization: Networks and Matroids*. Holt, Rinehart and Winston, 1976.
5. R. Morin. On regular message sequence chart languages and relationships to Mazurkiewicz trace theory. In *Proc. of FoSSaCS'01*, LNCS 2030, pp. 332–346, 2001.
6. M. Mukund, K. N. Kumar, and M. A. Sohoni. Synthesizing distributed finite-state systems from MSCs. In *Proc. of CONCUR'00*, LNCS 1877, pp. 521–535, 2000.
7. A. Muscholl, D. Peled, and Z. Su. Deciding properties for message sequence charts. In *Proc. of FoSSaCS'98*, LNCS 1378, pp. 226–242, 1998.
8. C. H. Papadimitriou. *Computational Complexity*. Addison Wesley, 1994.
9. R. Sethi. Complete register allocation problems. *SIAM Journal on Computing*, 4(3):226–248, 1975.
10. K. Simon. On minimum flow and transitive reduction. In *Proc. of ICALP'88*, LNCS 317, pp. 535–546, 1988.

The Informatic Derivative at a Compact Element

Keye Martin

Oxford University Computing Laboratory
Wolfson Building, Parks Road, Oxford OX1 3QD
kmartin@comlab.ox.ac.uk
http://web.comlab.ox.ac.uk/oucl/work/keye.martin

Abstract. We extend the informatic derivative to compact elements in domains. This allows one to quantitatively analyze processes which manipulate both continuous and discrete data in a *uniform* manner.

1 Introduction

One of the important aspects of the measurement formalism in domain theory is its informatic derivative: Given a map $f : D \to D$ on a domain with a measurement (D, μ), its informatic derivative is given by

$$df_\mu(p) := \lim_{x \to p} \frac{\mu f(x) - \mu f(p)}{\mu x - \mu p},$$

where the limit is taken in the μ topology at a point p which is not isolated in the μ topology on D.

As one might expect, this idea was applied to establish the first relationship between domain theory and the differential calculus [2], where it was shown that it could be used to give a purely domain theoretic account of C^1 mappings on the real line. But it has other applications which appear to be more promising. One of these is that it allows us to make sense of the idea "rate of change" with respect to a measurement. For instance, one can discuss the rate at which a mapping on a domain converges to its fixed point. This has natural applications in the study of what one might term continuous phenomena, like in numerical analysis, where it provides a uniform approach to calculating rates of convergence – while some rates of convergence may be determined using the classical derivative (an example of an informatic derivative), some of the most well-known methods for zero finding in all of numerical analysis have rates of convergence that arise as informatic derivatives which are *not* classical (in the sense of calculus).

But if one looks closely at the definition of the informatic derivative above, it has a computationally restrictive aspect: The requirement that p not be isolated in the μ topology. This is equivalent to saying that p must not be a *compact* element of D. From the mathematical viewpoint, one does not object to this: Mathematics offers us no way of obtaining unique 'limits' at isolated points of topological spaces. Nevertheless, computationally, it is easy to write down simple examples of mappings on domains, which *should have* derivatives, but are excluded simply because they work only with compact elements.

M. Nielsen and U. Engberg (Eds.): Fossacs 2002, LNCS 2303, pp. 310–325, 2002.

For instance, on the domain of lists $[S]$, the map rest: $[S] \to [S]$ which removes the first element from a nonempty list, and sends the empty list to itself, satisfies

$$\mu \operatorname{rest}(x) = \mu(x) - 1$$

for $x \neq [\,]$, where μ is the length measurement. Thus, we ought to be able to say that $d(\operatorname{rest})_\mu(x) = 1$ for $x \neq [\,]$.

In this paper, we offer an extension of the definition of informatic derivative which applies at compact elements (as long as they are not minimal). One of the benefits of this work is that we are finally able to understand the sense in which the asymptotic notions of complexity used in numerical analysis (rates of convergence) are the same as those used in the analysis of 'discrete' algorithms (for example, list processing). Another is that we have identified ideas which allow us to systematically calculate both of these complexity notions in a uniform manner. But what appears more pertinent than either of these is that we are (slowly but surely) developing a very real understanding of informatic rates of change.

2   Background

2.1   Domain Theory

Let $(P, \sqsubseteq)$ be a partially ordered set or *poset* [1]. A nonempty subset $S \subseteq P$ is *directed* if $(\forall x, y \in S)(\exists z \in S)\, x, y \sqsubseteq z$. The *supremum* $\bigsqcup S$ of $S \subseteq P$ is the least of its upper bounds when it exists. A *dcpo* is a poset in which every directed set has a supremum.

For elements x, y of a dcpo D, we write $x \ll y$ iff for every directed subset S with $y \sqsubseteq \bigsqcup S$, we have $x \sqsubseteq s$, for some $s \in S$. In the special case that this occurs for $x = y$, we call x *compact*. The set of compact elements in D is $K(D)$.

Definition 1. Let $(D, \sqsubseteq)$ be a dcpo. We set

- $\mathord{\downarrow} x := \{y \in D : y \ll x\}$ and $\mathord{\uparrow} x := \{y \in D : x \ll y\}$
- $\mathord{\downarrow} x := \{y \in D : y \sqsubseteq x\}$ and $\mathord{\uparrow} x := \{y \in D : x \sqsubseteq y\}$

and say D is *continuous* if $\mathord{\downarrow} x$ is directed with supremum x for each $x \in D$. A *domain* is a continuous dcpo.

The *Scott topology* on a domain D has as a basis all sets of the form $\mathord{\uparrow} x$ for $x \in D$. A function $f : D \to E$ between domains is *Scott continuous* if it reflects Scott open sets. This is equivalent to saying that f is *monotone*,

$$(\forall x, y \in D)\, x \sqsubseteq y \Rightarrow f(x) \sqsubseteq f(y),$$

and that it *preserves directed suprema*:

$$f\Big(\bigsqcup S\Big) = \bigsqcup f(S),$$

for all directed $S \subseteq D$.

Definition 2. A subset B of a dcpo D is a *basis* for D if $B \cap \downarrow x$ contains a directed subset with supremum x, for each $x \in D$. A dcpo is *algebraic* if its compact elements form a basis. A dcpo is ω-*continuous* if it has a countable basis.

The next definition is fundamental in this paper: Splittings model the recursive part of an algorithm [4].

Definition 3. A *splitting* on a poset D is a function $s : D \to D$ with $x \sqsubseteq s(x)$ for all $x \in D$.

2.2   Examples of Domains

In this section, we give examples of domains that we will use in this paper.

Example 1. Orders on the naturals.

(i) The naturals $\mathbb{N}^\infty = \mathbb{N} \cup \{\infty\}$ in their usual order with a top element ∞:
$$(\forall x, y \in \mathbb{N}^\infty)\ x \sqsubseteq y \Leftrightarrow (x \le y\ \&\ x, y \in \mathbb{N})\ \text{or}\ y = \infty.$$

(ii) The naturals $\mathbb{N}^* = \mathbb{N}$ in their dual order: $x \sqsubseteq y \Leftrightarrow y \le x$.
(iii) The naturals $\mathbb{N}^\flat = \mathbb{N}$ ordered flatly: $x \sqsubseteq y \Leftrightarrow x = y$.

Example 2. The *interval domain* is the collection of compact intervals of the real line
$$\mathbb{IR} = \{[a, b] : a, b \in \mathbb{R}\ \&\ a \le b\}$$
ordered under reverse inclusion
$$[a, b] \sqsubseteq [c, d] \Leftrightarrow [c, d] \subseteq [a, b]$$
is an ω-continuous dcpo. The supremum of a directed set $S \subseteq \mathbb{IR}$ is $\bigcap S$, while the approximation relation is characterized by $I \ll J \Leftrightarrow J \subseteq \text{int}(I)$. A countable basis for $\mathbb{IR}$ is given by $\{[p, q] : p, q \in \mathbb{Q}\ \&\ p \le q\}$.

Our final example is the domain $[S]$ of finite lists over a poset $(S, \le)$.

Definition 4. A *list* over S is a function $x : \{1, ..., n\} \to S$, for $n \ge 0$. The *length* of a list x is $|\text{dom } x|$. The set of all (finite) lists over S is $[S]$. A list x is *sorted* if x is monotone as a map between posets.

A list x can be written as $[x(1), ..., x(n)]$, where the *empty list* (the list of length 0) is written $[\ ]$. We also write lists as $a :: x$, where $a \in S$ is the *first element* of the list $a :: x$, and $x \in [S]$ is the *rest* of the list $a :: x$. For example, the list $[1, 2, 3]$ is written $1 :: [2, 3]$.

Definition 5. A set $K \subseteq \mathbb{N}$ is *convex* if $a, b \in K\ \&\ a \le x \le b \Rightarrow x \in K$. Given a finite convex set $K \subseteq \mathbb{N}$, the map $\text{scale}(K) : \{1, ..., |K|\} \to K$ given by
$$\text{scale}(K)(i) = \min K + i - 1$$
relabels the elements of K so that they begin with one.

Definition 6. For $x, y \in [S]$, x is a *sublist* of y iff there is a convex subset $K \subseteq \{1, \ldots, \text{length } y\}$ such that $y \circ \text{scale } K = x$.

Example 3. If $L = [1, 2, 3, 4, 5, 6]$, then $[1, 2, 3], [4, 5, 6], [3, 4, 5], [2, 3, 4], [3, 4], [5]$ and $[]$ are all sublists of L. However, $[1, 4, 5, 6], [1, 3]$ and $[2, 4]$ are *not* sublists of L.

Lemma 1 (Martin [2]). *The finite lists $[S]$ over a set S, ordered under reverse convex containment,*

$$x \sqsubseteq y \Leftrightarrow y \text{ is a sublist of } x,$$

form an algebraic dcpo with $[S] = K([S])$. Thus, $[S]$ is ω-continuous iff S is countable.

The order on $[S]$ is based on computational progress: Intuitively, it is easier to solve a problem on input $[]$ than for any other input x, hence $x \sqsubseteq []$.

2.3 Content and the μ Topology

It is during the study of measurement [2] that one encounters for the first time the μ topology on a domain. Let $[0, \infty)^*$ denote the domain of nonnegative reals in the order opposite to their natural one.

Definition 7. A Scott continuous map $\mu : D \to [0, \infty)^*$ on a domain *measures* the elements in a set $X \subseteq D$ when for all $x \in X$, if (x_n) is a sequence with $x_n \ll x$ then

$$\lim_{n \to \infty} \mu x_n = \mu x \Rightarrow \bigsqcup_{n \in \mathbb{N}} x_n = x,$$

and this supremum is directed. We write this as $\mu \to \sigma_X$.

The terminology used in [2] and [5] is different, but the ideas are identical. The next result is fundamental and we use it often (implicitly).

Proposition 1 (Martin [2]). *Let $\mu : D \to [0, \infty)^*$ be a map that measures $X \subseteq D$. Then for all $x \in D$ and $y \in X$, we have $x \sqsubseteq y$ and $\mu x = \mu y \Rightarrow x = y$.*

For the sake of formality, we mention the following.

Definition 8. A *measurement* is a map $\mu : D \to [0, \infty)^*$ which measures the set $\ker \mu := \{x \in D : \mu x = 0\}$.

If x is an approximation of r, that is, $x \ll r$, then $|\mu x - \mu r|$ is a measure of how closely x approximates r, while μx is a measure of the uncertainty in x. If we obtain an improved approximation y of r, $x \sqsubseteq y \ll r$, then y should be more certain than x. Hence $\mu x \geq \mu y$.

Definition 9. The μ *topology* on a continuous dcpo D has as a basis all sets of the form $\uparrow x \cap \downarrow y$ where $x, y \in D$. It is denoted μ_D.

To clarify the relation between the two ideas, given a measurement $\mu \to \sigma_D$, consider the elements ε-close to $x \in D$, for $\varepsilon > 0$, given by

$$\mu_\varepsilon(x) := \{y \in D : y \sqsubseteq x \ \& \ |\mu x - \mu y| < \varepsilon\}.$$

Regardless of the measurement we use, these sets are *always* a basis for the μ topology.

Theorem 1 (Martin [2]). *For a Scott continuous mapping $\mu : D \to [0, \infty)^*$, $\mu \to \sigma_D$ iff $\{\mu_\varepsilon(x) : x \in D \ \& \ \varepsilon > 0\}$ is a basis for the μ topology on D.*

This also turns out to be the topology one needs to define rates of change on a domain. This comes as something of a surprise since the μ topology is *always zero-dimensional and Hausdorff*. In the next definition, the limit is taken with respect to the μ topology.

Definition 10. Let D be a domain with a map $\mu : D \to [0, \infty)^*$ that measures $X \subseteq D$. If $f : D \to \mathbb{R}$ is a map and $p \in X$ is not a compact element of D, then

$$df_\mu(p) := \lim_{x \to p} \frac{f(x) - f(p)}{\mu x - \mu p}$$

is called *the informatic derivative* of f at p with respect to μ, provided that it exists.

If the limit above exists, then it is unique, since the μ topology is Hausdorff, and we are taking a limit at a point that is not *isolated*: It is not difficult to show that $\{p\}$ is μ open iff p is compact. Notice too the importance of strict monotonicity of μ in Prop. 1: Without it, we could not define the derivative.

Definition 11. Let $f : D \to D$ be a function on a domain (D, μ) with a map μ that measures D at $p \in D \setminus K(D)$. If

$$df_\mu(p) := d(\mu f)_\mu(p)$$

exists, then we call this number *the informatic derivative* of f at p with respect to μ.

Our first example of this comes from calculus, and in fact provided the first relationship between domain theory and the differential calculus [2].

Theorem 2 (Martin [2]). *Let $f : \mathbb{R} \to \mathbb{R}$ be a continuous map on the real line with $p \in \mathbb{R}$. If $f'(p)$ exists, then*

$$d\bar{f}_\mu[p] = |f'(p)|$$

where $\bar{f}(x) = f(x)$ is the canonical extension of f to $\mathbb{IR}$ and $\mu[a, b] = b - a$.

In particular, any iterative process with a classical derivative has an informatic derivative, and from the complexity viewpoint, they are equal. Here is an example of a process with an informatic derivative that is *not* classical.

Example 4. The Bisection Method. To a continuous map $f : [a, b] \to \mathbb{R}$, we may assign the splitting

$$\text{split}_f : \mathbf{IR} \to \mathbf{IR}$$

$$\text{split}_f(x) = \begin{cases} \text{left}(x) & \text{if left}(x) \in C(f); \\ \text{right}(x) & \text{otherwise;} \end{cases}$$

where $C(f) = \{[a, b] \in \mathbf{IR} : f(a) \cdot f(b) \leq 0\}$, $\text{left}[x, y] = [x, (x + y)/2]$ and $\text{right}[x, y] = [(x + y)/2, y]$. At any $[r] \in \text{fix}(\text{split}_f)$, its rate of convergence is given by

$$d(\text{split}_f)[r] = 1/2.$$

Notice that this informatic derivative is *not* a classical derivative.

Other examples appear in [2], [6] and [5]. To be brief, let us say this: The *smaller* the derivative of a map on a domain at a fixed point, the quicker the convergence.

3   The Derivative at an Isolated Point

The reason that the informatic derivative requires points which are not isolated is that there must be enough *nontrivial* μ open sets around p so that we can take a limit in the formal sense of topology – without enough nontrivial open sets, a limit may not be unique.

However, any point $p \notin \min(D) := \{x \in D : \downarrow x = \{x\}\}$ can be approximated from below using the nontrivial μ open subsets of D which are contained in $\downarrow p$ and which themselves contain p and at least one other element:

$$\text{approx}_\mu(p) = \{V \in \mu D : p \in V \subseteq \downarrow p \text{ and } V \neq \{p\}\}.$$

Thus, the existence of approximations is not the problem – the problem is that we need a concept more applicable than 'limit'.

Definition 12. Let $f : D \to \mathbb{R}$ be a function and $p \in D$. We set

$$d^+ f_\mu(p) := \sup\{c : (\exists V \in \text{approx}_\mu(p))(\forall x \in V) \, f(x) - f(p) \geq c \cdot (\mu x - \mu p)\}$$

and

$$d^- f_\mu(p) := \inf\{c : (\exists V \in \text{approx}_\mu(p))(\forall x \in V) \, f(x) - f(p) \leq c \cdot (\mu x - \mu p)\},$$

provided p is not a *minimal element* of D, i.e., $p \notin \min(D)$.

Trying to conceptualize these quantities isn't such a good idea, so we resort to theorem proving.

Theorem 3. *Let $f : D \to \mathbb{R}$ be a function with $p \in D \setminus K(D)$. Then $df_\mu(p)$ exists iff $d^+ f_\mu(p)$ exists, $d^- f_\mu(p)$ exists and $d^- f_\mu(p) \leq d^+ f_\mu(p)$. In either case, we have $df_\mu(p) = d^+ f_\mu(p) = d^- f_\mu(p)$.*

Proof. First suppose that $df_\mu(p)$ exists. Then by definition, for each $\varepsilon > 0$ there is a $\delta > 0$ such that

$$(\forall x)\, x \sqsubseteq p \ \& \ 0 < |\mu x - \mu p| < \delta \Rightarrow \left| \frac{f(x) - f(p)}{\mu x - \mu p} - df_\mu(p) \right| < \varepsilon.$$

Because μ measures D at p and p is not compact,

$$\mu_\delta(p) := \{x : x \sqsubseteq p \ \& \ |\mu x - \mu p| < \delta\} \in \mathrm{approx}_\mu(p).$$

Thus, the sets used in the definition of $d^+ f_\mu(p)$ and $d^- f_\mu(p)$ are nonempty since for the set $V = \mu_\delta(p)$, we can write

$$(\forall x \in V)\, f(x) - f(p) \geq c^+ \cdot (\mu x - \mu p) \ \& \ f(x) - f(p) \leq c^- \cdot (\mu x - \mu p),$$

where $c^+ = df_\mu(p) - \varepsilon$ and $c^- = df_\mu(p) + \varepsilon$. But now *if* we can show that $d^+ f_\mu(p)$ and $d^- f_\mu(p)$ exist, the argument just given applies to give

$$d^- f_\mu(p) \leq df_\mu(p) + \varepsilon \ \text{ and } \ df_\mu(p) - \varepsilon \leq d^+ f_\mu(p),$$

for each $\varepsilon > 0$, and hence that $d^- f_\mu(p) \leq df_\mu(p) \leq d^+ f_\mu(p)$.

With this last remark in mind, suppose we have numbers c^+, c^- and μ open sets $V^+, V^- \in \mathrm{approx}_\mu(p)$ such that

$$(\forall x \in V^+)\, f(x) - f(p) \geq c^+ \cdot (\mu x - \mu p)$$

and

$$(\forall x \in V^-)\, f(x) - f(p) \leq c^- \cdot (\mu x - \mu p).$$

Because p is not compact, we have $V = V^+ \cap V^- \in \mathrm{approx}_\mu(p)$ and

$$c^+ \leq \frac{f(x) - f(p)}{\mu x - \mu p} \leq c^-$$

for all $x \in V \setminus \{p\}$. Letting $x \to p$ in the μ topology, we have $c^+ \leq df_\mu(p) \leq c^-$. Then $d^- f_\mu(p)$ and $d^+ f_\mu(p)$ both exist and satisfy $d^+ f_\mu(p) \leq df_\mu(p) \leq d^- f_\mu(p)$. Now our earlier remark applies, leaving $d^+ f_\mu(p) = df_\mu(p) = d^- f_\mu(p)$.

For the other direction, suppose $d^- f_\mu(p)$ and $d^+ f_\mu(p)$ both exist and satisfy $d^- f_\mu(p) \leq d^+ f_\mu(p)$. First we show that $d^- f_\mu(p) = d^+ f_\mu(p)$. Let $\varepsilon > 0$. Then there are numbers c^+, c^- and μ open sets $V^+, V^- \in \mathrm{approx}_\mu(p)$ such that

$$d^+ f_\mu(p) - \varepsilon/2 < c^+ \leq d^+ f_\mu(p) \ \text{ and } \ (\forall x \in V^+)\, f(x) - f(p) \geq c^+ \cdot (\mu x - \mu p)$$

and

$$d^- f_\mu(p) \leq c^- < d^- f_\mu(p) + \varepsilon/2 \ \text{ and } \ (\forall x \in V^-)\, f(x) - f(p) \leq c^- \cdot (\mu x - \mu p).$$

Let $V = V^+ \cap V^- \in \mathrm{approx}_\mu(p)$. Then the inequality

$$d^+ f_\mu(p) - \varepsilon/2 < c^+ \leq \frac{f(x) - f(p)}{\mu x - \mu p} \leq c^- < d^- f_\mu(p) + \varepsilon/2$$

holds for all x in the *nonempty* set $V \setminus \{p\}$. Using this inequality once, we obtain $d^+ f_\mu(p) < d^- f_\mu(p) + \varepsilon$ for each $\varepsilon > 0$ and hence $d^+ f_\mu(p) \leq d^- f_\mu(p)$, which gives $d^- f_\mu(p) = d^+ f_\mu(p)$. But going back to the inequality a second time reveals that the number $d := d^+ f_\mu(p) = d^- f_\mu(p)$ has the following property: For all $\varepsilon > 0$ there is a μ open set $V \in \text{approx}_\mu(p)$ such that

$$(\forall x \in V)\ x \neq p \implies d - \varepsilon < \frac{f(x) - f(p)}{\mu x - \mu p} < d + \varepsilon.$$

This is precisely the statement that $df_\mu(p)$ exists and is equal to d.   □

The previous theorem justifies the following definition.

Definition 13. Let $f : D \to \mathbb{R}$ be a function on a domain D with a measurement μ which measures D at $p \in D \setminus \min(D)$. If $d^- f_\mu(p)$ exists, $d^+ f_\mu(p)$ exists and $d^- f_\mu(p) \leq d^+ f_\mu(p)$, then we define

$$df_\mu(p) := d^+ f_\mu(p)$$

and call this number the *informatic derivative* of f at p.

By Theorem 3, the new definition and the old definition agree in the continuous case $(p \notin K(D))$. We now turn our attention to the discrete case $(p \in K(D))$.

Theorem 4. *Let $f : D \to \mathbb{R}$ be a function on an algebraic domain D with a measurement μ that measures D at $p \in K(D) \setminus \min(D)$. Then the following are equivalent:*

(i) *The derivative $df_\mu(p)$ exists.*
(ii) *The supremum*

$$\sup\left\{ \frac{f(x) - f(p)}{\mu x - \mu p} : x \in K(D) \cap {\downarrow} p, x \neq p \right\}$$

exists and the infimum

$$\inf\left\{ \frac{f(x) - f(p)}{\mu x - \mu p} : x \in K(D) \cap {\downarrow} p, x \neq p \right\}$$

exists.

In either case, the value of $d^+ f_\mu(p)$ is the supremum in (ii), while the value of $d^- f_\mu(p)$ is the infimum in (ii).

Proof. (i) $\Rightarrow$ (ii): By assumption, $d^+ f_\mu(p)$ and $d^- f_\mu(p)$ both exist. We first show that the supremum exists. Let $x \in K(D)$ with $x \sqsubseteq p$ and $x \neq p$. Then

$$f(t) - f(p) \geq c \cdot (\mu t - \mu p)$$

for all $t \in V = \{x, p\} \in \operatorname{approx}_\mu(p)$, where $c = (f(x) - f(p))/(\mu x - \mu p)$. Since $d^+ f_\mu(p)$ exists, we have $c \leq d^+ f_\mu(p)$. But then the set of all such c is bounded from above by $d^+ f_\mu(p)$. Thus, its supremum satisfies

$$\sup \left\{ \frac{f(x) - f(p)}{\mu x - \mu p} : x \in K(D) \cap \downarrow p, x \neq p \right\} \leq d^+ f_\mu(p).$$

Similarly, since $d^- f_\mu(p)$ exists, the same argument gives $d^- f_\mu(p) \leq c$, which implies that the set of all such c has an infimum which satisifes

$$d^- f_\mu(p) \leq \inf \left\{ \frac{f(x) - f(p)}{\mu x - \mu p} : x \in K(D) \cap \downarrow p, x \neq p \right\}.$$

(ii) $\Rightarrow$ (i): To show that $df_\mu(p)$ exists, we must show that $d^+ f_\mu(p)$ exists, $d^- f_\mu(p)$ exists and that $d^- f_\mu(p) \leq d^+ f_\mu(p)$. We establish this by proving that $d^+ f_\mu(p)$ is the supremum in (ii), while $d^- f_\mu(p)$ is the infimum in (ii).

First the case of $d^+ f_\mu(p)$. To start, recall the definition of $d^+ f_\mu(p)$,

$$d^+ f_\mu(p) := \sup\{c : (\exists V \in \operatorname{approx}_\mu(p))(\forall x \in V)\, f(x) - f(p) \geq c \cdot (\mu x - \mu p)\}$$

Because D is algebraic and p is a compact element that is not minimal, the set of all such c is nonempty. To see why, let $y \sqsubseteq p$ be an element with $y \neq p$, which exists since p is not minimal. By algebraicity of D, y can be approximated by some compact element $x \ll y \sqsubseteq p$. Then as in the proof of (i) $\Rightarrow$ (ii), we have a μ open set $V = \{x, p\} \in \operatorname{approx}_\mu(p)$ such that

$$(\forall t \in V)\, f(t) - f(p) \geq c \cdot (\mu t - \mu p),$$

where $c = (f(x) - f(p))/(\mu x - \mu p)$.

Now that we know this set is nonempty, let $V \in \operatorname{approx}_\mu(p)$ and c be any constant such that $f(x) - f(p) \geq c \cdot (\mu x - \mu p)$ for all $x \in V$. Let $y \in V$ be some element with $y \neq p$, which exists since $V \neq \{p\}$. By the algebraicity of D, y is the supremum of compact elements, and since V is μ open, there is some compact element $x \ll y$ with $x \in V$. Then $x \sqsubseteq p$ since $V \subseteq \downarrow p$, and $x \neq p$, since $y \neq p$. But this means

$$\frac{f(x) - f(p)}{\mu x - \mu p} \geq c,$$

and since we know that the set of all such elements has a supremum,

$$c \leq \sup \left\{ \frac{f(x) - f(p)}{\mu x - \mu p} : x \in K(D) \cap \downarrow p, x \neq p \right\},$$

which means that the set of all such c is bounded from above, and thus that $d^+ f_\mu(p)$ exists and satisifes

$$d^+ f_\mu(p) \leq \sup \left\{ \frac{f(x) - f(p)}{\mu x - \mu p} : x \in K(D) \cap \downarrow p, x \neq p \right\}.$$

The other inequality was established in the proof of (i) $\Rightarrow$ (ii), assuming only the existence of $d^+ f_\mu(p)$. The dual argument handles the case of $d^- f_\mu(p)$. $\square$

Finally, the definition of derivative for selfmaps on a domain D.

Definition 14. Let $f : D \to D$ be a function on a domain (D, μ) with a map μ that measures D at $p \in D \setminus \min(D)$. If $d(\mu f)_\mu(p)$ exists, then we write

$$df_\mu(p) := d(\mu f)_\mu(p)$$

and call this number the *informatic derivative* of f at p with respect to μ. We also set $d^* f_\mu(p) := d^*(\mu f)_\mu(p)$ for $* \in \{+, -\}$.

It is easy to extend this definition for a map $f : (D, \mu) \to (E, \lambda)$, as was done for the original formulation of the derivative in the continuous case [2], but in the present paper there are no applications warranting such an abstraction.

Example 5. Derivatives of list operations.

(i) The map first : $[S] \to [S]$, first$(a :: x) = [a]$, first$[] = []$. Using Theorem 4,

$$d(\text{first})_\mu(x) = d^+(\text{first})_\mu(x) = d^-(\text{first})_\mu(x) = 0,$$

for all $x \neq []$. At $x = []$, $d(\text{first})_\mu(x) = d^+(\text{first})_\mu(x) = 1 \geq 0 = d^-(\text{first})_\mu(x)$.

(ii) The map rest : $[S] \to [S]$, rest$(a :: x) = x$, rest$[] = []$. Using Theorem 4,

$$d(\text{rest})_\mu(x) = d^+(\text{rest})_\mu(x) = d^-(\text{rest})_\mu(x) = 1,$$

for all $x \neq []$. At $x = []$, $d(\text{rest})_\mu(x) = d^+(\text{rest})_\mu(x) = 1 \geq 0 = d^-(\text{rest})_\mu(x)$.

There is something worth pointing out before we focus on the derivative in the discrete case. The definition of $df_\mu(p)$ splits into two cases, the continuous $(p \notin K(D))$ and the discrete $(p \in K(D))$. From this bifurcation appears a remarkable duality: In the continuous case the inequality $df_\mu^+(p) \leq df_\mu^-(p)$ always holds, but $df_\mu^-(p) \leq df_\mu^+(p)$ may not; in the discrete case the opposite is true, $df_\mu^-(p) \leq df_\mu^+(p)$ always holds, but $df_\mu^+(p) \leq df_\mu^-(p)$ may not.

The results of this section allow for only one interpretation of this phenomenon: In the continuous case, the derivative is determined by *local* properties of the function; in the discrete case, the derivative is determined by *global* properties of the function.

4   Measuring the Length of an Orbit

Throughout this section, we assume that (D, μ) is an algebraic domain whose compact elements form a lower set. Some important examples of this are $\mathbb{N}^*$, $\mathbb{N}^\infty$, $[S]$, $\mathcal{P}\omega$, Σ^∞, and $[\mathbb{N} \to \mathbb{N}_\perp]$. Computationally, this is not much of an assumption.

Theorem 5 (The Mean Value Theorem). *Let $f : D \to D$ be a function on (D, μ) such that $df_\mu(p)$ exists at a compact element p. Then*

$$(\mu x - \mu p) \cdot d^- f_\mu(p) \leq \mu f(x) - \mu f(p) \leq d^+ f_\mu(p) \cdot (\mu x - \mu p),$$

for all $x \sqsubseteq p$.

Proof. Immediate by Theorem 4, in view of our assumption that the compact elements of D form a lower set. □

If a splitting r has a compact fixed point p reachable by iteration $\bigsqcup r^n(x) = p$, then the derivative of r at p can be used to provide a precise measure of the number of iterations required to get to p from an input of x. Later we will see that such quantities can play an integral role in determining the complexity of certain algorithms.

Definition 15. Let $r : D \to D$ be a splitting. An *orbit* is a sequence of iterates $(r^n x)$. An orbit is *compact* if

$$\bigsqcup_{n \geq 0} r^n(x) \in K(D).$$

The *length* of a compact orbit $(r^n x)$ is

$$|(r^n x)| := \inf\{n \geq 0 : r^{n+1}(x) = r^n(x)\}.$$

A compact orbit is *nontrivial* when $|(r^n x)| > 0$; otherwise it is a *fixed point*.

In this new language, we can say that we are interested in determining the length of nontrivial compact orbits of splittings. If $(r^n x)$ is a compact orbit, then $r^l(x)$ is a fixed point of r where $l = |(r^n x)|$. For this reason, we say that the orbit $(r^n x)$ *ends* at $p = r^l(x)$.

Lemma 2. *If a splitting $r : D \to D$ has a nontrivial compact orbit which ends at $p \in K(D)$, and $dr_\mu(p)$ exists, then $0 \leq dr_\mu(p) \leq 1$.*

Proof. By assumption, there is an $x \neq p$ with $\bigsqcup r^n(x) = p$. Since $dr_\mu(p)$ exists, by Theorem 4, we have

$$dr_\mu(p) = \sup \left\{ \frac{\mu r(x) - \mu(p)}{\mu x - \mu p} : x \in K(D) \cap \downarrow p, x \neq p \right\}.$$

Because r is a splitting, $\mu r(x) \leq \mu x$ for all x, which means that the supremum on the right is bounded above by 1. Hence $dr_\mu(p) \leq 1$.

To see that $dr_\mu(p) \geq 0$, we use the fact that $x \neq p$ and $rx \in K(D) \cap \downarrow p$, to deduce

$$0 \leq \frac{\mu r(x) - \mu p}{\mu x - \mu p} \leq dr_\mu(p),$$

which finishes the proof. □

Theorem 6. *Let r be a splitting with a nontrivial compact orbit $(r^n x)$ that ends at p. If $dr_\mu(p) = 0$, then $r(x) = p$. If $0 < dr_\mu(p) < 1$, then*

$$n \geq \left\lceil \frac{\log((\mu x - \mu p)/\varepsilon)}{\log(1/dr_\mu(p))} \right\rceil + 1 \Rightarrow |\mu r^n(x) - \mu p| < \varepsilon,$$

for any $\varepsilon > 0$.

Proof. First the case $dr_\mu(p) = 0$. Because $rx \sqsubseteq p$, we can apply the monotonicity of μ followed by the mean value theorem (5) to derive

$$0 \leq \mu r(x) - \mu p \leq 0 \cdot (\mu x - \mu p).$$

Then since μ measures the domain at p and $\mu r(x) = \mu p$, we must have $r(x) = p$.
For the other case, we simply apply the mean value theorem to obtain

$$0 \leq \mu r^n(x) - \mu p \leq (dr_\mu(p))^n (\mu x - \mu p),$$

and then the rest follows from arithmetic.   □

By the compactness of p, there is a choice of $\varepsilon > 0$ which will ensure that $|\mu r^n(x) - \mu p| < \varepsilon \Rightarrow r^n(x) = p$, but at this level of generality we cannot give a precise description of it. It depends on μ. For lists, the value is $\varepsilon = 1$.

Example 6. Let r be a splitting on $[S]$ with $0 < dr_\mu(p) < 1$ at any fixed point p. Then for any x, there is some $k \geq 0$ such that $r^k(x) = p$ is a fixed point. By the last result, doing

$$n > \left\lceil \frac{\log(\mu x - \mu p)}{\log(1/dr_\mu(p))} \right\rceil$$

iterations implies that $r^n(x) = p$.

Let's consider an important example of this type.

Example 7. Contractive list operations. For a positive integer $x > 0$, define

$$m(x) = \begin{cases} x/2 & \text{if } x \text{ even;} \\ (x+1)/2 & \text{if } x \text{ odd.} \end{cases}$$

Consider the splittings

$$\text{left}(x) = [x(1), \cdots, x(m(\mu x) - 1)]$$

$$\text{right}(x) = [x(m(\mu x) + 1), \cdots, x(\mu x)]$$

each of which takes lists of length one or less to the empty list $[\,]$. Each has a derivative at its unique fixed point $[\,]$ as follows.

First, since both of these maps are splittings and $p = [\,]$ has measure $\mu p = 0$, each has a derivative at p – it is simply a matter of determining d^+ at $[\,]$ in each case. For this, if $x \neq [\,]$, then

$$\frac{\mu \text{left}(x)}{\mu x} \leq \frac{(\mu x/2) - (1/2)}{\mu x} = \frac{1}{2} \cdot \left(1 - \frac{1}{\mu x}\right) \leq \frac{1}{2}$$

$$\frac{\mu \text{right}(x)}{\mu x} \leq \frac{\mu x/2}{\mu x} = \frac{1}{2}$$

which means $d(\text{left})_\mu[\,] = d(\text{right})_\mu[\,] = 1/2$.

Notice that the case of 'left' is much more interesting than the case of 'right.' In the former, the value of the derivative is never attained by any of the quotients $\mu \text{left}/\mu$ – it is determined by a 'limit' process which extracts global information about the mapping left.

Already we notice a relationship to processes in numerical analysis: The case $dr_\mu(p) = 0$ is an extreme form of *superlinear* convergence (extreme since in one iteration the computation finishes), while the case $0 < dr_\mu(p) < 1$ behaves just like ordinary *linear* convergence. However, unlike numerical analysis, we can actually say something about the case $dr_\mu(p) = 1$.

To do this is nontrivial, and in what follows, we seek only to illustrate the value of the informatic derivative in the discrete case by showing that the precise number of iterations required to calculate a fixed point p by iteration of a map r can be determined when $dr_\mu(p) = 1$ – a case in which classical derivatives are notorious for yielding no information.

We exploit the nature of the discrete: Given a compact element p that is not minimal, it has a natural set of *predecessors,* these are formally defined as the set of maximal elements in the dcpo $\downarrow p \setminus \{p\}$:

$$\mathrm{pred}(p) = \max(\downarrow p \setminus \{p\}).$$

To see that this makes sense, notice that $\downarrow p \setminus \{p\}$ is nonempty since p is not minimal, and is closed in the μ topology, as the intersection of μ closed sets. But a μ closed set is closed under directed suprema, and so must have at least one maximal element.

Theorem 7. *Let $r : D \to D$ be a splitting on (D, μ) with a compact fixed point $p = r(p)$ such that*

$$(\forall x) \, x \sqsubseteq p \Rightarrow \bigsqcup_{n \geq 0} r^n(x) = p.$$

If $d^+ r_\mu(x) = 1$ for all $x \sqsubseteq p$ and $d^- r_\mu(x) = 1$ for all $x \sqsubseteq p$ with $x \neq p$, then for all $x \sqsubseteq p$ with $x \neq p$, there is $q \in \mathrm{pred}(p)$ such that

$$r^n(x) = p \Leftrightarrow n = \frac{\mu x - \mu p}{\mu q - \mu p}.$$

Proof. Let $x \sqsubseteq p$ with $x \neq p$. Let $m \geq 0$ be the least integer with $r^{m+1}(x) = p$. Set $q = r^m(x)$. This element belongs to $\mathrm{pred}(p)$. To see this, first note that q belongs to the dcpo $\downarrow p \setminus \{p\}$, and so there is $z \in \mathrm{pred}(p)$ with $q \sqsubseteq z$. By assumption, $d^+ r_\mu(z) = d^- r_\mu(z) = 1$, so applying the mean value theorem at z yields

$$\mu r(q) - \mu r(z) = \mu q - \mu z.$$

But $\bigsqcup r^n(z) = p$ and $z \in \mathrm{pred}(p)$, so $r(z) = p$. And since $r(q) = p$ by definition, the expression on the left is zero, leaving $\mu q = \mu z$. Hence $q = z \in \mathrm{pred}(p)$ by strict monotonicity of μ at the point z. Now we find the length of this orbit.

By the mean value theorem applied at q, we have $\mu r(x) - \mu r(q) = \mu x - \mu q$ for $x \sqsubseteq q$. By induction, we obtain

$$\mu r^{k+1}(x) - \mu r(q) = k \cdot \mu r(q) + \mu x - (k + 1) \cdot \mu q$$

for $k \geq 0$ whenever $r^k(x) \sqsubseteq q$. Because $r(q) = p$, we can see that $r^n(x) = p$ iff $n = k + 1$, where $\mu r^{k+1}(x) - \mu r(q) = 0$. Setting the equation above to zero and solving for k yields

$$k = \frac{\mu x - \mu q}{\mu q - \mu p},$$

which means that $n = k + 1 = (\mu x - \mu p)/(\mu q - \mu p)$.   □

It is interesting to notice in the last result that if $d^- r_\mu(p) = 1$, then we *must* have $r(x) = x$ for all $x \sqsubseteq p$. Of course, our hypotheses on r rule this out since the fixed point p must be an attractor on $\downarrow p$.

Example 8. In Example 5, we saw that the map rest : $[S] \to [S]$ is an example of the sort hypothesized in Theorem 7 with $p = [\,]$. The predecessors of p are the one element lists

$$\mathrm{pred}(p) = \{[x] : x \in S\}.$$

Thus, the last theorem says that

$$\mathrm{rest}^n(x) = [\,] \Leftrightarrow n = \mu x,$$

for any $x \neq [\,]$.

5   Complexity

Due to space limitations, we cannot go into great detail about how it is that algorithms can be represented in a manner favorable to the theory presented here. However, the interested reader can consult [2] and [4]. Nevertheless, we can still give the reader a good feel for how it is that our study of the informatic derivative gives us a new perspective on the complexity of algorithms.

Example 9. Linear search. To search a list x for a key k consider

$$\mathrm{search} : [S] \times S \to \{\bot, \top\}$$

given by

$$\begin{aligned}
\mathrm{search}([\,], k) &= \bot \\
\mathrm{search}(x, k) &= \top & \text{if first } x = k, \\
\mathrm{search}(x, k) &= \mathrm{search}(\mathrm{rest}\, x, k) \text{ otherwise.}
\end{aligned}$$

Let $D = [S] \times S^\flat$ – the product of $[S]$ with the set S ordered flatly. We measure this domain as $\mu(x, k) = \mu x$. Let $r : D \to D$ be the splitting $r(x, k) = (\mathrm{rest}\, x, k)$.

On input (x, k) in the *worst case*, the number of comparisons n done by this algorithm is the same as the number of iterations needed to compute $r^n(x, k) = ([\,], k)$. Since $d^+ r_\mu(x) = 1$ for all x and $d^- r_\mu(x) = 1$ for all $x \neq ([\,], k)$, Theorem 7 applies to give

$$r^n(x, k) = ([\,], k) \Leftrightarrow n = \mu(x, k) = \mu x,$$

which helps us understand how the complexity of a discrete algorithm can be determined by the derivative of a splitting which models its iteration mechanism.

Example 10. Binary search. To search a sorted list x for a key k, we use the partially defined

$$\mathrm{bin} : [S] \times S \to \{\bot, \top\}$$

is given by

$$\mathrm{bin}([\,], k) = \bot$$
$$\mathrm{bin}(x, k) = \top \qquad\quad \text{if } \mathrm{mid}\, x = k,$$
$$\mathrm{bin}(x, k) = \mathrm{bin}(\mathrm{left}\, x, k) \quad \text{if } \mathrm{mid}\, x > k,$$
$$\mathrm{bin}(x, k) = \mathrm{bin}(\mathrm{right}\, x, k) \text{ otherwise.}$$

Again $D = [S] \times S^\flat$ and $\mu(x, k) = \mu x$. This time we consider the splitting $r : D \to D$ by

$$r(x, k) = \begin{cases} (\mathrm{left}\, x, k) & \text{if } \mathrm{mid}\, x > k; \\ (\mathrm{right}\, x, k) & \text{otherwise.} \end{cases}$$

On input (x, k) in the *worst case,* the number of comparisons n must satisfy $r^n(x, k) = ([\,], k)$. In this case, we have $dr_\mu([\,], k) = 1/2$, so by Theorem 6,

$$n \leq \left\lceil \frac{\log(\mu x)}{\log(2)} \right\rceil + 1 = \lceil \log_2(\mu x) \rceil + 1,$$

since we know that the number on the right will *guarantee* that $r^n(x, k) = ([\,], k)$.

To summarize these simple examples: We have two different algorithms which solve the same problem recursively by iterating splittings r and s, respectively, on a domain (D, μ) in an effort to compute a fixed point p. If $dr_\mu(p) < ds_\mu(p)$, then the algorithm using r is faster than the one which uses s. In the case of linear search we have $ds_\mu(p) = 1$, while for binary search we have $dr_\mu(p) = 1/2$. As we have already mentioned, this is identical to the way one compares zero finding methods in numerical analysis – by comparing the derivatives of mappings at fixed points.

6   Presentation

First, we have worked with total mappings, though the derivative works just as well on partial mappings [2]. The reason for this choice was our emphasis on the discrete setting: In it, the partial maps encountered in practice tend to have domains which are μ closed as well as μ open (hence domains in their own right).

Another issue concerns the very definition of df_μ itself. Theorem 3 is crucial in that it characterizes differentiability *independent* of its continuous component. Taking only this result as motivation for the definition of derivative leaves a few distinct possibilities. For instance, if we had called the derivative the interval $[d^- f_\mu(p), d^+ f_\mu(p)]$, we might notice more clearly (as in probability theory) the tendency of continuous information to collapse at a point. Another possibility is to say that the derivative is $d^- f_\mu(p)$. The author chose $d^+ f_\mu$ because it makes the most sense from an applied perspective. As an illustration, consider the intuitions we have established about it in this paper: Algorithms r with $dr_\mu(p) = 0$ belong to $O(1)$, those with $0 < dr_\mu(p) < 1$ belong to $O(\log n)$, while $dr_\mu(p) = 1$ indicates a process is in $O(n)$.

7   Conclusion

At first glance, an extension of the informatic derivative to the case of discrete data (compact elements) seems like an absurd idea. To begin, we have to confront the issue of essentially defining unique limits at isolated points. But even if we assume we have this, we need the new formulation to extend the previous, which means spotting a relationship between limits in the continuous world versus finite sequences of discrete objects. But what we are *taught* is that the continuous and discrete are 'fundamentally different,' and that the essence of this distinction is to be found in the sensibility of the limit concept for continuous objects, as compared to the discrete case where 'limit' has no meaning.

The existence of a derivative in the discrete case means much more than it does in the continuous case. Most results on discrete derivatives do not hold in the continuous case. Just consider a quick example: Let $r : D \to D$ be any continuous map with $p = r(p) \in K(D)$ and $dr_\mu(p) = 0$. If $x \sqsubseteq p$, then $r(x) = p$. Now compare this to the continuous case (like calculus on the real line), where one can only conclude that there is an $a \ll p$ such that $r^n(x) \to p$ for all x with $a \ll x \sqsubseteq p$. Again, this sharp contrast is due to the fact that discrete derivatives make use of *global* information, while continuous derivatives use only *local* information. Nevertheless, each is an instance of a common theme.

Finally, let us put this work in its proper perspective. It is evidence that the idea of an "informatic rate of change" is real – it is equally meaningful for understanding processes which manipulate information, the nature of the information is irrelevant (continuous/discrete) in this regard. We hope to inspire others to take a closer look at the idea. One feels certain that better approaches are possible, that much more can be said, and that many new and exciting applications await us.

References

1. S. Abramsky and A. Jung, *Domain theory*. In S. Abramsky, D. M. Gabbay, T. S. E. Maibaum, editors, Handbook of Logic in Computer Science, vol. III. Oxford University Press, 1994.
2. K. Martin, *A foundation for computation*. Ph.D. Thesis, Department of Mathematics, Tulane University, 2000.
   http://web.comlab.ox.ac.uk/oucl/work/keye.martin
3. K. Martin, *A principle of induction*. Lecture Notes in Computer Science, vol. 2142, Springer-Verlag, 2001.
4. K. Martin, *A renee equation for algorithmic complexity*. Lecture Notes in Computer Science, vol. 2215, Springer-Verlag, 2001.
5. K. Martin, *The measurement process in domain theory*. Proceedings of the 27th International Colloquium on Automata, Languages and Programming (ICALP), Lecture Notes in Computer Science, vol. 1853, Springer-Verlag, 2000.
6. K. Martin, *Powerdomains and zero finding*. Electronic Notes in Theoretical Computer Science, vol 59.3, 2001, to appear.
7. K. Martin, *Unique fixed points in domain theory*. Proceedings of MFPS XVII, Electronic Notes in Theoretical Computer Science, vol. 45, 2001.

Heterogeneous Development Graphs and Heterogeneous Borrowing

Till Mossakowski

BISS, Dept. of Computer Science, University of Bremen
till@tzi.de

Abstract. Development graphs are a tool for dealing with structured specifications in a formal program development in order to ease the management of change and reusing proofs. Often, different aspects of a software system have to be specified in different logics, since the construction of a huge logic covering all needed features would be too complex to be feasible. Therefore, we introduce *heterogeneous development graphs* as a means to cope with heterogeneous specifications.
We cover both the semantics and the proof theory of heterogeneous development graphs. A proof calculus can be obtained either by combining proof calculi for the individual logics, or by representing these in some "universal" logic like higher-order logic in a coherent way and then "borrowing" its calculus for the heterogeneous language.

1 Introduction

In an evolutionary software development process using formal specifications, typically not only implementations evolve over time, but during attempts to prove correctness (of implementations), also the *specifications* may turn out to be incorrect and therefore have to be revised. Development graphs [3] with hiding [13] have been introduced as a tool for dealing with the necessary management of change in structured formal specifications, with the goal of re-using proofs as much as possible. In this work, we extend these to deal with *heterogeneous* specifications, consisting of parts written in different logics. This is needed, since complex problems have different aspects that are best specified in different logics, while a combination of all these would become too complex in many cases. Moreover, we also aim at formal interoperability among different *tools*.

Consider the following sample specification, written in CASL-LTL [18], an extension of the Common algebraic specification language CASL [17] with a labeled transition logic. The behaviour of a buffer and a user writing into and reading from that buffer is described at a very abstract requirements level using temporal logic (cf. [2], chapter 13).

%CASL-LTL
spec SYSTEM = BUFFER **and** USER
then **dsort** *system*
     free **types** *system* ::= __ || __ (*buffer*; *user*)
             lab_system ::= *START* | *OK* | *ERROR* | *tau*

M. Nielsen and U. Engberg (Eds.): Fossacs 2002, LNCS 2303, pp. 326–341, 2002.
© Springer-Verlag Berlin Heidelberg 2002

∀s,s':SYSTEM

- $\nabla(s, \square\langle\lambda l.\neg l = ERROR\rangle)$

%% there is always a possible correct behaviour

- $s \xrightarrow{START} s' \Rightarrow \nabla(s', \diamond(\langle OK\rangle \vee \langle ERROR\rangle))$

%% after starting, always the system will eventually send out either OK
or ERROR

- $(s \xrightarrow{OK} s' \vee s \xrightarrow{ERROR} s' \Rightarrow \nabla(s', \square\langle\lambda l.\neg l = OK \vee l = ERROR\rangle))$

%% OK and ERROR are sent at most once, and it cannot happen
that both are sent

. . .

Typically, within the development process, one will need to refine the abstract
requirements and pass over to a concrete design. This could, for example, be expressed in SB-CASL [5], a state based extension of CASL following the paradigm
of abstract state machines. Here, it is possible to use assignments and sequential
and parallel composition, such that the passage to an imperative program is no
longer a big step. In order to be able to interface the SB-CASL specification with
the CASL-LTL specification above, we here use labeled transition system signature as above, which is projected from CASL-LTL to CASL with **hide** *LTL-keep*,
which means that the labeled transition system is kept (while the temporal logic
formulae are dropped). Thus, we get a heterogeneous specification, consisting
of parts written in different logics, and of inter-logic translations and inter-logic
projections (we here denote logic translations by **with** and logic projections by
hide, in analogy to CASL's translations and hidings *within* one logic).

%**SB-CASL**

System BIT
use   VALUE **then**
        {   %**CASL-LTL**
             dsort *system*
             free types *system* ::= $\_\_ || \_\_ (buffer;\ user)$
                       lab_system ::= $START \mid OK \mid ERROR \mid tau$ }
      hide   *LTL-keep*
dynamic func $Buf\_Cont : buffer$; $User\_State : user\_state$;
proc $proc\_START$; $proc\_OK$; $proc\_ERROR$; $proc\_tau$;

- $proc_START = $ **seq** $User\_State := Putting\_0$; $Buf\_Cont := Empty$ **end**
- $proc_tau = $ *if* $User\_State = Putting\_0$ *then*
                seq $User\_State := Putting\_1$;
                       $Buf\_Cont := Put(0, Buf\_Cont')$ **end**
              elseif . . .

post $proc\_tau : (Buf\_Cont || User\_State) \xrightarrow{tau} (Buf\_Cont' || User\_State')$

%%   Specify the generated LTL relation

We then have that BIT actually is a refinement of SYSTEM, which can be
expressed in the following form in SB-CASL:

view   v : { SYSTEM **hide** LTL-keep **with** SB-CASL } **to** BIT **end**
        %% BIT is a possible run of SYSTEM

The first specification within this refinement is again heterogeneous: SYS-TEM is projected from LTL-CASL to CASL (using **hide** LTL-keep) and then translated from CASL to SB-CASL (using **with** SB-CASL).

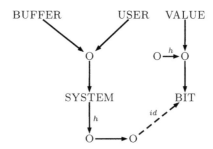

Fig. 1. Development graph for the refinement of SYSTEM into BIT

In Fig. 1 we present the development graph expressing the above refinement. Development graphs concentrate on the (homogeneous and heterogeneous) structuring of specifications and proofs, independently of the particular structuring or module-building constructs of the input language. In order to be able to use heterogeneous development graphs for performing proofs, we introduce the notion of *heterogeneous borrowing*, which is a generalization to the heterogeneous case of the notion of borrowing [8], which allows to re-use theorem provers. As an application, we will sketch how to represent various extensions of CASL within higher-order logic in a coherent way, such that heterogeneous borrowing becomes applicable. This means that we can re-use any theorem prover for higher-order logic to do theorem proving in the heterogeneous logic consisting of CASL and some of its extensions.

2   Preliminaries

When studying heterogeneous development graphs, we want to focus on the structuring and abstract from the details of the underlying logical systems. Therefore, we recall the abstract notion of institution [10].

Definition 1. *An institution* $I = (\mathbf{Sign}, \mathbf{Sen}, \mathbf{Mod}, \models)$ *consists of*

- *a category* **Sign** *of signatures,*
- *a functor* **Sen**: **Sign** $\longrightarrow$ **Set** *giving the set of sentences* **Sen**(Σ) *over each signature* Σ, *and for each signature morphism* $\sigma: \Sigma \longrightarrow \Sigma'$, *the sentence translation map* **Sen**$(\sigma):$ **Sen**$(\Sigma) \longrightarrow$ **Sen**(Σ'), *where often* **Sen**$(\sigma)(\varphi)$ *is written as* $\sigma(\varphi)$,

- a functor **Mod**: **Sign**^{op} $\longrightarrow$ $\mathcal{CAT}$ *giving the category of* models *over a given signature, and for each signature morphism* $\sigma: \Sigma \longrightarrow \Sigma'$, *the* reduct functor **Mod**(σ): **Mod**$(\Sigma') \longrightarrow$ **Mod**(Σ), *where often* **Mod**$(\sigma)(M')$ *is written as* $M'|_\sigma$,
- *a satisfaction relation* $\models_\Sigma \subseteq |\mathbf{Mod}(\Sigma)| \times \mathbf{Sen}(\Sigma)$ *for each* $\Sigma \in \mathbf{Sign}$,

such that for each $\sigma: \Sigma \longrightarrow \Sigma'$ *in* **Sign**,

$$M' \models_{\Sigma'} \sigma(\varphi) \Leftrightarrow M'|_\sigma \models_\Sigma \varphi$$

holds for each $M' \in \mathbf{Mod}(\Sigma')$ *and each* $\varphi \in \mathbf{Sen}(\Sigma)$ *(satisfaction condition).*

A *logic* is an institution equipped with an *entailment system* consisting of an entailment relation $\vdash_\Sigma \subseteq |\mathbf{Sen}(\Sigma)| \times \mathbf{Sen}(\Sigma)$, for each $\Sigma \in |\mathbf{Sign}|$, such that the following conditions are satisfied:

1. *reflexivity:* for any $\varphi \in \mathbf{Sen}(\Sigma)$, $\{\varphi\} \vdash_\Sigma \varphi$,
2. *monotonicity:* if $\Gamma \vdash_\Sigma \varphi$ and $\Gamma' \supseteq \Gamma$ then $\Gamma' \vdash_\Sigma \varphi$,
3. *transitivity:* if $\Gamma \vdash_\Sigma \varphi_i$, for $i \in I$, and $\Gamma \cup \{\varphi_i \mid i \in I\} \vdash_\Sigma \psi$, then $\Gamma \vdash_\Sigma \psi$,
4. $\vdash$*-translation:* if $\Gamma \vdash_\Sigma \varphi$, then for any $\sigma: \Sigma \longrightarrow \Sigma'$ in **Sign**, $\sigma[\Gamma] \vdash_{\Sigma'} \sigma(\varphi)$,
5. *soundness:* for any $\Sigma \in |\mathbf{Sign}|$, $\Gamma \subseteq \mathbf{Sen}(\mathbf{Sign})$ and $\varphi \in \mathbf{Sen}(\Sigma)$,

$$\Gamma \vdash_\Sigma \varphi \text{ implies } \Gamma \models_\Sigma \varphi.$$

A logic will be called *complete* if, in addition, the converse of the soundness implication holds.

We will at times need the assumption that a given institution $I = (\mathbf{Sign}, \mathbf{Sen}, \mathbf{Mod}, \models)$ has *composable signatures*, i.e. **Sign** has finite colimits, and moreover, I admits *weak amalgamation*, i.e. **Mod** maps finite colimits to weak limits. Informally, this means that if a diagram of signatures is glued together, then it is also possible to glue together families of models that are compatible w.r.t. the morphisms in the diagram.

Examples of logics that can be formalized in this sense are many-sorted equational logic, many-sorted first-order logic, higher-order logic, various lambda calculi, various modal, temporal, and object-oriented logics etc.

3   Development Graphs with Hiding

Development graphs, as introduced in [3], represent the actual state of a formal program development. They are used to encode the structured specifications in various phases of the development and make them amenable to theorem proving. Roughly speaking, each node of such a graph represents a theory such as BIT in the above example. The links of the graph define how theories can make use of other theories. Leaves in the graph correspond to basic specifications, which do not make use of other theories (e.g. VALUE). Inner nodes correspond to structured specifications which define theories importing other theories (e.g. BIT using VALUE). The corresponding links in the graph are called *definition links.* If only part of a theory shall be imported, one can use a *hiding link.* With these kinds of links, one can express a wide variety of formalisms for structured specification. E.g., there is a translation from CASL structured specifications (as used in the examples) to development graphs [3].

Fix an arbitrary institution $I = (\mathbf{Sign}, \mathbf{Sen}, \mathbf{Mod}, \models)$.

Definition 2. *A* development graph *is an acyclic directed graph $\mathcal{S} = \langle \mathcal{N}, \mathcal{L} \rangle$.*

$\mathcal{N}$ is a set of nodes. Each node $N \in \mathcal{N}$ is a tuple (Σ^N, Γ^N) such that Σ^N is a signature and $\Gamma^N \subseteq \mathbf{Sen}(\Sigma^N)$ is the set of **local axioms** *of N.*

$\mathcal{L}$ is a set of directed links, so-called **definition links***, between elements of $\mathcal{N}$. Each definition link from a node M to a node N is either*

- **global**[1] *(denoted $M \overset{\sigma}{\longrightarrow} N$), annotated with a signature morphism $\sigma : \Sigma^M \to \Sigma^N$, or*
- **hiding** *(denoted $M \overset{\sigma}{\underset{h}{\longrightarrow}} N$), annotated with a signature morphism $\sigma : \Sigma^N \to \Sigma^M$ going against the direction of the link. Typically, σ will be an inclusion, and the symbols of Σ^M not in Σ^N will be hidden.*

Definition 3. *Given a node $N \in \mathcal{N}$, its associated class $\mathbf{Mod}_S(N)$ of models (or N-models for short) consists of those Σ^N-models n for which*

- *n satisfies the local axioms Γ^N,*
- *for each $K \overset{\sigma}{\longrightarrow} N \in \mathcal{S}$, $n|_\sigma$ is a K-model,*
- *for each $K \overset{\sigma}{\underset{h}{\longrightarrow}} N \in \mathcal{S}$, n has a σ-expansion k (i.e. $k|_\sigma = n$) which is a K-model.*

Complementary to definition and hiding links, which *define* the theories of related nodes, we introduce the notion of a *theorem link* with the help of which we are able to *postulate* relations between different theories. (Global) theorem links (denoted by $N \overset{\sigma}{\dashrightarrow} M$) are the central data structure to represent proof obligations arising in formal developments. The semantics of theorem links is given by the next definition.

Definition 4. *Let $\mathcal{S}$ be a development graph and N, M be nodes in $\mathcal{S}$. $\mathcal{S}$* **implies** *a global theorem link $N \overset{\sigma}{\dashrightarrow} M$ (denoted $\mathcal{S} \models N \overset{\sigma}{\dashrightarrow} M$) iff for all $m \in \mathbf{Mod}_S(M)$, $m|_\sigma \in \mathbf{Mod}_S(N)$.*

A sound and complete (relative to an oracle for proving conservative extension) set of proof rules for deriving entailments of form

$$\mathcal{S} \vdash N \overset{\sigma}{\dashrightarrow} M$$

has been introduced in [13] (based on the assumption that the underlying logic is complete and two further technical assumptions, namely composable signatures and weak amalgamation).

Based on this, there is a development graph tool MAYA [4], keeping track of specifications, proof goals and proofs, and also supporting a management of

---

[1] There are also local links, which are omitted since they are not so essential here.

change. The tool is parameterized over a tool for the entailment system of the underlying logic, and only assumes the abstract properties of entailment systems given in their definition above.

E.g. consider the development graph of the running example (cf. Fig. 1): The theorem link from $SYSTEM$ to BIT expresses the postulation that the latter is a refinement of the former. Note that this development graph is heterogeneous because it involves different logics – hence it goes beyond the above formalization of development graphs over *one* arbitrary but fixed logic. The main goal of this paper is hence to provide a formal basis for *heterogeneous development graphs*. But before coming to this, let us first examine how to use translations between logics to *prove* theorem links.

4   Borrowing

Often, for a given logic, there is no direct proof support available. Then, a way to obtain proof support is to *encode* the logic into another logic that has good tool support. For encoding logics, we use the notion of *institution representation*.

Definition 5. *Given institutions I and J, a simple institution representation [20] (also called simple map of institutions [11]) $\mu = (\Phi, \alpha, \beta) : I \longrightarrow J$ consists of*

- *a functor $\Phi : \mathbf{Sign}^I \longrightarrow \mathbf{Pres}^{J\,2}$,*
- *a natural transformation $\alpha : \mathbf{Sen}^I \longrightarrow \mathbf{Sen}^J \circ \Phi$,*
- *a natural transformation $\beta : \mathbf{Mod}^J \circ \Phi^{op} \longrightarrow \mathbf{Mod}^I$*

such that the following representation condition *is satisfied for all $\Sigma \in \mathbf{Sign}^I$, $M' \in \mathbf{Mod}^J(\Phi(\Sigma))$ and $\varphi \in \mathbf{Sen}^I(\Sigma)$:*

$$M' \models^J_{Sig[\Phi(\Sigma)]} \alpha_\Sigma(\varphi) \Leftrightarrow \beta_\Sigma(M') \models^I_\Sigma \varphi.$$

In more detail, this means that each signature $\Sigma \in \mathbf{Sign}^I$ is translated to a presentation $\Phi(\Sigma) \in \mathbf{Pres}^J$, and each signature morphism $\sigma : \Sigma \longrightarrow \Sigma' \in \mathbf{Sign}^I$ is translated to a presentation morphism $\Phi(\sigma) : \Phi(\Sigma) \longrightarrow \Phi(\Sigma') \in \mathbf{Pres}^J$. Moreover, for each signature $\Sigma \in \mathbf{Sign}^I$, we have a sentence translation map $\alpha_\Sigma : \mathbf{Sen}^I(\Sigma) \longrightarrow \mathbf{Sen}^J(\Phi(\Sigma))$ and a model translation functor $\beta_\Sigma : \mathbf{Mod}^J(\Phi(\Sigma)) \longrightarrow \mathbf{Mod}^I(\Sigma)$. Naturality of α and β means that for any signature morphism

---

[2] A *presentation* $P = \langle \Sigma, \Gamma \rangle \in \mathbf{Pres}$ consists of a signature Σ and a finite set of sentences $\Gamma \subseteq \mathbf{Sen}(\Sigma)$ (we set $Sig[P] = \Sigma$ and $Ax[P] = \Gamma$). *Presentation morphisms* are those signature morphisms that map axioms to logical consequences.

$\sigma\colon \Sigma \longrightarrow \Sigma' \in \mathbf{Sign}^I$,

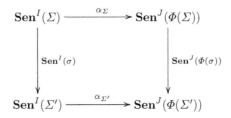

and

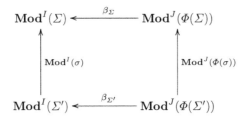

commute.

Example 1. The logic of CASL (subsorted partial first-order logic with sort generation constraints) can be encoded with a simple institution representation into second-order logic [12]. This representation can be described as a composite of three representations: The first one encodes partiality via error elements living in a supersort, the second one encodes subsorting via injections, and the third one encodes sort generation constraints via second-order induction axioms. The details can be found in [12].

Definition 6. *Given a simple institution representation* $\mu = (\Phi, \alpha, \beta)\colon I \longrightarrow J$, *we can extend it to a translation* $\hat{\mu}$ *of development graphs with hiding as follows: Given a development graph* $\mathcal{S}$, $\hat{\mu}(\mathcal{S})$ *has the same structure as* $\mathcal{S}$, *but the signature of a node* N *is changed from* Σ^N *to* $Sig[\Phi(\Sigma^N)]$, *the set of local axioms is changed from* Γ^N *to* $\alpha_{\Sigma^N}(\Gamma^N) \cup Ax[\Phi(\Sigma^N)]$. *Moreover, a signature morphism* σ *occurring in a link (of any type) is replaced by* $\Phi(\sigma)$. *Note that* $\Phi(\sigma)$ *as used above is a morphism between presentations, but as such it also is a signature morphism.*

An important use of (simple) institution representations is the re-use (also called borrowing) of entailment systems along the lines of [8,6]. Therefore, we need two preparatory notions.

A simple institution representation $(\Phi, \alpha, \beta)\colon I \longrightarrow J$ *admits model expansion* if β is pointwise surjective on objects (i.e., each β_Σ is surjective on objects). Informally, this means that each model of the source institution has a model representing it in the target institution.

Let a class $\mathcal{D}$ of signature morphisms in I be given. An institution representation $\mu\colon I \longrightarrow J$ *admits weak* $\mathcal{D}$-*amalgamation*, if for signature morphisms in $\mathcal{D}$, the β-naturality diagrams shown above are weak pullbacks. Informally, this means that each representation of a reduct of a model can be extended to a representation of the whole model (for reducts along signature morphisms in $\mathcal{D}$).

Theorem 1 (Local borrowing [8]). *Let $\mu = (\Phi, \alpha, \beta): I \longrightarrow J$ be a simple institution representation admitting model expansion into a (complete) logic J. Then we can turn I into a (complete) logic by putting*

$$\Gamma \vdash_{\Sigma} \varphi \quad \textit{iff} \quad Ax[\Phi(\Sigma)] \cup \alpha_{\Sigma}[\Gamma] \vdash_{Sign(\Phi(\Sigma))} \alpha_{\Sigma}(\varphi).$$

Theorem 2 (Global borrowing). *Let $\mu = (\Phi, \alpha, \beta): I \longrightarrow J$ be an institution representation admitting model expansion and weak $\mathcal{D}$-amalgamation, and let J be a complete logic. Then μ admits global borrowing, i.e. if we put*

$$\mathcal{S} \vdash M \overset{\sigma}{-\rightarrow} N \quad \textit{iff} \quad \hat{\mu}(\mathcal{S}) \vdash M \overset{\Phi(\sigma)}{-\rightarrow} N.$$

we get an entailment relation which is sound and complete (relative to an oracle for proving conservative extension) for a subset of development graphs over I (namely the set of all those development graphs with all hiding links along signature morphisms in $\mathcal{D}$).

Example 2. The institution representation from Example 1 admits model expansion and weak (injective)-amalgamation. Hence, it admits global borrowing for development graphs over the CASL logic that contain hiding links only along injective signature morphisms. That is, to prove a theorem link of such a development graph, it suffices to prove the translation of the link in the translated development graph over second-order logic.

5   Logic Morphisms and a CoFI Logic Graph

How can we give a precise semantics to the development graph in Fig. 1? As a prerequisite, we need to relate the underlying institutions somehow. In the previous section, we have introduced institution representations serving the purpose of *encoding* an institution within another one. But they are not so appropriate for dealing with heterogeneity (a motivation for this is given in [21]). Rather, we need *institution morphisms* [10], expressing the fact that a "larger" institution *is built upon* a "smaller" institution by *projecting* the "larger" institution onto the "smaller" one.

Given institutions I and J, an *institution morphism* [10] $\mu = (\Phi, \alpha, \beta): I \longrightarrow J$ consists of

- a functor $\Phi: \mathbf{Sign}^I \longrightarrow \mathbf{Sign}^J$,
- a natural transformation $\alpha: \mathbf{Sen}^J \circ \Phi \longrightarrow \mathbf{Sen}^I$ and
- a natural transformation $\beta: \mathbf{Mod}^I \longrightarrow \mathbf{Mod}^J \circ \Phi^{op}$,

such that the following *satisfaction condition* is satisfied for all $\Sigma \in \mathbf{Sign}^I$, $M \in \mathbf{Mod}^I(\Sigma)$ and $\varphi' \in \mathbf{Sen}^J(\Phi(\Sigma))$:

$$M \models^I_\Sigma \alpha_\Sigma(\varphi') \Leftrightarrow \beta_\Sigma(M) \models^J_{\Phi(\Sigma)} \varphi'.$$

If I and J are also logics, an institution morphism $\mu \colon I \longrightarrow J$ is called a *logic morphism*, if for any $\Sigma \in \mathbf{Sign}^I$, and $\{\varphi\}, \Gamma \subseteq \mathbf{Sen}^J(\Phi(\Sigma))$,

$$\Gamma \vdash^J_{\Phi(\Sigma)} \varphi \quad \text{implies} \quad \alpha_\Sigma[\Gamma] \vdash^I_\Sigma \alpha_\Sigma(\varphi).$$

Note that this condition always holds if I is complete.

This leads to a category *Log* of logics and logic morphisms.

As an example, consider the graph of logics and logic morphisms shown in Fig. 2. CASL extends first-order logic with partiality, subsorting and generation constraints (some form of induction). CASL-LTL [18] is an extension of CASL with a CTL-like labeled transition logic. LB-CASL [1] extends CASL with late binding, and SB-CASL [5] is an extension of CASL following the abstract state machine paradigm, where states correspond to algebras. HO-CASL [14] extends CASL with higher-order functions, and HasCASL [19] further adds shallow polymorphism and type constructors. (We here use the extensional variants ExtHO-CASL and ExtHasCASL of these logics, in order to be able to embed them into classical higher-order logic later on.) $FOL^=$ is the restriction of CASL to first-order logic, $SubPHorn^=$ [12] the restriction to Horn logic, and $Horn^=$ is the intersection of both restrictions. The definition of the logic morphisms is quite straightforward, except that for projecting CASL-LTL and LB-CASL onto CASL, we have two choices: since the dynamic structure can be represented in CASL itself, we either can choose to keep it or to drop it. Note that in Example 1 we have chosen the keep-morphism for going from CASL-LTL to CASL in order to be able to keep the labeled transition system also in SB-CASL and thus provide a true interaction between the two worlds.

6   Heterogeneity through Grothendieck Logics

With a given (arbitrary but fixed) graph of logics and morphisms as exhibited in the last section, we are now able to define heterogeneous development graphs. We could introduce new types of definition link to capture the heterogeneity, similarly to [21]. However, a more elegant way is to flatten the graph of logics, and then use the usual constructions for the thus obtained logic. This leads to the notion of Grothendieck logic, extending Diaconescu's Grothendieck institutions [9].

Definition 7. *An* indexed logic *is a functor* $\mathcal{L} \colon Ind^{op} \longrightarrow Log$ *into the category of logics and logic morphisms.*

For example, the graph of logics from Fig. 2 can be easily considered to be an indexed logic. (Any graph of logics can be extended to an indexed logic by taking Ind^{op} to be the free category over the graph, basically consisting of paths.)

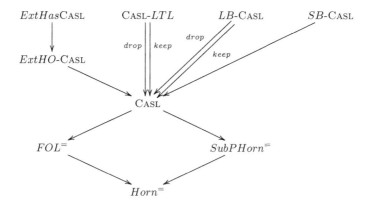

Fig. 2. A first CoFI logic graph

An indexed logic can now be flattened, using the so-called *Grothendieck construction*. The basic idea here is that all signatures of all logics are put side by side, and a signature morphism in this large realm of signatures consists of an intra-logic signature morphism plus an inter-logic translation (along some logic morphism from the graph). The other components are then defined in a straightforward way.

Definition 8. *Given an* indexed logic $\mathcal{L}: Ind^{op} \longrightarrow \underline{Log}$, *define the* Grothendieck logic $\mathcal{L}^{\#}$ *as follows:*

- *signatures in $\mathcal{L}^{\#}$ are pairs (Σ, i), where $i \in |Ind|$ and Σ a signature in the logic $\mathcal{L}(i)$,*
- *signature morphisms $(\sigma, d): (\Sigma_1, i) \longrightarrow (\Sigma_2, j)$ consist of a morphism $d: i \longrightarrow j \in Ind$ and a signature morphism $\sigma: \Sigma_1 \longrightarrow \Phi^{\mathcal{L}(d)}(\Sigma_2)$ (here, $\mathcal{L}(d): \mathcal{L}(j) \longrightarrow \mathcal{L}(i)$ is the logic morphism corresponding to the arrow $d: i \longrightarrow j$ in the logic graph, and $\Phi^{\mathcal{L}(d)}$ is its signature translation component),*
- *the (Σ, i)-sentences are the Σ-sentences in $\mathcal{L}(i)$, and sentence translation along (σ, d) is the composition of sentence translation along σ with sentence translation along $\mathcal{L}(d)$,*
- *the (Σ, i)-models are the Σ-models in $\mathcal{L}(i)$, and model reduction along (σ, d) is the composition of model translation along $\mathcal{L}(d)$ with model reduction along σ, and*
- *satisfaction (resp. entailment) w.r.t. (Σ, i) is satisfaction (resp. entailment) w.r.t. Σ in $\mathcal{L}(i)$.*

Now we can just define heterogeneous development graphs over $\mathcal{L}$ to be usual development graphs over the logic $\mathcal{L}^{\#}$. Hence, the graph shown in Fig 1 now becomes a development graph in the formal sense. Proving in such heterogeneous development graphs is then heterogeneous proving: the goal of deriving a global theorem link is decomposed (using the proof rules from [13]) into local goals that refer to the entailment relation of the Grothendieck logic, which in turn is defined in terms of the entailment relations of the individual logics.

However, there is one obstacle with this approach: in order to be able to use the calculus for the development graphs with hiding in a sound and relatively complete way, one needs weak amalgamation for the Grothendieck logic $\mathcal{L}^{\#}$ (note that with the calculus for structured specifications given in [6], one even needs Craig interpolation). Diaconescu [9] gives necessary and sufficient conditions for this. However, he points out that in many cases not all of these conditions will be satisfied (and this also is the case for our graph of logics). Therefore, we also will pursue a different way of obtaining proof support for heterogeneous logics.

7   Grothendieck Representations and Heterogeneous Borrowing

Often, heterogeneous proving in the Grothendieck logic is not feasible. One problem is a possible lack of weak amalgamation as indicated in the previous section. Another problem with a logic graph covering a variety of logics is that one needs to implement a proof tool for each individual logic. Therefore, we now show how to translate heterogeneous proof goals into homogeneous ones (i.e. over *one* logic), using heterogeneous borrowing.

To this end, we need the notion of institution representation map [20,16]. Fix a logic $U = (\mathbf{USign}, \mathbf{USen}, \mathbf{UMod}, \models, \vdash)$ which we will very informally view as a "universal" logic (with sufficient expressiveness to represent many logics, and with suitable tool support). We will also denote the institution $(\mathbf{USign}, \mathbf{USen}, \mathbf{UMod}, \models)$ by U.

Definition 9. *Let* $I = (\mathbf{Sign}, \mathbf{Sen}, \mathbf{Mod}, \models)$ *and* $I' = (\mathbf{Sign}', \mathbf{Sen}', \mathbf{Mod}', \models')$ *be institutions and* $\rho = (\Phi, \alpha, \beta) \colon I \to U$ *and* $\rho' = (\Phi', \alpha', \beta') \colon I' \to U$ *be their representations in* U. *A representation map from* ρ *to* ρ' *consists of:*

- *an institution morphism* $\mu = (\bar{\Phi}, \bar{\alpha}, \bar{\beta}) \colon I \to I'$, *and*
- *a natural transformation* $\theta \colon \Phi' \circ \bar{\Phi} \to \Phi$,

such that

- $\alpha \circ \bar{\alpha} = (\mathbf{USen} \cdot \theta) \circ (\alpha' \cdot \bar{\Phi})$,
- $\bar{\beta} \cdot \beta = (\beta' \cdot \bar{\Phi}^{op}) \circ (\mathbf{UMod} \cdot \theta^{op})$, *i.e., that for each signature* $\Sigma \in |\mathbf{Sign}|$ *the following diagram commutes:*

$$
\begin{array}{ccc}
\mathbf{Mod}(\Sigma) & \xleftarrow{\quad \beta_{\Sigma} \quad} & \mathbf{UMod}(\Phi(\Sigma)) \\
{\scriptstyle \bar{\beta}_{\Sigma}} \downarrow & & \downarrow {\scriptstyle \mathbf{UMod}(\theta_{\Sigma})} \\
\mathbf{Mod}'(\bar{\Phi}(\Sigma)) & \xleftarrow{\quad \beta'_{\bar{\Phi}(\Sigma)} \quad} & \mathbf{UMod}(\Phi'(\bar{\Phi}(\Sigma)))
\end{array}
$$

Moreover, we say that (μ, θ) *admits weak amalgamation, if for each signature* $\Sigma \in |\mathbf{Sign}|$, *the above diagram is a weak pullback in* $\mathcal{CAT}$.

With an obvious composition, this gives us a category $Repr(U)$ of institution representations into U and representation maps. An indexed representation *then is just a functor $\mathcal{R} \colon Ind^{op} \longrightarrow Repr(U)$. We now have:*

Theorem 3. *Given an indexed institution representation $\mathcal{R} \colon Ind^{op} \longrightarrow Repr(U)$, we can form its* Grothendieck representation *$\mathcal{R}^{\#} \colon (\Pi_1 \circ \mathcal{R})^{\#} \longrightarrow U$, which is a representation of the Grothendieck institution of the indexed institution $\Pi_1 \circ \mathcal{R}$ formed from the source institutions and morphisms involved in $\mathcal{R}$.*

Proposition 1. *Given an indexed representation $\mathcal{R} \colon Ind^{op} \longrightarrow Repr(U)$, if all the individual representations $\mathcal{R}(i)$ admit model expansion, then also $\mathcal{R}^{\#}$ admits model expansion.*

Definition 10. *Given an indexed representation $\mathcal{R} \colon Ind^{op} \longrightarrow Repr(U)$ and a class of signature morphisms $\mathcal{D}$ in $(\Pi_1 \circ \mathcal{R})^{\#}$, $\mathcal{R}$ is said to* admit weak $\mathcal{D}$-amalgamation *if*

- *for each $i \in Ind$, $\mathcal{R}(i)$ admits weak $\mathcal{C}$-amalgamation, where $\mathcal{C} = \{\sigma \mid (\sigma, d) \in \mathcal{D}$ for some $d \colon i \longrightarrow j \in Ind\}$, and*
- *for each $d \in Ind$ such that $(\sigma, d) \in \mathcal{D}$ for some σ, $\mathcal{R}(d)$ admits weak amalgamation.*

Proposition 2. *Given an indexed representation $\mathcal{R} \colon Ind^{op} \longrightarrow Repr(U)$ and a class of signature morphisms $\mathcal{D}$ in $(\Pi_1 \circ \mathcal{R})^{\#}$, if $\mathcal{R}$ admits weak $\mathcal{D}$-amalgamation, then also $\mathcal{R}^{\#}$ admits weak $\mathcal{D}$-amalgamation.*

Corollary 1. *Given an indexed representation $\mathcal{R} \colon Ind^{op} \longrightarrow Repr(U)$, if all the individual representations $\mathcal{R}(i)$ admit model expansion, and moreover $\mathcal{R}$ admits weak $\mathcal{D}$-amalgamation, then $\mathcal{R}^{\#}$ admits global borrowing for development graphs containing hiding links only along signature morphisms in $\mathcal{D}$.*

This means that global theorem links in heterogeneous development graphs can be derived using only the entailment relation of U (and the proof rules for development graphs from [13]).

Theorem 4. *The underlying indexed institution from Fig. 2 can be extended to an indexed representation $\mathcal{COFI} \colon Ind^{op} \longrightarrow Repr(HOL)$, as indicated in Fig. 3. Moreover, if $\mathcal{INJ}$ is the set of all signature morphisms that are injective in the first (intra-institution) component, then $\mathcal{COFI}$ admits weak $\mathcal{INJ}$-amalgamation.*

Proof. (Sketch) CASL is represented in HOL by Example 1. CASL-LTL and LB-CASL are represented in CASL by construction, hence we can compose this with the representation of CASL in HOL. ExtHO-CASL can be represented in HOL by an easy extension of the representation of CASL in HOL (for representing

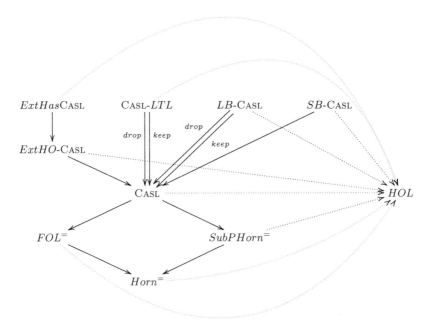

Fig. 3. The embedding to the CoFI logic graph into HOL

ExtHasCASL, we need a variant of HOL supporting type constructors and shallow polymorphism). The most complicated representation is that of SB-CASL: we have to represent the static part as with the standard CASL representation in HOL in order to get a representation map, while we need a set-theoretic representation for dynamic part (which involves whole algebras as states). The link between the static and the dynamic part is done by lifting functions which lift the static part into set theory.   □

By Corollary 1, $\mathcal{COFI}^{\#}$ admits global borrowing for development graphs containing hiding links only along signature morphisms in $\mathcal{INJ}$.

8   Conclusion and Related Work

Multi-logic systems can be studied in the context of an arbitrary but fixed graph of logics and logic morphisms (formalized as an indexed logic). In such a setting, we have generalized development graphs with hiding [13] to the heterogeneous case, using the Grothendieck construction of Diaconescu [9]. We then have extended the Grothendieck construction form institutions (and morphisms) to institution representations (and representation maps). We also have studied conditions under which Grothendieck representations admit the re-use ("borrowing") of theorem provers for proving global theorem links in heterogeneous development graphs. Our work is related to the introduction of heterogeneous notions in [21], which here occur more naturally through the Grothendieck construction.

As a first application, we have sketched a graph of institutions consisting of institutions for the Common Algebraic Specification Language CASL and some of its extensions and sublanguages. We also have extended this to a graph of representations and representation maps in higher-order logic. By the construction of the associated Grothendieck representation, any theorem prover for higher-order logic, together with the development graph tool based on the calculus for development graphs with hiding introduced in [13], can be used for theorem proving in the heterogeneous language over the above mentioned institution graph. As a first practical step, the development graph tool MAYA has been connected with the Isabelle/HOL theorem prover [4]. Other provers will follow, with the possibility of multi-prover proofs. We also have made the static analysis of CASL in-the-large institution independent [15], which is a step towards an analysis tool for the heterogeneous input language.

We have also presented a sample heterogeneous specification involving a refinement of an abstract requirement specification in CASL-LTL using temporal logic to a design specification in SB-CASL following paradigm of abstract state machines. With this, we have indicated that heterogeneous development graphs are indeed useful for dealing with interaction of different formalisms. It should be noted though that this interaction is possible because we use an institution morphism form CASL-LTL to CASL that keeps the dynamic structure. In order to have an interaction also in cases where it is not possible to keep some structure, one has to use parchments [16,7], which allow a true "interleaved" feature interaction. However, the theory of parchments is not ripe yet to deal with a combination of all the logics in our sample institution graph.

In the future, one should, of course, further explore the applicability of this approach. Concerning tool support, we have presented two extremes: either each logic comes with individual proof support, or all logics are encoded into one "universal" logic like HOL. Possibly it will be desirable to find some way between these extremes by allowing a large variety of input logics which is then mapped into a smaller variety of proof logics (for example, MAYA already supports both HOL and HOL plus TLA). The details of how to construct a logic representation between the induced Grothendieck logics need to be worked out yet. Another line of future work concerns the application of the ideas presented here to *programming* languages, which can also be considered to be institutions [20].

Acknowledgments

This work came out of both a cooperation with Andrzej Tarlecki on the semantic aspects and with Serge Autexier and Dieter Hutter on the proof theoretic aspects of specifications. This work has been supported by the *Deutsche Forschungsgemeinschaft* under Grant KR 1191/5-1.

References

1. D. Ancona, M. Cerioli, and E. Zucca. Extending CASL by late binding. In C. Choppy, D. Bert, and P. Mosses, editors, *Recent Trends in Algebraic Development Techniques, 14th International Workshop, WADT'99, Bonas, France*, volume 1827 of *Lecture Notes in Computer Science*. Springer-Verlag, 2000.
2. E. Astesiano, H.-J. Kreowski, and B. Krieg-Brückner. *Algebraic Foundations of Systems Specification*. Springer, 1999.
3. S. Autexier, D. Hutter, H. Mantel, and A. Schairer. Towards an evolutionary formal software-development using CASL. In C. Choppy and D. Bert, editors, *Recent Trends in Algebraic Development Techniques, 14th International Workshop, WADT'99, Bonas, France*, volume 1827 of *Lecture Notes in Computer Science*, pages 73–88. Springer-Verlag, 2000.
4. S. Autexier and T. Mossakowski. Integrating HOL-CASL into the development graph manager MAYA. FroCoS 2002, to appear.
5. H. Baumeister and A. Zamulin. State-based extension of CASL. In *Proceedings IFM 2000*, volume 1945 of *Lecture Notes in Computer Science*. Springer-Verlag, 2000.
6. T. Borzyszkowski. Logical systems for structured specifications. *Theoretical Computer Science*, to appear.
7. C.Caleiro, P.Mateus, J.Ramos, and A.Sernadas. Combining logics: Parchments revisited. In M. Cerioli and G. Reggio, editors, *Recent Trends in Algebraic Development Techniques, 15th International Workshop, WADT'01, Genova, Italy*, Lecture Notes in Computer Science. Springer-Verlag. To appear.
8. M. Cerioli and J. Meseguer. May I borrow your logic? (transporting logical structures along maps). *Theoretical Computer Science*, 173:311–347, 1997.
9. R. Diaconescu. Grothendieck institutions. *Applied categorical structures*. to appear.
10. J. A. Goguen and R. M. Burstall. Institutions: Abstract model theory for specification and programming. *Journal of the Association for Computing Machinery*, 39:95–146, 1992. Predecessor in: LNCS 164, 221–256, 1984.
11. J. Meseguer. General logics. In *Logic Colloquium 87*, pages 275–329. North Holland, 1989.
12. T. Mossakowski. Relating CASL with other specification languages: the institution level. *Theoretical Computer Science*. To appear.
13. T. Mossakowski, S. Autexier, and D. Hutter. Extending development graphs with hiding. In H. Hußmann, editor, *Fundamental Approaches to Software Engineering*, volume 2029 of *Lecture Notes in Computer Science*, pages 269–283. Springer-Verlag, 2001.
14. T. Mossakowski, A. Haxthausen, and B. Krieg-Brückner. Subsorted partial higher-order logic as an extension of CASL. In C. Choppy, D. Bert, and P. Mosses, editors, *Recent Trends in Algebraic Development Techniques, 14th International Workshop, WADT'99, Bonas, France*, volume 1827 of *Lecture Notes in Computer Science*, pages 126–145. Springer-Verlag, 2000.
15. T. Mossakowski and B. Klin. Institution independent static analysis for CASL. In M. Ceriolo and G. Reggio, editors, *Recent Trends in Algebraic Development Techniques, 15th International Workshop, WADT'01, Genova, Italy*, Lecture Notes in Computer Science. Springer-Verlag. To appear.
16. T. Mossakowski, A. Tarlecki, and W. Pawłowski. Combining and representing logical systems using model-theoretic parchments. In F. Parisi Presicce, editor,

Recent trends in algebraic development techniques. Proc. 12th International Workshop, volume 1376 of *Lecture Notes in Computer Science*, pages 349–364. Springer, 1998.

17. P. D. Mosses. CoFI: The Common Framework Initiative for Algebraic Specification and Development. In *TAPSOFT '97, Proc. Intl. Symp. on Theory and Practice of Software Development*, volume 1214 of *LNCS*, pages 115–137. Springer-Verlag, 1997.

18. G. Reggio and L. Repetto. CASL-CHART: a combination of statecharts and of the algebraic specification language CASL. In *Proc. AMAST 2000*, volume 1816 of *Lecture Notes in Computer Science*. Springer Verlag, 2000.

19. L. Schröder and T. Mossakowski. HasCASL: Towards integrated specification and development of Haskell programs. Submitted.

20. A. Tarlecki. Moving between logical systems. In M. Haveraaen, O. Owe, and O.-J. Dahl, editors, *Recent Trends in Data Type Specifications. 11th Workshop on Specification of Abstract Data Types*, volume 1130 of *Lecture Notes in Computer Science*, pages 478–502. Springer Verlag, 1996.

21. A. Tarlecki. Towards heterogeneous specifications. In D. Gabbay and M. d. Rijke, editors, *Frontiers of Combining Systems 2, 1998*, Studies in Logic and Computation, pages 337–360. Research Studies Press, 2000.

Notions of Computation Determine Monads

Gordon Plotkin and John Power[*]

Division of Informatics, University of Edinburgh, King's Buildings,
Edinburgh EH9 3JZ, Scotland

Abstract. We model notions of computation using algebraic operations and equations. We show that these generate several of the monads of primary interest that have been used to model computational effects, with the striking omission of the continuations monad. We focus on semantics for global and local state, showing that taking operations and equations as primitive yields a mathematical relationship that reflects their computational relationship.

1 Introduction

Eugenio Moggi, in [14,16], introduced the idea of giving a unified category theoretic semantics for what he called notions of computation, but which we call computational effects. He modelled each computational effect in the Kleisli category for an appropriate strong monad T on a base category C with finite products. The perspective of this paper is that computational effects *determine* monads but are not identified with monads. We regard a computational effect as being realised by families of operations, with a monad being generated by their equational theory.

Examples of computational effects are: exceptions, interactive input/output, nondeterminism, probabilistic nondeterminism, side-effects and continuations. Moggi's unified approach to modelling them has proved useful, for example in functional programming [2], but there has not been a precise mathematical basis on which to compare and contrast the various effects.

For instance, continuations are computationally of a different character to other computational effects, being an inherently non-local phenomenon. Again, computationally, the introduction of global state is a first step towards the introduction of local state. So we seek a mathematical description of features of the various monads that reflects the comparisons between the corresponding computational phenomena.

An immediate observation is that the monad for continuations $R^{(R^-)}$ does not have a rank (see [9] for a definition), while the monads for all the other above-mentioned computational effects do. There is a theorem to the effect that monads are derivable from algebraic operations and equations if and only if they have bounded rank [10]. So consideration of operations and equations might provide a way to describe features of the computational effects. The equations

---

[*] This work is supported by EPSRC grant GR/M56333 and a British Council grant.

M. Nielsen and U. Engberg (Eds.): Fossacs 2002, LNCS 2303, pp. 342–356, 2002.
© Springer-Verlag Berlin Heidelberg 2002

may also prove useful when manipulating programs, e.g., for optimisation. We regard it as positive that there are no algebraic operations and equations in the sense of the theorem yielding the continuations monad, taking that as reflecting its differing computational nature.

There are computationally natural families of operations associated with several of the above monads: one has 'raise' operations for exceptions; one has 'read' and 'write' operations associated with interactive input/output; one has a nondeterministic binary 'choice' operation when modelling nondeterminism; one has a 'random choice' operation for probabilistic nondeterminism; and one has 'lookup' and 'update' operations when modelling global state. An analysis of several of these families of operations appears in [20]: they are regarded as *algebraic families of operations* associated with an already given monad, and are characterised in terms of generic effects: e.g., to give a generic effect $e : \underline{n} \longrightarrow T\underline{m}$ is equivalent to giving m n-ary algebraic families of operations, where m and n need not be finite ($\underline{m}$ is the m-fold coproduct of 1 in C). Crucially when a monad is given by algebraic operations and equations in the sense of [10], the algebraic families of operations associated with it are given by the derived operations.

In programming languages, effects are obtained using syntactic constructs corresponding to the operations or the generic effects. Some examples with finitary operations were considered in [19], which considered suitable extensions of call-by-value PCF, itself an extension of Moggi's computational λ-calculus, and gave a unified treatment of operational semantics. Although infinitary operations, as we study here, do not appear directly in programming languages, the corresponding generic effects do, and we sketch appropriate extensions of call-by-value PCF incorporating them.

The present paper investigates whether the monads are given by computationally natural equations for the above naturally occurring families of operations. This is already well known to be so in the case of some of the above examples, notably those associated with nondeterminism; other cases, such as those of exceptions and interactive input/output, are easy; but global and local state required considerable thought. So most of the technical detail is devoted to the situation for state. At this point, we should like to thank Eugenio Moggi for suggesting to us that the monad for global state may be derived from (possibly infinitary) computationally natural operations and equations, and we should like to thank Peter O'Hearn for showing us a monad for local state suited to call-by-value. Two new features emerge in characterising local state. First, the arities must be allowed to be not just sets but presheafs; and second, the block operation, in contrast to lookup and update, is linear, using symmetric monoidal closed structure rather than cartesian closed structure.

The paper is organised as follows. In Section 2, we give a general explanation of the notions of signature, operations, and equations, and we present the straightforward examples discussed above. In Section 3, we give a careful explanation of how the monad $(S \otimes -)^S$ for global state is generated by operations for lookup and update subject to computationally natural equations. And in Section 4, we extend the definitions of Section 3 to see how the addition of block subject to natural additional equations generates the monad for local state. The central point here is that this gives precise mathematics that reflects the computational relationship between global and local state. For future work, having made some progress in understanding individual computational effects, one can consider their combinations; we address that issue in [6].

2   Operations and Equations

Given a finitary signature Σ in the usual universal algebraic sense, one can speak of a Σ-algebra in any category C with finite products: it consists of an object A of C together with, for each σ in Σ, a map

$$a_\sigma : A^{ar(\sigma)} \longrightarrow A$$

in C, where $ar(\sigma)$ is the arity of σ. One can speak of Σ-equations and their satisfaction in a Σ-algebra, obtaining the notion of a (Σ, E)-algebra in C. This, with the evident definition of homomorphism of algebras, generates a category (Σ, E)-Alg with a forgetful functor

$$U : (\Sigma, E) - Alg \longrightarrow C$$

which, if C is locally presentable, has a left adjoint F, inducing a monad $T = UF$ on C. The category (Σ, E)-Alg is isomorphic to the category T-Alg of algebras for the monad T.

This is a considerably simplified version of the work in [10], but the above version is sufficient here. One illuminating view is in terms of models for a Lawvere theory in a category other than Set, cf [20,21]. There is nothing special about the finitariness of Σ: everything holds equally for infinitary operations, providing C has correspondingly infinitary products, as all our examples do. It is, moreover, routine to verify that the induced monad T always has a natural associated strength, induced by the universal property of products. Leading examples of interesting categories C are Set, $Poset$, ω-Cpo, presheaf categories $[W, Set]$, and functor categories of the form $[W, \omega$-$Cpo]$ for a small category of worlds W, cf [17].

Example 1. Exceptions The monad $- + E$ for exceptions on Set is induced by E nullary operations, with no equations. These operations model the raising of exceptions, but do not model a 'handle' operation. This distinction is consistent with the fact that raising exceptions is algebraic [20], while (significantly!) handling exceptions is not. In this paper, we only consider algebraic operations; non-algebraic operations such as handle are of a different character, which remains to be understood.

Example 2. Interactive Input/Output The monad $TX = \mu Y.(O \times Y + Y^I + X)$ for interactive I/O on Set is induced by operations $read : X^I \longrightarrow X$ (which is infinitary) and $write : X \longrightarrow X^O$, with no equations [15]. The corresponding generic effects are $e_r : 1 \longrightarrow TI$ and $e_w : O \longrightarrow T1$; the corresponding extension of call-by-value PCF would have datatypes In and Out (they could both be $Char$, a character type) and programs **read** $: In$ and **write** $M : 1$ for $M : Out$.

Example 3. Nondeterminism Let C be the category of ω-cpo's. Then the category of algebras for the convex power-domain [5,18,1] is the category of semi-lattices in C (i.e., structures with an associative, commutative, idempotent binary operation), equipped with a least element $\perp$. Similar facts are true of the upper and lower power-domains, except that each requires an additional equational axiom in the setting of [10].

Example 4. Probabilistic Nondeterminism The probabilistic power-domain [7], [8,4] can be treated algebraically in several equivalent ways. One is via a random choice operator $x +_r y$ meaning "do x with probability r, or y with probability $1-r$." Taken together with a bottom element this has an axiomatisation over the category of ω-cpo's that fits within the framework of [10]. The equivalent generic effect is $(e_p)_r : 1 \to T(2)$. In programming languages considered in the literature one sees both explicit choice operators and a random 'die' **rand**$_r$: *Bool*.

3   Global State

In this section, we show how the side-effects monad, which is used to model global state, is generated by operations for lookup and update subject to computationally natural equations.

Let L be a finite set, to be regarded as a set of locations, and let V be a countable set, to be regarded as the set of values. For instance, V may be taken to be the set of natural numbers. One defines the set S of states of a language to be the set V^L of functions from locations to values. So S is a countable set. The restriction to finite L is deliberate and is needed for the proofs of our results; rather than use an infinite set to deal with the availability of an unbounded number of locations, we prefer to use a presheaf semantics as in Section 4. Observe that one includes the case of any countable set S by putting $L = 1$ and $V = S$; we shall need L explicit in order to analyse local state.

Now assume we have a category C with countable products and coproducts. Consider the monad T on C given by $(S \otimes -)^S$, where A^X means the product of X copies of the object A of C, and $X \otimes A$ means the coproduct of X copies of A. A map in the Kleisli category from A to B is equivalent to giving a map in C from $S \otimes A$ to $S \otimes B$, thus allowing a change of state.

We seek to express the category $(S \otimes -)^S$-Alg as the category of (Σ, E)-algebras, for computationally natural Σ and E, in the category C. In order to give this result, we define a category $GS(C)$, which, by its description, is the category of (Σ, E)-algebras in C for evident (Σ, E), so that the evident forgetful functor $U : GS(C) \longrightarrow C$ has a left adjoint given by $(S \otimes -)^S$. It follows that (Σ, E)-Alg is isomorphic to $(S \otimes -)^S$-Alg.

Our operations will consist of a lookup operation $l : A^V \longrightarrow A^L$ and an update operation $u : A \longrightarrow A^{L \times V}$; these are equivalent to families of operations as previously considered. Given a V-indexed family of elements of A, the infinitary lookup operation takes a location *loc*, finds out what its value is in the current state of the computation, and computes the element of A determined by that value. Given an element of A together with a location loc and a value v, the update operation updates the state by insisting that loc take value v, and then allowing the computation to run. The corresponding generic effects are $e_l : \underline{L} \longrightarrow T\underline{V}$ and $e_u : \underline{L} \times \underline{V} \longrightarrow T1$, where $\underline{L} = L \otimes 1$ and $\underline{V} = V \otimes 1$. In a corresponding extension of call-by-value PCF, one would have datatypes Loc and Val (the latter might be Nat) and program constructions $!M : Val$ for $M : Loc$ and $(M := N) : 1$ for $M : Loc$ and $N : Val$.

We take care here to give the result for a category C with axiomatic structure rather than just for Set, as we expect the more general result to be required for modelling the combination of side effects with other computational effects. Our results also extend routinely to the situation where C is a V-category (see [9]) and the set of values is replaced by an object of V. It remains to be seen how best to handle complex situations such as storable procedures [11] or linked lists.

Definition 1. *Given a category C with countable products, a finite set L, and a countable set V, we define the category $GS(C)$ as follows: an object consists of*

- *an object A of C*
- *a lookup map $l : A^V \longrightarrow A^L$, and*
- *an update map $u : A \longrightarrow A^{L \times V}$*

subject to commutativity of two classes of diagrams. First, we have four inter-action diagrams as follows:

$$
\begin{array}{ccccc}
A & \xrightarrow{\;u\;} & A^{L \times V} & \xrightarrow{\;\cong\;} & (A^V)^L \\
{\scriptstyle A^t}\big\downarrow & & & & \big\downarrow{\scriptstyle l^L} \\
A^L & \xleftarrow{\;A^\delta\;} & A^{L \times L} & \xleftarrow{\;\cong\;} & (A^L)^L
\end{array}
$$

where $\delta : L \longrightarrow L \times L$ and $t : L \longrightarrow 1$ are the diagonal and terminal maps, and the lower unlabelled isomorphism matches the outer L of $(A^L)^L$ with the first L of $A^{L \times L}$,

$$
\begin{array}{ccccc}
(A^V)^V & \xrightarrow{\;l^V\;} & (A^L)^V & \xrightarrow{\;\cong\;} & (A^V)^L \\
{\scriptstyle \cong}\big\downarrow & & & & \big\downarrow{\scriptstyle l^L} \\
A^{V \times V} & & & & (A^L)^L \\
{\scriptstyle A^\delta}\big\downarrow & & & & \big\downarrow{\scriptstyle \cong} \\
A^V & \xrightarrow{\;l\;} & A^L & \xleftarrow{\;A^\delta\;} & A^{L \times L}
\end{array}
$$

where the unlabelled isomorphisms match the outer V of $(A^V)^V$ with the first V of $A^{V \times V}$ and similarly for L, cf [9],

$$
\begin{array}{ccccc}
A & \xrightarrow{\ u\ } & A^{L \times V} & \xrightarrow{\ u^{L \times V}\ } & (A^{L \times V})^{L \times V} \\[2pt]
\Big\downarrow{\scriptstyle u} & & & & \Big\downarrow{\scriptstyle \cong} \\[2pt]
A^{L \times V} & \xrightarrow{\ A^{L \times \pi_1}\ } & A^{L \times V \times V} & \xleftarrow{\ A^{\delta \times V \times V}\ } & A^{L \times L \times V \times V}
\end{array}
$$

where the unlabelled isomorphism matches the outside L with the first L and similarly for V, and

$$
\begin{array}{ccccc}
A^V & \xrightarrow{\ l\ } & A^L & \xrightarrow{\ u^L\ } & (A^{L \times V})^L \\[2pt]
\Big\downarrow{\scriptstyle u^V} & & & & \Big\downarrow{\scriptstyle A^{\delta \times V}} \\[2pt]
(A^{L \times V})^V & & \xrightarrow{\quad A^{L \times \delta}\quad} & & A^{L \times V}
\end{array}
$$

suppressing two isomorphisms. We also have three commutation diagrams as follows:

$$
\begin{array}{ccccccc}
(A^V)^V & \xrightarrow{\ l^V\ } & (A^L)^V & \xrightarrow{\ \cong\ } & (A^V)^L & \xrightarrow{\ l^L\ } & (A^L)^L \\[2pt]
\Big\downarrow{\scriptstyle s} & & & & & & \Big\downarrow{\scriptstyle s} \\[2pt]
(A^V)^V & & & & & & (A^L)^L \\[2pt]
\Big\downarrow{\scriptstyle l^V} & & & & & & \Big\downarrow{} \\[2pt]
(A^L)^V & \xrightarrow{\ \cong\ } & (A^V)^L & \xrightarrow{\ l^L\ } & (A^L)^L & \xrightarrow{\quad} & A^{L_2}
\end{array}
$$

where s signifies 'swap' maps and L_2 denotes the set of ordered pairs of distinct elements of L, with the unlabelled maps both given by the same canonical map,

$$
\begin{array}{ccccccc}
A & \xrightarrow{\ u\ } & A^{L \times V} & \xrightarrow{\ u^{L \times V}\ } & (A^{L \times V})^{L \times V} & \xrightarrow{\ s\ } & (A^{L \times V})^{L \times V} \\[2pt]
\Big\downarrow{\scriptstyle u} & & & & & & \Big\downarrow{} \\[2pt]
A^{L \times V} & & \xrightarrow{\quad u^{L \times V}\quad} & & (A^{L \times V})^{L \times V} & \xrightarrow{\quad} & A^{L_2 \times V \times V}
\end{array}
$$

where s again signifies a swap map and with the unlabelled maps again given by the same canonical map, and

$$A^V \xrightarrow{\ l\ } A^L \xrightarrow{\ u^L\ } (A^{L\times V})^L \xrightarrow{\ \cong\ } (A^L)^{L\times V}$$

$$u^V \downarrow \qquad\qquad\qquad\qquad\qquad\qquad \downarrow$$

$$(A^{L\times V})^V \underset{\cong}{\rightarrow} (A^V)^{L\times V} \xrightarrow{\ l^{L\times V}\ } (A^L)^{L\times V} \longrightarrow A^{L_2\times V}$$

where, again, the unlabelled maps are given by the same canonical map. The rest of the structure of $GS(C)$ as a category is evident: for instance, a map from (A,u,l) to (A',u',l') is a map $f : A \longrightarrow A'$ in C subject to commutativity of f with l and l' and commutativity of f with u and u'.

The above constitutes our formal definition of the category of algebras. For any category C with countable products, one can routinely give an equational language for which equations between infinitary terms of the language correspond to commutative diagrams in the category. One has a V-ary function symbol l_{loc} for each loc in L and a unary function symbol $u_{loc,v}$ for each loc in L and v in V. The seven commutative diagrams in the definition of $GS(C)$ can be expressed equationally as the following seven axiom schema involving infinitary expressions respectively:

1. $l_{loc}(u_{loc,v}(x))_v = x$
2. $l_{loc}(l_{loc}(t_{vv'})_v)_{v'} = l_{loc}(t_{vv})_v$
3. $u_{loc,v}(u_{loc,v'}(x)) = u_{loc,v'}(x)$
4. $u_{loc,v}(l_{loc}(t_{v'})_{v'}) = u_{loc,v}(t_v)$
5. $l_{loc}(l_{loc'}(t_{vv'})_{v'})_v = l_{loc'}(l_{loc}(t_{vv'})_v)_{v'}$ where $loc \neq loc'$
6. $u_{loc,v}(u_{loc',v'}(x)) = u_{loc',v'}(u_{loc,v}(x))$ where $loc \neq loc'$
7. $u_{loc,v}(l_{loc'}(t_{v'})_{v'}) = l_{loc'}(u_{loc,v}(t_{v'}))_{v'}$ where $loc \neq loc'$.

It can be shown that this axiom system is *Hilbert-Post complete*, meaning that it has no equationally consistent extensions; thus we have all the equations for global state. The schema induce program assertions. Here are those corresponding to the third and sixth:

3*. $(l := x; \textbf{let } y \textbf{ be } !l \textbf{ in } M) = (l := x; M[x/y])$

6*. $(l \neq m) \supset (l := x; m := y) = (m := y; l := x)$

where $x, y : Val$, $l, m : Loc$ and $M; N$ abbreviates $(\lambda x : 1.N)(M)$ with x fresh.

Proposition 1. *For any object (A, l, u) of $GS(C)$, the diagram*

commutes.

Proof. Use two applications of the first axiom and one application of the second axiom.

In the equational logic, this proposition is: $l_{loc}(x)_v = x$.

We henceforth assume that C has both countable products and countable coproducts.

Proposition 2. *For any object X of C, the object $(S \otimes X)^S$ together with the maps*

$$u : (S \otimes X)^S \longrightarrow ((S \otimes X)^S)^{L \times V}$$

determined by composition with the function from $L \times V \times V^L$ to V^L that, given (loc, v, σ), "updates" $\sigma : L \longrightarrow V$ by replacing its value at loc by v and

$$l : ((S \otimes X)^S)^V \longrightarrow ((S \otimes X)^S)^L$$

determined by composition with the function from $L \times V^L$ to $V \times V^L$ that, given (loc, σ), "looks up" loc in $\sigma : L \longrightarrow V$ to determine its value, and is given by the projection to V^L, satisfy the commutative diagrams required to give an object of $GS(C)$.

The definitions of u and l in the proposition correspond to the equations

$$u(loc, v, x)(\sigma) = x(\sigma[v/loc])$$

and

$$l(loc, (x_v)_v)(\sigma) = x_{\sigma(loc)}(\sigma).$$

Theorem 1. *The forgetful functor $U : GS(C) \longrightarrow C$ exhibits the category $GS(C)$ as monadic over C, with monad $(S \otimes -)^S$.*

Proof. We first show that the left adjoint to U is the functor $(S \otimes -)^S$, with algebra structure on $(S \otimes X)^S$ given by the proposition, and with the unit of the adjunction given by the canonical map $\eta_X : X \longrightarrow (S \otimes X)^S$. Given an algebra (A, l, u) and a natural number n, let

$$u_n : (L \times V)^n \otimes A \longrightarrow A$$

denote the canonical map induced by n applications of u, and let

$$l_n : A^{V^n} \longrightarrow A^{L^n}$$

denote the canonical map induced by n applications of l.

Given an arbitrary map $f : X \longrightarrow A$, and recalling that $S = V^L$, define $\overline{f} : (S \otimes X)^S \longrightarrow A$ to be the composite of $(S \otimes f)^S : (S \otimes X)^S \longrightarrow (S \otimes A)^S$ with

$$(V^L \otimes A)^{V^L} \longrightarrow ((L \times V)^L \otimes A)^{V^L} \xrightarrow{u_L^{V^L}} A^{V^L} \xrightarrow{l_L} A^{L^L} \longrightarrow A$$

where the unlabelled maps are the evident structural maps. We need to prove four commutativities: one showing that $\overline{f}$ composed with η_X is f, two to show that $\overline{f}$ is an algebra map, and a final one to show that, given any algebra map $g : (S \otimes X)^S \longrightarrow A$, the map $\overline{g\eta}$ equals g.

For the unit axiom, first observe that the commutation axioms generalise to allow l and u to be replaced by l_n and u_m for arbitrary natural numbers n and m. The unit axiom follows by induction on the size of L using these generalised versions of the first two commutation axioms and the first interaction axiom.

One can see the proof of commutativity of $\overline{f}$ with u by first considering the case where L has precisely one element, when the proof is easy using the third and fourth interaction axioms, and Proposition 1. The proof for arbitrary L is essentially the same, but also requires the generalised commutation axioms.

Commutativity of $\overline{f}$ with l is straightforward: it requires the second interaction diagram together with generalised versions of the first commutation diagram. And the final commutativity follows from routine calculation, just using naturality. So $(S \otimes -)^S$ is indeed left adjoint to U.

Finally, it follows routinely from Beck's monadicity theorem that U is monadic.

4   Local State

We now consider local state in terms of operations and equations, extending those for global state in a principled fashion. In order to do that, we first discuss how to model local state. Following [17], as further studied in [12], we do not model local state in terms of a category with axiomatically given structure as we have done for global state, but rather restrict attention to a particular presheaf category $[I, Set]$ where I is the category of finite sets and injections. We hope that our results will generalise to functor categories $[I, C]$ where C has axiomatically given structure.

Note that I is equivalent to the category of natural numbers and monomorphisms; I does not have finite coproducts, and in particular, the sum of two natural numbers does not act as their binary coproduct. However, I does have an initial object, so by duality, I^{op} has a terminal object. The Yoneda embedding embeds I^{op} into the presheaf category $[I, Set]$, which is cartesian closed as a locally presentable category, allowing us to use the general theory of operations and equations of [10].

Finite products in $[I, Set]$ are given pointwise, and the closed structure, given functors $X, Y : I \longrightarrow Set$, is given by

$$(Y^X)n = [I, Set](X - \times I(n, -), Y-)$$

i.e., the set of natural transformations from $X - \times I(n, -)$ to Y. The terminal object of $[I, Set]$ is $I(0, -)$. There is a convenient additional 'convolution' symmetric monoidal closed structure on $[I, Set]$. The closed structure $[X, Y]$ corresponding to the convolution monoidal product is

$$[X, Y]n = [I, Set](X-, Y(n + -))$$

In particular, by the Yoneda lemma, $[I(m, -), Y]n = Y(n + m)$. Moreover, the functor $[X, -]$ has a canonical strength with respect to the cartesian closed structure of $[I, Set]$. We shall use a combination of both symmetric monoidal closed structures here.

We no longer model state by a set; instead, we index it according to the world in which it is defined. So, given a set of values V, state is modelled by the functor $S : I^{op} \longrightarrow Set$ given by $Sn = V^n$. Note that S is not an object of $[I, Set]$. Observe that the functor S is the composite of the inclusion $I^{op} \longrightarrow Set^{op}$ with $V^{(-)} : Set^{op} \longrightarrow Set$.

The monad for local state is

$$(TX)n = \left(\int^{m\epsilon(n/I)} (Sm \times Xm) \right)^{Sn}$$

where $\int$ denotes a coend, which is a complicated form of colimit involving a universal dinatural map [9,13]. This construction is a simplified version of one in Levy's thesis [12]; the idea is that in a state with n locations, a computation can create $m - n$ new locations and return a value (e.g., a function) that depends on them (and so one also needs to know S at all of m). In the case $V = 1$ it reduces to the monad for local names in [23]; it would be interesting to know the relationship with the monads for local state in [22]. The behaviour of T on injective maps $f : n \longrightarrow n'$ is as follows: decompose n' as the sum $n + n''$, note that $S(p + n'') = Sp \times Sn''$, and use covariance of X. So the map

$$\left(\int^{m\epsilon(n/I)} (Sm \times Xm) \right)^{Sn} \times Sn \times Sn'' \longrightarrow \int^{m'' \epsilon((n+n'')/I)} (Sm'' \times Xm'')$$

evaluates at Sn, then maps the m-th component of the first coend into the $(m + n'')$-th component of the second, using the above isomorphism for S and functoriality of X. The monad T routinely has strengths with respect to both symmetric monoidal closed structures.

We denote the inclusion of I into Set, which is $I(1, -)$, by the notation L, as it represents locations, and we overload notation by letting $V : I \longrightarrow Set$ denote the constant functor at V, representing values. As L is not a mere set but rather a set indexed by a world, we need more refined notions of signature, operations, and equations in order to allow L and V to be arities as we had for global state. Note that our definition of L_2 as in the previous section extends here, where L_2 may be seen as the functor from I to Set that sends a finite set to the set of ordered pairs of distinct elements.

Ideally, we should like to use either the cartesian closed structure or the convolution monoidal closed structure of $[I, Set]$ in order to present the monad T as generated by algebraic structure as in [10]. But the equations we need for l and u are those for global state, and they are inherently cartesian, using diagonals and projections. So, if we were to use only one of the structures, it would need to be the cartesian closed one. But our construction of a lifting, as is essential to our proof of the main theorem, requires the block map b to have domain $[L, A]$ given by the linear convolution closed structure (and this is computationally natural as $[L, A](n) \cong A(n + 1)$). So, we use a combination of the two kinds of structure here. Such a combination is not considered in [10], but that theory does apply in that, from our description, one can routinely induce unenriched algebraic structure, albeit complicated. However, it may ultimately be better to develop the theory of [10] to allow for a pair of enrichments interacting with each other, as here, then use that generalised theory in describing such phenomena as local state or as arise in modelling the π-calculus [3].

For this paper, we proceed by analogy with global state, by defining a category $LS([I, Set])$ which should be of the form (Σ, E)-Alg in a sense to be made precise in one of the ways outlined above. The relationship between our modelling of global and local state will be clear. Observe that, as $V : I \longrightarrow Set$ is a constant functor, we have

$$(A^V)- = [V, A]- = (A-)^V$$

We shall only use the notation A^V.

Definition 2. *We define the category $LS([I, Set])$ as follows: an object consists of*

- *an object A of $[I, Set]$*
- *a lookup map $l : A^V \longrightarrow A^L$*
- *an update map $u : A \longrightarrow A^{L \times V}$*
- *a block map $b : [L, A] \longrightarrow A^V$*

subject to commutativity of six interaction diagrams and six commutativity diagrams. The interaction diagrams consist of the four interaction diagrams for global state, together with

$$
\begin{array}{ccccc}
[L, A] & \xrightarrow{[L, u]} & [L, A^{L \times V}] & \xrightarrow{\cong} & [L, A^L]^V \longrightarrow [L \times L, A]^V \\
\downarrow{\scriptstyle b} & & & & \downarrow{\scriptstyle [\delta, A]^V} \\
A^V & \xrightarrow[(A^t)^V]{} & (A^V)^V & \xleftarrow[b^V]{} & [L, A]^V
\end{array}
$$

where the horizontal unlabelled map is given by a canonical distributivity law of $X \otimes -$ over product together with the fact that the unit for the tensor product is *the terminal object, and*

$$
\begin{array}{ccc}
[L, A^V] \xrightarrow{[L,l]} [L, A^L] \longrightarrow [L \times L, A] \\
\cong \Big\downarrow \qquad\qquad\qquad \Big\downarrow [\delta, A] \\
[L, A]^V \qquad\qquad\qquad [L, A] \\
b^V \Big\downarrow \qquad\qquad\qquad \Big\downarrow b \\
(A^V)^V \xrightarrow[\cong]{} A^{V \times V} \xrightarrow{A^\delta} A^V
\end{array}
$$

where the horizontal unlabelled map is determined as in the first diagram.
The commutation diagrams are those for global state together with

$$
\begin{array}{ccc}
[L, [L, A]] \xrightarrow{[L,b]} [L, A^V] \xrightarrow{\cong} [L, A]^V \\
s \Big\downarrow \qquad\qquad\qquad\qquad \Big\downarrow b^V \\
[L, [L, A]] \qquad\qquad\qquad (A^V)^V \\
{[L,b]} \Big\downarrow \qquad\qquad\qquad\qquad \Big\downarrow s \\
[L, A^V] \xrightarrow[\cong]{} [L, A]^V \xrightarrow{b^V} (A^V)^V
\end{array}
$$

$$
\begin{array}{ccc}
[L, A] \xrightarrow{[L,u]} [L, A^{L \times V}] \longrightarrow [L, A]^{L \times V} \\
b \Big\downarrow \qquad\qquad\qquad\qquad \Big\downarrow b^{L \times V} \\
A^V \xrightarrow{u^V} (A^{L \times V})^V \xrightarrow{\cong} (A^V)^{L \times V}
\end{array}
$$

and

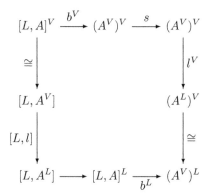

We do not have a formal syntactic analogue of these diagrams as equations, but we intend to produce one in further work. In outline, for the diagrams inherited from global state, we imagine interpreting the previous equations internally, as regards the *loc* indices. And for the new diagrams, we could imagine something along the lines of introducing operations b_v and expressing the above equations syntactically as

1. $b_v \langle u_{loc,v'}(t) \rangle_{loc} = b_{v'} \langle t \rangle_{loc}$
2. $b_v \langle l_{loc}(t_{v'})_{v'} \rangle_{loc} = b_v \langle t_v \rangle_{loc}$
3. $b_v \langle b_{v'} \langle t \rangle_{loc'} \rangle_{loc} = b_{v'} \langle b_v \langle t \rangle_{loc} \rangle_{loc'}$
4. $b_v \langle u_{loc',v'}(t) \rangle_{loc} = u_{loc',v'}(b_v \langle t \rangle_{loc})$
5. $b_v \langle l_{loc'}(t_{v'})_{v'} \rangle_{loc} = l_{loc'}(b_v \langle t_{v'} \rangle_{loc})_{v'}$

notationally differentiating linear abstraction and cartesian indexing (note that the terms t may contain occurrences of variables such as *loc*).

For an extension of call-by-value PCF we can add a block construct

block new $l := x; M$ **end** $: \sigma$

for $M : \sigma$. A construct corresponding to the generic effect $e_b : V \to TL$ (see below) appears in [22], viz **ref** $M : Loc$ for $M : Val$, creating a new reference. One can also add an equality test on locations. Here is a sample program assertion, corresponding to the fourth equation:

(**block new** $l := x; m := y; M$ **end**) = ($m := y;$ **block new** $l := x; M$ **end**)

In order to prove that the free algebra is given by the monad for local state, we need to put an algebra structure on TX for arbitrary X in $[I, Set]$. It is simplest to express this, using the theory of [20], in terms of generic effects. So we give maps $e_l : L \longrightarrow TV$, $e_u : L \times V \longrightarrow T1$ and $e_b : V \longrightarrow TL$ with the understanding that $l : (TX)^V \longrightarrow (TX)^L$ is defined using composition with e_l in the Kleisli category $Kl(T)$, and similarly for e_u and e_b. They are defined as follows:

$$(e_l)_n : n \longrightarrow [Sn, Sn \times V]$$

is defined by $(e_l)_n(p, \sigma) = (\sigma, \sigma(p))$

$$(e_u)_n : n \times V \longrightarrow [Sn, Sn]$$

is defined by $(e_u)_n(p, v, \sigma) = \sigma[v/p]$, and

$$(e_b)_n : V \longrightarrow (\int^{m\epsilon(n/I)} (Sm \times m))^{Sn}$$

is defined by $(e_b)_n(v, \sigma) = ((\sigma, v), 1)\epsilon S(n + 1) \times (n + 1)$.

Proposition 3. *For any object X of $[I, Set]$, the object TX together with the maps l, u and b as defined above, satisfy the commutative diagrams required to give an object of $LS([I, Set])$.*

Theorem 2. *The forgetful functor $U : LS([I, Set]) \longrightarrow [I, Set]$ exhibits the category $LS([I, Set])$ as monadic over $[I, Set]$ with monad T as above.*

Proof. The proof is essentially the same as that for Theorem 1. The key construction is that given a map $f : X \longrightarrow A$ where A is an algebra, f extends to an algebra map $\overline{f}$ given by the composite of $Tf : TX \longrightarrow TA$ with, on the n-th component,

- a structural map

$$(\int^{m\epsilon(n/I)} (V^m \times Am))^{V^n} \longrightarrow (\int^{m\epsilon(n/I)} (V^{m-n} \times (m \times V)^n \times Am))^{V^n}$$

- a map $(\int^{m\epsilon(n/I)}(V^{m-n} \times (m \times V)^n \times Am))^{V^n} \longrightarrow (\int^{m\epsilon(n/I)}(V^{m-n} \times Am))^{V^n}$ given by n applications of u_m
- a map $(\int^{m\epsilon(n/I)}(V^{m-n} \times Am))^{V^n} \longrightarrow (An)^{V^n}$ given on the $(i : n \to m)$-th component by a composite of applications of b_p as p varies from n to $m - 1$
- a map $(An)^{V^n} \longrightarrow (An)^{n^n}$ given by n applications of l_n, and
- a structural map $(An)^{n^n} \longrightarrow An$.

The two new interaction axioms are used to prove that $\overline{f}$ respects b.

Unlike the case of global state there is a further natural sixth axiom for block, viz: $b_v \langle x \rangle_l = x$. This is *false* in our model, although the corresponding program assertion (**block new** $l := x; M$ **end**) $= M$ (l not free in M) does hold operationally. Relevant logical relation techniques for finding a monadic semantics are given in [22,23]; we conjecture that, with the additional axiom, the axioms for local state will prove Hilbert-Post complete.

References

1. S. O. Anderson and A. J. Power, A Representable Approach to Finite Nondeterminism, in *Theoret. Comput. Sci.*, Vol. 177, No. 1, pp. 3–25, 1997.
2. N. Benton, J. Hughes, and E. Moggi, *Monads and Effects*, APPSEM '00 Summer School, 2000.
3. M. P. Fiore, E. Moggi, and D. Sangiorgi, A Fully-Abstract Model for the pi-Calculus, in *Proc. LICS '96*, pp. 43–54, Washington: IEEE Press, 1996.
4. R. Heckmann, Probabilistic Domains, in *Proc. CAAP '94*, LNCS, Vol. 136, pp. 21-56, Berlin: Springer-Verlag, 1994.
5. M. C. B. Hennessy and G. D. Plotkin, Full Abstraction for a Simple Parallel Programming Language, in *Proc. MFCS '79* (ed. J. Bečvář), LNCS, Vol. 74, pp. 108-120, Berlin: Springer-Verlag, 1979.
6. J. M. E. Hyland, G. D. Plotkin, and A. J. Power, Combining Computataional Effects: Commutativity and Sum, submitted, 2002.
7. C. Jones, *Probabilistic Non-Determinism*, Ph.D. Thesis, University of Edinburgh, Report ECS-LFCS-90-105, 1990.
8. C. Jones and G. D. Plotkin, A Probabilistic Powerdomain of Evaluations, in *Proc. LICS '89*, pp. 186–195, Washington: IEEE Press, 1989.
9. G. M. Kelly, *Basic Concepts of Enriched Category Theory*, Cambridge: Cambridge University Press, 1982.
10. G. M. Kelly and A. J. Power, Adjunctions whose Counits are Coequalizers, and Presentations of Finitary Enriched Monads, in *J. Pure Appl. Algebra*, Vol. 89, pp. 163–179, 1993.
11. P. B. Levy, Call-by-Push-Value: A Subsuming Paradigm, Ph.D. thesis, Queen Mary College, 2001.
12. P. B. Levy, Call-by-Push-Value, in *Proc. TLCA '99* (ed. J.-Y. Girard), LNCS, Vol. 1581, pp. 228-242, Berlin: Springer-Verlag, 1999.
13. S. Mac Lane, *Categories for the Working Mathematician*, Springer-Verlag, 1971.
14. E. Moggi, Computational Lambda-Calculus and Monads, in *Proc. LICS '89*, pp. 14–23, Washington: IEEE Press, 1989.
15. E. Moggi, *An Abstract View of Programming Languages*, University of Edinburgh, Report ECS-LFCS-90-113, 1989.
16. E. Moggi, Notions of computation and monads, *Inf. and Comp.*, Vol. 93, No. 1, pp. 55–92, 1991.
17. P. W. O'Hearn and R. D. Tennent, *Algol-like Languages*, Progress in Theoretical Computer Science, Boston: Birkhauser, 1997.
18. G. D. Plotkin, *Domains*, URL: http://www.dcs.ed.ac.uk/home/gdp, 1983.
19. G. D. Plotkin and A. J. Power, Adequacy for Algebraic Effects, in *Proc. FOSSACS 2001* (eds. F. Honsell and M. Miculan), LNCS, Vol. 2030, pp. 1–24, Berlin: Springer-Verlag, 2001.
20. G. D. Plotkin and A. J. Power, Semantics for Algebraic Operations (extended abstract), in *Proc. MFPS XVII* (eds. S. Brookes and M. Mislove), ENTCS, Vol. 45, Amsterdam: Elsevier, 2001.
21. A. J. Power, Enriched Lawvere Theories, in *Theory and Applications of Categories*, pp. 83–93, 2000.
22. I. Stark, *Names and Higher-Order Functions*, Ph.D. thesis, University of Cambridge, 1994.
23. I. Stark, Categorical Models for Local Names, in *Lisp and Symbolic Computation*, Vol. 9, No. 1, pp. 77–107, 1996.
and

A Calculus of Circular Proofs
and Its Categorical Semantics*

Luigi Santocanale**

Department of Computer Science
University of Calgary
luigis@cpsc.ucalgary.ca

Abstract. We present a calculus of "circular proofs": the graph underlying a proof is not a finite tree but instead it is allowed to contain a
certain amount of cycles. The main challenge in developing a theory for
the calculus is to define the semantics of proofs, since the usual method
by induction on the structure is not available. We solve this problem
by associating to each proof a system of equations – defining relations
among undetermined arrows of an arbitrary category with finite products and coproducts as well as constructible initial algebras and final
coalgebras – and by proving that this system admits always a unique
solution.

1 Introduction

In this paper we introduce a *calculus of proofs* for a simple fixed point logic.
The proofs of the calculus are *circular* in that their underlying graph is not
a tree but it is allowed to contain a certain amount of cycles. We present the
semantics of the calculus and show how to interpret proof terms as arrows in
categories. We also discuss a form of cut elimination theorem that holds for the
calculus. Before discussing further our work, we relate it to two distinct topics
in computer science.

Fixed Points Logics. The originating ground for the present work are fixed
point logics [6, 13] and μ-calculi [4]; as a particular μ-calculus we count our work
on free μ-lattices [20, 21]. Roughly speaking, these frameworks are obtained from
previously existing logical or algebraic frameworks by the addition of least and
greatest fixed point operators. For example, the propositional modal μ-calculus
[15] arises in this way from modal logic. Usually cut free proofs in sequent calculi are inherently finite because premiss sequents are always strictly smaller
than conclusions. However, in settings where the propositions themselves can be
circular or infinite (as for fixed point propositions) there exists the possibility
of having circular or infinite proofs as well. Remarkably these proofs happen

---

* Work developed at BRICS, Centre of the Danish National Research Foundation.
** Supported by Canada's NSERC and the Pacific Institute for the Mathematical Sciences.

M. Nielsen and U. Engberg (Eds.): Fossacs 2002, LNCS 2303, pp. 357–371, 2002.
© Springer-Verlag Berlin Heidelberg 2002

to be the most useful in the theories so far developed. Examples from the literature are the refutations of the propositional μ-calculus [26] and the proofs with guarded induction of type theory [9]. A major challenge when dealing with circular proofs is to prove their soundness, since the usual method by induction on the well founded structure of the proof tree is not available. Soundness is the main content of Walukiewicz's proof of the completeness of Kozen's axiomatization of the propositional μ-calculus [26]: there the refutations are translated into more common tree like proofs characterized by the presence of a specific inference rule for fixed points.

We propose a categorical semantics of circular proofs and in this way we give a strong solution to the problem of soundness. It is our opinion that lifting the point of view from the theory of provability to proof theory – and from posets to categories – is of substantial help in clarifying the principles behind circular proofs. Recall that a recursively defined function is uniquely determined by its defining system of equations. In the spirit of categorical logic we analyze proofs as sort of recursively defined functions and obtain an immediate hint on the reasons for which proof terms should look like fixed point expressions.

Semantics of Computation. Often a programming language is given and one seeks for adequate algebraic models. If the language is typed, then the interesting models usually are structured categories. We follow an opposite direction as our aim is to extract a programming language from a given mathematical model. The present work is part of a more general investigation of categories with finite products, finite coproducts, "enough" initial algebras and final coalgebras; we call a category with these properties μ-bicomplete, since it generalizes a posetal μ-lattice to a categorical setting. Our primary interest are those categories that possess this structure in a canonical way, the free μ-bicomplete categories. Syntactical constructions of free categories are always possible, however these constructions turn out to be useful only if the syntax has good proof theoretic properties like cut elimination or normalization. Thus our goal is to find a good syntax for a given semantic world. With respect to analogous logical and algebraic settings [8, 11, 12], with μ-bicomplete categories the focus is on initial algebras and final coalgebras of functors. Initial algebras of functors, which naturally generalize least fixed points of order preserving functions, are a categorical formulation of induction and recursion and model inductive types [10]. On the other hand, final coalgebras – generalizing greatest fixed points – are a counterpart of coinduction and corecursion; they are related to bisimilarity in that they classify the observable behavior of systems [17, 18]. The use of coalgebraic methods is now a well established practice to deal with infinite objects by means of their defining equations [2].

As it is usually the case in proof theoretic contexts, it is possible to give a computational interpretation to proofs. The interpretation of circular proofs we shall propose stems from the game theoretical setting of free μ-lattices [19, 20, 21] and the link we have established [23] between the theory of μ-bicomplete categories and parity games [4]. The interpretation is consistent with the well known analogy proposed in [1] between games and winning strategies on the one hand, and systems' specifications and correct programs on the other. Given two μ-lattice terms S, T (the directed systems of section 2 are essentially μ-lattice terms), the witnesses that a relation $S \vdash T$ holds are the winning strategies for one player in a game $S \multimap T$ with possibly infinite plays. A useful lemma allows to replace arbitrary winning strategies with bounded memory winning strategies; more explicitly, if we represent a winning strategy as an infinite tree, we can always assume that this tree is the unraveling of a finite graph. After we have translated our intuitions on games and strategies into a proof theoretic framework, we have rediscovered infinite and circular proofs: the first corresponding to infinite winning strategies, the latter corresponding to bounded memory winning strategies. Therefore the circular proofs presented here are meant to describe bounded memory deterministic strategies. The computational interpretation takes a game or a μ-term into the description of a bidirectional synchronous communication channel. Given two μ-terms S and T, a circular proof witness of $S \vdash T$ can be understood as a protocol for letting the left user of the channel S to communicate with the right user of T in a constrained but asynchronous way.

Our contribution. The calculus of circular proofs would be uninteresting if not supported by good properties. As one of these properties, we account the existence of a canonical semantics of proof terms. The main purpose of this paper is that of illustrating this point. The semantics establishes equivalences between proofs and an obvious consequence of the way the semantics will be defined is that proofs in the form of tree with back edges can be partially unraveled to obtain equivalent proofs, and that "bisimilar" proofs are equivalent. To define the semantics we proceed as follows: once the propositions (the types, in the terminology of type theory) of the calculus are interpreted in the obvious way by means of products, coproducts, initial algebras and final coalgebras, it is then possible to associate to a circular proof a system of equations defining relations among undetermined arrows of an arbitrary μ-bicomplete category. Theorem 3.7 states that the systems of equations arising from circular proofs admit always a unique solution. This is not an obvious result and depends strongly on the combinatorial condition by which we constrain cycles in circular proofs. To obtain this result, we need to improve the semantical tools that relate the theory of initial algebras to the theory of fixed points – known in type theory as Mendler's recursion [24] – in order to account for parameterized fixed points. This is the content of proposition 3.2.

A second property of the calculus, stated in 4.2, asserts that circular proofs are composable. This result is analogous to a cut elimination theorem in that it asserts the existence of an algorithm to produce a new cut free finite circular proof out of two given ones. This is an essential property of the calculus as it allows to consider circular proofs as concrete algorithms. To this end it would have been enough to observe that a lazy cut elimination holds (that is, a cut can indefinitely often be pushed up to a tree, producing an infinite tree). However our result is stronger, for example, under the given computational interpretation, it implies that there is a way of synthesizing a program without explicit substitution out of two programs with the same property. As far as we know, the most similar result concerns program transformation techniques [25]. The semantics allows to easily see that this sort of cut elimination is sound: two proofs can be composed into a proof the interpretation of which is the categorical composition of the interpretations of the two original proofs. Finally, we observe that the calculus is not powerful enough to describe all the arrows of a free μ-bicomplete category. This reflects the fact that there are strategies that use an unbounded amount of memory, nonetheless, are computable. This observation suggests that some kind of step has to be done in order to describe free μ-bicomplete categories; on the other hand, we expect that the ideas and tools presented in this paper will be helpful in future researches.

The paper is organized as follows. In section 2 we describe the syntactical part of the calculus, defining first the terms and then the proofs. In section 3 we state the main technical proposition which on the other hand is the key to define the semantics of proofs. The semantics is then implicitly defined by observing that the systems of equations associated to proofs admit unique solutions. In section 4, as concluding remarks, we state a cut elimination theorem, discuss the fact that the calculus is not enough expressive with respect to its intended models, and suggest a natural relation with automata theory. Full proofs of the statements presented here can be found in [22] and its extended version. The author is grateful to Robin Cockett for stimulating conversations on the subject.

Notation. With Set we shall denote the category of sets and functions; for a function $f : A \longrightarrow B$ we shall use both the notations f_a and $f(a)$ for the result of applying f to a. With $[n]$ we shall denote the set $\{1, \ldots, n\}$. Composition in categories, say $A \xrightarrow{f} B \xrightarrow{g} C$, will be denoted in two different ways, that is, $g \circ f$ and $f \cdot g$. Sometimes we shall omit the symbol $\circ$ and write gf, but we always write the symbol $\cdot$. We shall use id for identities, $\langle \rangle$ and pr for tuples and projections, $\{\}$ and in for cotuples and injections, for every kind of categorical products and coproducts. If $f : C \times A \longrightarrow C$ is a function (or a system of equations), we shall denote by $f^\dagger : A \longrightarrow C$ its unique parameterized fixed point (unique solution) whenever this exists. Our conventions on variables are as follows: each variable $x, y, z, \ldots$ can be in two states, either it is free or it is bound to some value. As a general rule, we shall use the usual style $x, y, z, \ldots$ for free variables and the overlined typewriter style $\overline{\mathtt{x}}, \overline{\mathtt{y}}, \overline{\mathtt{z}}, \ldots$ for bound variables.

2   The Calculus of Circular Proofs

Before we formally present the calculus, we shall point out its essential properties by inspecting the following "circular proof". We observe that:

- It is a proof in a sort of a Gentzen system: there are sequents $\Gamma \vdash \Delta$, where the expressions Γ and Δ are simple formulas.
- The usual inference rules for disjunction and conjunction apply (true and false are treated as empty conjunction and disjunction respectively).
- There are inference rules (regenerations) allowing to replace variables with their values according to the set of equations on the left.

$$\left\{\begin{array}{l} \overline{x} =_\mu \overline{y} \vee \overline{x} \\ \overline{y} =_\mu \top \vee \overline{y} \end{array}\right\}$$

```
                                   ——————— RΛ_∅
                                   ⊤ ⊢ ⊤
                          ————————————————— RV_{l,r}_l         ⟩ȳ ⊢ ȳ⟨_{10}
                          ⊤ ⊢ ⊤ ∨ ȳ                     ————————————— RV_{l,r}_r
                                                         ȳ ⊢ ⊤ ∨ ȳ
                          ————————————————————————————————————————— LV_{l,r}
                                     ⊤ ∨ ȳ ⊢ ⊤ ∨ ȳ
                                  ——————————————— Rȳ_μ
                                     ⊤ ∨ ȳ ⊢ ȳ
                                  ——————————— Lμȳ
                                     ȳ ⊢ ȳ
                                  ————————————— RV_{l,r}_r
                                     ȳ ⊢ ⊤ ∨ ȳ
                                  ——————————— Rȳ_μ
                                     ȳ ⊢ ȳ                            ⟩x̄ ⊢ x̄⟨_4
                                  ————————————— RV_{l,r}_l       ————————————— RV_{l,r}_r
                                     ȳ ⊢ ȳ ∨ x̄                  x̄ ⊢ ȳ ∨ x̄
          ——————— RΛ_∅             ———————————————————————————————————————— LV_{l,r}
          ⊤ ⊢ ⊤                               ȳ ∨ x̄ ⊢ ȳ ∨ x̄
      ————————————— RV_{l,r}_l              ———————————————— Rx̄_μ
      ⊤ ⊢ ⊤ ∨ ȳ                                ȳ ∨ x̄ ⊢ x̄
      ——————————— Rȳ_μ                       ——————————— Lμx̄
      ⊤ ⊢ ȳ                                     x̄ ⊢ x̄
      ————————————— RV_{l,r}_l               ————————————— RV_{l,r}_r
      ⊤ ⊢ ȳ ∨ x̄                              x̄ ⊢ ȳ ∨ x̄
      ——————————— Rx̄_μ                       ——————————— Rx̄_μ
      ⊤ ⊢ x̄                                     x̄ ⊢ x̄
      ———————————————————————————————————————————————————— LV_{l,r}
                        ⊤ ∨ x̄ ⊢ x̄
```

- Regeneration rules make it possible to construct infinite proof trees. We consider only regular trees and thus introduce the notation $\rangle\ldots\langle_n$ that you can see on some leaf. Its meaning is comparable to a `goto` command: "go back to the n-th node on the path from the root to this leaf, where you can find the same pair of formulas".

This circular proof has the following dynamic interpretation (which we have derived from the game theoretic setting): if $\top$ is read on the left, then no $\overline{x}$ is produced on the right and then no new $\overline{y}$ is produced on the right. If $\overline{x}$ is read on the left, then $\overline{x}$ is produced on the right and then as many $\overline{x}$s are produced on the right as they are received from the left. After this cycle, a $\overline{y}$ is produced on the right and then as many $\overline{y}$s are produced on the right as they are received.

We shall abstract from regular infinite trees and consider simply properly labeled finite graphs. Not every such graph will be a circular proof. We observe in the above proof that on every cycle we can find a variable which is regenerated on the left side of the sequent symbol. We shall discuss this point in more details after the formal definition of the calculus.

2.1 Directed Systems of Labeled Equations

We fix a signature Ω and by writing $H \in \Omega_n$, $n \geq 0$, we mean that H is a function symbol from Ω of arity n; we assume that the symbols $\bigwedge_I, \bigvee_I$ do not belong to Ω, for each finite set I. We let X be a countable set of variables, and let $\mathcal{C}$ be a category. We form terms as usual.

Definition 2.1. *The collection of terms $\mathcal{T}(\mathcal{C})$ and the free variables function* $\mathrm{fv} : \mathcal{T}(\mathcal{C}) \longrightarrow P(X)$ *are defined by induction by the following clauses:*

- *If $x \in X$, then $x \in \mathcal{T}(\mathcal{C})$ and $\mathrm{fv}(x) = \{x\}$.*
- *If c is an object of $\mathcal{C}$, then $c \in \mathcal{T}(\mathcal{C})$ and $\mathrm{fv}(c) = \emptyset$.*
- *If I is a finite set and $s : I \longrightarrow \mathcal{T}(\mathcal{C})$ is a function, then $\bigwedge_I s \in \mathcal{T}(\mathcal{C})$ and $\bigvee_I s \in \mathcal{T}(\mathcal{C})$. Moreover $\mathrm{fv}(\bigwedge_I s) = \mathrm{fv}(\bigvee_I s) = \bigcup_{i \in I} \mathrm{fv}(s_i)$.*
- *If $H \in \Omega_n$ and $s : [n] \longrightarrow \mathcal{T}(\mathcal{C})$ is a function, then $Hs \in \mathcal{T}(\mathcal{C})$ and $\mathrm{fv}(Hs) = \bigcup_{i \in [n]} \mathrm{fv}(s_i)$.*

If $Y \subseteq X$, we denote by $\mathcal{T}(\mathcal{C}, Y)$ the collection of terms $s \in \mathcal{T}(\mathcal{C})$ such that $\mathrm{fv}(s) \subseteq Y$. For a function $s : \{l, r\} \longrightarrow \mathcal{T}(\mathcal{C})$ we use the standard notation and write $s_l \wedge s_r, s_l \vee s_r$ for $\bigwedge_{\{l,r\}} s, \bigvee_{\{l,r\}} s$, respectively. Similarly, $\top$ stands for $\bigwedge_\emptyset$ and $\bot$ stands for $\bigvee_\emptyset$.

Definition 2.2. *A polarized system of equations over $\mathcal{C}$ is a tuple $\langle \overline{X}, q, \epsilon \rangle$ where*

- *$\overline{X} \subseteq X$ is a finite subset of X, the set of bound variables.*
- *$q : \overline{X} \longrightarrow \mathcal{T}(\mathcal{C})$ is a function associating a value to each bound variable.*
- *$\epsilon : \overline{X} \longrightarrow \{\mu, \nu\}$ is a labeling of bound variables.*

Given a polarized system of equations $\langle \overline{X}, q, \epsilon \rangle$, the relation $\rightarrow$ on the set of variables X is defined by saying that $\overline{x} \rightarrow y$ if and only if $\overline{x} \in \overline{X}$ and $y \in \mathrm{fv}(q_{\overline{x}})$.

Definition 2.3. *A tuple $S = \langle \overline{X}_S, q_S, \epsilon_S, \overline{X}_{0,S} \rangle$ is said to be a directed system over $\mathcal{C}$ if $\langle \overline{X}_S, q_S, \epsilon_S \rangle$ is a polarized system of equations, $\overline{X}_{0,S} \subseteq \overline{X}_S$ and moreover for each $\overline{x} \in \overline{X}_S$ there exists a unique simple path in the graph $\langle \overline{X}_S, \rightarrow \rangle$ from an element $r(\overline{x}) \in \overline{X}_{0,S}$ to $\overline{x}$. For $\overline{x}, \overline{y} \in \overline{X}_S$, we write $\overline{x} \leq_S \overline{y}$ if $\overline{x}$ lies on the simple path from $r(\overline{y})$ to $\overline{y}$; we write $\overline{x} <_S \overline{y}$ if $\overline{x} \leq_S \overline{y}$ and $\overline{x} \neq \overline{y}$. We let $\mathrm{fv}(S)$ be the set $(\bigcup_{\overline{x} \in \overline{X}_S} \mathrm{fv}(q_{\overline{x}})) \setminus \overline{X}_S$ and by $\mathrm{V}(S)$ we denote the collection of finite subsets Y of X such that $\mathrm{fv}(S) \subseteq Y$ and $Y \cap \overline{X}_S = \emptyset$. With $\mathcal{S}(\mathcal{C})$ we denote the collection of directed systems over $\mathcal{C}$.*

The notation $\{\overline{x} =_{\epsilon_{\overline{x}}} q_{\overline{x}}\}_{\overline{x} \in \overline{X}}$ is used to represent a polarized system of equations $\langle \overline{X}, q, \epsilon \rangle$. Roughly speaking, directed systems stand for μ-terms, for example the μ-term $\mu_x.\nu_y.(x \wedge \mu_z.(z \vee y))$ is translated into the directed system on the right which comes with the graph structure on bound variables; the induced order is

$$\left\langle \left\{ \begin{array}{l} \overline{x} =_\mu \overline{y} \\ \overline{y} =_\nu \overline{x} \wedge \overline{z} \\ \overline{z} =_\mu \overline{z} \vee \overline{y} \end{array} \right\}, \{\overline{x}\} \right\rangle$$

$\overline{x} < \overline{y} < \overline{z}$. Observe that the order does matter: the two directed systems on the right have the same underlying labeled system, however they represent the μ-terms $\mu_x.\nu_y.(x \wedge y)$

$$\left\langle \left\{ \begin{array}{l} \overline{x} =_\mu \overline{y} \\ \overline{y} =_\nu \overline{x} \wedge \overline{y} \end{array} \right\}, \{\overline{x}\} \right\rangle \quad \left\langle \left\{ \begin{array}{l} \overline{x} =_\mu \overline{y} \\ \overline{y} =_\nu \overline{x} \wedge \overline{y} \end{array} \right\}, \{\overline{y}\} \right\rangle$$

and $\nu_y.((\mu_x.y) \wedge y)$, respectively. In the category of sets, the interpretation of the first will be the empty set, where the interpretation of the second will be the set of unlabeled infinite binary trees, i.e. a singleton.

Let S be a directed system, with $(\overline{x})_{\downarrow S}$ we denote the set of variables $\overline{y}$ such that $\overline{y} \leq_S \overline{x}$. By S_x we denote the system obtained from S by freeing the variable

x: we let $\overline{X}_{S_x}$ be the set of variables $\overline{z}$ such that $\overline{x} <_S \overline{z}$ and let $\overline{X}_{0,S_x}, q_{S_x}$ and ϵ_{S_x} be the restrictions of $\overline{X}_{0,S}, q_S$ and ϵ_S to $\overline{X}_{S_x}$. It is easily verified that $\mathrm{fv}(S_x)$ is a subset of $\mathrm{fv}(S) \cup (\overline{x})_{\downarrow_S}$.

2.2   Circular Proofs

Let S, T be two directed systems over $\mathcal{C}$. The collection $\mathcal{R}_{S,T}$ of *rule symbols* over S, T, with their arity set, is defined by means of table on the right.

Definition 2.4. *A*   *tuple* $\langle G_0, \lambda, \rho, \sigma \rangle$, *where*

- G_0 *is a set of vertices,*
- $\lambda : G_0 \longrightarrow \mathcal{T}(\mathcal{C}) \times \mathcal{T}(\mathcal{C})$ *is a labeling of vertices by sequents,*
- $\rho : G_0 \longrightarrow \mathcal{R}_{S,T}$ *is a labeling of vertices by rule symbols over S, T,*
- $\sigma_g : \mathrm{Arity}(\rho(g)) \longrightarrow G_0$ *is a successor function associated to each $g \in G_0$,*

Rule	Range	Arity
A		$[0]$
Cf	f is an arrow of $\mathcal{C}$	$[0]$
CH	$H \in \Omega_n$	$[n]$
L$\bigwedge_{Ii}$	I is a finite set, $i \in I$	$[1]$
R$\bigwedge_{I}$	I is a finite set	I
L$\bigvee_{I}$	I is a finite set	I
R$\bigvee_{Ii}$	I is a finite set, $i \in I$	$[1]$
L$\mu\overline{x}$	$\overline{x} \in \overline{X}_S, \epsilon_S(\overline{x}) = \mu$	$[1]$
R$\overline{y}_\mu$	$\overline{y} \in \overline{X}_T, \epsilon_T(\overline{y}) = \mu$	$[1]$
L$\overline{x}_\nu$	$\overline{x} \in \overline{X}_S, \epsilon_S(\overline{x}) = \nu$	$[1]$
R$\nu\overline{y}$	$\overline{y} \in \overline{X}_T, \epsilon_T(\overline{y}) = \nu$	$[1]$

is said to be well typed *over S, T if the typing constraints, defined in the following, hold.*

We present typing constraints on the right. A typing constraint has the form

$$\frac{\{s_i \vdash t_i\}_{i \in \mathrm{Arity}(R)}}{s \vdash t} R$$

and stands for the following implication: *for all $g \in G_0$, if $\rho(g) = R$, then $\lambda(g)$ has the form $s \vdash t$ and for each $i \in \mathrm{Arity}(R)$ $\lambda(\sigma_{g,i})$ has the form $s_i \vdash t_i$.*

Typing constraints are analogous to inference rules. For technical reasons we need the rule A: a sequent justified by this rule has to be considered an assumption. Indeed, if $P = \langle G_0, \lambda, \rho, \sigma \rangle$ is a tuple well typed over S, T, we say that

$$\frac{}{s \vdash t} A$$

$$\frac{}{\mathrm{dom}\, f \vdash \mathrm{cod}\, f} Cf \qquad \frac{\{s_i \vdash t_i\}_{i \in [n]}}{Hs \vdash Ht} CH$$

$$\frac{s_i \vdash t}{\bigwedge_I s \vdash t} L\bigwedge_{Ii} \qquad \frac{\{s \vdash t_i\}_{i \in I}}{s \vdash \bigwedge_I t} R\bigwedge_I$$

$$\frac{\{s_i \vdash t\}_{i \in I}}{\bigvee_I s \vdash t} L\bigvee_I \qquad \frac{s \vdash t_i}{s \vdash \bigvee_I t} R\bigvee_{Ii}$$

$$\frac{q_{\overline{x}} \vdash t}{\overline{x} \vdash t} L\mu\overline{x} \qquad \frac{s \vdash q_{\overline{y}}}{s \vdash \overline{y}} R\overline{y}_\mu$$

$$\frac{q_{\overline{x}} \vdash t}{\overline{x} \vdash t} L\overline{x}_\nu \qquad \frac{s \vdash q_{\overline{y}}}{s \vdash \overline{y}} R\nu\overline{y}$$

a vertex $g \in G_0$ is a *conclusion* if $\rho(g) \neq \mathsf{A}$ and that it is an *assumption* if $\rho(g) = \mathsf{A}$. We denote by $\mathcal{C}_P$ and $\mathcal{A}_P$ the set of conclusions and the set of assumptions of P, respectively. Not every well typed tuple is going to be a circular proof. To define this concept we need to analyze the graph underlying such a tuple.

Definition 2.5. *Let $P = \langle G_0, \lambda, \rho, \sigma \rangle$ be a tuple which is well typed over S, T. The graph $\mathcal{G}(P) = \langle G_0, \rightarrow \rangle$ has as vertices the elements of G_0, and $g \rightarrow g'$ iff $g' = \sigma_{g,i}$ for some $i \in \mathrm{Arity}(\rho(g))$. Let $\gamma_0 \rightarrow \gamma_1 \rightarrow \ldots \gamma_n = \gamma_0$, $n \geq 1$, be a proper cycle of $\mathcal{G}(P)$. We let*

$$\gamma_S = \{ \, \overline{\mathsf{x}} \in \overline{\mathsf{X}}_S \mid \exists i \in [n] \ s.t. \ \rho(\gamma_i) \in \{ \mathsf{L}\mu\overline{\mathsf{x}}, \mathsf{L}\overline{\mathsf{x}}_\nu \} \, \},$$
$$\gamma_T = \{ \, \overline{\mathsf{x}} \in \overline{\mathsf{X}}_T \mid \exists i \in [n] \ s.t. \ \rho(\gamma_i) \in \{ \mathsf{R}\overline{\mathsf{x}}_\mu, \mathsf{R}\nu\overline{\mathsf{x}} \} \, \}.$$

Observe that if γ is a proper cycle of $\mathcal{G}(P)$, then either $\gamma_S \neq \emptyset$ or $\gamma_T \neq \emptyset$. If $\gamma_S \neq \emptyset$, then γ_S is a strongly connected subgraph of the graph associated to S, hence we can find a minimum element with respect to the order $\leq_S$. A similar remark holds for γ_T.

Definition 2.6. *A tuple Π well typed over S, T is said to be a* circular proof *over S, T, if, for every proper cycle γ of $\mathcal{G}(\Pi)$, either $\gamma_S \neq \emptyset$ and $\epsilon(\min \gamma_S) = \mu$, or $\gamma_T \neq \emptyset$ and $\epsilon(\min \gamma_T) = \nu$.*

We refer to the first statement as $\mathsf{L}(\gamma)$, and to the second as $\mathsf{R}(\gamma)$, so that a tuple Π, well typed over S, T, is a circular proof over S, T if for every proper cycle γ of $\mathcal{G}(\Pi)$ either $\mathsf{L}(\gamma)$ holds or $\mathsf{R}(\gamma)$ holds. The above condition can be understood as follows: the systems S and T are translations of games for free μ-lattices, and a circular proof is meant to describe a bounded memory winning strategy in the compound game $S \multimap T$, which we described in [20, 21]. As in Blass' game semantics of Linear Logic [5] and in Joyal's games for communication [14], a chosen player has to win either on S or on T. On the other hand, the games S and T are parity games, cf. [4]. Henceforth, the condition $\mathsf{L}(\gamma)$ can be understood as stating the fact that the chosen player of S won't lose in this game by repeating infinitely often the instructions contained in the cycle γ of his winning strategy.

In the examples we consider circular proofs coming with a base point, i.e. a chosen conclusion, such that the underlying pointed graph is a tree with back edges. It is our goal to remark the analogy with the usual model of a proof as a finite tree and use existing tools for drawing proofs. It is a consequence of the theory presented here that every circular proof with a chosen conclusion is equivalent to another one having the tree-with-back-edges shape. Hence, we draw trees with some of the leaves anno-tated by a number, as exemplified on the right. With this notation we mean that there is a transition in $\mathcal{G}(\Pi)$ from the vertex g to the vertex that is at the n-th place on the path from the root to g.

$$\frac{\rangle s \vdash t \langle_n \quad \cdots}{\lambda(g)} \rho(g)$$
$$\vdots$$

In the data below, let S be the the directed system on the left and observe that the associated order is $\overline{\mathsf{x}} <_S \overline{\mathsf{y}}$. If T is the empty system of equations, then the two proof objects on the center and on the right below are both well typed over S and T:

$$\left\langle \left\{ \begin{array}{l} \overline{\mathbf{x}} =_\nu \overline{\mathbf{y}} \\ \overline{\mathbf{y}} =_\mu \overline{\mathbf{x}} \wedge \overline{\mathbf{y}} \end{array} \right\} , \{\overline{\mathbf{x}}\} \right\rangle \qquad \cfrac{\cfrac{\cfrac{\cfrac{\rangle \overline{\mathbf{y}} \vdash \bot \langle_2}{\overline{\mathbf{x}} \wedge \overline{\mathbf{y}} \vdash \bot} \, \mathsf{L}\!\bigwedge_{\{l,r\}r}}{\overline{\mathbf{y}} \vdash \bot} \, \mathsf{L}\mu\overline{\mathbf{y}}}{\overline{\mathbf{x}} \vdash \bot} \, \mathsf{L}\overline{\mathbf{x}}_\nu} \qquad \cfrac{\cfrac{\cfrac{\cfrac{\rangle \overline{\mathbf{x}} \vdash \bot \langle_1}{\overline{\mathbf{x}} \wedge \overline{\mathbf{y}} \vdash \bot} \, \mathsf{L}\!\bigwedge_{\{l,r\}l}}{\overline{\mathbf{y}} \vdash \bot} \, \mathsf{L}\mu\overline{\mathbf{y}}}{\overline{\mathbf{x}} \vdash \bot} \, \mathsf{L}\overline{\mathbf{x}}_\nu}$$

The one on the center is a circular proof over S,T. The one on the right is not, since it does not satisfy condition of definition 2.6 on cycles. Indeed, let γ be the only simple cycle on this graph. $\mathsf{R}(\gamma)$ does not hold, since $\gamma_T = \emptyset$. On the other hand $\mathsf{L}(\gamma)$ does not hold, since $\min \gamma_S = \overline{\mathbf{x}}$ and $\epsilon(\overline{\mathbf{x}}) = \nu$.

To end this section, we introduce some notation. Let Π be a circular proof over the directed systems S,T. We write s_g, t_g if g is a vertex of Π and $\lambda(g) = s_g \vdash t_g$. We let $\mathrm{fv}_l(\Pi)$ be the set $\mathrm{fv}(S) \cup (\bigcup_{g\in G_0} \mathrm{fv}(s_g)) \backslash \overline{\mathbf{X}}_S$ and let $\mathrm{fv}_r(\Pi)$ be the set $\mathrm{fv}(T) \cup (\bigcup_{g\in G_0} \mathrm{fv}(t_g)) \backslash \overline{\mathbf{X}}_T$. Observe that $\mathrm{fv}_l(\Pi) \in \mathsf{V}(S)$ and $\mathrm{fv}_r(\Pi) \in \mathsf{V}(T)$, and that, for $g \in G_0$, $s_g \in \mathcal{T}(\mathcal{C}, \overline{\mathbf{X}}_S \cup \mathrm{fv}_l(\Pi))$ and $t_g \in \mathcal{T}(\mathcal{C}, \overline{\mathbf{X}}_T \cup \mathrm{fv}_r(\Pi))$.

3   Semantics of the Calculus

The logical operators by which we have constructed terms and directed systems – that is, conjunction, disjunction, least prefixed point and greatest postfixed point – can be naturally interpreted in the category $\mathcal{C}$ provided $\mathcal{C}$ has finite products, finite coproducts and "enough" initial algebras and final coalgebras. We recall the definition of the latter two concepts and remind that these are categorical analogues of inductive and coinductive types.

Definition 3.1. *Let $S : \mathcal{C} \longrightarrow \mathcal{C}$ be an endofunctor, an S-algebra is a pair (c, γ) where c is an object of $\mathcal{C}$ and $\gamma : Sc \longrightarrow c$ is an arrow of $\mathcal{C}$. An S-algebra $(\overline{\mathbf{x}}, \chi)$ is initial if for each algebra (c, γ) there exists a unique arrow $f : \overline{\mathbf{x}} \longrightarrow c$ such that $\chi \cdot f = Sf \cdot \gamma$. We define S-coalgebras in the dual way; an S-coalgebra $\theta : \overline{\mathbf{y}} \longrightarrow S\overline{\mathbf{y}}$ is final if for each coalgebra $\gamma : c \longrightarrow Sc$ there exists a unique arrow $f : c \longrightarrow \overline{\mathbf{y}}$ such that $f \cdot \theta = \gamma \cdot Sf$.*

It is known [16] that the arrow χ of an initial S-algebra $(\overline{\mathbf{x}}, \chi)$ is invertible. The universal property of the initial algebra states the existence and uniqueness of a solution of the equation $f = \chi^{-1} \cdot Sf \cdot \alpha$ for each algebra $\alpha : Sa \longrightarrow a$. This equation is rephrased in a more compact way as the fixed point equation

$$f = \chi^{-1} \cdot \alpha_{\overline{\mathbf{x}}}(f) \,,$$

where the transformation (natural in the variable x) $\alpha_x : \mathcal{C}(x, a) \longrightarrow \mathcal{C}(Sx, a)$ is defined by the formula $\alpha_x(f) = Sf \cdot \alpha$. Henceforth, we shall approach initial algebras and final coalgebras from the point of view of fixed point theory [6]. In order to obtain the full power of this theory we need a parameterized version of the universal property, which can be deduced if the category $\mathcal{C}$ has products.

Proposition 3.2. *Let* $\mathcal{Z}, \mathcal{W}, \mathcal{C}$ *be three categories, of which* $\mathcal{C}$ *has finite products, and let* S, T *and* Q *be functors such that* $S : \mathcal{C} \times \mathcal{Z} \longrightarrow \mathcal{C}$, $T : \mathcal{W} \longrightarrow \mathcal{C}$, *and* $Q : \mathcal{C}^{op} \times \mathcal{Z}^{op} \times \mathcal{W} \longrightarrow$ Set. *Consider a natural transformation*

$$\alpha_{x,z,w} : \mathcal{C}(x, Tw) \times Q(x, z, w) \longrightarrow \mathcal{C}(S(x,z), Tw)$$

and let $(\overline{x}_z, \chi_z)$ *be a parameterized initial algebra of the functor* $S(x, z)$. *For each object* z *of* $\mathcal{Z}$, w *of* $\mathcal{W}$ *and each* $q \in Q(\overline{x}_z, z, w)$, *there exists a unique* $f : \overline{x}_z \longrightarrow Tw$ *that is a solution of the equation*

$$f = \chi_z^{-1} \cdot \alpha_{\overline{x}_z, z, w}(f, q) \,.$$

Unique solutions of the above equation make up a natural transformation

$$\beta_{z,w} : Q(\overline{x}_z, z, w) \longrightarrow C(\overline{x}_z, Tw) \,.$$

The above proposition leads to show that circular proofs, whenever interpreted as systems of equations, always admit a unique solution. The other tool needed is the Bekič lemma, cf. [6, §5.3.1.c], which can be stated in the form of a sufficient condition to determine whether a system admits a unique solution in terms of its subsystems. Before giving the formal semantics, we shall sketch our ideas with the circular proof of page 365. We can define the semantics of a directed system as for the μ-term $\nu_x.\mu_y.(x \wedge y)$. We let

$\|x \wedge y\| = \times : \mathcal{C} \times \mathcal{C} \longrightarrow \mathcal{C}$.

$\|\overline{y}\| = $ The initial algebra of the above functor, parameterized in the variable x. This makes up a functor:
$$\mu_{\overline{y}}.(x \times \overline{y}) : \mathcal{C} \longrightarrow \mathcal{C} \,.$$

$\|\overline{x}\| = $ The final coalgebra of the above functor:
$$\nu_{\overline{x}}.\mu_{\overline{y}}.(\overline{x} \times \overline{y}) : 1 \longrightarrow \mathcal{C} \,.$$

Observe that $\|\overline{x}\|$, corresponding to a closed μ-term, can be thought to be an object of $\mathcal{C}$. At this point, $\|\overline{y}\|$ and $\|\overline{x} \wedge \overline{y}\|$ can be closed too, so that they also become objects of $\mathcal{C}$:

$$\|\overline{y}\| = 1 \xrightarrow{\ \|\overline{x}\|\ } \mathcal{C} \xrightarrow{\ \|\overline{y}\|\ } \mathcal{C}$$

$$\|\overline{x} \wedge \overline{y}\| = 1 \xrightarrow{\ \langle \|\overline{x}\|, \|\overline{y}\| \rangle\ } \mathcal{C} \times \mathcal{C} \xrightarrow{\ \times = \|x \wedge y\|\ } \mathcal{C} \,.$$

In order to interpret the circular proof of page 365 we associate to it a system of equations. Recall that we have

$$\|\overline{x} \wedge \overline{y}\| = \|\overline{x}\| \times \|\overline{y}\| \xrightarrow{\ \mathrm{pr}_{\|\overline{y}\|}\ } \|\overline{y}\|$$
$$\text{product structure}$$

$$\|\overline{y}\| = \|\overline{y}\|(\|\overline{x}\|) \xleftarrow{\ \theta_{\|\overline{x}\|}\ } \|\overline{x}\| \times \|\overline{y}\|(\|\overline{x}\|) = \|\overline{x} \wedge \overline{y}\|$$
$$\text{initial algebra structure}$$

$$\|\overline{x}\| \xrightarrow{\ \chi\ } \|\overline{y}\|(\|\overline{x}\|) = \|\overline{y}\|$$
$$\text{final coalgebra structure} \,.$$

Thus we can transform the circular proof into a system of equations:

$$
\cfrac{\cfrac{\cfrac{\rangle \overline{y} \vdash \bot \langle_2}{\overline{x} \wedge \overline{y} \vdash \bot}{}_3\; \mathsf{L}\!\wedge_r}{\overline{y} \vdash \bot}{}_2\; \mathsf{L}\mu\overline{y}}{\overline{x} \vdash \bot}{}_1\; \mathsf{L}\overline{x}_\nu
\qquad \rightsquigarrow \qquad
\left\{
\begin{array}{l}
h_3 = \mathtt{pr}_{\|\overline{y}\|} \cdot h_2 \\[4pt]
h_2 = \theta_{\|\overline{x}\|}^{-1} \cdot h_3 \\[4pt]
h_1 = \chi \cdot h_2
\end{array}
\right\}
$$

We shall see that this system admits a unique solution.

3.1   Semantics of Systems

In the following $\mathcal{C}$ will be a fixed category and I, J will range over finite sets. A functor $S : \mathcal{C}^{\{x\} \cup J} \longrightarrow \mathcal{C}$ is said to *admit initial algebras* if, for each object z of $\mathcal{C}^J$, an initial algebra of the functor $S(-, z)$ exists. Observe that if $R : \mathcal{C}^I \longrightarrow \mathcal{C}^J$ is a functor and $S : \mathcal{C}^{\{x\} \cup J} \longrightarrow \mathcal{C}$ admits initial algebras, then also the functor

$$
S \circ (\mathtt{id}_\mathcal{C} \times R) : \mathcal{C}^{\{x\} \cup I} \longrightarrow \mathcal{C}
$$

admits initial algebras. A *choice of initial algebras* is a correspondence $(\overline{x}, \chi)$ that assigns to each pair (S, z), where $S : \mathcal{C}^{\{x\} \cup J} \longrightarrow \mathcal{C}$ admits initial algebras and z is an object of $\mathcal{C}^J$, an initial algebra $\chi_z : S(\overline{x}_z, z) \longrightarrow \overline{x}_z$. We shall require that a choice of initial algebras is stable under substitution, that is, if $\chi_z : S(\overline{x}_z, z) \longrightarrow \overline{x}_z$ is the initial algebra associated to the pair (S, z), then $\chi_{Ru} : S(\overline{x}_{Ru}, Ru) \longrightarrow \overline{x}_{Ru}$ is the initial algebra associated to the pair $(S \circ (\mathtt{id}_\mathcal{C} \times R), u)$. A *choice of final coalgebras* is defined in a similar way.

Definition 3.3. *An Ω-model is a pair $\langle \mathcal{C}, \mathcal{I} \rangle$ where $\mathcal{C}$ is a category with a given choice of finite products, finite coproducts, initial algebras and final coalgebras, and $\mathcal{I}$ is an interpretation of the signature, that is, a correspondence which assigns a functor $\mathcal{I}(H) : \mathcal{C}^n \longrightarrow \mathcal{C}$ to each symbol $H \in \Omega_n$, for each $n \geq 0$.*

We can avoid the use of choices if we allow uniqueness up to unique natural isomorphism in proposition 3.4. To ease the notation, we shall write simply $H : \mathcal{C}^n \longrightarrow \mathcal{C}$ for $\mathcal{I}(H) : \mathcal{C}^n \longrightarrow \mathcal{C}$ and say that $\mathcal{C}$ is an Ω-model. To understand properly the next proposition, recall that if $\mathcal{C}$ has products (coproducts), then the functor category $\mathcal{C}^J$ has products (coproducts), which are calculated pointwise. Hence, a choice of products (coproducts) gives rise to a choice of products (coproducts) in the category $\mathcal{C}^J$. In a similar way, a choice of initial algebras (final coalgebras) determines, for each functor $S : \mathcal{C}^{\{x\} \cup J} \longrightarrow \mathcal{C}$ admitting initial algebras, a unique extension of the collection of objects $\{\overline{x}_z\}_{z \in Obj(\mathcal{C}^J)}$ to a functor $\overline{x} : \mathcal{C}^J \longrightarrow \mathcal{C}$ such that χ_z is a natural transformation from $S(\overline{x}_z, z)$ to $\overline{x}_z$.

Proposition 3.4. *Let $\mathcal{C}$ be an Ω-model, let $S \in \mathcal{S}(\mathcal{C})$ and $Z \in \mathrm{V}(S)$. There exists at most one correspondence $\|-\|_S^Z$, defined on $\mathcal{T}(\mathcal{C}, \overline{x}_S \cup Z)$, with the following properties:*

- For each $s \in \mathcal{T}(\mathcal{C}, \overline{\mathbf{x}}_S \cup Z)$, $\|s\|_S^Z$ is a functor $\mathcal{C}^Z \longrightarrow \mathcal{C}$.
- For each $z \in Z$, $\|z\|_S^Z$ is the projection functor on the z component.
- For each object c of $\mathcal{C}$, $\|c\|_S^Z = c$, a constant functor.
- If $s : I \longrightarrow \mathcal{T}(\mathcal{C}, \overline{\mathbf{x}}_S \cup Z)$, then $\|\bigwedge_I s\|_S^Z = \prod_{i \in I} \|s_i\|_S^Z$ and $\|\bigvee_I s\|_S^Z = \coprod_{i \in I} \|s_i\|_S^Z$.
- If $H \in \Omega_n$ and $s : [n] \longrightarrow \mathcal{T}(\mathcal{C}, \overline{\mathbf{x}}_S \cup Z)$, then $\|Hs\|_S^Z = H \circ \langle \|s_i\|_S^Z \rangle_{i \in [n]}$.
- If the equation $\overline{\mathbf{x}} =_\mu q_{\overline{\mathbf{x}}}$ belongs to S, then $\|\overline{\mathbf{x}}\|_S^Z$ is the chosen initial algebra of the functor

$$\|q_x\|_{S_x}^{(\overline{\mathbf{x}})_{\downarrow_S} \cup Z} \circ \left(\mathrm{id}_{\mathcal{C}} \times \langle \|\overline{\mathbf{y}}\|_S^Z, \mathrm{id}_{\mathcal{C}^Z} \rangle_{\overline{\mathbf{y}} <_S \overline{\mathbf{x}}}\right) : \mathcal{C}^{\{x\} \cup Z} \longrightarrow \mathcal{C}.$$

- If the equation $\overline{\mathbf{x}} =_\nu q_{\overline{\mathbf{x}}}$ belongs to S, then $\|\overline{\mathbf{x}}\|_S^Z$ is the chosen final coalgebra of the above functor.

Observe that we need the relation $(\overline{\mathbf{x}})_{\downarrow_S} \cup Z \in \mathrm{V}(S_x)$ to hold, however it is not difficult to derive it. We can now introduce the following definition.

Definition 3.5. *An Ω-model $\mathcal{C}$ is said to be μ-bicomplete if, for each directed system $S \in \mathcal{S}(\mathcal{C})$ and $Z \in \mathrm{V}(S)$, there exists exactly one correspondence $\|-\|_S^Z$ with the above properties.*

Every complete lattice L with an interpretation of the signature Ω is a μ-bicomplete Ω-model. If Ω is the empty signature, then a lattice L is μ-bicomplete if and only if it is a μ-lattice [20]. We have proved in [23] that a model $\langle \mathcal{C}, \mathcal{I} \rangle$ is μ-bicomplete if (1) the interpretation of every function symbol is an accessible functor, and (2) the category $\mathcal{C}$ is locally presentable, cf. [3]. Assuming (1), it follows that a model is μ-bicomplete if its underlying category is the category of sets and functions or is a variety or quasivariety of algebras. For example, the category of sets and partial functions is μ-bicomplete, since this category is equivalent to the variety of pointed sets and functions that preserve the points.

3.2   Semantics of Circular Proofs

We shall suppose in the following that $\mathcal{C}$ is a μ-bicomplete Ω-model.

Definition 3.6. *Let $\Pi = \langle G_0, \lambda, \rho, \sigma \rangle$ be a circular proof over $S, T \in \mathcal{S}(\mathcal{C})$. If the equation $\overline{\mathbf{x}} =_\mu q_{\overline{\mathbf{x}}}$ is in S (resp. T), let χ be the arrow part of the chosen initial algebras of the functor $\|q_x\|_{S_x}^{(x)_{\downarrow_S} \cup Z}$ (resp. $\|q_x\|_{T_x}^{(x)_{\downarrow_T} \cup W}$). Similarly, let θ be the arrow part of a chosen final coalgebra associated to an equation of the form $\overline{\mathbf{y}} =_\nu q_{\overline{\mathbf{y}}}$ and to the analogous functorial expression. The (natural) system of equations $\|\Pi\|$ in the variables $\{h_g\}_{g \in G_0}$ has the form*

$$\left\{ h_g = \|\rho(g)\| (h_{\sigma_{g,i}})_{i \in \mathrm{Arity}(\rho(g))} \right\}_{g \in \mathcal{C}_\Pi}$$

where

$$\|\mathsf{C}f\| = f \qquad\qquad \|\mathsf{C}H\|(h_i)_{i\in[n]} = H(h_1,\ldots,h_n)$$

$$\|\mathsf{L}\bigwedge_{I\,i}\|(h) = \mathrm{pr}_i \cdot h \qquad\qquad \|\mathsf{R}\bigwedge_I\|(h_i)_{i\in I} = \langle h_i\rangle_{i\in I}$$

$$\|\mathsf{L}\bigvee_I\|(h_i)_{i\in I} = \{h_i\}_{i\in I} \qquad\qquad \|\mathsf{R}\bigvee_{I\,i}\|(h) = h \cdot \mathrm{in}_i$$

$$\|\mathsf{L}\mu\overline{\mathsf{x}}\|(h) = \chi^{-1} \cdot h \qquad\qquad \|\mathsf{R}\overline{\mathsf{x}}_\mu\|(h) = h \cdot \chi$$

$$\|\mathsf{L}\overline{\mathsf{y}}_\nu\|(h) = \theta \cdot h \qquad\qquad \|\mathsf{R}\nu\overline{\mathsf{y}}\|(h) = h \cdot \theta^{-1} \ .$$

Let $Z = \mathrm{fv}_l(\Pi)$ and and $W = \mathrm{fv}_r(\Pi)$. This system of equation can be seen as a natural transformation

$$\|\Pi\| : \prod_{g\in\mathcal{C}_\Pi} \mathcal{C}_{S,T}(g) \times \prod_{g\in\mathcal{A}_\Pi} \mathcal{C}_{S,T}(g) \longrightarrow \prod_{g\in\mathcal{C}_\Pi} \mathcal{C}_{S,T}(g),$$

where $\mathcal{C}_{S,T}(g)$ is the functor

$$\mathcal{C}(\|s_g\|_S^Z, \|t_g\|_T^W) : (\mathcal{C}^Z)^{op} \times \mathcal{C}^W \longrightarrow \mathrm{Set}.$$

We can now state our main result.

Theorem 3.7. *The system $\|\Pi\|$ admits a unique (natural) solution*

$$\|\Pi\|^\dagger : \prod_{g\in\mathcal{A}_\Pi} \mathcal{C}_{S,T}(g) \longrightarrow \prod_{g\in\mathcal{C}_\Pi} \mathcal{C}_{S,T}(g).$$

Consider the circular proof on the right. From the fact that the associated system admits a unique solution it is easy to deduce that the interpretation of μ-term $\mu_x.x$, corresponding to $\overline{\mathsf{x}}$, has to be an initial object. On the other hand, consideration of the second well typed tuple tells us that the condition on cycles is necessary. The interpretation of $\nu_x.x$ in the category of sets is any singleton set, which cannot be an initial object, i.e. the empty set.

$$\{\overline{\mathsf{x}} =_\mu \overline{\mathsf{x}}\} \qquad \dfrac{\,\rangle\overline{\mathsf{x}} \vdash y\langle_1}{\overline{\mathsf{x}} \vdash y}\,\mathsf{L}\mu\overline{\mathsf{x}}$$

$$\{\overline{\mathsf{x}} =_\nu \overline{\mathsf{x}}\} \qquad \dfrac{\,\rangle\overline{\mathsf{x}} \vdash y\langle_1}{\overline{\mathsf{x}} \vdash y}\,\mathsf{L}\overline{\mathsf{x}}_\nu$$

4   Further Remarks and Future Work

The calculus presented in this paper satisfies a form of cut elimination, in a sound way. This is made precise in what follows.

Let S, T be two directed systems, a *pointed circular proof* over S, T is a pair $\langle\Pi, g_0\rangle$ where $\Pi = \langle G_0, \lambda, \rho, \sigma\rangle$ is a circular proof over S, T and $g_0 \in G_0$. We say that a pointed circular proof $\langle\Pi, g_0\rangle$ is *reachable* if the pointed graph $\langle\mathcal{G}(\Pi), g_0\rangle$ is reachable. A pair (s, S), where $S \in \mathcal{S}(\mathcal{C})$ and $s \in \mathcal{T}(\mathcal{C})$, is closed if $\mathrm{fv}(S) = \emptyset$ and $\mathrm{fv}(s) \subseteq \overline{\mathsf{X}}_S$. By writing $\Pi_{g_0} : (s, S) \longrightarrow (t, T)$ we mean that $\Pi_{g_0} = \langle\Pi, g_0\rangle$ is a reachable pointed circular proof over S, T such that $\lambda(g_0) = s \vdash t$, $\mathcal{A}_\Pi = \emptyset$ and moreover $(s, S), (t, T)$ are closed. We define the semantics of pointed reachable circular proofs in the obvious way.

Definition 4.1. *For $\Pi_{g_0} : (s, S) \longrightarrow (t, T)$, we let $\|\Pi_{g_0}\|$ be $\|\Pi\|^\dagger \cdot \mathrm{pr}_{g_0}$.*

If a pair (s, S) is closed, then $\|s\|_S^\emptyset : \mathcal{C}^\emptyset \longrightarrow \mathcal{C}$ can be identified with an object of $\mathcal{C}$. Moreover, if $\Pi_{g_0} : (s, S) \longrightarrow (t, T)$, then $\mathcal{A}_\Pi = \emptyset$ and the domain of $\|\Pi_{g_0}\|$ is a singleton set. It follows that $\|\Pi_{g_0}\|$ can be identified with an arrow from the object $\|s\|_S^\emptyset$ to the object $\|t\|_T^\emptyset$.

Theorem 4.2. *Let $\Pi_{g_0} : (s, S) \longrightarrow (t, T)$ and $\Gamma_{h_0} : (t, T) \longrightarrow (u, U)$ be pointed circular proofs. There is an algorithm to construct a pointed circular proof $\Pi_{g_0} ; \Gamma_{h_0} : (s, S) \longrightarrow (u, U)$ with the property that $\|\Pi_{g_0} ; \Gamma_{h_0}\| = \|\Pi_{g_0}\| \cdot \|\Gamma_{h_0}\|$.*

Identities are also definable in the calculus so that, up to the equations induced by the semantics, the above construction can be extended to the construction of a category. This is a proper subcategory of a free μ-bicomplete category, since the calculus is not powerful enough to describe all the arrows that are needed. The diagonal $\Delta : \mathbb{N} \longrightarrow \mathbb{N}^2$ arises as the unique algebra morphism from the initial one to the algebra $\langle \langle 0, 0 \rangle, s \times s \rangle : 1 + \mathbb{N}^2 \longrightarrow \mathbb{N}^2$, which is definable in the calculus being the interpretation of the circular proof of page 361 (here s is the successor function on natural numbers). Let S be the directed system to be found at the same page, so that $\|\overline{x}\|_S^\emptyset = \mathbb{N}^2$ and $\|\overline{y}\|_S^\emptyset = \mathbb{N}$.

Proposition 4.3. *There is no pointed reachable circular proof $\Pi_g : (\overline{y}, S) \longrightarrow (\overline{x}, S)$ such that $\|\Pi_g\|$ is the diagonal.*

The above result is analogous to the well known fact that the set of words $\{ a^n b^n \mid n \geq 0 \}$ is not recognizable and indeed the computation which arises under the cut elimination is similar to computation with finite automata. The above result shows that the ideas presented in this paper and the syntax of the calculus have to be generalized in order to describe free μ-bicomplete categories. However, it seems likely that the calculus presented here describes all the computations requiring bounded space and thus it seems interesting to understand the structure of the arising category of circular proofs, in particular to understand whether it has some kind of universal property. To this end we expect the comparison with [7] to be useful, since in this work analogous ideas are presented without a necessary reference to the notion of initial algebra.

References

1. S. Abramsky and R. Jagadeesan. Games and full completeness for multiplicative linear logic. *J. Symbolic Logic*, 59(2):543–574, 1994.
2. P. Aczel. *Non-well-founded sets*. Stanford University Center for the Study of Language and Information, Stanford, CA, 1988.
3. J. Adámek and J. Rosický. *Locally presentable and accessible categories*. Cambridge University Press, Cambridge, 1994.
4. A. Arnold and D. Niwinski. *Rudiments of mu-calculus*. Number 146 in Studies in Logic and the Foundations of Mathematics. Elsevier (North-Holland), 2001.
5. A. Blass. A game semantics for linear logic. *Ann. Pure Appl. Logic*, 56(1-3):183–220, 1992.
6. S. L. Bloom and Z. Ésik. *Iteration theories*. Springer-Verlag, Berlin, 1993. The equational logic of iterative processes.

7. S. L. Bloom, Z. Ésik, A. Labella, and E. G. Manes. Iteration 2-theories. *Appl. Categ. Structures*, 9(2):173–216, 2001.
8. J.R.B. Cockett and R.A.G. Seely. Finite sum-product logic. *Theory and Applications of Categories*, 8:63–99, 2001.
9. T. Coquand. Infinite objects in type theory. In *Types for proofs and programs (Nijmegen, 1993)*, pages 62–78. Springer, Berlin, 1994.
10. T. Coquand and C. Paulin. Inductively defined types. In *COLOG-88 (Tallinn, 1988)*, pages 50–66. Springer, Berlin, 1990.
11. J.-Y. Girard. Linear logic. *Theoret. Comput. Sci.*, 50(1):101, 1987.
12. H. Hu and A. Joyal. Coherence completions of categories. *Theoret. Comput. Sci.*, 227(1-2):153–184, 1999. Linear logic, I (Tokyo, 1996).
13. A. J. C. Hurkens, M. McArthur, Y. N. Moschovakis, L. S. Moss, and G. T. Whitney. The logic of recursive equations. *J. Symbolic Logic*, 63(2):451–478, 1998.
14. A. Joyal. Free lattices, communication, and money games. In *Logic and scientific methods*, pages 29–68. Kluwer Academic Publishers, 1997.
15. D. Kozen. Results on the propositional μ-calculus. *Theoret. Comput. Sci.*, 27(3):333–354, 1983.
16. J. Lambek. A fixpoint theorem for complete categories. *Math. Z.*, 103:151–161, 1968.
17. M. Lenisa. A complete coinductive logical system for bisimulation equivalence on circular objects. In *Foundations of software science and computation structures (Amsterdam, 1999)*, pages 243–257. Springer, Berlin, 1999.
18. J. J. M. M. Rutten. Universal coalgebra: a theory of systems. *Theoret. Comput. Sci.*, 249(1):3–80, 2000.
19. L. Santocanale. The alternation hierarchy for the theory of μ-lattices. Technical Report RS-00-29, BRICS, November 2000. To appear in *Theory and Applications of Categories*.
20. L. Santocanale. Free μ-lattices. Technical Report RS-00-28, BRICS, November 2000. To appear in *Journal of Pure and Applied Algebra*.
21. L. Santocanale. *Sur les μ-treillis libres*. PhD thesis, Université du Québec à Montréal, July 2000.
22. L. Santocanale. A calculus of circular proofs and its categorical semantics. Technical Report RS-01-15, BRICS, May 2001. Extended version available from: http://www.cpsc.ucalgary.ca/~luigis/.
23. L. Santocanale. Parity functors and μ-bicomplete categories (extended abstract). In *Fixed Points in Computer Science 2001*, September 2001. Extended version submitted.
24. T. Uustalu and V. Vene. Mendler-style inductive types, categorically. *Nordic J. Comput.*, 6(3):343–361, 1999. Programming theory (Turku, 1998).
25. P. Wadler. Deforestation: transforming programs to eliminate trees. *Theoret. Comput. Sci.*, 73(2):231–248, 1990.
26. I. Walukiewicz. Completeness of Kozen's axiomatisation of the propositional μ-calculus. *Inform. and Comput.*, 157(1-2):142–182, 2000. LICS 1995 (San Diego, CA).

Verifying Temporal Properties
Using Explicit Approximants:
Completeness for Context-free Processes

Ulrich Schöpp and Alex Simpson

LFCS, Division of Informatics, University of Edinburgh
JCMB, King's Buildings, Edinburgh, EH9 3JZ

Abstract. We present a sequent calculus for formally verifying modal μ-calculus properties of concurrent processes. Building on work by Dam and Gurov, the proof system contains rules for the explicit manipulation of fixed-point approximants. We develop a new syntax for approximants, incorporating, in particular, modalities for approximant modification. We make essential use of this feature to prove our main result: the sequent calculus is complete for establishing arbitrary μ-calculus properties of context-free processes.

1 Introduction

In this paper, we present a proof system for establishing temporal properties, expressed in the modal μ-calculus [14], of concurrent processes. The proof system is a sequent calculus in which sequents have the form $\Gamma \vdash \Delta$, where Γ and Δ are sets of assertions. As usual, a derivation of $\Gamma \vdash \Delta$ will establish that if all the assertions in Γ hold then so does at least one assertion in Δ. The principal assertion form is $p : \varphi$, which is the syntactic expression of the relation $p \models \varphi$, stating that process p satisfies μ-calculus property φ. The sequent-based formalism has several virtues:

1. Ordinary verification goals are expressed by sequents of the form $\vdash p : \varphi$.
2. More generally, by allowing process variables, *parameterized* verification goals can be expressed by sequents of the form

$$x_1 : \psi_1, \ \ldots, \ x_n : \psi_n \vdash p(x_1, \ldots, x_n) : \varphi. \tag{1}$$

   Such a sequent states that the process p satisfies φ whenever its parameters $x_1, \ldots, x_n$ are instantiated with processes satisfying $\psi_1, \ldots, \psi_n$ respectively.
3. Such parameterized goals can be used to support *compositional* reasoning. Using cut and substitution, one obtains a derived rule:[1]

$$\frac{\vdash p(q_1, \ldots, q_n) : \varphi}{\vdash q_1 : \psi_1 \quad \cdots \quad \vdash q_n : \psi_n \quad x_1 : \psi_1, \ \ldots, \ x_n : \psi_n \vdash p(x_1, \ldots, x_n) : \varphi}$$

---

[1] In this paper, we write all inference rules and derivations in tableau form, i.e. with the goal (conclusion) on top and the subgoals (premises) underneath.

M. Nielsen and U. Engberg (Eds.): Fossacs 2002, LNCS 2303, pp. 372–386, 2002.

This rule reduces the goal of establishing a property φ of a compound process $p(q_1, \ldots, q_n)$ to the subgoals of establishing properties of its components $q_1, \ldots, q_n$ together with a further subgoal justifying the decomposition.

4. The proof system also supports a direct *structural* form of reasoning. The inference rules decompose logical connectives on the left and right of sequents in the familiar Gentzen style, allowing the construction of a derivation to be guided by the form of the goal sequent.

Such a sequent-based approach to process verification was proposed independently by Dam [4] and the second author [17], as a way of uniformly accounting for many specialist techniques for compositional reasoning that had appeared in the earlier literature, especially [18].

The paper [17] presents a sequent calculus, for establishing properties expressed in Hennessy-Milner logic [12], in which sequents contain a second form of assertion, *transition assertions* $p \xrightarrow{a} q$, expressing that process p evolves to process q under action a. This device allows the proof system to be adapted to any process calculus with an operational semantics in GSOS format [1]. The main results of [17] are strong completeness and cut-elimination for the system.

In [4,5,6,7,8,9,11], Dam and his co-workers address the interesting question of how best to incorporate fixed-point reasoning into such sequent-based proof systems. In their more recent research, see, in particular, [9], Dam and Gurov propose dealing with this issue by extending the μ-calculus with *ordinal variables*, κ, which are semantically interpreted as ordinals, and by introducing new formulae $\mu^\kappa X. \varphi$ and $\nu^\kappa X. \varphi$ standing for the κ-th iterations in the chain of approximations to the fixed-points $\mu X. \varphi$ and $\nu X. \varphi$ respectively. This machinery allows a sound notion of proof to be defined, by identifying certain repeats of sequents in a derivation tree and by imposing a global *discharge condition* on a derivation tree, formulated in terms of ordinal variables.

As the first contribution of the present paper, we provide a new proof system for incorporating fixed-point reasoning into the sequent-calculus approach. Our system is strongly based on Dam and Gurov's idea of using explicit fixed-point approximants. However, we provide an alternative formulation of these, not requiring ordinal variables. Instead, we use ordinary propositional variables X to range over approximants. To properly deal with such variables, we include an extra component on the left of sequents, a context D of approximant declarations. Such declarations have one of two forms: $X \leqslant \varphi$, which declares X to be an approximant of $\mu X. \varphi$; and $X \geqslant \varphi$, which declares X to be an approximant of $\nu X. \varphi$, see Sect. 2. Thus far, our approach can be seen as merely a less expressive reformulation of Dam and Gurov's syntax. However, we also extend the syntax of the μ-calculus in two significant ways. First, we allow explicit approximant declarations in formulae, introducing two new formula constructions: $\langle X \leqslant \varphi \rangle \, \psi$, which says that there exists an approximant X of $\mu X. \varphi$ such that ψ; and $[X \geqslant \varphi] \, \psi$, which says that ψ holds for all approximants X of $\nu X. \varphi$. Second, we incorporate modalities for approximant "modification" in formulae. If X is an approximant for $\mu X. \varphi$ then the formula $\langle -X \rangle \, \psi$ expresses that there exists another approximant X' of $\mu X. \varphi$ with $X' \subset X$ (proper inclusion) such that $\psi[X' / X]$. Dually, if X is an approximant for $\nu X. \varphi$ then $[+X] \, \psi$ expresses that, for all approximants X' of $\mu X.\varphi$ with $X' \supset X$ (proper containment), it holds that $\psi[X'/X]$.

The full proof system is presented in Sect. 3. The use of approximant variables and modifiers allows a straightforward definition of a global combinatorial condition for a derivation tree to be a proof. The soundness of the proof system is then established as Theorem 1.

It is our belief that the proof system we present provides a powerful and flexible tool for verifying a wide class of processes using a compositional style of reasoning. As the verification problem is, in general, undecidable, the proof system is necessarily incomplete, and so it is impossible to back up such a claim with an all-encompassing completeness theorem. Instead, there are two other avenues open for partially substantiating this belief. One is to demonstrate the effectivity of the system on a range of worked examples. Using proof systems closely related to ours, such an enterprise has already been undertaken by Dam, Gurov et al., who have presented applications to CCS [5,8], the π-calculus [6] and Erlang [7,11]. The second avenue is to obtain restricted completeness theorems. Once again, Dam, Gurov et al. have obtained such results, establishing completeness for sequents of the form $\vdash x:\varphi$, i.e. completeness with respect to μ-calculus validity [9], and proving completeness for finite-state processes [5].

As the main contribution of the paper, Theorem 2, we present a significant extension of the latter result. We show that our proof system is complete for establishing μ-calculus properties of arbitrary *context-free* processes, see e.g. [2].

Of course, many techniques for verifying context-free processes are already known. The decidability of the problem is a direct consequence of the work of Muller and Schupp, who established that full monadic second-order logic (MSOL) is decidable over the wider class of pushdown transition graphs [15]. The decision problem for MSOL is known to be of non-elementary complexity. However, for the special case of μ-calculus properties, elementary decision algorithms have been given in [20,3]. Also, Hungar and Steffen showed how alternation-free μ-calculus properties of context-free processes can be established by a tableau-style proof system embodying a form of compositional reasoning [13].

We stress, however, that the motivation behind the present paper is not merely to contribute one more method of verifying context-free processes to the literature. Indeed, in spite of their applications to dataflow analysis in languages with stack-based procedure calls [10], context-free processes are of limited relevance to the general problem of verifying concurrent systems. Rather, our motivation is to extend the scope of completeness results for proof systems whose full range of application is potentially much wider. Indeed, as far as we know, ours is the first completeness result for a general purpose proof system (i.e. one not tailored in advance to a restricted class of processes) with respect to any significant class of infinite state processes.

We would like to thank Dilian Gurov and the anonymous referees for their comments. For lack of space, in this conference version of the paper, proofs are either sketched or omitted.

2 Modal μ-Calculus and Explicit Approximants

Our treatment of the μ-calculus will be brief. The reader is referred to [19] for further details. We consider the μ-calculus in positive normal form, with formulae defined by the grammar:

$$\varphi ::= X \mid \textbf{ff} \mid \textbf{tt} \mid \varphi_1 \vee \varphi_2 \mid \varphi_1 \wedge \varphi_2 \mid \langle a \rangle \varphi \mid [a]\varphi \mid \mu X.\,\varphi \mid \nu X.\,\varphi.$$

Here a ranges over a given set A of action symbols. Free and bound variables are defined as usual, and we identify formulae up to renaming of bound variables. We write $FV(\varphi)$ for the set of free variables of φ, and we say that φ is *closed* if $FV(\varphi) = \emptyset$. The negation of a closed formula can be defined by induction on its structure using De Morgan duals.

Formulae are interpreted over a transition system $(T, \{\overset{a}{\to}\}_{a \in A})$ (here T is a set of states and each $\overset{a}{\to}$ is a binary relation on T). A formula φ is interpreted relative to an *environment* V mapping $FV(\varphi)$ to subsets of T, with its interpretation $\|\varphi\|_V \subseteq T$ defined as in [19].

Next we introduce approximants. Rather than invoking the set-theoretic machinery of ordinal indices, we give a definition that is directly interpretable in monadic third-order logic.

Definition 1 (μ- and ν-approximants). For any least-fixed-point formula $\mu X.\,\varphi$, its family of μ-*approximants* $\mathcal{A}_V^{\mu X.\,\varphi}$, relative to an environment V defined on $FV(\mu X.\,\varphi)$, is the smallest family of subsets of T satisfying:

1. if $\mathcal{A}' \subseteq \mathcal{A}_V^{\mu X.\,\varphi}$ then $\bigcup \mathcal{A}' \in \mathcal{A}_V^{\mu X.\,\varphi}$, and
2. if $S \in \mathcal{A}_V^{\mu X.\,\varphi}$ then $\|\varphi\|_{V[S/X]} \in \mathcal{A}_V^{\mu X.\,\varphi}$.

For any greatest-fixed-point formula $\nu X.\,\varphi$, its family of ν-*approximants* $\mathcal{A}_V^{\nu X.\,\varphi}$ relative to V is the smallest family of subsets of T satisfying:

1. if $\mathcal{A}' \subseteq \mathcal{A}_V^{\nu X.\,\varphi}$ then $\bigcap \mathcal{A}' \in \mathcal{A}_V^{\nu X.\,\varphi}$, and
2. if $S \in \mathcal{A}_V^{\nu X.\,\varphi}$ then $\|\varphi\|_{V[S/X]} \in \mathcal{A}_V^{\nu X.\,\varphi}$.

Note that, by taking $\mathcal{A}' = \emptyset$ we have that $\emptyset \in \mathcal{A}_V^{\mu X.\,\varphi}$, and $T \in \mathcal{A}_V^{\nu X.\,\varphi}$ (because $T = \bigcap \emptyset$ when $\emptyset$ is considered as the empty family of subsets of T).

As discussed in the introduction, the proof system will use a class of *extended formulae* containing declarations and modifiers for approximant variables:

$$\Phi ::= \varphi \mid \langle X \leqslant \varphi \rangle\, \Phi \mid [X \geqslant \varphi]\, \Phi \mid \langle -X \rangle\, \Phi \mid [+X]\, \Phi$$

In this definition, and henceforth, we use lower case Greek letters $\varphi, \psi, \ldots$ to range over ordinary μ-calculus formulae, and upper case letters $\Phi, \Psi, \ldots$ to range over extended formulae.

The sets of free variables of extended formulae are defined by:

$$\begin{aligned}
FV(\langle X \leqslant \varphi \rangle\, \Phi) &= FV([X \geqslant \varphi]\, \Phi) = (FV(\varphi) \cup FV(\Phi)) \backslash \{X\} \\
FV(\langle -X \rangle\, \Phi) &= FV([+X]\, \Phi) \quad = FV(\Phi) \cup \{X\}
\end{aligned}$$

Extended formulae are again identified up to renaming of bound variables.

The semantic interpretation of extended formulae is given relative to a finite set, D, of approximant *declarations*, each of the form $X \leqslant \varphi$ or $X \geqslant \varphi$. The former is a μ-*approximant* declaration, the latter a ν-*approximant* declaration, and in each case the *declared variable* is X. We write $DV(D)$ for the set of all variables declared in D.

The *declaration contexts* are produced as follows: (i) the empty set is a declaration context; (ii) if D is a declaration context, X is a variable not declared in D, and φ is a μ-calculus formula with $FV(\varphi) \subseteq DV(D) \cup \{X\}$ then $D, X \leqslant \varphi$ and $D, X \geqslant \varphi$ are both declaration contexts (where we write comma for union). The set of *used variables* in a declaration context is defined by:

$$UV(X \leqslant \varphi) = UV(X \geqslant \varphi) = FV(\varphi) \backslash \{X\}$$
$$UV(D) \qquad = \bigcup \{UV(\delta) \mid \delta \in D\}$$

We next define the notion of an extended formula Φ being *well-formed* relative to a declaration context D. First, any μ-calculus formula φ is well-formed relative to any declaration context D with $FV(\varphi) \subseteq DV(D)$. Second, the extended formula $\langle X \leqslant \varphi \rangle \Phi$ (respectively $[X \geqslant \varphi] \Phi$) is well-formed relative to D if $D, X \leqslant \varphi$ (respectively $D, X \geqslant \varphi$) is a declaration context, where $X \notin DV(D)$ (which can be always assumed, by the identification of formulae up to renaming of bound variables), and Φ is well-formed relative to it. Finally, the extended formula $\langle -X \rangle \Phi$ (respectively $[+X] \Phi$) is well-formed relative to D if D contains a declaration $X \leqslant \varphi$ (respectively $X \geqslant \varphi$), $X \notin UV(D)$ and also Φ is well-formed relative to D. By this definition, we have that $FV(\Phi) \subseteq DV(D)$ whenever Φ is well-formed relative to D.

Given a declaration context D, a D-*environment* is a function V mapping $DV(D)$ to subsets of T such that: for each declaration $X \leqslant \varphi$ (respectively $X \geqslant \varphi$) in D, it holds that $V(X) \in \mathcal{A}_V^{\mu X. \varphi}$ (respectively $V(X) \in \mathcal{A}_V^{\nu X. \varphi}$). To give a semantics to extended formulae, we define subsets $\| \Phi \|_V^D \subseteq T$ whenever D is a declaration context, Φ is well-formed relative to D, and V is a D-environment.

$$\| \varphi \|_V^D = \| \varphi \|_V$$

$$\| \langle X \leqslant \varphi \rangle \Phi \|_V^D = \bigcup \{ \| \Phi \|_{V[S/X]}^{D, X \leqslant \varphi} \mid S \in \mathcal{A}_V^{\mu X. \varphi} \} \quad \text{where } X \notin DV(D)$$

$$\| [X \geqslant \varphi] \Phi \|_V^D = \bigcap \{ \| \Phi \|_{V[S/X]}^{D, X \geqslant \varphi} \mid S \in \mathcal{A}_V^{\nu X. \varphi} \} \quad \text{where } X \notin DV(D)$$

$$\| \langle -X \rangle \Phi \|_V^D = \bigcup \{ \| \Phi \|_{V[S/X]}^D \mid S \subset V(X) \text{ and } S \in \mathcal{A}_V^{\mu X. \varphi} \text{ where } X \leqslant \varphi \in D \}$$

$$\| [+X] \Phi \|_V^D = \bigcap \{ \| \Phi \|_{V[S/X]}^D \mid S \supset V(X) \text{ and } S \in \mathcal{A}_V^{\nu X. \varphi} \text{ where } X \geqslant \varphi \in D \}$$

3   The Proof System

The proof system we present is general purpose in the sense that, following the approach of [17], it can be easily adapted to give a sound system for reasoning about any process algebra whose operational semantics is given in the GSOS format [1]. However, for brevity of exposition, we present proof rules for the special case of context-free processes only.

Definition 2 (Context-free system). A *context-free system* is specified by a finite set of *nonterminals* $\Sigma = \{P_1, \ldots, P_k\}$ together with a finite set $\mathcal{P}$ of *productions*, each of the form $P_i \xrightarrow{a} p$, where p ranges over Σ^* (the set of finite words over Σ) and a ranges over a finite set of action symbols A. The transition system $(T, \{\xrightarrow{a}_T\}_{a \in A})$ determined by the specification is defined as follows.

$$T = \Sigma^*$$

$s \xrightarrow{a}_T t$ iff $s = P_i q$ and $t = pq$ for some production $P_i \xrightarrow{a} p \in \mathcal{P}$.

Here, as usual, a juxtaposition pq means the concatenation of words p and q.

Example 1. As a running example, consider the system with a single nonterminal P, set of actions $A = \{a, b\}$, and with two productions: $P \xrightarrow{a} PP$ and $P \xrightarrow{b} \varepsilon$, where ε is the empty word. This has as its transition system:

$$\varepsilon \xleftarrow{\quad} P \underset{b}{\overset{a}{\rightleftarrows}} P^2 \underset{b}{\overset{a}{\rightleftarrows}} P^3 \overset{a}{\underset{b}{\rightleftarrows}} \cdots$$

This is an infinite-state process in which no two distinct states are bisimilar.

Henceforth in this section we assume that we have a fixed specification of a context-free system, as in Definition 2, and we write $(T, \{\xrightarrow{a}_T\}_{a \in A})$ for the transition system it determines.

The proof system uses process terms containing free process variables $x, y, \ldots$

Definition 3 (Process term). A *process term* is a word of one of two forms: either $p\,x$, where $p \in \Sigma^*$ and x is a process variable; or p where $p \in \Sigma^*$.

We use $p, q, \ldots$ to range over process terms. By a *process substitution* we shall mean a mapping θ from process variables to process terms. The substituted term $p[\theta]$ is defined in the obvious way.

Process terms are interpreted relative to *process environments* ρ mapping process variables to states in the transition system T. We extend ρ to a function (also called ρ) from process terms to T by: $\rho(p\,x) = p\,\rho(x)$ and $\rho(p) = p$.

Sequents will be built from two forms of assertion: *verification assertions* of the form $p : \Phi$, where Φ is an extended formula, as in Sect. 2; and *transition assertions* of the form $p \xrightarrow{a} q$. We use $J, K, \ldots$ to range over assertions. Given a declaration context D, an assertion is a D-*assertion* if it is either a verification assertion $p : \Phi$ with Φ well-formed relative to D, or a transition assertion.

Definition 4 (Sequent). *Sequents* have the form $D ; \Gamma \vdash \Delta$ where D is a declaration context and Γ and Δ are finite sets of D-assertions.

Semantically, assertions and sequents will always be interpreted relative to the transition system $(T, \{\xrightarrow{a}_T\}_{a \in A})$. Given a D-environment V and a process environment ρ, the relation $\models_{V\rho} J$, for D-assertions J, is defined by:

$$\models_{V\rho} p : \Phi \quad \text{iff} \quad \rho(p) \in \|\Phi\|_V^D$$
$$\models_{V\rho} p \xrightarrow{a} q \quad \text{iff} \quad \rho(p) \xrightarrow{a}_T \rho(q)$$

General rules

$$(\text{Axiom}) \ \frac{}{\mathsf{D}\,;\,\Gamma \vdash \Delta} \ \Gamma \cap \Delta \neq \emptyset \qquad (\text{Weak}) \ \frac{\mathsf{D}\,;\,\Gamma \vdash \Delta}{\mathsf{D}'\,;\,\Gamma' \vdash \Delta'}, \ \mathsf{D}' \subseteq \mathsf{D},\ \Gamma' \subseteq \Gamma,\ \Delta' \subseteq \Delta$$

$$(\text{Cut}) \ \frac{\mathsf{D}\,;\,\Gamma \vdash \Delta}{\mathsf{D}\,;\,\Gamma \vdash \Delta,\ J \qquad \mathsf{D}\,;\,\Gamma,\ J \vdash \Delta} \qquad (\text{Sub}) \ \frac{\mathsf{D}\,;\,\Gamma[\theta] \vdash \Delta[\theta]}{\mathsf{D}\,;\,\Gamma \vdash \Delta}$$

Logical rules

$$(\mathtt{ff}\text{L}) \ \frac{}{\mathsf{D}\,;\,\Gamma,\ p\!:\!\mathtt{ff} \vdash \Delta} \qquad (\mathtt{tt}\text{R}) \ \frac{}{\mathsf{D}\,;\,\Gamma \vdash \Delta,\ p\!:\!\mathtt{tt}}$$

$$(\vee\text{L}) \ \frac{\mathsf{D}\,;\,\Gamma,\ p\!:\!\varphi_1 \vee \varphi_2 \vdash \Delta}{\mathsf{D}\,;\,\Gamma,\ p\!:\!\varphi_1 \vdash \Delta \qquad \mathsf{D}\,;\,\Gamma,\ p\!:\!\varphi_2 \vdash \Delta} \qquad (\vee\text{R}) \ \frac{\mathsf{D}\,;\,\Gamma \vdash \Delta,\ p\!:\!\varphi_1 \vee \varphi_2}{\mathsf{D}\,;\,\Gamma \vdash \Delta,\ p\!:\!\varphi_1,\ p\!:\!\varphi_2}$$

$$(\wedge\text{L}) \ \frac{\mathsf{D}\,;\,\Gamma,\ p\!:\!\varphi_1 \wedge \varphi_2 \vdash \Delta}{\mathsf{D}\,;\,\Gamma,\ p\!:\!\varphi_1,\ p\!:\!\varphi_2 \vdash \Delta} \qquad (\wedge\text{R}) \ \frac{\mathsf{D}\,;\,\Gamma \vdash \Delta,\ p\!:\!\varphi_1 \wedge \varphi_2}{\mathsf{D}\,;\,\Gamma \vdash \Delta,\ p\!:\!\varphi_1 \qquad \mathsf{D}\,;\,\Gamma \vdash \Delta,\ p\!:\!\varphi_2}$$

Modal rules

$$(\langle a\rangle\text{L})^* \ \frac{\mathsf{D}\,;\,\Gamma,\ p\!:\!\langle a\rangle\varphi \vdash \Delta}{\mathsf{D}\,;\,\Gamma,\ p \xrightarrow{a} x,\ x\!:\!\varphi \vdash \Delta} \qquad (\langle a\rangle\text{R}) \ \frac{\mathsf{D}\,;\,\Gamma \vdash \Delta,\ p\!:\!\langle a\rangle\varphi}{\mathsf{D}\,;\,\Gamma \vdash \Delta,\ p \xrightarrow{a} q \qquad \mathsf{D}\,;\,\Gamma \vdash \Delta,\ q\!:\!\varphi}$$

$$([a]\text{L}) \ \frac{\mathsf{D}\,;\,\Gamma,\ p\!:\![a]\varphi \vdash \Delta}{\mathsf{D}\,;\,\Gamma \vdash \Delta,\ p \xrightarrow{a} q \qquad \mathsf{D}\,;\,\Gamma,\ q\!:\!\varphi \vdash \Delta} \qquad ([a]\text{R})^* \ \frac{\mathsf{D}\,;\,\Gamma \vdash \Delta,\ p\!:\![a]\varphi}{\mathsf{D}\,;\,\Gamma,\ p \xrightarrow{a} x \vdash \Delta,\ x\!:\!\varphi}$$

* Restriction on $(\langle a\rangle\text{L})$ and $([a]\text{R})$: x must not occur free in the goal.

Operational rules

$$(\mathsf{P_i}\text{L}) \ \frac{\mathsf{D}\,;\,\Gamma,\ \mathsf{P_i}\,q \xrightarrow{a} x \vdash \Delta}{\{\mathsf{D}\,;\,\Gamma[\mathsf{p}\,q\,/\,x] \vdash \Delta[\mathsf{p}\,q\,/\,x]\}_{\mathsf{P_i} \xrightarrow{a} \mathsf{p} \in \mathcal{P}}} \ x \text{ does not occur in } q$$

$$(\varepsilon\text{L}) \ \frac{\mathsf{D}\,;\,\Gamma,\ \varepsilon \xrightarrow{a} x \vdash \Delta}{} \qquad (\mathsf{P_i}\text{R}) \ \frac{}{\mathsf{D}\,;\,\Gamma \vdash \Delta,\ \mathsf{P_i}\,q \xrightarrow{a} \mathsf{p}\,q} \ \mathsf{P_i} \xrightarrow{a} \mathsf{p} \in \mathcal{P}$$

Fig. 1. Basic rules

We write $\mathsf{D}\,;\,\Gamma \models_{V\rho} \Delta$ to mean that if $\models_{V\rho} J$, for all $J \in \Gamma$, then there exists $K \in \Delta$ such that $\models_{V\rho} K$. We write $\mathsf{D}\,;\,\Gamma \models \Delta$ to mean that $\mathsf{D}\,;\,\Gamma \models_{V\rho} \Delta$ for all V and ρ.

Fixed-point rules

$$(\mu L)\ \frac{\mathsf{D}\,;\,\Gamma,\ p\!:\!\mu X.\,\varphi \vdash \Delta}{\mathsf{D}\,;\,\Gamma,\ p\!:\!\langle X\!\leqslant\!\varphi\rangle\,\varphi \vdash \Delta} \qquad\qquad (\mu R)\ \frac{\mathsf{D}\,;\,\Gamma \vdash \Delta,\ p\!:\!\mu X.\,\varphi}{\mathsf{D}\,;\,\Gamma \vdash \Delta,\ p\!:\!\langle X\!\leqslant\!\varphi\rangle\,\varphi}$$

$$(\leqslant\text{-}\mu L)\ \frac{\mathsf{D}\,;\,\Gamma,\ p\!:\!\langle X\!\leqslant\!\varphi\rangle\,\Phi \vdash \Delta}{\mathsf{D}\,;\,\Gamma,\ p\!:\!\Phi[\mu X.\,\varphi\,/\,X] \vdash \Delta} \qquad\qquad (\leqslant\text{-}\mu R)\ \frac{\mathsf{D}\,;\,\Gamma \vdash \Delta,\ p\!:\!\langle X\!\leqslant\!\varphi\rangle\,\Phi}{\mathsf{D}\,;\,\Gamma \vdash \Delta,\ p\!:\!\Phi[\mu X.\,\varphi\,/\,X]}$$

$$(\nu L)\ \frac{\mathsf{D}\,;\,\Gamma,\ p\!:\!\nu X.\,\varphi \vdash \Delta}{\mathsf{D}\,;\,\Gamma,\ p\!:\![X\!\geqslant\!\varphi]\,\varphi \vdash \Delta} \qquad\qquad (\nu R)\ \frac{\mathsf{D}\,;\,\Gamma \vdash \Delta,\ p\!:\!\nu X.\,\varphi}{\mathsf{D}\,;\,\Gamma \vdash \Delta,\ p\!:\![X\!\geqslant\!\varphi]\,\varphi}$$

$$(\geqslant\text{-}\nu L)\ \frac{\mathsf{D}\,;\,\Gamma,\ p\!:\![X\!\geqslant\!\varphi]\,\Phi \vdash \Delta}{\mathsf{D}\,;\,\Gamma,\ p\!:\!\Phi[\nu X.\,\varphi\,/\,X] \vdash \Delta} \qquad\qquad (\geqslant\text{-}\nu R)\ \frac{\mathsf{D}\,;\,\Gamma \vdash \Delta,\ p\!:\![X\!\geqslant\!\varphi]\,\Phi}{\mathsf{D}\,;\,\Gamma \vdash \Delta,\ p\!:\!\Phi[\nu X.\,\varphi\,/\,X]}$$

Approximant rules

$$(\leqslant\text{-}XL)^{*}\ \frac{\mathsf{D}\,;\,\Gamma,\ p\!:\!\langle X\!\leqslant\!\varphi\rangle\,\Phi \vdash \Delta}{\mathsf{D},\ X\!\leqslant\!\varphi\,;\,\Gamma,\ p\!:\!\Phi \vdash \Delta} \qquad\qquad (\leqslant\text{-}XR)\ \frac{\mathsf{D}\,;\,\Gamma \vdash \Delta,\ p\!:\!\langle X\!\leqslant\!\varphi\rangle\,\Phi}{\mathsf{D}\,;\,\Gamma \vdash \Delta,\ p\!:\!\Phi}\ X\!\leqslant\!\varphi \in \mathsf{D}$$

$$(X_{\mu}L)\ \frac{\mathsf{D}\,;\,\Gamma,\ p\!:\!X \vdash \Delta}{\mathsf{D}\,;\,\Gamma,\ p\!:\!\langle -X\rangle\,\varphi \vdash \Delta}\ X\!\leqslant\!\varphi \in \mathsf{D} \qquad (X_{\mu}R)\ \frac{\mathsf{D}\,;\,\Gamma \vdash \Delta,\ p\!:\!X}{\mathsf{D}\,;\,\Gamma \vdash \Delta,\ p\!:\!\langle -X\rangle\,\varphi}\ X\!\leqslant\!\varphi \in \mathsf{D}$$

$$(\langle -X\rangle)\ \frac{\mathsf{D}\,;\,\langle -X\rangle\,\Gamma,\ \Gamma' \vdash \langle -X\rangle\,\Delta,\ \Delta'}{\mathsf{D}\,;\,\Gamma,\ \Gamma' \vdash \Delta,\ \Delta'}\ \Gamma \neq \emptyset,\ X \notin UV(\mathsf{D}) \cup FV(\Gamma')$$

$$(\geqslant\text{-}XL)\ \frac{\mathsf{D}\,;\,\Gamma,\ p\!:\![X\!\geqslant\!\varphi]\,\Phi \vdash \Delta}{\mathsf{D}\,;\,\Gamma,\ p\!:\!\Phi \vdash \Delta}\ X\!\geqslant\!\varphi \in \mathsf{D} \qquad (\geqslant\text{-}XR)^{*}\ \frac{\mathsf{D}\,;\,\Gamma \vdash \Delta,\ p\!:\![X\!\geqslant\!\varphi]\,\Phi}{\mathsf{D},\ X\!\geqslant\!\varphi\,;\,\Gamma \vdash \Delta,\ p\!:\!\Phi}$$

$$(X_{\nu}L)\ \frac{\mathsf{D}\,;\,\Gamma,\ p\!:\!X \vdash \Delta}{\mathsf{D}\,;\,\Gamma,\ p\!:\![+X]\,\varphi \vdash \Delta}\ X\!\geqslant\!\varphi \in \mathsf{D} \qquad (X_{\nu}R)\ \frac{\mathsf{D}\,;\,\Gamma \vdash \Delta,\ p\!:\!X}{\mathsf{D}\,;\,\Gamma \vdash \Delta,\ p\!:\![+X]\,\varphi}\ X\!\geqslant\!\varphi \in \mathsf{D}$$

$$([+X])\ \frac{\mathsf{D}\,;\,[+X]\,\Gamma,\ \Gamma' \vdash [+X]\,\Delta,\ \Delta'}{\mathsf{D}\,;\,\Gamma,\ \Gamma' \vdash \Delta,\ \Delta'}\ \Delta \neq \emptyset,\ X \notin UV(\mathsf{D}) \cup FV(\Delta')$$

* Restriction on $(\leqslant\text{-}XL)$ and $(\geqslant\text{-}XR)$: X must not occur free in the goal.

Fig. 2. Fixed-point and approximant rules

The proof system provides a means of verifying sequents $\mathsf{D}\,;\,\Gamma \vdash \Delta$ for which $\mathsf{D}\,;\,\Gamma \models \Delta$. The rules are presented in Figs. 1 and 2. The rules in Fig. 1 concern the modal fragment of the logic, and are essentially from [17]. Figure 2 presents the crucial rules for fixed points and explicit approximants. We emphasise again that we write the rules in tableau style with the *goal* sequent above the line and its (possibly empty) set of *subgoals* below the line. Rules are applicable only in instances in which the subgoals produced are indeed sequents according to Definition 4. Certain rules have additional side conditions, written on the right. In the rules, we use the abbreviations:

$$\Gamma[\theta] = \{\, p[\theta]\!:\!\Phi \mid p\!:\!\Phi \in \Gamma\,\} \cup \{\, p[\theta] \xrightarrow{a} q[\theta] \mid p \xrightarrow{a} q \in \Gamma\,\},$$
$$\langle -X\rangle\,\Gamma = \{\, p\!:\!\langle -X\rangle\,\Phi \mid p\!:\!\Phi \in \Gamma\,\}, \quad [+X]\,\Gamma = \{\, p\!:\![+X]\,\Phi \mid p\!:\!\Phi \in \Gamma\,\},$$

where, whenever we write $\langle -X\rangle\,\Gamma$ and $[+X]\,\Gamma$, we tacitly assume that Γ contains only verification assertions. We briefly explain the rule $(\langle -X\rangle)$ which, along with $([+X])$, is probably the most obscure. Suppose we have V and ρ invalidating the goal, i.e. such that $\mathsf{D}\,;\,\langle -X\rangle\,\Gamma,\ \Gamma' \not\models_{V\rho} \langle -X\rangle\,\Delta,\ \Delta'$. We show that the subgoal is also invalid. Because the goal is invalidated, we have that $\rho(p_j) \in \|\,\langle -X\rangle\,\Phi_j\,\|_V^\mathsf{D}$, for each $p_j\!:\!\Phi_j \in \Gamma = \{p_1\!:\!\Phi_1,\ldots,p_l\!:\!\Phi_l\}$. So, for each $p_j\!:\!\Phi_j$, there exists $S_j \subset V(X)$ with $S_j \in \mathcal{A}_V^{\mu X.\,\varphi}$ such that $\rho(p_j) \in \|\,\Phi_j\,\|_{V[S_j\,/\,X]}^\mathsf{D}$. As approximants are linearly ordered and $\Gamma \neq \emptyset$, we can take the largest such $S_k \subset V(X)$, and, by monotonicity considerations, simultaneously satisfy $\rho(p_j) \in \|\,\Phi_j\,\|_{V[S_k\,/\,X]}^\mathsf{D}$ for all $p_j\!:\!\Phi_j \in \Gamma$. Define $V' = V[S_k\,/\,X]$. We claim that $\mathsf{D}\,;\,\Gamma,\ \Gamma' \not\models_{V'\rho} \Delta,\ \Delta'$. We have seen that the assertions in Γ are satisfied. Those in Γ' are because $X \notin UV(\mathsf{D}) \cup FV(\Gamma')$. The assertions in Δ are not satisfied under V' because those in $\langle -X\rangle\,\Delta$ weren't under V. Finally, by monotonicity considerations, the assertions in Δ' are also not satisfied under V', because they weren't under V.

The above justification for the $(\langle -X\rangle)$ rule modifies a D-environment on X by mapping it to a strictly smaller μ-approximant. Dually, the $([+X])$ rule results in X being mapped to a strictly larger ν-approximant. By well-foundedness considerations, neither event can occur infinitely often. This observation motivates the definitions below, which formulate when a derivation tree constitutes a proof.

By a *leaf* in a derivation tree, we mean a sequent occurrence in the tree such that no rule has been applied with that sequent occurrence as its goal (thus sequents to which a rule with an empty set of subgoals has been applied *do not* count as leaves, even though they have no child sequents).

Definition 5 (Repeat). In a derivation tree, a leaf $\mathsf{D}\,;\,\Gamma \vdash \Delta$ is a *repeat* of another sequent occurrence $\mathsf{D}'\,;\,\Gamma' \vdash \Delta'$ if $\mathsf{D}' \subseteq \mathsf{D}$ and there exists a process substitution θ such that $\Gamma'[\theta] \subseteq \Gamma$ and $\Delta'[\theta] \subseteq \Delta$.

Definition 6 (Pre-proof). A *pre-proof* is a derivation tree in which, to each leaf $\mathsf{D}\,;\,\Gamma \vdash \Delta$, there is an assigned sequent occurrence $\mathsf{D}'\,;\,\Gamma' \vdash \Delta'$ (the *companion* of the leaf) such that $\mathsf{D}\,;\,\Gamma \vdash \Delta$ is a repeat of $\mathsf{D}'\,;\,\Gamma' \vdash \Delta'$.

In the above definitions, it is worth noting that the companion is not required to appear on the branch from the root sequent to the leaf.

We consider a pre-proof as a directed graph whose vertices are sequent occurrences in the pre-proof, and with edges of two kinds: (i) edges from the goal
of a rule application to each subgoal (if any) of the goal; (ii) an edge from each
leaf to its companion. By a (finite or infinite) *path* through a pre-proof, we mean
a sequence $(\mathcal{S}_i)_{0 \leq i < n \leq \infty}$ of sequent occurrences forming a directed path through
the graph. We say that a rule is *applied along* a path $(\mathcal{S}_i)$ if the path contains
two consecutive sequents $\mathcal{S}_i$ and $\mathcal{S}_{i+1}$ with $\mathcal{S}_i$ the goal of the rule and $\mathcal{S}_{i+1}$ one
of its subgoals.

Definition 7 (Preservation). A path *preserves* an approximant variable X
if, for every sequent $\mathsf{D} ; \varGamma \vdash \varDelta$ occurring on the path, $X \in DV(\mathsf{D})$.

Definition 8 (Progress). A μ-approximant variable X *progresses* on a path
if it is preserved by the path and the rule $(\langle -X \rangle)$ is applied along the path.
Similarly, a ν-approximant variable X *progresses* if it is preserved and the rule
$([+X])$ is applied.

We say that X progresses *infinitely often* on an infinite path $(\mathcal{S}_i)_{i \geq 0}$ if, for all
$n \in \mathbb{N}$, it holds that X progresses on the tail path $(\mathcal{S}_i)_{i \geq n}$.

Definition 9 (Proof). A pre-proof is a *proof* if, for every infinite path $(\mathcal{S}_i)_{i \geq 0}$
through it, there exist an approximant variable X and a tail $(\mathcal{S}_i)_{i \geq n}$ on which
X progresses infinitely often.

We remark that this condition is necessarily global, in the sense that it cannot
be reformulated as a condition to be satisfied by each repeat individually.

Proposition 1. *It is decidable whether a pre-proof is a proof or not.*

Theorem 1 (Soundness). *If $\mathsf{D} ; \varGamma \vdash \varDelta$ has a proof then $\mathsf{D} ; \varGamma \models \varDelta$.*

In Fig. 3 we give an example proof in the system, showing that the process P,
from Example 1, satisfies the property $\nu X. \mu Y. [a]X \wedge [b]Y$, stating that action a
occurs infinitely often along any infinite path of a and b actions. The identified
repeats determine a pre-proof, which is easily seen to be a proof.

4   Completeness for Context-Free Processes

We assume a fixed specification of a context-free system, as in Definition 2.

Theorem 2 (Context-free completeness). *For any $\mathsf{p} \in \varSigma^*$ and closed μ-
calculus formula φ, if $\mathsf{p} \in \| \varphi \|$ then the sequent $\vdash \mathsf{p} : \varphi$ has a proof.*

The proof uses a variant of the property-checking games described in [19]. In
a transition system $(T, \{\xrightarrow{a}_T\}_{a \in A})$, the property-checking game $\mathsf{G}(s, \varphi)$, where
$s \in T$ and φ is a closed μ-calculus formula, is a game played by two players, Veri-
fier and Refuter. Verifier aims to show that $s \in \| \varphi \|$ whereas Refuter attempts to
refute this. We use an asymmetric variant of property-checking games, designed
to facilitate translating properties of games into the sequent calculus.

Abbreviations: $V \equiv \nu X.\, \mu Y.\, [a]X \wedge [b]Y,\quad U \equiv \mu Y.\, [a]X \wedge [b]Y.$

$$
\cfrac{
\cfrac{
\cfrac{
\cfrac{
\cfrac{
\cfrac{\vphantom{X}}{\vdash \varepsilon:[X \geqslant U]\,U}
}{X \geqslant U\,;\ \vdash \varepsilon:U}
}{X \geqslant U\,;\ \vdash \varepsilon:\langle Y \leqslant [a]X \wedge [b]Y\rangle\,[a]X \wedge [b]Y}
}{X \geqslant U\,;\ \vdash \varepsilon:[a]X \wedge [b]U}
}{
\cfrac{X \geqslant U\,;\ \vdash \varepsilon:[a]X}{X \geqslant U\,;\ \varepsilon \overset{a}{\to} x \vdash x:X}
\qquad
\cfrac{X \geqslant U\,;\ \vdash \varepsilon:[b]U}{X \geqslant U\,;\ \varepsilon \overset{b}{\to} x \vdash x:U}
}
\qquad
\cfrac{
\cfrac{
\cfrac{
\cfrac{\vdash P:V \qquad \varepsilon:[X \geqslant U]\,U \vdash P:V}{x:[X \geqslant U]\,U \vdash P\,x:V}\ \text{(Cut)}
}{x:[X \geqslant U]\,U \vdash P\,x:[X \geqslant U]\,U}
}{X \geqslant U\,;\ x:[X \geqslant U]\,U \vdash P\,x:U}
}{\vdots}\ \text{(Sub)}
}{}
$$

We continue with the right-hand branch.

$$
\cfrac{
\cfrac{
\cfrac{
\cfrac{\vdots}{X \geqslant U\,;\ x:U \vdash P\,x:U}\ (\star)
}{X \geqslant U\,;\ x:U \vdash P\,x:\langle Y \leqslant [a]X \wedge [b]Y\rangle\,[a]X \wedge [b]Y}
}{X \geqslant U\,;\ x:U \vdash P\,x:[a]X \wedge [b]U}
}{
\cfrac{X \geqslant U\,;\ x:U \vdash P\,x:[a]X}{X \geqslant U\,;\ x:U,\ P\,x \overset{a}{\to} y \vdash y:X}\ \vdots
\qquad
\cfrac{X \geqslant U\,;\ x:U \vdash P\,x:[b]U}{\cfrac{X \geqslant U\,;\ x:U,\ P\,x \overset{b}{\to} y \vdash y:U}{X \geqslant U\,;\ x:U \vdash x:U}}
}
$$

We continue with the left-hand branch.

$$
\cfrac{
\cfrac{
\cfrac{\vdots}{X \geqslant U\,;\ x:U \vdash P\,P\,x:X}
}{
\cfrac{X \geqslant U\,;\ x:U \vdash P\,x:[+X]\,U}{X \geqslant U\,;\ x:U \vdash P\,x:U}\ ([+X])
}
\qquad
\cfrac{
\cfrac{X \geqslant U\,;\ P\,x:[+X]\,U \vdash P\,P\,x:X}{X \geqslant U\,;\ P\,x:[+X]\,U \vdash P\,P\,x:[+X]\,U}
}{X \geqslant U\,;\ P\,x:U \vdash P\,P\,x:U}\ ([+X])
}{}\ \text{(Cut)}
$$

Both leaves are repeats of the sequent $(\star)$.

Fig. 3. Example Proof

For technical convenience, we assume representations of formulae in which all bound variables have different names, and we assume that we only encounter fixed-point formulae $\mu X.\,\varphi$, $\nu X.\,\varphi$ with $X \in FV(\varphi)$. We use sequences, E, of greatest-fixed-point definitions called ν-*contexts*, together with their sets of *declared variables* $DV(\mathsf{E})$. These are defined by: (i) the empty sequence () is a ν-context with the empty set of declared variables; (ii) if E is a ν-context, $X \notin DV(\mathsf{E})$ and $FV(\varphi) \subseteq DV(\mathsf{E}) \cup \{X\}$ then $\mathsf{E},\, X = \varphi$ is a ν-context with $DV(\mathsf{E}) \cup \{X\}$ as its set of declared variables. The equality $X = \varphi$ in a ν-context declares X to be the greatest fixed-point $\nu X.\,\varphi$.

Definition 10 (Position). A *position* is a triple (s, E, φ) where $s \in T$ is any state, E is a ν-context and φ is a formula such that $FV(\varphi) \subseteq DV(\mathsf{E})$ but, for all proper prefixes E' of E, $FV(\varphi) \not\subseteq DV(\mathsf{E}')$.

Definition 11 (Move). The legitimate *moves* from one position (s, E, φ) to another are defined by case analysis on φ:

ff: It is Verifier's move, but she is stuck.

tt: It is Refuter's move, but he is stuck.

$\psi_1 \vee \psi_2$: Verifier chooses a disjunct ψ_j where $j \in \{1, 2\}$, and the next position is (s, E', ψ_j), where E' is the smallest prefix of E with $FV(\psi_j) \subseteq DV(\mathsf{E}')$.

$\psi_1 \wedge \psi_2$: Refuter chooses a conjunct ψ_j where $j \in \{1, 2\}$, and the next position is (s, E', ψ_j), where E' is the smallest prefix of E with $FV(\psi_j) \subseteq DV(\mathsf{E}')$.

$\langle a \rangle \psi$: Verifier chooses a transition $s \xrightarrow{a}_T t$, and the next position is (t, E, ψ).

$[a]\psi$: Refuter chooses a transition $s \xrightarrow{a}_T t$, and the next position is (t, E, ψ).

$\mu X. \psi$: Verifier moves to the next position $(s, \mathsf{E}, \psi[\mu X. \psi / X])$.

$\nu X. \psi$: Refuter moves to the next position (s, E', ψ), where E' is $\mathsf{E}, X = \psi$.

X: Refuter moves to the next position (s, E, ψ), where $X = \psi \in \mathsf{E}$.

Definition 12 (Play). A *play* is a finite or infinite sequence $(s_i, \mathsf{E}_i, \varphi_i)_i$ of positions where each position $(s_{k+1}, \mathsf{E}_{k+1}, \varphi_{k+1})$ is produced from $(s_k, \mathsf{E}_k, \varphi_k)$ by following one of the moves above.

Definition 13 (Preservation). We say that a play $(s_i, \mathsf{E}_i, \varphi_i)_i$ *preserves* a variable X if, for each E_i in the play, $X \in DV(\mathsf{E}_i)$.

Definition 14 (Progress). We say that a fixed-point variable X *progresses* along a play if it is preserved by the play and the play contains a move away from a position (s, E, X).

Definition 15 (Winning play). The Verifier *wins* a play either if the play is finite and its last position is one at which it is Refuter's move, or if the play is infinite and there exist a variable X and a tail of the play such that X progresses infinitely often along the tail.

Definition 16 (The game $\mathsf{G}(s, \varphi)$). The *game* $\mathsf{G}(s, \varphi)$, where φ is a closed formula, is played on the set of all positions reachable from the *initial position* $(s, (), \varphi)$. The game is a two player game, played by Verifier and Refuter, with play starting from the initial position.

For ordinary property-checking games, the following result appears in [19, §6.3]. The adaptation to our games is straightforward.

Proposition 2. *If $s \in \| \varphi \|$ then Verifier has a history-free winning strategy for the game $\mathsf{G}(s, \varphi)$.*

We now begin the proof of Theorem 2. Henceforth, suppose that $p_0 \in \Sigma^*$ is such that $p_0 \in \| \varphi_0 \|$. We use the game $G(p_0, \varphi_0)$ to construct a proof of the sequent $\vdash p_0 : \varphi_0$.

Henceforth, all plays will be of the game $G(p_0, \varphi_0)$. By Proposition 2, Verifier has a history-free winning strategy for this game. We henceforth fix on one such strategy, and we call a play a *V-play* if all Verifier's moves in the play follow the strategy. We write $\mathbf{u}_0$ for the initial position $(p_0, (), \varphi_0)$. From now on, we shall only consider those positions that arise in some V-play from $\mathbf{u}_0$. We use $\mathbf{u}, \mathbf{v}, \mathbf{w}, \ldots$ to range over such positions, and $\pi, \tau \ldots$ to range over V-plays starting from any such position. Note that Verifier wins any infinite V-play. We write $\mathbf{u}\pi$ and $\pi\mathbf{v}$ to mean that $\mathbf{u}$ and $\mathbf{v}$ are the first and last positions in π respectively. Given two V-plays $\pi_1\mathbf{v}$ and $\mathbf{v}\pi_2$, we write $\pi_1\pi_2$ for the evident concatenation of the two plays.

We give a brief summary of the proof structure. Similar to [13], we consider "canonical" sequents of the restricted form:

$$D \,;\, x : \Psi_1, \ \ldots, \ x : \Psi_k \vdash \mathsf{P}\, x : \varphi, \tag{2}$$

where P is a nonterminal. Each such sequent is constructed with reference to a position of the form $\mathbf{u} = (\mathsf{P}\,\mathsf{q}, \mathsf{E}, \varphi)$, with each assumption $x : \Psi_i$ being determined by a V-play π from $\mathbf{u}$ to some position $\mathbf{v}$ whose state is q. Importantly, the extended formula Ψ_i contains ν-approximant declarations and modifiers that reflect preservation and progress properties of the play π. We use Verifier's strategy to construct a derivation tree in which individual rule applications can be combined into larger steps between sequents of the form (2). Crucially, only finitely many distinct such sequents occur in the constructed derivation, enabling the derivation tree to terminate in repeats. Moreover, paths in the derivation tree reflect preservation and progress properties of the V-plays used to construct the derivation, which allows the choice of repeats to be made so that the resulting pre-proof is a proof.

To define canonical sequents, we need various auxiliary definitions. Given a play π ending in the position (s, E, φ), we define functions $dec_\pi(\mathsf{E}', \Phi)$ and $pro_\pi(\mathsf{E}', \Phi)$ for prefixes E' of E and extended formulae Φ with $FV(\Phi) \subseteq DV(\mathsf{E}')$.

$$pro_\pi(\mathsf{E}', \Phi) = \begin{cases} dec_\pi(\mathsf{E}', [+X]\,\Phi) & \text{if } \mathsf{E}' \text{ is } \mathsf{E}'', X = \varphi \text{ and } X \text{ progresses on a tail of } \pi \\ dec_\pi(\mathsf{E}', \Phi) & \text{otherwise} \end{cases}$$

$$dec_\pi(\mathsf{E}', \Phi) = \begin{cases} pro_\pi(\mathsf{E}'', [X \geqslant \varphi]\,\Phi) & \text{if } \mathsf{E}' \text{ is } \mathsf{E}'', X = \varphi \text{ and } \pi \text{ does not preserve } X \\ \Phi & \text{otherwise} \end{cases}$$

Definition 17 (Characteristic formula). For any play π ending in (s, E, φ), its *characteristic formula* $\chi(\pi)$ is $pro_\pi(\mathsf{E}, \varphi)$.

Definition 18 (Assumption set). For any position $\mathbf{u} = (p, \mathsf{E}, \varphi)$, its *assumption set* relative to q is the set

$$AS(\mathbf{u}, \mathsf{q}) = \{ \chi(\pi) \mid \mathbf{u}\pi\mathbf{v} \text{ is a V-play with } \mathbf{v} = (\mathsf{q}, \mathsf{E}', \psi) \}.$$

Definition 19 (Canonical sequent). For any position $\mathbf{u} = (\mathsf{p\,q}, \mathsf{E}, \varphi)$, the *canonical sequent* relative to p is the sequent

$$\mathcal{S}(\mathbf{u}, \mathsf{p}) = \mathsf{D_E} ; \{x : \Psi \mid \Psi \in AS(\mathbf{u}, \mathsf{q})\} \vdash \mathsf{p}\,x : \varphi,$$

where $\mathsf{D_E} = \{X \geqslant \psi \mid X = \psi \text{ occurs in } \mathsf{E}\}$.

This is a good definition because the set $AS(\mathbf{u}, \mathsf{q})$ is finite.

The next two lemmas show how to build up derivation trees between canonical sequents of the form $\mathcal{S}(\mathbf{u}, \mathsf{P})$, where P is nonterminal, providing the "larger steps" between such sequents discussed above.

Lemma 1. *Given a position* $\mathbf{u} = (\mathsf{Q_1} \ldots \mathsf{Q_k\,r}, \mathsf{E}, \varphi)$, *where* $\mathsf{Q_1}, \ldots, \mathsf{Q_k}$ *are nonterminals, the sequent* $\mathcal{S}(\mathbf{u}, \mathsf{Q_1} \ldots \mathsf{Q_k})$ *occurs as the root of a derivation tree in which each leaf has the form* $\mathcal{S_\pi} = \mathcal{S}(\mathbf{v_\pi}, \mathsf{Q_i})$, *where* $\mathbf{u}\pi\mathbf{v_\pi}$ *is a V-play and* $\mathbf{v_\pi} = (\mathsf{Q_i} \ldots \mathsf{Q_k\,r}, \mathsf{E_\pi}, \psi_\pi)$ *for some* i. *Moreover, if the play* π *preserves (respectively progresses on)* X *then so does the unique path from the root to* $\mathcal{S_\pi}$.

The proof repeatedly uses (Cut) and (Sub) to remove each nonterminal $\mathsf{Q_i}$ from the sequence $\mathsf{Q_i} \ldots \mathsf{Q_k}$, applying appropriate proof rules to convert the induced subgoal for $\mathsf{Q_{i+1}} \ldots \mathsf{Q_k}$ into the required form for the process to be repeated.

Lemma 2. *Given a position* $\mathbf{u} = (\mathsf{Q\,r}, \mathsf{E}, \varphi)$, *where* Q *is nonterminal, the sequent* $\mathcal{S}(\mathbf{u}, \mathsf{Q})$ *occurs as the root of a derivation tree in which each leaf has the form* $\mathcal{S_\pi} = \mathcal{S}(\mathbf{v_\pi}, \mathsf{Q_\pi})$, *where* $\mathsf{Q_\pi}$ *is nonterminal,* $\mathbf{v_\pi} = (\mathsf{Q_\pi\,q_\pi\,r}, \mathsf{E_\pi}, \psi_\pi)$ *and* $\mathbf{u}\pi\mathbf{v_\pi}$ *is a V-play containing at least one move. If the play* π *preserves (respectively progresses on)* X *then so does the unique path to* $\mathcal{S_\pi}$ *in the derivation tree.*

The proof is by case analysis on φ using the sequent rules to mimic the possible moves of any V-play. In the case of the modal rules, Lemma 1 is used to break down any sequence of nonterminals produced.

Lemma 2 builds derivation trees between canonical sequents and relates preservation and progress properties of paths through the trees to analogous properties of the V-plays used to construct them. As discussed above, these properties allow the derivation trees to be combined into a proof, yielding:

Lemma 3 (Main lemma). *For any position* $\mathbf{u} = (\mathsf{p\,q}, \mathsf{E}, \varphi)$ *the canonical sequent* $\mathcal{S}(\mathbf{u}, \mathsf{p})$ *has a proof.*

The proof of Theorem 2 is now concluded by using (Cut) and (Sub) to combine Lemma 3 above with the relatively straightforward:

Lemma 4. *For any position* $\mathbf{u} = (\mathsf{p}, \mathsf{E}, \varphi)$ *and* Ψ *in the assumption set* $AS(\mathbf{u}, \varepsilon)$ *the sequent* $\vdash \varepsilon : \Psi$ *has a proof.*

5   Discussion and Future Work

Our proof of completeness for context-free processes makes essential use of ν-approximant declarations and modifiers. These features can be incorporated into Dam and Gurov's proof system [9], by extending their syntax with ordinal quantifiers $\forall \kappa. \varphi$ and $\forall \kappa' < \kappa. \varphi$. Indeed, the completeness proof for context-free processes was originally developed in this context in the first author's MSc dissertation [16]. We do not know whether context-free completeness holds for Dam and Gurov's system without ordinal quantifiers.

It is natural to ask whether the approach in this paper might extend to obtain completeness for richer classes of processes, such as pushdown processes [15,20,3]. In a different direction, it would be very interesting to ascertain to what extent one can obtain completeness results for parameterized verification goals of the form (1), see Sect. 1.

References

1. B. Bloom, S. Istrail, and A.R. Meyer. Bisimulation can't be traced. *J. Assoc. Comput. Mach.*, 42:232–268, 1995.
2. O. Burkart, D. Caucal, F. Moller, and B. Steffen. Verification over infinite states. In *Handbook of Process Algebra*, pages 545–623. Elsevier, 2001.
3. O. Burkart and B. Steffen. Model checking the full modal mu-calculus for infinite sequential processes. *Theoretical Computer Science*, 221(1–2):251–270, 1999.
4. M. Dam. Compositional proof systems for model checking infinite state processes. In *International Conference on Concurrency Theory*, pages 12–26, 1995.
5. M. Dam. Proving properties of dynamic process networks. *Information and Computation*, 140(2):95–114, 1998.
6. M. Dam. Proof systems for π-calculus logics. In R. de Queiroz, editor, *Logic for Concurrency and Synchronisation*. OUP, 2001.
7. M. Dam, L. Fredlund, and D. Gurov. Toward parametric verification of open distributed systems. In A. Pnueli H. Langmaack and W.-P. de Roever, editors, *Compositionality: the Significant Difference*. Springer, 1998.
8. M. Dam and D. Gurov. Compositional verification of CCS processes. In *Proceedings of PSI'99*. Springer LNCS 1755, 1999.
9. M. Dam and D. Gurov. μ-calculus with explicit points and approximations. *Journal of Logic and Computation*, to appear, 2001. Abstract in Proceedings of FICS 2000.
10. J. Esparza and J. Knoop. An automata-theoretic approach to interprocedural dataflow analysis. In *Proceedings of FOSSACS'99*. Springer LNCS 1578, 1999.
11. L. Fredlund. A framework for reasoning about Erlang code. PhD Thesis, Swedish Institute of Computer Science, 2001.
12. M. Hennessy and R. Milner. Algebraic laws for nondeterminism and concurrency. *J. Assoc. Comput. Mach.*, 32:137–161, 1985.
13. H. Hungar and B. Steffen. Local model checking for context-free processes. *Nordic Journal of Computing*, 1(3):364–385, Fall 1994.
14. D. Kozen. Results on the propositional μ-calculus. *Theoretical Computer Science*, 27:333–354, 1983.
15. D.E. Muller and P.E. Schupp. The theory of ends, pushdown automata, and second-order logic. *Theoretical Computer Science*, 37:51–75, 1985.
16. U. Schöpp. Formal verification of processes. MSc Dissertation, University of Edinburgh, 2001. Available as `http://www.dcs.ed.ac.uk/home/us/th.ps.gz`.
17. A.K. Simpson. Compositionality via cut-elimination: Hennessy-Milner logic for an arbitrary GSOS. In *Logic in Computer Science*, pages 420–430, 1995.
18. C.P. Stirling. Modal logics for communicating systems. *Theoretical Computer Science*, 49:311–347, 1987.
19. C.P. Stirling. *Modal and temporal properties of processes*. Texts in Computer Science. Springer, 2001.
20. I. Walukiewicz. Pushdown processes: games and model-checking. *Information and Computation*, 164(2):234–263, January 2001.

Note on the Tableau Technique
for Commutative Transition Systems

Jiří Srba[*]

BRICS[**], Department of Computer Science, University of Aarhus,
Ny Munkegade bldg. 540, 8000 Aarhus C, Denmark
srba@brics.dk

Abstract. We define a class of transition systems called effective commutative transition systems (ECTS) and show, by generalising a tableau-based proof for BPP, that strong bisimilarity between any two states of such a transition system is decidable. It gives a general technique for extending decidability borders of strong bisimilarity for a wide class of infinite-state transition systems. This is demonstrated for several process formalisms, namely BPP process algebra, lossy BPP processes, BPP systems with interrupt and timed-arc BPP nets.

1 Introduction

Semantics of various formalisms for description of concurrent processes like process algebra, Petri nets, pushdown systems and many others is usually given in terms of labelled transition systems. This provides a common ground for studying such systems, and the usually considered problems as *model checking* and *equivalence checking* (see e.g. [8]) can be defined purely in terms of labelled transition systems. In this paper we focus on the equivalence checking problem and show a general approach for extending known decidability borders of strong bisimilarity for commutative-based process formalisms. In particular, we examine the class of transition systems generated by algebras with the operator of parallel composition and we discuss its extensions with lossiness, interrupt and with time features.

It is known that strong bisimilarity is undecidable for a typical representative of fully parallel models — Petri nets [15]. Nevertheless, in [9,10] Christensen, Hirshfeld and Moller proved using a tableau technique, that bisimilarity is decidable for an important fragment of Petri nets called *communication free Petri nets.* The complexity of this algorithm is still open — no primitive recursive upper bound is known. PSPACE-hardness of the problem was recently shown in [23]. The class of transition systems definable by communication free Petri nets can be equivalently described in terms of process algebra with a commutative operator for parallel composition and recursion. It is this formalism, usually

---

[*] The author is supported in part by the GACR, grant No. 201/00/0400.
[**] **B**asic **R**esearch in **C**omputer **S**cience,
Centre of the Danish National Research Foundation.

M. Nielsen and U. Engberg (Eds.): Fossacs 2002, LNCS 2303, pp. 387–401, 2002.

called *Basic Parallel Processes* (BPP), that is used in the original tableau-based proof in [10]. For an overview on the tableau technique consult e.g. [16].

We abstract from the specific BPP syntax and generalise the proof for a class of transition systems called *effective commutative transition systems* (ECTS). We give six simple conditions on a transition system to be an ECTS and if all of them are satisfied, bisimilarity between any two states of the transition system is decidable. There is no need to know the syntactic description of the system. Moreover, the generalisation is achieved in several ways: (i) states can be tuples of bounded multisets of natural numbers and not only tuples of natural numbers, (ii) we do not insist on a specific computation of successors of a given state — any effectively computable and finite set of successors is acceptable, and (iii) an auxiliary equivalence relation on states is introduced in order to check invariants for pairs in a bisimulation relation.

Semantics of many formalisms can be defined as an ECTS and this yields immediately decidability of bisimilarity. We demonstrate this on four examples — BPP process algebra, lossy BPP processes, BPP systems with interrupt and timed-arc BPP nets — thus extending in several ways the known decidability border which lies somewhere between BPP systems and state-extended BPP systems (state-extended BPP systems are a strict subclass of Petri nets where bisimilarity is still undecidable [8,16]).

Note: full version of this paper appears as [22].

2   General Method

Let $\mathbb{N}_0 = \{0, 1, \ldots\}$ be the set of natural numbers. A *multiset* of $\mathbb{N}_0$ is a function $M : \mathbb{N}_0 \to \mathbb{N}_0$. Let $i \in \mathbb{N}_0$, then $M(i)$ denotes the number of occurrences of i in the multiset M. The *empty multiset* $\emptyset$ is a function such that $\emptyset(i) = 0$ for all $i \in \mathbb{N}_0$. The *multiset union* of two multisets M_1 and M_2 is defined by $(M_1 \uplus M_2)(i) = M_1(i) + M_2(i)$ for all $i \in \mathbb{N}_0$. By $\mathcal{B}_\infty$ we denote the set of all multisets of $\mathbb{N}_0$. Let $m \in \mathbb{N}_0$. We define a set $\mathcal{B}_m$ of all multisets of $\{0, 1, \ldots, m\}$, i.e., $M \in \mathcal{B}_m$ iff $M \in \mathcal{B}_\infty$ and $M(i) = 0$ for all $i \in \mathbb{N}_0$ such that $i > m$. We call a multiset $M \in \mathcal{B}_\infty$ *finite* if there is some $m \in \mathbb{N}_0$ such that $M \in \mathcal{B}_m$. For finite multisets we sometimes use an alternative set-like notation: e.g. a multiset $\{0, 1, 1, 4, 4, 4\}$ is the same as a multiset M such that $M(0) = 1$, $M(1) = 2$, $M(4) = 3$ and $M(i) = 0$ for $i \in \mathbb{N}_0 \smallsetminus \{0, 1, 4\}$.

Let $M, N \in \mathcal{B}_m$. We write $M \prec_\ell N$ iff there is k, $0 \le k \le m$, such that $M(k) < N(k)$ and $M(i) = N(i)$ for all i, $0 \le i < k$. Let $M, N \in \mathcal{B}_m$ then $M \neq N$ implies that either $M \prec_\ell N$ or $N \prec_\ell M$. We write $M \preceq_c N$ iff $M(i) \le N(i)$ for every i, $1 \le i \le m$, i.e., iff there is $M' \in \mathcal{B}_m$ such that $N = M \uplus M'$.

Let $m, n \in \mathbb{N}_0$ and $n > 0$. We define a structure $S = (\mathcal{B}_m^n, \oplus, \emptyset^n)$ where $\mathcal{B}_m^n$ is a set of n-tuples of elements from $\mathcal{B}_m$. Let $\alpha = (M_1, M_2, \ldots, M_n) \in \mathcal{B}_m^n$ and $\beta = (N_1, N_2, \ldots, N_n) \in \mathcal{B}_m^n$, then $\alpha \oplus \beta = (M_1 \uplus N_1, M_2 \uplus N_2, \ldots, M_n \uplus N_n)$. Of course, $\alpha \oplus \beta \in \mathcal{B}_m^n$. The structure S is a commutative monoid. If $\alpha \in \mathcal{B}_m^n$ then α_i, $1 \le i \le n$, is the i'th coordinate of α. We introduce two orderings on $\mathcal{B}_m^n$.

Let $\alpha, \beta \in \mathcal{B}_m^n$, then $\alpha <_\ell \beta$ iff there is k, $1 \leq k \leq n$, such that $\alpha_k \prec_\ell \beta_k$ and $\alpha_i = \beta_i$ for every i, $1 \leq i < k$; and $\alpha \leq_c \beta$ iff $\alpha_i \preceq_c \beta_i$ for every i, $1 \leq i \leq n$.

Observe that $<_\ell$ is a well-founded ordering (there is no infinite sequence $\alpha_1, \alpha_2, \ldots$ such that $\alpha_1 >_\ell \alpha_2 >_\ell \ldots$) since $\prec_\ell$ is well-founded. Moreover for any $\alpha \neq \beta$ either $\alpha <_\ell \beta$ or $\beta <_\ell \alpha$. Also notice that $\alpha \leq_c \beta$ iff there is $\alpha' \in \mathcal{B}_m^n$ such that $\beta = \alpha \oplus \alpha'$. We write $\alpha <_c \beta$ iff $\alpha \leq_c \beta$ and $\alpha \neq \beta$. The following lemma is a simple generalisation of Dickson's Lemma [12].

Lemma 1. *Every infinite sequence from $\mathcal{B}_m^n$ has an infinite nondecreasing subsequence w.r.t. $\leq_c$.*

A *labelled transition system* is a 4-tuple $(S, \mathcal{A}ct, \longrightarrow, \mathcal{E}qv)$ where S is a set of *states* (or *processes*), $\mathcal{A}ct$ is a set of *labels* (or *actions*), $\longrightarrow \subseteq S \times \mathcal{A}ct \times S$ is a *transition relation*, written $\alpha \xrightarrow{a} \beta$, for $(\alpha, a, \beta) \in \longrightarrow$, and $\mathcal{E}qv \subseteq S \times S$ is an *equivalence relation* on states.

Our definition of labelled transition systems is a generalisation of labelled transition systems with final states — see an overview paper [8]. Let $F \subseteq S$ be a set of final states. In order to recover the definition from [8] we define $(\alpha, \beta) \in \mathcal{E}qv$ iff $\alpha \in F$ and $\beta \in F$, or $\alpha \notin F$ and $\beta \notin F$.

Let $\alpha \in S$. We write $\alpha \not\rightarrow$ whenever there is no $\beta \in S$ and $a \in \mathcal{A}ct$ such that $\alpha \xrightarrow{a} \beta$. As usual we extend the transition relation to the elements of $\mathcal{A}ct^*$. We define a *norm* of $\alpha \in S$ by $\mathcal{N}(\alpha) = \min\{|w| \mid w \in \mathcal{A}ct^* \text{ such that } \exists \beta \in S. \ \alpha \xrightarrow{w} \beta \not\rightarrow\}$. By definition $\min \emptyset = \infty$.

Let $T = (S, \mathcal{A}ct, \longrightarrow, \mathcal{E}qv)$ be a labelled transition system. A binary relation $R \subseteq S \times S$ is a *bisimulation* iff whenever $(\alpha, \beta) \in R$ then for each $a \in \mathcal{A}ct$: if $\alpha \xrightarrow{a} \alpha'$ then $\exists \beta' \in S$ such that $\beta \xrightarrow{a} \beta'$ and $(\alpha', \beta') \in R$; if $\beta \xrightarrow{a} \beta'$ then $\exists \alpha' \in S$ such that $\alpha \xrightarrow{a} \alpha'$ and $(\alpha', \beta') \in R$; and $(\alpha, \beta) \in \mathcal{E}qv$.

States $\alpha, \beta \in S$ are *bisimulation equivalent* or *bisimilar* in a transition system T, written $\alpha \sim_T \beta$, iff $(\alpha, \beta) \in R$ for some bisimulation R. If T is clear from the context, we write only $\alpha \sim \beta$ instead of $\alpha \sim_T \beta$.

Remark 1. Sometimes the bisimilarity checking problem is formulated in this way: we are given a pair of labelled transition systems T_1 and T_2 with states α_1 from T_1 and α_2 from T_2, and the question $\alpha_1 \sim \alpha_2$ is asked. In this case, we can consider a disjoint union of T_1 and T_2 (i.e. the sets of states of T_1 and T_2 are disjoint) as a new transition system T and ask the question $\alpha_1 \sim_T \alpha_2$.

Let $(S, \mathcal{A}ct, \longrightarrow, \mathcal{E}qv)$ be a labelled transition system. The *stratified bisimulation relations* [19] $\sim_k \subseteq S \times S$ for $k \in \mathbb{N}_0$ are defined as follows:

 - $\alpha \sim_0 \beta$ for all $\alpha, \beta \in S$ such that $(\alpha, \beta) \in \mathcal{E}qv$, i.e., $\sim_0 = \mathcal{E}qv$
 - $\alpha \sim_{k+1} \beta$ iff for each $a \in \mathcal{A}ct$: if $\alpha \xrightarrow{a} \alpha'$ then $\exists \beta' \in S$ such that $\beta \xrightarrow{a} \beta'$ and $\alpha' \sim_k \beta'$; if $\beta \xrightarrow{a} \beta'$ then $\exists \alpha' \in S$ such that $\alpha \xrightarrow{a} \alpha'$ and $\alpha' \sim_k \beta'$; and $(\alpha, \beta) \in \mathcal{E}qv$.

Given a labelled transition system $T = (S, \mathcal{A}ct, \longrightarrow, \mathcal{E}qv)$ we define $\mathsf{next}(\alpha, a) = \{\beta \in S \mid \alpha \xrightarrow{a} \beta\}$ for $\alpha \in S$ and $a \in \mathcal{A}ct$. We also define $\mathsf{next}(\alpha, *) = \bigcup_{a \in \mathcal{A}ct} \mathsf{next}(\alpha, a)$. The system T is *image-finite* iff the set $\mathsf{next}(\alpha, a)$ is finite for every $\alpha \in S$ and $a \in \mathcal{A}ct$. The following lemma is a standard one.

Lemma 2. *Let $(S, \mathcal{A}ct, \longrightarrow, \mathcal{E}qv)$ be an image-finite labelled transition system and $\alpha, \beta \in S$. Then $\alpha \sim \beta$ iff $\alpha \sim_k \beta$ for all $k \in \mathbb{N}_0$.*

Definition 1 (Effective Commutative Transition System). *A labelled transition system $T = (S, \mathcal{A}ct, \longrightarrow, \mathcal{E}qv)$ is an effective commutative transition system (ECTS) iff there exist $n, m \in \mathbb{N}_0$, $n > 0$ such that the following conditions are satisfied:*

(1) $S = \mathcal{B}_m^n$,
(2) $\mathcal{A}ct$ is a finite set,
(3) given $\alpha, \beta \in S$ it is decidable whether $(\alpha, \beta) \in \mathcal{E}qv$,
(4) $\mathsf{next}(\alpha, a)$ is effectively constructible for every $\alpha \in \mathcal{B}_m^n$ and $a \in \mathcal{A}ct$,
(5) T is image-finite,
(6) if $\alpha \sim_k \beta$ then $(\alpha \oplus \gamma) \sim_k (\beta \oplus \gamma)$ for every $\alpha, \beta, \gamma \in \mathcal{B}_m^n$ and $k \in \mathbb{N}_0$.

Let us call the elements of $\mathcal{B}_m^n$ *processes*. Since any ECTS is image-finite (5), the fact that $\sim_k$ are congruences (6) together with Lemma 2 implies: *(6')* if $\alpha \sim \beta$ then $(\alpha \oplus \gamma) \sim (\beta \oplus \gamma)$ for every $\alpha, \beta, \gamma \in \mathcal{B}_m^n$.

Theorem 1. *Let $T = (\mathcal{B}_m^n, \mathcal{A}ct, \longrightarrow, \mathcal{E}qv)$ be an ECTS. Given $A, B \in \mathcal{B}_m^n$, it is decidable whether $A \sim B$.*

Proof. The proof is by tableau-technique and it is a generalisation of the tableau-based proof used by Christensen, Hirshfeld and Moller in order to demonstrate decidability of bisimilarity for BPP [9,10].

A tableau for $(A, B) \in \mathcal{B}_m^{2n}$ is a maximal proof tree rooted with (A, B) and built according to the following rules. Let (α, β) be a node in the tree. A node (α, β) is either *terminal (leaf)* or *nonterminal*. The following nodes are terminal:

- (α, α) is a *successful leaf* for any $\alpha \in \mathcal{B}_m^n$ (note that always $(\alpha, \alpha) \in \mathcal{E}qv$),
- (α, β) is a *successful leaf* if $\mathsf{next}(\alpha, *) \cup \mathsf{next}(\beta, *) = \emptyset$ and $(\alpha, \beta) \in \mathcal{E}qv$,
- (α, β) is an *unsuccessful leaf* if for some $a \in \mathcal{A}ct$ it is the case that $\mathsf{next}(\alpha, a) \cup \mathsf{next}(\beta, a) \neq \emptyset$, and either $\mathsf{next}(\alpha, a) = \emptyset$ or $\mathsf{next}(\beta, a) = \emptyset$,
- (α, β) is an *unsuccessful leaf* if $(\alpha, \beta) \notin \mathcal{E}qv$.

We say that a node is an *ancestor* of (α, β) if it is on the path from the root to (α, β) and at least one application of the rule EXPAND (defined later) separates them. If (α, β) is not a leaf then we reduce it using the following RED rules as long as possible.

$$\mathrm{RED}_L \quad \frac{(\alpha, \beta)}{(\gamma \oplus \omega, \beta)} \quad \begin{array}{l} \text{if there is an ancestor } (\gamma, \delta) \text{ or } (\delta, \gamma) \text{ of } (\alpha, \beta) \text{ such that} \\ \gamma <_\ell \delta \text{ and } \alpha = \delta \oplus \omega \text{ for some } \omega \in \mathcal{B}_m^n \end{array}$$

$$\mathrm{RED}_R \quad \frac{(\alpha, \beta)}{(\alpha, \gamma \oplus \omega)} \quad \begin{array}{l} \text{if there is an ancestor } (\gamma, \delta) \text{ or } (\delta, \gamma) \text{ of } (\alpha, \beta) \text{ such that} \\ \gamma <_\ell \delta \text{ and } \beta = \delta \oplus \omega \text{ for some } \omega \in \mathcal{B}_m^n \end{array}$$

If no other reduction RED is applicable and the resulting node is not a leaf, we apply the rule EXPAND for a set of relations S_a, $a \in \mathcal{A}ct$, where $S_a \subseteq$

$\mathsf{next}(\alpha, a) \times \mathsf{next}(\beta, a)$ such that $\forall \alpha' \in \mathsf{next}(\alpha, a).\exists \beta' \in \mathsf{next}(\beta, a). (\alpha', \beta') \in S_a$ and $\forall \beta' \in \mathsf{next}(\beta, a).\exists \alpha' \in \mathsf{next}(\alpha, a). (\alpha', \beta') \in S_a$.

$$\text{EXPAND} \quad \frac{(\alpha, \beta)}{\{(\alpha', \beta') \mid a \in \mathcal{A}ct \ \wedge \ (\alpha', \beta') \in S_a\}}$$

The set notation used in the rule EXPAND means that each element (α', β') in the conclusion of the rule becomes a new child in the proof tree. Now, we start again applying the RED-rules to every such child (which is not a leaf) as long as possible. Note that reduction rules are applicable to a node iff the node is not terminal (leaf).

Lemma 3. *Any tableau for (A, B) is finite and there are only finitely many tableaux.*

Proof. Observe that any tableau for (A, B) is finitely branching because of the assumption (5) and the condition that $\mathcal{A}ct$ is finite (2), which implies that for a given $a \in \mathcal{A}ct$ any relation S_a is finite and there are finitely many such relations. Should the tableau be infinite, there is an infinite branch, which gives an infinite sequence of vectors from $\mathcal{B}_m^{2n}$. Since the rules RED can be used only finitely many times in a sequence (they decrease the $<_\ell$ order, which is well founded), there must be an infinite subsequence of vectors on which the rule EXPAND was applied. Using Lemma 1, this sequence must contain an infinite nondecreasing subsequence $p_1 \leq_c p_2 \leq_c \ldots$. However, the rule EXPAND cannot be applied on p_2 since one of the rules RED is applicable. This is a contradiction.

Since there are only finitely many relations S_a for an $a \in \mathcal{A}ct$ available for the EXPAND rule and finitely many possibilities for an application of the RED rule, there are always finitely many possibilities how to extend already existing partial tableau. Suppose that there are infinitely many tableaux starting from (A, B). Then there must be a tableau for (A, B) with an infinite branch, which contradicts that every tableau is finite.   □

We call a tableau for (A, B) *successful* if it is maximal (no further rules are applicable) and all its leaves are successful.

Lemma 4 (Completeness). *If $A \sim B$ then there is a successful tableau for (A, B).*

Proof. We construct a tableau from the root (A, B) such that every node (α, β) in the tableau satisfies $\alpha \sim \beta$. Hence this tableau cannot contain any unsuccessful leaf and it must be finite because of Lemma 3. Suppose that (α, β) is already a node in the tableau such that $\alpha \sim \beta$ and consider the rule RED_L applied on (α, β). We may assume that $\gamma \sim \delta$, which means using (6') that $(\gamma \oplus \omega) \sim (\delta \oplus \omega) = \alpha \sim \beta$. Hence $(\gamma \oplus \omega) \sim \beta$. Similarly for RED_R. From the definition of $\sim$ follows that the rule EXPAND is also forward sound, i.e., if $\alpha \sim \beta$ then we can choose for every $a \in \mathcal{A}ct$ a relation S_a such that $(\alpha', \beta') \in S_a$ implies that $\alpha' \sim \beta'$.   □

Lemma 5 (Soundness). *If there is a successful tableau for (A, B) then $A \sim B$.*

Proof. For the sake of contradiction assume that there is a successful tableau for (A, B) and $A \not\sim B$. We show that we can construct a path from the root (A, B) to some leaf, such that for any pair (α, β) on this path $\alpha \not\sim \beta$.

If $A \not\sim B$ then using Lemma 2 there is a minimal k such that $A \not\sim_k B$. Notice that if $\alpha \not\sim_k \beta$ such that k is minimal and we apply the rule EXPAND, then at least one of its children (α', β') satisfies that $\alpha' \not\sim_{k-1} \beta'$. We choose such a child to extend our path from the root.

If we apply RED_L on (α, β) where $\alpha \not\sim_k \beta$ and k is minimal, then the corresponding ancestor (γ, δ) is separated by at least one application of EXPAND and so $\gamma \sim_k \delta$. This implies that $(\gamma \oplus \omega) \not\sim_k \beta$, otherwise using the assumption (6) we get that $\alpha = (\delta \oplus \omega) \sim_k (\gamma \oplus \omega) \sim_k \beta$, which is a contradiction with $\alpha \not\sim_k \beta$. The same is true for RED_R. Thus there must be a path from the root to some leaf such that for any pair (α, β) on this path $\alpha \not\sim \beta$. This is a contradiction with the fact that the path contains a successful leaf.   □

We have proved that it is decidable whether $A \sim B$, since it is the case iff there is a successful tableau for (A, B). There are only finitely many tableaux and all of them are finite, moreover the conditions (3) and (4) ensure that they are effectively constructible.   □

3   Applications

In this section we consider several specific classes of commutative transition systems. We study in particular BPP and lossy BPP processes, interrupt BPP systems and timed-arc BPP nets.

3.1   BPP and Deadlock-Sensitive BPP

The class of Basic Parallel Processes (BPP) [9] is a natural subclass of PA (Process Algebra) where only the operator of parallel composition is used. It is a well known fact that bisimilarity is decidable for BPP [9,10]. We give the definition of BPP by means of process rewrite systems [17], which is more convenient for our purposes than the usual one by process equations used by Milner [19]. We remind the reader of the fact that these two definitions are equivalent in the sense that they define the same class of processes up to bisimilarity.

Let $\mathcal{A}ct$ and $\mathcal{V}ar$ be countable sets of *actions* and *process constants* such that $\mathcal{A}ct \cap \mathcal{V}ar = \emptyset$. We define a class of *process expressions* $\mathcal{E}^{\mathcal{V}ar}$ over $\mathcal{V}ar$ by the following abstract syntax $E ::= \epsilon \mid X \mid E\|E$, where ϵ is the *empty process* and X ranges over $\mathcal{V}ar$. The operator '$\|$' stands for a *parallel composition*. We do not distinguish between process expressions related by a *structural congruence* $\equiv \subseteq \mathcal{E}^{\mathcal{V}ar} \times \mathcal{E}^{\mathcal{V}ar}$, which is the smallest congruence over process expressions such that '$\|$' is associative and commutative, and 'ϵ' is a unit for '$\|$'.

A BPP *process rewrite system* (PRS) [17] is a finite set $\Delta \subseteq \mathcal{V}ar \times \mathcal{A}ct \times \mathcal{E}^{\mathcal{V}ar}$ of *rules*, written $X \xrightarrow{a} E$ for $(X, a, E) \in \Delta$. Let us denote the set of actions and process constants that appear in Δ as $\mathcal{A}ct(\Delta)$ resp. $\mathcal{V}ar(\Delta)$ (note that these sets

$$\frac{(X \xrightarrow{a} E) \in \Delta}{X \xrightarrow{a} E} \qquad \frac{E \xrightarrow{a} E'}{E\|F \xrightarrow{a} E'\|F}$$

Fig. 1. SOS rules for BPP

are finite). A process rewrite system Δ determines a labelled transition system $T(\Delta) = (\mathcal{E}^{\mathcal{V}ar(\Delta)}/\equiv, \mathcal{A}ct(\Delta), \longrightarrow, \mathcal{E}qv)$ where states are $\equiv$-equivalence classes of process expressions over $\mathcal{V}ar(\Delta)$, $\mathcal{A}ct(\Delta)$ is the set of labels, the transition relation $\longrightarrow$ is the least relation satisfying the SOS rules in Figure 1 (recall that '$\|$' is commutative and in what follows we often abuse the notation and write only E instead of $[E]_\equiv$, i.e., the equivalence class represented by E). There are two possibilities for defining the equivalence relation $\mathcal{E}qv$. In the usual setting $\mathcal{E}qv = (\mathcal{E}^{\mathcal{V}ar(\Delta)}/\equiv) \times (\mathcal{E}^{\mathcal{V}ar(\Delta)}/\equiv)$ is the universal relation (thus it is in fact unused) and we call this class BPP. Another possibility is to define $\mathcal{E}qv$ by

$$\mathcal{E}qv = \{(E, F) \in (\mathcal{E}^{\mathcal{V}ar(\Delta)}/\equiv) \times (\mathcal{E}^{\mathcal{V}ar(\Delta)}/\equiv) \mid E = [\epsilon]_\equiv \iff F = [\epsilon]_\equiv\}.$$

We call this class *deadlock-sensitive* BPP. A study of strict (deadlock-sensitive) and nonstrict (deadlock-nonsensitive) bisimilarity for a sequential analogue of BPP called Basic Process Algebra (BPA) is provided in [21].

We show that given a BPP system Δ, we can interpret its semantics as a commutative transition system such that states are elements of $\mathcal{B}_{n-1} = \mathcal{B}_{n-1}^1$ where $n = |\mathcal{V}ar(\Delta)|$. Because of the structural congruence $\equiv$, any process expression E over $\mathcal{V}ar(\Delta)$ can be represented by a vector of n natural numbers. Suppose a fixed ordering on $\mathcal{V}ar(\Delta) = \{X_0, X_1, \ldots, X_{n-1}\}$. Then the corresponding vector contains on i'th coordinate the number of occurrences of the variable X_i in E. Formally, we define a mapping $\phi : \mathcal{E}^{\mathcal{V}ar(\Delta)} \to \mathcal{B}_{n-1}^1$ by

$$\begin{aligned} \phi(\epsilon) &= \emptyset \\ \phi(X_i) &= M \text{ such that } M(i) = 1 \text{ and } M(j) = 0 \text{ for } j \neq i \\ \phi(E_1\|E_2) &= \phi(E_1) \oplus \phi(E_2). \end{aligned}$$

The following proposition is an easy observation.

Proposition 1. *Let* $E, F \in \mathcal{E}^{\mathcal{V}ar(\Delta)}$. *Then* $E \equiv F$ *if and only if* $\phi(E) = \phi(F)$.

Hence any rule $(X \xrightarrow{a} E) \in \Delta$ can be represented by $\phi(X) \xrightarrow{a} \phi(E)$. The system Δ, where $n = |\mathcal{V}ar(\Delta)|$, generates a commutative labelled transition system $T^c(\Delta) = (\mathcal{B}_{n-1}^1, \mathcal{A}ct(\Delta), \longrightarrow, \mathcal{E}qv)$, where $\alpha \xrightarrow{a} \beta$ iff there exists a rule $(X \xrightarrow{a} E) \in \Delta$ such that $\alpha = \phi(X) \oplus \omega$ and $\beta = \phi(E) \oplus \omega$ for some $\omega \in \mathcal{B}_{n-1}^1$. The relation $\mathcal{E}qv$ for BPP and deadlock-sensitive BPP is defined in the same fashion as above.

Example 1. Let $\Delta = \{X_0 \xrightarrow{a} X_0\|X_1\|X_2\|X_1, \; X_0 \xrightarrow{a} \epsilon, \; X_1 \xrightarrow{b} \epsilon, \; X_2 \xrightarrow{c} \epsilon\}$. Then $n = 3$ and e.g. $\phi(X_0) = \{0\}$, $\phi(X_0\|X_1\|X_2\|X_1) = \{0, 1, 2\}$ and $\phi(\epsilon) = \emptyset$. A sequence of transitions $X_0 \xrightarrow{a} X_0\|X_1\|X_2\|X_1 \xrightarrow{a} X_0\|X_1\|X_2\|X_1\|X_1\|X_2\|X_1$

$$\frac{(X \xrightarrow{a} E) \in \Delta}{X \xrightarrow{a} E} \qquad \frac{E \xrightarrow{a} E'}{E\|F \xrightarrow{a} E'\|F} \qquad \frac{}{E \xrightarrow{drop} F} \text{ if } \exists F' \neq \epsilon \text{ s.t. } E = F\|F'$$

Fig. 2. SOS rules for lossy BPP

$\xrightarrow{b} X_0\|X_2\|X_1\|X_1\|X_2\|X_1 \xrightarrow{c} X_0\|X_1\|X_1\|X_2\|X_1$ has a straightforward analogue in $\mathcal{B}_2^1$: $\{0\} \xrightarrow{a} \{0,1,1,2\} \xrightarrow{a} \{0,1,1,1,1,2,2\} \xrightarrow{b} \{0,1,1,1,2,2\} \xrightarrow{c} \{0,1,1,1,2\}$.

Obviously, $T(\Delta)$ and $T^c(\Delta)$ are isomorphic labelled transition systems.

Theorem 2. *Given a BPP^1 process rewrite system Δ (or a deadlock-sensitive BPP process rewrite system Δ) and a pair of processes $P_1, P_2 \in \mathcal{E}^{Var(\Delta)}/\equiv$, it is decidable whether $P_1 \sim_{T(\Delta)} P_2$.*

Proof. By Theorem 1 and the fact that $T^c(\Delta)$ defined above is an ECTS. $\square$

3.2   Lossy BPP

The notion of unreliability, in particular lossiness, has been intensively studied with a number of interesting results. Let us mention e.g. *Lossy Channel Systems* [1] and *Lossy Vector Addition Systems* [7,18]. Lossy BPP systems were studied in [18] in the context of model checking problems. In lossy BPP we allow process constants disappear spontaneously at any time. We give a formal definition of lossy BPP systems first.

A *lossy* BPP *process rewrite system* is a finite set $\Delta \subseteq Var \times Act \times \mathcal{E}^{Var}$ of *rules*, written $X \xrightarrow{a} E$ for $(X, a, E) \in \Delta$. A process rewrite system Δ determines a labelled transition system $T(\Delta) = (\mathcal{E}^{Var(\Delta)}/\equiv, Act(\Delta) \cup \{drop\}, \longrightarrow, \mathcal{E}qv)$ where states are $\equiv$-equivalence classes of process expressions over $Var(\Delta)$, $Act(\Delta) \cup \{drop\}$ is the set of labels with a distinguished label $drop \notin Act(\Delta)$ modelling lossiness, the transition relation $\longrightarrow$ is defined by the SOS rules in Figure 2 (we again abuse the notation and write only E instead of $[E]_\equiv$) and $\mathcal{E}qv$ for lossy BPP can be defined as in the case of BPP — deadlock sensitive or deadlock nonsensitive.

Example 2. Let $\Delta = \{X_0 \xrightarrow{a} X_0\|X_0, X_0 \xrightarrow{b} \epsilon\}$. Then $X_0 \longrightarrow^* X_0^k$ for any $k \in \mathbb{N}_0$ where $X_0^0 = \epsilon$ and $X_0^{k+1} = X_0\|X_0^k$. Also, $X_0^k \xrightarrow{drop} X_0^{k'}$ for any k', $0 \leq k' < k$, in particular, $X_0^k \xrightarrow{drop} \epsilon$ and $\epsilon \nrightarrow$. This means that any reachable state in $T(\Delta)$ has norm at most 1. Moreover, $X_0^k \nsim_{T(\Delta)} X_0^{k'}$ for any $k \neq k'$. Hence there cannot be any BPP process bisimilar to X_0 (there are only finitely many nonbisimilar BPP states of norm less or equal to 1). On the other hand this property in general disallows to find a bisimilar lossy BPP process for a given BPP process. Thus the classes BPP and lossy BPP are, as expected, incomparable w.r.t. bisimilarity.

---

[1] For BPP this is already proved in [9,10]. We repeat the theorem in order to demonstrate that our technique is general enough to cover already known results.

We are now ready to define semantics of lossy BPP in terms of commutative transition systems, similarly as for BPP. Let Δ be a lossy BPP system, where $n = |Var(\Delta)|$. By $T^c(\Delta) = (\mathcal{B}_{n-1}^1, Act(\Delta) \cup \{drop\}, \longrightarrow, \mathcal{E}qv)$ we denote a commutative transition system, where $\alpha \xrightarrow{a} \beta$ iff either (i) there is a rule $(X \xrightarrow{a} E) \in \Delta$ such that $\alpha = \phi(X) \oplus \omega$ and $\beta = \phi(E) \oplus \omega$ for some $\omega \in \mathcal{B}_{n-1}^1$, or (ii) $\beta <_c \alpha$ and $a = drop$. The relation $\mathcal{E}qv$ for lossy BPP is defined in the same fashion as mentioned above (deadlock sensitive or deadlock nonsensitive).

Obviously, $T(\Delta)$ and $T^c(\Delta)$ are isomorphic labelled transition systems. This implies the following decidability theorem for lossy BPP systems.

Theorem 3. *Given a lossy BPP process rewrite system Δ (either deadlock sensitive or deadlock nonsensitive) and a pair of processes $P_1, P_2 \in \mathcal{E}^{Var(\Delta)}/_\equiv$, it is decidable whether $P_1 \sim_{T(\Delta)} P_2$.*

Proof. By showing that $T^c(\Delta)$ is an ECTS and then by using Theorem 1 and the isomorphism between $T(\Delta)$ and $T^c(\Delta)$. Details can be found in [22]. □

3.3   Interrupt BPP

In this subsection we investigate *mode transfer operators* in BPP process algebra, in particular the interrupt operator. Quoting [3]: "A useful feature in programming languages and specification languages is the ability to denote mode switches. In particular, most languages have means to describe the disrupt and interrupt of the normal execution of a system." Various mode transfer operators were considered in the literature [2,3,5,11,13]. We define interrupt BPP systems that extend the pure BPP systems with an interrupt vector and a mechanism for handling the interrupt. The motivation is that every state is annotated with a set of allowed interrupts and if no interrupt appears, a normal execution of the process is performed. At any time an interrupt can be raised by performing the action *int*. A normal execution of the process is interrupted and the raised interrupt is handled. During this all interrupts are disallowed. After the interrupt is finished, the action *iret* is performed and a normal execution of the interrupted process continues.

Formally, an *interrupt* BPP *process rewrite system* Δ is a pair (Δ_1, Δ_2) where Δ_1 is a finite set $\Delta_1 \subseteq Var \times Act \times \mathcal{E}^{Var} \times 2^{Var(\Delta_2)}$ and Δ_2 is a BPP system. We write $(X \xrightarrow{a} E, enable)$ for $(X, a, E, enable) \in \Delta_1$. By $Var(\Delta_1)$ we denote the set of variables that occur in the first and the third component of Δ_1. A process rewrite system $\Delta = (\Delta_1, \Delta_2)$ determines a labelled transition system $T(\Delta) = ((\mathcal{E}^{Var(\Delta_1)}/_\equiv) \times 2^{Var(\Delta_2)} \times \{0,1\} \times (\mathcal{E}^{Var(\Delta_2)}/_\equiv), Act(\Delta_1) \cup Act(\Delta_2) \cup \{int, iret\}, \longrightarrow, \mathcal{E}qv^u)$ where states are 4-tuples (E_1, IV, IF, E_2) such that E_1 is a BPP process, IV is an *interrupt vector*, IF is an *interrupt flag* (0 means normal execution and 1 means interrupt call) and E_2 is ϵ if $IF = 0$ or it contains the interrupt handling process in the case $IF = 1$. We assume that $int, iret \notin Act(\Delta_1) \cup Act(\Delta_2)$. The SOS rules for $\longrightarrow$ are defined in Figure 3 (E again represents $[E]_\equiv$ and '$\|$' is commutative) and for the sake of simplicity let us assume that $\mathcal{E}qv^u$ is the universal relation on states.

$$\frac{(X \xrightarrow{a} E_1, enable) \in \Delta_1}{(X, IV, 0, \epsilon) \xrightarrow{a} (E_1, IV \cup enable, 0, \epsilon)}$$

$$\frac{(E_1, IV, 0, \epsilon) \xrightarrow{a} (E_1', IV', 0, \epsilon)}{(E_1 \| F_1, IV, 0, \epsilon) \xrightarrow{a} (E_1' \| F_1, IV', 0, \epsilon)}$$

$$\frac{X \in IV}{(E_1, IV, 0, \epsilon) \xrightarrow{int} (E_1, IV, 1, X)} \qquad \frac{}{(E_1, IV, 1, \epsilon) \xrightarrow{iret} (E_1, IV, 0, \epsilon)}$$

$$\frac{(X \xrightarrow{a} E_2) \in \Delta_2}{(E_1, IV, 1, X) \xrightarrow{a} (E_1, IV, 1, E_2)} \qquad \frac{(E_1, IV, 1, E_2) \xrightarrow{a} (E_1, IV, 1, E_2')}{(E_1, IV, 1, E_2 \| F_2) \xrightarrow{a} (E_1, IV, 1, E_2' \| F_2)}$$

Fig. 3. SOS rules for interrupt BPP

Example 3. Let $\Delta = \Big(\{(X_0 \xrightarrow{a} X_0 \| X_0, \{Y_0\}), (X_0 \xrightarrow{b} \epsilon, \{Y_1\})\}, \{Y_0 \xrightarrow{c} \epsilon, Y_1 \xrightarrow{d} Y_1\} \Big)$. Consider an initial state $(X_0, \emptyset, 0, \epsilon)$. Then the following sequence of transitions is possible in $T(\Delta)$: $(X_0, \emptyset, 0, \epsilon) \xrightarrow{a} (X_0 \| X_0, \{Y_0\}, 0, \epsilon) \xrightarrow{b} (X_0, \{Y_0, Y_1\}, 0, \epsilon) \xrightarrow{int} (X_0, \{Y_0, Y_1\}, 1, Y_0) \xrightarrow{c} (X_0, \{Y_0, Y_1\}, 1, \epsilon) \xrightarrow{iret} (X_0, \{Y_0, Y_1\}, 0, \epsilon) \xrightarrow{int} (X_0, \{Y_0, Y_1\}, 1, Y_1) \xrightarrow{d} (X_0, \{Y_0, Y_1\}, 1, Y_1) \xrightarrow{d} (X_0, \{Y_0, Y_1\}, 1, Y_1) \xrightarrow{d} \cdots$. It is an easy observation that there is no BPP process bisimilar to the initial state $(X_0, \emptyset, 0, \epsilon)$ of $T(\Delta)$ — we use similar arguments as in Example 2.

We remind the reader of the fact that for any BPP system we can find a bisimilar interrupt BPP system simply by disallowing interrupts at all — we define $enable = \emptyset$ in every rule of the BPP system. Hence the class of interrupt BPP is strictly more expressive (w.r.t. bisimilarity) than the class of BPP.

We demonstrate now, how to give an alternative semantics in terms of a commutative transition system T^c. The idea is that the normal process execution is simulated one-to-one in T^c and the interrupt calls are checked using the relation $\mathcal{E}qv$ — thus there are no actions int and $iret$. Let $\Delta = (\Delta_1, \Delta_2)$ be an interrupt BPP system such that $Var(\Delta_1) = \{X_0, \ldots, X_{n_1-1}\}$ and $Var(\Delta_2) = \{Y_0, \ldots, Y_{n_2-1}\}$. In what follows we denote by $T(\Delta_2)$ the deadlock sensitive transition system generated by the BPP process Δ_2. Since bisimilarity in $T(\Delta_2)$ is decidable (Theorem 2), we may assume w.l.o.g. that $Y_i \not\sim_{T(\Delta_2)} Y_j$ for all i, j such that $0 \leq i < j \leq n_2 - 1$. Let $n = \max\{n_1 - 1, n_2 - 1\}$.

Let $T^c(\Delta) = (\mathcal{B}_n^2, Act(\Delta_1) \cup Act(\Delta_2), \longrightarrow, \mathcal{E}qv)$. The intuition is that in the first component of a state $(M, N) \in \mathcal{B}_n^2$ we remember a BPP expression of normal process execution and in the second component we remember an interrupt vector IV in the following sense: $N(i) = 0$ if $Y_i \notin IV$, and $N(i) > 0$ if $Y_i \in IV$. For $\alpha = (M, N) \in \mathcal{B}_n^2$, let $IV(\alpha) = \{Y_i \mid 0 \leq i \leq n_2 - 1 \wedge N(i) > 0\}$ and let $cut(\alpha) = (M, N') \in \mathcal{B}_n^2$ such that

$$N'(i) = \begin{cases} 0 & \text{if } N(i) = 0 \\ 1 & \text{if } N(i) > 0 \end{cases}$$

for all $i \in \mathbb{N}_0$. We define $\alpha = (M, N) \xrightarrow{a} (M', N') = \alpha'$ iff $(E, IV(\alpha), 0, \epsilon) \xrightarrow{a} (E', IV(\alpha'), 0, \epsilon)$ such that $a \notin \{int, iret\}$, $\phi(E) = M$, $\phi(E') = M'$, and $cut(\alpha') = \alpha'$. The last condition $(cut(\alpha') = \alpha')$ ensures that $T^c(\Delta)$ becomes image-finite. Finally we define $\mathcal{E}qv$ as such a relation that for states $\alpha, \beta \in \mathcal{B}_n^2$: $(\alpha, \beta) \in \mathcal{E}qv$ iff $IV(\alpha) = IV(\beta)$.

The following property is an immediate consequence of the definition.

Property 1. Let $\alpha \in \mathcal{B}_n^2$. Then $\alpha \sim_{T^c(\Delta)} cut(\alpha)$.

Proposition 2. *Let $\Delta = (\Delta_1, \Delta_2)$ be an interrupt BPP system. Then it holds that $(E, \emptyset, 0, \epsilon) \sim_{T(\Delta)} (F, \emptyset, 0, \epsilon)$ iff $(\phi(E), \emptyset) \sim_{T^c(\Delta)} (\phi(F), \emptyset)$ for any $E, F \in \mathcal{E}Var(\Delta_1)$.*

Proof. It is obvious that any transition under a where $a \notin \{int, iret\}$ in $T(\Delta)$ can be simulated naturally in the system $T^c(\Delta)$ and vice versa. An interrupt call in $T(\Delta)$ is checked using the relation $\mathcal{E}qv$ and whenever $(\alpha, \beta) \notin \mathcal{E}qv$ in $T^c(\Delta)$ then we can distinguish the corresponding states in $T(\Delta)$ by an appropriate interrupt call.   □

Theorem 4. *Given an interrupt BPP process rewrite system Δ and a pair of processes $(E, \emptyset, 0, \epsilon)$, $(F, \emptyset, 0, \epsilon)$ in $T(\Delta)$, it is decidable whether $(E, \emptyset, 0, \epsilon) \sim_{T(\Delta)} (F, \emptyset, 0, \epsilon)$.*

Proof. By Proposition 2 it is enough to show that $T^c(\Delta)$ is an ECTS and then we use Theorem 1. Details can be found in [22].   □

Remark 2. We used BPP processes for interrupt handling (the system Δ_2). In fact, any process algebra where bisimilarity is decidable can be used.

3.4   Timed-Arc BPP

In this subsection we establish decidability of bisimilarity for a timed extension of BPP systems, called timed-arc BPP. It is worth mentioning another positive decidability result for timed BPP. The authors in [4] show that performance equivalence (a version of timed bisimilarity) is decidable in a polynomial time for BPP processes where actions have a certain time duration. However, their definition of timed BPP does not allow to interpret ordinary BPP systems as timed ones since a duration of an action cannot be equal to 0 and must be strictly positive. We define timed-arc BPP as a natural subclass of timed-arc Petri nets where time (age) is associated to tokens and transitions are labelled by time intervals, which restrict the age of tokens available for firing a transition — see e.g. [6,14]. Our definition implies that timed-arc BPP are a strict extension (w.r.t. bisimilarity) of ordinary BPP systems, as it is demonstrated later.

First, we introduce *labelled timed-arc Petri nets*, following definitions from [20] and then we define timed-arc BPP as its subclass where each transition has exactly one input place. A *labelled timed-arc Petri net* (LTAPN) is a tuple

$N = (P, T, F, c, L, \lambda, \Sigma)$, where P is a finite set of *places*, T is a finite set of *transitions* such that $T \cap P = \emptyset$, $F \subseteq (P \times T) \cup (T \times P)$ is a *flow relation*, $c : F|_{P \times T} \to \mathbb{N}_0 \times (\mathbb{N}_0 \cup \{\infty\})$ is a *time constraint* on transitions such that for each arc $(p, t) \in F$ holds that $t_1 \leq t_2$ where $c(p, t) = (t_1, t_2)$, L is a finite set of *labels*, $\lambda : T \to L$ is a *labelling function*, and $\Sigma \subseteq \mathbb{N}_0$ is a recursive set of allowed *time-elapsing steps*.

Let $x \in \mathbb{N}_0$ and $c(p, t) = (t_1, t_2)$. We write $x \in c(p, t)$ whenever $t_1 \leq x \leq t_2$. We also define $^\bullet t = \{p \mid (p, t) \in F\}$ and $t^\bullet = \{p \mid (t, p) \in F\}$. A *marking* M on N is a function $M : P \to \mathcal{B}$ where $\mathcal{B}$ denotes the set of all finite multisets on $\mathbb{N}_0$. Each place is thus assigned a certain number of tokens, and each token is annotated with a natural number (*age*). Let $x \in \mathcal{B}$ and $a \in \mathbb{N}_0$. We define $x \oplus a$ such that we add the value a to every element of x, i.e., $x \oplus a = \{b + a \mid b \in x\}$.

Let us now define the dynamics of LTAPNs. We introduce two types of transition rules: *firing* of a transition and *time-elapsing*. Let $N = (P, T, F, c, L, \lambda, \Sigma)$ be a LTAPN, M a marking and $t \in T$. We say that t is *enabled* by M iff $\forall p \in {}^\bullet t. \exists x \in M(p). x \in c(p, t)$. If t is enabled by M then it can be *fired*, producing a marking M' (written $M[t\rangle M'$) such that $\forall p \in P. M'(p) = \left(M(p) \smallsetminus C^-(p, t) \right) \cup C^+(t, p)$ where C^- and C^+ are chosen to satisfy the following equations (note that there may be more possibilities and that all the operations are on multisets):

$$C^-(p, t) = \begin{cases} \{x\} & \text{such that } x \in M(p) \text{ and } x \in c(p, t) & \text{if } p \in {}^\bullet t \\ \emptyset & & \text{otherwise} \end{cases}$$

$$C^+(t, p) = \begin{cases} \{0\} & \text{if } p \in t^\bullet \\ \emptyset & \text{otherwise.} \end{cases}$$

Note that the tokens added to places $t^\bullet$ are of age 0. We define also *time-elapsing* transitions τ_k, $k \in \Sigma$, as follows: $M[\tau_k\rangle M'$ iff $\forall p \in P. M'(p) = M(p) \oplus k$.

Let $N = (P, T, F, c, L, \lambda, \Sigma)$ be a LTAPN. We define the corresponding labelled transition system $T(N) = ([P \to \mathcal{B}], L \cup \{\tau_k \mid k \in \Sigma\}, \longrightarrow, \mathcal{E}qv^u)$, where states are markings of N, actions are labels from L together with symbols for time-elapsing, and $M \xrightarrow{a} M'$ iff either $M[t\rangle M'$ and $a = \lambda(t)$, or $M[\tau_k\rangle M'$ and $a = \tau_k$ for some $k \in \Sigma$. For simplicity we define $\mathcal{E}qv^u$ to be the universal relation.

Definition 2. *A* timed-arc BPP *is a LTAPN such that* $|^\bullet t| = 1$ *for all* $t \in T$.

Example 4. Consider a timed-arc BPP net $(\{p_1, p_2\}, \{t_1, t_2\}, F, c, \{a, b\}, \lambda, \{1\})$ where F, c and λ are defined in Figure 4. Names of places (circles) are p_1 and p_2 (from left to right) and names of transitions (squares) are t_1 and t_2 (from left to right) such that $\lambda(t_1) = a$ and $\lambda(t_2) = b$. Notice that $^\bullet t_1 = \{p_1\}$ and $^\bullet t_2 = \{p_2\}$, so the net is indeed a timed-arc BPP. Let $(\{0\}, \emptyset)$ be an initial marking — since $|P| = 2$ we can identify any marking $M : P \to \mathcal{B}$ with a pair $(M(p_1), M(p_2))$. Now e.g. $(\{0\}, \emptyset) \xrightarrow{a} (\{0\}, \{0\}) \xrightarrow{a} (\{0\}, \{0, 0\}) \xrightarrow{b} (\{0\}, \{0\}) \xrightarrow{\tau_1} (\{1\}, \{1\}) \xrightarrow{\tau_1} (\{2\}, \{2\}) \xrightarrow{\tau_1} \dots$. Using similar arguments as in Example 2, there cannot be any BPP process bisimilar to the initial marking. On the other hand, for any BPP process there is a timed-arc BPP net bisimilar

Fig. 4. A timed-arc BPP net

to it — we use the fact that any BPP process is essentially a Petri net where $|{}^\bullet t| = 1$ for every transition t and then we define all the time constrains as $[0, \infty]$ and set $\Sigma = \emptyset$. So the class of timed-arc BPP is strictly more expressive (w.r.t. bisimilarity) than the BPP class.

Assuming a fixed ordering on $P = \{p_1, \ldots, p_n\}$, there is a natural one-to-one correspondence between $[P \to \mathcal{B}]$ and $\mathcal{B}^n$. Let $M : P \to \mathcal{B}$ then we define $(N_1, \ldots, N_n) \in \mathcal{B}^n$ by $N_i = M(p_i)$ for $1 \le i \le n$ and vice versa. In what follows we freely interchange these equivalent notations.

The system $T(N)$ is almost a commutative labelled transition system. There are only two problems: (i) states are not elements from $\mathcal{B}_m^n$ for some fixed $m \in \mathbb{N}_0$ and (ii) the set of actions can be infinite. The following arguments show how to avoid these problems.

Definition 3. *Let* $N = (P, T, F, c, L, \lambda, \Sigma)$ *be a LTAPN. We define its* maximal guard $mg(N) \in \mathbb{N}_0$ *as the maximal time constraint that appears in* N*, i.e.,* $mg(N) = \max\left(\{t_1, t_2 \mid \exists f \in F|_{P \times T}.\ c(f) = (t_1, t_2)\} \setminus \{\infty\}\right)$. *Let* $M \in [P \to \mathcal{B}]$. *We define a* compression *of* M*,* $C_M \in [P \to \mathcal{B}_{mg(N)+1}]$*, by*

$$C_M(p)(k) = \begin{cases} M(p)(k) & \text{if } k < mg(N) + 1 \\ \sum_{i=mg(N)+1}^{\infty} M(p)(i) & \text{if } k = mg(N) + 1 \\ 0 & \text{if } k > mg(N) + 1. \end{cases}$$

Lemma 6. *Let* $N = (P, T, F, c, L, \lambda, \Sigma)$ *be a LTAPN and* $M_1, M_2 \in [P \to \mathcal{B}]$. *If* $C_{M_1} = C_{M_2}$ *then* $M_1 \sim_{T(N)} M_2$.

Proof. It is a routine exercise to verify that $R = \{(M_1, M_2) \in [P \to \mathcal{B}] \times [P \to \mathcal{B}] \mid C_{M_1} = C_{M_2}\}$ is a bisimulation. □

Let $N = (P, T, F, c, L, \lambda, \Sigma)$ be a LTAPN. By m we denote the number $mg(N) + 1$. We define a commutative transition system $T^c(N) = (\mathcal{B}_m^n, L \cup \{\tau_k \mid k \in \Sigma \wedge k < m\} \cup T_m, \longrightarrow, \mathcal{E}qv^u)$ where $T_m = \{\tau_m\}$ if there is $k \in \Sigma$ such that $k \ge m$, otherwise $T_m = \emptyset$ (note that the construction of T_m is effective since Σ is a recursive set). We define $M \xrightarrow{a} M'$ for $M, M' \in \mathcal{B}_m^n$ iff either (i) $M[t\rangle M'$ and $a = \lambda(t)$, or (ii) $M[\tau_k\rangle M''$ where $m > k \in \Sigma$ or $\tau_k \in T_m$, such that $M' = C_{M''}$ and $a = \tau_k$.

Proposition 3. *Let* N *be a LTAPN and* M_1, M_2 *a pair of markings on* N*. Then* $M_1 \sim_{T(N)} M_2$ *iff* $C_{M_1} \sim_{T^c(N)} C_{M_2}$.

Proof. Immediately from Lemma 6. Also note that in $T(N)$ for any $k \ge m = mg(N) + 1$ holds that if $M \xrightarrow{\tau_m} M'$ and $M \xrightarrow{\tau_k} M''$, then $C_{M'} = C_{M''}$. □

Theorem 5. *Given a timed-arc BPP net $N = (P, T, F, c, L, \lambda, \Sigma)$ and a pair of markings M_1, M_2 on N, it is decidable whether $M_1 \sim_{T(N)} M_2$.*

Proof. First show that $T^c(N)$ is an ECTS. Then by Proposition 3 and Theorem 1. For details see [22]. □

Remark 3. It remains an open problem whether bisimilarity is decidable for timed-arc BPP with continuous time, i.e., if we allow e.g. $\Sigma = \mathbb{R}_0^+$.

4   Conclusion

We suggested a subclass of labelled transition systems called effective commutative transition systems (ECTS) where bisimilarity is decidable, and we showed that semantics of many extensions of BPP process algebra can be defined within the ECTS class. This approach seems to be feasible also for other natural extensions of BPP: the crucial condition to be satisfied is probably (6), saying that $\sim_k$ are congruences. This condition fails e.g. for Petri nets, and indeed strong bisimilarity becomes undecidable here [15].

Decidability of weak bisimilarity of BPP is still a well known open problem. Here the problematic condition is (5), stating that the transition system is image-finite, which is not the case for weak bisimilarity. Nevertheless, we can still instead of potentially infinite set of successors $\mathsf{next}(\alpha, a)$ examine only its finite subset such that soundness and completeness of the tableau system is preserved. This possibility was exploited by Stirling in [24] for weak bisimilarity of normed BPP, however, with additional technical restrictions. To design finite subsets of $\mathsf{next}(\alpha, a)$ preserving soundness and completeness even in the general case might be a reasonable way to attack this problem.

Acknowledgement

I would like to thank my advisor Mogens Nielsen for his kind supervision. I also thank Daniel Polansky, Jan Strejcek and the referees for their comments and suggestions.

References

1. P.A. Abdulla and B. Jonsson. Verifying programs with unreliable channels. *Information and Computation*, 127(2):91–101, 1996.
2. J.C.M. Baeten, J.A. Bergstra, and J.W. Klop. Syntax and defining equations for an interrupt mechanism in process algebra. *Fundamenta Informaticae*, IX(2):127–168, 1986.
3. J.C.M. Baeten and J.A. Bergstra. Mode transfer in process algebra. Technical report CSR 00-01, Vakgroep Informatica, Technische Universiteit Eindhoven, 2000.
4. B. Berard, A. Labroue, and Ph. Schnoebelen. Verifying performance equivalence for timed basic parallel processes. In *Proc. of FOSSACS'2000*, volume 1784 of *LNCS*, p. 35–47. Springer-Verlag, 2000.

5. J.A. Bergstra. A mode transfer operator in process algebra. Technical report P8808b, University of Amsterdam, The Netherlands, 1989.

6. T. Bolognesi, F. Lucidi, and S. Trigila. From timed Petri nets to timed LOTOS. In *Proc. of the IFIP WG 6.1 10th International Symposium on Protocol Specification, Testing and Verification*, p. 1–14. Amsterdam, 1990.

7. A. Bouajjani and R. Mayr. Model checking lossy vector addition systems. In *Proc. of STACS'99*, volume 1563 of *LNCS*, p. 323–333. Springer-Verlag, 1999.

8. O. Burkart, D. Caucal, F. Moller, and B. Steffen. Verification on infinite structures. In J. Bergstra, A. Ponse, and S. Smolka, editors, *Handbook of Process Algebra*, chapter 9, p. 545–623. Elsevier Science, 2001.

9. S. Christensen. *Decidability and Decomposition in Process Algebras*. PhD thesis, The University of Edinburgh, 1993.

10. S. Christensen, Y. Hirshfeld, and F. Moller. Bisimulation is decidable for basic parallel processes. In *Proc. of CONCUR'93*, volume 715 of *LNCS*, p. 143–157. Springer-Verlag, 1993.

11. T. Cobben and A. Engels. Disrupt and interrupt in MSC: Possibilities and problems. In *Proc. of the 1st Workshop of the SDL Forum Society on SDL and MSC*, number 104 in Informatik-Berichte, p. 75–83. 1998.

12. L.E. Dickson. Finiteness of the odd perfect and primitive abundant numbers with distinct factors. *American Journal of Mathematics*, 35:413–422, 1913.

13. B. Diertens. New features in PSF I: Interrupts, disrupts, and priorities. Technical report P9417, University of Amsterdam, The Netherlands, 1994.

14. H.M. Hanisch. Analysis of place/transition nets with timed-arcs and its application to batch process control. In *Application and Theory of Petri Nets*, volume 691 of *LNCS*, p. 282–299, 1993.

15. P. Jancar. Undecidability of bisimilarity for Petri nets and some related problems. *Theoretical Computer Science*, 148(2):281–301, 1995.

16. P. Jancar and F. Moller. Techniques for decidability and undecidability of bisimilarity – an invited tutorial. In *Proc. of CONCUR '99*, volume 1664 of *LNCS*, p. 30–45. Springer-Verlag, 1999.

17. R. Mayr. Process rewrite systems. *Information and Comp.*, 156(1):264–286, 2000.

18. R. Mayr. Undecidable problems in unreliable computations. In *Proc. of LATIN'00*, volume 1776 of *LNCS*. Springer-Verlag, 2000.

19. R. Milner. *Communication and Concurrency*. Prentice-Hall, 1989.

20. V. Valero Ruiz, D. de Frutos Escrig, and O. Marroquin Alonso. Decidability of properties of timed-arc Petri nets. In *ICATPN 2000*, volume 1825 of *LNCS*, p. 187–206. Springer-Verlag, 2000.

21. J. Srba. Basic process algebra with deadlocking states. *Theoretical Computer Science*, 266(1–2):605–630, 2001.

22. J. Srba. Note on the tableau technique for commutative transition systems. Technical Report RS-01-50, BRICS Research Series, 2001.

23. J. Srba. Strong bisimilarity and regularity of basic parallel processes is PSPACE-hard. In *Proc. of STACS'02*, LNCS. Springer-Verlag, 2002. To appear.

24. C. Stirling. Decidability of weak bisimilarity for a subset of basic parallel processes. In *Proc. of FOSSACS'01*, volume 2030 of *LNCS*, p. 379–393. Springer-Verlag, 2001.

A Semantic Basis for Local Reasoning

Hongseok Yang[1] and Peter O'Hearn[2]

[1] ROPAS, KAIST
[2] Queen Mary, University of London

Abstract. We present a semantic analysis of a recently proposed formalism for local reasoning, where a specification (and hence proof) can concentrate on only those cells that a program accesses. Our main results are the soundness and, in a sense, completeness of a rule that allows frame axioms, which describe invariant properties of portions of heap memory, to be inferred automatically; thus, these axioms can be avoided when writing specifications.

1 Introduction

The need to say what memory cells or other resources are not changed, along with those that are, has always been a vexing problem in program specification.

Consider a specification of a program to copy a tree:

$$\{\mathtt{tree}\,\tau\,p\}\,\mathtt{CopyTree}(p;q)\,\{(\mathtt{tree}\,\tau\,p) * (\mathtt{tree}\,\tau\,q)\}.$$

Here, the parameter list indicates that p is a value and q a reference parameter. The predicate $\mathtt{tree}\,\tau\,p$ says that p is, or points to, a data structure representing a binary tree τ, and (anticipating the work to come) $(\mathtt{tree}\,\tau\,p)*(\mathtt{tree}\,\tau\,q)$ says that p and q both represent this tree, but that their representations utilize disjoint storage.

This specification certainly captures part of what we intend to say about the procedure. But a Hoare triple typically only describes the effects an action has on the portion of program store it explicitly mentions; it does not say what cells among those not mentioned remain unchanged. As a result, the specification of $\mathtt{CopyTree}(p;q)$ leaves open the possibility that the procedure alters a cell not in the data structure described in the precondition. To make a stronger specification we need to, in one way or another, take into account the notorious "frame axioms" [8], which describe cells that remain unchanged.

It might seem that this problem is just a nuisance, that we should be content for practical purposes to prove weak properties and not worry about frame axioms. This viewpoint is untenable, for the following reason. At a call site for $\mathtt{CopyTree}(p;q)$ there will often be more cells active than those in p's data structure. In that case the specification is not strong enough to use, unless we somehow take the frame axioms into account. A particular example of such a call site is in the body of a recursive definition of $\mathtt{CopyTree}(p;q)$, which uses recursive calls for each of two subtrees. As explained in [5], if we do not have

M. Nielsen and U. Engberg (Eds.): Fossacs 2002, LNCS 2303, pp. 402–416, 2002.
© Springer-Verlag Berlin Heidelberg 2002

some way of showing that each recursive call doesn't affect the other, then the specification will not be strong enough to use as an induction hypothesis when proving the program.

It might alternatively be thought that the problem can be easily solved, simply by listing the variables that a program might alter as part of the specification. This viewpoint is untenable when there are storage cells other than those directly named by variables, typically when there are pointers of one form or another. This solution is thus not applicable to realistic imperative languages.

Nonetheless, although much more than a nuisance, this frame problem is still irritating. It seems unfortunate to have to think up a general formula to function as a description of the cells left unchanged, covering all potential call sites, whenever we write a specification. And intuitively the specification of $\texttt{CopyTree}(p; q)$, for instance, seems to already carry enough information. The hitch is that for this intuition to be realized we need to somehow require that any state alteration not explicitly mandated by the specification is excluded.

Unfortunately, this last part, that "any state alteration not explicitly mandated by the specification is excluded" is difficult to make precise, and that difficulty has spawned hundreds of papers in AI and in program specification. Twice unfortunately, no completely convincing solution has emerged.

In this paper we study the semantics of an approach recently developed in an extension of Hoare's logic for reasoning about mutable data structures [5]. The scope of the approach is modest in intent, in that it is not put forward as a general solution to the frame problem. Rather, the suggestion is that, when certain assumptions are met, there is a natural and simple way to avoid frame axioms. Although, as we further demonstrate here, these assumptions are met in some natural models of imperative languages, there is no claim that they are universally applicable in reasoning about action.

The general idea is that by focusing on the idea of the memory footprint of a program we can get a concrete handle on the resources that a specification of a program needs to describe. More specifically, there are two components to the approach.

1. We interpret a specification $\{P\}\,C\,\{Q\}$ so that, when C is run in a state satisfying P, it must dereference only those cells guaranteed to exist by P or allocated during execution.

2. An inference rule, the Frame Rule, lets us obtain $\{P * R\}\,C\,\{Q * R\}$ from the initial specification $\{P\}\,C\,\{Q\}$ of a procedure or command, where $P * R$ is true just when P and R are true of separate areas of the current heap memory.

Point 1 is reminiscent of the old informal idea of a tight interpretation of specifications: we assume that a specification mentions all the resources relevant to understanding a program, that other resources are automatically unaffected. With it the specification of the $\texttt{CopyTree}$ procedure above implies that any active cell not in p's tree before execution will remain unchanged; this allows us to avoid explicit frame axioms and instead work with the simple specification. Point

2 then gives us a proof method that enables us to infer the invariant properties supported by tightness.

We stress that the first of these points does not depend on the second. Given the tight interpretation, a host of invariant properties are simply true, and this is independent of the language used to describe pre and postconditions. The * connective just gives us a direct way to exploit tightness, in a program logic.

The purpose of this paper is to provide a semantic analysis of these ideas. The basic conception of the interplay between points 1 and 2 above as a basis for local reasoning is due to the second author. Many of the semantic foundations, particularly those related to completeness described later, were first worked out thoroughly by the first author. We refer to the precursor papers [9,2,5] for examples of reasoning with the spatial formalism, for program logic axioms for specific heap-altering and accessing commands, and for references to the literature on program logic and on the frame problem (see also [8]).

The first problem we tackle is the soundness of the Frame Rule. This turns out to be surprisingly delicate, and it is not difficult to find situations where the rule doesn't work. So a careful treatment of soundness, appealing to the semantics of a specific language, is essential. We phrase our argument here in terms of a model devised by Reynolds [10,5], for an extension of the language of while programs with operations for pointer manipulation, including address arithmetic.

In the course of proving soundness we will attempt to isolate the properties on which it relies. Once these properties are established, much of the work in this paper can be carried out at a more abstract level and we sketch the appropriate definitions. But a thorough abstract account will be left for other work; here our goal is to remain concrete and provide a detailed analysis of a single language.

After showing soundness we move on to prove a completeness result, which shows a sense in which no frame axioms are missing. Our approach to completeness follows a line of work which goes under the name of sharpness or adaptation completeness [4]. There one of the main issues is always to conclude certain invariant properties of variables not free in a command. Our completeness result can be seen as extending such results to handle the heap as well, where there are other store locations than those associated with program variables. The key idea for proving completeness is to view commands as predicate transformers satisfying a locality property.

2   A Programming Language

The programming language is an extension of the language of while programs, with operations for manipulating pointers in a heap. The syntax and domains for the language are in Table 1.

The model has two components, the store and the heap. The store is a mapping from variables to integers, and the heap is a finite mapping from natural numbers (addresses) to integers. The heap is accessed using indirect addressing $[E]$ where E is an arithmetic expression.

Table 1. Syntax and Domains

SYNTAX

$$C \quad ::= x := E \mid x := [E] \mid [E] := F \mid x := \mathtt{cons}(E_1, ..., E_n) \mid \mathtt{dispose}(E)$$
$$\quad\quad \mid \; C; C \mid \mathtt{while}\ B\ C \mid \mathtt{if}\ B\ \mathtt{then}\ C\ \mathtt{else}\ C$$

$$E, F ::= x, y, ... \mid 0 \mid 1 \mid E + F \mid E \times F \mid E - F$$

$$B \quad ::= \mathtt{false} \mid B \Rightarrow B \mid E = F \mid E < F$$

DOMAINS

$$\mathtt{Nats} \stackrel{\Delta}{=} \{0, 1, ..., 17, ...\} \qquad \mathtt{Ints} \stackrel{\Delta}{=} \{..., -17, ..., -1, 0, 1, ..., 17, ...\}$$

$$\mathtt{Variables} \stackrel{\Delta}{=} \{x, y, ...\} \qquad \mathtt{Stores} \stackrel{\Delta}{=} \mathtt{Variables} \rightarrow \mathtt{Ints}$$

$$\mathtt{Heaps} \stackrel{\Delta}{=} \mathtt{Nats} \rightharpoonup_{fin} \mathtt{Ints} \quad \mathtt{States} \stackrel{\Delta}{=} \mathtt{Stores} \times \mathtt{Heaps}$$

FUNCTIONALITY OF EXPRESSIONS

$$[\![E]\!]s \in \mathtt{Ints} \qquad [\![B]\!]s \in \{true, false\} \qquad (\text{where } s \in \mathtt{Stores})$$

We assume the standard denotational semantics of integer and boolean expressions. Note that expressions are heap-independent.

The crucial operation on heaps is disjoint combination. We write $h \# h'$ to indicate that the domains $dom(h)$ and $dom(h')$ are disjoint. When $h \# h'$ holds, $h * h'$ is the heap obtained by taking the union of disjoint partial functions. When $h \# h'$ does not hold, $h * h'$ is undefined. The empty heap $[]$ is the unit of $*$. The notation $[n \mapsto m]$ describes the singleton heap which maps n to m and which is undefined everywhere else.

The operational semantics of commands defines a relation $\rightsquigarrow$ on configurations. Configurations include terminal configurations s, h, triples C, s, h, and a special configuration *fault* indicating a memory fault. The command $x := [E]$ reads the value at address E in the heap and places it in x. $[E] := F$ updates address E so that its content is F. $x := \mathtt{cons}(E_1, ..., E_n)$ allocates a sequence of n contiguous heap cells, initializes them to $E_1, ..., E_n$, and places the address of the first cell in the segment in x. $\mathtt{dispose}(E)$ removes address E from the heap. The commands $x := [E]$, $[E] := F$ and $\mathtt{dispose}(E)$ generate a memory fault, a particular kind of error, if E is not an active address. Notice that the number m is chosen non-deterministically in the rule for $\mathtt{cons}$. An example of a command that always faults is $\mathtt{dispose}(x); [x] := 42$. In typical implementations an attempt to dereference a disposed address might not always lead immediately to a fault. Generating these faults early in the semantics is a device that allows us to arrange the formalism in a conservative manner, where well-specified programs will never try to dereference a disposed address.

Table 2. The Programming Language: Syntax and Semantics

$$x := E, s, h \rightsquigarrow (s \mid x \mapsto [\![E]\!]s), h$$

$$\frac{[\![E]\!]s = n}{\text{dispose}(E), s, h * [n \mapsto m] \rightsquigarrow s, h} \qquad \frac{[\![E]\!]s = n \quad n \notin dom(h)}{\text{dispose}(E), s, h \rightsquigarrow fault}$$

$$\frac{[\![E]\!]s = n \in dom(h) \quad h(n) = m}{x := [E], s, h \rightsquigarrow (s \mid x \mapsto m), h} \qquad \frac{[\![E]\!]s \notin dom(h)}{x := [E], s, h \rightsquigarrow fault}$$

$$\frac{[\![E]\!]s = n \in dom(h)}{[E] := F, s, h \rightsquigarrow s, (h \mid n \mapsto [\![F]\!]s)} \qquad \frac{[\![E]\!]s \notin dom(h)}{[E] := F, s, h \rightsquigarrow fault}$$

$$\frac{m, ..., n + m - 1 \notin dom(h) \quad v_1 = [\![E_1]\!]s, ..., v_n = [\![E_n]\!]s}{x := \text{cons}(E_1, ..., E_n), s, h \rightsquigarrow (s \mid x \mapsto m), (h * [m \mapsto v_1, ..., n + m - 1 \mapsto v_n])}$$

$$\frac{C_1, s, h \rightsquigarrow C_1', s', h'}{(C_1; C_2), s, h \rightsquigarrow (C_1'; C_2), s', h'} \qquad \frac{C_1, s, h \rightsquigarrow s', h'}{(C_1; C_2), s, h \rightsquigarrow C_2, s', h'} \qquad \frac{C_1, s, h \rightsquigarrow fault}{(C_1; C_2), s, h \rightsquigarrow fault}$$

$$\frac{[\![B]\!]s = true}{\text{if } B \text{ then } C \text{ else } C', s, h \rightsquigarrow C, s, h} \qquad \frac{[\![B]\!]s = false}{\text{if } B \text{ then } C \text{ else } C', s, h \rightsquigarrow C', s, h}$$

$$\frac{[\![B]\!]s = false}{\text{while } B \text{ do } C \text{ od}, s, h \rightsquigarrow s, h} \qquad \frac{[\![B]\!]s = true}{\text{while } B \text{ do } C \text{ od}, s, h \rightsquigarrow (C; \text{while } B \text{ do } C \text{ od}), s, h}$$

In the semantics we use $(f \mid i \mapsto j)$ for the (perhaps partial) function like f except that i goes to j. This notation is used both when i is and is not in the domain of f.

3 Specifications

We treat predicates semantically in this paper, so a predicate is just a subset of the set of states.

$$\text{Pred} \stackrel{\Delta}{=} \mathcal{P}(\text{States})$$

To evoke the semantics of the assertion languages from [9,2,5], we sometimes use the satisfaction notation

$$s, h \models p$$

as an alternative to $(s, h) \in p$.

To define the semantics of Hoare triples first recall point 1 from the Introduction, where we guarantee that if $\{p\}C\{q\}$ holds then C must not access any cells not guaranteed to exist by p. We can formalize this by observing that if C did guarantee to access such a cell, then it could be made to fault by running it in a state in which that cell is not active. This is the role of the following notion of safety.

- "C, s, h is safe" when $C, s, h \not\rightsquigarrow^* fault$.

For partial correctness the interpretation of triples is the standard one, with an additional safety requirement.

Partial Correctness. $\{p\}C\{q\}$ is true just when, for all s, h,
   if $s, h \models p$ then
   $-$ C, s, h is safe, and
   $-$ if $C, s, h \leadsto^* s', h'$ then $s', h' \models q$.

This fault-avoiding interpretation of triples is not new, but the connection to the intuitive notion of tight specification does not seem to have been observed before (excepting [2,5]). To describe this, suppose $E \hookrightarrow F$ is a predicate saying that F is the contents of the active address E in the current heap. Suppose, further, that the triple

$$\{x \hookrightarrow 5\}C\{x \hookrightarrow 6\}$$

holds and that C does not alter any variables (though it might alter heap cells). Then we claim that, just from this information, we can infer that C does not modify any heap cell existing in the starting state, other than the one denoted by x. To see the reason, suppose that C does modify such a cell and call it y. Then the specification says that the program will not fault if it is run in the singleton state where x is the only active address (with contents 5). But we just said that C alters the address y, and so this attempt to dereference y must generate a fault starting from the singleton state.

We will also consider a total correctness form of specification. For total correctness, we do not need an explicit safety assumption, because total correctness is about "must termination" which itself includes a safety requirement.

$-$ "C, s, h must terminate normally" when C, s, h is safe and there is no infinite $\leadsto$-sequence starting from C, s, h.

Total Correctness. $\{p\}C\{q\}$ is true just when, for all s, h
   if $s, h \models p$ then
   $-$ C, s, h must terminate normally, and
   $-$ if $C, s, h \leadsto^* s', h'$ then $s', h' \models q$.

To formulate the Frame Rule we will need the $*$ connective; if p and q are predicates then

$$p * q \overset{\Delta}{=} \{(s, h * h') \mid s, h \models p \land s, h' \models q \land h\#h'\}$$

The statement of the Frame Rule from [2,5] is as follows.

FRAME RULE, SYNTACTIC VERSION

$$\frac{\{P\}\,C\,\{Q\}}{\{P * R\}\,C\,\{Q * R\}} \quad \mathrm{Modifies}(C) \cap \mathrm{Free}(R) = \{\ \}$$

where $\mathrm{Modifies}(C)$ denotes the set of variables updated in the command C, i.e., those appearing as the destination of an assignment statement in C. To be precise, the Modifies set of each of $x := \cdots$ is $\{x\}$, while for $[E] := F$ and $\mathtt{dispose}(E)$ it is empty; these latter two statements affect the heap but not the values of variables in the store. Since we are working semantically with predicates in this paper, we need to reformulate the rule slightly and replace the reference to the free variables of R in the side condition. We will precede this with a short discussion.

The condition for variables in the rule is straightforward; it simply checks whether any variables in R are modified by a command C. However, the condition for heap cells is more elaborate. With the spatial conjunction, it says that for every state satisfying $P * R$, the current heap can be split into two subheaps so that P holds for the one and R for the other; then, the tight interpretation of the Hoare triple $\{P\} C \{Q\}$ says that the command can only access the first part, i.e. the part for P, consequently making R an invariant during execution.

As an example, starting from the specification of $\mathtt{CopyTree}$ in the Introduction we can infer that copying p's tree does not affect a cell not in it's data structure.

$$\frac{\{\mathtt{tree}\,\tau\,p\}\,\mathtt{CopyTree}(p;q)\,\{(\mathtt{tree}\,\tau\,p) * (\mathtt{tree}\,\tau\,q)\}}{\{(\mathtt{tree}\,\tau\,p) * (x \hookrightarrow y)\}\,\mathtt{CopyTree}(p;q)\,\{(\mathtt{tree}\,\tau\,p) * (\mathtt{tree}\,\tau\,q) * (x \hookrightarrow y)\}}$$

Here, the Modifies set of $\mathtt{CopyTree}(p;q)$ is assumed to be $\{q\}$.

To describe a version of the rule which refers to semantic rather than syntactic predicates we utilize a notion $X \# p$ of independence of a predicate from a set of variables. This can be formulated simply in terms of quantification. If X is a set of variables then

$$\forall X.p \overset{\Delta}{=} \{(s, h) \mid \forall s_X \in [X \to \mathtt{Ints}].\, (s[s_X], h) \in p\}$$

where $s[s']$ denotes the update of s by s' defined by:

$$s[s'](y) \overset{\Delta}{=} \begin{cases} s'(y) & \text{if } y \in dom(s') \\ s(y) & \text{otherwise} \end{cases}$$

Then

- $X \# p$ holds just if $p = \forall X.p$.

FRAME RULE, SEMANTIC VERSION

$$\frac{\{p\}\,C\,\{q\}}{\{p * r\}\,C\,\{q * r\}}\,\mathrm{Modifies}(C) \# r$$

4   Soundness of the Frame Rule

The Frame Rule codifies a notion of local behaviour, and in this section we undertake to describe that notion in terms of the operational semantics.

It will be helpful to first consider a plausible property that does not hold.

If $C, s, h_0 \rightsquigarrow^* s', h_0'$ and $h_0 \# h_1$, then $C, s, h_0 * h_1 \rightsquigarrow^* s', h_0' * h_1$.

The intuition behind this property is just that we can add on extra state, and any execution that works for a smaller state can still go ahead. This property fails because of the behaviour of cons. An address that is allocated during an execution from a small state cannot be allocated starting in a bigger state where it is already active. For example,

$$x := \mathbf{cons}(2, 3), [x \mapsto m], [\,] \rightsquigarrow [x \mapsto 0], [0 \mapsto 2, 1 \mapsto 3]$$

but if we run $x := \mathbf{cons}(2, 3)$ in a heap where 0 is already active, then a different address than 0 must be chosen by $\rightsquigarrow$.

This is an example of where an action on a little state can be disabled when moving to bigger states. Such behaviour might make us doubt that the Frame Rule could be sound at all. However, it only indicates that the language does not behave locally with respect to "may" properties. With Hoare triples we are interested in a form of "must" property. If $\{p\}C\{q\}$ holds and, starting from a state satisfying p, the command terminates, then the final state must satisfy q. Put another way, it is not individual computations that we will judge local, but properties of classes of computations.

The correct property says that if a command is safe in a given state, then the result of executing it in a larger state can be tracked to *some* execution computation on the little state.

Lemma 1 (Safety and Termination Monotonicity).

1. *If C, s, h is safe and $h \# h'$, then $C, s, h * h'$ is safe.*
2. *If C, s, h must terminate normally and $h \# h'$, then $C, s, h * h'$ must terminate normally.*

Lemma 2 (Frame Property). *Suppose*

$$C, s, h_0 \text{ is safe, and } C, s, h_0 * h_1 \rightsquigarrow^* s', h'.$$

Then there is h_0' where

$$C, s, h_0 \rightsquigarrow^* s', h_0', \text{ and } h' = h_0' * h_1.$$

Proof. For $x := \mathbf{cons}(E_1, ..., E_n)$, consider $m, ..., n + m - 1 \notin dom(h_0 * h_1)$, The operational rule gives us $s' = (s \mid x \mapsto m)$ and $h' = h_0 * h_1 * [m \mapsto v_1, ..., m + n - 1 \mapsto v_n]$. Then since $m, ..., m + n - 1 \notin dom(h_0)$, this segment may be selected by the operational rule for cons applied in the smaller heap h_0. So $h_0' = h_0 * [m \mapsto v_1, ..., m + n - 1 \mapsto v_n]$ gives us the desired result.

For $[E] := F$, since $[E] := F, s, h_0$ is safe by assumption we know $[\![E]\!]s \in dom(h_0)$ and therefore $[\![E]\!]s \notin dom(h_1)$. Thus, the assignment leaves h_1 unchanged, and taking $h_0' = (h_0 \mid [\![E]\!]s \mapsto [\![F]\!]s)$ gives the result.

For $\mathbf{dispose}(E)$, if $[\![E]\!]s = n$ then $n \in dom(h_0)$ by safety, and h_0 decomposes as $h_0' * [n \mapsto m]$ for some m. This h_0' satisfies the requirement of the theorem.

For $x := [E]$, safety ensures that $[\![E]\!]s \in dom(h_0)$, and taking $h_0' = h_0$ gives the result.

To cover $C; C'$, `while` and `if`, we need to prove a slightly stronger result. We state the property, which is needed to get the right induction hypothesis, but omit the detailed proof. Consider a variant of the theorem which considers non-terminal configurations; specifically, where the terminal configurations s', h' and s', h_0' are replaced by C', s', h' and C', s', h_0'. The terminal and non-terminal variants are proven simultaneously, by induction on the derivation of $C, s, h_0 *$ $h_1 \leadsto^* s', h'$ or $C, s, h_0 * h_1 \leadsto^* C', s', h'$. The rules for atomic commands above were already considered above, and each of the rules for `while` and $C; C'$ has an immediate proof.   □

Theorem 1 (Soundness). *The* Frame Rule *is sound for both partial and total correctness.*

Proof. The proof uses the Frame Property, and the following locality property for variables.

If $C, s, h \leadsto^* s', h'$ and a variable x is not assigned in C, then $s(x) = s'(x)$.

For partial correctness, suppose the premise of the Frame Rule holds, and that $s, h_0 \models p$ and $s, h_1 \models r$. The premise gives us that C, s, h_0 is safe, and safety of $C, s, h_0 * h_1$ follows from Safety Monotonicity. If $C, s, h_0 * h_1 \leadsto^* s', h$, the Frame Property yields h_0' where $h = h_0' * h_1$ and $C, s, h_0 \leadsto^* s', h_0'$. The premise then ensures $s', h_0' \models q$. The variable locality property implies that s' agrees with s on all variables not in Modifies(C), so $s', h_1 \models r$ follows since we know $s, h_1 \models r$ and Modifies$(C)\#r$. The semantics of $*$ then yields $s', h \models q * r$.

The argument for total correctness appeals additionally to Termination Monotonicity.   □

4.1   The Scope and Delicacy of the Frame Rule

Some remarks are in order on the delicacy of the soundness result.

First, the non-deterministic nature of `cons` was relied on in an essential way. If we had interpreted `cons` so that, say, the smallest possible free address was always chosen for allocation, then adding memory would change what this new address was, and the difference could be detected with address arithmetic; this would invalidate the Frame Rule. Non-deterministic allocation is used to force a program proof not to depend on details of how the allocator might work. (In a language without address arithmetic, we could use invariance under location renaming rather than non-determinism in allocation to ensure this sort of independence.)

Second, suppose we were to add an operation for trapping a memory fault to our language. If we did this, without changing $*$, then the Frame Rule would be invalid; the reason is that we could branch on whether or not a cell is active, and this would contradict Safety Monotonicity. This does not necessarily mean that fault trapping is incompatible with the Frame Rule. We could perhaps change the interpretation of $*$ so that the undefinedness it introduces is regarded as introducing the possibility of a further kind of error, different from memory fault. (The way Calcagno puts it, we need a notion that is detectable in the program logic, but not in the programming language.)

Although delicate, the scope of the Frame Rule is wider than the specific programming language considered here. We briefly sketch an abstract setting. Suppose we have an arbitrary partial commutative monoid (pcm), in place of (Heaps, $*$, []), and an arbitrary set V of values, which we use to define Stores $=$ Variables $\rightarrow V$. Then a "local action" is a binary relation between States and States $\cup \{\perp, fault\}$ satisfying Safety and Termination Monotonicity, and the Frame Property. With this definition, the Frame Rule is sound for every local action.

An example somewhat removed from heap storage that fits this definition is given by Petri nets. A net without capacity $\mathcal{N} = (P, T, pre, post)$ consists of sets P and T of places and transitions, and two functions $pre, post: T \rightarrow \mathcal{M}$ from transitions to markings, where a marking is a finite multiset of places and $\mathcal{M}$ denotes the set of all markings. $\mathcal{M}$ forms a pcm whose commutative monoid structure comes from the multiset union and the empty set. This is a total commutative monoid. If we regard a transition that is not enabled as equivalent to faulting, then each transition $t \in T$ determines a local action[1] by the firing rule: $M [t] N$ iff $\exists t.\exists M'. M = pre(t) * M'$ and $N = post(t) * M'$.

Nets with capacity 1 provide a counterexample. Suppose that places in a net can hold at most one token; consequently, markings are simply subsets of places, and $pre, post$ map transitions to finite subsets of places. Transitions are fired in this case only when it is guaranteed that all the tokens to be produced do not violate the capacity requirement. We can define a pcm on the set of places, where $*$ is union of disjoint sets (which is undefined on sets that overlap). A transition t that violates Safety Monotonicity has $pre(t) = \{a\}$, $post(t) = \{b\}$, where $a \neq b$. t is enabled in $\{a\}$ but not in $\{a, b\}$ because the post-place of t is already filled in $\{a, b\}$. (It is possible to define a different pcm, for which transitions do correspond to local actions, by recording when a place is known to be unmarked; we can do this using $P \rightharpoonup \{full, empty\}$, with $*$ as union of partial functions with disjoint domains.)

These examples and counterexamples indicate that the Frame Rule is not something we expect to be automatically valid, in the way that we expect, say, the rule of Consequence always to be. Close attention must be paid to the interplay between the definition of $*$ and the kinds of operation present in a language.

5   Completeness of the Frame Rule

Suppose we are given a Hoare triple specification $\{p\}C\{q\}$ but we are not told exactly what C is. The question we are concerned with in this section is whether we can derive all other specifications that follow from it, without making use of knowledge of C.

To formulate this we consider Hoare triples $\{p\} - \{q\}$ with an unspecified command. Following [3,12,1], we call such a Hoare triple with a hole a *specifica-*

---

[1] We take Stores to be the singleton set [Variables $\rightarrow \{1\}$].

Table 3. Proof system for specification statements with Modifies set X

Consequence	Frame Rule
$\dfrac{p' \subseteq p \quad \{p\} - \{q\} \quad q \subseteq q'}{\{p'\} - \{q'\}}$	$\dfrac{\{p\} - \{q\}}{\{p * r\} - \{q * r\}} X \# r$

tion statement. Throughout this section we assume a given set X of variables, regarded as the Modifies set. To derive one specification statement from the other we use the usual rule of Consequence from Hoare logic, and the Frame Rule; see Table 3.

The completeness question, which is variously called sharpness or adaptation completeness, is whether this system lets us derive one specification statement from another just when this inference holds semantically. Since the rule of Consequence is itself treated semantically, in that it uses inclusion between predicates-as-sets rather than a provable implication, all of the stress in this question is placed on the Frame Rule: it is essentially asking whether we obtain enough frame axioms.

To show completeness we need to define a notion of semantic consequence between specification statements. There is a niggling problem here: Not all pre/post pairs determine a relation in a direct way. The traditional way around this problem in work on specification statements is to use predicate transformers, which correspond more directly to pre/post pairs. One then separately singles out special kinds of transformers and pre/post pairs that have a good correspondence with relations. In the remainder of the paper we just work with transformers. The tie-up with relations is possible, but omitted for lack of space; we refer the reader to Yang's thesis for further information [11].

5.1   Local Predicate Transformers

In a predicate transformer interpretation, a command C is interpreted as a mapping from a postcondition to a precondition. For instance, the predicate transformer induced by $x := 2$ maps $y = x$ to $y = 2$.

Mathematically, predicate transformers are monotone maps from predicates to predicates.

$$\text{PT} \triangleq \text{Pred} \to_{monotone} \text{Pred}$$

Given a predicate transformer t the Hoare triple "$\{p\}\, t\, \{q\}$" corresponds to the property $p \subseteq t(q)$. Then, the monotonicity requirement is equivalent to saying that the rule of Consequence is valid.

The domain PT contains predicate transformers which, when viewed operationally, don't exhibit the local behavior of commands as described in Section 4. For instance, the predicate transformer $\lambda q.\, \{(s, h) \in q \mid |dom(h)| \leq 3\}$ corresponds to a command which generates a memory fault when there are more than 3 active heap cells and skips otherwise;[2] this command doesn't satisfy Safety Monotonicity. So, it is not surprising that the Frame Rule is not valid for PT since the rule is closely related to the locality properties of Section 4.

We refine PT by requiring predicate transformers to satisfy a locality condition. Recall that in this section we are assuming a given set X of modifiable variables.

$$\text{Locality for } X \colon \forall r, q \in \text{Pred. } X \# r \Longrightarrow t(q) * r \subseteq t(q * r)$$

The condition is equivalent to saying that t satisfies the Frame Rule, which in predicate transformer terms is

$$\forall p, r, q \in \text{Pred. } X \# r \wedge p \subseteq t(q) \Longrightarrow p * r \subseteq t(q * r)$$

The domain $\text{LPT}(X)$ of *local predicate transformers with Modifies set X* is defined as:

$$\text{LPT}(X) \overset{\triangle}{=} \{t \in \text{PT} \mid t \text{ satisfies locality for } X\}.$$

$\text{LPT}(X)$ inherits the ordering from PT, which is just a pointwise ordering induced by the subset ordering of Pred. With such an ordering, $\text{LPT}(X)$ forms a complete lattice, in fact, a complete sublattice of PT.

Proposition 1. $\text{LPT}(X)$ *is a complete sublattice of* PT. *Therefore, given a set* $\{t_i\}_{i \in I}$ *of elements in* $\text{LPT}(X)$, *its least upper bound is given by* $\lambda q. \bigcup_{i \in I} t_i(q)$, *and its greatest lower bound is given by* $\lambda q. \bigcap_{i \in I} t_i(q)$.

Proof. Let r be a predicate such that $X \# r$. It suffices to show that $\bigcup_{i \in I} t_i(q * r)$ and $\bigcap_{i \in I} t_i(q * r)$ include $(\bigcup_{i \in I} t_i(q)) * r$ and $(\bigcap_{i \in I} t_i(q)) * r$, respectively. The first inclusion follows because $\bigcup_{i \in I}(t_i(q) * r) = (\bigcup_{i \in I} t_i(q_i)) * r$, and the second inclusion holds since $*$ is monotone with respect to the subset ordering.   □

5.2   Operational Sensibility

The locality condition in $\text{LPT}(X)$ has an operational explanation via mappings, *wp* and *wlp*, from commands to predicate transformers, which correspond to total correctness and partial correctness. Let C be a command and q a predicate. Then we define the weakest, and weakest liberal, precondition predicate

$$wp(C)(q) \overset{\triangle}{=} \{(s, h) \mid C, s, h \text{ must terminate normally} \\ \text{and if } C, s, h \rightsquigarrow^* s', h', \text{then } s', h' \models q\}$$
$$wlp(C)(q) \overset{\triangle}{=} \{(s, h) \mid C, s, h \text{ is safe} \\ \text{and if } C, s, h \rightsquigarrow^* s', h', \text{then } s', h' \models q\}$$

We can now establish the operational sensibility of local predicate transformers, which says that if $X \supseteq \text{Modifies}(C)$, both $wp(C)$ and $wlp(C)$ are local predicate transformers in $\text{LPT}(X)$.

---

[2] This command, call it C, makes $\{\{(s, h) \in q \mid |dom(h)| \leq 3\}\} C \{q\}$ true for all q in both total and partial correctness, and C is the smallest such in the sense that all other such commands satisfy more Hoare triples than C.

Proposition 2. *For a command C, both $wp(C)$ and $wlp(C)$ satisfy locality for X iff C satisfies Safety and Termination Monotonicity, Frame Property and the following locality property for variables:*

> *if C, s, h is safe and $C, s, h \rightsquigarrow^* s', h'$, then $s(y) = s'(y)$ for all $y \in$*
> `Variables` $- X$.

Notice that this proposition establishes as close a correspondence with the locality properties of Section 4 as we would expect; since both wp and wlp completely ignore all unsafe configurations we can not obtain any properties of unsafe configurations with predicate transformers.

5.3   Proof of Completeness

We have already given a proof system for specification statements in Table 3. This determines a notion of consequence between specification statements.

> $\{p\} - \{q\} \vdash_X \{p'\} - \{q'\}$ iff $\{p'\} - \{q'\}$ can be derived from $\{p\} - \{q\}$
> using the rules in Table 3.

The semantic interpretation of each specification statement is given by a satisfaction relation between local predicate transformers in $\mathbf{LPT}(X)$ and specification statements. For t in $\mathbf{LPT}(X)$

> $t \models_X \{p\} - \{q\}$ iff $p \subseteq t(q)$.

We can now define the semantic consequence relation $\models$ by requiring that any transformer satisfying the antecedent also satisfies the consequent.

> $\{p\} - \{q\} \models_X \{p'\} - \{q'\}$ iff for all $t \in \mathbf{LPT}(X)$,
> $t \models_X \{p\} - \{q\}$ implies $t \models_X \{p'\} - \{q'\}$.

The proof system is sound with respect to this interpretation since the monotonicity condition in **PT** ensures that the rule of Consequence is sound and the locality condition for X guarantees that the Frame Rule is sound.

Proposition 3 (Soundness, II). *If $\{p\} - \{q\} \vdash_X \{p'\} - \{q'\}$, then $\{p\} - \{q\} \models_X \{p'\} - \{q'\}$.*

In the remainder of this section we concentrate on the proof of the converse.

Theorem 2 (Completeness). *If $\{p\} - \{q\} \models_X \{p'\} - \{q'\}$, then $\{p\} - \{q\} \vdash_X \{p'\} - \{q'\}$.*

The proof of completeness proceeds by finding the smallest local predicate transformer t in $\mathbf{LPT}(X)$, amongst those that satisfy a given specification. To describe this transformer it will be convenient to use a notation for the spatial implication $\twoheadrightarrow$ of predicates in pointer logic [2,5], which is itself taken from the logic of Bunched Implications [6,7].

$$p \twoheadrightarrow q \overset{\Delta}{=} \{(s, h) \mid \forall h'. \, h' \# h \wedge s, h' \models p \Longrightarrow (s, h * h') \models q\}$$

In words, $p \twoheadrightarrow q$ holds of a given heap if, whenever we are given new or fresh heap satisfying p, the combined new and current heap satisfies q.

Lemma 3. *Given predicates $p, q \in \mathtt{Pred}$, the predicate transformer $t = \lambda r.\, p *$ $\forall X.\,(q \twoheadrightarrow r)$ is in $\mathtt{LPT}(X)$ and satisfies $p \subseteq t(q)$. Moreover, it is the smallest such in $\mathtt{LPT}(X)$ with respect to the pointwise ordering.*

Proof. It is straightforward to see that t is monotone. To see that t satisfies the locality condition for X, pick predicate r, r' with $X \# r'$. Then, we have:

$$
\begin{aligned}
t(r * r') &= p * (\forall X.\,(q \twoheadrightarrow r * r')) & &\supseteq p * (\forall X.\,(q \twoheadrightarrow r) * r') \\
&\supseteq p * (\forall X.\,(q \twoheadrightarrow r)) * (\forall X.\, r') & &= p * (\forall X.\,(q \twoheadrightarrow r)) * r' = t(r) * r'
\end{aligned}
$$

The condition $p \subseteq t(q)$ is also easily verified as follows:

$$
\begin{aligned}
t(q) &= p * (\forall X.\,(q \twoheadrightarrow q)) \supseteq p * (\forall X.\,\mathsf{emp}) \\
&\supseteq p * \mathsf{emp} & &\supseteq p
\end{aligned}
$$

where $\mathsf{emp} = \{(s, [\,]) \mid s \in \mathtt{Stores}\}$ is the unit of $*$. Finally, t is the smallest satisfying $p \subseteq t(q)$ because for any other $t' \in \mathtt{LPT}(X)$ with $p \subseteq t'(q)$,

$$
t'(r) \supseteq t'(q * \forall X.\,(q \twoheadrightarrow r)) \supseteq t'(q) * \forall X.\,(q \twoheadrightarrow r) \supseteq p * \forall X.\,(q \twoheadrightarrow r).
$$

$\square$

We denote the smallest local predicate transformer in Lemma 3 by $smallest(p, q, X)$.

To prove completeness, first note that for predicates p, q, r, the precondition $smallest(p, q, X)(r)$ can be calculated with the Frame Rule and the rule of Consequence:

$$
\cfrac{\cfrac{\{p\} - \{q\}}{\{p * \forall X.(q \twoheadrightarrow r)\} - \{q * \forall X.(q \twoheadrightarrow r)\}} \qquad q * \forall X.(q \twoheadrightarrow r) \subseteq r}{\{p * \forall X.(q \twoheadrightarrow r)\} - \{r\}}
$$

The right-hand inclusion is just an application of the usual rule of $\forall$-elimination, together with a monotonicity rule for $*$ and the version of modus ponens that connects $*$ and $\twoheadrightarrow$.

Now, let $\{p'\} - \{q'\}$ be a specification statement with $\{p\} - \{q\} \models_X \{p'\} - \{q'\}$. Then, we have $p' \subseteq smallest(p, q, X)(q')$ by Lemma 3, and $\{p'\} - \{q'\}$ can be derived from $\{p\} - \{q\}$ as follows:

$$
\cfrac{p' \subseteq p * \forall X.(q \twoheadrightarrow q') \qquad \cfrac{\{p\} - \{q\}}{\{p * \forall X.(q \twoheadrightarrow q')\} - \{q'\}}}{\{p'\} - \{q'\}}
$$

This finishes the proof of Theorem 2.

To sum up, in this paper we have shown the soundness of a rule for automatically inferring frame axioms, and we have also shown a sense in which the rule gets all the frame axioms we need. We did this by appealing to the operational semantics of a specific programming language: Perhaps the main unresolved question is whether the approach here and in [9,2,5] can be adapted to problems further afield. We outlined a more abstract setting for the work, and a range of other models do fit the abstract definitions, but pointer models are the only ones whose program logic has been examined in detail so far. Particularly worthwhile would be to attempt to apply the notion of local action, mentioned in Section 4.1, in an AI setting, where the frame problem originally arose and where it continues to be intensely studied [8].

Acknowledgments

Thanks to David Naumann and Uday Reddy for advice on predicate transformers, to John Reynolds for discussions on the significance of fault avoidance in specifications, and to the anonymous referees for suggesting improvements to the presentation. Yang was supported by the US NSF under grant INT-9813854 and by Creative Research Initiatives of the Korean Ministry of Science and Technology. O'Hearn was supported by the EPSRC under the Local Reasoning about State project.

References

1. R.-J. R. Back. *On the Correctness of Refinement Steps in Program Development.* PhD thesis, Department of Computer Science, University of Helsinki, 1978. Report A-1978-4.
2. S. Ishtiaq and P. O'Hearn. BI as an assertion language for mutable data structures. In *Principles of Programming Languages*, pages 14–26, January 2001.
3. C. C. Morgan. The specification statement. *ACM Transactions on Programming Languages and Systems*, 10(3), Jul 1988.
4. D. Naumann. Calculating sharp adaptation rules. *Information Processing Letters*, 2000. To appear.
5. P. O'Hearn, J. Reynolds, and H. Yang. Local reasoning about programs that alter data structures. In L. Fribourg, editor, *Proceedings of 15th Annual Conference of the European Association for Computer Science Logic: CSL 2001*, pages 1–19. Springer-Verlag. LNCS 2142.
6. P. W. O'Hearn and D. J. Pym. The logic of bunched implications. *Bulletin of Symbolic Logic*, 5(2):215–244, June 99.
7. D. J. Pym. *The Semantics and Proof Theory of the Logic of Bunched Implications.* Kluwer Academic Publishers, Boston/Dordrecht/London, 2002. To appear.
8. R. Reiter. *Knowledge in Action.* MIT Press, 2001.
9. J. C. Reynolds. Intuitionistic reasoning about shared mutable data structure. In Jim Davies, Bill Roscoe, and Jim Woodcock, editors, *Millennial Perspectives in Computer Science*, pages 303–321, Houndsmill, Hampshire, 2000. Palgrave.
10. J. C. Reynolds. Lectures on reasoning about shared mutable data structure. *IFIP Working Group 2.3 School/Seminar on State-of-the-Art Program Design Using Logic.* Tandil, Argentina, September 2000.
11. H. Yang. *Local Reasoning for Stateful Programs.* Ph.D. thesis, University of Illinois, Urbana-Champaign, Illinois, USA, 2001.
12. H. Yang and U. S. Reddy. On the semantics of refinement calculi. In *Foundations of Software Science and Computation Structures*, pages 359–374. Springer-Verlag, 2000.

Linearity and Bisimulation

Nobuko Yoshida[1,*], Kohei Honda[2,**], and Martin Berger[2,**]

[1] University of Leicester, U.K.
[2] Queen Mary, University of London, U.K.

Abstract. We introduce a theory of weak bisimilarity for the π-calculus with linear type structure [35] in which we abstract away not only τ-actions but also non-τ actions which do not affect well-typed environments. This gives an equivalence far larger than the standard bisimilarity while retaining semantic soundness. The congruency of the bisimilarity relies on a liveness property at linear channels ensured by typing. The theory is consistently extendible to settings which involve nontermination, nondeterminism and state. As an application we develop a behavioural theory of secrecy for the π-calculus which ensures secure information flow for a strictly greater set of processes than the type-based approach in [20, 23].

1 Introduction

Linearity is a fundamental concept in semantics with many applications to both sequential and concurrent computation. This paper studies how a linear type structure, close to those of Linear Logic [12] and game semantics [4, 22, 24], can be used to give a powerful extension of a basic process equivalence, bisimilarity. We use a linear π-calculus, introduced in [35], which, among others, satisfies a basic liveness property in linear interaction: actions on linear channels always eventually fire. A central idea of our construction is that observables, an underpinning of any behavioural semantics, can be given a radical change in the presence of this liveness and other properties ensured by linear typing: a class of visible interactions with the environment which a typed process is actually engaged in, can be completely abstracted (neglected) away in terms of their semantic effects.

Let us briefly explain the key technical ideas, using a process encoding of a λ-calculus. We first recall that the linear π-calculus in [35] can fully abstractly embed $\lambda_{()\times+}$, the simply typed λ-calculus with unit, products and sums. The encoding $[\![M : \alpha]\!]_u$ for a λ-term $M : \alpha$ in [35] is a typed version of Milner's encoding [26]. We also recall that in $\lambda_{()\times+}$, the following equation is semantically sound: $\Gamma \vdash M_1 = M_2 : \texttt{unit}$ for any $\Gamma \vdash M_{1,2} : \texttt{unit}$. In particular, any term of this type is always equated with its unique constant, which we write $\star$. As an example we have the following equation.

$$y : \texttt{unit} \Rightarrow \texttt{unit} \vdash (y\star) = \star : \texttt{unit}$$

* Partially supported by EPSRC grant GR/R33465/01.
** Partially supported by EPSRC grant GR/N/37633.

M. Nielsen and U. Engberg (Eds.): Fossacs 2002, LNCS 2303, pp. 417–433, 2002.

If we apply the encoding in [35] to this, we obtain the following two processes:

$$[\![(y\star)]\!]_u \overset{\text{def}}{=} !u(c).\overline{y}(e)e.\overline{c} \qquad\qquad [\![\star]\!]_u \overset{\text{def}}{=} !u(c).\overline{c}.$$

Here $x(y)$ is an input of y via x, $\overline{x}(y)$ is an (asynchronous) output of a fresh name y via x, and ! indicates replication. Thus, the process $[\![(y\star)]\!]_u$, when invoked at u with a continuation c, first asks at y and, after receiving an answer at e, returns to c; while $[\![\star]\!]_u$ immediately answers at the continuation after the invocation. Because of the obvious difference in these actions, we know $[\![(y\star)]\!]_u \not\approx [\![\star]\!]_u$ where $\approx$ is the standard weak bisimilarity. However, since the encoding is fully abstract, the contextual equivalence $\cong_\pi$ in [35] for the linear π-calculus does equate them. Intuitively, this is because the linear type structure allows us to abstract away the additional non-τ-actions in the following way:

1. The action $\overline{y}(e)$ is typed as an output to replication: thus it just replicates a process in the environment without affecting it.
2. The action e is typed as a linear input: hence it necessarily receives its dual output, neither receiving nor emitting non-trivial information.

For these reasons, the additional actions in $[\![(y\star)]\!]_u$ never affect the environment in a way well-typed observers could detect, and are automatically executable, so they behave "as if they were τ-actions", allowing them to be neglected. This suggests the following principle of behavioural semantics in linear processes.

> *Categorise some of the typed actions as "non-affecting", and abstract away non-affecting actions as if they were τ-actions.*

The type structure plays a crucial role in this principle.

Following [6, 11, 15, 18, 33], the linear π-calculus in [35] includes branching and selection, which correspond to sums in the λ-calculus and additives in Linear Logic [12]. A *branching* is an input with I-indexed branches of form $x[\&_{i \in I}(\vec{y_i}).P_i]$, while a *selection* is an output of form $\overline{x}\mathtt{in}_j(\vec{z})Q$. These constructs have the following dynamics: $x[\&_i(\vec{y_i}).P_i]\|\overline{x}\mathtt{in}_j(\vec{y_j})Q \longrightarrow (\nu\,\vec{y_j})(P_j|Q)$. Now consider another equation in $\lambda_{()\times+}$, which uses sums this time. Let $\mathtt{bool} \overset{\text{def}}{=} \mathtt{unit+unit}$ below.

$$y : \mathtt{bool} \vdash \mathtt{case}\ y\ \mathtt{of}\ \{\mathtt{in}_i() : \mathtt{in}_1(\star)\}_{i\in\{1,2\}} = \mathtt{in}_1(\star) : \mathtt{bool}$$

These terms are translated as follows:

$$[\![\mathtt{case}\ y\ \mathtt{of}\ \{\mathtt{in}_i() : \mathtt{in}_1(\star)\}_{i\in\{1,2\}}]\!]_u \overset{\text{def}}{=} !u(c).\overline{y}(e)e[\&_{1,2}.\overline{c}\mathtt{in}_1]$$

$$[\![\mathtt{in}_1(\star)]\!]_u \overset{\text{def}}{=} !u(c).\overline{c}\mathtt{in}_1.$$

Both processes are equated by $\cong_\pi$. Intuitively this is because an input at e in the first process surely arrives (due to liveness at the linear channel e), and regardless of a selected branch, it leads to $\overline{c}\mathtt{in}_1$. We can thus augment the previous principle as follows.

> *We may abstract away linear branching inputs as far as they lead to the same action in all possible branches.*

The precise formulation of this idea is given in Section 2.

Applications. The bisimilarity based on these ideas, which we hereafter call linear bisimilarity, can justify the equations mentioned above, as well as many equations used for definability arguments to prove full abstraction of $\lambda_{()\times+}$ in [35]. As another application, Section 5 discusses a behavioural theory of secure information flow for the π-calculus, which uses a secrecy-sensitive bisimilarity built on the top of linear bisimilarity. The theory ensures secrecy through semantic means for a strictly larger set of processes than the syntactic theory in [23], which itself is powerful enough to embed representative secrecy calculi such as [3, 32]. As a simple example, the theory can justify the safety of the following λ-term via encoding ($\top$ and $\bot$ are high and low secrecy levels, respectively).

$$\texttt{case } y^\top \texttt{ of } \{\texttt{in}_i() : \texttt{in}_1(\star)\}_{i \in \{1,2\}} : \texttt{bool}^\bot$$

which is untypable in standard secrecy typing systems, cf. [3, 32].

One of the technical contributions of the present work is a proof technique for establishing congruency of linear bisimilarity which, among others, uses liveness at linear channels. The proof method is applicable when we extend linear bisimilarity to other type structures involving nontermination [6], nondeterminism [20] and state [23], as well as to their secrecy enhancement. Such extensions are briefly discussed at the end of in Section 5.

Related Work. Since the introduction of Linear Logic [12], linearity has been studied in various semantic and syntactic contexts. In the setting of the π-calculus, linearity and its relationship to contextual equivalences [21, 27] are studied in [25, 30, 34]. In each case, it is shown that linearity induces a strictly larger contextual equivalence than the standard bisimilarities. [30] as well as [5] study typed bisimilarities in which two processes whose actions are equivalent up to forwarding of names are equated. [19] studies an untyped bisimulation in which visible actions can be ignored due to asynchronous observables. [13] studies a process equivalence in which certain actions are ignored due to capabilities assigned to channels via subtyping. While sharing the common orientation towards a larger equality by a refined treatment of observables, the nature of abstraction offered by the present theory differs from these works in two aspects. First, the introduced behavioural equivalence allows us to treat visible interactions which do take place between the process and the environment as if they were internal (silent) actions. Since the use of liveness in linear actions is essential for this abstraction (as shown by the examples above), it would be difficult to apply these existing techniques to obtain the same effect. The second significance of using linear type structures for a behavioural equivalence is that it enables precise embedding of semantics of language constructs including functional [6, 35] and imperative ones [23], which is important for applications. This direction may not have been pursued in the foregoing studies. Combination of existing techniques and the present one would be an interesting subject for further study.

In the analysis of secure information flow, equality over programs often plays a central role, cf. [2, 3, 10, 14, 31]. Among them, [9, 10] present a bisimulation for cryptographic protocols where high-level actions are abstracted away, preceding the behavioural theory of secrecy in Section 5. The main difference from our approach is that [9, 10] are based on CCS without using type structure, which would limit expressiveness of the resulting theory. [1] establishes a secrecy theorem for the spi-calculus based on may-equivalence, using type information to control the interface of the attacker. Our approach differs in that it first uses linearity to limit environments, then applies it to information flow analysis by a simple elaboration of channels with security levels. [14] uses a secrecy-sensitive may-equivalence for noninterference in the π-calculus. The use of linear type structure in the present work is the main difference. Finally, the first two present authors proposed, in [20] (with Vasconcelos) and in [23], type systems for the π-calculus which ensures secrecy. The present paper gives a semantic theory of secrecy, extending and complementing the syntactic approach in [20, 23].

Outline of the paper. Section 2 briefly reviews the linear π-calculus in [35]. Section 3 introduces linear bisimilarity, whose proof of congruency is given in Section 4. Section 5 discusses an application of the linear bisimilarity to secure information flow analysis. For details of the results and motivation of the syntax and types used in the paper, the reader may refer to [6, 35]. The omitted proofs and definitions of this paper can be found in [36].

Acknowledgements. The authors thank Martin Abadi and anonymous referees for their useful comments and suggestions on an early version of this paper.

2   Preliminaries

2.1   Processes and Channel Types

The set of *processes* is given by the following grammar [6, 35]. Below and henceforth $x, y, \ldots$ range over a countable set of names.

$$P ::= x(\vec{y}).P \mid \overline{x}(\vec{y})P \mid x[\&_{i \in I}(\vec{y}_i).P_i] \mid \overline{x}\mathtt{in}_i(\vec{y})P \mid P|Q \mid (\boldsymbol{\nu}\, x)P \mid \mathbf{0} \mid !P.$$

$x(\vec{y}).P$ (resp. $\overline{x}(\vec{y})P$) is a unary input (resp. unary output), while $x[\&_{i \in I}(\vec{y}_i).P_i]$ (resp. $\overline{x}\mathtt{in}_i(\vec{y})P$) is a branching (resp. selection). Bound name passing has essentially equivalent expressive power as free name passing [17, 29], and is convenient for obtaining precise correspondence with functional type structures [6, 35]. $P|Q$ is a parallel composition, $(\boldsymbol{\nu}\, x)P$ is a restriction, and $!P$ is a replication. In $!P$ we assume P is either a unary or branching input. The reduction relation $\longrightarrow$ is generated from the following rules, closed under output prefix, restriction and parallel composition modulo $\equiv$ [36]. We also set $\twoheadrightarrow \overset{\text{def}}{=} \longrightarrow^* \cup \equiv$.

$$x(\vec{y}).P|\overline{x}(\vec{y})Q \longrightarrow (\boldsymbol{\nu}\, \vec{y})(P|Q)$$
$$!x(\vec{y}).P|\overline{x}(\vec{y})Q \longrightarrow !x(\vec{y}).P|(\boldsymbol{\nu}\, \vec{y})(P|Q)$$
$$x[\&_i(\vec{y}_i).P_i]|\overline{x}\mathtt{in}_j(\vec{y}_j)Q \longrightarrow (\boldsymbol{\nu}\, \vec{y}_j)(P_j|Q)$$
$$!x[\&_i(\vec{y}_i).P_i]|\overline{x}\mathtt{in}_j(\vec{y}_j)Q \longrightarrow !x[\&_i(\vec{y}_i).P_i]|(\boldsymbol{\nu}\, \vec{y}_j)(P_j|Q)$$

Action modes, ranged over by $p, \ldots$, are from the sets $\{\downarrow, !\}$ (written $p_\mathrm{I}, \ldots$), and $\{\uparrow, ?\}$ (written $p_\mathrm{O}, \ldots$). $\downarrow$ (resp. $\uparrow$) represents linear input (resp. output).

! means a unique server associated with input replication. Dually **?** represents client requests to **!**. We also use the mode $*$ to indicate uncomposability. The *dual* $\bar{p}$ of p is given by $\bar{\downarrow} =\uparrow$, $\bar{!} = ?$ and $\bar{\bar{p}} = p$. Then *channel types* are given by the following grammar. For simplicity we assume indices i range over $\{1, 2\}$.

$$\tau ::= \tau_{\mathrm{I}} \mid \tau_{\mathrm{O}} \mid * \qquad \tau_{\mathrm{I}} ::= (\vec{\tau})^{p_{\mathrm{I}}} \mid [\&_i \vec{\tau}_i]^{p_{\mathrm{I}}} \qquad \tau_{\mathrm{O}} ::= (\vec{\tau})^{p_{\mathrm{O}}} \mid [\oplus_i \vec{\tau}_i]^{p_{\mathrm{O}}}$$

Above, $\vec{\tau}$ denotes a vector of channel types. A branching type is sometimes written $[\tau_1 \& \tau_2]^p$ and similarly for selection. We define $\bar{\tau}$, the *dual* of τ, by dualising the action modes and exchanging $\oplus$ and $\&$ in τ. $\mathsf{md}(\tau)$ is $*$ if $\tau = *$, otherwise the outermost action mode of τ.

On types $\odot$ is the least commutative partial operation such that

(1) $\tau \odot \bar{\tau} = *$ $(\mathsf{md}(\tau) =\downarrow)$ $\qquad$ (2) $\tau \odot \tau = \tau$ and $\tau \odot \bar{\tau} = \bar{\tau}$ $(\mathsf{md}(\tau) = ?)$.

Intuitively, (1) says once we compose input-output linear channels it becomes uncomposable (for example, $x.0 \mid \bar{x}$ has mode $*$ at x, which is uncomposable with any process which has x). (2) says that a server should be unique, to which an arbitrary number of clients can request interactions (for example, $!x.0 \mid !x.0$ is never typed because of $()^! \not\asymp ()^!$, while $\bar{x} \mid \bar{x}$ is typable by $()^?$ at x, and $!x.0 \mid \bar{x} \mid \bar{x}$ is so by $()^!$ at x). If $\tau \odot \tau'$ is defined we say they *compose*.

Following $[6, 22, 35]$, we assume the following *sequentiality constraint* (IO-alternation and a unique answer $\uparrow$ in each server type **!**), which comes from game semantics $[4, 22, 24]$. We state the constraint only for unary types: for branching/selection types, we require the same constraint for each summand.

- In $(\vec{\tau})^{\downarrow}$, $\mathsf{md}(\tau_i) = ?$ for each $1 \leq i \leq n$. Dually for $(\vec{\tau})^{\uparrow}$.
- In $(\vec{\tau})^!$, $\mathsf{md}(\tau_i) \in ?$ for each $1 \leq i \leq n$ except at most one j for which $\mathsf{md}(\tau_j) =\uparrow$. Dually for $(\vec{\tau})^?$.

2.2   Typing and Typed Processes

An *action type* is a finite acyclic directed graph whose nodes have the form $x : \tau$ such that no names occur twice and each edge is of form $x : \tau \to x' : \tau'$ with either $\mathsf{md}(\tau) =\downarrow$ and $\mathsf{md}(\tau') =\uparrow$, or $\mathsf{md}(\tau) = !$ and $\mathsf{md}(\tau') = ?$. We write $A(x)$ for the channel type assigned to x occurring in A. The partial operator $A \odot B$ is defined iff channel types with common names compose and the adjoined graph does not have a cycle. This avoids divergence. For example, $x : \tau_1 \to y : \tau_2$ and $y : \bar{\tau_2} \to x : \bar{\tau_1}$ are not composable, hence a process such as $!x.\bar{y} \mid !y.\bar{x}$ is untypable.[1] $\mathsf{fn}(A)$ and $\mathsf{md}(A)$ denote the sets of free names and modes in A, respectively. $A \asymp B$ indicates $A \odot B$ is defined.

Sequents of the linear typing system have the form $\vdash P \triangleright A$.[2] The rules are given in Appendix A. If $\vdash P \triangleright A$ is derivable, we say P *is typable with* A. We sometimes write P^A instead of $\vdash P \triangleright A$. Typable processes are often called *linear processes*.

---

[1] See Section 2 in [35] or Appendix B in [36] for detailed examples and definitions.

[2] In [35], the main sequent has the shape $\Gamma \vdash P \triangleright A$. This is equivalent to the present one by adjoining Γ to the right-hand side.

Example 1. (linear processes)

1. $\vdash \overline{x} \triangleright x : ()^{\uparrow}$ and $\vdash x.\mathbf{0}|\overline{x} \triangleright x : *$. The former can also be typed with $x : ()^{?}$.
2. $\vdash !u(c).\overline{c} \triangleright u : (()^{\uparrow})^!$ and $\vdash !u(c).\overline{x}(e).\overline{c} \triangleright u : (()^{\uparrow})^! \to x : (()^{\downarrow})^{?}$.
3. Let $\mathbb{B} = [\varepsilon \oplus \varepsilon]^{\uparrow}$ (where ε is the empty vector). Then $\vdash !u(c).\overline{x}(e)e[.\overline{c}\mathtt{in}_1 \& .\overline{c}\mathtt{in}_2] \triangleright u : (\mathbb{B})^! \to x : (\overline{\mathbb{B}})^{?}$. Other terms typable with this type include $!u(c).\overline{c}\mathtt{in}_1$ and $!u(c).\overline{x}(e)e[.\overline{c}\mathtt{in}_1 \& .\overline{c}\mathtt{in}_1]$ as well as their symmetric variants.

The following properties of typed terms are from [35]. (2) is a consequence of strong normalisability of linear processes and will play an important role later.

Proposition 1. *1.* (subject reduction) *If* $\vdash P \triangleright A$ *and* $P \twoheadrightarrow Q$ *then* $\vdash Q \triangleright A$.
2. (liveness) *Let* $\vdash P \triangleright A \otimes x : \tau$ *with* $\mathsf{md}(\tau) = \uparrow$ *and* $\mathsf{md}(A) \subseteq \{!, *\}$ *($\otimes$ is disjoint graph union). Then* $P \twoheadrightarrow P'$ *such that* $P' \equiv \overline{x}(\vec{y})R$ *or* $P' \equiv \overline{x}\mathtt{in}_j(\vec{y})R$.

2.3   Contextual Congruence and Bisimilarity

A relation $\mathcal{R}$ over typed processes is *typed* when $P_1^{A_1} \mathcal{R} P_2^{A_2}$ implies $A_1 = A_2$. We write $P_1 \mathcal{R}^A P_2$ when P_1^A and P_2^A are related by a typed relation $\mathcal{R}$. A *typed congruence* is a typed relation which is an equivalence, closed under all typed contexts. The *contextual congruence* $\cong_\pi$ is the maximum typed congruence satisfying the following condition ($\mathbb{B}$ appeared in Example 1).

$$\text{If } P \Downarrow_x^i \text{ and } P \cong_\pi^{x:\mathbb{B}} Q, \text{ then } Q \Downarrow_x^i \qquad (i = 1, 2)$$

where $P \Downarrow_x^i$ means $P \twoheadrightarrow \overline{x}\mathtt{in}_i(\vec{y})P'$. $\cong_\pi$ is maximally consistent in the sense that any addition of equations leads to inconsistency. A more restricted and tractable equality is obtained by labelled transition. Let $l, l', \ldots$ be given by:

$$l ::= \tau \mid x(\vec{y}) \mid \overline{x}(\vec{y}) \mid x\mathtt{in}_i(\vec{y}) \mid \overline{x}\mathtt{in}_i(\vec{y})$$

If $l \neq \tau$, we write $\mathsf{sbj}(l)$ for the initial free name of l. Using these labels, the typed transition $P^A \xrightarrow{l} Q^B$ is defined as in Appendix B. The weak bisimilarity induced by the transition is denoted $\approx$.

As indicated in the introduction, $\cong_\pi$ is strictly greater than $\approx$. One of the aims of the present work is to fill the gap between $\approx$ and $\cong_\pi$, at least partially, without losing the ease of reasoning of $\approx$.

3   Linear Bisimilarity

3.1   Categorising Actions

We begin our path towards the definition of linear bisimilarity with classifying types according to the following criteria: whether actions typed with these types affect the environment non-trivially; and whether the typed actions are guaranteed to take place. One of the significant aspects of our linear type structure is that types are informative enough to allow this classification.

Definition 1. (affecting and enabled types)

1. τ is *affecting* iff there exist $\vdash P_{1,2} \triangleright x : \tau$ and a typed context $C[\,\cdot\,]$ such that $\vdash C[P_i] \triangleright u : \mathbb{B}$, $C[P_1] \Downarrow_u^1$ and $C[P_2] \Downarrow_u^2$.
2. τ is *enabling* iff $\vdash P \triangleright x : \tau$ implies $P \twoheadrightarrow P' \xrightarrow{l}$ such that $\mathsf{sbj}(l) = x$. τ is *enabled* if $\overline{\tau}$ is enabling.

Example 2. (affecting and enabled types)

1. $\mathbb{B}$, $(\mathbb{B})^!$ and $((\mathbb{B})^!)^\uparrow$ are affecting but $((\mathbb{B})^!)^?$ and $(((\mathbb{B})^!)^?)^\downarrow$ are not. It is notable that no τ such that $\mathsf{md}(\tau) \in \{?, \downarrow\}$ is affecting.
2. Any τ such that $\mathsf{md}(\tau) \in \{\downarrow, \uparrow, !\}$ is enabling, while any τ such that $\mathsf{md}(\tau) = ?$ is not. Hence all and only enabled types are τ such that $\mathsf{md}(\tau) = \{\downarrow, \uparrow, ?\}$.

As suggested in the above example, we have an easy rule to determine whether a type is affecting or not, based on the shape of types.

Proposition 2. *Define* Aff *as the smallest set of types generated by:*

- $[\oplus_{1,2}\vec{\tau}_i]^\uparrow \in \mathsf{Aff}$.
- $(\tau_1..\tau_n)^\uparrow \in \mathsf{Aff}$ *and* $(\tau_1..\tau_n)^! \in \mathsf{Aff}$ *when* $\tau_i \in \mathsf{Aff}$ *for some* i $(1 \le i \le n)$.
- $[\&_{1,2}\tau_{i1}..\tau_{in_i}]^! \in \mathsf{Aff}$ *when* $\tau_{ij} \in \mathsf{Aff}$ *for some* i *and* j $(i \in \{1,2\}, 1 \le j \le n_i)$.

Then τ *is affecting iff* $\tau \in \mathsf{Aff}$.

Using the classification of types given above, we can classify actions of well-typed processes. First, an action annotated with an action type, say l^A, is called a *typed action* if the shape of l conforms to A. For example, if $l = \overline{x}\mathsf{in}_1$ then l^A is a typed action iff $A(x) = \mathbb{B}$. τ^A is a typed action for an arbitrary A. If $l \ne \tau$ and l^A is typed, the *type of* l^A is $A(\mathsf{sbj}(l))$. Then we say:

Definition 2. (affecting and enabled typed actions) l^A is *affecting* if $l \ne \tau$ and the type of l^A is affecting; l^A is *non-affecting* if it is not affecting. Further l^A is *enabled* if $l = \tau$ or the type of l^A is enabled.

Table 1 illustrates the classification of actions, writing $\tau, \downarrow(), \uparrow(), \downarrow\&, \uparrow\oplus, !$ and $?$ for (respectively) the τ-action, unary linear input, unary linear output, linear branching, linear selection, replicated unary/branching input, and its dual.[3]

Table 1. Classification of Actions

	τ	$\downarrow()$	$\uparrow()$	$\downarrow\&$	$\uparrow\oplus$	$!$	$?$
affecting	no	no	yes	no	yes	yes	no
enabled	yes	yes	yes	yes	yes	no	yes

We can now introduce invisibility under the linear type structure which dictates the "τ-like" nature of certain non-τ-actions in the typed setting. Below and henceforth $\Delta, \Gamma, \ldots$ range over finite sets of names. $\mathsf{fn}(l)$ is the set of free names in l while $\mathsf{bn}(l)$ is the set of free names in l.

---

[3] We classify unary linear outputs $\uparrow()$ as affecting in Table 1 even though they are sometimes not, as is seen from Proposition 2. A simplest example is $()^\uparrow$.

Definition 3. 1. (invisible actions) A typed action l^A is Δ-*invisible* (Δ-i.) when either $\mathsf{fn}(l) \cap \Delta = \emptyset$ or, if not, l^A is an output which is non-affecting.[4] If l^A is Δ-invisible and is enabled, then l^A is Δ-*strongly invisible* (Δ-s.i.).

2. (abstracted transitions) $P^A \overset{\hat{l}}{\longrightarrow}_\Delta Q^B$ when either: (1) $P^A \overset{l}{\longrightarrow} Q^B$ or (2) $B = A$, $Q = P$ and l^A is Δ-invisible. $P^A \Longrightarrow_\Delta Q^B$ denotes $P^A \overset{l_1 \ldots l_n}{\longrightarrow} Q^B$ ($n \geq 0$) where each l_i is strongly Δ-invisible; then $P^A \overset{l}{\Longrightarrow}_\Delta Q^B$ denotes $P^A \Longrightarrow_\Delta \overset{l}{\longrightarrow}_\Delta \Longrightarrow_\Delta Q^B$; finally $P^A \overset{\hat{l}}{\Longrightarrow}_\Delta Q^B$ denotes either $P^A \overset{l}{\Longrightarrow}_\Delta Q^B$ or $P^A \Longrightarrow_\Delta Q^B$ where l is invisible and $\mathsf{fn}(B) \cap \mathsf{bn}(l) = \emptyset$. if $P^A \Longrightarrow_\Delta Q^B$ is induced by $P^A \overset{l_1 \ldots l_n}{\longrightarrow} Q^B$, we say the latter *underlies* the former.

Note the standard abstracted transitions are a special case of those defined above.

3.2   Semi-typed Relation and Branching Closure

The invisibility of non-τ-actions necessitates one fundamental change in the notion of bisimulation. As an illustration we go back to the initial example in the introduction. The two typed processes concerned were $!x(c).\bar{c}^A$ and $!x(c).\bar{y}(e)e.\bar{c}^A$ with $A = x : ((\,)^\uparrow)^! \to y : ((\,)^\downarrow)^?$. After the common initial action, the typing becomes $A \otimes c : (\,)^\uparrow$. But if $\bar{y}(e)e.\bar{c}^A$ has an output action (which should and can be abstracted away), then e becomes free in the residual and appears in its type environment. This state should be related to the other process which still has type $A \otimes c : (\,)^\uparrow$. Consequently, a bisimulation needs to relate processes with distinct action types.

Definition 4. A relation $\mathcal{R}$ on typed processes is *semi-typed* when $P^A \mathcal{R} Q^B$ implies that the projections of A and B on $\mathsf{fn}(A) \cap \mathsf{fn}(B)$ coincide. We write $P^A \mathcal{R}^\Delta Q^B$ if $\mathcal{R}$ is semi-typed and $\mathsf{fn}(A) \cap \mathsf{fn}(B) = \Delta$, in which case we say P^A and Q^B are *related by* $\mathcal{R}$ *at* Δ. The maximum typed subrelation of a semi-typed $\mathcal{R}$ is called its *centre*.

Using semi-typed relation, a natural way to define a bisimulation would be as follows: a semi-typed $\mathcal{R}$ such that, whenever $P_1^{A_1} \mathcal{R} P_2^{A_2}$ with $\Delta = \mathsf{fn}(A_1) \cap \mathsf{fn}(A_2)$, we have the following and its symmetric case:

$$\text{whenever } P_1^{A_1} \overset{l}{\longrightarrow} Q_1^{B_1}, \text{ there is } P_2^{A_2} \overset{\hat{l}}{\Longrightarrow}_\Delta Q_2^{B_2} \text{ such that } Q_1^{B_1} \mathcal{R} Q_2^{B_2}.$$

However the following shows that congruency is lost if we allow branching.

Example 3. $\bar{x}\mathsf{in}_1^{x:\mathbb{B}}$ and $\bar{y}\mathsf{in}_2^{y:\mathbb{B}}$ are bisimilar at $\emptyset$ in the above definition. Similarly $x[\&_{1,2}\bar{z}\mathsf{in}_i]$ and $y[\&_{1,2}\bar{z}\mathsf{in}_i]$ are bisimilar at z. However when we compose them in pairs, $(\bar{x}\mathsf{in}_1 | x[\&_{1,2}\bar{z}\mathsf{in}_i])$ and $(\bar{y}\mathsf{in}_2 | y[\&_{1,2}\bar{z}\mathsf{in}_i])$ are *not* bisimilar: in fact these terms can be regarded as, up to redundant reduction, $\bar{z}\mathsf{in}_1$ and $\bar{z}\mathsf{in}_2$, which would not be equated under any reasonable semantic criteria.

---

[4] We can consistently abstract away linear input at Δ. For simplicity and because this may not significantly change the resulting equality, we use the present definition.

The problem in this example is in the second equation: intuitively, $x[\&_{1,2}\overline{z}\text{in}_i]$ and $y[\&_{1,2}\overline{z}\text{in}_i]$ cannot be equated because, at disparate interfaces (here x and y), we should expect anything can happen: thus it is possible, at x, the first process receives the left selection, while, at y, the second process receives the right selection (which is precisely what happens in the composition). This indicates that we should say "for every possible branching at disparate channels, the behaviours of two processes at common channels coincide." This idea is formalised in the following definition. Below $t, t_i, \ldots$ range over sequences of typed transitions. A *branching variant* of, say, $x\text{in}_1(\vec{y})$ is $x\text{in}_2(\vec{z})$ (conforming to the given typing), taken up to α-equality.

Definition 5. (branching closure) A set $\{P^A \xrightarrow{t_i} Q_i^{B_i}\}_{i \in I}$ of sequences of typed transitions is Δ-*branching closed* (Δ-b.c.) iff: whenever $t_i = sls' \in S$ with l being a linear branching input such that $\text{fn}(l) \cap \text{fn}(\Delta) = \emptyset$, there is $t_j = sl's''$ $(j \in I)$ for each branching variant l' of l.

Accordingly we say $\{P^A \xRightarrow{\hat{l}}_\Delta Q_i^{B_i}\}_{i \in I}$ is Δ-branching closed if there exists a Δ-branching closed set $\{P^A \xrightarrow{t_i} Q_i^{B_i}\}_{i \in I}$ where $P^A \xrightarrow{t_i} Q_i^{B_i}$ underlies $P^A \xRightarrow{\hat{l}}_\Delta Q_i^{B_i}$ for each i. Similarly for other forms of abstracted transitions.

3.3   Linear Bisimulation

We can now introduce a bisimilarity on linear processes.

Definition 6. (linear bisimulation) A semi-typed $\mathcal{R}$ is a *linear bisimulation* when $P_1^{A_1} \mathcal{R} P_2^{A_2}$ with $\Delta = \text{fn}(A_1) \cap \text{fn}(A_2)$ implies the following and its symmetric case: whenever $P_1^{A_1} \xrightarrow{l} Q_1^{B_1}$, there is a Δ-closed $\{P_2^{A_2} \xRightarrow{\hat{l}}_\Delta Q_{2i}^{B_{2i}}\}_{i \in I}$ such that $Q_1^{B_1} \mathcal{R} Q_{2i}^{B_{2i}}$ for all $i \in I$. The maximum linear bisimulation exists, denoted $\approx_{\text{L}}$.

Simple examples of (non-)bisimilarity follow. Below and henceforth we omit obvious type annotations, assuming all processes are well-typed. We often annotate $\approx_{\text{L}}$ as $\approx_{\text{L}}^{x,y}$ (which follows Definition 4) to make intersecting channels explicit.

Example 4. 1. $x.\mathbf{0} \approx_{\text{L}}^{\emptyset} \mathbf{0}$ and $!x.\mathbf{0} \approx_{\text{L}}^{\emptyset} \mathbf{0}$ and $\overline{x}|\overline{x} \approx_{\text{L}}^{x} \overline{x} \approx_{\text{L}}^{x} \mathbf{0}$.
  2. $x.\overline{y}\text{in}_1 \approx_{\text{L}}^{y} \overline{y}\text{in}_1$. Intuitively this is because an output at x will surely arrive in which case the former process has the same observable as the latter.
  3. Because of the lack of branching closure, we have $x[\&_{1,2}\overline{z}\text{in}_i] \not\approx_{\text{L}}^{z} y[\&_{1,2}\overline{z}\text{in}_i]$. On the other hand, we have $x[\&_{1,2}\overline{z}\text{in}_1] \approx_{\text{L}}^{z} y[\&_{1,2}\overline{z}\text{in}_1] \approx_{\text{L}}^{z} \overline{z}\text{in}_1$.

We prove the following result in the next section.

Theorem 1. *The centre of $\approx_{\text{L}}$ is a congruence.*

Since an action of $\mathbb{B}$-type is always visible, we immediately obtain:

Corollary 1. *The centre of $\approx_{\text{L}}$ is a subrelation of $\cong_\pi$.*

We give simple applications of the linear bisimilarity. Below in (1) $?A$ in the condition indicates $\mathsf{md}(A) = ?$. (1) says processes which are entirely typed with $?$-types (which in particular includes $\mathbf{0}$) are mutually equated with each other even if they may be engaged in arbitrarily long interactions with the environments. (2) says there is essentially a unique inhabitant in the translation of the unit type of $\lambda_{()\times+}$. (3) uses Theorem 1 and (2), combined with Theorem 5.9 (full abstraction) in [35], to derive the equality in $\lambda_{()\times+}$.

Proposition 3. *1.* (innocuous actions [20]) *If* $\vdash P_{1,2} \triangleright ?A$ *then* $P_1 \approx_{\mathrm{L}}^{\mathsf{fn}(A)} P_2$.
   2. (unit inhabitation, 1) $\vdash P \triangleright A$ *with* $A = x : (()^{\uparrow})^! \to A_0$ *implies* $P \approx_{\mathrm{L}}^x {!}x(c).\bar{c}$.
   3. (unit inhabitation, 2) *If* $\Gamma \vdash M : \mathtt{unit}$ *in* $\lambda_{()\times+}$ *then* $\Gamma \vdash M \cong \star : \mathtt{unit}$
   where $\cong$ *is the standard contextual equivalence in* $\lambda_{()\times+}$.

4   Congruency of Linear Bisimilarity

The purpose of this section is to briefly illustrate a proof method for congruency of $\approx_{\mathrm{L}}$. A central difficulty of the proof lies in the existence of strong invisibility when we prove a closure of parallel compositions. This is overcome by the analysis of the operational structures ensured by linear typing, which involve liveness.

   Suppose we wish to prove the relation $\mathcal{R} \stackrel{\text{def}}{=} \{(P_1|Q_1, \ P_2|Q_2) \mid P_1 \approx P_2, \ Q_1 \approx Q_2\}$ to be a bisimulation in order to show that $\approx$ is closed under $|$. Assume $P_1 \mid Q_1 \stackrel{l}{\longrightarrow} P_1' \mid Q_1$; then by assumption, there exists $P_2 \stackrel{\hat{l}}{\Longrightarrow} P_2' \approx P_1'$, hence in the standard proof, we easily have: $P_2 \mid Q_2 \stackrel{\hat{l}}{\Longrightarrow} P_2' \mid Q_2$, and $P_1' \mid Q_1 \ \mathcal{R} \ P_2' \mid Q_2$. However, due to strong invisibility, the same reasoning does not work for $\approx_{\mathrm{L}}$ even in the above trivial case. Recall the example in the Introduction, $P_1 \stackrel{\text{def}}{=} {!}u(x).\overline{x}\mathtt{in}_1$ and $P_2 \stackrel{\text{def}}{=} {!}u(x).\overline{y}(e)e.\overline{x}\mathtt{in}_1$. Then we know $P_1 \approx_{\mathrm{L}} P_2$ because $\overline{y}(e)$ and e are both invisible, so we have $P_1 \stackrel{u(x)}{\longrightarrow}_{uy} P_1' \stackrel{\text{def}}{=} \overline{x}\mathtt{in}_1 \mid P_1$ and $P_2 \stackrel{u(x)}{\Longrightarrow}_{uy} P_2' \stackrel{\text{def}}{=} \overline{x}\mathtt{in}_1 \mid P_2$ with P_1' and P_2' bisimilar. Suppose we compose them with $Q \stackrel{\text{def}}{=} {!}y(e).Q_0$ for some Q_0 such that $P_1 \mid Q$ and $P_2 \mid Q$ are typable. Then we have $P_1 \mid Q \stackrel{u(x)}{\longrightarrow}_{uy} P_1' \mid Q$, while we cannot have $P_2 \mid Q \stackrel{u(x)}{\Longrightarrow}_{uy} P_2' \mid Q$, because the only possible transition is $P_2 \mid Q \stackrel{u(x)}{\longrightarrow} \stackrel{\tau}{\longrightarrow} (\boldsymbol{\nu} e)(e.\overline{x}\mathtt{in}_1 \mid Q_0) \mid P_2 \mid Q$. In order to achieve $P_2' \stackrel{\text{def}}{=} \overline{x}\mathtt{in}_1 \mid P_2$ from this process, $e.\overline{x}\mathtt{in}_1$ needs an acknowledgement $\overline{e}$ from Q_0. At this point, however, we can use a liveness property which extends Proposition 1 (2): if Q_0 has a linear output type at e, then there *always* exist a finite sequence of strong invisible transitions to emit e such that $Q_0 \stackrel{\overline{e}}{\Longrightarrow}_{uy} Q_0'$ and $Q \approx_{\mathrm{L}} Q_0' \mid Q$.

   In the following we define such a chain, called *call-sequence*. Let us assume $P \stackrel{l_1 \cdot l_2}{\Longrightarrow} Q$. We write: $l_1 \frown_{\mathsf{b}} l_2$ (l_1 *binds* l_2) when the subject of l_2 is bound by l_1 (e.g. $x(y) \frown_{\mathsf{b}} \overline{y}$) and $l_1 \frown_{\mathsf{p}} l_2$ (l_1 *prefixes* l_2) when the action l_2 is input-prefixed by l_1 (e.g. $x(y) \frown_{\mathsf{p}} \overline{z}$ in $x(y).\overline{z}$). Define $\frown = \frown_{\mathsf{b}} \cup \frown_{\mathsf{p}}$. We write $\tau \frown l_2$ if $P \stackrel{l_2}{\Longrightarrow} Q$ and P has subterms Q_1 and Q_2 such that $Q_1 \stackrel{l}{\Longrightarrow} Q_1'$ and $Q_2 \stackrel{\overline{l} \cdot l_2}{\Longrightarrow} Q_2'$ with $\overline{l} \frown l_2$; similarly we define $l_1 \frown \tau$; we extend this to a chain $l_1 \frown \tau^* \frown l_2$ and denote it

$l_1 \curvearrowright^+ l_2$ ([6, Appendix F] gives a detailed definition using occurrences of terms). Then a *call-sequence (c.s.) to l under A* is a sequence of actions which has the following shape.

$$(l_0 \curvearrowright^+) \, l_1 \curvearrowright_{\mathsf{b}} l_2 \curvearrowright^+ l_3 \curvearrowright_{\mathsf{b}} l_4 \curvearrowright^+ \cdots \curvearrowright^+ l_{2n-1} \curvearrowright_{\mathsf{b}} l_{2n} \curvearrowright_{\mathsf{p}} l$$

where $\mathsf{md}(l^A_{2k-1}) = \,?$ and $\mathsf{md}(l^A_{2k}) = \,\downarrow$.

Lemma 1. *1.* (shortest c.s.) *Suppose* $\vdash P \triangleright A$ *and* $P \overset{l}{\Longrightarrow}_\Gamma$ *with l output. Then there is a shortest c.s. $l_1 \curvearrowright \cdots \curvearrowright l_n$ to l under A such that* $P \overset{l_1 \cdots l_n}{\longrightarrow} \overset{l}{\longrightarrow}$.

2. (extended liveness) *If* $\vdash P \triangleright A \otimes e : \tau$ *with* $\mathsf{md}(\tau) = \,\uparrow$, *then* $P \Longrightarrow_{A \otimes e : \tau} \overset{l}{\longrightarrow}$ *with* $\mathsf{sbj}(l) = e$.

Note (2) does not restrict the shape of A, cf. Proposition 1 (2). Together with (1), we know there is always a shortest strongly invisible call sequence to each linear output.

We now turn to the congruency of $\approx_{\mathsf{L}}$. First, reflexivity and symmetry of $\approx_{\mathsf{L}}$ are immediate by definition; it also satisfies transitivity on the centre ($P^{A_1}_1 \approx^\Gamma_{\mathsf{L}} P^{A_2}_2$ and $P^{A_2}_2 \approx^\Delta_{\mathsf{L}} P^{A_3}_3$ with $\mathsf{fn}(A_1) \cap \mathsf{fn}(A_3) = \Gamma \cap \Delta$ imply $P^{A_1}_1 \approx^{\Gamma \cap \Delta}_{\mathsf{L}} P^{A_3}_3$). Hence $\approx_{\mathsf{L}}$ is an equivalence. For compatibility, we use the following characterisation of $\approx_{\mathsf{L}}$, which reduces the conditions needed for a bisimulation closure. The form of the resulting relation is similar to the branching bisimulation studied in (untyped) confluent processes [28].

Lemma 2. (context lemma) *Suppose $\mathcal{R}$ is semi-typed such that $P^{A_1}_1 \mathcal{R} P^{A_2}_2$ with $\Delta = \mathsf{fn}(A_1) \cap \mathsf{fn}(A_2)$ implies the following and its symmetric case:*

- *whenever $P^{A_1}_1 \overset{l}{\longrightarrow} Q^{B_1}_1$ where l is Δ-invisible and $\mathsf{fn}(l) \cap \Delta = \emptyset$ then $Q^{B_1}_1 \mathcal{R} P^{A_2}_2$.*
- *whenever $P^{A_1}_1 \overset{l}{\longrightarrow} Q^{B_1}_1$ with l input such that $\mathsf{sbj}(l) \in \Delta$, then there is $P^{A_2}_2 \overset{l}{\longrightarrow}_\Delta Q^{B_2}_2$ such that $Q^{B_1}_1 \mathcal{R} Q^{B_2}_2$.*
- *whenever $P^{A_1}_1 \overset{l}{\longrightarrow} Q^{B_1}_1$ with l Δ-visible linear output such that $\mathsf{sbj}(l) \in \Delta$, then there is a Δ-closed call sequence to l $\{P^{A_2}_2 \Longrightarrow_\Delta \overset{l}{\longrightarrow} Q^{B_{2i}}_{2i}\}_{i \in I}$ such that $Q^{B_1}_1 \mathcal{R} Q^{B_{2i}}_{2i}$ for all $i \in I$.*
- *whenever $P^{A_1}_1 \overset{l}{\longrightarrow} Q^{B_1}_1$ with $\mathsf{md}(l^{A_1}) = \,?$ and $\mathsf{sbj}(l) \in \Delta$, there is a Δ-closed call sequence to l, $\{P^{A_2}_2 \Longrightarrow_\Delta Q^{B_{2i}}_{2i}\}_{i \in I}$, such that either $Q^{B_1}_1 \mathcal{R} Q^{B_{2i}}_{2i}$ or $Q^{B_{2i}}_{2i} \overset{l}{\longrightarrow} Q'^{B'_{2i}}_{2i}$ such that $Q^{B_1}_1 \mathcal{R} Q'^{B'_{2i}}_{2i}$.*

Then the maximum such relation, denoted by $\overset{\bullet}{\approx}_{\mathsf{L}}$, coincides with $\approx_{\mathsf{L}}$.

Using the characterisation, the closure under prefixes and restriction is easy. For parallel composition, using extended liveness repeatedly, we can prove if whenever $P \overset{l}{\longrightarrow}_\Delta P'$ and $P | Q$ is typable, there exists a Δ-b.c. $\{P | Q \Longrightarrow_\Delta \overset{l}{\longrightarrow}_\Delta (\boldsymbol{\nu} \, \vec{v}_i)(P''_i | Q''_i)\}_{i \in I}$ such that $P''_i \approx P'$ and $Q''_i \approx Q$. Using this and Lemma 2, we can prove the closure under the parallel composition on the centre ($P^A_1 \approx_{\mathsf{L}} P^A_2$ and $Q^B_1 \approx_{\mathsf{L}} Q^B_2$ with $A \asymp B$ imply $P_1 | Q^{A \odot B}_1 \approx_{\mathsf{L}} P_2 | Q^{A \odot B}_2$). Thus the centre of $\approx_{\mathsf{L}}$ is a congruence. Finally $\equiv \subset \approx_{\mathsf{L}}$ is proved easily by using weakening and strengthening of base A of $\approx^A_{\mathsf{L}}$. Since the observability predicate given in § 2.3 is easily satisfied by $\approx_{\mathsf{L}}$, we conclude that $\approx_{\mathsf{L}} \subseteq \cong_\pi$.

5   Applications to Secrecy

In linear bisimulations, we abstract away non-affecting typed actions as if they were τ-actions. If we assign a secrecy level to each channel and stipulate a level of observation, then we can further abstract away those actions which should not be visible from the stipulated level. For example, from a low-level viewpoint, actions at high-level channels should be invisible. The technical development of this secrecy enhancement closely follows that of the linear bisimilarity, and offers a powerful tool for reasoning about secrecy in processes.

Assume given a complete lattice of *secrecy levels* $(s, s', \ldots)$ with the ordering $\sqsubseteq$. $\top$ (the most secret) and $\bot$ (the most public) denote the top and bottom of the lattice, respectively. Channel types are annotated with these levels:

$$\tau ::= \tau_{\mathrm{I}} \mid \tau_{\mathrm{O}} \mid *_s \qquad \tau_{\mathrm{I}} ::= (\vec{\tau})_s^{p_1} \mid [\&_{i \in I} \vec{\tau}_i]_s^{p_1} \qquad \tau_{\mathrm{O}} ::= (\vec{\tau})_s^{p_0} \mid [\oplus_{i \in I} \vec{\tau}_i]_s^{p_0}$$

The same sequential constraints (cf. §2.1) apply to channel types. In $\overline{\tau}$, we require each dualised occurrence to own identical secrecy levels. Action types are given precisely as before, using secrecy annotated types. Then we set:

1. l^A is *s-affecting* if it is affecting in the preceding sense and, if l is a linear selection, then $\mathsf{sec}(A(x)) \sqsubseteq s$ ($\mathsf{sec}(\tau)$ is the outermost secrecy level of τ).
2. l^A is *s-Δ-invisible* when either $\mathsf{fn}(l) \cap \Delta = \emptyset$ or, if not, l^A is an output which is not s-affecting. If l^A is s-Δ-invisible and, moreover, is enabled, then l^A is s-Δ *strongly invisible*. The abstracted transitions $P^A \Longrightarrow_{\Delta,s} Q^B$, $P^A \overset{l}{\Longrightarrow}_{\Delta,s} Q^B$ and $P^A \overset{\hat{l}}{\Longrightarrow}_{\Delta,s} Q^B$ are defined accordingly.

In (1), we only count linear selections among secrecy-sensitive observable actions since in the linear type structure no other typed actions directly emit information (note, in Proposition 2, a type is affecting only when it is or contains linear selection). We can now introduce a secrecy-sensitive bisimilarity.

Definition 7. (*s-bisimulation*) A semi-typed relation $\mathcal{R}$ is a *s-bisimulation* when $P_1^{A_1} \mathcal{R} P_2^{A_2}$ with $\Delta = \mathsf{fn}(A_1) \cap \mathsf{fn}(A_2)$ implies the following and its symmetric case: whenever $P_1^{A_1} \overset{l}{\longrightarrow} Q_1^{B_1}$, there is a Δ-closed $\{P_2^{A_2} \overset{\hat{l}}{\Longrightarrow}_{\Delta,s} Q_{2i}^{B_{2i}}\}$ such that $Q_1^{B_1} \mathcal{R} Q_{2i}^{B_{2i}}$. The maximum s-bisimulation exists for each s, which we write $\approx_s$.

By definition, $P^A \approx_{\mathrm{L}} Q^B$ implies $P^A \approx_s Q^B$ for any s. Further $P^A \approx_\top Q^B$ implies $P^A \approx_{\mathrm{L}} Q^B$. A simple example of s-bisimilarity:

Example 5. (*s-bisimilarity*) $\vdash \overline{x}\mathsf{in}_1 \triangleright x : \mathbb{B}_\top \not\approx_\top \vdash \overline{x}\mathsf{in}_2 \triangleright x : \mathbb{B}_\top$ but we have $\vdash \overline{x}\mathsf{in}_1 \triangleright x : \mathbb{B}_\top \approx_\bot \vdash \overline{x}\mathsf{in}_2 \triangleright x : \mathbb{B}_\top$.

A basic observation on $\approx_s$ is that it alone does not form a coherent notion of process equivalence.

Fact 1. *Suppose $\vdash P \triangleright A$ is derived as Section 2 using secrecy annotated types. Then the centre of $\approx_s$ is not closed under parallel composition.*

Proof. Take $\overline{x}\mathrm{in}_i^{x:\tau_1}$ ($i = 1, 2$) with $\tau_1 = \mathbb{B}_\top$. Then $\overline{x}\mathrm{in}_1 \approx_\perp \overline{x}\mathrm{in}_2$. However if we compose these processes with $x[.\overline{u}\mathrm{in}_1\&.\overline{u}\mathrm{in}_2]^{x:\tau_2 \to u:\tau_3}$ where $\tau_2 = \overline{\tau_1}$ and $\tau_3 = \mathbb{B}_\perp$, then $(\boldsymbol{\nu}\,x)(P_1|Q)^{u:\tau_3} \not\approx_\perp (\boldsymbol{\nu}\,x)(P_2|Q)^{u:\tau_3}$.   ∎

The example in the proof above suggests that, for regaining compositionality in $\approx_s$, we need to restrict the set of processes to those which do not transfer information at some high-level to lower levels. In other words, we require information flow in processes to be *secure* [8]. Below we say l^A is *receiving at s* if l^A is a linear branching and moreover $\mathsf{sec}(A(\mathsf{sbj}(l))) = s$.

Definition 8. (behavioural secrecy) A set of typed processes $\mathcal{S}$ is a *secrecy witness* if the following holds: whenever $P^A \in \mathcal{S}$ and $P^A \xrightarrow{l} Q^B$, we have (1) $Q^B \in \mathcal{S}$ and (2) if l^A is receiving at s then $P^A \approx_{s'} Q^B$ for each s' such that $s \not\sqsubseteq s'$. P^A is *behaviourally secure* iff P^A is in some secrecy witness.

Only linear branching counts as "receiving", which is an exact dual of $\approx_s$ (where we consider abstraction by secrecy levels only for linear selection). Intuitively, a process is behaviourally secure iff, whenever it receives non-trivial information at some level, it behaves, to a lower-level observer, as if the action had not taken place. Some examples of (non-)secure processes follow.

Example 6. $\boldsymbol{0}^\emptyset$ is secure. If P^A is secure and $(\boldsymbol{\nu}\,x)P^{A/x}$ is well-typed, the latter is secure. If $P^{\overline{y}:\overline{\tau}\otimes?A}$ is secure and $!x(\overline{y}).P^{x:(\overline{\tau})^! \to A}$ is well-typed, the latter is secure. Finally, given $A \stackrel{\mathrm{def}}{=} x : \mathbb{B}_\top \to y : \overline{\mathbb{B}}_\perp$, $x[.\overline{y}\mathrm{in}_1\&.\overline{y}\mathrm{in}_2]^A$ is not secure but $x[.\overline{y}\mathrm{in}_1\&.\overline{y}\mathrm{in}_1]^A$ is secure (the latter is because $x[.\overline{y}\mathrm{in}_1\&.\overline{y}\mathrm{in}_1]^A \approx_\perp^y \overline{y}\mathrm{in}_1^{A/x}$).

The following is proved precisely as Theorem 1 except that the use of s-invisibility is compensated by behavioural secrecy.

Proposition 4. *The centre of $\approx_s$ over behaviourally secure processes is compatible with all operators except linear branching.*

Without using a syntactic type discipline for secrecy, Proposition 4 offers a framework for fully compositional reasoning for secure processes (we can further close $\approx_s$ under linear branching using the following condition: $x[\&_i(\overline{y}_i).P_i]$ is secure with x given level s if $P_i \approx_{s'} P_j$ for any s' such that $s \not\sqsubseteq s'$).

    To investigate the relationship with the present theory of secrecy and the type-based approach in [23], we introduce $\mathsf{tamp}(A)$ (the lowest possible effect level of A), a type discipline for secrecy $\vdash_{\mathsf{sec}} P \rhd A$ (which we read: P is securely typed by A) and $\cong_s$ (a secrecy-sensitive contextual congruence), all from [23].

Definition 9. (tamper level and secure typing [23]) The *tamper level* of τ, denoted $\mathsf{tamp}(\tau)$, is defined as follows. (1) $\mathsf{tamp}(\tau) = \top$ if τ is not affecting; (2) $\mathsf{tamp}((\overline{\tau})_s^\uparrow) = \sqcap_i \mathsf{tamp}(\tau_i)$, $\mathsf{tamp}([\oplus_i \overline{\tau}_i]_s^\uparrow) \stackrel{\mathrm{def}}{=} s$, $\mathsf{tamp}((\overline{\tau})_s^!) \stackrel{\mathrm{def}}{=} \sqcap_i \mathsf{tamp}(\tau_i)$, $\mathsf{tamp}([\&_i\overline{\tau}_i]_s^!) \stackrel{\mathrm{def}}{=} \sqcap_{ij}\mathsf{tamp}(\tau_{ij})$. Then $\mathsf{tamp}(A) \stackrel{\mathrm{def}}{=} \sqcap\{\mathsf{tamp}(A(x)) \mid x \in \mathsf{fn}(A)\}$. Sequents of the security typing have the form $\vdash_{\mathsf{sec}} P \rhd A$, whose rules are left to Appendix A. If $\vdash_{\mathsf{sec}} P \rhd A$, we say P *is securely typable with* A.

Note that $\mathsf{tamp}(\tau) = \top$ whenever τ is not affecting.

Definition 10. (secrecy-sensitive contextual equality) For each s, s-*contextual congruence* $\cong_s$ is defined as the maximum typed congruence satisfying the following condition: if $P \Downarrow_x^i$ and $P \cong_\pi^{x:\mathbb{B}_s} Q$ with $s' \sqsubseteq s$, then $Q \Downarrow_x^i$ (i=1,2).

Proposition 5. *1. If $\vdash_{\mathsf{sec}} P_{1,2} \triangleright A$ and $\mathsf{tamp}(A) \not\sqsubseteq s$ then $P_1^A \approx_s P_2^A$.*
2. If $\vdash_{\mathsf{sec}} P \triangleright A$, then P is behaviourally secure.
3. $\approx_s$ is congruent over securely typed processes, i.e. it is an equivalence closed under typed contexts given by the secure typing $\vdash_{\mathsf{sec}}$ in Definition 9.

Note that, in (2), the other direction does not hold (for the proof, we can use the last process in Example 6). This proposition allows us to consistently integrate the secrecy typing of [20, 23] with the present behavioural theory, for the purpose of secrecy analysis in processes and, via embeddings, in programs. For example, given a $\lambda_{()\times+}$-term MN, we can check the secrecy of $[\![M]\!]_m$ by typing, $[\![N]\!]_n$ by behavioural secrecy, and finally verify their combination using typing. Another consequence of Proposition 5 is a simple proof of the following noninterference result, first given in [23].

Corollary 2. (noninterference) *Let $\vdash_{\mathsf{sec}} P_{1,2} \triangleright A$ and $\mathsf{tamp}(A) \not\sqsubseteq s$. Then we have $\vdash P_1 \cong_s P_2 \triangleright A$.*

We conclude our technical development with a simple example of reasoning about secrecy, guaranteeing the λ-term mentioned in the introduction is indeed secure.

Example 7. (secrecy via encoding) Let $M \stackrel{\mathrm{def}}{=} \mathsf{case}\, y^\top \,\mathsf{of}\, \{\mathsf{in}_i() : \mathsf{in}_1(\star)\}_{i\in\{1,2\}}$. We show $[\![M : \mathsf{bool}_\top]\!]_u \stackrel{\mathrm{def}}{=} !u(c).\overline{y}(e)e[.\overline{c}\mathsf{in}_1\&.\overline{c}\mathsf{in}_1] \triangleright u : (\mathbb{B}_\perp)^! \to y : (\overline{\mathbb{B}_\top})^?$ is secure. By Proposition 4, it suffices to show $e[.\overline{c}\mathsf{in}_1\&.\overline{c}\mathsf{in}_1] \triangleright e : \overline{\mathbb{B}}_\top \to c : \mathbb{B}_\perp$ is secure. But this has already been shown in Example 6, hence done.

Extensions to Other Type Structures. We have presented a theory of behavioural secrecy focussing on the pure linear π-calculus. First, the same results can be obtained for the free name passing linear calculus via a fully abstract encoding [17]. The framework is also systematically extendible to other type structures which integrate linearity with affinity (nontermination) [6], statefulness (references) [23] and nondeterminism [20]. In each case, the only necessary extensions are (1) the incorporation of a new s-affecting action into s-bisimilarity and its dual receiving action into behavioural secrecy, and (2) when affinity is in the type structure, we change Definition 1 as follows: $\mathbb{B}$ becomes $()^{\uparrow_A}$ ($\uparrow_A$ indicates possibly diverging, or affine, output), and the condition "$C[P_1] \Downarrow_u^1$ and $C[P_2] \Downarrow_u^2$" becomes "$C[P_i] \Downarrow_x$ and $C[P_j] \Uparrow_x$ with $i \neq j$" (here $\Downarrow_x$ iff $P \longrightarrow^* \overline{x}|P'$ for some P', and $\Uparrow_x$ iff not $\Downarrow_x$). Except for these two changes, Definitions 1–8 can be used as they are. Because we have the same liveness property for call sequences (Lemma 1 (2)) in each extension, the same proof methods can be used to obtain the corresponding results such as Theorem 1 and Proposition 4. Together with full abstraction, the framework offers a uniform basis for behavioural analysis of secrecy in programming languages.

References

1. Abadi, M., Secrecy by typing in security protocols. *Journal of the ACM*, 46(5):749–786, 1999.
2. Abadi, M., Secrecy in programming-language semantics, *MFPS XV*, ENTCS, 20 (April 1999).
3. Abadi, M., Banerjee, A., Heintze, N. and Riecke, J., A core calculus of dependency, *POPL'99*, ACM, 1999.
4. Abramsky, S., Jagadeesan, R. and Malacaria, P., Full Abstraction for PCF. *Info. & Comp.* 163 (2000), 409–470.
5. Boreale, M. and Sangiorgi, D. Bisimulation in name-passing calculi without matching. *LICS'98*, IEEE, 1998.
6. Berger, M., Honda, K. and Yoshida, N., Sequentiality and the π-Calculus, *TLCA'01*, LNCS 2044, 29–45, Springer, 2001. The full version available at www.dcs.qmw.ac.uk/~kohei.
7. Boudol, G. and Castellani, I., Noninterference for Concurrent Programs, *ICALP'01*, LNCS, Springer, 2001.
8. Denning, D. and Denning, P., Certification of programs for secure information flow. *Communication of ACM*, ACM, 20:504–513, 1997.
9. Focardi, R. and Gorrieri, R., The compositional security checker: A tool for the verification of information flow security properties. *IEEE Transactions on Software Engineering,* 23(9), 1997.
10. Focardi, R., Gorrieri, R. and Martinelli, F., Non-interference for the analysis of cryptographic protocols. *ICALP'00*, LNCS 1853, Springer, 2000.
11. Gay, S. and Hole, M., Types and Subtypes for Client-Server Interactions, *ESOP'99*, LNCS 1576, 74–90, Springer, 1999.
12. Girard, J.-Y., Linear Logic, *TCS*, 50, 1–102, 1987.
13. Hennessy, M. and Rathke, J., Typed behavioural equivalences for processes in the presence of subtyping, To appear in Proc. *CATS 2002*.
14. Hennessy, M. and Riely, J., Information flow vs resource access in the asynchronous pi-calculus, *ICALP'00*, LNCS 1853, 415–427, Springer, 2000.
15. Honda, K., Types for Dyadic Interaction. *CONCUR'93*, LNCS 715, 509–523, 1993.
16. Honda, K., Composing Processes, *POPL'96*, 344–357, ACM, 1996.
17. Honda, K., Notes on Linear Typing for Free Outputs, May, 2001.
18. Honda, K., Kubo, M. and Vasconcelos, V., Language Primitives and Type Discipline for Structured Communication-Based Programming. *ESOP'98*, LNCS 1381, 122–138. Springer-Verlag, 1998.
19. Honda, K. and Tokoro, M. An object calculus for asynchronous communication. *ECOOP'91*, LNCS 512, 133–147, 1991.
20. Honda, K., Vasconcelos, V. and Yoshida, N., Secure Information Flow as Typed Process Behaviour, *ESOP'00*, LNCS 1782, 180–199, 2000.
21. Honda, K. and Yoshida, N. On Reduction-Based Process Semantics. *TCS*, 151, 437–486, 1995.
22. Honda, K. and Yoshida, N., Game-theoretic analysis of call-by-value computation. *TCS*, 221 (1999), 393–456, 1999.
23. Honda, K. and Yoshida, N., A uniform type structure for secure information flow, To appear in *POPL'02*, ACM, 2002.
24. Hyland, M. and Ong, L., "On Full Abstraction for PCF": I, II and III. *Info. & Comp.* 163 (2000), 285–408, 2000.

25. Kobayashi, N., Pierce, B., and Turner, D., Linearity and the π-calculus, *POPL'96*, 358–371, 1996.

26. Milner, R., Functions as Processes. *MSCS*, 2(2), 119–146, CUP, 1992.

27. Milner, R. and Sangiorgi, D., Barbed Bisimulation, *ICALP'92*, LNCS 623, 685–695, Springer, 1992.

28. Philippou, A. and Walker, D., On confluence in the π-Calculus, *ICALP'97*, LNCS 1256, 314–324, Springer, 1997.

29. Sangiorgi, D. π-calculus, internal mobility, and agent-passing calculi. *TCS*, 167(2):235–271, 1996.

30. Sangiorgi, D., The name discipline of uniform receptiveness, *TCS*, 221, 457–493, 1999.

31. Sabelfield, A. and Sands, D. A per model of secure information flow in sequential programs. *ESOP'99*, LNCS 1576, Springer, 1999.

32. Smith, G. and Volpano, D., Secure information flow in a multi-threaded imperative language, 355–364, *POPL'98*, ACM, 1998.

33. Vasconcelos, V., Typed concurrent objects. *ECOOP'94*, LNCS 821, 100–117. Springer, 1994.

34. Yoshida, N. Graph Types for Mobile Processes. *FST/TCS'16*, LNCS 1180, 371–386, Springer, 1996.

35. Yoshida, N., Berger, M. and Honda, K., Strong Normalisation in the π-Calculus, *LICS'01*, IEEE, 2001. The full version as MCS technical report, 2001-09, University of Leicester, 2001. Available at www.mcs.le.ac.uk/~nyoshida/paper.html.

36. A full version of this paper. MCS technical report, 2001-48, University of Leicester, 2001. Available at www.mcs.le.ac.uk/~nyoshida/paper.html.

A   Typing Rules

In the following rules, $A\langle \vec{y} : \vec{\tau} \rangle$ indicates each $y_i : \tau_i$ occurs in A. $\otimes$ is disjoint union. $x : \tau \to A$ adds new edges from $x : \tau$ to the non-suppressed nodes in A. A^{-x} indicates $x \notin \mathsf{fn}(A)$. pA indicates $p \in \mathsf{md}(A)$. We also assume $\uparrow A$ in $(\mathsf{In}^{\downarrow})$ and $(\mathsf{Bra}^{\downarrow})$ is either a singleton or empty ("unique-answer-per-thread").

	(Par)	(Res)	(Weak-*, ?)
(Zero)	$\vdash P_i \triangleright A_i \quad (i = 1, 2)$	$\vdash P \triangleright A\langle x : \tau \rangle$	$\vdash P \triangleright A^{-x}$
	$A_1 \asymp A_2$	$\mathsf{md}(\tau) \in \{*, !\}$	$\mathsf{md}(\tau) \in \{*, ?\}$
$\overline{\vdash \mathbf{0} \triangleright \_}$	$\overline{\vdash P_1 \mid P_2 \triangleright A_1 \odot A_2}$	$\overline{\vdash (\boldsymbol{\nu} x) P \triangleright A/x}$	$\overline{\vdash P \triangleright A \otimes x : \tau}$

(In$^{\downarrow}$)	(In$^!$)	(Out) $(p \in \{\uparrow, ?\})$
		$\vdash P \triangleright C\langle \vec{y} : \vec{\tau} \rangle$
$\vdash P \triangleright \vec{y} : \vec{\tau} \otimes \uparrow A^{-x} \otimes ? B^{-x}$	$\vdash P \triangleright \vec{y} : \vec{\tau} \otimes ? A^{-x}$	$C/\vec{y} = A \asymp x : (\vec{\tau})^p$
$\overline{\vdash x(\vec{y}).P \triangleright (x : (\vec{\tau})^{\downarrow} \to A) \otimes B}$	$\overline{\vdash\, !\, x(\vec{y}).P \triangleright x : (\vec{\tau})^! \to A}$	$\overline{\vdash \overline{x}(\vec{y}) P \triangleright A \odot x : (\vec{\tau})^p}$

(Bra$^{\downarrow}$)	(Bra$^!$)	(Sel) $(p \in \{\uparrow, ?\})$
		$\vdash P \triangleright C\langle \vec{y} : \vec{\tau}_j \rangle$
$\vdash P_i \triangleright \vec{y}_i : \vec{\tau}_i \otimes \uparrow A^{-x} \otimes ? B^{-x}$	$\vdash P_i \triangleright \vec{y}_i : \vec{\tau}_i \otimes ? A^{-x}$	$C/\vec{y} = A \asymp x : [\oplus_i \vec{\tau}_i]^p$
$\overline{\vdash x[\&_i(\vec{y}_i).P_i] \triangleright (x : [\&_i \vec{\tau}_i]^{\downarrow} \to A) \otimes B}$	$\overline{\vdash\, !\, x[\&(\vec{y}_i).P_i] \triangleright x : [\&_i \vec{\tau}_i]^! \to A}$	$\overline{\vdash \overline{x}\mathsf{in}_j(\vec{y}) P \triangleright A \odot x : [\oplus_i \vec{\tau}_i]^p}$

In Section 5, we consider a secrecy enhancement of typed terms. This is done in two stages. First we simply annotate channels with secrecy levels, leaving the rules themselves precisely as above except types are now annotated by secrecy levels (which the rules simply ignore). Second we consider *securely typed processes*, which are the set of sequents of form $\vdash_{\text{sec}} P \rhd A$ which are derived from the above rules except the rule $(\mathsf{Bra}^\downarrow)$ is replaced by the following one, using the channel types annotated by secrecy levels and using the sequent $\vdash_{\text{sec}} P \rhd A$ instead of $\vdash P \rhd A$.

$$(\mathsf{Bra}^\downarrow) \quad \frac{\vdash_{\text{sec}} P_i \rhd \vec{y}_i : \vec{\tau}_i \otimes \uparrow A^{-x} \otimes ? B^{-x} \quad s \sqsubseteq \mathsf{tamp}(A)}{\vdash_{\text{sec}} x[\&_i(\vec{y}_i).P_i] \rhd (x : [\&_i \vec{\tau}_i]^\downarrow_s \multimap A) \otimes B}$$

B   Transition Rules

We assume all l.h.s. processes are well-typed. A allows l unless: (1) $A(\mathsf{sbj}(l)) = *$ or (2) l is output and $\mathsf{md}(A(\mathsf{sbj}(l))) = {!}$, cf. [6]. $\mathsf{n}(l)$ is the set of names in l.

$$x[\&_i \vec{y}_i.P_i]^A \xrightarrow{x\,\mathsf{in}_i(\vec{y}_i)} P_i^{\vec{y}_i : \vec{\tau}_i \otimes A/x} \qquad (x : [\&\vec{\tau}_i]^\downarrow \in A)$$

$$!x[\&_i \vec{y}_i.P_i]^A \xrightarrow{x\,\mathsf{in}_i(\vec{y}_i)} !x[\&_i \vec{y}_i.P_i] | P_i^{\vec{y}_i : \vec{\tau}_i \otimes A} \quad (x : [\&\vec{\tau}_i]^! \in A)$$

$$\overline{x}\,\mathsf{in}_i(\vec{y})P^A \xrightarrow{\overline{x}\,\mathsf{in}_i(\vec{y})} P^{\vec{y} : \vec{\tau}_i \otimes A/x} \qquad (x : [\oplus_i \vec{\tau}_i]^\uparrow \in A)$$

$$\overline{x}\,\mathsf{in}_i(\vec{y})P^A \xrightarrow{\overline{x}\,\mathsf{in}_i(\vec{y})} P^{\vec{y} : \vec{\tau}_i \otimes A} \qquad (x : [\oplus_i \vec{\tau}_i]^? \in A)$$

$$\frac{P_1' \equiv_\alpha P_1 \quad P_1^{A_1} \xrightarrow{l} P_2^{A_2} \quad P_2 \equiv_\alpha P_2'}{P_1'^{A_1} \xrightarrow{l} P_2'^{A_2}} \qquad \frac{P_1^{A_1} \xrightarrow{l} P_2^{A_2} \quad x \notin \mathsf{n}(l)}{(\boldsymbol{\nu} x)P_1^{A_1/x} \xrightarrow{l} (\boldsymbol{\nu} x)P_2^{A_2/x}}$$

$$\frac{P_1^{A_1} \xrightarrow{l} P_2^{A_2} \quad A_1 \odot B \text{ allows } l}{P_1|Q^{A_1 \odot B} \xrightarrow{l} P_2|Q^{A_2 \odot B}} \qquad \frac{P_1^{A_1} \xrightarrow{l} P_2^{A_2} \quad Q_1^{B_1} \xrightarrow{\overline{l}} Q_2^{B_2}}{P_1|Q_1^{A_1 \odot B_1} \xrightarrow{\tau} (\boldsymbol{\nu}\,\mathsf{bn}(l))(P_2|Q_2)^{A_2 \odot B_2/\mathsf{bn}(l)}}$$

$$\frac{P_1^{A_1} \xrightarrow{l} P_2^{A_2} \quad \mathsf{n}(l) \cap \{\vec{y}\} = \emptyset}{\overline{x}\,\mathsf{in}_i(\vec{y})P_1^{A_1/\vec{y} \odot x : [\oplus_i \vec{\tau}_i]^p} \xrightarrow{l} \overline{x}\,\mathsf{in}_i(\vec{y})P_2^{A_2/\vec{y} \odot x : [\oplus_i \vec{\tau}_i]^p_i}}$$

$$\frac{P_1^{A_1} \xrightarrow{x\,\mathsf{in}_i(\vec{z})} P_2^{A_2}}{\overline{x}\,\mathsf{in}_i(\vec{y})P_1^{A_1/\vec{y} \odot x : [\oplus_i \vec{\tau}_i]^p} \xrightarrow{\tau} (\boldsymbol{\nu}\,\vec{y})P_2\{\vec{y}/\vec{z}\}^{A_2/\vec{z}}}$$

We omit rules for unary actions and symmetric case of $|$. The rules are well-typed in the sense that if $P_1^{A_1}$ is well-typed and $P_1^{A_1} \xrightarrow{l} P_2^{A_2}$ then $P_2^{A_2}$ is well-typed.

Author Index

Lecture Notes in Computer Science

For information about Vols. 1–2228
please contact your bookseller or Springer-Verlag

Vol. 2266: S. Reich, M.T. Tzagarakis, P.M.E. De Bra (Eds.), Hypermedia: Openness, Structural Awareness, and Adaptivity. Proceedings, 2001. X, 335 pages. 2002.

Vol. 2267: M. Cerioli, G. Reggio (Eds.), Recent Trends in Algebraic Development Techniques. Proceedings, 2001. X, 345 pages. 2001.

Vol. 2268: E.F. Deprettere, J. Teich, S. Vassiliadis (Eds.), Embedded Processor Design Challenges. VIII, 327 pages. 2002.

Vol. 2269: S. Diehl (Ed.), Software Visualization. Proceedings, 2001. VIII, 405 pages. 2002.

Vol. 2270: M. Pflanz, On-line Error Detection and Fast Recover Techniques for Dependable Embedded Processors. XII, 126 pages. 2002.

Vol. 2271: B. Preneel (Ed.), Topics in Cryptology – CT-RSA 2002. Proceedings, 2002. X, 311 pages. 2002.

Vol. 2272: D. Bert, J.P. Bowen, M.C. Henson, K. Robinson (Eds.), ZB 2002: Formal Specification and Development in Z and B. Proceedings, 2002. XII, 535 pages. 2002.

Vol. 2273: A.R. Coden, E.W. Brown, S. Srinivasan (Eds.), Information Retrieval Techniques for Speech Applications. XI, 109 pages. 2002.

Vol. 2274: D. Naccache, P. Paillier (Eds.), Public Key Cryptography. Proceedings, 2002. XI, 385 pages. 2002.

Vol. 2275: N.R. Pal, M. Sugeno (Eds.), Advances in Soft Computing – AFSS 2002. Proceedings, 2002. XVI, 536 pages. 2002. (Subseries LNAI).

Vol. 2276: A. Gelbukh (Ed.), Computational Linguistics and Intelligent Text Processing. Proceedings, 2002. XIII, 444 pages. 2002.

Vol. 2277: P. Callaghan, Z. Luo, J. McKinna, R. Pollack (Eds.), Types for Proofs and Programs. Proceedings, 2000. VIII, 243 pages. 2002.

Vol. 2278: J.A. Foster, E. Lutton, J. Miller, C. Ryan, A.G.B. Tettamanzi (Eds.), Genetic Programming. Proceedings, 2002. XI, 337 pages. 2002.

Vol. 2279: S. Cagnoni, J. Gottlieb, E. Hart, M. Middendorf, G.R. Raidl (Eds.), Applications of Evolutionary Computing. Proceedings, 2002. XIII, 344 pages. 2002.

Vol. 2280: J.P. Katoen, P. Stevens (Eds.), Tools and Algorithms for the Construction and Analysis of Systems. Proceedings, 2002. XIII, 482 pages. 2002.

Vol. 2281: S. Arikawa, A. Shinohara (Eds.), Progress in Discovery Science. XIV, 684 pages. 2002. (Subseries LNAI).

Vol. 2282: D. Ursino, Extraction and Exploitation of Intensional Knowledge from Heterogeneous Information Sources. XXVI, 289 pages. 2002.

Vol. 2283: T. Nipkow, L.C. Paulson, M. Wenzel, Isabelle/HOL. XIII, 218 pages. 2002.

Vol. 2284: T. Eiter, K.-D. Schewe (Eds.), Foundations of Information and Knowledge Systems. Proceedings, 2002. X, 289 pages. 2002.

Vol. 2285: H. Alt, A. Ferreira (Eds.), STACS 2002. Proceedings, 2002. XIV, 660 pages. 2002.

Vol. 2286: S. Rajsbaum (Ed.), LATIN 2002: Theoretical Informatics. Proceedings, 2002. XIII, 630 pages. 2002.

Vol. 2287: C.S. Jensen, K.G. Jeffery, J. Pokorny, Saltenis, E. Bertino, K. Böhm, M. Jarke (Eds.), Advances in Database Technology – EDBT 2002. Proceedings, 2002. XVI, 776 pages. 2002.

Vol. 2288: K. Kim (Ed.), Information Security and Cryptology – ICISC 2001. Proceedings, 2001. XIII, 457 pages. 2002.

Vol. 2289: C.J. Tomlin, M.R. Greenstreet (Eds.), Hybrid Systems: Computation and Control. Proceedings, 2002. XIII, 480 pages. 2002.

Vol. 2291: F. Crestani, M. Girolami, C.J. van Rijsbergen (Eds.), Advances in Information Retrieval. Proceedings, 2002. XIII, 363 pages. 2002.

Vol. 2292: G.B. Khosrovshahi, A. Shokoufandeh, A. Shokrollahi (Eds.), Theoretical Aspects of Computer Science. IX, 221 pages. 2002.

Vol. 2293: J. Renz, Qualitative Spatial Reasoning with Topological Information. XVI, 207 pages. 2002. (Subseries LNAI).

Vol. 2296: B. Dunin-Kęplicz, E. Nawarecki (Eds.), From Theory to Practice in Multi-Agent Systems. Proceedings, 2001. IX, 341 pages. 2002. (Subseries LNAI).

Vol. 2299: H. Schmeck, T. Ungerer, L. Wolf (Eds.), Trends in Network and Pervasive Computing – ARCS 2002. Proceedings, 2002. XIV, 287 pages. 2002.

Vol. 2300: W. Brauer, H. Ehrig, J. Karhumäki, A. Salomaa (Eds.), Formal and Natural Computing. XXXVI, 431 pages. 2002.

Vol. 2301: A. Braquelaire, J.-O. Lachaud, A. Vialard (Eds.), Discrete Geometry for Computer Imagery. Proceedings, 2002. XI, 439 pages. 2002.

Vol. 2302: C. Schulte, Programming Constraint Services. XII, 176 pages. 2002. (Subseries LNAI).

Vol. 2303: M. Nielsen, U. Engberg (Eds.), Foundations of Software Science and Computation Structures. Proceedings, 2002. XIII, 435 pages. 2002.

Vol. 2304: R.N. Horspool (Ed.), Compiler Construction. Proceedings, 2002. XI, 343 pages. 2002.

Vol. 2305: D. Le Métayer (Ed.), Programming Languages and Systems. Proceedings, 2002. XII, 331 pages. 2002.

Vol. 2306: R.-D. Kutsche, H. Weber (Eds.), Fundamental Approaches to Software Engineering. Proceedings, 2002. XIII, 341 pages. 2002.

Vol. 2308: I.P. Vlahavas, C.D. Spyropoulos (Eds.), Methods and Applications of Artificial Intelligence. Proceedings, 2002. XIV, 514 pages. 2002. (Subseries LNAI).

Vol. 2309: A. Armando (Ed.), Frontiers of Combining Systems. Proceedings, 2002. VIII, 255 pages. 2002. (Subseries LNAI).

Vol. 2314: S.-K. Chang, Z. Chen, S.-Y. Lee (Eds.), Recent Advances in Visual Information Systems. Proceedings, 2002. XI, 323 pages. 2002.

Vol. 2315: F. Arhab, C. Talcott (Eds.), Coordination Models and Languages. Proceedings, 2002. XI, 406 pages. 2002.

Vol. 2322: V. Mařík, O. Stěpánková, H. Krautwurmová, M. Luck (Eds.), Multi-Agent Systems and Applications II. Proceedings, 2001. XII, 377 pages. 2002. (Subseries LNAI).